Payroll Accounting

2008 EDITION

Bernard J. Bieg
Bucks County Community College
Judith A. Toland
Bucks County Community College

THOMSON
SOUTH-WESTERN

Australia · Brazil · Canada · Mexico · Singapore · Spain · United Kingdom · United States

THOMSON
SOUTH-WESTERN

Payroll Accounting, 2008 Edition

Bernard J. Bieg and Judith A. Toland

VP/Editorial Director
Jack W. Calhoun

Editor-in-Chief
Rob Dewey

Acquisitions Editor
Keith Chassé

Associate Developmental Editor
Jessica Kempf

Marketing Manager
Kristen Hurd

Senior Content Project Manager
Tim Bailey

Manager of Technology, Editorial
John Barans

Technology Project Manager
Robin Browning

Web Site Project Manager
Brian Courter

Senior Frontlist Buyer
Doug Wilke

Production House
LEAP Publishing Services, Inc.

Compositor
GGS Book Services, Inc.

Printer
Quebecor World
Dubuque, IA

Art Director
Linda Helcher

Internal Designer
Chris Miller

Cover Designer
Chris Miller

Cover Image
© PhotoDisc Collection/Getty Images

Photography Manager
John Hill

Photo Researcher
Rose Alcorn

Printed in the United States of America

1 2 3 4 5 10 09 08 07

Student Edition
ISBN-13: 978-0-324-65856-9
ISBN-10: 0-324-65856-7

Student Edition with CD
ISBN-13: 978-0-324-64554-5
ISBN-10: 0-324-64554-6

Library of Congress Control Number: 2007934904

For more information about our products, contact us at:

Thomson Learning Academic Resource Center

1-800-423-0563

Thomson Higher Education
5191 Natorp Boulevard
Mason, OH 45040
USA

AS WE GO TO PRESS...

Chapter 3

AMENDED 941

Beginning in 2008, the new form replacing Form 941c will be Form 941x, *Amended Employer's Quarterly Federal Tax Return*. This is a stand alone form and only one can be filed each quarter.

Chapter 4

TAX-FREE FRINGE BENEFIT

The cost of an employee's lodging will qualify as a working condition fringe (not taxable) if:

- lodging is on a temporary basis.
- lodging is an ordinary and necessary business expense.
- lodging is needed for the employee to be available for business meetings or functions of the employer.

PREFACE

Payroll Accounting and Today's Business Environment

Today's payroll accountant is a major player on a company's management team. Management's need for timely and accurate payroll cost data as a part of the total planning step has moved payroll from a disbursement and recording function to an integral part of the management process.

With constant changes in the legal environment, technology advancements in the administration of payroll functions and with tax withholding responsibilities, the payroll accounting occupation has become proactive. During this time when the need for accurate information is so critical, ***Payroll Accounting*** has established a record of being the most thorough book on the market. Each edition has been updated with the most current data available.

The 2008 edition of ***Payroll Accounting*** continues to provide the most user-friendly payroll accounting coverage in addition to significant resources that will aid instructors and students alike in their mastery of payroll accounting.

Payroll and Technology

In this edition, we have further incorporated technology to give instructors full support for today's teaching options and students hands-on experience based on the practices of payroll specialists.

Computerized Payroll Project

Students can solve the payroll project with Klooster & Allen's Computerized Payroll Accounting Software, free with the purchase of the text. The software is updated with the most current tax information. The payroll project takes students through payroll periods within a 3-month time period. Appendix A includes step-by-step instructions for completing the Computerized Payroll Project.

New! SHORTENED PAYROLL PROJECT

In response to requests from users, the 2008 edition of ***Payroll Accounting*** includes a Shortened Payroll Project which is found in Klooster & Allen's Computerized Payroll Accounting Software. The Shortened Payroll Project takes students through payroll periods for one month only. It is offered as an option for instructors who want to assign a Payroll Project but do not have the time to do the full version. The Shortened Payroll Project can also be completed using Excel Spreadsheets, found on the Web site.

Extra! ADP's PC/PAYROLL TUTORIAL FOR WINDOWS

ADP, the number one provider of payroll outsourcing products and services in the industry, has produced a tutorial that will teach users how to start a new payroll cycle, enter employee and payroll information, transmit a payroll, and verify payroll with output reports. Upon successful completion of the tutorial, users can print a résumé quality certificate of completion, perfect for demonstrating an established knowledge of the most popular payroll service in the industry. And best of all, the tutorial CD-ROM is included with each new copy of the 2008 edition!

CHECK FIGURES INCLUDED AT THE END OF THIS TEXT

Check figures provide help and assist users in staying on track as they learn the intricacies of payroll accounting.

COMPANION WEB SITE (www.thomsonedu.com/accounting/bieg)

This comprehensive and easy to use Web site offers a complete Interactive Study Center for students containing Interactive Quizzes, Check Figures, Excel Spreadsheet Templates, Net Activities, Web Links, Computerized Payroll Accounting User's Guide, and Controlling Costs. In addition to these useful tools, instructors can access materials online including the Solutions Manual, PowerPoint Presentations, Excel Solutions, Achievement Test Solutions, and more.

EXCEL TEMPLATES

Excel templates for selected end of chapter problems, the Computerized Payroll Project, and the Continuing Payroll Problem provide students with additional practice. An Excel primer is located on the Web site.

A Great Study Tool for the Payroll Certification Examination

The 2008 edition of ***Payroll Accounting*** continues to offer the course content and tutorials to help users prepare for the American Payroll Association's Fundamental Payroll Certification (FPC) designation exam.

UP-TO-THE-MINUTE TAX LAW CHANGES

Up-to-date knowledge is especially important for today's payroll specialists. This edition has been completely updated to reflect the tax law changes that affect payroll accounting. Users can find these changes listed on the "As We Go To Press" page in the text and on the Web site.

COMPREHENSIVE PAYROLL PROJECT

Using the latest payroll software—available in Windows® format and packaged FREE with each text—users can review key concepts in a comprehensive review problem at the end of the book.

November 20 Payroll

The step-by-step instructions for completing the November 20 payroll (for the period ending November 14) follow.

Step 1: Answer the questions for the November 20 payroll on the Student Project Audit Test as you complete processing for the pay period.

Step 2: If you quit the software after processing the previous pay period, perform the following steps:
a. Start up the *Integrated Accounting for Payroll* software.
b. Load your file containing the last pay period data *(11-13 your name).*

Step 3: Enter and post the following transactions:
November 16: Deposited with City Bank the amount of FICA taxes and federal income taxes for the October payrolls.
Hint: Display the general ledger report to obtain these amounts from the FICA Taxes Payable—OASDI, FICA Taxes Payable—HI, and the Employees FIT payable account balances.

INTEGRATED PAYROLL LAW AND PRACTICE

Payroll laws are presented next to their respective practices—making it easy for learners to understand the ***reasoning*** behind confusing federal, state, and local regulations.

Outstanding Pedagogy

Learning Objectives are enumerated at the beginning of each chapter and the numbers repeated next to the start of the applicable text coverage.

Fair Labor Standards Act

1 LEARNING OBJECTIVE

FLSA (referred to as the Federal Wage and Hour Law) is covered in Chapter 2. The outline of the law deals with:

- Minimum wage ($5.85 per hour—end of 2007) and overtime pay requirements. In addition, equal pay for equal work, employment of child labor, public service contracts, and wage garnishment.
- Coverage of employers engaged in interstate commerce or in production of goods and services for interstate commerce.
- Maintaining records that explain the basis of wage differentials paid to employees of opposite sex for equal work.
- Displaying a poster (from the regional office of the Wage and Hour division) informing employees of the provisions of the law.
- States' Minimum Wage and Maximum Hour Laws that also establish minimum wage rates for covered employees. Where both federal and state laws cover the same employee, the higher of two rates prevails (e.g., Oregon—$7.80 per hour).
- The State's wage orders that also can affect pay periods, pay for call-in and waiting times, rest and meal periods, absences, meals and lodging, uniforms, etc.

2 LEARNING OBJECTIVE

Self-Study Quizzes appear throughout each chapter and test the understanding of major concepts.

SELF-STUDY QUIZ 5-3 *The FUTA taxable wages of Davies Company during 2008 follow. List the amount and the due date of each deposit of FUTA taxes for the year.*

	Amount	Due Date
1st Quarter—$66,000	$________	________
2nd Quarter—$64,000	$________	________
3rd Quarter—$42,000	$________	________
4th Quarter—$25,000	$________	________

Use of Marginal Icons ("On the Net," "News Alert," "IRS Connection," and "On the Job") helps integrate the real world applications of this facts-intensive area of study. "On the Net" icons allow optional integration of Internet research sites for learners, like the example that follows:

on the *NET*

http://www.eeoc.gov/ This **EEOC Homepage** overviews guidelines and services of the Equal Employment Opportunity Commission (EEOC).

The **icons** in each chapter highlight the most current forms, instructions, and wage and tax laws available.

MATCHING QUIZ

_____ 1. Employee's earnings record
_____ 2. Payroll register
_____ 3. Executive orders
_____ 4. Fair Labor Standards Act
_____ 5. Immigration Reform and Control Act
_____ 6. Unemployment insurance taxes
_____ 7. Vesting
_____ 8. Disability benefits
_____ 9. Income tax
_____ 10. Hiring notice

A. Also known as the Federal Wage and Hour Law.
B. Record used in preparing employee's W-2.
C. Protection against losses due to work-related injuries.
D. Multicolumn form used to summarize data needed each paydate.
E. Levy on earnings of most employees and deducted from their gross pay.
F. Antidiscrimination orders for employers with contracts involving federal funds.
G. Form sent to Payroll Department so that new employee is added to the payroll.
H. Form I-9 to be completed by all new employees.
I. Levied by both federal and state governments.
J. Conveys to employees the right to share in a retirement fund.

Thorough End-of-Chapter Materials include matching exercises, review questions, discussion questions, practical problems, and case problems.

CONTINUING PAYROLL PROBLEM

Refer to the partially completed payroll register that you worked on at the end of Chapter 4. You will now compute the employer's liability for unemployment taxes (FUTA and SUTA) for the pay of January 14. These computations will be used at the end of Chapter 6 in recording the payroll tax entries.

To compute the employer's liability for unemployment taxes, proceed as follows:

1. Enter each employee's gross earnings in the Taxable Earnings—FUTA and SUTA columns.
2. Total the Taxable Earnings—FUTA and SUTA columns.
3. At the bottom of your payroll register, compute the following for the total payroll:

a. Net FUTA tax. Since this is the first pay period of the year, none of the employees are near the $7,000 ceiling; therefore, each employee's gross earnings is subject to the FUTA tax.

b. SUTA tax. Since Kipley Company is a new employer, Pennsylvania has assigned the company a contribution rate of 3.5% on the first $8,000 of each employee's earnings. Employees pay 0.09% on total gross pay.

NOTE: Retain your partially completed payroll register for use at the end of Chapter 6.

The final payroll project can be completed manually (Chapter 7) or by using the computer (Appendix A). A Payroll CD, now in Windows, is free with the purchase of the text. Additionally, the payroll project can be completed on Excel templates. For the Computerized Payroll Project and the Excel Templates, there is a short version available.

Instructor Resources

SOLUTIONS MANUAL/TEST BANK/ACHIEVEMENT TESTS (ISBN: 0-324-65628-9)

The Solutions Manual/Test Bank contains the Learning Objectives, Chapter Contents and the solutions to the End-of-Chapter material, including the Payroll Project. The Achievement Tests and Key are included in the Solutions Manual and are available for reprinting.

INSTRUCTOR'S RESOURCE CD-ROM WITH Exam*View* (ISBN: 0-324-65630-0)

This complete instructor resource on CD-ROM contains the downloadable Solutions Manual, Test Bank, Achievements Test and Key, Excel Solutions, PowerPoint Presentation, and [ExamView] Computerized Testing Software.

WEB SITE

The Bieg Web site provides the instructor password-protected access to the Solutions Manual, the Achievement Tests and Key, and the PowerPoint Presentations. Visit today at www.thomsonedu.com/accounting/bieg.

Student Resources

WEB SITE—www.thomsonedu.com/accounting/bieg

The Bieg Web site also offers downloadable supplements, crossword puzzles, payroll and tax Web links, and interactive quizzes.

ACKNOWLEDGEMENTS

Our sincere appreciation is due to the many instructors and students who have contributed suggestions to make the textbook more interesting, understandable, and practical to those who pursue the study of payroll accounting. As a result of their very helpful recommendations, the textbook will better satisfy the learning needs of students and the teaching needs of instructors. Reviewers for the current edition of the textbook include:

Ali Anwar
Heald College

Donna Ascenzi
Bryant & Stratton College

Catherine Barton
Cecil Community College

Judy Benish
Fox Valley Technical College

Anne Bikofsky
The College of Westchester

Charles Black
Heald College, Stockton

Margaret Black
San Jacinto College North

Maryann Bolton
Central Community College—Hastings

Judi Chowen
Cerritos Community College

Robbin Richard Clouser, J.D.
Penn Commercial Business & Technical School

Diane Clugston
Cambria-Rowe Business College

Chris P. Crosby
York Technical College

Barbara Dickson
MTI College

Rebecca M. Floor
Greenville Technical College

Kathleen Fratianne
Blackhawk Technical College

Joseph M. Galante, CPA
King's College

Janet Garver
Mid Michigan Community College—Harrison

Barbara Gershowitz
Nashville State Technical Community College

Florence Godat
Northeast State Technical Community College

Susan Greene
Cloud County Community College

Patrick Haggerty
Lansing Community College

Ken Haling
Gateway Technical College

Scott Hanson
Empire College

Merrily Hoffman
San Jacinto College—Central

Carol Hutchinson
Asheville-Buncombe Technical Community College

Deb Jones
Iowa Lakes Community College

George Kippenhan
Gateway Technical College—Kenosha

Brenda Lauer
Northeastern Junior College

Anne C. Lewis
Edgecombe Community College

Diane Litynski
Mildred-Elley

Claudette Milligan
Trident Technical College

Norma R. Montague
Central Carolina Community College

Karen Mozingo
Pitt Community College

Tim Nygaard
Madisonville Community College

Stephen E. Paris
The College of Westchester

Charles Parks
Central Carolina Community College

Shirley Powell
Arkansas State University—Beebe

Jeanne Reed
American River College

Carol Rogers
Central New Mexico Community College

Belinda Sasala
Bohecker College

Billy Sexton
York Technical College

Karen Spray
Northeast Community College

Robert L. Taylor
Mayland Community College

Paul Vanderbosch, CPA
Southwestern College

Scott Wallace
Blue Mountain Community College

Debra Walsh
Carteret Community College

Karen Willcut
Mendocino College

Carol Wilhelm
San Joaquin Valley College

David L. Zagorodney
Heald College

Prior reviewers of the textbook include:

Dawn Addington
Central New Mexico Community College

Donna Atkins
Bee County College—Kingsville

Richard Barden
Southwestern Community College

Catherine Barton
Cecil Community College

Jan Batman
Indian Hills Community College

Judy Benish
Fox Valley Technical College

Donna Bersch
Fox Valley Technical College—OshKosh

Margaret Black
San Jacinto College North

Maryann Bolton
Central Community College—Hastings

LeRoy Bowman
Ivy Technical State College

Walt Boyll
Central Community College

James Bronder, CPA, CMA
The University of Northwestern Ohio

Linda Carey
Mid-State Technical College

James Carriger, PhD
Ventura College

Judi Chowen
Cerritos Community College

Karen G. Collins
Horry-Georgetown Technical College

Don Craig
Del Mar College

Chris P. Crosby
York Technical College

Giles Dail
Edgecombe Community College

Lee Daugherty
Lorain County Community College

Howard Director
Nassau Community College

Martin L. Epstein, CPA, MBA
Albuquerque TVI Community College

Walter Erickson
St. Cloud Technical College

Rebecca M. Floor
Greenville Technical College

Kathleen Fratianne
Blackhawk Technical College

Janet Garver
Mid Michigan Community College—Harrison

Barbara Gershowitz
Nashville State Technical Community College

Florence Godat
Northeast State Technical Community College

Harry Gray
Ivy Technical State College—Indianapolis

Susan Greene
Cloud County Community College

Darwin Grimm
Iowa Lakes Community College

Dale Guimont
Anoka Technical College

Patrick Haggerty
Lansing Community College

Ken Haling
Gateway Technical College

Jillane Halverson
Winona Technical College

Sara Harris
Arapahoe Community College

Paul Haugen
Wisconsin Indianhead Technical College

Ron Haugen
St. Cloud Technical College

Kay Hauser
Beaufort County Community College

Rebecca Helms
Ivy Technical State College

Brenda Hester
Volunteer State Community College

Linda Hischke
Northeast Wisconsin Technical College

Merrily Hoffman
San Jacinto College—Central

Japan Holmes, Jr.
Savannah Technical Institute

Jerry Hoogers
Hennepin Technical College

Sharon Hoover
Scott Community College

Carol Hutchinson
Asheville-Buncombe Technical Community College

Dawn A. Humburg, CPA
Iowa Central Community College

Verne Ingram
Red Rocks Community College

Betty Jolly
Caldwell Community College

Deb Jones
Iowa Lakes Community College

George Kippenhan
Gateway Technical College—Kenosha

Ronald Kremer
Wright State University

Brenda Lauer
Northeastern Junior College

Anne C. Lewis
Edgecombe Community College

Rosemary Lint
Umpqua Community College

J. Thomas Love
Walters State Community College

Dorinda Lynn
Pensacola Junior College

Patricia Lynn
Pasadena City College

David Mack
Atlanta Area Technical College

Dennis Mackey
Gogebic Community College

Robert Maloney
University of Alaska—Anchorage

Cynthia Mascola
Trumbull Business College

David Miller
Community College of San Francisco

Claudette Milligan
Trident Technical College

Norma R. Montague
Central Carolina Community College

Carol Moore
Northwest State Community College

Paul Morgan
Mississippi Gulf Coast Community College

Karen Mozingo
Pitt Community College

Jim Murray
Western Wisconsin Technical College

Lanny Nelms
Gwinnett Technical Institute

Jon Nitschke
Montana State University, Great Falls Campus

Tim Nygaard
Madisonville Community College

John Palafox
Ventura College

Charles Parks
Central Carolina Community College

Keith Patterson
Ricks College

Barbara Jeanne Pauer BS, MBA, CMA
Gateway Technical College

David Peterson
Madison Area Technical College

Shirley Powell
Arkansas State University—Beebe

Barbara Prince
Cambridge Community College

Alan Ransom
Cypress College

Jeanne Reed
American River College

Joe Rivkin
Harper College

Teresa Roberts
Wilson Technical Community College

Pam Sager
North Central Missouri College

Carol Schroeder
Fox Valley Technical College

William Serafin
Community College of Alleghany County—South Campus

Billy Sexton
York Technical College

Jon Smith
Vermillion Community College

Rene Smith
Horry-Georgetown Technical College

Albert Spencer
Kauai Community College

Karen Spray
Northeast Community College

Lyle Stelter
Red Wing/Winona Technical College

Kellie A. Storrer, CPA
Golden West College and Cypress College

Larry Swisher
Muskegon Community College

Stella Tavares
Hawaii Community College

Robert L. Taylor
Mayland Community College

Lynette E. Teal, BS, MS
Western Wisconsin Technical College

Vicki Vorell
Cuyahoga Community College

Philip Waits
Harry Ayers State Technical College

Scott Wallace
Blue Mountain Community College

Debra Walsh
Carteret Community College

Alison Watkins
Valdosta Technical Institute

Carole Weber
Alexandria Technical College

Michael Welser
Feather River College

Mary AnnWhitehurst
GriffinTechnical Institute

Karen Willcut
Mendocino College

In addition, the authors would like to thank the following content-providers and author-contributors to the 2008 edition:

Bernie Hill, *Spokane Falls Community College*, Spokane, WA, for preparing the Excel spreadsheet templates for the text problems and Continuing Payroll Problem, and for verifying the text and all elements of the Web site.

Mark Sears for preparing the spreadsheet templates that accompany the Payroll Project as well as the Excel primer.

Tim Nygaard, *Madisonville Community College*, Madisonville, KY, for authoring the Internet Activities in the text and providing the Payroll Tax Internet links.

Lisa Swallow, *University of Montana, College of Technology*, Missoula, MT, for preparing the PowerPoint Lectures available on the Web site.

ABOUT THE AUTHORS

Bernard J. Bieg

After receiving his Masters in Business Administration from the University of Notre Dame and passing the Certified Public Accountants' exam in the early 1970's, Bernard Bieg turned his attention toward a career in teaching. He has been a professor at Bucks County Community College for more than 30 years. During that time, he has taught the whole spectrum of accounting offerings, including payroll accounting. He has maintained his ties with the business world by working as an internal auditor for a local non-profit organization.

His association with this textbook began in 1977 as a co-author with one of the originators of the book, Bill Keeling.

Judith A. Toland

Judith Toland received her Masters Degree in Education from Temple University in 2002, her Bachelors Degree in Business Administration—Accounting from Bloomsburg University in 1981 and her Associate's Degree from Bucks County Community College in Business Administration in 1979. Judy has taught Accounting courses at BCCC since 1989 and is currently an Associate Professor.

CONTENTS

chapter

1

The Need for Payroll and Personnel Records

LEARNING OBJECTIVES

After studying this chapter, you should be able to:

① Identify the various laws that affect employers in their payroll operations.

② Examine the recordkeeping requirements of these laws.

③ Explain the importance of a thorough recordkeeping system.

④ Describe the employment procedures generally followed in a Human Resources Department.

⑤ Recognize the various personnel records used by businesses and know the type of information shown on each form.

⑥ Outline the procedures employed in a typical payroll accounting system.

⑦ Identify the *payroll register* and the *employee's earnings record.*

As an employee, your favorite day of the week is probably *Payday*! However, your paycheck is the last step in a process that starts with the employment application, the interview, the testing, the hiring, the wage rates, the withholding taxes, and the payroll records.

As an employer, knowledge of tax compliance can save you time, can free you of levies for penalties and interest, and can help you avoid unnecessary lawsuits.

What kind of information can be asked of job applicants? Is it worthwhile to check references? Can credit reports be considered? The impact that various federal laws have on personnel and payroll operations will be explored in this chapter, and you will get a brief look at topics that are covered in detail in subsequent chapters.

No matter the size of the company, the profitability, the product or service being sold, the type of organization, employees have to be paid. This task has become more difficult as numerous regulations have been passed. The payroll person is no longer the employee stuck in the corner who only appears on payday to distribute paychecks. The job responsibilities have multiplied and now require persons with advanced knowledge in the area of payroll to handle the position.

Payroll professionals are responsible for processing over four billion pay statements each year to over a hundred million people in the workforce of the United States. The processing of payrolls allows no margin for error. Employees, employers, and government agencies monitor the work performed by payroll professionals. A payroll accounting system is the only operation in a business that is almost completely governed by various federal, state, and local laws and regulations. Rules establish who is an employee, what is time worked, when overtime is to be paid, what deductions are made, when to pay an employee, and when taxes are paid. Lack of compliance with these laws and regulations can result in both fines and back-pay awards.

The payroll professional has risen in the ranks of the accounting profession and now demands salaries commensurate with his or her peers. The confidentiality of the payroll information from each employee's pay rate to the garnishments imposed on some employees has tightened the link to the upper management teams. The confidence and trust that must be placed in payroll professionals have made them an integral part of the "inner circle." This chapter briefly examines the various laws that affect employers in their payroll operations and the payroll and personnel records that they use to meet the requirements of the laws. First, however, let's take a brief look at payroll accounting as a profession.

The Payroll Profession

A 2005 biennial survey conducted for the American Payroll Association revealed that the average salary of senior payroll managers was $69,280, while that of entry-level payroll clerks was $28,935.

Typically, an entry-level payroll clerk collects, reviews, approves, and records time records. The clerk also updates attendance records, including vacation, sick, and personal days. Once a payroll is processed, the clerk reviews the information to ensure the accuracy of each employee's pay statement. Subsequent job responsibilities will include entering the following information into the payroll system:

1. Time-worked data.
2. Pay rate changes.
3. Tax rate changes.
4. Employee-authorized payroll deductions.
5. New employee information.
6. Marital and employee allowance changes.

Providing information to the Finance Department concerning the amounts to be paid for taxes, health insurance premiums, retirement plans, etc., may also be part of the evolving duties of the advancing payroll professional. One of the final stages involves the completion of payroll tax returns, employee information returns, federal and state census returns, and fringe benefit and welfare plan returns.

Payroll professionals must keep abreast of the changes in their field so that they can remain technically proficient. This need has been met by an association of payroll practitioners—the American Payroll Association (APA). Membership in the association is open to anyone interested in or engaged in the support of payroll accounting. The APA offers professional training seminars and various publications to its members. Each year, the APA administers an examination for the payroll accountant and awards a certificate to those who pass the exam (Certified Payroll Professional). This testing and certification process has

FIGURE 1–1

APA Code of Ethics

1. To be mindful of the personal aspect of the payroll relationship between employer and employee and to ensure that harmony is maintained through constant concern for the Payroll Professional's fellow employees.
2. To strive for perfect accuracy and timeliness of all payroll activities.
3. To keep abreast of the state of the payroll art with regard to developments in payroll technologies.
4. To be current with legislative developments, actions on the part of regulatory bodies, and the like, in so far as they affect payroll.
5. To maintain the absolute confidentiality of the payroll, within the procedures of the employer.
6. To refrain from using Association activities for one's personal self-interest or financial gain.
7. To take as one's commitment the enhancement of one's professional abilities through the resources of the American Payroll Association.
8. To support one's fellow Payroll Professionals, both within and outside one's organization.

helped the payroll profession to gain recognition in the business community. The APA has also established guidelines for the conduct of the payroll professional. This "Code of Ethics," shown in Figure 1–1, sets the direction for the profession.[1]

One of a number of publications designed to provide current information to the practitioner is published by the Research Institute of America, Inc. This biweekly publication is entitled ***Payroll Guide,*** and it is a comprehensive review of changes in regulations affecting payroll reporting.[2]

Fair Labor Standards Act

1 LEARNING OBJECTIVE

FLSA (referred to as the Federal Wage and Hour Law) is covered in Chapter 2. The outline of the law deals with:

- Minimum wage ($5.85 per hour—end of 2007) and overtime pay requirements. In addition, equal pay for equal work, employment of child labor, public service contracts, and wage garnishment.
- Coverage of employers engaged in interstate commerce or in production of goods and services for interstate commerce.
- Maintaining records that explain the basis of wage differentials paid to employees of opposite sex for equal work.
- Displaying a poster (from the regional office of the Wage and Hour division) informing employees of the provisions of the law.
- States' Minimum Wage and Maximum Hour Laws that also establish minimum wage rates for covered employees. Where both federal and state laws cover the same employee, the higher of two rates prevails (e.g., Oregon—$7.80 per hour).
- The State's wage orders that also can affect pay periods, pay for call-in and waiting times, rest and meal periods, absences, meals and lodging, uniforms, etc.

NEWS // ALERT //

Recent legislation raised the minimum wage in a series of three steps (the last one in 2009) to $7.25 per hour.

2 LEARNING OBJECTIVE

on the NET

http://www.dol.gov/esa/minwage/america.htm This Web site contains the minimum wage laws by state in map and text form.

1 For more information on the organization, write to American Payroll Association, 660 North Main Avenue, Suite 100, San Antonio, TX 78205-1217; Tel: 210-224-6406.

2 *Payroll Guide* is published by the Research Institute of America, Inc., 395 Hudson Street, New York, NY 10014; Tel: 1-800-431-9025.

Federal Insurance Contributions Act

Chapter 3 covers FICA (social security) in detail; however, the basic provisions of the act deal with:

- Tax on employees (set percent of their gross wages) and employers (match of the employees' contributions) for the Federal Old-Age and Survivors' Trust Fund and the Federal Disability Insurance Trust Fund.
- Separate tax on employers and employees to finance the Health Insurance Plan—Medicare.
- Tax on net earnings of the self-employed individual (Self-Employment Contributions Act—SECA).
- Making payments to persons who are entitled to benefits under these social security taxes.

Income Tax Withholding Laws

Chapter 4 covers income tax withholding, but basically:

- **Income tax** is levied on the earnings of most employees and is deducted from their gross pay.
- Income taxes can be imposed by the federal, the state, and the local governments.
- Federal Income Tax (FIT) employs a percentage formula used by each employer to withhold a specified amount from each wage payment.
- State tax rates vary from state to state.

on the *NET*

http://www.payroll-taxes.com/ *Payroll Tax Information Site.* This site contains addresses, phone numbers, form numbers (with explanations), and filing dates for federal and state taxing authorities.

Unemployment Tax Acts

Chapter 5 covers unemployment taxes with a detailed discussion of:

- Tax levied on employers (Federal Unemployment Tax Act—FUTA) that is used to pay state and federal administrative expenses of the unemployment program.
- A credit granted against most of the FUTA tax if the employer pays a state unemployment tax.
- State unemployment taxes (SUTA) on employers imposed by all states. These taxes are used to pay unemployment benefits.
- Standards set by the Social Security Act that result in a high degree of uniformity in the requirements of state unemployment laws.
- Employers' need to be aware of the SUTA laws in the states where they operate.

Recordkeeping Requirements

Although the laws do impose recordkeeping requirements on employers, no specific form of record is mandated. Figure 1–2 lists the specific information needed and the retention time periods required.

Fair Employment Laws

Federal and state legislations have been enacted to enforce **fair employment practices**. Many of these laws deal with discrimination on the basis of age, race, color, religion, gender, or national origin.

on the *JOB*

The Supreme Court has ruled that the Civil Rights Act does not protect U.S. citizens working abroad.

CIVIL RIGHTS ACT OF 1964

Title VII of the Civil Rights Act of 1964, entitled "Equal Employment Opportunity," provides for several fair employment practices. The act, as amended, forbids employers to discriminate in hiring, firing, promoting, compensating, or in any other condition of employment on the basis of race, color, religion, gender, or national origin. Guidelines,

FIGURE 1–2

Summary of Information Required by Major Federal Payroll Laws

	Item	Fair Labor Standards Act	Social Security	Income Tax Withholding	Unemployment Tax
EMPLOYEE DATA	Name	Yes	Yes	Yes	Yes
	Address	Yes	Yes	Yes	Yes
	Gender	Yes	....	....	....
	Date of birth	Yes	....	....	....
	Social Security Number	Yes	Yes	Yes	Yes
	Withholding allowances claimed	....	....	Yes	....
	Occupation	Yes	Yes	Yes	Yes
	Period employed	....	Yes	Yes	Yes
	State where services rendered	....	Yes	....	Yes
EMPLOYMENT DATA	Beginning and ending dates of employee's employment	....	Yes	Yes	....
	Day and time of day when workweek begins	Yes	....	....	....
	Regular hourly rate of pay	Yes	....	....	....
	Basis of wage payments; e.g., $9.25 per hour; $74.00 per day	Yes	....	....	....
	Hours worked each day	Yes	....	....	....
	Hours worked each week	Yes	....	....	....
	Daily or weekly straight-time pay, exclusive of overtime pay	Yes	....	....	....
	Amount and nature of exempt pay	Yes	....	....	....
	Weekly overtime pay	Yes	....	....	....
	Total additions to or deductions from wages	Yes	....	....	....
	Total remuneration for payroll period	Yes	Yes	Yes	....
	Total remuneration for calendar year	....	Yes	....	Yes
	Date of payment	Yes	Yes	Yes	Yes
	Payroll period	Yes	Yes	Yes	Yes
TAX DATA	Employee's wages subject to tax for payroll period	....	Yes	Yes	....
	Employee's wages subject to tax for calendar year	....	Yes	....	Yes
	Taxable remuneration—if different from total remuneration, reason for difference	....	Yes	Yes	Yes
	Tax deductions from employee's wages	....	Yes	Yes	Yes
	Date tax collected if other than date of payment	....	Yes	Yes	....
	Tax paid by employer but not deducted from employee's wages	....	Yes	Yes	Yes
GEN'L	Specific form of records	No	No	No	No
	Number of years records must be kept	2–3	4*	4*	4*

*Four years after the due date of the payment of the tax to which the records relate.

on the *NET*

http://www.eeoc.gov/ This **EEOC Homepage** overviews guidelines and services of the Equal Employment Opportunity Commission (EEOC).

established by the Equal Employment Opportunity Commission (EEOC), also include physical characteristics in the definition of national origin discrimination. For example, unnecessary height or weight requirements could exclude some individuals on the basis of their national origin. The EEOC has also declared that sexual harassment violates the Civil Rights Act. Unwelcome sexual advances, requests for sexual favors, and other verbal or physical conduct of a sexual nature can constitute sexual harassment.

The EEOC prohibits unions from excluding or segregating their members on these bases, and employment agencies may not refer or refuse to refer applicants for employment on the basis of race, color, religion, gender, or national origin.

This act covers all employers who engage in an industry "affecting commerce" and who employ 15 or more workers for each working day in each of 20 or more weeks in the current or preceding calendar year. Employers specifically excluded from coverage of the fair employment practices include the U.S. government (state and local governments are covered), a corporation wholly owned by the United States, Indian tribes, private membership clubs (other than labor unions) exempt from federal income tax, and religious societies in the employment of members of a particular religion to work on the societies' religious activities. Although the U.S. government is classified as an exempt employer, the act states that the policy of the U.S. government provides equal employment opportunities without discrimination and that the president should use his existing authority to implement this policy.

Title VII does not protect an employee from arbitrary treatment or dismissal. As long as the employer applies these policies in a nondiscriminatory manner, Title VII requirements have not been violated.

To accomplish the purpose of eliminating discrimination, the EEOC tries to obtain voluntary compliance with the law before filing a court action for an injunction. It can institute court proceedings for an injunction if it believes that any person or group of persons is not complying with the law. Where a state or local law forbids discriminatory practices, relief must first be sought under the state or local law before a complaint is filed with the Commission. In most states, a special commission or the state Department of Labor administers the laws and may authorize cease-and-desist orders that are enforceable in the courts.

EXECUTIVE ORDERS

Employers not subject to the Title VII coverage discussed above may come within the scope of the Civil Rights Act by reason of a contract or a subcontract involving federal funds. In a series of **executive orders,** the federal government has banned, in employment on government contracts, discrimination based on race, color, religion, gender, or national origin.

AGE DISCRIMINATION IN EMPLOYMENT ACT

on the *JOB*

The EEOC has approved the use of "Help Wanted" ads targeting older workers. It was ruled that these ads do not violate the age discrimination laws.

The Age Discrimination in Employment Act of 1967 (ADEA) prohibits employers, employment agencies, and labor unions from discriminating on the basis of age in their employment practices. The act covers employers engaged in an industry affecting interstate commerce (who employ 20 or more workers), employment agencies, and labor unions. The act also covers federal, state, and local government employees, other than elected officials and certain aides not covered by civil service. The ADEA provides protection for virtually all workers over 40. A key exception is executives who are 65 or older and who have held high policy-making positions during the two-year period prior to retirement. If such an employee is entitled to an annual retirement benefit from the employer of at least $44,000, the employee can be forcibly retired.

In order to prove compliance with the various fair employment laws, employers must keep accurate personnel and payroll records. All employment applications, along with notations as to their disposition and the reasons for the disposition, should be retained. All records pertaining to promotions, discharges, seniority plans, merit programs, incentive payment plans, etc., should also be retained.

AMERICANS WITH DISABILITIES ACT

The Americans with Disabilities Act of 1990 (ADA) prohibits employers with 15 or more employees, employment agencies, labor organizations, or joint labor-management committees from discriminating against qualified persons with disabilities because of their disability.

The prohibition of disability-based discrimination applies to job application procedures, hiring, advancement, termination, compensation, job training, and other conditions of employment. In addition, reasonable accommodations, such as wheelchair-accessible restrooms and ramps for qualified disabled job applicants and workers, must be provided.

Other Federal Laws Affecting the Need for Payroll and Personnel Records

Generally, the payroll and personnel records and reports that a business prepares and retains to meet the requirements of the laws already discussed provide sufficient information needed under the laws outlined in Figure 1–3, on page 1-10, and discussed below.

FEDERAL PERSONAL RESPONSIBILITY AND WORK OPPORTUNITY RECONCILIATION ACT OF 1996

The Federal Personal Responsibility and Work Opportunity Reconciliation Act of 1996 (PRWORA) mandates that all states must establish new-hire reporting programs. Every employer is required to report the name, address, and social security number on each new employee and the employer's name, address, and federal employer identification number *within 20 days of hire* to the appropriate state agency. In many states, submission of a copy of the employee's W-4 form (Employee's Withholding Allowance Certificate) will satisfy the reporting requirement. This information must then be forwarded by the state to the federal Office of Child Support Enforcement (OCSE) for entry into the National Directory of New Hires.

Employers with operations in more than one state may file one report with the state of their choice. That state is then to share the information with the other states.

The main reason for this requirement is to help in the enforcement of child support obligations. In addition, it will reduce fraud in the unemployment, workers' compensation, and public assistance programs. Failure to report this information can result in fines of up to $25.00 per new hire. Even though under federal law employers do not have to report this same information on independent contractors, some states (California, Iowa, and New Hampshire) do require such reporting.

IMMIGRATION REFORM AND CONTROL ACT OF 1986

The Immigration Reform and Control Act of 1986 (IRCA) bars employers from hiring and retaining aliens unauthorized to work in the United States. It also requires all employers to verify employment eligibility for all individuals by examining the employee's verification documents and having the employee complete ***Form I-9, Employment Eligibility Verification*** (not illustrated). Form I-9 lists the documents that an employee must furnish to the employer. These documents identify the employee and, if an alien, verify authorization to work in the United States. Photocopying new employees' I-9 documents is permitted but not required. If done, photocopying should apply to ***all*** new employees.

Form I-9 must be completed ***within three business days*** of the date the employee starts work. The process of collecting, filing, and retaining I-9 forms should be a centralized function so that inconsistencies are eliminated. The forms (I-9) should be filed separately from other personnel records so that the information contained in the forms is kept private. The form must be retained for three years after the date of hiring or for one year after the date the employment is terminated, whichever is later. Terminated employees who are rehired within three years of the date of the initially filed Form I-9 need only reverify the information to the employer.

NEWS// ALERT//

Legislation now permits electronic completion and storage of Forms I-9.

FIGURE 1–3

Federal Laws Affecting the Need for Payroll and Personnel Records

Law	Coverage	Contract Dollar Minimum	Major Provisions
Davis-Bacon Act (1931)	Laborers for contractors or subcontractors on federal government contracts for construction, alteration, or repair of public buildings or works.	$2,000	Minimum wage set by Secretary of Labor (weight is given to union wage scale prevailing in the project area).
Walsh-Healey Public Contracts Act (1936)	Laborers for contractors who furnish materials, supplies, articles, and equipment to any agency of the United States.	$10,000	Single minimum wage determined by Secretary of Labor for all covered employees in a given industry.
McNamara-O'Hara Service Contract Act (1965)	Service employees on contracts with the United States or the District of Columbia for the furnishing of services.	$2,500	Minimum wage set by Secretary of Labor based on minimum wage found to be prevailing in that locality.
Occupational Safety and Health Act (OSHA) (1970)	Any business involved in interstate commerce.	-0-	Sets specific occupational and health standards for employers; requires that records be kept of work-related injuries, illnesses, and deaths.
Vocational Rehabilitation Act (1973)	Companies with federal agency contracts.	$2,500	Must include in the contract an affirmative action clause requiring that the handicapped applicant or employee will be given appropriate consideration.
Vietnam Era Veterans' Readjustment Act (1974)	Government contractors with federal contracts or subcontracts.	$10,000	Requires contractors to take affirmative action to employ and advance in employment qualified veterans of the Vietnam era and disabled veterans.

The U.S. Citizenship and Immigration Services (USCIS) can levy fines if an audit uncovers recordkeeping violations. Civil penalties range from $100 to $1,000 for each violation. Any person or entity found to have unlawfully employed an unauthorized alien is subject to civil fines ranging from $250 to $11,000. Criminal penalties are assessed where a pattern of discriminatory practice is found.

FAMILY AND MEDICAL LEAVE ACT OF 1993

The Family and Medical Leave Act of 1993 (FMLA) requires employers that have 50 or more employees within a 75-mile radius, for at least 20 weeks in the current or preceding calendar year, to grant workers unpaid leave for a family or medical emergency. In cases of childbirth, adoption, or serious illness of the employee or the employee's child, spouse, or parent, the employer must offer the worker as many as 12 weeks of unpaid leave. The leave may be used all at once, or in separate weeks, days, or hours. However, the leave must be taken within 12 months of the qualifying event.

During the leave, employers must continue health-care coverage, and they must also guarantee that the employee will return to the same job or to a comparable position. The employer can substitute an employee's earned paid leave for any part of the 12-week family leave.

Employers can exempt the following:

1. The highest-paid 10 percent of their workforce.
2. Those who have not worked at least one year and at least 1,250 hours in the previous 12 months for the company.

NEWS // ALERT //

A survey by the Labor Department found that only 2 to 4 percent of eligible workers have taken time off under FMLA. Of these, more than half did so to attend to their own health needs.

UNIFORMED SERVICES EMPLOYMENT AND REEMPLOYMENT RIGHTS ACT OF 1994

The Uniformed Services Employment and Reemployment Rights Act (USERRA) gives military personnel the right to take leaves of absences from their civilian jobs for active military service and to return to their jobs with accrued seniority. The reinstatement must be to the employee's original position or its equivalent, except for the dishonorably discharged. In addition, the return must be granted within two weeks of the job request, and health benefits must be started without any waiting period.

EMPLOYEE RETIREMENT INCOME SECURITY ACT OF 1974

The Employee Retirement Income Security Act of 1974 (ERISA) covers employee pension and welfare plans established or maintained by any employer or employee organization representing employees engaged in commerce or in any industry or activity affecting commerce. The legislation safeguards pension funds by regulating how the funds are to be raised and disbursed, who controls them, and what is to be done when funds are insufficient to pay promised benefits. The law ***does not*** require every employer to establish a pension plan; however, if there is an employer's pension plan, every employee is eligible *after reaching age 21 or completing one year of service*, whichever is later.

ERISA was designed primarily to ensure that workers covered by private pension plans receive benefits from those plans in accordance with their credited years of service with their employers. **Vesting** conveys to employees the right to share in a retirement fund if they are terminated before the normal retirement age. The vesting process is linked to the number of years needed for workers to earn an equity in their retirement plans and to become entitled to full or partial benefits at some future date if they leave the company before retirement. Once vested, a worker has the right to receive a pension at retirement age, based on years of covered service, even though the worker may not be working for the firm at that time. Currently, the law provides for full vesting of the employer's contributions in *three years or gradually over six years* (20 percent after two years and 20 percent a year for the next four years). The plan administrator must file an annual report (Form 5500) with the federal government by the end of the seventh month following the close of the plan year.

To protect against potential benefit losses because of a plan's termination, ERISA set up a government insurance program, the Pension Benefit Guaranty Corporation, to pay any benefits that could not be met with funds from the plan.

DISCLOSURE REQUIREMENTS The reporting and disclosure requirements set forth by ERISA have tremendous implications on the recordkeeping requirements of employers. Informational reports must be filed with the U.S. Department of Labor, the IRS, and the government insurance program. In general, the reports consist of descriptions of the plans and the annual financial data. The plan descriptions include the eligibility requirements for participation and for benefits; provisions for nonforfeitable pension benefits; circumstances that may result in disqualification, loss, or denial of benefits; and procedures for presenting claims. The annual reports include financial statements and schedules showing the current value of plan assets and liabilities, receipts and disbursements, and employer contributions; the assets held for investment purposes; insurance data; and an opinion by an independent qualified public accountant. Upon written request from the participants, the administrator must also furnish a statement, not more than once in a 12-month period, of the total benefits accrued, accrued benefits that are vested, if any, or the earliest date on which accrued benefits will become vested.

Other State Laws Affecting the Need for Payroll and Personnel Records

States have enacted other laws that have a direct bearing on the payroll and personnel records that an employer must maintain and on the rights that must be extended to employees.

WORKERS' COMPENSATION LAWS

Workers' compensation insurance protects employees and their dependents against losses due to work-related injury, illness, or death. Most states have passed laws that require employers to provide workers' compensation insurance through one of the following plans:

1. Contribution to a state compensation insurance fund administered by an insurance department of the state.
2. Purchase of workers' compensation insurance from a private insurance company authorized by the state to issue this type of policy.
3. Establishment of a self-insurance plan, approved by the state, under which the company bears all risk itself.

Benefits are paid to cover medical bills and also to provide a percentage of the worker's regular wages during the time that the employee is unable to work.

The employer bears the cost of the workers' compensation insurance premiums, except in Montana, New Mexico, Oregon, and Washington, where both the employer and the employee contribute to the workers' compensation fund.

The insurance premiums are often based upon the total gross payroll of the business and may be stated in terms of an amount for each $100 of weekly wages paid to employees. The premium rates vary among types of jobs.

EXAMPLE

The rate for the office workers of the Volpe Parts Company is $0.30 per $100 of payroll, while the rate for machine-shop workers is $1.90 per $100 of payroll.

Because the premium rates vary according to the different degrees of danger in various classes of jobs, payroll records must indicate job classifications for rate purposes. If the employer has low accident experience, the rates may be reduced to a certain minimum.

STATE DISABILITY BENEFIT LAWS

California, Hawaii, New Jersey, New York, Rhode Island, and Puerto Rico have passed laws to provide **disability benefits** to employees absent from their jobs because of illness, accident, or disease ***not arising out of their employment.*** Chapter 5 presents further discussion of state disability benefit laws.

Human Resources and Payroll Accounting Systems

LEARNING OBJECTIVE 3

Up to this point, we have seen that a business must keep human resources and payroll records to meet the requirements of the various laws under which it operates. In addition, these records form an integral part of an effective business system. In developing its human resources and payroll accounting systems, a business should design basic forms and records that satisfy the requirements of all the laws applicable to that organization. Properly designed forms and records, as described later in this chapter, not only supply the information required by the various laws but also provide management with information needed in its decision-making process. They also result in savings in both time and work because the necessary information is recorded, stored, retrieved, and distributed economically, efficiently, and quickly.

Before studying the employment process, it is important to examine the close relationship between the Payroll Department and the Human Resources Department. Some businesses consider payroll to be strictly an accounting function and, as such, place it under the direct control of the chief financial officer. However, because of the need for frequent interchange of information between the Payroll and Human Resources departments, the recent trend has been to place payroll under the control of the director of human resources. This movement toward centralization eliminates the duplication of many tasks. With the required information in one department, the process of completing these forms is shortened. Further, questions from employees concerning sick pay, vacation pay, and other benefits can be answered from one source.

Individual computer programs have been developed for the combined needs of payroll and human resources. Information concerning such diverse activities as attendance, retirement benefits, health insurance coverages, and bonus pay is now available to designated employees in the Human Resources Department through a computer terminal.

Human Resources System

4 LEARNING OBJECTIVE

In many medium-size and large companies, the **human resources system** embodies all those procedures and methods related to recruiting, selecting, orienting, training, and terminating personnel. Extensive recordkeeping procedures are required in order to:

1. Provide data for considering promotions and changes in the status and earnings of workers.
2. Provide the information required by various federal, state, and local laws.
3. Justify company actions if investigated by national or state labor relations boards.
4. Justify company actions in discussions with local unions or plant committees.

Before the Payroll Department can pay newly hired employees, the Human Resources Department must process those employees. Figure 1–4, on page 1-14, charts the procedure that the Human Resources Department follows in this hiring process.

A number of companies that manufacture business forms have available standard personnel forms and records that may be successfully used if a business does not care to design its own special forms. In small companies, an application form or an employee history record may be the only document needed. Throughout the remainder of this chapter, several illustrations augment the discussion of the various human resources and payroll records. In these examples, we shall follow Cheryl Crowson from her initial application for employment with the Palmero Maintenance Company to her entry onto the company's payroll records.

REQUISITION FOR PERSONNEL

The **requisition for personnel** form notifies the Human Resources Department of the need for additional or replacement employees. The requisition for new employees can be initiated in a number of ways. Some companies utilize a memo that is forwarded to the Human Resources Department stating the title of the position to be filled, a brief description of the duties of the job, and the salary range. Other companies may use preprinted forms. A preprinted form should indicate the type and number of persons needed, the position to be filled, the rate of pay for the job, the salary range, the date the employee is needed, a summary of any special qualifications, and whether the position is permanent or temporary.

This process can also be completed electronically, through the use of a company's e-mail system. This will help to eliminate unnecessary paperwork. Since some of the information might be considered confidential, the transmission of the request must be safeguarded.

FIGURE 1–4

Human Resources Department Procedure in the Hiring Process

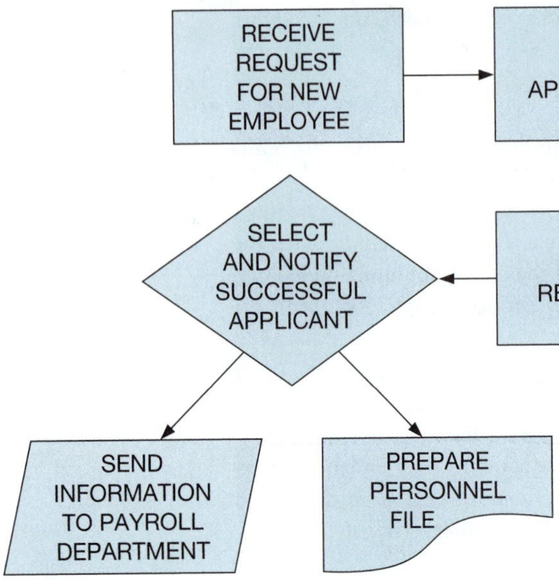

APPLICATION FOR EMPLOYMENT

Every business, regardless of size, should have an application form (similar to that in Figure 1–5 on pages 1-15 and 1-16) to be filled out by a person seeking employment. The **application form** gives the applicant an opportunity to provide complete information as to:

1. Personal information including the name, address, telephone number, and social security number of the applicant.
2. Educational background including a summary of the schools attended, whether the applicant graduated, and degrees conferred.
3. Employment and experience record.
4. Type of employment desired.
5. References.

The application form also provides information for the checking of references, serves as a guide to effective interviewing, and provides information for correlation with data obtained from employment tests. It serves as a permanent record for the business. This form can also be set up to be completed electronically by the applicant.

Employers subject to fair employment laws must make certain that all aspects of the prehire inquiries are free of discrimination on the basis of race, color, religion, gender, national origin, or age. **Prehire inquiries** include questions asked in the employment interview and on application forms, résumés of experience or education required of an applicant, and any kind of written testing. None of the federal civil rights laws specifically outlaws questions concerning the race, color, religion, gender, national origin, or age of an applicant. However, if the employer can offer no logical explanation for asking such questions, the EEOC and the Wage and Hour Administrator view such questions as discriminatory. Of course, prehire questions pertaining to religion, gender, national origin, or age are allowed when these factors are bona fide occupational qualifications for a job.

Asking an applicant's age or date of birth may tend to deter the older worker. Thus, if an application form calls for such information, a statement should appear on that form notifying the applicant that the ADEA prohibits discrimination on the basis of age with respect to individuals who are at least 40.

on the *JOB*

A survey by the American Management Association International found that 38 percent of employers performed psychological testing on job applicants. The tests were directed toward cognitive abilities, analytical thinking, and moral character.

FIGURE 1–5

APPLICATION FOR EMPLOYMENT

An Affirmative Action/Equal Opportunity Employer

POSITION APPLIED FOR *Payroll Accounting Clerk*

This job application is valid only for the position you have listed above. If you wish to be considered for other positions, you will need to complete and/or submit a separate application for each position.

PERSONAL

Name *Cheryl Crowson*

Address *1630 West End Ave.* *Huntington, WV 25703*
STREET CITY STATE ZIP

Telephone *(304) 555-2192* *(304) 555-1618*
WORK HOME OTHER

Social Security Number *199-00-6357*

Have you worked for Palmero Maintenance Company before? YES ☐ NO ☑
If Yes, when? __________

If hired, can you provide proof of identity and eligibility to work in the U.S.? YES ☑ NO ☐

Have you ever been convicted of a felony? YES ☐ NO ☑ If Yes, describe. __________

EDUCATION

NAMES	ADDRESS	ACADEMIC MAJOR	NO. OF YEARS ATTENDED	DEGREE
HIGH SCHOOL *Centennial Senior*	*Stanford Road* *Huntington, WV*	*Business*	*4*	*Yes*
COLLEGE, JUNIOR COLLEGE, OR UNIVERSITY *Huntington Community College*	*Swamp Road* *Huntington, WV*	*Business—Occupational*	*2*	*Associate*
TECHNICAL OR VOCATIONAL				

Other details of training: (Courses) (Cert.)

(Continued)

FIGURE 1–5 (Concluded)

Application for Employment (page 2)

EMPLOYMENT HISTORY

List in sequence all employers, beginning with present/most recent employer, including military experience and apprenticeship. Explain any gaps in employment in comments section below. If additional space is needed, please attach sheet(s).

EMPLOYER	TELEPHONE	DATES EMPLOYED FROM Month Year	TO Month Year	Summarize the nature of the work performed and job responsibilities
Brennan Shipping Co.	(304) 555-1119			
ADDRESS 193 Mountain Blvd., Huntington, WV		5/00	Present	Input time worked
JOB TITLE Payroll Assistant		Hourly Rate/Salary		information, checked
IMMEDIATE SUPERVISOR AND TITLE Helen Young—Payroll Manager		$ 2,850	Per Month	payroll, distributed
REASON FOR LEAVING Want to have more responsibility		Full-time ✓	Part-time	checks
MAY WE CONTACT FOR REFERENCE? ☑ YES ☐ NO ☐ LATER				

EMPLOYER	TELEPHONE	DATES EMPLOYED FROM Month Year	TO Month Year	Summarize the nature of the work performed and job responsibilities
AVS Drug	(304) 555-0101			
ADDRESS Broad & Cherry Sts., Huntington, WV		9/98	5/00	Served as head cashier
JOB TITLE Clerk/Cashier		Hourly Rate/Salary		and maintained inventory
IMMEDIATE SUPERVISOR AND TITLE John Stumley—Manager		$ 8.15	Per Hour	
REASON FOR LEAVING Graduated college—Full-time position		Full-time	Part-time ✓	
MAY WE CONTACT FOR REFERENCE? ☑ YES ☐ NO ☐ LATER				

REFERENCES

Give names of persons we may contact to verify your qualifications for the position:

Name	(Title)	(Occupation)	(Organization)
Edna White	Instructor	Teacher	Huntington Community College

Swamp Road, Huntington, WV (Address) Bus. No.: (304) 555-8000 Home No.: (304) 555-2111

Name	(Title)	(Occupation)	(Organization)
Henry Stone	Controller	Finance	Brennan Shipping Co.

193 Mountain Blvd., Huntington, WV (Address) Bus. No.: (304) 555-1119 Home No.: (304) 555-8710

I hereby certify that all statements made in this application (and accompanying résumé, if any) are true and complete. I understand that any false or misleading statement on this application constitutes sufficient grounds for dismissal, if hired. I further certify that I may lawfully be employed in this country and, if employed, will provide required documentation to verify identity and employment eligibility. In addition, in making this application for employment, I understand that the Company may investigate my employment and educational records. I hereby authorize my current and/or former employer(s) and school(s) to furnish the information requested by the Palmero Maintenance Company.

Signature of Applicant *Cheryl Crowson* Date *June 10, 20--*

REFERENCE INQUIRY

5 LEARNING OBJECTIVE

Before employing an applicant, a company may check some of the references given on the application. Many businesses use a standard **reference inquiry form,** which is usually mailed to the person or company given as a reference. Other companies prefer a telephone reference check because they feel that a more frank opinion of the candidate is received over the telephone. Some companies prefer not to check on personal references given by the job applicant, since these tend to be less objective than business references (e.g., prior employers).

Today, any type of reference checking has taken on new meaning—expensive litigation. In most cases, respondents to these inquiries will verify dates of employment only, with no information on former employees' work habits. Because of this, many human resources departments give references only a cursory glance.

Some companies have made an "Employment Reference Release" part of the employment application. By signing the form, the applicant authorizes prior employers to release all information regarding employment with them, and the applicant releases the former employer from any legal liability for any damages that may result from the disclosure of this information.

The Fair Credit Reporting Act of 1968 subjects employers to certain disclosure obligations when they seek an **investigative consumer report** from a consumer reporting agency on a job applicant or in certain instances on present employees. An investigative consumer report usually contains information about the individual's character, general reputation, and mode of living. Generally, the employer must notify the applicant or the employee in writing that such a report is being sought. Also, the employer must notify the applicant or employee that he or she may request information from the employer about the nature and scope of the information sought. In the event employment is denied because of the consumer report information, the employer must inform the individual that this was the reason or part of the reason for denying employment. Also, the employer must furnish the applicant with the name and address of the consumer reporting agency that made the report.

NEWS // ALERT //

A survey conducted by the Society for Human Resource Management found that 53 percent of employers have been subject to employment-related lawsuits. The majority of lawsuits were filed by former or current employees; only 5 percent were from prospective employees.

HIRING NOTICE

After the successful applicant is notified of employment and the starting date, time, and to whom to report, a **hiring notice** is sent to the Payroll Department so that the new employee can be added properly to the payroll. A hiring notice such as that shown in Figure 1–6, on page 1-18, usually gives the name, address, and telephone number of the new employee, the department in which employed, the starting date, the rate of pay, the number of withholding allowances claimed, and any other information pertaining to deductions that are to be made from the employee's wages.

on the JOB

According to the U.S. Chamber of Commerce, 30 percent of all business failures are due to employee theft and dishonesty. This puts a premium on a company's prehiring screening process.

EMPLOYEE HISTORY RECORD

Although many businesses keep no personnel records other than the application, a more detailed record is needed to provide a continuous record of the relationship between the employer and the employee. The **employee history record** is such a record and, in addition to providing personal and other information usually found on an application, provides space to record the employee's progress, attendance, promotions, performance appraisals, and salary increases. As with most records, the individual employee must have access to his or her own human resource files.

CHANGE IN PAYROLL RATE

The **change in payroll rate form** notifies the proper departments of a change in the employee's rate of remuneration. The change in rate may originate in the Human Resources Department or with the head of the department in which the employee works. In either event, the Payroll Department must be informed of the change for the employee so that the rate change is put into effect at the proper time and so that the records reflect the new rate. Figure 1–7, on page 1-18, shows a form that may be used for this purpose.

IRS CONNECTION

In 2007, April 30 was the day on which the average American worker's income, since the beginning of the year, equaled the tax obligations to federal, state, and local governments.

FIGURE 1–6

Hiring Notice

HIRING NOTICE

NO. 220

SOCIAL SECURITY NO. 199-00-6357

DATE June 28, 20--

NAME Cheryl Crowson CLOCK NO. 418

ADDRESS 1630 West End Ave., Huntington, WV ZIP 25703 PHONE NO. 555-1618

OCCUPATION Payroll Clerk DEPT. Accounting GROUP NO. --

STARTING DATE July 1, 20-- TIME 8:00 A.M. P.M. RATE $36,000 yr.

MARRIED | SINGLE x | BIRTH DATE 8/1/--

LAST EMPLOYMENT Brennan Shipping Co. LOCATION Huntington, WV

DATE LEFT June 30, 20-- REASON Advancement

NO. OF WITHHOLDING ALLOWANCES 1

IN EMERGENCY NOTIFY Robert Crowson PHONE NO. 555-5136

EMPLOYEE'S SIGNATURE IN FULL *Cheryl Crowson*

SUPERVISOR'S SIGNATURE *Margaret T. Johnson*

EMPLOYMENT DEPARTMENT

ORIGINAL TO PAYROLL DEPT.
DUPLICATE RETAINED BY HUMAN RESOURCES DEPT.

FIGURE 1–7

Change in Status Form

CHANGE OF STATUS

Please enter the following change(s) as of January 1, 20--

Name Cheryl Crowson Clock or Payroll No. 418 Soc. Sec. Number 199-00-6357

FROM

Job	Dept.	Shift	Rate
Payroll Clerk	Acct.	--	$36,000

TO

Job	Dept.	Shift	Rate
Accounting Clerk	Acct.	--	$38,500

REASON FOR CHANGE:

- ☐ Hired
- ☐ Re-hired
- ☒ Promotion
- ☐ Demotion
- ☐ Transfer
- ☐ Merit Increase
- ☐ Leave of Absence to ________ Date
- ☐ Length of Serv. Increase
- ☐ Re-eval. of Existing Job
- ☐ Resignation
- ☐ Retirement
- ☐ Layoff
- ☐ Discharge

Other reason or explanation: ____________________

AUTHORIZED BY *Margaret T. Johnson* APPROVED BY *E. J. Dunn*

Prepare in triplicate: (1) Human Resources (2) Payroll (3) Employee's Department

EMPLOYEE ACCESS—PERSONNEL FILES

Even though personnel files are the property of the employer, employees may have the right to view and receive a copy of their own files. More than half of the states allow current employees access to their records.

Even with this right, some documents are considered confidential, and employers should not allow employees to view anything that would be considered an invasion of privacy (e.g., reference letters, investigative notes, etc.). Before granting access to personnel files, the payroll professional should check all applicable state laws and their own company's written policy.

Payroll Accounting System

6 LEARNING OBJECTIVE

A **payroll accounting system** embodies all those procedures and methods related to the disbursement of pay to employees. A typical payroll accounting system includes the procedures shown in Figure 1–8. The nature of the payroll records depends to a great extent on the size of the workforce and the degree to which the recordkeeping is automated. This course describes and illustrates manual payroll accounting systems. Appendix A describes computerized payroll accounting systems, along with operating instructions for using the software available with this text. In most payroll systems—manual or automated—the payroll register and the employee's earnings record are the two basic records that are utilized.

FIGURE 1–8

Procedures in a Payroll Accounting System

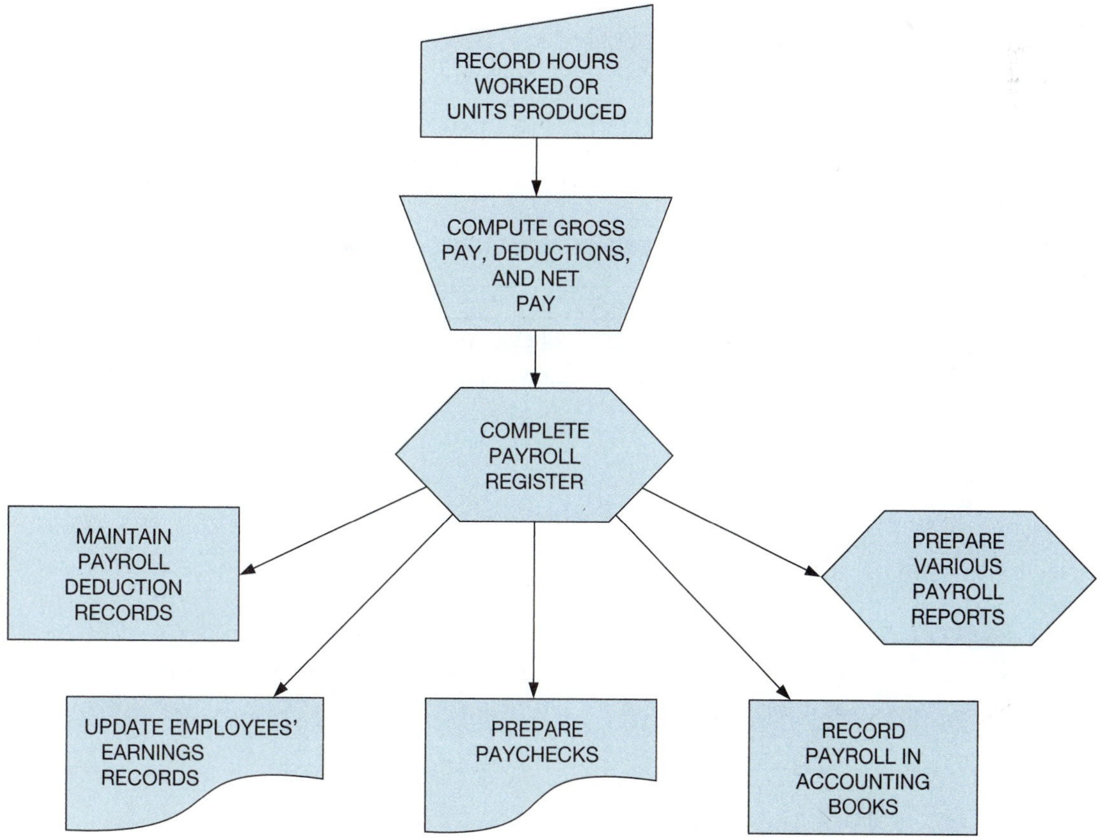

PAYROLL REGISTER

The **payroll register** is a multicolumn form used to assemble and summarize the data needed at the end of each payroll period. It provides a detailed listing of a company's complete payroll for that particular pay period. Thus, the payroll register lists all the employees who earned remuneration, the amount of remuneration, the deductions, and the net amount paid. The information provided in the payroll register is used primarily to meet the requirements of the Fair Labor Standards Act. However, the register also provides information for recording the payroll entries in the journal and for preparing reports required by other federal, state, and local laws. Figure 1–9 shows one form of payroll register. Another form, used in the Continuing Payroll Problem at the end of Chapters 2 through 6, is shown in the fold-out at the back of this book. Chapter 6 presents further discussion of the payroll register.

on the *JOB*

Payroll schemes account for almost 10 percent of all reported business frauds. Companies become most vulnerable when employees have access to check-writing software and hardware and when outsiders have access to company checks that are distributed to employees.

EMPLOYEE'S EARNINGS RECORD

LEARNING OBJECTIVE 7

In addition to the information contained in the payroll register, businesses must provide more complete information about the accumulated earnings of each employee. For that reason, it is necessary to keep a separate payroll record on each employee—the **employee's earnings record**. Each payday, after the information has been recorded in the payroll register, the information for each employee is transferred, or posted, to the employee's earnings record. The employee's earnings record provides the information needed to prepare periodic reports required by the withholding tax laws, the FICA tax law, and state unemployment or disability laws. Employers also use the employee's earnings record in preparing **Form W-2, Wage and Tax Statement**. This form shows the amount of wages paid each worker in the course of the trade or business of the employer. Figure 1–10 shows an example of the employee's earnings record. Chapter 6 presents a more detailed discussion of the preparation and use of the earnings record.

on the *JOB*

The retention requirements imposed on employers by various government agencies set a limit of seven years on payroll registers and eight years on employees' earnings records.

PAYCHECK

When employees are paid by check, a check is written for each worker, using as the amount of net pay that figure appearing in the Net Paid column of the payroll register. Most paychecks, such as that depicted in Figure 1–11, carry a stub, or voucher, that shows the

FIGURE 1–9

Payroll Register

PAYROLL REGISTER

FOR WEEK ENDING *January 19* 20 - -

	No.	Name	Total Hours Worked	Regular Earnings Hrs.	Regular Earnings Rate	Regular Earnings Amount	Overtime Earnings Hrs.	Overtime Earnings Rate	Overtime Earnings Amount	Total Earnings	Deductions OASDI Tax	Deductions HI Tax	Deductions Fed. Income Tax	Deductions State Income Tax	Net Paid Check No.	Net Paid Amount
1	*403*	*Springs, Carl A.*	*40*	*40*	*7.75*	*310.00*				*310.00*	*19.22*	*4.50*	*32.00*	*11.00*	*504*	*243.28*
2	*409*	*Wiegand, Sue T.*	*42*	*40*	*7.20*	*288.00*	*2*	*10.80*	*21.60*	*309.60*	*19.20*	*4.49*	*9.00*	*9.00*	*505*	*267.91*
3	*412*	*O'Neill, John B.*	*38*	*38*	*9.10*	*345.80*				*345.80*	*21.44*	*5.01*	*13.00*	*10.00*	*506*	*296.35*
4	*413*	*Bass, Marie S.*	*44*	*40*	*8.80*	*352.00*	*4*	*13.20*	*52.80*	*404.80*	*25.10*	*5.87*	*46.00*	*14.00*	*507*	*313.83*
5	*418*	*Crowson, Cheryl*	*40*	*40*	*S*	*740.38*				*740.38*	*45.90*	*10.74*	*91.00*	*29.00*	*508*	*563.74*
47		*Totals*				*3,895.75*			*317.20*	*4,212.95*	*261.20*	*61.09*	*808.00*	*224.00*		*2,858.66*

FIGURE 1–10

Employee's Earnings Record

EMPLOYEE'S EARNINGS RECORD

Week	Week Ending	Total Hours Worked	Regular Earnings			Overtime Earnings			Total Earnings	Deductions				Net Paid		Cumulative Earnings
			Hrs.	Rate	Amount	Hrs.	Rate	Amount		OASDI Tax	HI Tax	Fed. Income Tax	State Income Tax	Check No.	Amount	
1	*1/5*	*40*	*40*	*S*	*740.38*				*740.38*	*45.90*	*10.74*	*91.00*	*29.00*	*419*	*563.74*	*740.38*
2	*1/12*	*42*	*40*	*S*	*740.38*	*2*	*27.77*	*55.54*	*795.92*	*49.35*	*11.54*	*103.00*	*30.00*	*463*	*602.03*	*1536.30*
3	*1/19*	*40*	*40*	*S*	*740.38*				*740.38*	*45.90*	*10.74*	*91.00*	*29.00*	*508*	*563.74*	*2276.68*

Sex		Department	Occupation	State Employed	S.S.No.	Name—Last First Middle	No. W/H Allow.
F	M	*Accounting*	*Accounting Clerk (A)*	*West Virginia*	*199-00-6357*	*Crowson, Cheryl*	*1*
√							Marital Status *S*

FIGURE 1–11

Paycheck with Stub Showing Current and Year-to-Date Earnings and Deductions

REGULAR HOURS	O.T.B. HOURS	REGULAR EARNINGS	O.T.B. EARNINGS	GROSS EARNINGS	OASDI	HI	FIT	SIT
40		740.38		740.38	45.90	10.74	91.00	29.00

DEDUCTIONS

1. MISC.	5. SPECIAL INSURANCE	9. TOOLS
2. BONDS	6. WELFARE FUND	10. RELIEF ASSOC.
3. CREDIT UNION	7. ADVANCES	11. SHOES
4. GROUP INSURANCE	8. UNIFORMS	12.

CLOCK NO.	RATE	PERIOD ENDING	GROSS EARNINGS	OASDI	HI	FIT	SIT
418	S	1 19	2,276.68	141.15	33.02	285.00	88.00
			YEAR TO DATE				

CODE	DEDUCTIONS
	563.74
NET PAY ↑	

RETAIN THIS STUB
IT IS A STATEMENT OF YOUR EARNINGS AND DEDUCTIONS

Palmero Maintenance

CLOCK NO. 418

Palmero Maintenance
Huntington, WV

69-21
513

DATE January 19, 20--

No. 508

PAYROLL ACCOUNT

PAY TO THE ORDER OF Cheryl Crowson 563.74

DOLLARS	CENTS
563	74

the 1st national bank
Huntington, WV

BY *S. Hollis Stevenson*

⑆0513002⑆2⑆ 6139⑈

earnings and deductions. Paying workers in cash, by check, or by means of electronic transfer is discussed in Chaper 6.

Many states have laws that affect the frequency of wage payments. In Connecticut, for example, employees must be paid on a weekly basis unless the labor commission has approved an exception.

OUTSOURCING PAYROLL

on the *JOB*

Surveys have found that 50 percent of mid-market companies (those with 500–4,999 employees) outsource their payrolls.

With the increased need for up-to-the-minute information concerning changes in payroll tax laws, the trend toward outsourcing payroll operations has grown stronger. This is especially true with small to midsize companies. Many businesses have found that processing payroll by using an outside payroll company is more cost effective than doing the processing in-house. Other benefits realized are increased quality, improved efficiency, and a quicker release time, all of which enable the company to concentrate on its other operations.

Basically, the payroll operations at the company's site need only deal with the entry of new employee information and the number of hours worked by each employee. This information is sent to the payroll processing company electronically. The input is then processed by the outside firm. Once the processing is completed, the output package (paychecks, payroll, and management reports) is returned to the company.

Leading companies in the industry, such as ADP,[3] will custom-make a comprehensive and integrated program that will meet the needs of each individual business at a cost that many businesses find affordable.

3 The ADP Logo is a registered trademark of ADP (Automatic Data Processing) of North America, Inc.

KEY TERMS

Application form *(p. 1-14)*
Change in payroll rate form *(p. 1-17)*
Disability benefits *(p. 1-12)*
Employee history record *(p. 1-17)*
Employee's earnings record *(p. 1-20)*
Executive orders *(p. 1-8)*
Fair employment practices *(p. 1-6)*
Form W-2, Wage and Tax Statement *(p. 1-20)*
Hiring notice *(p. 1-17)*
Human resources system *(p. 1-13)*
Income tax *(p. 1-6)*
Investigative consumer report *(p. 1-17)*
Payroll accounting system *(p. 1-19)*
Payroll register *(p. 1-20)*
Prehire inquiries *(p. 1-14)*
Reference inquiry form *(p. 1-17)*
Requisition for personnel *(p. 1-13)*
Vesting *(p. 1-11)*
Workers' compensation insurance *(p. 1-12)*

CHAPTER SUMMARY

A brief introduction is presented in the laws affecting payroll—from determining gross pay (FLSA), to taxing for social security (FICA), to withholding for income taxes (FIT), to charging employers to cover the costs of the unemployment programs (FUTA and SUTA).

The laws dealing with discrimination in the workplace (Civil Rights Act, Age Discrimination in Employment, and Americans with Disabilities) were examined. These have a profound effect on every phase of the employment process.

New-hire reporting requirements and the verification of employment eligibility (Form I-9) were discussed as part of the general topic of the need for personnel records—internally and legally.

The chapter concluded with a review of records that are employed in a human resource system. The employment records started with the requisition for personnel, followed by the application form, the reference inquiry, the hiring notice, and, finally, the employment history record. The two major payroll accounting records (the payroll register and the employee's earnings record) recap the calculation of every employee's pay, and they are the source for the payroll accounting entries and the completion of each employee's W-2.

MATCHING QUIZ

______ 1. Employee's earnings record
______ 2. Payroll register
______ 3. Executive orders
______ 4. Fair Labor Standards Act
______ 5. Immigration Reform and Control Act
______ 6. Unemployment insurance taxes
______ 7. Vesting
______ 8. Disability benefits
______ 9. Income tax
______10. Hiring notice

A. Also known as the Federal Wage and Hour Law.
B. Record used in preparing employee's W-2.
C. Protection against losses due to work-related injuries.
D. Multicolumn form used to summarize data needed each paydate.
E. Levy on earnings of most employees and deducted from their gross pay.
F. Antidiscrimination orders for employers with contracts involving federal funds.
G. Form sent to Payroll Department so that new employee is added to the payroll.
H. Form I-9 to be completed by all new employees.
I. Levied by both federal and state governments.
J. Conveys to employees the right to share in a retirement fund.

QUESTIONS FOR REVIEW

1. Which act sets the minimum wage, and what is the current wage rate?
2. Under the FLSA, what information concerning employees' wages earned must be maintained by the employer?
3. Who pays the social security taxes that are levied by the Federal Insurance Contributions Act?
4. How are the funds used which are provided by FUTA and SUTA?
5. What types of unfair employment practices are prohibited by the Civil Rights Act of 1964 as amended?
6. What is the purpose of the Age Discrimination in Employment Act (ADEA)?
7. Are there any exceptions to the protection afforded older workers by the Age Discrimination in Employment Act?
8. Who is covered by the Walsh-Healey Public Contracts Act?
9. What are the major provisions of the Occupational Safety and Health Act (OSHA)?
10. Under the Family and Medical Leave Act, what is the maximum number of weeks of unpaid leave that a covered employer is required to offer an employee whose spouse is seriously ill?
11. What is the primary purpose of the Employee Retirement Income Security Act (ERISA)?
12. Explain the concept of vesting.
13. Under ERISA, if requested in writing, what information must the administrator of the pension fund supply to the participants?
14. Summarize the procedure that may be followed by the Human Resources Department in hiring new employees.
15. What information is commonly provided by a jobseeker on the application for employment form?
16. What is the significance of the Civil Rights Act of 1964 and the Age Discrimination in Employment Act in the employer's use of prehire inquiries?
17. What obligations are imposed upon the employer by the Fair Credit Reporting Act of 1968?
18. What procedures are usually included in a typical payroll accounting system?
19. What two basic records are generated in most payroll accounting systems?
20. What uses are made of the information shown in the employee's earnings record?

QUESTIONS FOR DISCUSSION

1. What personnel records would you suggest for a small retailer with three employees?
2. What kind of problem can be encountered when requesting references from previous employers of job applicants?
3. In staffing their offices, some firms encourage in-house referrals (recommendations of their present employees). What are some possible objections to this practice as a means of obtaining job applicants? What advantages may be realized by the firm that uses in-house referrals?

4. The main office of a large bank has an annual turnover of 500 office workers. As an employment officer of this bank, discuss the sources you would use in obtaining replacement employees.
5. Among the questions asked on the application for employment form of Horner Company are the following:
   a. What is the name of your church and what religious holidays do you observe?
   b. What is the name of your birthplace?
   c. Are you a citizen of the United States?
   d. What foreign languages can you read, write, or speak fluently?

   In view of federal and state civil rights laws, do you believe that Horner Company is acting legally or illegally in asking each of the questions listed above?

CASE PROBLEM

C1. Paychecks Kept Coming.

Ken, a salaried employee, was terminated from his company in April of this year. Business had been slow since the beginning of the year, and each of the operating plants had laid off workers.

Ken's dismissal was processed through the Human Resources Department, but the information was not relayed to the corporate payroll office.

As had been the policy, checks for workers at remote sites were mailed to the employees. The mailing of Ken's checks continued for the next four weekly paydays. It wasn't until the monthly payroll reports were sent to Ken's supervisor that the error was detected.

Ken refused to return the four extra checks. What actions should the company take?[4]

4 Reprinted with permission from *Payroll Guide Newsletter.* Volume 60, No. 21, Copyright © 2001 by Research Institute of America, 395 Hudson Street, New York, NY 10014. All rights reserved.

chapter

2

Computing Wages and Salaries

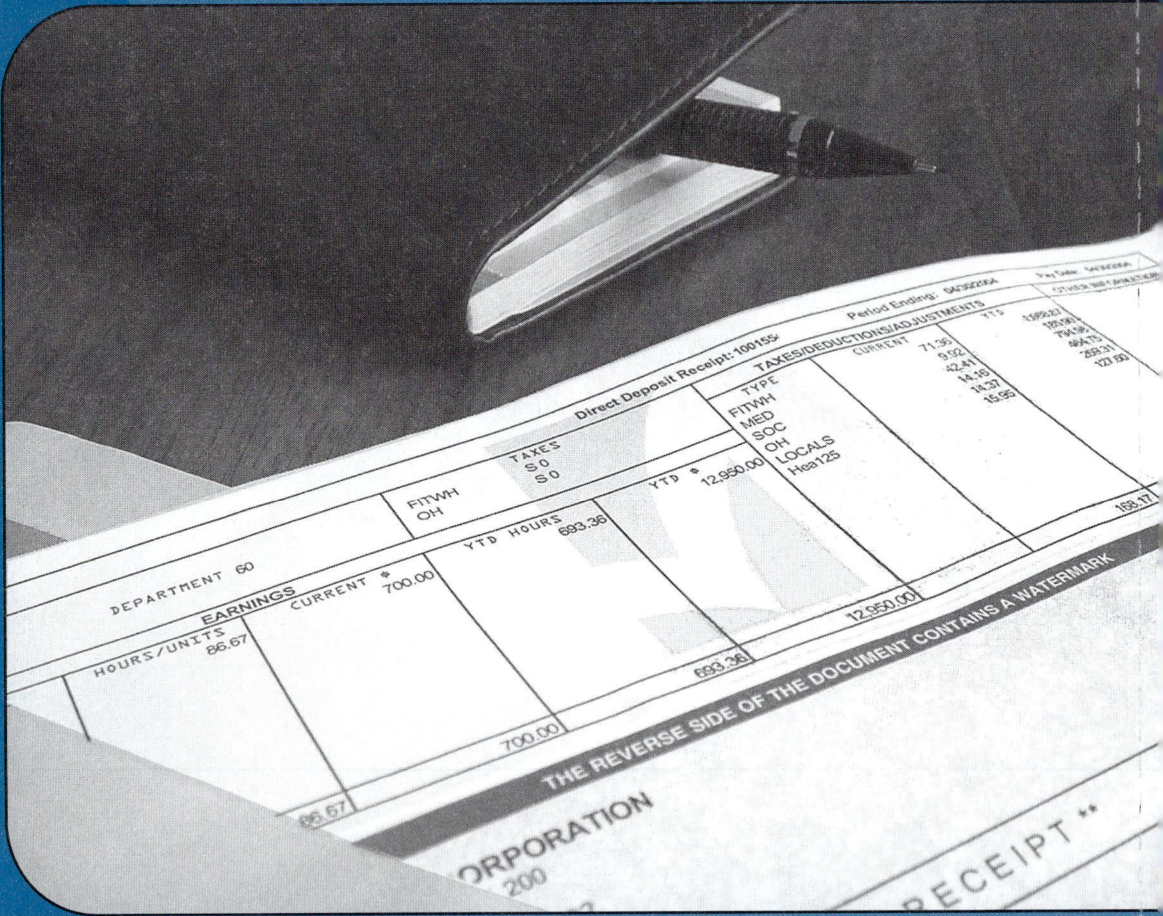

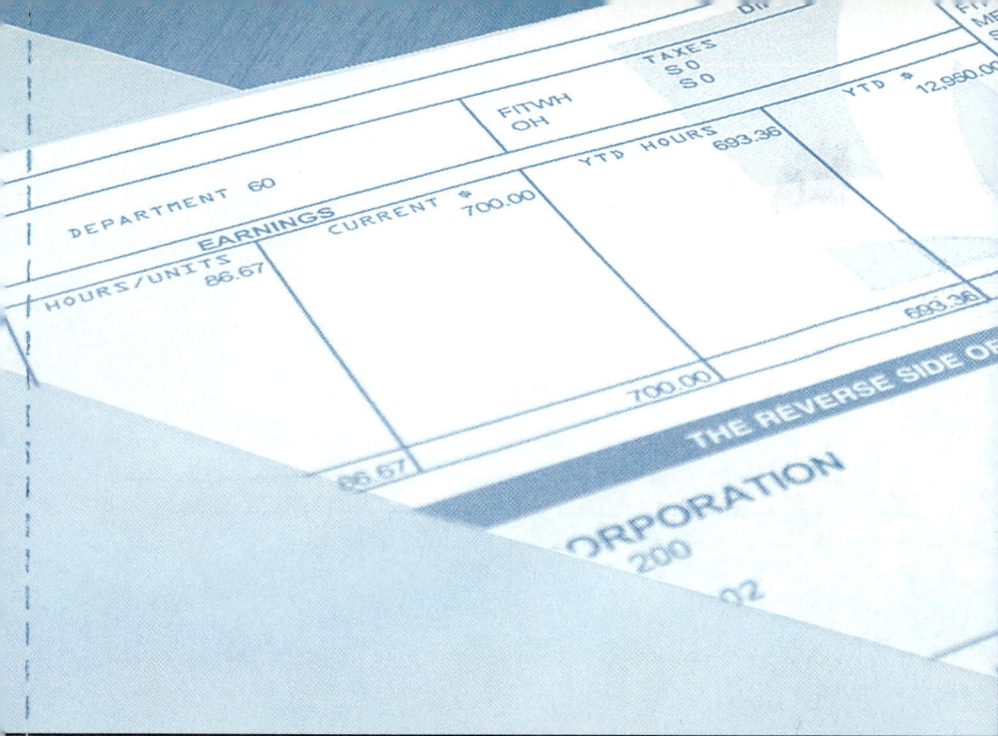

What difference does it make—employee or independent contractor? What do you mean—"exempt"? Do we have to pay them for that time? Do we really have to pay overtime? Isn't she a salaried employee? What do you mean that the minimum wage has changed? It's time to discuss the law that affects the determination of gross pay. Rev up your calculators. You will now learn to calculate employees' pays.

LEARNING OBJECTIVES

After studying this chapter, you should be able to:

① Explain the major provisions of the Fair Labor Standards Act.

② Distinguish between the employees' *principal* activities and their *preliminary* and *postliminary* activities.

③ Describe the main types of records used to collect payroll data.

④ Calculate regular and overtime pay.

⑤ Perform the following computations:

a. Convert weekly wage rates to hourly wage rates.

b. Convert monthly and annual salary rates to hourly rates.

c. Compute regular earnings and overtime earnings to arrive at total gross earnings.

d. Compute overtime payments for pieceworkers using two different methods.

e. Compute earnings under incentive, commission, and bonus plans.

This chapter examines the major provisions of the Fair Labor Standards Act, how to determine hours worked by employees, commonly used methods to record time worked, and the major methods of computing salaries and wages. Tracing its origin back to the 1930s, the Fair Labor Standards Act is the most encompassing of all the labor laws. However, it is also the one most violated.

The Fair Labor Standards Act

LEARNING OBJECTIVE 1

The Fair Labor Standards Act (FLSA), commonly known as the Federal Wage and Hour Law, contains provisions and standards concerning minimum wages, equal pay for equal work regardless of sex, overtime pay, recordkeeping, and child labor. The Wage and Hour Division of the U.S. Department of Labor (DOL) administers the act.

COVERAGE

The FLSA provides for two bases of coverage—enterprise coverage and individual employee coverage.

on the *JOB*

A National Call Center has been established by the Department of Labor to answer employees' and employers' questions on a range of employment issues. The toll-free number is 1-866-4-USA-DOL.

ENTERPRISE COVERAGE **Enterprise coverage** includes all employees of an enterprise if:

1. At least two employees engage in interstate commerce or produce goods for interstate commerce. Interstate commerce refers to the trade, transportation, or communication among several states or between a state and any place outside that state. The law also covers employees if they handle, sell, or otherwise work on goods or materials that have been moved in or produced for interstate commerce, and
2. The business has annual gross sales of at least $500,000.

Coverage extends, ***without regard to annual sales volume,*** to those who operate:

1. A hospital.
2. A nursing home.
3. An institution for the mentally ill.
4. A school for mentally or physically handicapped or gifted children.
5. A preschool, elementary, or secondary school.
6. An institution of higher education.
7. A public agency.

on the *NET*

http://www.dol.gov/esa/ *U.S. Department of Labor Employment Standards Administration homepage.* This site contains various codes sections, such as affirmative action and workers' compensation. To find the most useful information, choose the ESA program that interests you.

The enterprise coverage under the FLSA does not apply to family establishments, often referred to as "mom and pop stores." Thus, if the only regular employees of an establishment include the owner, parent, spouse, child, or other immediate family members, the establishment is exempt from FLSA coverage.

INDIVIDUAL EMPLOYEE COVERAGE Under **individual employee coverage,** the FLSA covers a worker if the employee either engages in interstate commerce or produces goods for such commerce. Coverage also includes employment in a fringe occupation closely related and directly essential to the production of goods for interstate commerce. Coverage depends on the activities of the individual employee and not on the work of fellow employees, the nature of the employer's business, or the character of the industry as a whole. Thus, even though a business does not meet the enterprise coverage test, it must pay FLSA wages to those workers eligible for individual coverage.

EXAMPLE

Glenn Morris works for a small manufacturing firm that has an annual sales volume of $370,000. Although the firm does not meet the $500,000 volume-of-sales requirement for enterprise coverage, Morris is *individually* covered since he operates machinery used to produce goods for interstate commerce.

EMPLOYER

The FLSA defines an employer as "any person acting directly or indirectly in the interest of an employer" in relation to an employee. In order to protect employees, courts have defined "employers" in the broadest sense. Co-owners who control the day-to-day operations of the business are employers who are individually liable for violations of the law.

EMPLOYEE

An individual is an **employee** if he or she performs services in a covered employment. As long as the common-law relationship of employer and employee exists and the employment is not exempt from the provisions of the law, both are covered and must observe its provisions. No differentiation is made between regular, temporary, substitute, or part-time workers.

A **common-law relationship** of employer and employee exists when the employer has the right to control both what work will be done and how it will be done. How the relationship is labeled is immaterial; it is the substance of the relationship that governs the worker's status.

To determine if a worker may be classified as an employee and if the employer has the right to control, the Internal Revenue Service uses a "24-factor" test based on behavioral control, financial control, and the relationship between the worker and the employer.

A shortened "ABC test" defines an independent contractor (nonemployee) as one who:

1. is free of direction and control in the performance of the work.
2. performs services outside the usual course of business of the company that has hired the contractor.
3. customarily engages in an independent occupation.

Several other factors to consider would be the amount of instruction or training given to the worker, the amount of the worker's investment in the business, the ability to hire and supervise others, and the worker's offering of services to the public.

> ***IRS* CONNECTION**
>
> If you want the IRS to determine whether a worker is an employee, file **Form SS-8, Determination of Employee Work Status** for purposes of Federal Employment Taxes and Income Tax Withholding. Over 90 percent of these filed forms were determined to be for *employees.*

EMPLOYEES OF A CORPORATION

Managers, superintendents, supervisors, department heads, and other executives of a corporation are considered employees under the FICA tax law. All officers, such as the president, vice president, secretary, and treasurer, are also employees of the corporation. Their salaries are taxable the same as the wages paid to other employees. A director of a corporation who performs no services other than attending and participating in meetings of the board of directors is not an employee.

DOMESTICS

Domestic workers also must be paid the minimum wage if:

1. They perform services in one or more homes for a total of more than eight hours in any workweek, ***or if***
2. They earn wages of at least $1,000 from an employer in a calendar year.

Domestic service consists of services of a household nature performed in or about a private home of the person who employs the domestic. Some typical domestics include cooks, butlers, maids, caretakers, gardeners, and chauffeurs. The term also includes a baby sitter employed on other than a casual basis, such as a person who sits for a child five days a week. If the domestics do not live in the household, they must be paid overtime compensation as well as the minimum wage. However, live-in domestics do not have to be paid overtime. A casual baby sitter (one employed on an irregular or intermittent basis) or a companion for the aged or infirm is not covered.

PARTNERSHIPS

Partners generally are not employees of the partnership. In some cases, however, a partnership may operate as an association that may be classified as a corporation. In such situations, any partner who renders services similar to those of corporate officers would be an employee.

on the JOB

Today, nearly 25 percent of the workforce is made up of temporary workers, consultants, and independent contractors.

STATUTORY NONEMPLOYEES There are two categories of statutory nonemployees—direct sellers and licensed real estate agents. For federal tax purposes, they are considered to be self-employed as long as their earnings are based on the amount of sales and their services are performed under a written contract stating that they will not be treated as employees for federal tax purposes.

WAGES

Wages include the remuneration or compensation paid employees. The terms wages and salaries are commonly used interchangeably. However, **wage** usually refers to remuneration paid on an hourly or a piecework basis. **Salary** usually refers to the remuneration paid on a weekly, **biweekly** (every two weeks), **semimonthly** (twice a month), monthly, or yearly basis.

THE MINIMUM WAGE

The FLSA of 1938 established a minimum wage of 25 cents per hour for a straight-time workweek of 44 hours. With the objective of improving the purchasing power of covered workers, succeeding amendments to the FLSA increased the minimum hourly rate and reduced the workweek. The Fair Minimum Wage Act of 2007 increased the minimum wage in a three-step program as follows:

$5.85 until July 24, 2008, then to
$6.55 until July 24, 2009, then to
$7.25

In this 2008 text, we will use the rate established for the first part of this year—$5.85.

There is also a provision for a training wage that allows employers to pay $4.25 per hour to newly hired employees under 20 years of age (opportunity wage). This only applies to the first 90 calendar days of employment.

Included in the regular rate of pay is all remuneration for employment paid to or on behalf of the employee. Some examples are:

1. Commission payments.
2. Earned bonuses (**nondiscretionary bonus**—which is a bonus normally based on hours worked, units produced, production efficiency, or work quality).
3. Severance pay.
4. On-call pay.
5. Shift or weekend differentials.

A **discretionary bonus,** which is a bonus not agreed upon, announced, or promised before payment, is *not* included in an employee's regular rate of pay. The employer retains discretion both to the granting and to the amount of the bonus until close to the end of the period for which the bonus is paid.

The law also allows employers to credit the reasonable cost of housing, meals, and transportation to work that they provide towards payment of the minimum wage. To qualify, these facility credits must be furnished for the employer's benefit and must be accepted voluntarily by the employee.

Some other payments are not included in the regular rate of pay. Examples are:

1. Gifts made as a reward for service.
2. Payments for a bona fide profit-sharing or savings plan.
3. Payments for periods when no work is performed—vacations, holidays, sick days, or jury duty days.
4. Payments reported as part of a guaranteed minimum number of hours paid that are more than the actual hours worked.

PAYING LESS THAN THE MINIMUM WAGE

Under certain conditions, wages lower than the minimum wage may be paid to some employees.

1. Retail or service establishments and farms may employ full-time students at 85 percent of the minimum wage ($4.97 per hour).
2. Institutions of higher education may employ their own full-time students at 85 percent of the minimum wage.
3. Student-learners may be employed at 75 percent of the minimum wage if they are participating in a bona fide vocational training program conducted by an accredited school ($4.39 per hour).
4. Persons whose earning capacity is impaired by age, physical or mental deficiency, or injury may be employed at special minimum wage rates. However, a certificate authorizing employment at such rates must first be obtained.

NEWS // ALERT//

The Department of Labor has ruled that illegal aliens must also be paid at least the minimum wage and overtime as stipulated in the FLSA.

SELF-STUDY QUIZ 2-1 *Indicate which of the following statements regarding the Fair Labor Standards Act are false.*

______ **1.** Under the FLSA, wages include sales commissions and bonuses paid for employee performance.

______ **2.** Domestic workers must always be paid overtime compensation in addition to the minimum wage.

______ **3.** A son working for his parents in a family-owned business is not covered under the FLSA.

______ **4.** Individual employee coverage under the FLSA applies only if fellow employees are engaged in similar activities.

______ **5.** A college may pay its own full-time students less than the minimum wage.

Note: Answers at back of book.

PAYING A "LIVING WAGE"

Over 100 cities have enacted local ordinances to require employers who do business with the government to pay a "living wage" to their low-wage workers. The movement, started by local advocates, grew out of the failure to keep the national minimum wage on pace with the needs of the working poor. Recently, some "living wage" laws have been passed that also include private industry doing business within the cities' jurisdiction. In Miami, all city workers and workers for companies that have contracts (over $100,000) with the city must be paid $10.58 per hour with health insurance coverage or $11.83 per hour without coverage. In Santa Fe, New Mexico, the living wage rate is set at $10.50 per hour with the value of any employer-provided health benefits credited against this minimum.

TIPS

A **tip** (to ensure promptness) is a gift or gratuity given by a customer in recognition of some service performed for him or her. A **tipped employee** is one who engages in an occupation in which tips of more than $30 a month are customarily and regularly received. An employer may consider, within prescribed limits, the tips received by a tipped employee as part of the employee's wages. In 1996, the Small Business Job Protection Act froze the minimum cash wage required for tipped employees at $2.13 per hour. Tips received by the employee are credited toward the remainder ($3.72) of the total minimum wage ($5.85 less $2.13). If tips received do not amount to at least $3.72 per hour, the employer must increase the hourly rate of pay so that the hourly wage plus the equivalent hourly rate of tips received equal, at a minimum, $5.85 per hour.

Service charges imposed on patrons by the employer do not count toward the tip credit. To be included for the credit, the tip must be voluntarily paid by a customer.

NEWS // ALERT//

The DOL has ruled that credit card tips must be paid to the employee by the next payday. The amount of these tips can be reduced by the amount that the credit card company charges the employer.

In cases of two jobs performed by one worker, the tip credit can only be applied to the job that qualifies as tipped employment.

EXAMPLE

Karl Marx worked for the Hilton Hotel in Las Vegas as a waiter. In addition, on his days off, he worked on Hilton's maintenance crew. Hilton can only claim the tip credit against Marx's wages on his waiter job.

Under state laws, the states' tip credit percentage (different in each state) is applied to the federal minimum wage to calculate the actual tip credit and the resulting minimum wage required under state law. In states where the tip credit differs from the federal, employers must determine the credit and the resulting minimum wage under both federal and state law and pay their employees the higher cash wage.

EXAMPLE

James Rudolph, a waiter, earns a weekly wage of $100.00 for a 40-hour workweek and receives tips of $100.00 each week. Even though the hourly rate paid to Rudolph ($100.00 ÷ 40 hours = $2.50) exceeds the minimum wage rate of $2.13, the employer must pay Rudolph an extra $34.00 so that the tips received plus the wages paid equal the minimum wage of $5.85 per hour.

$5.85 × 40 =	$234.00
Weekly wage	(100.00)*
Tips received	(100.00)
Extra weekly pay	$ 34.00*

*$100.00 + $34.00 = $134.00; $134.00 ÷ 40 hours = $3.35/hour

SELF-STUDY QUIZ 2-2 *Genna Harrison, a waitress, earns $85.20 a week for a 40-hour workweek. During one week, Harrison received tips of $90.*

1. What hourly rate is being paid to Harrison?
   $__________

2. How much must the employer pay Harrison in addition to her $85.20 weekly wage?
   $__________

WORKWEEK

The FLSA defines a **workweek** as a fixed and regularly recurring period of 168 hours—seven consecutive 24-hour periods. The individual employee's workweek is the statutory or contract number of hours to be worked regularly during that period. The workweek may begin on any day of the week and need not coincide with the calendar week. An employer may establish the same workweek for the business operations as a whole or assign different workweeks to individual workers or groups of workers.

An employer may change the day a workweek begins if intended to be a permanent change and not just to evade the overtime pay requirements of the FLSA. If, however, a union contract fixes the workweek, the employer's right to change the workweek depends upon the wording in the contract. Each workweek stands alone, and the overtime hours worked in one week may not be shifted to another workweek. Thus, each workweek is a separate unit for the purpose of computing overtime pay.

OVERTIME HOURS AND OVERTIME PAY The FLSA requires overtime pay for all hours worked in excess of 40 in a workweek. The FLSA requires no overtime pay for daily hours worked in excess of any given number or for work on Saturdays, Sundays, holidays, or other special days. The law requires overtime pay to be one and one-half times the employee's regular hourly rate of pay, which must not be less than the statutory minimum.

With some restrictions, employees covered under the FLSA can be required by their employers to work overtime. If they refuse, they can be fired under the law. There is also no limit on the overtime that can be required. However, in these cases, the state laws may be the governing force.

EXAMPLE

If an employee's regular rate of pay is $8.40 an hour, the overtime rate must be at least $8.40 × 1.5, or $12.60 an hour.

If an hourly-rate employee works in pay periods of two weeks or longer, the employer can elect to give the employee 1.5 hours off for every overtime hour. However, the time off must be in the same pay period as the overtime hours worked.

In the case of tipped employees, the same tip credit also applies to overtime hours. The regular rate of pay for a tipped employee is the current minimum wage—$2.13 plus $3.72 tip credit = $5.85/hour. Time and one-half of $5.85 is $8.78. Since the employer can use the same tip credit for overtime hours, the employee's overtime cash wages are $5.06/hour ($8.78 − $3.72).

on the JOB

California defines overtime as any hours worked over eight in one day, and 40 in a workweek, and also, provides for double-time pay for hours over 12 in one day.

EXCEPTIONS TO OVERTIME HOURS AND OVERTIME PAY PROVISIONS An exception to overtime hours and overtime pay applies to ***hospital employees.*** Hospitals may enter into an agreement with their employees under which a 14-day period, rather than a workweek, becomes the basis for computing overtime pay. Employees entering such an agreement must receive overtime pay at not less than one and one-half times their regular hourly rate for hours worked in excess of eight hours in any workday or in excess of 80 hours in a 14-day period, whichever is the greater number of overtime hours. Although employers have the option of using the normal workweek or the 14-day period, they cannot change from one method to the other arbitrarily.

EXAMPLE

Donna Maloney, a lab technician, agreed that a 14-day period would be used to figure her overtime pay. Maloney works 12 hours in one day during the period and 8 hours in each of the 9 other days during the period, a total of 84 hours.

Maloney is entitled to 80 hours of straight-time pay and 4 hours of overtime pay for the 14-day period.

If Maloney worked only 7 hours in each of the 9 other days during the period, or a total of 75 hours, she would be entitled to 71 hours of straight-time pay and 4 hours of overtime pay for the 14-day period.

Employees in retail or service industries are exempt from the overtime provisions as long as their regular weekly rate of pay, including commissions, is at least one and one-half times the federal minimum wage rate and more than half of their pay over a monthly period comes from commissions.

Minimum wage legislation also provides an exception for ***employees receiving remedial education.*** Under this law, employees who receive remedial education offered by their employers are permitted to work up to 10 hours overtime each week without receiving overtime compensation. The remedial training, which does not include training for a specific job, must be designed to provide reading and other basic skills at an eighth-grade level or below.

COMPENSATORY TIME OFF A state, a political subdivision of a state, or an interstate governmental agency may grant employees compensatory time off in lieu of overtime compensation. Employees working in public safety, emergency response, or seasonal activities may accumulate compensatory time off up to 480 hours. (The 480-hour limit represents 320 hours of overtime actually worked at the one and one-half overtime rate.) Employees may "bank" their hours and use them later as time off at time and one-half during the course of their employment.

Employees whose work does not include the preceding activities may bank 240 hours for compensatory time off. Upon reaching the 480- or 240-hour limit, an employee must receive either cash for additional hours of overtime worked or use some compensatory time before receiving further overtime compensation in the form of compensatory time off. Note that not all 480 or 240 hours have to be accrued before compensatory time off may be used. The FLSA also provides for the payment of cash for unused comp time when the employee terminates employment.

EXEMPTIONS FROM FLSA REQUIREMENTS

Exempt employees (see Figure 2–1) are those workers exempt from some, or all, of the FLSA requirements, such as minimum wages, equal pay, and overtime pay.

FIGURE 2–1

Exemption Status of Workers Under FLSA

Employee Job Description	Minimum Wage Exemption	Equal Pay Exemption	Full Overtime Exemption
Agricultural employees.			X
Agricultural workers who are members of the employer's immediate family.	X	X	X
Air carrier employees if the carrier is subject to Title II of the Railway Labor Act.			X
Amusement or recreational establishment employees, provided the business has seasonal peaks.	X	X	X
Announcers, news editors, and chief engineers of radio or television stations in small communities.			X
Baby sitters (casual) and companions to ill or aged persons unable to care for themselves.	X	X	X
Drivers and drivers' helpers who make local deliveries and are paid on a trip-rate or similar basis following a plan approved by the government.			X
Executive, administrative, and professional employees, including teachers and academic administrative personnel in schools.	X		X
Fruit and vegetable employees who are engaged in the local transportation of these items or of workers employed or to be employed in the harvesting of fruits or vegetables.			X
Household domestic service employees who reside in the household.			X
Motion picture theater employees.			X
Motor carrier employees if the carrier is subject to regulation by the secretary of transportation.			X
Newspaper employees if the newspaper is published on a weekly, semiweekly, or daily basis and if the circulation is less than 4,000 copies, with the major circulation in the county of publication or contiguous counties.	X	X	X
Railroad, express company, and water carrier employees if the companies are subject to Part I of the Interstate Commerce Act.			X
Salespersons for automobile, truck, or farm implement dealers; parts stock clerks or mechanics; salespersons for boat, trailer, or aircraft dealers.			X
Taxicab drivers.			X

FIGURE 2-2

Indications of Exempt Status

Executive	Administrative	Professional	Business Owner
1. Primary duty—managing 2. Supervises two or more employees 3. Authority to hire, fire, promote	1. Primary duty—performs office work 2. Regularly uses discretion and independent judgment	**Learned Professional** 1. Work requires advanced knowledge (science or learning) 2. Knowledge acquired by prolonged course of instruction	1. Owns at least 20% of equity 2. Actively manages business operations
Highly Compensated	**Computer Professionals**	**Creative Professional**	**Outside Salespeople**
1. Earns $100,000 or more 2. Performs nonmanual work 3. Regularly performs one of the exempt duties of an executive, professional, or administrative employee	1. Salary of at least $455/week or $27.63/hour 2. Duties consist of system analysis techniques, design of computer systems or programs	1. Requires talent in an artistic or a creative endeavor	1. Primary duty—makes sales or obtains orders for services or use of facilities 2. Regularly away from the employer's place of business 3. No salary test

WHITE-COLLAR WORKERS The FLSA exempts some workers, such as executives, administrators, professional employees, highly compensated employees, computer professionals, and outside salespersons, from the minimum wage and overtime pay provisions if they satisfy certain tests.

TEST OF EXEMPTION To be eligible for this exemption, the employee must be paid on a ***salary basis,*** must be paid at least $455 per week, and must meet the "primary duty" requirements as listed in Figure 2–2. Employees paid by the hour are not exempt from the minimum wage and overtime pay requirements and thus do not qualify for the salary test even if their total weekly compensation exceeds the limits specified.

on the *NET*

http://www.aphis.usda.gov/mrpbs/forms/mrp/flsaworksheet.pdf. The FLSA has a worksheet that you can use to determine your exempt status.

SALARY BASIS These white-collar employees must be paid their full salary in any week in which any work is performed without regard to the number of hours worked. However, deductions can be made from the salary if an exempt employee misses one or more full days of work for personal reasons, other than sickness or accident. If the employee does not qualify for the employer's sick pay plan or has used up all available sick time, deductions can also be made for these full-day absences. However, if there is not a bona fide sick leave plan, an employer cannot make deductions from the salaries of exempt employees for absences due to sickness.

A proportionate share of an exempt employee's salary for the time actually worked is allowed only for the employee's first or last week of employment.

Partial-day absences cannot be deducted from the exempt employee's salary. However, the Wage and Hour Division has stated that the employer can require the employee to use any accumulated leave time to offset the time absent. Employers may also require exempt employees to record and track hours worked and to work a specified schedule.

on the *JOB*

The Department of Labor has ruled that these FLSA-exempt employees can be required by their employers for business purposes to record their work time on an hourly basis.

BLUE-COLLAR WORKERS The exemption from overtime pay based on the duties and salary tests does not apply to blue-collar workers (manual workers). No matter how highly paid, these workers are still entitled to overtime pay. This also applies to police officers, firefighters, paramedics, emergency medical technicians, and licensed practical nurses.

EQUAL PAY ACT

The Equal Pay Act amended the FLSA to require that men and women performing equal work receive equal pay. The Equal Pay Law applies to any employer having workers subject to the minimum pay provisions of the Wage and Hour Law. The equal-pay requirements also apply to white-collar workers and outside salespersons, even though they are exempt from the minimum wage standards.

The Equal Pay Law prohibits an employer from discriminating by paying wages to employees of one sex at a lower rate than those paid the opposite sex for equal work on jobs that require equal skill, effort, and responsibility and that are performed under similar working conditions. However, wage differentials between sexes are allowable if based on a seniority system, a merit system, a payment plan that measures earnings by quantity or quality of production, or any factor other than sex. If an unlawful pay differential between men and women exists, the employer must raise the lower rate to equal the higher rate.

on the *JOB*

The Department of Labor prohibits occupational driving for minors except on an occasional or incidental basis. Permitted driving can only be done during daylight hours and in vehicles not exceeding 6,000 pounds. In New York state, 16- and 17-year-olds are prohibited from driving in Manhattan.

CHILD-LABOR RESTRICTIONS

The FLSA prohibits a business from the interstate shipment of its goods or services if it employs child labor unlawfully. Under the FLSA, the Secretary of Labor issues regulations that restrict the employment of individuals under the age of 18. The restrictions divide child employment into nonfarm occupations and agricultural occupations.

NONFARM OCCUPATIONS The basic minimum age for most jobs is 16 years. This is the minimum age for work in manufacturing and processing jobs or in any other occupations except those declared by the secretary of labor as hazardous for minors under 18. The FLSA lists 17 occupations that are considered too dangerous. These include mining, forestry, excavation, roofing work, operation of certain power-driven tools, and most on-the-job driving.

Within certain limits, 14- and 15-year-olds may be employed in retail, food service, and gasoline service establishments. For example, this age group may be employed in office and clerical work, including the operation of office machines; cashiering; selling; price marking and tagging by hand or by machine; errand and delivery work; kitchen work and other work involved in preparing and serving food and beverages; dispensing gasoline and oil; and car cleaning.

The employment of minors between the ages of 14 and 16 cannot interfere with their schooling, health, and well-being. In addition, the following conditions must be met:

1. All work must be performed outside school hours.
2. There is a maximum three-hour day and 18-hour week when school is in session (eight hours and 40 hours when not in session).
3. All work must be performed between 7 A.M. and 7 P.M. (9 P.M. during the summer).

AGRICULTURAL OCCUPATIONS The employment of children under age 12 is generally prohibited in agricultural occupations, as described below.

1. During hours when school is in session.
2. Outside school hours on farms, including conglomerates, that used more than 500 man-days of labor in any quarter of the preceding calendar year.
3. Outside school hours on noncovered farms without parental consent.

However, children may work on farms owned or operated by their parents or guardians. Children 10 and 11 years old can work as hand harvest laborers outside school hours for up to eight weeks between June 1 and October 15, with a number of strict conditions on the employer. Children aged 12 and 13 may be employed only during hours when school is not in session provided there is parental consent or the employment is on a farm where the parents are employed. Children aged 14 and 15 may be employed, but only during hours when school is not in session. No child under the age of 16 may be employed in a hazardous farm occupation, such as operating large tractors, corn pickers, cotton pickers, grain combines, and feed grinders.

CERTIFICATE OF AGE Employers cannot be charged with having violated the child-labor restrictions of the law if they have on file an officially executed ***certificate of age*** which shows that the minor has reached the stipulated minimum age. In most states, a state employment or age certificate, issued by the Federal Wage and Hour Division or by a state agency, serves as proof of age. In some states, a state or federal certificate of age, a state employment certificate, or a work permit may not be available. In such cases, the employer may rely on any one of the following documents as evidence of age for minor employees:

1. Birth certificate (or attested transcript thereof) or a signed statement of the recorded date and place of birth issued by a registrar of vital statistics or other officer charged with the duty of recording births.
2. Record of baptism (or attested transcript thereof) showing the date of birth of the minor.
3. Statement on the census records of the Bureau of Indian Affairs and signed by an administrative representative thereof showing the name, date, and place of the minor's birth.

The employer should maintain a copy of the document or indicate in the payroll records which document verified the minor's age.

PENALTIES

The U.S. government may bring civil or criminal actions against employers who violate the FLSA. Employers who willfully violate the wage and hour provisions of the law or the wage orders fixed by the Administrator of the Wage and Hour Division of the Department of Labor will be prosecuted and will be subject to a fine of not more than $10,000, or imprisonment for up to six months, or both. However, no person may be imprisoned for a first offense violation. If an imposed fine goes unpaid, however, the courts have the power to order imprisonment as an incident to the nonpayment. Violators of the child-labor provisions of the Act are subject to fines of $11,000 for each violation. Payroll managers should read the Fair Labor Standards Act and its amendments very carefully.

AREAS NOT COVERED BY THE FLSA

The FLSA does not require employers to:

1. Pay extra wages for work on Saturdays, Sundays, or holidays.
2. Pay for holidays, vacations, or severance.
3. Limit the number of hours or work for persons 16 years of age or over.
4. Give holidays off.
5. Grant vacation time.
6. Grant sick leave.

Determining Employee's Work Time

To avoid paying for time not actually spent on the job and to eliminate payment for unnecessary overtime work, employers must know what types of employee activities count as working time under the law. Generally, the hours counted as working time include all the time that employees actually work or must be on duty. A distinction must

2 LEARNING OBJECTIVE

be made between an employee's principal activities and the preliminary and postliminary activities.

PRINCIPAL ACTIVITIES

The **principal activities** of employees include those tasks employees must perform and include any work of consequence performed for the employer. Principal activities include those indispensable to the performance of productive work and those that are an integral part of a principal activity.

EXAMPLE

Chad Quinn is a lathe operator who oils and cleans his machines at the beginning of each workday and installs new cutting tools. These activities performed by Quinn are part of his principal activity.

The test of compensability with respect to principal activities requires that there be physical or mental exertion, controlled or required by the employer and performed for the employer's benefit.

CLOTHES-CHANGING TIME AND WASH-UP Because of the nature of their work, some employees change clothes or wash on the employer's premises. Statutes or ordinances may require clothes changing or washing. Employees who spend time changing clothes or washing on the employer's premises regard this time as part of their principal activities. However, even where the nature of the job or the law requires clothes changing or wash-up, it may be excluded from time worked either expressly or by custom and practice under a collective bargaining contract. In the case of meat and poultry processing workers, the "putting on and taking off" of protective gear in the locker room was ruled to be part of their principal activities; and, therefore, the subsequent walks to and from the production area were part of the workday under the "continuous workday rule."

TRAVEL TIME The time spent by employees in traveling to and from work needs to be counted as time worked only if contract, custom, or practice so requires. In some situations, however, travel time between home and work counts as time worked. If an employee who regularly works at a fixed location is given a special one-day work assignment in another city, time worked includes the travel time.

EXAMPLE

Dana MacAvoy receives an emergency call outside regular working hours and must travel a substantial distance to perform a job away from MacAvoy's usual work site for one of the employer's customers. The travel time counts as time worked.

When performed during the workday as part of an employee's principal activities, the travel time counts as time worked.

EXAMPLE

Rena Thorpe travels throughout the city to various job sites during regular working hours, 9 A.M. to 5 P.M., Mondays through Fridays. Such travel time counts as work time.

When Thorpe travels between workdays from one city to another, the travel time counts as working time when the hours correspond to regular working hours, even though the hours may occur on Saturday and Sunday.

For example, if Thorpe is sent on a trip requiring travel on Saturday and Sunday to be at a job the first thing Monday morning, the travel time on Saturday and Sunday between the hours of 9 A.M. and 5 P.M. counts as time worked, but travel time before 9 A.M. and after 5 P.M. does not count.

IDLE TIME Readiness to serve can also be considered employment. If the time spent while idle was primarily for the benefit of the employer, this time must be compensated. However, if workers are required to carry a beeper, pager, or cell phone, this on-call time is not compensable, provided they can use this time for their own purposes.

WAITING TIME If an employee is "engaged to wait," this is work time. For example, an employee who is reading a magazine while waiting for an assignment is considered to be working. On the other hand, if an employee is "waiting to be engaged," this is not work time. An employee completely relieved from duty until a certain hour is not working during the time spent waiting for that hour.

REST PERIODS AND COFFEE BREAKS The FLSA does not require that an employer give employees a rest period or a coffee break. However, the employer may grant such rest periods voluntarily; or the union contract or municipal or state legislation may require them. In these cases, the time spent on a rest period of 20 minutes or less counts as part of the hours worked. If longer than 20 minutes, the compensability for the time depends upon the employee's freedom during that time or upon the provisions of the union contract.

MEAL PERIODS Bona fide meal periods (not including coffee breaks or snack times) during which the employee is completely relieved from duty are not considered working time. Lunch periods during which the employee must perform some duties while eating are not bona fide meal periods. The general rule sets a bona fide meal period at 30 minutes or longer.

In cases where the employer and employee agree that it is sufficient, a 15-minute lunch period can be considered a bona fide meal period. However, the lunchroom facilities must be readily accessible.

on the *JOB*

California requires a 30-minute break (unpaid) after five hours. If nonexempt employees do not get this break, they must be given an additional hour of pay.

EXAMPLE

Virginia Sherr, an office worker, must eat at her desk and operate the switchboard at lunch time. Sherr must be paid for the lunch period.

TAKING WORK HOME With more and more employees taking work home with them, it is important to understand that this is compensable time. Nonexempt employees must be paid for ***all hours worked,*** even those outside the regular workplace. This holds true whether the work was assigned or the employees took on the extra workload themselves.

SLEEP TIME If required to be on duty for less than 24 hours, the employee is considered to be working even though the employee is sleeping or engaging in other personal activities. If over 24 hours, an agreement to exclude a sleeping period of not more than eight hours from time worked is binding. Adequate sleeping facilities must be provided, and the employee must be permitted at least five hours of uninterrupted sleep.

TRAINING SESSIONS Generally, working time includes the time spent by employees in attending lectures and meetings for training purposes.

EXAMPLE

The working time spent by postal clerks in learning mail distribution practices and the operation of letter-sorting machines counts as compensable time because it is (a) controlled and required by the employer, (b) for the primary benefit of the employer, and (c) an integral and indispensable part of the employees' principal work activities.

However, time spent in training sessions need not be counted as working time if ALL the following conditions are met:

1. Attendance by the employee is voluntary.
2. The employee does not produce any goods or perform any other productive work during the meeting or lecture.
3. The meeting or lecture takes place outside regular working hours.
4. The meeting or lecture is not directly related to the employee's work.

PRELIMINARY AND POSTLIMINARY ACTIVITIES

Activities regarded as ***preliminary*** and ***postliminary*** need not be counted as time worked unless required by contract or custom. Under the ***Portal-to-Portal Act,*** these activities are not compensated unless they are an "integral and indispensable part of the employee's principal activities and not specifically excluded by the Act." Some examples of activities regarded as preliminary and postliminary include: walking, riding, or traveling to or from the actual place where employees engage in their principal activities; checking in and out at the plant or office and waiting in line to do so; changing clothes for the convenience of the employee, washing up and showering unless directly related to the specific type of work the employee is hired to perform; and waiting in line to receive paychecks.

Activities that qualify as "work time" but the time spent on them is so short that they are considered ***de minimis*** (insignificant) need not be compensated.

FRACTIONAL PARTS OF AN HOUR

The FLSA requires that employees be paid for ***all*** time worked, including fractional parts of an hour. An employer cannot use an arbitrary formula or an estimate as a substitute for determining precisely the compensable working time which is part of an employee's fixed or regular hours. The Wage and Hour Division allows employers to round off employees' worktime as shown on their time cards (to the nearest five, six, or fifteen minutes). The round-off process must be applied consistently so that over time employees are compensated for all time worked.

Uncertain and indefinite working periods beyond the scheduled working hours cannot be practicably determined. Therefore, a few seconds or minutes may be disregarded. Some courts have allowed from 10 to 20 minutes to be ignored, while other courts have refused to apply the law to periods as small as 10 minutes. Generally, a few minutes of time spent by employees on the company premises for their own convenience before or after their workdays are not included in the hours worked.

A general rule that has been applied is the **7-minute rule.** This rule allows companies to set a policy of rounding seven minutes or less to zero and eight minutes or more to a quarter-hour. This rule must be administered fairly and consistently.

In the case of union or other employment contracts, the method of computing regular and overtime rates may be prescribed in the contracts.

ABSENCES

The FLSA does not require an employer to pay an employee for hours not worked because of illness. For employees on an hourly wage basis, the time card shows the exact hours worked. In addition, the time off for absences does not count toward the 40 hours for overtime pay purposes even if the employee is paid for the absences. Employees on a salary basis are frequently paid for a certain number of days of excused absences after they have been employed by their company for a certain length of time.

TARDINESS

Employers may handle tardiness in many ways. Frequently, when an employee is late or leaves early, causing the time clock to print in red, the supervisor must O.K. the time card. Some companies require the employee to sign a special slip indicating the reason for being late or leaving early. Some companies keep time according to the decimal system, whereby each hour is divided into units of tens (six minutes times 10 periods in each hour). An employee who is late one through six minutes is penalized or "docked" one-tenth of an hour. One who is seven through 12 minutes late is "docked" one-fifth of an hour, etc.

Records Used for Timekeeping

3 LEARNING OBJECTIVE

The FLSA requires employers subject to the law to keep certain time and pay records. For example, employers must keep records that indicate the hours each employee worked each workday and each workweek.

How the employer chooses the methods of keeping time records depends on the size of the company and whether employees are paid on an hourly, weekly, biweekly, semimonthly, or monthly basis. Employees on a salary basis usually work a given number of hours each day and can be required to record and track their hours and to work a specified schedule. Employees on an hourly wage basis may work a varying number of hours with some "down time" and layoffs and some overtime work. All of this time must be recorded in some way.

TIME SHEETS

A **time sheet** provides the information required by law and the data used to compute the payroll. Many small businesses that must keep a record of time worked by each employee require each person to submit and sign a sign time sheet, indicating the times of arrival and departure from work. These time reports are approved by the appropriate supervisor or department head at the end of the pay period. They are then forwarded to the Payroll Department for entry into the payroll system. Time sheets offer a simple method of accumulating employees' working times.

TIME CARDS

Under this timekeeping system, each employee receives a **time card** on which the time worked is recorded manually by the employee or automatically by a time clock. The time card is designed to fit various lengths of pay periods. Figure 2–3 shows one type of time card frequently used for a weekly pay period. The card provides space to record the hours worked, the rate of pay, deductions, and net pay. The Payroll Department inserts the handwritten figures to be used in computing total earnings, deductions, and net pay for the payroll period.

Some time clocks use the **continental system** of recording time, where each day consists of one 24-hour period, instead of two 12-hour periods. The time runs from 12 midnight to 12 midnight. Eight o'clock in the morning is recorded as 800; eight o'clock in the evening, as 2000.

COMPUTERIZED TIME AND ATTENDANCE RECORDING SYSTEMS

The main kinds of computerized time and attendance recording systems include:

1. ***Card-generated systems***—employees use time cards similar to the traditional time cards illustrated earlier. Daily and weekly totals are calculated and printed on the time cards for data entry into the firm's computer system.

FIGURE 2–3

Time Card

No. **312** Pay Ending October 17, 20--

NAME GARY A. SCHNEIDER 262-09-7471

	Hours	Rate	Amount	
Reg.	40	10.75	430	00
O/T	6	16.13	96	78
Total Earnings			526	78
Less Deductions			141	59
NET PAY			385	19

DEDUCTIONS		
OASDI	32	66
HI	7	64
FIT	81	00
SIT	10	54
Group Life Ins.	1	60
Hospital Ins.	3	15
U.S. Sav. Bonds	5	00
Other		
Total	141	59

Days	MORNING IN	MORNING OUT	AFTERNOON IN	AFTERNOON OUT	OVERTIME IN	OVERTIME OUT	Daily Totals
1	M 759	M 1203	M 100	M 505			8
2	TU 750	TU 1204	TU 1259	TU 507			8
3	W 751	W 1201	W 1250	W 504	W 529	W 735	10
4	TH 800	TH 1202	TH 1258	TH 503			8
5	FR 800	FR 1205	FR 101	FR 506			8
6	SA 755	SA 1204					4
7							

Signature *Gary A. Schneider*

2. ***Badge systems***—employees are issued plastic laminated badges containing punched holes or having magnetic strips or bar codes. The badges are used with electronic time clocks that collect and store data, which later become input to the computer system.
3. ***Cardless and badgeless systems***—employees enter only their personal identification numbers (PIN) on a numerical or alphanumerical key pad. This system, like the badge system, uses time clocks to collect and store data for transmission to, and processing by, the firm's computer system.
4. ***Personal computer-based systems***—employees swipe their identification cards across bar code readers connected to personal computers for easy recording of time worked.

For example, the Timekeeper, a self-contained, wall-mounted time clock, contains a computer system.[1] This time clock accepts time and attendance data from time cards and

1 Information supplied by Kronos, Incorporated.

computes complex payroll and on-the-job information. Time-clock systems, such as the Timekeeper, eliminate most manual payroll processing operations. Employees receive their own time cards that show their daily attendance record, thus complying with federal, state, and union regulations. The Timekeeper also totals employee hours and rounds out employee time to fractions of an hour in accordance with the payroll practice of the firm.

The Timekeeper card, shown in Figure 2–4, is similar to the time card illustrated previously. The mark-sense field at the bottom of the card identifies each employee or supervisor and authorizes access to and use of the Timekeeper.

When an employee places the card in the time clock, the computer scans the card, optically verifies the employee's number, and locates the last print line on the card. The time of entry is then printed on the next line. Simultaneously, the computer stores the

FIGURE 2–4

Mark-Sense Time Card Used in the Timekeeper Computerized System

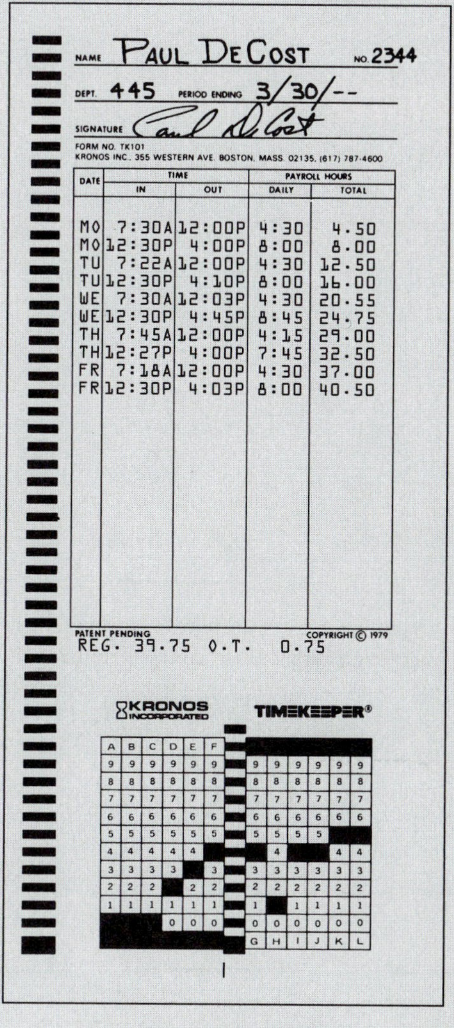

NAME PAUL DE COST NO. 2344

DEPT. 445 PERIOD ENDING 3/30/--

SIGNATURE Paul DeCost

FORM NO. TK101
KRONOS INC., 355 WESTERN AVE. BOSTON, MASS. 02135, (617) 787-4600

DATE	TIME IN	TIME OUT	PAYROLL HOURS DAILY	PAYROLL HOURS TOTAL
MO	7:30A	12:00P	4:30	4.50
MO	12:30P	4:00P	8:00	8.00
TU	7:22A	12:00P	4:30	12.50
TU	12:30P	4:10P	8:00	16.00
WE	7:30A	12:03P	4:30	20.55
WE	12:30P	4:45P	8:45	24.75
TH	7:45A	12:00P	4:15	29.00
TH	12:27P	4:00P	7:45	32.50
FR	7:18A	12:00P	4:30	37.00
FR	12:30P	4:03P	8:00	40.50

PATENT PENDING COPYRIGHT © 1979
REG. 39.75 O.T. 0.75

KRONOS INCORPORATED TIMEKEEPER®

Source: Kronos, Inc.

punch-in time in the system's memory. When an employee punches out, the Timekeeper again verifies the employee's identification number and computes and rounds off the daily and cumulative payroll hours. Next, the actual punch-out time and the computed cumulative hours are printed on the card and stored within the Timekeeper for transmission to a computer for payroll processing. Figure 2–5 charts a computerized time and attendance recording system.

FIGURE 2–5

A Computerized Time and Attendance Recording System

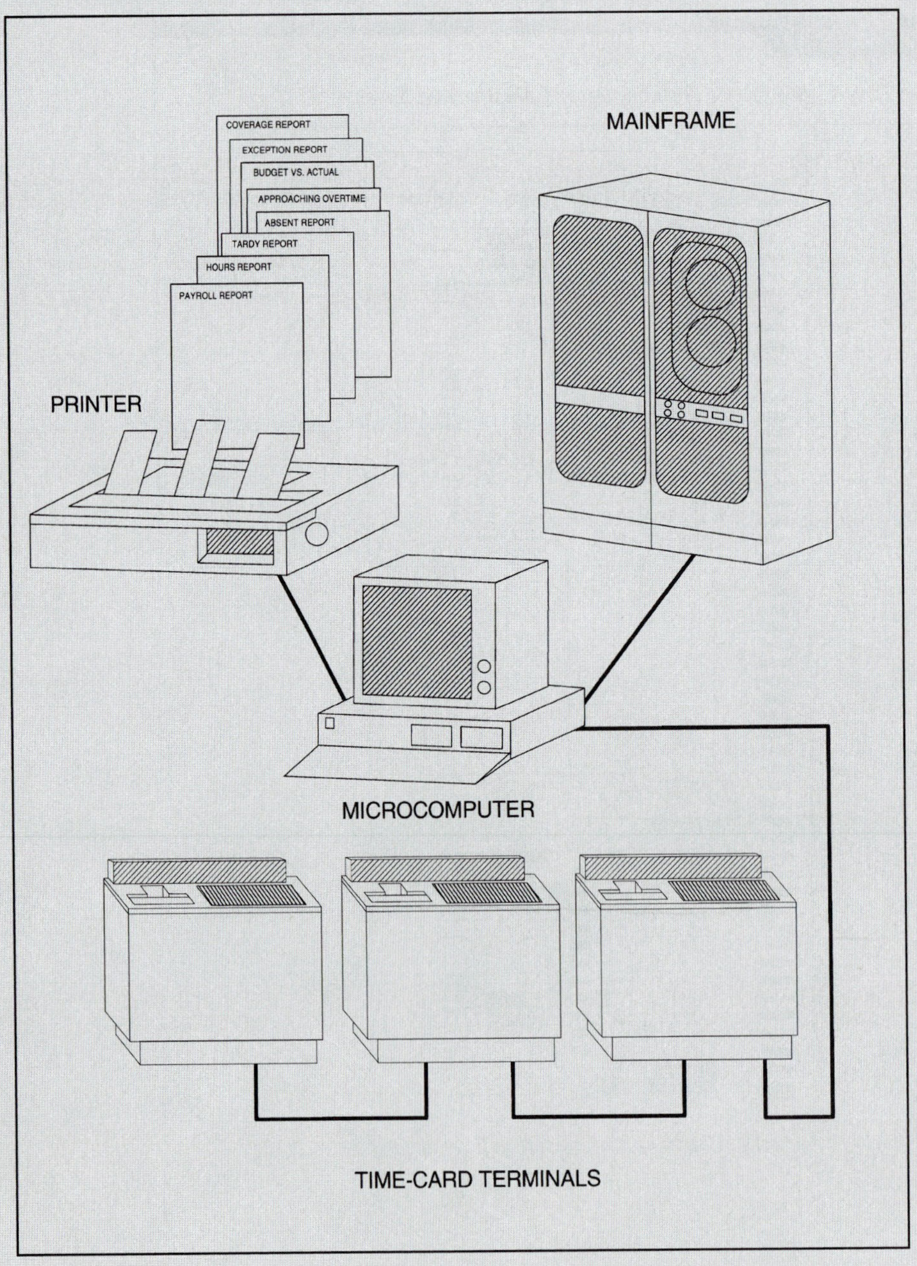

NEXT GENERATION

With more and more employees working outside the traditional office environment, the time clock has not been able to keep up with most companies' needs for time and attendance information. Many companies have been forced to acquire more automated systems.

TOUCH-SCREEN TECHNOLOGY In this system, data can be collected and processed instantaneously. The system requires employees to punch in and out on touch-screen personal computers (PCs), which are connected to the company's main computer server. These touch-screen kiosks are also used to provide information back to the employee regarding the organization.

INTERNET Some Web-based time accounting systems now allow employees to "clock" in and out via the Internet. Employees use passwords to log on to a secured Web site. This site can also be used by the employees to check their hours worked, vacation time accrued, and messages from the Human Resources Department. This can also be accomplished through the use of mobile and wireless data collection devices (cell phones and Personal Digital Assistants). Without ever visiting their office, employees can enter time and labor information.

BIOMETRICS The need for greater security and precision has recently produced a more affordable alternative to companies that are searching for time and attendance systems. A biometric time system uses a time clock that reads an employee's unique fingerprint or hand geometry (size and shape) to validate the employee. This technology is also available in other forms—voice recognition and iris scan. Figure 2–6 illustrates a biometric time clock.

on the NET

http://www.timeclockeshop.com/
In this era of heightened attention to security, biometric time recording systems are becoming reasonably priced and more easily accepted.

FIGURE 2–6

Biometric Time Clock

Photo provided by Recognition Systems, Inc.

Methods of Computing Wages and Salaries

LEARNING OBJECTIVE 4

Employees are usually paid for time worked at a time rate, such as hourly, weekly, biweekly, semimonthly, or monthly. The employee may also be paid at a piece rate, incentive rate, commission basis, or a combination of these rates.

TIME RATE

To compute the wages of employees on an hourly basis, multiply the total regular hours worked by the regular hourly rate. If the employee works overtime, multiply the total overtime hours by the overtime rate. By adding the total regular earnings and the total overtime earnings, we obtain the **gross earnings.** (In the examples that follow, if needed, rates have been rounded to two decimal places.)

EXAMPLE

Joanne French works a 40-hour week at $12.40 an hour with overtime hours paid at 1½ times the regular rate.

Regular weekly earnings are........................... $496.00 (40 × $12.40)
The overtime rate is................................... $18.60 ($12.40 × 1.5)
If French works 4 hours overtime, additional earnings for the 4 hours are........................ $74.40 (4 × $18.60)
French's weekly gross earnings are.................... $570.40 ($496.00 + $74.40)
If paid only for time actually worked and she works only 36 hours during a week, French earns........... $446.40 (36 × $12.40)

The employee's regular rate of pay includes ***all payments*** given for working a particular job. This does not include discretionary bonuses, gifts on special occasions, and contributions to certain welfare plans (see page 2-6).

In the case of factory workers, many factories compute the actual time spent on a certain job so that amount can be charged to that job.

EXAMPLE

Sonja Patel spent 100 minutes on a certain job. The wages chargeable to that job at the regular hourly rate of $11.58 would be computed as follows:

$$\$11.58 \times \frac{100}{60} = \$19.30$$

CALCULATING OVERTIME PAY

In calculating the gross pay of an employee who worked overtime, one of two methods can be used, both of which will result in the same total gross pay.

The most common method is to calculate the gross pay for the 40 hours and then calculate the overtime pay by multiplying the number of hours over 40 by a pay rate of one and one-half times the employee's regular rate of pay.

EXAMPLE

John Dilcher is paid an hourly rate of $18.50 per hour and he worked 49 hours this week. His gross pay is:

40 hours × $18.50	=	$740.00
9 hours × $27.75 ($18.50 × 1.5)	=	249.75
Total gross pay	=	$989.75

The other method is the **overtime premium** approach. In this case, the total hours worked (including overtime hours) are multiplied by the regular rate of pay. Then the overtime premium pay is calculated by multiplying the overtime hours by an overtime premium rate of one-half the regular hourly rate.

EXAMPLE

John Dilcher's (the prior example) pay would be calculated as follows:

49 hours × $18.50	=	$906.50
9 hours × $9.25 ($18.50 × 0.5)	=	83.25
Total gross pay	=	$989.75

By using the overtime premium approach, an employer could save on the calculation of workers' compensation insurance. Most states do not include the overtime premium in the determination of the workers' compensation insurance costs to employers.

Plans in which overtime is **paid in advance** do not violate the pay requirements of the FLSA. In these plans, in weeks in which an employee works less than the applicable statutory workweek (e.g., 40 hours), the employer will advance the difference in pay to raise it to the standard for the statutory workweek. When overtime is worked, the advances (computed at the time and one-half rate) will offset the overtime pay. A running account must be maintained for each employee, and if the prepayment credits are not sufficient to cover the overtime compensation, the difference must be paid on the following payday.

In cases where an employee works at **different rates for different jobs** during the same workweek, the employers can, at their option, calculate the overtime in one of three ways. (1) One could pay at the higher rate for the overtime hours. (2) It may be calculated by taking the total earnings for both jobs, dividing by the total hours worked, then taking one-half of this rate, and multiplying by the overtime hours. (3) One could use an overtime rate based on the rate for the job performed after the 40th hour (the employee must have agreed to this in advance).

on the *JOB*

In 2005, the average employer cost for employee compensation was $26.05. Wages made up 70 percent of this total.

EXAMPLE

Steve Timko worked at two different pay rates during the past week. His main job paid $17.30/hour, while the extra job rate was $20.50. He worked the first 36 hours at Job "A" and 8 hours at Job "B."

Method (1)

Regular earnings	$622.80 (36 × $17.30)
Job B	$164.00 (8 × $20.50)
Overtime rate (higher rate)	$ 10.25 (0.5 × $20.50)
Overtime pay	$ 41.00 (4 × $10.25)
Total pay	$827.80 ($622.80 + $164.00 + $41.00)

Method (2)

Job A	$622.80 (36 × $17.30)
Job B	$164.00 (8 × $20.50)
Overtime rate (1/2)	$ 8.94 ($786.80 ÷ 44 × 0.5)
Extra overtime pay	$ 35.76 (4 × $8.94)
Total pay	$822.56 ($622.80 + $164.00 + $35.76)

Method (3)

Job A	$622.80 (36 × $17.30)
Job B	$164.00 (8 × $20.50)
Overtime pay (Job B)	$ 41.00 (4 × $10.25)
Total pay	$827.80 ($622.80 + $164.00 + $41.00)

5 LEARNING OBJECTIVE

CONVERTING WEEKLY WAGE RATES TO HOURLY RATES When paying on a weekly basis, sometimes employers must convert the weekly wage rate to an hourly rate, especially to figure overtime earnings. To do this, divide the weekly wage rate by the number of hours in the regular workweek.

EXAMPLE

John Hazelton earns $412 a week for a workweek consisting of 40 hours. If Hazelton worked 43 hours in a particular week, compute gross pay as follows:

$412.00 ÷ 40 hours = $10.30 hourly wage rate
$10.30 hourly wage rate × 1.5 = $15.45 overtime wage rate
Gross pay = $412 + (3 hours × $15.45) = $458.35

CONVERTING BIWEEKLY WAGE RATES TO HOURLY RATES If paying employees biweekly, divide the biweekly earnings by 2 to arrive at the weekly rate, and divide the weekly rate by the standard number of hours.

EXAMPLE

Glenda Rome earns $980 biweekly and works a standard 40-hour workweek. Compute Rome's hourly and overtime rates as follows:

$980.00 ÷ 2 = $490.00 regular weekly earnings
$490.00 ÷ 40 = $12.25 regular hourly rate
$12.25 × 1.5 = $18.38 overtime hourly rate

CONVERTING MONTHLY SALARY RATES TO HOURLY RATES If workers paid on a monthly basis earn overtime pay for work beyond a 40-hour week, compute the hourly overtime rate by converting the monthly salary rate to an hourly rate. To do this correctly, you must extend the monthly salary to an annual figure, divide by 52, and then divide by the regular number of hours worked each week.

EXAMPLE

Al Carmen earns $5,200 per month and works a standard 40-hour week. During one week, Carmen earned 6 hours of overtime.

Step 1

Convert the monthly salary rate to a weekly rate by first annualizing the monthly salary. Then divide the annual salary by 52 weeks. →

$5,200 monthly salary × 12 months = $62,400 annual salary
$62,400 annual salary ÷ 52 weeks = $1,200 weekly salary

Step 2

Divide the weekly rate by the standard number of hours in the workweek. →

$1,200 weekly salary ÷ 40 hours = $30.00 hourly rate

Step 3

Compute the overtime rate by multiplying the hourly rate by 1.5. →

$30.00 hourly rate × 1.5 = $45.00 overtime rate

Step 4

Compute the *gross pay* for the week by adding the overtime earnings to the regular weekly earnings. →

Regular weekly earnings	$1,200.00
Overtime earnings (6 × $45.00)	270.00
Gross pay	$1,470.00

CONVERTING SEMIMONTHLY SALARY RATES TO HOURLY RATES Semimonthly salary rates are converted the same as monthly rates except semimonthly earnings are multiplied by 24 instead of by 12 to compute the annual earnings.

EXAMPLE

Margaret Johnson earns $1,175 semimonthly.

Step 1

Annualize the salary. → $1,175 × 24 = $28,200 annual rate

Step 2

Compute the weekly salary. → $28,200 ÷ 52 = $542.31 weekly rate

Step 3

Compute the hourly rate. → $542.31 ÷ 40 = $13.56 hourly rate

Step 4

Compute the overtime rate. → $13.56 × 1.5 = $20.34 overtime rate

Numerous tables of decimal equivalents, such as the one shown in Figure 2–7, help in converting wages to an hourly rate.

EXAMPLE

Weekly salary $550: $550 × 0.025 = $13.75 hourly rate; $550 × 0.0375 = $20.63 hourly overtime rate

Monthly salary $1,800: $1,800 × 0.00577 = $10.39 hourly rate; $1,800 × 0.00866 = $15.59 hourly overtime rate

SALARIED NONEXEMPT EMPLOYEES In order to cut administrative costs, salaries can be paid to nonexempt employees; however, these employees are still subject to FLSA's overtime rules. The employee's ***regular rate*** of pay is found by dividing the number of ***hours expected to be worked*** each week into the weekly salary. The employee is then entitled to be paid at the regular rate of pay for the first 40 hours and at one and one-half times the regular rate of pay for the hours over 40.

If an employee's normal workweek is less than 40 hours, as long as an agreement exists between the employee and the employer that the salary covers all hours worked up to and including 40 hours, the employer does not have to pay for the "overtime hours" up to the 40 hours.

FIGURE 2–7

Table of Decimal Equivalents to Convert into Weekly, Hourly, and Hourly Overtime Salary Rates

To convert into:	Weekly Salary Rate	Hourly Salary Rate	Hourly Overtime Salary Rate
Multiply the:			
Weekly salary rate by	. . . .	0.025	0.0375
Semimonthly salary rate by	0.4615	0.01154	0.0173
Monthly salary rate by	0.2308	0.00577	0.00866
Yearly salary rate by	0.01923	0.00048	0.000721

EXAMPLE

Rob Hau, a nonexempt employee, works a standard 35-hour week and is paid a salary of $1,080.00. Last week, Hau worked 39 hours and was paid his normal salary of $1,080.00 since he has an agreement with his employer that the salary covers all hours worked with the exception of the work hours over 40.

If he had worked 43 hours, his pay would have been:

Regular (up to 40 hours) = $1,080.00
Overtime pay:
$1,080.00 ÷ 35 = $ 30.86 per hour
$30.86 × 1.5 = $ 46.29
$46.29 × 3 = $ 138.87
$1,080.00 + $138.87 = $1,218.87 gross pay

on the JOB

This calculation also applies to employees who receive a day rate compensation. The total pay for the week would be divided by the hours worked. The extra half rate would then be applied to the hours worked over 40 to determine the overtime pay.

SALARIED WITH FLUCTUATING WORKWEEK Employers may pay employees who work fluctuating schedules a fixed salary, regardless of the number of hours worked.

Both parties must agree, prior to the workweek, that this pay calculation method will be used. In such cases, overtime pay is found by dividing the normal salary by the total hours worked. An ***extra half rate*** is then paid for all hours worked over 40. Some states prohibit or limit the use of this method of payment.

EXAMPLE

Matt Leonard earns $739.20 a week with fluctuating workweek hours. If he worked 48 hours in one week, his gross pay would be calculated as follows:

$739.20 ÷ 48 hours = $ 15.40 regular rate
$15.40 × 0.5 = $ 7.70 extra half pay rate
8 hours O.T. × $7.70 = $ 61.60 extra pay
$739.20 + $61.60 = $800.80 weekly gross pay

An alternative method of calculating the overtime is to use the fixed salary divided by 40 hours to determine the regular rate of pay. This way, the overtime premium will be the same no matter how many hours are worked. This method eliminates the need to recalculate the regular rate of pay each week as the number of hours worked changes.[2]

EXAMPLE

Same as the example above.

$739.20 ÷ 40 hours = $ 18.48 regular rate
$18.48 × 0.5 = $ 9.24 extra half pay rate
8 hours O.T. × $9.24 = $ 73.92 extra pay
$739.20 + $73.92 = $813.12 weekly gross pay

As a true "fixed salary arrangement," employers cannot make deductions from the salary for absences occasioned by the employee. The exception would apply to disciplinary deductions.

BELO Plan. An alternative salary method to compensate employees working fluctuating schedules is the BELO plan. It is more restrictive than the fluctuating workweek method, and the following conditions must be met:

- Irregular work hours are the nature of the job.
- There are large variations in weekly hours above and below 40 hours.
- Rate of pay cannot include additional forms of compensation—bonuses, commissions, etc.

2 Robert Ditmer, "Using a Fluctuating Worksheet May Save You Money," *PAYTECH*, April 2003, pp. 42–44.

- Guaranteed compensation cannot be for more than 60 hours—beyond 60 hours requires one-and-a-half times the regular rate.
- Agreement must exist between the employer and the employee.

Basically, the salary is figured by calculating the wages for the maximum number of hours at straight time and then adding 50 percent (one-half) of the regular rate for the overtime hours.

EXAMPLE

The agreement between John Kalas and his employer provides for a pay rate of $14 per hour with a maximum of 48 hours per week.

48 hours × $14 =	$672.00
8 hours × 0.5 × $14 =	56.00
John's weekly salary =	$728.00

No matter how many hours John works each week (above and below 40), his gross pay would be $728.00. However, if John works beyond the agreed-upon maximum of 48 hours, he must be paid at one-and-a-half times his regular rate of pay (1.5 × $14 = $21) for the hours over 48.

SELF-STUDY QUIZ 2-3 *Compute the hourly and overtime rates for a standard 40-hour workweek for the following amounts:*

		Hourly Rate	Overtime Rate
1.	$525.00 weekly	13.12	19.68
2.	$892.00 biweekly	11.15	16.72
3.	$1,450.00 semimonthly	16.73	25.09
4.	$1,600.00 monthly	9.23	13.84

PIECE RATE

Under the **piece-rate system**, the employer pays workers according to their output, such as an amount for each unit or piece produced. Thus, the wages increase as production increases. The employer keeps production records for each employee so that these records will be available when computing the wages earned by each employee. The Fair Labor Standards Act specifies that under a piece-rate system, the regular hourly rate of pay is computed as shown in the following example.

EXAMPLE

Sally Ray produced 13,000 items during a 40-hour workweek. Ray is paid 4 cents per unit and receives a bonus 2 cents for each unit over 12,000 in a week. Ray's weekly earnings are:

Step 1

Add the total weekly earnings from piece rates and all other sources, such as incentive bonuses. →

Regular earnings	13,000 × $0.04 =	$520.00
Incentive earnings	1,000 × $0.02 =	20.00
Total weekly earnings		$540.00

Step 2

Divide the weekly earnings by total number of hours worked in the week for which such compensation was paid. →

$$\frac{\text{Total weekly earnings}}{\text{Total hours worked}} = \frac{\$540.00}{40} = \$13.50 \text{ per hour}$$

The piece rate must at least equal the statutory minimum wage rate. In some instances, an employer may pay a worker an hourly rate for some hours and a piece rate for other hours during the week. In such cases, both the hourly rate and the piece-rate earnings must be at least the minimum rate.

OVERTIME EARNINGS FOR PIECEWORKERS—METHOD A For overtime work, the pieceworker is entitled to be paid, in addition to piecework earnings for the entire period, a sum equal to one-half the regular hourly rate of pay multiplied by the number of hours worked in excess of 40 in the week.

EXAMPLE

Paul Fritz produced 3,073 pieces in a 44-hour workweek and is paid 14¾ cents for every unit produced.

Step 1

Compute the total regular weekly earnings. → 3,073 × \$0.1475 = \$453.27 regular weekly earnings

Step 2

Compute the regular hourly rate of pay. → \$453.27 ÷ 44 hours = \$10.30 regular hourly rate of pay

Step 3

Compute the overtime rate of pay and compute the overtime earnings. The regular earnings include the pay for the overtime hours at the regular rate. This is for the extra one-half time. → 0.5 × \$10.30 = \$5.15 overtime rate of pay
4 hours × \$5.15 = \$20.60 overtime earnings

Step 4

Compute the total regular and overtime earnings for the week. → \$453.27 + \$20.60 = \$473.87 piecework and overtime earnings

OVERTIME EARNINGS FOR PIECEWORKERS—METHOD B Another method of computing overtime payment for pieceworkers complies with the requirements of the FLSA. Before doing the work, piece-rate employees may agree with their employer, in advance of the work being done, to be paid at a rate not less than one and one-half times the piece rate for each piece produced during the overtime hours. No additional overtime pay will be due to the employees.

EXAMPLE

Assume that in the preceding example, Fritz earned overtime at a piece rate of one and one-half times the regular rate for all pieces produced during overtime hours. Of the total 3,073 pieces produced, 272 were produced in the 4 overtime hours. Fritz's total piecework and overtime earnings are as follows:

2,801 × \$0.1475 = \$413.15 piecework earnings
272 pieces × 0.2213 (\$0.1475 × 1.5) = \$60.19 overtime earnings
\$413.15 + \$60.19 = \$473.34 piecework and overtime earnings

SELF-STUDY QUIZ 2-4 *Bruce Eaton is paid 5 cents per unit under the piece-rate system. During one week, Eaton worked 46 hours and produced 5,520 units. Compute the following:*

1. The piecework earnings $________
2. The regular hourly rate $________
3. The overtime hourly rate $________
4. The overtime earnings $________
5. The total earnings $________

SPECIAL INCENTIVE PLANS

Most wage systems involving special incentives are modifications of the piece-rate system described previously. Under many incentive plans, the company determines a standard for the quantity that an average worker can produce in a certain period of time. Workers failing to reach the standard earn a lower piece rate, while those who produce more than the standard receive a higher rate. With incentive plans, the computation of the payroll is usually more complicated than under the time-rate or piece-rate systems. Records of time worked as well as the production of each employee must be available in computing wages under most incentive plans.

on the NET

http://www.incentivelogic.com
There are companies that specialize in setting up different forms of employee incentive plans.

EXAMPLE

Chu Wang, Inc., pays its blade polishers according to the following piece-rate incentive plan:

No. of Blades Polished per 8-Hour Workday	Earnings per Blade Polished
less than 1,850	0.0150
1,850 to 1,999	0.0165
2,000 (Daily Standard)	0.0180
2,001 to 2,100	0.0198
2,101 to 2,250	0.0217
over 2,250	0.0240

COMMISSIONS

The entire remuneration, or at least part of the remuneration, of certain employees may be on a commission basis. A **commission** is a stated percentage of revenue paid to an employee who transacts a piece of business or performs a service. Thus, a salesperson working in a certain territory may have a fixed salary each year plus a bonus for sales in excess of a certain amount.

EXAMPLE

Kate Kline receives an annual $35,000 base salary for working a certain territory. A sales quota of $800,000 has been set for that territory for the current year. Kline will receive a 6 percent commission on all sales in excess of $800,000. For the current year, the sales in the territory are $1,030,000. The bonus paid Kline would be:

$13,800 (6% of $230,000)

Kline's total earnings for the year would be:

$48,800 ($35,000 + $13,800)

There are numerous variations of the commission method of remuneration. Some businesses offer special premiums or bonuses for selling certain merchandise. For example, to help move merchandise in a ready-to-wear department, a department store will frequently pay a premium or a bonus to the salesperson who sells specific items of merchandise. Commissions are considered to be payments for hours worked and must be included in determining the regular hourly rate. This applies regardless of whether the commission is the sole source of the employee's compensation or is paid in addition to a salary or hourly rate. It does not matter whether the commission earnings are computed daily, weekly, monthly, or at some other interval. However, in the case of outside salespeople who are exempt from the FLSA, commissions paid to them do not have to meet the minimum wage criteria.

Commissions are treated as straight-time pay. To calculate overtime, the weekly commission is divided by the *total hours* worked. This is the employee's regular rate of pay. The overtime pay would be one-half the regular rate of pay for all hours worked over 40 in the workweek.

NONDISCRETIONARY BONUSES

A bonus that is part of employees' wage rates must be allocated to the wages for the period covered by the bonus. Bonuses that are known in advance, or that are set up as inducements to achieve goals, would fit into this category. The employer has only to add the bonus to the wages for the week and divide the sum by the *total* hours worked to determine the regular rate of pay. One-half of the regular rate would be the premium needed to apply to the overtime hours.

EXAMPLE

Garrison Heard earns $9.00 per hour and has earned a production bonus this week of $27.60. Since Heard worked 46 hours this week, his gross pay would be:

46 hours × $9.00 = $414.00 + $27.60 = $441.60
$441.60 ÷ 46 hours = $9.60 regular rate of pay
$9.60 × 0.5 = $4.80 × 6 hours = $28.80
$441.60 + $28.80 = $470.40 gross pay

PROFIT-SHARING PLANS

Many businesses have developed **profit-sharing plans** whereby the employer shares with the employees a portion of the profits of the business. Generally, profit-sharing plans include the following three types:

1. Cash payments based upon the earnings of a specified period.
2. Profits placed in a special fund or account to be drawn upon by employees at some future time. This plan may be in the form of a savings account, a pension fund, or an annuity.
3. Profits distributed to employees in the form of capital stock.

The payments made pursuant to a bona fide profit-sharing plan that meets the standards fixed by the secretary of labor's regulations are not deemed wages in determining the employee's regular rate of pay for overtime purposes.

VIOLATIONS AND REMEDIES

In a situation where an employer fails to pay an employee the minimum wage or the proper amount of overtime pay, the Wage and Hour Division will require the employer to pay enough backpay to satisfy the requirements of the law. In cases where the violations were willful, the FLSA provides for the payment of additional "liquidated damages" which will be equal to the amounts of the backpay and overtime awards. In cases of incorrect classification of an employee as exempt, the employee is entitled to retroactive overtime pay. The statute of limitations in these cases is two years unless the violation is willful. In that case, the government can go back three years.

on the *JOB*

In fiscal 2005, the Wage and Hour Division recovered over $166 million in back wages for 241,000 workers.

KEY TERMS

Biweekly *(p. 2-6)*
Commission *(p. 2-29)*
Common-law relationship *(p. 2-5)*
Continental system *(p. 2-17)*
Discretionary bonus *(p. 2-6)*
Domestic service *(p. 2-5)*
Employee *(p. 2-5)*
Enterprise coverage *(p. 2-4)*
Exempt employees *(p. 2-10)*
Gross earnings *(p. 2-22)*
Individual employee coverage *(p. 2-4)*
Nondiscretionary bonus *(p. 2-6)*
Overtime premium *(p. 2-22)*
Piece-rate system *(p. 2-27)*
Principal activities *(p. 2-14)*
Profit-sharing plans *(p. 2-30)*
Salary *(p. 2-6)*
Semimonthly *(p. 2-6)*
7-minute rule *(p. 2-16)*
Time card *(p. 2-17)*
Time sheet *(p. 2-17)*
Tip *(p. 2-7)*
Tipped employee *(p. 2-7)*
Wage *(p. 2-6)*
Wages *(p. 2-6)*
Workweek *(p. 2-8)*

CHAPTER SUMMARY

The focus of this chapter deals with the calculation of employees' gross pays. This must start with a review of the Fair Labor Standards Act, which sets the minimum wage ($5.85 per hour/$2.13 for tipped employees) and the standard for overtime pay (over 40 hours at time-and-one-half). Exemptions from these requirements do apply to white-collar workers who are paid on a salary basis of at least $455 per week and meet the "primary duty" requirements. The FLSA coverage also included a review of the Equal Pay Act and the Child Labor Laws.

In examining the employees' work time, the principal activities were defined with a look at the "gray areas"—clothes- changing, travel, rest periods, meal periods, training, etc.

The calculations in this chapter involved the regular pay (hours worked × hourly rate of pay), overtime pay (hours over 40 × time-and-one-half the hourly rate of pay), and conversions of weekly, biweekly, monthly, and semimonthly wage rates to hourly rates.

To determine the overtime of the nonexempt salaried employee who works fluctuating schedules involves dividing the fixed salary by the hours worked to get the regular rate of pay. An extra half of this rate is then paid for all hours worked over 40. This also applies to the BELO plan that instead of using hours worked, divides the salary by a set maximum number of hours.

The chapter ends with a review of three other compensation plans—piece rate, commissions, and bonuses.

MATCHING QUIZ

D 1. Biweekly
G 2. Commission
F 3. Tipped employee
E 4. Common-law relationship
H 5. Gross earnings
C 6. Individual employee coverage
J 7. Overtime premium
B 8. Exempt employees
I 9. Piece-rate system
A 10. Semimonthly

A. Remuneration paid twice a month
B. Exempt from some or all of the FLSA requirements
C. Employee engages in interstate commerce or produces goods for such commerce
D. Remuneration paid every two weeks
E. Employer has the right to control both what work will be done and how it will be done
F. Engaged in a job in which tips of more than $30 a month are regularly received
G. Payment to employee based on a stated percentage of revenue
H. Regular earnings plus overtime earnings
I. Pay system based on an amount paid to the employee per units produced
J. One-half the regular hourly rate

QUESTIONS FOR REVIEW

1. Explain the two bases of coverage provided by the FLSA.
2. In determining the existence of an employer/employee relationship, the IRS groups the items of evidence into which general categories?
3. What kinds of establishments may employ full-time students at 85% of the minimum wage?
4. What is Miami's living wage rate?
5. To what extent are tips considered wages under the FLSA?
6. Explain how a state employee working in the area of public safety may use compensatory time off in lieu of overtime compensation.
7. Under what conditions would an employee of a state receive cash for his or her compensatory time off?
8. The following employees are exempt from various requirements of the FLSA. Indicate from which requirement or requirements each of the following employees is exempt:
   a. Amusement park employee
   b. Taxicab driver
   c. Casual baby sitter
   d. Elementary school teacher
   e. Outside salesperson
9. What are the types of exempt white-collar employees?
10. What requirements need be met in order to be classified as a "highly compensated" employee?
11. In order not to interfere with the schooling and well-being of minors between the ages of 14 and 16, employers of these minors must satisfy what three conditions?
12. In determining the working time of employees, how are the principal activities of employees defined?
13. Under what conditions is travel time counted as time worked?
14. What is the difference between "engaged to wait" and "waiting to be engaged" as far as working time?
15. In order to get caught up, an employee takes work home. Must the employee be paid for this extra time?
16. When is time spent by employees in attending lectures and meetings for training purposes not counted as working time?
17. Under what conditions would preliminary and postliminary activities be counted as time worked?
18. How does a biometric time system identify an employee?
19. What is the Wage and Hour Division's position on the rounding off of fractional parts of an hour in determining an employee's time worked?
20. If the ***overtime premium*** approach is used, how is the overtime premium pay calculated?
21. Explain how to calculate the overtime hourly rate for employees who are paid biweekly.
22. In the case of a salaried nonexempt employee, how is the regular rate of pay determined?
23. How is overtime pay calculated for a nonexempt employee who works on fluctuating schedules and is paid a fixed salary?
24. Are commissions included in determining an employee's regular rate of pay?
25. In cases of willful failure to pay employees the minimum wage or the correct amount of overtime, the Wage and Hour Division will require the employer to take what kind of corrective action?

QUESTIONS FOR DISCUSSION

1. Abreu Company allows employees the option of carrying over unused vacation days or "cashing" them out. If they cash out, does the employer count the time or earnings when calculating overtime for these nonexempt employees?[3]
2. Along with many other companies, Sanchez Printers observes the Friday after Thanksgiving as a paid holiday. The company requires each employee to make up Friday's lost hours in the following workweek by working extra hours without pay. Is Sanchez Printers proceeding legally by requiring its employees to work extra hours without compensation to make up for the hours lost on the Friday holiday? Explain.
3. Lidle Company needs time to calculate employees' overtime payments by the end of the pay period in which the overtime is worked. Can they pay the overtime payments with the following period's paycheck?
4. The Payroll Department of DuMont has a policy of waiting one full week before correcting any paycheck errors of $30 or less. However, any pay shortages that exceed $30 are made up the same day. Also, any amounts less than $30 are made up the same day when the particular circumstances of the employees indicate that it would place an undue hardship on them to wait until the next pay one week later.

   Denise Harris, an order checker in DuMont's Shipping Department, discovered an error of $28.34 in her weekly check. When Harris reported the error, a payroll clerk informed her that she would have to wait until the next week's paycheck to recover the amount, since the underpayment was less than $30.

   What is your reaction to DuMont's policy of providing for paycheck corrections? Assume that Harris protests the delay and in court argues that her earned wages

3 *Payroll Currently*, June 25, 2004, Issue #13, p. 3.

should be paid on the date due. As the judge hearing the case, how would you decide?

5. Mack Banta, a nonexempt account representative, worked extra hours this week as a call operator. A number of operators were out for the week and Banta was asked to pick up some of their hours. Can the company pay Banta at a lower pay rate for the hours he worked as an operator? These extra hours also pushed Banta's work time over 40 hours. How should the company calculate Banta's overtime pay?

DATE ______________ NAME ______________________________

PRACTICAL PROBLEMS—SERIES A

Special forms required to solve the Practical Problems are provided along with the problems in each chapter.

> *Note:* In this chapter and in all succeeding work throughout the course, ***unless instructed otherwise,*** calculate hourly rates and overtime rates as follows:
>
> **1.** Carry the hourly rate and the overtime rate to 3 decimal places and then round off to 2 decimal places.
> **2.** If the third decimal place is 5 or more, round to the next higher cent.
> **3.** If the third decimal place is less than 5, simply drop the third decimal place.
>
> *Examples:* \$6.765 should be rounded to \$6.77.
> \$6.764 should be rounded to \$6.76.
>
> Also, use the minimum hourly wage of \$5.85 in solving these problems and all that follow.

2-1A LO 1.

Eleanor Wu, a full-time student at Southwestern University, is employed by Gifford's Dress Shop as a salesperson. Her hourly rate is \$3.95. One week Wu worked 32¾ hours.

a. Wu's earnings for the week are . . . . \$ __________

b. Is the hourly rate in violation of the FLSA? Explain.

____

____

c. If the hourly rate is in violation of the FLSA, the amount the dress shop should pay Wu is . . . . \$ __________

2-2A LO 1.

Ben Lieber is a waiter at the Harbor House, where he receives a weekly wage of \$80 plus tips for a 40-hour workweek. Lieber's weekly tips usually range from \$180 to \$200.

a. Under the Fair Labor Standards Act, the minimum amount of wages that Lieber must receive for a 40-hour workweek is . . . . \$ __________

b. Since it is in violation of the FLSA, the additional amount it should pay Lieber each week to meet the minimum wage requirement for a tipped employee is . . . . \$ __________

2-3A LO 4.

The hours worked and the hourly wage rates for five employees of Kagan Company for the week ended September 10 follow.

a. For each employee, compute the gross earnings.
b. Compute the total gross earnings for all employees.

Employee	Hours Worked	Regular Hourly Wage Rate	(a) Gross Earnings
Darley, R.	38	\$9.70	\$ __________
Waxman, B.	40	8.35	__________
Isaac, J..	37	9.00	__________
Bruner, H.	40	7.75	__________
Kellogg, P.	32½	8.40	__________
		(b) Total gross earnings.	\$ __________

2-4A LO 4.

The wages and hours information for five employees of McNeese Enterprises for the week ended July 5 is given below. Employees work a standard 40-hour workweek and are paid time and one-half for all hours over 40 in each workweek.

a. For each employee, compute the regular earnings, overtime rate, overtime earnings, and total gross earnings.
b. Compute the total gross earnings for all employees.

(a)

Employee	Hours Worked	Regular Hourly Wage Rate	Regular Earnings	Overtime Rate	Overtime Earnings	Total Gross Earnings
Carman, T.	47	$ 9.45	$ 378	$ 14.18	$ 99.26	$ 477.26
Galasso, A.	42	11.90	476	17.85	35.70	511.70
Jones, B.	48	8.85	354	13.28	106.24	460.24
Rodna, G.	44	8.25	330	12.38	49.52	379.52
Wilmon, W.	45½	7.40	296	11.10	61.05	357.05
				(b) Total gross earnings		$ 2185.77

2-5A LO 1.

George Dixon, a white-collar exempt employee, started working for Duffy Company on Wednesday of this week. He worked 8 hours on Wednesday and 10 hours on both Thursday and Friday. His annual salary is $85,000, and he is paid weekly for a 5-day week. Determine his gross pay for his first partial week of work.

Gross pay . . . . $________

2-6A LO 2.

John Porter is an hourly employee of Motter Company located in New York City. This week, Porter had to travel to the company's regional office in Albany. He left Sunday at noon and arrived in Albany at 3:00 P.M. During the week, he worked his normal 40 hours in the Albany office (Monday through Friday—9 A.M. to 5 P.M.). In addition, he attended the company's 4-hour work training session on Wednesday evening. Porter's hourly rate of pay is $14.80 per hour.

a. Porter's overtime earnings for the week are . . . . $________

b. Porter's total earnings for the week are . . . . $________

2-7A LO 4.

Joseph Cavato is paid $12.96 per hour. During the past week, he worked 46 hours, and he is a covered employee who must be paid for overtime. Calculate his gross pay using the overtime premium approach.

a. Regular pay (46 hours) . . . . $________

b. Overtime premium pay . . . . . . ________

c. Gross pay . . . . $________

2-8A LO 3, 4.

The following time card shows the time worked one week by Pat Skea. The employer disregards any time before 8:00 A.M. or between 12:00 and 1:00 P.M. and after 5:00 P.M. Employees do not begin work until 8:00 A.M. or 1:00 P.M., and do not work beyond 5:00 P.M., unless they are asked to work overtime. Hours worked beyond the regular 8-hour day and on Saturday are paid at one and one-half times the regular rate. Hours worked on Sunday are paid double the regular rate. Fractions of the hour for time worked are based on full quarter-hour increments.

2-8A (concluded)

No. 72 Name Pat Skea							(a)
Day	Morning		Afternoon		Overtime		Hours Worked
	In	Out	In	Out	In	Out	
M	7:50	12:00	12:50	5:01			
T	7:56	12:01	12:49	5:02	5:30	7:31	
W	7:59	12:02	12:58	5:03			
T	7:45	12:00	12:55	5:00	5:29	8:02	
F	8:01	12:01	1:00	5:01	6:00	7:30	
S	7:48	12:02					
S			2:00	6:03			
(b)	Total Hours Worked						
Remarks____							

Skea's regular wage rate is $11.50 per hour, and the regular workweek is 40 hours with five 8-hour days. Compute:

a. The hours worked each day. (Ignore the one-minute tardiness on Friday.) . . . . ____________

b. The total hours worked. . . . . . . ____________

c. The regular earnings . . . . $____________

d. The overtime earnings . . . . ____________

e. The total earnings . . . . $____________

2-9A LO 3.

Under the decimal system of computing time worked at Timmerman Company, production workers who are tardy are "docked" according to the schedule shown below.

Minutes Late in Ringing in	Fractional Hour Deducted
1 through 6	1/10
7 through 12	2/10
13 through 18	3/10
19 through 24	4/10
etc.	

The regular hours of work, Monday through Friday, are from 7:30 to 11:30 A.M. and from 12:30 to 4:30 P.M. During one week, Henry Vanderhoff, who earns $12.15 an hour, reports in and checks out as shown below. Employees are not paid for ringing in a few minutes before 7:30 and 12:30 nor for ringing out a few minutes after 11:30 and 4:30.

(a)

DAY	AM		PM		HRS WORKED
	In	Out	In	Out	
M	7:28	11:31	12:29	4:31	
T	7:35	11:30	12:30	4:30	
W	7:50	11:33	12:27	4:32	
Th	7:27	11:31	12:50	4:33	
F	7:28	11:32	12:40	4:30	

2-9A (concluded)

Refer to the partial time card and compute:

a. The hours worked each day. . . . __________

b. The total hours worked . . . . . . __________

c. The gross earnings for the week . . . . $__________

2-10A LO 3, 4.

Potts, Inc., recently converted from a 5-day, 40-hour workweek to a 4-day, 40-hour workweek, with overtime continuing to be paid at one and one-half times the regular hourly rate for all hours worked beyond 40 in the week. In this company, time is recorded under the continental system, as shown on the time card at the right.

Sue Ellen Boggs is part of the Group B employees whose regular workweek is Tuesday through Friday. The working hours each day are 800 to 1200; 1230 to 430; and 600 to 800. The company disregards any time before 800, between 1200 and 1230, and between 430 and 600, and permits employees to ring in up to 10 minutes late before any deduction is made for tardiness. Deductions are made to the nearest 1/4 of an hour for workers who are more than 10 minutes late in ringing in.

No. 160 Hr. Rate $8.45
Name Sue Ellen Boggs O.T. Rate $12.675

Time		Mon	Tues	Wed	Thurs	Fri	Sat	
Evening	Out		802	801	805	800		
Evening	In		601	609	602	600		
Afternoon	Out		430	431	430	435		
Afternoon	In		1230	1231	1230	1238		
Morning	Out		1200	1202	1200	1203	1201	
Morning	In		755	750	813	759	800	Total for Week
Daily Totals		(a)						(b)

Remarks *13 minutes late Thursday - deduct ¼ hr.*

Refer to the time card and compute:

a. The daily total hours. . . . . __________

b. The total hours for the week. . . . . . . __________

c. The regular weekly earnings . . . . $__________

d. The overtime earnings (company rounds O/T rate to 3 decimal places) . . . . __________

e. The total weekly earnings . . . . $__________

2-11A LO 1.

Kyle Forman worked 47 hours during the week for Erickson Company at two different jobs. His pay rate was $14.00 for the first 40 hours, and his pay rate was $11.80 for the other 7 hours. Determine his gross pay for that week if the company uses the one-half average rate method.

a. Gross pay . . . . $__________

b. If prior agreement existed that overtime would be paid at the rate for the job performed after the 40th hour, the gross pay would be . . . . $__________

2-12A LO 4.

Charlene Harris, a nonexempt employee, receives $595 for a regular 40-hour week and time and one-half for overtime. For a workweek of 46 hours, compute:

a. The regular earnings . . . . $__________

b. The overtime earnings . . . . __________

c. The total earnings . . . . $__________

2-13A LO 4.

Cal DiMangino earns $2,875 each month and works 40 hours each week. Compute:

a. The hourly rate . . . . $ ________

b. The overtime rate at time and one-half . . . . $ ________

2-14A LO 4.

Sheila Williams, a medical secretary, earns $2,575 monthly for a 35-hour week. For overtime work, she receives extra pay at the regular hourly rate up to 40 hours and time and one-half beyond 40 hours in any week. During one semimonthly pay period, Williams worked 10 hours overtime. Only 2 hours of this overtime were beyond 40 hours in any one week. Compute:

a. The regular semimonthly earnings $ ________

b. The overtime earnings . . . . ________

c. The total earnings . . . . $ ________

2-15A LO 4.

Kenneth Caplan is a salaried employee who normally works a 37½ hour week and is paid a weekly salary of $675.00. The agreement that he has with his employer states that his salary is to cover all hours worked up to and including 40. This week, Caplan worked 42 hours. Calculate his gross pay.

Gross pay . . . . $ ________

2-16A LO 4.

Bernardette Pellini is a salaried employee who works fluctuating work schedules. She is paid a fixed salary of $915 each week, with an agreement with her employer that overtime (over 40 hours) will be paid at an extra half-rate, based on the actual hours worked. This week she worked 52 hours. Compute:

a. The overtime earnings . . . . $ ________

b. The total earnings . . . . $ ________

c. If this was a BELO plan with a pay rate of $22.00 per hour and a maximum of 53 hours, how much would Pellini be paid for 52 hours? . . . . $ ________

2-17A LO 4.

During the first week in November, Erin Mills worked 45½ hours and produced 1,275 units under a piece-rate system. The regular piece rate is $0.35 a unit. Mills is paid overtime according to the FLSA ruling for overtime work under a piece-rate system. Compute:

a. The piecework earnings . . . . $ ________

b. The regular hourly rate . . . . $ ________

The overtime hourly rate . . . . $ ________

c. The overtime earnings . . . . ________

d. The total earnings . . . . $ ________

2-18A LO 4.

Refer to Problem 2–17A. Assume that Mills had agreed with her employer prior to the performance of the work that she would be paid one and one-half times the regular piece rate for all pieces produced during the overtime hours. Assume that her production totals for the week were 1,075 pieces during regular hours and 200 pieces during overtime hours. Compute:

a. The piecework earnings . . . . . . $ ________

b. The overtime earnings . . . . ________

c. The total earnings . . . . $ ________

2-19A **LO 4.**

Wendy Epstein, a sales representative, earns an annual salary of $29,500 and receives a commission on that portion of her annual sales that exceeds $150,000. The commission is 8.5% on all sales up to $50,000 above the quota. Beyond that amount, she receives a commission of 10%. Her total sales for the past year were $295,000. Compute:

a. The regular annual salary . . . . . $__________

b. The commission . . . . __________

c. The total annual earnings . . . . . $__________

2-20A **LO 4.**

Joyce Sand is employed as a salesperson in the men's department of Lukens Fashions. In addition to her weekly base salary of $240, Sand is paid a commission of 1% on her total net sales for the week (total gross sales less any customer returns). During the past week, to promote the sale of its fine cashmere sweaters, Lukens agreed to pay Sand an additional PM (push money) of 2% of the total net sales of cashmere sweaters. Sand's weekly sales tally is given below.

Item	Gross Sales	Customer Returns
Regular sweaters	$400	$48
Cashmere sweaters	995	75
Ties	190	-0-
Dress shirts	445	39
Sports shirts	185	25

Compute Sand's total weekly earnings, showing her (a) weekly base salary, (b) commission, (c) PM, and (d) total weekly earnings.

a. Weekly base salary		$ 240.00
Weekly gross sales	$2215	
Less customer returns	187	
Weekly net sales	$ 2028	
b. Commission: $ 2028 × 1%		20.28
Weekly gross sales of cashmere sweaters	$ 995	
Less customer returns	75	
Weekly net sales of cashmere sweaters	$ 920	
c. PM: $ 920 × 2%		18.40
d. Total weekly earnings		$ 278.68

PRACTICAL PROBLEMS—SERIES B

Special forms required to solve the Practical Problems are provided along with the problems in each chapter.

> *Note:* In this chapter and in all succeeding work throughout the course, ***unless instructed otherwise,*** calculate hourly rates and overtime rates as follows:
>
> 1. Carry the hourly rate and the overtime rate to 3 decimal places and then round off to 2 decimal places.
> 2. If the third decimal place is 5 or more, round to the next higher cent.
> 3. If the third decimal place is less than 5, simply drop the third decimal place.
>
> *Examples:* \$6.765 should be rounded to \$6.77.
> \$6.764 should be rounded to \$6.76.
>
> Also, use the minimum hourly wage of \$5.85 in solving these problems and all that follow.

2-1B LO 1.

Kathy Kirby, a full-time student at Canton University, is employed by Garland's Dress Shop as a salesperson. Her hourly rate is \$4.25. One week, Kirby worked 33¼ hours.

a. Kirby's earnings for the week are . . . . \$ ____________

b. Is the hourly rate in violation of the FLSA? Explain.

____

____

c. If the hourly rate is in violation of the FLSA, the amount the dress shop should pay Kirby is . . . . . \$ ____________

2-2B LO 1.

Bert Garro is a waiter at the La Bron House, where he receives a weekly wage of \$75 plus tips for a 40-hour workweek. Garro's weekly tips usually range from \$200 to \$250.

a. Under the Fair Labor Standards Act, the minimum amount of wages that Garro must receive for a 40-hour workweek is . . . . \$ ____________

b. Since it is in violation of the FLSA, the additional amount it should pay Garro each week to meet the minimum wage requirement for a tipped employee is . . . . \$ ____________

2-3B LO 4.

The hours worked and the hourly wage rates for five employees of Koogel Company for the week ended June 9 follow.

a. For each employee, compute the gross earnings.

b. Compute the total gross earnings for all employees.

Employee	Hours Worked	Regular Hourly Wage Rate	(a) Gross Earnings
Duffy, M.	35	\$11.90	\$ ________
Hazleton, G.	28	14.15	________
Inman, T.	39½	10.90	________
Palmer, C.	24½	16.40	________
Diaz, O.	31	12.90	________
		(b) Total gross earnings.	\$ ________

2-4B **LO 4.**

The wages and hours information for five employees of Somja Enterprises for the week ended April 3 is given below. Employees work a standard 40-hour workweek and are paid time and one-half for all hours over 40 in each workweek.

a. For each employee, compute the regular earnings, overtime rate, overtime earnings, and total gross earnings.

b. Compute the total gross earnings for all employees.

(a)

Employee	Hours Worked	Regular Hourly Wage Rate	Regular Earnings	Overtime Rate	Overtime Earnings	Total Gross Earnings
Wilson, H.	43	$11.90	$ ______	$ ______	$ ______	$ ______
Aha, C.	42	14.20	______	______	______	______
Shoup, K.	47	9.90	______	______	______	______
Carlyn, D.	41½	10.70	______	______	______	______
McMurray, J.	45	17.10	______	______	______	______
			(b) Total gross earnings			$ ______

2-5B **LO 1.**

Cam Fitzer, a white-collar exempt employee, started working for Villan Company on Thursday of this week. He worked 9 hours on both Thursday and Friday. His annual salary is $77,000, and he is paid weekly for a 5-day week. Determine his gross pay for his first partial week of work.

Gross pay . . . . $ ______

2-6B **LO 2.**

Jamie Kerr is an hourly employee of Noonan Company located in Los Angeles. This week, Kerr had to travel to the company's regional office in Santa Fe. He left Sunday at noon and arrived in Santa Fe at 3:30 P.M. During the week, he worked his normal 40 hours in the Santa Fe office (Monday through Friday—9 A.M. to 5 P.M.). In addition, he attended the company's 3½-hour work training session on Wednesday evening. Kerr's hourly rate of pay is $16.90 per hour.

a. Kerr's overtime earnings for the week are . . . . $ ______

b. Kerr's total earnings for the week are . . . . $ ______

2-7B **LO 4.**

Peter Case is paid $13.76 per hour. During the past week, he worked 44 hours, and he is a covered employee who must be paid for overtime. Calculate his gross pay using the overtime premium approach.

a. Regular pay (44 hours) . . . . $ ______

b. Overtime premium pay . . . . . . ______

c. Gross pay . . . . $ ______

2-8B **LO 3, 4.**

The following time card shows the time worked one week by John Sherm. The employer disregards any time before 8:00 A.M. or between 12:00 and 1:00 P.M. and after 5:00 P.M. Employees do not begin work until 8:00 A.M. or 1:00 P.M., and do not work beyond 5:00 P.M., unless they are asked to work overtime. Hours worked beyond the regular 8-hour day and on Saturday are paid at one and one-half times the regular rate. Hours worked on Sunday are paid double the regular rate. Fractions of the hour for time worked are based on full quarter-hour increments.

2-8B (concluded)

No. 72								
Name John Sherm								(a)
Day	Morning		Afternoon		Overtime		Hours Worked
	In	Out	In	Out	In	Out	
M	7:47	12:00	12:50	5:01			
T	7:50	12:01	12:49	5:02	5:30	8:31	
W	8:05	12:02	12:58	5:03			
T	7:45	12:00	12:55	5:00	5:29	7:35	
F	8:01	12:01	1:00	5:01	6:00	8:01	
S	7:48	12:02					
S			2:00	6:03			
(b)	Total Hours Worked						
Remarks______							

Sherm's regular wage rate is $13.80 per hour, and the regular workweek is 40 hours with five 8-hour days. Compute:

a. The hours worked each day. (Ignore the one-minute tardiness on Friday.) . . . . ______________

b. The total hours worked. . . . . . . ______________

c. The regular earnings . . . . $______________

d. The overtime earnings . . . . ______________

e. The total earnings . . . . $______________

2-9B LO 3.

Under the decimal system of computing time worked at Carman's Company, production workers who are tardy are "docked" according to the schedule shown below.

Minutes Late in Ringing in	Fractional Hour Deducted
1 through 6	1/10
7 through 12	2/10
13 through 18	3/10
19 through 24	4/10
etc.	

The regular hours of work, Monday through Friday, are from 7:30 to 11:30 A.M. and from 12:30 to 4:30 P.M. During one week, Bernard Hoskins, who earns $12.95 an hour, reports in and checks out as shown below. Employees are not paid for ringing in a few minutes before 7:30 and 12:30 nor for ringing out a few minutes after 11:30 and 4:30.

(a)

DAY	AM		PM		HRS WORKED
	In	Out	In	Out	
M	7:28	11:31	12:50	4:31	
T	7:35	11:30	12:30	4:30	
W	7:44	11:33	12:27	4:32	
Th	7:27	11:31	12:32	4:33	
F	7:34	11:32	12:40	4:30	

2-9B (concluded)

Refer to the partial time card and compute:

a. The hours worked each day. . . . __________

b. The total hours worked . . . . . . __________

c. The gross earnings for the week . . . . $__________

2-10B LO 3, 4.

Costa, Inc., recently converted from a 5-day, 40-hour workweek to a 4-day, 40-hour workweek, with overtime continuing to be paid at one and one-half times the regular hourly rate for all hours worked beyond 40 in the week. In this company, time is recorded under the continental system, as shown on the time card at the right.

Barbara Bansta is part of the Group B employees whose regular workweek is Tuesday through Friday. The working hours each day are 800 to 1200; 1230 to 430; and 600 to 800. The company disregards any time before 800, between 1200 and 1230, and between 430 and 600, and permits employees to ring in up to 10 minutes late before any deduction is made for tardiness. Deductions are made to the nearest 1/4 of an hour for workers who are more than 10 minutes late in ringing in.

No. 160 Hr. Rate $9.35
Name Barbara Bansta O.T. Rate $14.025

Time		Mon	Tues	Wed	Thurs	Fri	Sat	
Evening	Out		802	801	805	800		
Evening	In		601	609	602	600		
Afternoon	Out		430	431	430	435		
Afternoon	In		1230	1231	1230	1238		
Morning	Out		1200	1202	1200	1203	1201	
Morning	In		755	750	825	759	800	Total for Week
Daily Totals		(a)						(b)

Remarks 25 minutes late Thursday - deduct ½ hr.

Refer to the time card and compute:

a. The daily total hours. . . . . __________

b. The total hours for the week. . . . . . . __________

c. The regular weekly earnings . . . . $__________

d. The overtime earnings (company rounds O/T rate to 3 decimal places) . . . . __________

e. The total weekly earnings . . . . $__________

2-11B LO 1.

Kenneth Johanson worked 49 hours during the week for Luben Company at two different jobs. His pay rate was $15.00 for the first 40 hours, and his pay rate was $13.10 for the other 9 hours. Determine his gross pay for that week if the company uses the one-half average rate method.

a. Gross pay . . . . $__________

b. If prior agreement existed that overtime would be paid at the rate for the job performed after the 40th hour, the gross pay would be . . . . $__________

2-12B LO 4.

Pam Patrone, a nonexempt employee, receives $695 for a regular 40-hour week and time and one-half for overtime. For a workweek of 43 hours, compute:

a. The regular earnings . . . . $__________

b. The overtime earnings . . . . __________

c. The total earnings . . . . $__________

2-13B LO 4.

Carl La Duca earns $3,875 each month and works 40 hours each week. Compute:

a. The hourly rate .... $ __________
b. The overtime rate at time and one-half .... $ __________

2-14B LO 4.

Stefani Wilson, a medical secretary, earns $2,650 monthly for a 37½-hour week. For overtime work, she receives extra pay at the regular hourly rate up to 40 hours and time and one-half beyond 40 hours in any week. During one semimonthly pay period, Wilson worked 6 hours overtime. Only 2 hours of this overtime were beyond 40 hours in any one week. Compute:

a. The regular semimonthly earnings $ __________
b. The overtime earnings .... __________
c. The total earnings .... $ __________

2-15B LO 4.

Jody Baush is a salaried employee who normally works a 35-hour week and is paid a weekly salary of $735.00. The agreement that he has with his employer states that his salary is to cover all hours worked up to and including 40. This week, Baush worked 42 hours. Calculate his gross pay.

Gross pay .... $ __________

2-16B LO 4.

Toni Peroglin is a salaried employee who works fluctuating work schedules. She is paid a fixed salary of $840 each week, with an agreement with her employer that overtime (over 40 hours) will be paid at an extra half-rate, based on the actual hours worked. This week she worked 42 hours. Compute:

a. The overtime earnings .... $ __________
b. The total earnings .... $ __________
c. If this was a BELO plan with a pay rate of $21 per hour and a maximum of 45 hours, how much would Peroglin be paid for 42 hours? .... $ __________

2-17B LO 4.

During the first week in April, Courtney Nelson worked 46 hours and produced 1,450 units under a piece-rate system. The regular piece rate is $0.38 a unit. Nelson is paid overtime according to the FLSA ruling for overtime work under a piece-rate system. Compute:

a. The piecework earnings .... $ __________
b. The regular hourly rate .... $ __________
The overtime hourly rate .... $ __________
c. The overtime earnings .... __________
d. The total earnings .... $ __________

2-18B LO 4.

Refer to Problem 2–17B. Assume that Nelson had agreed with her employer prior to the performance of the work that she would be paid one and one-half times the regular piece rate for all pieces produced during the overtime hours. Assume that her production totals for the week were: 1,120 pieces during regular hours and 330 pieces during overtime hours. Compute:

a. The piecework earnings ...... $ __________
b. The overtime earnings .... __________
c. The total earnings .... $ __________

2-19B LO 4.

Warrenda Spuhn, a sales representative, earns an annual salary of $34,500 and receives a commission on that portion of her annual sales that exceeds $150,000. The commission is 9.5% on all sales up to $50,000 above the quota. Beyond that amount, she receives a commission of 12%. Her total sales for the past year were $315,000. Compute:

a. The regular annual salary . . . . . $__________

b. The commission . . . . __________

c. The total annual earnings . . . . . $__________

2-20B LO 4.

June Maron is employed as a salesperson in the men's department of Lista Fashions. In addition to her weekly base salary of $320, Maron is paid a commission of 1% on her total net sales for the week (total gross sales less any customer returns). During the past week, to promote the sale of its fine cashmere sweaters, Lista agreed to pay Maron an additional PM (push money) of 2% of the total net sales of cashmere sweaters. Maron's weekly sales tally is given below.

Item	Gross Sales	Customer Returns
Regular sweaters	$600	$58
Cashmere sweaters	895	75
Ties	190	-0-
Dress shirts	445	39
Sports shirts	585	45

Compute Maron's total weekly earnings, showing her (a) weekly base salary, (b) commission, (c) PM, and (d) total weekly earnings.

a. Weekly base salary		$ 320.00
Weekly gross sales	$________	
Less customer returns	________	
Weekly net sales	$________	
b. Commission: $________ × 1%		________
Weekly gross sales of cashmere sweaters	$________	
Less customer returns	________	
Weekly net sales of cashmere sweaters	$________	
c. PM: $________ × 2%		________
d. Total weekly earnings		$________

CONTINUING PAYROLL PROBLEM

In the Continuing Payroll Problem, presented at the end of succeeding chapters, you will gain experience in computing wages and salaries and preparing a payroll register for Kipley Company, Inc., a newly formed corporation. At the end of subsequent chapters, information will be presented so that the payroll register can be completed step by step as you proceed through the discussion material relating to that particular section of the payroll register.

Kipley Company is a small manufacturing firm located in Pittsburgh, Pennsylvania. The company has a work force of both hourly and salaried employees. Each employee is paid for hours actually worked during each week, with the time worked being recorded in quarter-hour increments. The standard workweek consists of 40 hours, with all employees being paid time and one-half for any hours worked beyond the 40 regular hours.

Wages are paid every Friday, with one week's pay being held back by the company. Thus, the first payday for Kipley Company is January 14 for the workweek ending January 8.

The information below will be used in preparing the payroll for the pay period ending January 8.

Time Card No.	Employee Name	Hourly Wage or Salary
11	Fran M. Carson	$ 7.50 per hour
12	William A. Wilson	7.25 per hour
13	Harry T. Utley	8.10 per hour
21	Lawrence R. Fife	7.90 per hour
22	Lucy K. Smith	9.75 per hour
31	Gretchen R. Fay	515 per week
32	Glenda B. Robey	1,700 per month
33	Thomas K. Schork	2,350 per month
51	Barbara T. Hardy	1,510 per month
99	Carson C. Kipley	52,000 per year

Ms. Glenda B. Robey prepares the time clerk's report for each pay period. Her report for the first week of operations is given below.

TIME CLERK'S REPORT NO. 1
For Period Ending January 8, 20--

Time Card No.	Employee	Time Record M	T	W	T	F	S	Time Worked	Time Lost
11	Fran M. Carson	8	8	8	8	8	—	40	
12	William A. Wilson	8	8	8	8	8	8	48	
13	Harry T. Utley	8	5½	8	8	8	—	37½	2½ hrs. tardy
21	Lawrence R. Fife	10	10	8	8	10	—	46	
22	Lucy K. Smith	8	8	8	8	8	—	40	
31	Gretchen R. Fay	8	8	8	8	8	1¼	41¼	
32	Glenda B. Robey	8	8	8	8	8	—	40	
33	Thomas K. Schork	8	8	8	8	8	—	40	
51	Barbara T. Hardy	8	8	8	8	8	4	44	
99	Carson C. Kipley	8	8	8	8	8	—	40	

Using the payroll register for Kipley Company, which is reproduced on a fold-out at the back of the book (PR-1), proceed as follows:

1. Enter each employee's time card number and name in the appropriate columns.
2. Record the regular hours and the overtime hours worked for each employee, using the time clerk's report as your reference.
3. Complete the Regular Earnings columns (Rate per Hour and Amount) and the Overtime Earnings columns (Rate per Hour and Amount) for each hourly employee. For salaried workers, complete the regular weekly earnings column and show the hourly overtime rate and earnings only if overtime was worked.
4. Record the Total Earnings for each employee by adding the Regular Earnings and the Overtime Earnings.

Note: Retain your partially completed payroll register for use at the end of Chapter 3.

CASE PROBLEMS

C1. Reducing the Cost of Compensated Leave Time. LO 1.

For the past several weeks, Adele Delgado, payroll manager for Petrillo Packing Company, has been studying the mounting costs of accrued vacations and sick leave. Most of her firm's employees are entitled to two weeks' vacation each year and the privilege of accruing their vacation time for future use. Also, the workers have a generous sick-leave plan that reimburses them while they are ill at home or in the hospital.

Scanning the employees' accrued vacation times on the computer printout, Delgado notes the line entry for John Mannick. Mannick recently retired and cashed in 14 weeks of accrued vacation—all paid at his current wage, which was much more than when he originally earned the vacations. And of course, the firm's payroll taxes for the accrued vacation payout were significantly increased.

Delgado also knows that some workers feel short-changed if they do not use their sick leave each year. They realize that if the leave is not used, they lose it for that year. Probably, she thinks, this accounts for those who regularly become ill on Mondays or Fridays.

What solutions can you offer to limit the cost of and more effectively manage the firm's policies for compensated leave time?

C2. Payment of Personal Time off at Year-End. LO 4.

Huche Company allows its employees to carry over unused personal time off (PTO) days (vacation, sick days, etc.) from year to year. In addition, employees have the option to "cash out" their unused days at the end of the year.

John Keevens was just paid $685 for his unused PTO days. Since he is a nonexempt employee, John has questioned the amount of his last paycheck (which includes the $685). The PTO days push the paid hours over 40, and he wants to be paid for his overtime hours.

What would you tell John?

chapter

3

Social Security Taxes

© PHOTODISC COLLECTION/GETTY IMAGES

LEARNING OBJECTIVES

After studying this chapter, you should be able to:

1. Identify, for social security purposes, those persons covered under the law and those services that make up employment.
2. Identify the types of compensation that are defined as wages.
3. Apply the current tax rates and wage base for FICA and SECA purposes.
4. Explain the importance of obtaining and correctly using the Employer's Identification Number and the Employee's Social Security Number.
5. Describe the different requirements and procedures for depositing FICA taxes and income taxes withheld from employees' wages.
6. Complete Form 941, Employer's Quarterly Federal Tax Return, and Form 8109, Federal Tax Deposit Coupon.
7. Recognize that, as collection agents for the government, employers may be subject to civil and criminal penalties if they fail to carry out their duties.

Now that we have determined employees' gross pays, is there anything we have to take out of their pay?

How about social security taxes? Is everything taxed? What is the rate? What do we do with the money that we collect from employees? Are there any tax returns we have to file? Welcome to the world of social security taxes! To employees, it is a pay-now–collect-later system.

This chapter covers the government's old-age, survivors, and disability insurance benefits program (OASDI) and the retirees' health insurance program (HI). These programs are funded by Social Security and Medicare taxes imposed on employees and their employers. The taxes are calculated at a standard flat rate for every employee and employer. The statutes that provide the taxes include:

1. **Federal Insurance Contributions Act (FICA)**, which imposes two taxes on employees and two taxes on employers. One of the taxes finances the federal old-age, survivors, and disability insurance program (OASDI). The other finances the hospital insurance (HI), or Medicare, program.
2. **Self-Employment Contributions Act (SECA)**, which levies a tax upon the net earnings of the self-employed.

Coverage Under FICA

LEARNING OBJECTIVE 1

The retirement and disability parts of the social security program cover most workers in the United States. However, before an individual is considered to be "covered" for social security purposes, the following must be determined:

1. If the individual is an "employee," as defined by the common-law relationship of employer and employee.
2. If the service the individual renders is "employment," as defined by FICA tax law.
3. If the compensation the individual receives is "taxable wages," as defined by FICA tax law.

By identifying a "covered" employee and "covered" employment, it can then be determined who pays the tax and who will be entitled to benefits. An employee who is receiving social security benefits must pay the tax on his or her current earned wages. Part-time employees and seasonal employees are taxed in the same way as full-time employees.

EMPLOYER

Every **person** is an **employer** if the person employs one or more individuals for the performances of services in the United States, unless such services or employment are specifically exempted by the law. The term "person," as defined in the law, means an individual, a trust or estate, a partnership, or a corporation.

The term **employment** applies to any service performed by employees for their employer, regardless of the citizenship or residence of either. FICA covers most types of employment, but there are specific exclusions. Some types of employment are wholly exempt from coverage, and others are exempt only if the cash wages received are less than a stipulated dollar amount, as shown in Figure 3–1.

If an employee's services performed during one-half or more of any period constitute covered employment, then all the employee's services for that pay period must be counted as covered employment, and vice versa. In these cases, a pay period cannot exceed 31 consecutive days.

EMPLOYEE

As explained in Chapter 2, the test used by the IRS to determine a worker's classification is the Common-Law Test. Basically, if a business tells, or has a right to tell, a worker how, when, and where to work, then the worker is an employee.

OCCUPATIONS SPECIFICALLY COVERED BY FICA In addition to the Common-Law Test, FICA law also provides specific coverage for the following list of four occupations. Even though these workers are independent contractors under common law, they are treated by statute as employees. However, such persons are not covered by FICA

FIGURE 3–1

Exempt Employment

Employment Type	Conditions of Exclusion
Agricultural services	Compensation of all farm workers is less than $2,500 in any calendar year, or compensation is less than $150 for each worker in a calendar year. Remuneration other than cash is not taxed.
Domestic service	Service performed in a local college club or a chapter of a college fraternity or sorority by a student who is *enrolled* and *regularly attending classes* at the school, college, or university.
Services performed by civilians for the U.S. government	Of any of its agencies if such agencies are specifically exempt from the employer portion of the FICA tax, or if such services are covered by a retirement system established by law.
Service performed by railroad workers	For employers covered by the Railroad Retirement Tax Act.
Services performed in the employment of foreign governments	Ambassadors, ministers, and other diplomatic officers and employees.
Services performed by an individual under the age of 18, as a newspaper distributor	Delivery or distribution of newspapers or shopping news, excluding delivery or distribution to a point for subsequent delivery or distribution.
Services performed by student nurses	In the employ of a hospital or a nurses' training school chartered or approved under state law, and the nurses are *enrolled* and *regularly attending classes* in that school. FICA exempts only the pay received by student nurses if the pay is nominal and their work is part-time and an integral part of the curriculum.
Services performed by students for their public or private school, college, or university	Working as "noncareer" employees while enrolled academically at least half-time (for undergraduates, at least six credit hours). This student FICA exception does not apply to an employee who regularly works 40 or more hours a week.

if they have a substantial interest in the facilities used in connection with their jobs or if the services consist of a single transaction. The list includes:

1. *Agent-drivers* and *commission-drivers* who distribute food and beverage products or handle laundry or dry cleaning.
2. Full-time *life insurance salespersons.*
3. Full-time *traveling or city salespersons* for one firm or person.
4. An individual who works *at home* on materials or goods that you supply and that must be returned to you or to a person you name if you also furnish specifications for the work to be done.

GOVERNMENT EMPLOYEES Different rules apply.

- Federal Hired after 1983—full coverage.
  Hired prior to 1984—only Medicare (HI) applies.

- State and local — Work done after July 1, 1991, and not in public retirement plan—full coverage.
  Hired after March 31, 1986, and covered by a public retirement plan—Medicare (HI) only.
- Military — Basic pay—full FICA taxes.
  Excess of basic pay—not subject to FICA tax.
  Temporary service with National Guard—difference in pay covered by civilian employer—subject to FICA tax.

INTERNATIONAL AGREEMENTS Totalization agreements with over 20 foreign countries have eliminated dual taxation and dual coverage. In-patriates who are working in the United States from one of these countries will not have social security taxes withheld on U.S.-sourced income. If the worker is from a country that has no such agreement, social security tax must be withheld.

Expatriates will be subject to U.S. social security tax and could also be subject to foreign social security taxes.

FAMILY EMPLOYMENT Work performed for a parent by a child under the age of 18 is exempt from FICA. If the work is not in the course of the parent's business and the child is under 21, the exemption also applies. However, if the child's services are done for a corporation, a partnership (unless each partner is a parent of the child), or an estate, the exemption does not apply.

on the *JOB*

Some examples of workers who may be household employees include:

- Baby sitters
- Caretakers
- Cooks
- Drivers
- Gardeners
- Governesses
- Housekeepers
- Maids

HOUSEHOLD EMPLOYEE If a worker performs household services in or around your home subject to your will and control, as to both what must be done and how it will be done, that worker is your household employee. It does not matter whether you exercise this control as long as you have the legal right to control the method and result of the work.

However, in order for the household employee and the employer to be liable for the FICA taxes, the household employee must receive ***$1,500 or more in cash wages*** from any one employer in the year. Household employees do not include people (a) who work for you in your business; (b) who follow an independent trade, business, or profession in which they offer services to the general public; and (c) who are under the age of 18 unless their principal occupation is household employment.

EXEMPT EMPLOYEES Employees of not-for-profit organizations are subject to FICA taxes. Some services, such as those performed by duly ordained ministers of churches, remain exempt from FICA taxes, but the individuals are then subject to self-employment tax on their net earnings. Ministers, certain members of religious orders, and Christian Science practitioners previously electing exemption from social security coverage may now be covered by filing a waiver form with the IRS. Once an election to be covered by social security is made, it is irrevocable.

The following are also exempt from both the OASDI and HI portions of the tax:

- Medical interns.
- Student nurses.
- Inmates of U.S. penal institutions.
- Those serving temporarily in case of emergency (storm, flood, etc.).

VOLUNTARY COVERAGE Coverage under FICA can be extended to certain classes of services that otherwise would be excluded. For example, service in the employ of a state or local government that began prior to April 1, 1986, is still exempt for the OASDI portion of the FICA tax. However, coverage can be extended to these employees by means of a voluntary agreement entered into by the state and secretary of health and human services. When a state elects voluntary coverage, it becomes responsible for the collection and payment of the FICA tax as if it were covered employment.

SELF-STUDY QUIZ 3-1 *Which of the following are covered by FICA (indicate Yes or No)?*

Yes 1. Andrian Mitchell, a full-time life insurance salesperson.
Yes 2. John Sain, a federal government employee, hired in 1990.
No 3. Bonnie Stone, a real estate agent.
No 4. Stuart Schuck, who offers lawn care service to homeowners in the neighborhood.

INDEPENDENT CONTRACTOR

The FICA tax law identifies **independent contractors** as persons who follow an independent trade, business, or profession where they offer their services to the public. The Small Business Administration estimates that nearly 5 million workers are independent contractors. The test in Figure 3–2 determines independent contractor status.

Employers do not pay or withhold payroll taxes on payments made to independent contractors. However, the individual contractors are liable for social security taxes (self-employment taxes) on the net earnings of their businesses.

on the JOB

Intentionally misclassifying an employee as an independent contractor may result in the employer being liable for 100 percent of the worker's FICA and federal income taxes, in addition to other penalties for failure to file returns and pay taxes.

TAXABLE WAGES

2 LEARNING OBJECTIVE

The amount of wages paid by employers to their employees during the calendar year determines the amount of OASDI/HI taxes. The basis of payment may be hourly, daily, weekly, biweekly, semimonthly, monthly, annually, piece rate, or a percentage of profits. Wages include the following:

1. Actual money received by employees, whether called wages or salaries.
2. Cash value of meals and lodging provided for the convenience of the ***employees.***
3. Bonuses and commissions paid by the employer with respect to employment.

Other common types of payments that are considered wages under FICA are listed in Figure 3–3 (on page 3-8).

TIPS FICA considers cash tips of $20 or more in a calendar month to be taxable wages. Employees must report their tips in writing to their employers by the 10th of the month following the month in which the tips were received. Employers can require more frequent reporting. Rules for reporting tips by employees and employers are summarized on page 3-9.

FIGURE 3–2

Test for Independent Contractor Status

Workers *may* be classified as independent contractors if they:

1. Hire, supervise, and pay assistants.
2. Determine the sequence of their work.
3. Set their own hours of work.
4. Work for as many employers as they wish.
5. Are paid by the job.
6. Make their services available to the public.
7. Have an opportunity for profit or loss.
8. Furnish their own tools.
9. Have a substantial investment in their trade.
10. May be dismissed only under terms of contract.

FIGURE 3–3

Other Types of Taxable Wages

Type of Wage	Conditions
Advance payments	For future work to be done by the individual receiving the advance where the employer considers the work satisfaction for the advance.
Back-pay awards	Pay received in one period for employment in an earlier period, unless it is a settlement for failure to employ workers.
Bonuses	For services rendered by employees for an employer.
Cash and noncash prizes and awards	For outstanding work, exceeding sales quotas, contributing suggestions that increase productivity or efficiency.
Christmas gifts	Except gifts of nominal value (such as a turkey or a ham).
Commissions	On sales or insurance premiums paid as compensation for services performed.
Death benefits	Wage payments (not gratuity) to an employee's beneficiaries or estate after the employee's death. Payments made after the calendar year in which the employee died and employer-provided death-benefit plans are not taxed.
Dismissal pay	Payments by employer for involuntary separation of an employee from the employer's service.
Employees' federal income and social security taxes paid for by the employer	Payment of the employee portion of the FICA tax by the employer for domestics working in the employer's home and for agricultural laborers is an exception to this rule.
Fringe benefits—noncash	Personal use of company car, employer-provided vehicles for commuting, flights on employer-provided airplanes, and free or discounted flights on commercial airlines.
Guaranteed annual wage payments	Union contract agreements whereby an employer guarantees certain employees will either work during or be paid for each normal workweek in a calendar year.
Idle time or standby payments	Amounts paid workers who are at the beck and call of an employer but who are performing no work.
Insurance premiums paid by the employer for an employee's group-term life insurance coverage	Exceeding $50,000 of coverage. For retired workers, their group-term life insurance that exceeds $50,000 is also subject to FICA.
Jury duty pay	The difference between the employee's regular wages and the amount received for jury duty, paid by employers.
Moving expense reimbursements	Unless the employee will be entitled to deduct these moving expenses in determining taxable income for federal income tax purposes.
Retroactive wage increases	Treated as wages in the period paid.
Sick pay—first six months	For sickness or accident disability. Payments under a state temporary disability law are also subject to FICA taxes.
Stock payments	The fair market value of stock transferred by employers to employees as remuneration for services.
Vacation pay	Whether the leave is taken or not.

FIGURE 3–4

Form 4070, Employee's Report of Tips to Employer

Form **4070** Department of the Treasury Internal Revenue Service	**Employee's Report of Tips to Employer** ▶ For Paperwork Reduction Act Notice, see back of form.	OMB No. 1545-0065
Employee's name and address Carmen T. Perez 1704 Elm St., San Diego, CA 92121-8837		**Social security number** 269 ⋮ 21 ⋮ 7220
Employer's name and address (include establishment name, if different) Holland House Inn 9 Fairway, San Diego, CA 92123-1369		1 Cash tips received $389.10
		2 Credit card tips received —
		3 Tips paid out —
Month or shorter period in which tips were received from July 1, 20__, to July 31, 20__		4 Net tips (lines 1 + 2 - 3) $389.10
Signature *Carmen T. Perez*		Date August 10, 20__

1. Employees can report tips on ***Form 4070, Employee's Report of Tips to Employer,*** shown in Figure 3–4.
2. Employees failing to report tips to their employers may be penalized 50 percent of the FICA tax due on the tips. The Tax Court may rule that the nonreporting of tip income constitutes fraud.
3. Employers must collect the employee's FICA tax on the tips that each employee reports. The employer deducts the employee's FICA tax from the wages due the employee or from other funds the employee makes available. The employer should deduct the FICA taxes (on the reported tips plus the wage payment) from the first pay after the reporting of the previous month's tips.
4. Employers are also liable for their share of the FICA tax on any tips subject to the employee's FICA tax.
5. Large food and beverage establishments (11 or more employees where tipping is customary) are required to allocate to their tipped employees the excess of 8 percent of the establishment's gross receipts over the tips actually reported by their employees. However, employers withhold FICA taxes only on the tips reported by employees, not from tips that are allocated. The amount of allocated tip income is shown separately on the employee's ***Wage and Tax Statement (Form W-2),*** explained in Chapter 4.
6. Every large food or beverage establishment must report the amount of its receipts from food and beverage operations annually to the IRS and the amount of tips reported by its employees. [***Form 8027, Employer's Annual Information Return of Tip Income and Allocated Tips*** (not illustrated)]

EXEMPT PAYMENTS FICA tax only applies to types of compensation considered taxable under the law. Examples of compensation that the law excludes from the tax follow.

Meals and Lodging. FICA exempts the value of meals or lodging furnished to employees for the ***convenience of the employer.*** The value of meals or lodging not meeting this test will be subject to FICA tax. The IRS places no specific value on meals or lodging furnished by employers to employees. Instead, the IRS relies on state valuations. Where a state has no law or regulation on the subject, fair value is defined as the reasonable prevailing value of the meals or lodging.

on the *JOB*

Many restaurants now use software to help in tracking tips. Some programs add a "prompt" that freezes the computer screen as employees try to clock out if they have not entered their tips for the day.

on the *NET*

http://www.ssa.gov/
Social Security Online.
Maintained by the Social Security Administration, it contains general FICA information.

http://www.ssa.gov/employer/how.htm
"Employer Reporting Instructions & Information."

Sick Pay. The ***first six months of sick pay*** an employee receives is considered wages and is subject to FICA tax. Payments made ***after*** the expiration of the six consecutive calendar months following the last month in which the employee worked for the employer are not taxed. The period off the job must be continuous for six months. Any return to work starts a new six-month period. FICA defines **sick pay** as any payment made to individuals due to personal injury or sickness that does not constitute wages. Sick pay payments must be part of a plan to which the employer is a party. Sick pay must not include amounts paid to individuals who are permanently disabled.

Sick pay payments may also be made by a third party, including insurance companies, trusts providing sick and accident benefits, and employers' associations funded to pay sickness and accident benefits. The third party is treated as a separate employer and must withhold and deposit the employees' FICA taxes. However, the third party may be relieved of the liability for the employer's share of the FICA taxes if the third party fulfills each of these requirements:

1. Withholds and deposits the employee portion of the FICA tax.
2. Notifies the employer of the amount of wages or compensation involved.

The liability for that share of the taxes then reverts back to the employer. For convenience, an employer may contract to have the third party deposit the employer portion of the tax as well as the employee portion.

Generally, payments made to employees or their dependents for medical or hospital expenses in connection with sickness or accident disability are not considered wages. However, these payments must be part of a plan established by the employer for all employees or for a particular class of employees.

Makeup Pay for Military Duty. Wage supplements paid by employers to cover the difference between employees' salary and their military pay or payment of their full salary are exempt from FICA and Medicare taxes. This applies to active-duty soldiers and reservists activated for *more than 30 days.*

CONTRIBUTIONS TO DEFERRED COMPENSATION PLANS

Employee pretax (federal income tax) contributions under a qualified cash or deferred compensation arrangement (***Tax-Deferred Retirement Plans,*** as discussed in Chapter 4) are subject to FICA tax. However, the *employers' matching* contributions are tax-free.

PAYMENTS FOR EDUCATIONAL ASSISTANCE

Educational assistance refers to the expenses that an employer pays for an employee's education, such as tuition, fees, and payments for books, supplies, and equipment. Also, educational assistance includes the cost of employer-provided courses of instruction (books, supplies, and equipment). Educational assistance excludes payment for tools or supplies that employees keep after they complete a course of instruction. Payments for job-related educational expenses are not subject to FICA taxes if the education maintains or improves skills required by the individual's employment. Payments for non–job-related educational expenses up to *$5,250* are also exempt from FICA taxes.

SELF-STUDY QUIZ 3-2 *Which of the following are subject to FICA tax (indicate Yes or No)?*

No 1. A $15 gift certificate for a local grocery store given to employees as a Christmas gift.
Yes 2. Sales representatives using their company cars for personal use on weeknights and weekends.
No 3. Employer's contributions to a Simplified Employee Pension Plan for its employees.
No 4. A tuition reimbursement plan that pays tuition for employees successfully completing job-related courses.
Yes 5. Severance pay made to an employee discharged for theft.

TAX RATES

3 LEARNING OBJECTIVE

The Social Security Act, as amended, imposes a separate tax on employers and employees for old-age, survivors, and disability insurance (OASDI) benefits and for hospital insurance (HI) benefits. The 2008 tax rates for both the employer and the employee portions of the tax follow:

	Rate	*Wage Base*
OASDI	6.20%	$102,300 (estimated)
HI	1.45%	None

IRS CONNECTION

The Social Security Administration projects the base to be $141,900 by 2016. The actual OASDI taxable wage base for the following year is published in the *Federal Register* by November 1.

TAXABLE WAGE BASE The employer must consider the **taxable wage base** when computing the OASDI portion of the FICA tax. The law exempts wages that exceed this base during the calendar year (*$102,300 estimated for 2008*). Once the OASDI taxable wage base has been reached, all payments made to the employee during the remainder of the year are not taxable. The wage base applies to amounts ***paid*** employees in a calendar year and not to the time when the services were performed by the employees. The HI portion of the FICA tax does ***not*** have a ceiling; thus, employers compute this tax on the total wages and salaries paid during the year. Just as social security benefits increase each year based on changes in the Consumer Price Index, the taxable wage base is increased also.

This means that an employee who makes $34,000 would pay the FICA tax (6.2% + 1.45%) on his or her total earnings, while an employee who makes $1 million would pay the HI portion (1.45%) on his or her total earnings but only $102,300 of the $1 million would be taxed at 6.2 percent.

Determining OASDI Tax:

If:

Cumulative Wages	+	Current Wage Payment	< OASDI Wage Base, then
$52,400	+	$3,000	= $55,400

compute the OASDI tax on the entire wage payment. ($3,000 × 0.062 = $186.00)

If:

Cumulative Wages	+	Current Wage Payment	> OASDI Wage Base, then
$101,600	+	$3,000	= $104,600

compute the OASDI tax on the part of the current wage payment that brings the cumulative wages up to the OASDI taxable wage limit. ($700 × 0.062 = $43.40)

Cumulative Wages	+	Taxable Wages	= Cumulative Limit
$101,600	+	$700	= $102,300

IRS CONNECTION

In 1950, there were 16 workers paying into the Social Security system for every one person collecting benefits. By 2042, the projection is a ratio of 2 to 1.

EMPLOYEES' FICA (OASDI/HI) TAXES AND WITHHOLDINGS FICA requires employers to collect the OASDI/HI taxes from their employees and pay the taxes to the IRS at the same time they pay their own tax. The employer deducts the tax from the wages at the time of payment. The amount of each tax to be withheld is computed by applying to the employee's taxable wages the tax rate in effect at the time that the wages are received. In calculating the amounts of FICA taxes to withhold from employees' pays, the employer may disregard any fractional part of a cent, unless it is one-half cent or more, which must be rounded up one cent.

EXAMPLE

Ruth Engle receives pay on January 4, 2008, for work done during the last week of December 2007. The wages would be taxed as income in the calendar year 2008, using 2008 tax rates.

The liability for the tax extends to both the employee and the employer, but after the employer has collected the tax, the employee's liability ceases. The following examples illustrate the computation of the FICA taxes to be withheld.

EXAMPLE

1. Casey Berra, employed by the Gobel Company, earned $460 during the week ended February 1, 2008. Prior to February 1, Berra's cumulative gross earnings for the year were $2,765.70. FICA taxes to be withheld on $460 are computed as follows:

OASDI		*HI*	
Taxable Wages	$ 460	Taxable Wages	$ 460
Tax Rate	× 6.2%	Tax Rate	× 1.45%
OASDI Tax to Be Withheld	$ 28.52	HI Tax to Be Withheld	$ 6.67

2. Francis Aha, a salaried employee of the Wilson Advertising Agency, is paid every Friday. She earned $1,925 for this pay. Prior to the pay of November 14, 2008, she had earned $101,850. The FICA taxes to be withheld from Aha's pay on November 14 are computed as follows:

OASDI		*HI*	
Taxable Wage Limit	$102,300	Taxable Wage Limit	NONE
Wages Paid to Date	101,850	Wages Paid to Date	$ 101,850
Taxable Wages This Pay	$ 450	Taxable Wages This Pay	$ 1,925
Tax Rate	× 6.2%	Tax Rate	× 1.45%
OASDI Tax to Be Withheld	$ 27.90	HI Tax to Be Withheld	$ 27.91

3. Marc Todd, president of Uni-Sight, Inc., is paid $4,200 semimonthly. Prior to his last pay on December 26, 2008, Todd had earned $104,000. The FICA taxes to be withheld from Todd's pay on December 26 are computed as follows:

OASDI		*HI*	
Taxable Wage Limit	$102,300	Taxable Wage Limit	NONE
Wages Paid to Date	104,000	Wages Paid to Date	$ 104,000
Taxable Wages This Pay	-0-	Taxable Wage This Pay	$ 4,200
OASDI Tax to Be Withheld	-0-	Tax Rate	× 1.45%
		HI Tax to Be Withheld	$ 60.90

Sometimes an employee has paid FICA taxes on wages in excess of the taxable base because of having worked for more than one employer. If so, the employee is entitled to a refund for the overpayment. The amount of the overpayment is credited against the employee's federal income taxes for that year. Instructions are given on the ***Individual Income Tax Return (Form 1040)*** that explain how the overpayment should be treated.

EMPLOYER'S FICA (OASDI) TAXES In addition to withholding the correct amount of FICA tax from the employees' taxable earnings, the employer must make contributions to the program. The employer's portion of the tax is based on the wages paid to the employees. The employer's taxes, however, are not computed on the wages paid each employee, but on the total taxable wages paid all employees. As with employee withholdings, once the OASDI taxable wage base is reached, the employer no longer contributes for that particular employee. The OASDI tax is 6.2 percent of each employee's wages paid, and the HI tax is 1.45 percent of each employee's wages paid.

EXAMPLE

The Wallington Company has 100 employees, each earning $375.25 a week.

OASDI		
Amount of OASDI tax withheld from each employee's paycheck each week:	$23.27	(6.2% × $375.25)
Total tax withheld from the 100 employees' wages:	$2,327.00	($23.27 × 100)
Tax on employer:	$2,326.55	(6.2% × $37,525)

HI

Amount of HI tax withheld from each employee's paycheck each week:	$5.44	(1.45% × $375.25)
Total tax withheld from the 100 employees' wages is:	$544.00	($5.44 × 100)
Tax on employer:	$544.11	(1.45% × $37,525)

SUCCESSOR EMPLOYER Wages paid by the prior employer can be counted towards the annual OASDI wage base by a successor employer if all the following criteria are met:

1. The successor has acquired all the property used in the prior employer's business.
2. The affected employees were employed immediately before and continued working right after the transfer of the business.
3. Wages were paid by the prior employer during the calendar year of acquisition.

SELF-STUDY QUIZ 3-3 *Patrick's Fine Foods employs five people. For each person, compute the amount of OASDI and HI tax for the first week in January.*

Employee	Weekly Wage	OASDI	HI
Tammy Wolf	$225.00	13.95	3.26
Bill Young	300.00	18.60	4.35

Employee	Weekly Wage	OASDI	HI
Howard Feldman	$ 175.00	10.87	2.54
Carin Clever	1,000.00	62.00	14.50
Bud McAvoy	2,200.00	136.40	31.90

Compute the employer's portion of the FICA taxes, based on the payroll data above.

Will any of the employees exceed the taxable wage base during the year? If yes, on which payday will it occur? Bud Week 47

A Self-Employed Person

The Self-Employment Contributions Act (SECA) extended coverage under the social security system to the self-employed in 1951. Over the years, most self-employed persons have become covered by the law.

SELF-EMPLOYMENT INCOME

SECA uses an individual's **self-employment income** as the basis for levying taxes and for determining the amount of income to credit toward OASDI insurance benefits or HI coverage. Self-employment income generally consists of the net earnings derived by individuals from a business or profession carried on as a sole proprietorship or as a partnership. Self-employed persons determine their net earnings by finding the sum of the following:

1. The ***gross income*** derived by an individual from any business or profession carried on, less allowable deductions attributable to such a business or profession, and
2. The ***individual's distributive share*** (whether or not distributed) of the ordinary net income or loss from any business or profession carried on by a partnership of which the individual is a member.

on the NET

http://www.irs.gov/taxtopics/tc762.html Lists IRS criteria for determining employee versus independent contractor status.

SELF-EMPLOYMENT OASDI/HI TAXES The self-employed tax rate for 2008 on the net earnings is 15.3 percent—12.4 percent for OASDI and 2.9 percent for HI (double the employee rate).

EXAMPLE

Svetlana Priosky's net self-employment earnings for the year were $63,210. Her self-employment tax would be:

$63,210 × 0.153 = $9,671.13

Usually, the net business income of individuals, as shown in their income tax returns, makes up their net earnings from self-employment for the purpose of the Social Security Act. Earnings of less than $400 from self-employment are ignored. For computing the OASDI taxes, the maximum self-employment taxable income of any individual for 2008 is $102,300 (estimated). For the HI taxes, however, the total self-employment income is taxable. If the individual is also an employee of another company, the wages received can reduce the amount of self-employment income that is taxed for OASDI (wages + self-employment income > $102,300).

EXAMPLE

Roberta Wurst receives wages of $103,000 from her job in 2008. She also earned $15,000 in net self-employment income during the year. In computing her OASDI taxes, none of her self-employment income is considered, since her wages exceed the taxable wage base of $102,300. However, in computing her HI taxes, all of her earnings from self-employment are taxed.

If the wages received in 2008 amount to less than $102,300, any net self-employment earnings amounting to $400 or more must be counted as self-employment income up to an aggregate amount of $102,300 for OASDI taxes.

EXAMPLE

George Talbot receives wages in 2008 amounting to $79,100. His net earnings from self-employment amount to $24,600. Talbot must count $23,200 of his earnings in determining taxable self-employment income for OASDI taxes.

FICA Taxable Wage Base	–	Wages Rec'd in 2008	=	Taxable Self-Employment Income
$102,300	–	$79,100	=	$23,200

TAXABLE YEAR In computing the taxes on self-employment income, sole proprietors use the same taxable year as that used for income tax purposes. In the case of a partnership, the taxable year of the partners may not correspond with that of the partnership. In such instances, the partners are required to include in computing net earnings from self-employment their distributive share of the income or loss from the partnership for any taxable year ending with or within their taxable year.

REPORTING SELF-EMPLOYMENT INCOME Sole proprietors report their self-employment income by transferring certain data from ***Schedule C (Form 1040), Profit or Loss from Business*** to ***Schedule SE (Form 1040), Self-Employment Tax.*** SECA requires self-employed persons to include SECA taxes in their quarterly payment of estimated income taxes. The taxpayer's estimated tax is the sum of the estimated income taxes and SECA taxes less any credits against the tax.

SELF-STUDY QUIZ 3-4 *Lori Kinmark works as a jeweler for a local company. She earns $1,000 per week, plus a year-end bonus of $2,000. Kinmark also earns an additional net self-employment income of $28,000 per year.*

$__________ 1. Compute Kinmark's annual earnings from employment.

$__________ 2. Compute Kinmark's total earnings from job and from self-employment income.

$__________ 3. How much self-employment income should Kinmark include in computing taxable self-employment income for OASDI taxes?

$__________ 4. What are the total FICA taxes on her self-employment earnings?

Application for Employer Identification Number (Form SS-4)

Every employer of one or more persons must file an application for an identification number, ***Form SS-4,*** available from any IRS or social security office. Figure 3–5 shows a filled-in copy of Form SS-4. The employer should file this form early enough to allow for processing, preferably four to five weeks before the identification number (EIN) is needed. The employer files the application with the IRS service center where the federal tax returns are filed. If the employer has no legal residence, principal place of business, or principal office in any IRS district, the application should be sent to the Internal Revenue Service, Entity Control, Philadelphia, PA 19255-0005.

The employer must enter this EIN on all returns, forms, and correspondence sent to the District Director of Internal Revenue that relate to the taxes imposed under FICA. The employer uses the EIN in any correspondence with the Social Security Administration (SSA) and enters the number on forms issued by the SSA. Regardless of how many different business locations are operated, the employer receives only one EIN. The penalty for failing to supply the identification number is discussed later in this chapter. If the owner sells or otherwise transfers a business, the new owner must file an application for a new identification number.

The Internal Revenue Service also offers employers a toll-free number (800-829-4933) where they can request an employer identification number. This method can be used instead of filing Form SS-4.

Identification numbers can also be obtained directly from the IRS Web site. Once the business completes the application form (online), the system issues an employer identification number.

IRS CONNECTION

Some states allow employers to register with the state and get an Employer ID Number by e-filing a single form.

4 LEARNING OBJECTIVE

on the NET

An EIN can be obtained directly from https://www.irs.gov/businesses/small/article/0,,id=102767,00.html.

Employee's Application for Social Security Card (Form SS-5)

Under the Social Security Act, every employee and every self-employed person must have a social security number (SSN). The application for a SSN is available at any social security or IRS office. The ***Application for a Social Security Card (Form SS-5)*** can be filed with any field office of the SSA. Figure 3–6 shows a filled-in copy of Form SS-5.

The Social Security Act requires applicants for a social security card to furnish evidence of their age, identity, and U.S. citizenship or lawful alien status. Applicants may either apply by mailing the required documents and forms to their nearest social security office or apply in person. If they are age 18 or older and have never had a social security card, or are aliens whose immigration documents should not be sent through the mail, they must apply in person. After filing Form SS-5, the applicant will receive from the SSA a card showing the assigned social security number.

Upon receipt of their SSN, employees should inform their employers of the number assigned them. If employees change positions, they must notify the new employer of their SSN when they begin employment. If an employee changes his or her name by court order or by marriage, the individual should request a new social security card by completing Form SS-5.

on the JOB

The employer must obtain each employee's SSN to enter on Form W-2 (discussed in Chapter 4). If the employer does not provide the correct name and SSN, he or she may owe a penalty.

If the employee's name is not correct as shown on the card, including a name change due to marriage or divorce, the employee should request a new card.

FIGURE 3–5

Form SS-4, Application for Employer Identification Number

Form **SS-4** (Rev. February 2006) Department of the Treasury Internal Revenue Service

Application for Employer Identification Number

(For use by employers, corporations, partnerships, trusts, estates, churches, government agencies, Indian tribal entities, certain individuals, and others.)

▶ See separate instructions for each line. ▶ Keep a copy for your records.

OMB No. 1545-0003

EIN

Type or print clearly.

1 Legal name of entity (or individual) for whom the EIN is being requested
Myers Payroll Services, Inc.

2 Trade name of business (if different from name on line 1)

3 Executor, administrator, trustee, "care of" name
Care of Martin Myers

4a Mailing address (room, apt., suite no. and street, or P.O. box)
P.O. Box 212

5a Street address (if different) (Do not enter a P.O. box.)
3401 Atrium Way

4b City, state, and ZIP code
Sacramento, CA 95814-1212

5b City, state, and ZIP code
Sacramento, CA 95814-0340

6 County and state where principal business is located
Orange County, California

7a Name of principal officer, general partner, grantor, owner, or trustor
Catherine Myers

7b SSN, ITIN, or EIN
311-07-6119

8a **Type of entity** (check only one box)
- ☐ Sole proprietor (SSN)
- ☐ Partnership
- ☒ Corporation (enter form number to be filed) ▶ 1120
- ☐ Personal service corporation
- ☐ Church or church-controlled organization
- ☐ Other nonprofit organization (specify) ▶
- ☐ Other (specify) ▶
- ☐ Estate (SSN of decedent)
- ☐ Plan administrator (SSN)
- ☐ Trust (SSN of grantor)
- ☐ National Guard ☐ State/local government
- ☐ Farmers' cooperative ☐ Federal government/military
- ☐ REMIC ☐ Indian tribal governments/enterprises
- Group Exemption Number (GEN) ▶

8b If a corporation, name the state or foreign country (if applicable) where incorporated — State: California — Foreign country:

9 **Reason for applying** (check only one box)
- ☒ Started new business (specify type) ▶ Payroll Processing
- ☐ Hired employees (Check the box and see line 12.)
- ☐ Compliance with IRS withholding regulations
- ☐ Other (specify) ▶
- ☐ Banking purpose (specify purpose) ▶
- ☐ Changed type of organization (specify new type) ▶
- ☐ Purchased going business
- ☐ Created a trust (specify type) ▶
- ☐ Created a pension plan (specify type) ▶

10 Date business started or acquired (month, day, year). See instructions.
July 3, 20--

11 Closing month of accounting year
December

12 First date wages or annuities were paid (month, day, year). **Note.** If applicant is a withholding agent, enter date income will first be paid to nonresident alien. (month, day, year) . . . . ▶ July 15, 20--

13 Highest number of employees expected in the next 12 months (enter -0- if none).
Do you expect to have $1,000 or less in employment tax liability for the calendar year? ☐ **Yes** ☐ **No.** (If you expect to pay $4,000 or less in wages, you can mark yes.)

Agricultural	Household	Other
		6

14 Check **one** box that best describes the principal activity of your business.
- ☐ Health care & social assistance ☐ Wholesale–agent/broker
- ☐ Construction ☐ Rental & leasing ☐ Transportation & warehousing ☐ Accommodation & food service ☐ Wholesale–other ☐ Retail
- ☐ Real estate ☐ Manufacturing ☐ Finance & insurance ☒ Other (specify) Payroll Services

15 Indicate principal line of merchandise sold, specific construction work done, products produced, or services provided.
Payroll Processing

16a Has the applicant ever applied for an employer identification number for this or any other business? . . . . ☐ **Yes** ☒ **No**
Note. If "Yes," please complete lines 16b and 16c.

16b If you checked "Yes" on line 16a, give applicant's legal name and trade name shown on prior application if different from line 1 or 2 above.
Legal name ▶ Trade name ▶

16c Approximate date when, and city and state where, the application was filed. Enter previous employer identification number if known.
Approximate date when filed (mo., day, year) | City and state where filed | Previous EIN

Third Party Designee

Complete this section **only** if you want to authorize the named individual to receive the entity's EIN and answer questions about the completion of this form.

Designee's name — Designee's telephone number (include area code) ( )

Address and ZIP code — Designee's fax number (include area code) ( )

Under penalties of perjury, I declare that I have examined this application, and to the best of my knowledge and belief, it is true, correct, and complete.

Name and title (type or print clearly) ▶ Catherine Myers, President

Applicant's telephone number (include area code) (919) 555-2111

Applicant's fax number (include area code) (919) 555-2119

Signature ▶ *Catherine Myers* Date ▶ *7/31/--*

For Privacy Act and Paperwork Reduction Act Notice, see separate instructions. Cat. No. 16055N Form **SS-4** (Rev. 2-2006)

FIGURE 3–6

Form SS-5, Application for a Social Security Card

SOCIAL SECURITY ADMINISTRATION
Application for a Social Security Card

Form Approved
OMB No. 0960-0066

1	NAME → TO BE SHOWN ON CARD	First: Helen	Full Middle Name: Dolores	Last: Jennings
	FULL NAME AT BIRTH IF OTHER THAN ABOVE	First	Full Middle Name	Last
	OTHER NAMES USED			
2	MAILING ADDRESS → Do Not Abbreviate	Street Address, Apt. No., PO Box, Rural Route No.: 719 Second Street		
		City: Stockton	State: California	Zip Code: 95204
3	CITIZENSHIP → (Check One)	[X] U.S. Citizen; [ ] Legal Alien Allowed To Work	[ ] Legal Alien **Not** Allowed To Work (See Instructions On Page 1)	[ ] Other (See Instructions On Page 1)
4	SEX →	[ ] Male	[X] Female	
5	RACE/ETHNIC DESCRIPTION → (Check One Only - Voluntary)	[ ] Asian, Asian-American or Pacific Islander; [ ] Hispanic	[X] Black (Not Hispanic); [ ] North American Indian or Alaskan Native	[ ] White (Not Hispanic)
6	DATE OF BIRTH: 8/7/-- (Month, Day, Year)	7 PLACE OF BIRTH (Do Not Abbreviate): Stockton, California (City; State or Foreign Country)		Office Use Only; FCI
8	A. MOTHER'S MAIDEN NAME →	First / Full Middle Name / Last Name At Her Birth: Dolores Alicia Ames		
	B. MOTHER'S SOCIAL SECURITY NUMBER →	719–16–5411		
9	A. FATHER'S NAME →	First / Full Middle Name / Last: Allen Steven Jennings		
	B. FATHER'S SOCIAL SECURITY NUMBER →	919–86–3715		

10 Has the applicant or anyone acting on his/her behalf ever filed for or received a Social Security number card before?
[ ] Yes (If "yes", answer questions 11-13.) [X] No (If "no", go on to question 14.) [ ] Don't Know (If "don't know", go on to question 14.)

11 Enter the Social Security number previously assigned to the person listed in item 1. → ☐☐☐–☐☐–☐☐☐☐

12 Enter the name shown on the most recent Social Security card issued for the person listed in item 1. → First / Middle Name / Last

13 Enter any different date of birth if used on an earlier application for a card. → x (Month, Day, Year)

14 TODAY'S DATE: 10/11/-- (Month, Day, Year) **15** DAYTIME PHONE NUMBER: (909) 555-1793 (Area Code, Number)

16 I declare under penalty of perjury that I have examined all the information on this form, and on any accompanying statements or forms, and it is true and correct to the best of my knowledge.
YOUR SIGNATURE ▸ *Allen S. Jennings*

17 YOUR RELATIONSHIP TO THE PERSON IN ITEM 1 IS: [ ] Self [X] Natural Or Adoptive Parent [ ] Legal Guardian [ ] Other (Specify)

DO NOT WRITE BELOW THIS LINE (FOR SSA USE ONLY)

NPN		DOC	NTI	CAN		ITV
PBC	EVI	EVA	EVC	PRA	NWR	DNR	UNIT

EVIDENCE SUBMITTED

SIGNATURE AND TITLE OF EMPLOYEE(S) REVIEWING EVIDENCE AND/OR CONDUCTING INTERVIEW

DATE

DCL DATE

Form **SS-5** (10-2003) EF (12-2004) Destroy Prior Editions Page 5

Employees may have their SSN changed at any time by applying to the SSA and showing good reasons for a change. Otherwise, only one number is assigned to an employee, and the employee will continue to use that number regardless of the changes in positions or employers.

For aliens who must file U.S. tax returns but are not eligible to receive a social security number, the IRS has instituted ***Form W-7, Application for IRS Individual Taxpayer Identification Number (ITIN)***. An ITIN (begins with the number 9) is intended for tax purposes only. Even though employers can verify individuals' names and social security numbers over the Internet, this feature only applies to people who have already been hired.

on the JOB

Over 400 million social security numbers have been issued since 1936.

The secretary of health and human services is authorized to ensure that SSNs are issued to or on behalf of children who are below school age at the request of their parents or guardians and to children of school age when they first enroll in school. Further, SSNs must be obtained for children age one or over who are claimed as dependents on federal income tax returns. Taxpayers must list on their tax returns the taxpayer identification numbers of any claimed dependents. The secretary also ensures that SSNs are assigned to aliens when they are admitted to the United States under conditions that permit them to work.

Criminal penalties (of up to $5,000 or imprisonment of up to five years, or both) exist for persons involved in the following situations:

1. Knowingly and willfully using a SSN obtained with false information.
2. Using someone else's SSN.
3. Altering a social security card.
4. Buying or selling a card claimed to be issued by the secretary.
5. Possessing a card or counterfeit card with the intent to sell or alter it.

Returns Required for Social Security Purposes

Employers covered under FICA are liable for their own FICA taxes and their employees' FICA and income taxes withheld from wages. Withholding of income taxes is discussed in Chapter 4. Every employer (except those employing agricultural workers) who is required to withhold income taxes from wages or who is liable for social security taxes must file:

1. A ***quarterly*** or an ***annual*** tax and information return (Form 941 or 944). This return shows the total FICA wage paid and the total FICA taxes (employer and employee contributions) and federal income taxes withheld.
2. An ***annual*** return of withheld federal income taxes (Form 945). This return covers ***nonpayroll*** items such as backup withholding, withholding on gambling winnings, pensions, annuities, IRAs, and military retirement.

Generally, an employer must either electronically transfer to the IRS or deposit in an authorized depository the income taxes and social security taxes withheld and the employer's matching social security taxes.

Any employer who fails to pay the withheld income taxes and FICA taxes, fails to make deposits and payments, or does not file the tax returns as required by law may be required to deposit such taxes in a special trust account for the U.S. government and file monthly tax returns. Figure 3–7 lists and briefly describes the major forms used to prepare FICA tax returns and deposits.

LEARNING OBJECTIVE 5

DEPOSIT REQUIREMENTS (NONAGRICULTURAL WORKERS)

The requirements for depositing *FICA taxes and income taxes withheld* from employees' wages vary according to the amount of such taxes reported during a **lookback period.** Depending on the total amount of taxes involved (federal income tax and FICA tax withheld from employees' earnings plus the employer's portion of the FICA tax), employers

FIGURE 3–7

Major Forms for Preparing FICA Tax Returns and Deposits

Form 941, Employer's Quarterly Federal Tax Return	Required of all covered employers, except employers of household and agricultural employees, who withhold income tax and social security taxes (see Figure 3–10).
Form 941c, Supporting Statement to Correct Information	Used to correct income and social security tax information previously reported on Forms 941, 941-M, 941-SS, 943, 945.
Form 941-V, Form 941 Payment Voucher	Filled in by employers with a total tax liability of less than $2,500 for the quarter who are making payment with Form 941.
Form 941-M, Employer's Monthly Federal Tax Return	Required of employers who have not complied with the requirements for filing returns or paying or depositing all taxes reported on quarterly returns. Notification to file Form 941-M is received from the District Director, and pre-addressed forms are mailed to the employer monthly.
Form 941-PR, Employer's Quarterly Federal Tax Return	Required of employers to report social security taxes for workers in Puerto Rico.
Form 941-SS, Employer's Quarterly Federal Tax Return	Required of employers to report social security taxes for workers in American Samoa, Guam, the Northern Mariana Islands, and the Virgin Islands.
Form 943, Employer's Annual Tax Return for Agricultural Employees	Used by employers of agricultural workers for reporting FICA and income taxes on wages paid.
Form 944, Employer's Annual Federal Tax Return	Can be used by employers who owe $1,000 or less in employment taxes each year (in place of Form 941).
Form 945, Annual Return of Withheld Federal Income Tax	Required of employers to report income tax withheld from nonpayroll payments.
Form 8109, Federal Tax Deposit Coupon	Completed at the time of depositing various types of taxes such as withheld income and FICA (Form 941), agricultural withheld income and FICA (Form 943), and federal unemployment (Form 940, as will be discussed in Chapter 5).

may have to pay their taxes several times a month or monthly. Some employers may not have to make any deposits but, instead, may pay their taxes at the time of filing their quarterly return, Form 941, discussed later in this chapter.

The amount of employment taxes that the employer reported on the quarterly returns for the *four quarters in the lookback period* determines if the employer is a monthly or a semiweekly depositor. A lookback period consists of four quarters beginning July 1 of the second preceding year and ending June 30 of the prior year. These four quarters are the employer's lookback period even if no taxes were reported for any of the quarters. Figure 3–8 shows the lookback period for 2008. Each November, the IRS notifies employers whether they will be a monthly or a semiweekly depositor for the next calendar year.

FIGURE 3–8

Lookback Period for Calendar Year 2008

2006		2007	
July–Sept.	Oct.–Dec.	Jan.–Mar.	Apr.–June

Monthly Depositor	Reported—$50,000 or less in lookback period. Required deposits—By the 15th of the following month (if not a banking day, next banking day).
Semiweekly Depositor	Reported—More than $50,000 in lookback period. Required deposits—Payday on Wednesday, Thursday, or Friday—due following Wednesday. —Payday on Saturday, Sunday, Monday, or Tuesday—due following Friday. Separate liabilities and deposits—When deposit period spans two separate quarters.
One-Day Rule	Reported—$100,000 or more in undeposited taxes on any day during a deposit period. Required deposit—Close of the next banking day. Semiweekly status—If an employer falls under the one-day rule at any time during this year or last year.
No Deposits	Reported—Accumulated employment taxes of less than $2,500 for the whole calendar quarter. Required deposit—Pay with the filing of quarterly Form 941 or deposit by the end of month following the calendar quarter. Unsure of $2,500 total—Use the appropriate rules above.

MONTHLY

EXAMPLE

1. The Robart Company's deposit status for 2008 was determined by using the lookback period shown in Figure 3–8. During the two quarters of 2006, Robart reported employment taxes (FICA & Employees' Income Tax) of $16,000. For each of the two quarters in 2007, the company reported taxes of $10,000. Since the taxes reported by Robart during the lookback period do not exceed $50,000, the company is classed as a monthly depositor and follows the monthly rule for the current year, 2008.
2. Vu-Tu, Inc., is a monthly depositor. For July taxes of $11,000, Vu-Tu must deposit the $11,000 on or before August 15, 2008 (Friday).

SEMIWEEKLY

EXAMPLE

1. The Meyer Company's deposit status for 2008 was determined by using the lookback period shown in Figure 3–8. In the two quarters of 2006, Meyer reported taxes of $35,000. The taxes reported in the two quarters of 2007 totaled $30,000. **Since the total taxes reported during the four quarters of the lookback period exceeded $50,000, Meyer is subject to the semiweekly rule for the current year, 2008.**

2. The employees of Franchild, a semiweekly depositor, are paid every Monday. On September 29, 2008, Franchild has accumulated taxes totaling $24,000. Franchild is required to deposit the $24,000 on or before the following Friday, October 3.
3. Xeria Inc., a semiweekly depositor, has accumulated taxes on Wednesday, December 31, 2008, and on Friday, January 2, 2009. The company needs to make two separate deposits on Wednesday, January 7, 2009, even though they are part of the same semiweekly deposit period.

ONE-DAY

EXAMPLE

1. On Tuesday, January 8, 2008, Wycheck Company accumulated $105,000 in employment taxes for wages paid on that day. Regardless of Wycheck's deposit status, the firm is required to deposit the $105,000 by the next banking day, Wednesday, January 9. Note that if Wycheck was not subject to the semiweekly rule on January 8, 2008, the company would become subject to that rule as of January 9, 2008.
2. The Blastein Company is subject to the semiweekly rule. On Monday, February 4, 2008, Blastein accumulated $120,000 in employment taxes. The firm is required to deposit the $120,000 by the next banking day, Tuesday, February 5.

   On Tuesday, February 5, Blastein accumulates $30,000 more in employment taxes. Even though Blastein had a previous $120,000 deposit obligation that occurred earlier in the semiweekly period, Blastein now has an additional and separate deposit obligation that must be met by the following Friday, February 8.

A ***new employer*** becomes a monthly depositor until a lookback period that can be used to determine deposit frequency is established. However, if an unsatisfied deposit of $100,000 or more triggers the $100,000 one-day rule (discussed on page 3-20) at any time during the year, the new employer becomes a semiweekly depositor for the remainder of the current calendar year and the subsequent calendar year.

THE SAFE HARBOR RULE (98 PERCENT RULE) The amount deposited by an employer may be affected by the **safe harbor rule**. Under this rule, an employer satisfies the deposit obligations provided:

1. The amount of any shortfall (under deposit) does not exceed the greater of $100 or 2 percent of the amount of employment taxes required to be deposited.
2. The employer deposits the shortfall on or before the shortfall makeup date.

A **shortfall** is the excess of the amount of employment taxes required to be deposited over the amount deposited on or before the last date prescribed for the deposit. The shortfall makeup rules follow:

1. ***Monthly depositors:*** The shortfall must be deposited or remitted by the quarterly return due date, in accordance with the applicable form and instruction.
2. ***Semiweekly depositors and those subject to the $100,000 one-day rule:*** The shortfall must be deposited on or before the first Wednesday or Friday, whichever is earlier, falling on or after the 15th day of the month following the month in which the deposit was required to be made.

EXAMPLE

1. On Friday, June 6, 2008, Rogers, Ltd., a semiweekly depositor, pays wages and accumulates employment taxes. Rogers makes a deposit on Wednesday, June 11, in the amount of $4,000. Later it was determined that Rogers was actually required to deposit $4,080 by Wednesday.

   Rogers has a shortfall of $80. The shortfall is less than the greater of $100 or 2 percent of the amount required to be deposited. Therefore, Rogers satisfies the safe harbor rule so long as the $80 shortfall is deposited by Wednesday, July 16.

2. On Friday, October 17, 2008, Vargan Company, a semiweekly depositor, pays wages and accumulates employment taxes. Vargan makes a deposit of $30,000 but later finds that the amount of the deposit should have been $32,000.

   The $2,000 shortfall ($32,000 − $30,000) exceeds the greater of $100 or 2 percent of the amount required to be deposited (2% × $32,000 = $640). Thus, the safe harbor rule was not met. As a result, Vargan is subject to a failure-to-deposit penalty, as described later in this chapter.

DEPOSIT REQUIREMENTS FOR EMPLOYERS OF AGRICULTURAL WORKERS

The deposit-making rules that apply to employers of agricultural laborers resemble those for employers of nonagricultural workers. However, there are exceptions, explained in the instructions accompanying ***Form 943, Employer's Annual Tax Return for Agricultural Employees.***

DEPOSIT REQUIREMENTS FOR EMPLOYERS OF HOUSEHOLD EMPLOYEES

Household or domestic employees are usually not subject to federal income tax withholding, but they may voluntarily request that federal income taxes be withheld from their wages. Even though federal income taxes are not withheld from their wages, they are subject to FICA taxes if each worker has been paid cash wages of $1,500 or more in a calendar year. Noncash items given to household employees are not subject to FICA tax.

Employers who withhold and pay FICA taxes and federal income taxes for household services must report these taxes on ***Form W-2, Wage and Tax Statement,*** for each household employee.

DEPOSIT REQUIREMENTS FOR STATE AND LOCAL GOVERNMENT EMPLOYERS

Each state and local government employer must file its return on Form 941 with the IRS and deposit its FICA taxes through the federal deposit system. State and local government employers must make their tax deposits according to the same deposit schedule used by private employers.

PROCEDURES FOR MAKING DEPOSITS There are two methods of depositing employment taxes. The original paper-based system is being replaced over time by an electronic depositing system.

Electronic Deposits. Many employers must now make their deposits via the Electronic Federal Tax Payment System (EFTPS). Any employer who made more than $200,000 in aggregate deposits (not just employment tax deposits) in 2006 or was required to use EFTPS in 2007 must make electronic deposits in 2008. A deposit using this system must be initiated at least one business day before it is due in order to be considered timely.

This system is a communications network that facilitates the direct transfer of funds from the employer's bank to the Treasury Department. Generally, these transfers are transacted by touch-tone phone, personal computer, or online.

To use the online option, the employer must have Internet access. Enrollment in EFTPS-Online can be done at http://www.eftps.gov.

Once enrolled in the EFTPS program, an employer can switch between computer software or online methods anytime. The linkage on all the methods is provided by the company's employer identification number.

There are two electronic methods of deposit. The employer can instruct the Treasury Financial Agent for the area to withdraw funds from the employer's bank account and route them to the Treasury's account at the Federal Reserve Bank (ACH Debit Method). The employer could also instruct the bank to send each payment directly to the Treasury's account at the Federal Reserve Bank (ACH Credit Method).

To enroll, an employer must complete ***Form 9779, EFTPS Business Enrollment Form.*** Enrollment takes from three to six weeks, and a confirmation package will be sent by the IRS to the employer with a personal identification number (PIN) and payment instructions.

In an effort to encourage the use of the electronic system, the IRS will automatically pre-enroll in the EFTPS all employers who receive a new employer identification number. After obtaining their EIN, new employers will receive in the mail an EFTPS identification number and instructions for activating their enrollment.

Employers who are mandated to use this system will be assessed a *10 percent penalty* on every tax deposit that is not made through EFTPS.

FTD Coupons. Businesses not making deposits by EFTPS will use preprinted ***Federal Tax Deposit Coupons, Form 8109,*** to make payments at an authorized federal depository. Employers indicate on the coupon the type of tax being deposited. Figure 3–9

FIGURE 3–9

Form 8109, Federal Tax Deposit Coupon, and a Portion of the Accompanying Instructions[1]

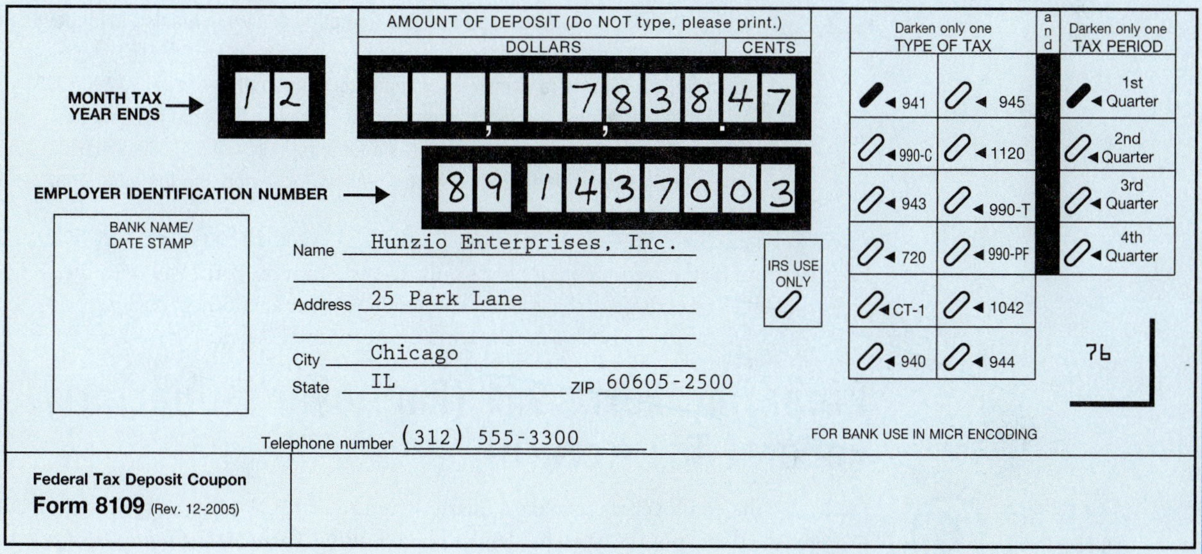
AMOUNT OF DEPOSIT (Do NOT type, please print.)
DOLLARS | CENTS
MONTH TAX YEAR ENDS → 12
7838 47
EMPLOYER IDENTIFICATION NUMBER → 89 1437003
BANK NAME/ DATE STAMP
Name Hunzio Enterprises, Inc.
Address 25 Park Lane
City Chicago
State IL ZIP 60605-2500
Telephone number (312) 555-3300
IRS USE ONLY
Darken only one TYPE OF TAX: 941, 945, 990-C, 1120, 943, 990-T, 720, 990-PF, CT-1, 1042, 940, 944
and
Darken only one TAX PERIOD: 1st Quarter, 2nd Quarter, 3rd Quarter, 4th Quarter
76
FOR BANK USE IN MICR ENCODING
Federal Tax Deposit Coupon
Form 8109 (Rev. 12-2005)

1 Form 8109-B is used by employers when (1) preprinted deposit coupons (Forms 8109) have not been received or (2) the employer is a new entity and the initial supply of preprinted deposit coupons has not been received.

on the JOB

If a deposit is required and the employer has not yet received the Employer Identification Number, the deposit must be mailed directly to the Internal Revenue Service with an explanation attached.

shows a sample coupon. The "TYPE OF TAX" section on the form is completed by darkening the 941 block.

Employers must make their deposits of taxes either at a Treasury Tax and Loan institution or by mailing it to Financial Agent, Federal Tax Deposit Processing, P.O. Box 970030, St. Louis, Missouri, 63917. They must make payment with an ***immediate credit item.*** An **immediate credit item** is a check or other instrument of payment for which the receiving bank gives immediate credit in accordance with its check-collection schedule. If a deposit is not made with an immediate credit item, the bank stamps the coupon to reflect the name of the bank and the date on which the proceeds of the accompanying payment instrument are collected. This date determines the timeliness of the payment.

The timeliness of deposits is determined by the date received by the institution. A deposit will be considered timely if the employer establishes that it was mailed at least two days before the due date. Deposits of $20,000 by an employer required to deposit tax more than once a month must be received by the due date to be timely.

on the JOB

According to a study conducted by the IRS, EFTPS has a 99.9 percent accuracy rate, which is more than 19 times better than paper coupons.

Each FTD coupon has a stub that the employer keeps as a record of payment. The canceled check, bank receipt, or money order is the employer's receipt. The FTD coupon is not returned to the employer but is used to credit the employer's tax account, identified by the employer's identification number entered on the coupon. The bank stamps the date and bank name on the coupon and forwards the tax deposit to the IRS for posting to the taxpayer's account. The IRS reconciles the tax deposits with the payments claimed by the employer on each quarterly return (Form 941). At this point, settlement of the employer's tax liability is made.

SELF-STUDY QUIZ 3-5

______ **1.** Johnson Industries, a semiweekly depositor, pays its employees every Friday. When should the company deposit the employment taxes for each weekly payday?

______ **2.** What rule should Bartlett Repair, a new company, follow in making its deposits for accumulated employment taxes?

______ **3.** Quail Hollow Motors (a semiweekly depositor) accumulates taxes of $105,000 on Monday and must deposit this amount on Tuesday, the next banking day. On Tuesday, the company accumulates additional taxes of $20,000. What deposit rule should Quail Hollow Motors follow for depositing the additional $20,000?

Preparing Form 941 (Employer's Quarterly Federal Tax Return)

LEARNING OBJECTIVE 6

Generally, the employer must make a quarterly return of FICA taxes and withheld income taxes for the three months of each calendar quarter, using ***Form 941, Employer's Quarterly Federal Tax Return.*** Figure 3–10, on pages 3-25 and 3-26, shows a completed copy of Form 941. Once the form has been filed, the employer receives preaddressed forms every three months. If the employer has not received the form, the employer should request one from an IRS office in time to file the return when due.

All nonpayroll items (backup withholding and withholding from pensions, annuities, IRAs, military retirement and gambling winnings) are reported on ***Form 945, Annual Return of Withheld Federal Income Tax*** (Chapter 4).

FIGURE 3–10

Form 941, Employer's Quarterly Federal Tax Return (Page 1)

Form **941 for 20--: Employer's QUARTERLY Federal Tax Return** 990107
(Rev. January 2007) Department of the Treasury — Internal Revenue Service OMB No. 1545-0029

(EIN) Employer identification number	89–1787779
Name (not your trade name)	JOHN GRANATELLI
Trade name (if any)	GRANATELLI MOTORS
Address (Number, Street, Suite or room number)	3709 FIFTH
City / State / ZIP code	CHICAGO / IL / 60605

Report for this Quarter of 20-- (Check one.)

- ☑ **1:** January, February, March
- ☐ **2:** April, May, June
- ☐ **3:** July, August, September
- ☐ **4:** October, November, December

Read the separate instructions before you fill out this form. Please type or print within the boxes.

Part 1: Answer these questions for this quarter.

Line	Description	Column 1	Column 2	Amount
1	**Number of employees who received wages, tips, or other compensation for the pay period including:** ***Mar. 12*** **(Quarter 1),** ***June 12*** **(Quarter 2),** ***Sept. 12*** **(Quarter 3),** ***Dec. 12*** **(Quarter 4)**			26
2	**Wages, tips, and other compensation**			74895.92
3	**Total income tax withheld from wages, tips, and other compensation**			12372.13
4	**If no wages, tips, and other compensation are subject to social security or Medicare tax**			☐ Check and go to line 6.
5	**Taxable social security and Medicare wages and tips:**			
5a	**Taxable social security wages**	74895.92 × .124 =	9287.09	
5b	**Taxable social security tips**	. × .124 =	.	
5c	**Taxable Medicare wages & tips**	74895.92 × .029 =	2171.98	
5d	**Total social security and Medicare taxes** (*Column 2,* lines 5a + 5b + 5c = line 5d)			11459.07
6	**Total taxes before adjustments** (lines 3 + 5d = line 6)			23831.20
7	**TAX ADJUSTMENTS** (Read the instructions for line 7 before completing lines 7a through 7h.):			
7a	**Current quarter's fractions of cents**		– .15	
7b	**Current quarter's sick pay**		.	
7c	**Current quarter's adjustments for tips and group-term life insurance**		.	
7d	**Current year's income tax withholding** (attach Form 941c)		.	
7e	**Prior quarters' social security and Medicare taxes** (attach Form 941c)		.	
7f	**Special additions to federal income tax** (attach Form 941c)		.	
7g	**Special additions to social security and Medicare** (attach Form 941c)		.	
7h	**TOTAL ADJUSTMENTS** (Combine all amounts: lines 7a through 7g.)			– .15
8	**Total taxes after adjustments** (Combine lines 6 and 7h.)			23831.05
9	**Advance earned income credit (EIC) payments made to employees**			.
10	**Total taxes after adjustment for advance EIC** (line 8 – line 9 = line 10)			23831.05
11	**Total deposits for this quarter, including overpayment applied from a prior quarter**			23831.05
12	**Balance due** (If line 10 is more than line 11, write the difference here.) Follow the Instructions for Form 941-V, Payment Voucher.			.
13	**Overpayment** (If line 11 is more than line 10, write the difference here.)		.	Check one ☐ Apply to next return. ☐ Send a refund.

▶ You **MUST** fill out both pages of this form and **SIGN** it.

Next ➡

For Privacy Act and Paperwork Reduction Act Notice, see the back of the Payment Voucher. Cat. No. 17001Z Form **941** (Rev. 1-2007)

FIGURE 3–10 (Concluded)

Form 941, Employer's Quarterly Federal Tax Return (Page 2)

990207

Name (not your trade name)	Employer identification number (EIN)
JOHN GRANATELLI	89-1787779

Part 2: Tell us about your deposit schedule and tax liability for this quarter.

If you are unsure about whether you are a monthly schedule depositor or a semiweekly schedule depositor, see *Pub. 15 (Circular E)*, section 11.

14 [I] [L] **Write the state abbreviation for the state where you made your deposits** OR **write "MU" if you made your deposits in *multiple* states.**

15 Check one: ☐ **Line 10 is less than $2,500.** Go to Part 3.

☐ **You were a monthly schedule depositor for the entire quarter. Fill out your tax liability for each month.** Then go to Part 3.

Tax liability: **Month 1** [.]

Month 2 [.]

Month 3 [.]

Total liability for quarter [.] **Total must equal line 10.**

☑ **You were a semiweekly schedule depositor for any part of this quarter.** Fill out *Schedule B (Form 941): Report of Tax Liability for Semiweekly Schedule Depositors,* and attach it to this form.

Part 3: Tell us about your business. If a question does NOT apply to your business, leave it blank.

16 If your business has closed or you stopped paying wages . . . . ☐ Check here, and

enter the final date you paid wages [/ /].

17 If you are a seasonal employer and you do not have to file a return for every quarter of the year . . ☐ Check here.

Part 4: May we speak with your third-party designee?

Do you want to allow an employee, a paid tax preparer, or another person to discuss this return with the IRS? (See the instructions for details.)

☐ Yes. Designee's name [ ]

Select a 5-digit Personal Identification Number (PIN) to use when talking to IRS. ☐☐☐☐☐

☑ No.

Part 5: Sign here. You MUST fill out both pages of this form and SIGN it.

Under penalties of perjury, I declare that I have examined this return, including accompanying schedules and statements, and to the best of my knowledge and belief, it is true, correct, and complete.

X Sign your name here *John Granatelli*

Print your name here: JOHN GRANATELLI

Print your title here: OWNER

Date: 04 / 30 / 08

Best daytime phone: (773) 555 - 2119

Part 6: For paid preparers only *(optional)*

Paid Preparer's Signature [ ]

Firm's name [ ]

Address [ ] EIN [ ]

ZIP code [ ]

Date [/ /] Phone ( ) – SSN/PTIN [ ]

☐ Check if you are self-employed.

Page **2** Form **941** (Rev. 1-2007)

COMPLETING THE RETURN

In making entries on the form:

a. Dollar signs and decimal points—not used.
b. Zero value line item—leave blank.
c. Negative amounts—use "minus" sign.

PART 1 Most of the entries required on this part are self-explanatory. Other sources of information are shown in Figure 3-12 (see page 3-29). The tax adjustments on line 7 relate to:

7a. Fractions of cents—employees' share (one-half) of amounts on lines 5(a)–5(c) may differ slightly from amounts actually withheld (due to rounding).
7b. Sick pay—adjustment for employees' share of FICA taxes that were withheld by third-party sick pay payer.
7c. Tips and group-term insurance—uncollected FICA taxes on tips and group-term life insurance premiums.
7d. Income tax withholding—adjustments for errors in income tax withholdings for earlier quarters in this year.
7e. Prior quarters' taxes—adjustments for prior quarters' FICA taxes.
7f. and 7g. Special additions—reserved for employers with special circumstances.
7h. Total—combine lines 7a through 7g.

PART 2

14. Use the Postal Service two-letter state abbreviation for the state where taxes are deposited. If deposits were made in more than one state enter "MU" in the box.
15. Check the appropriate box. If the monthly schedule applies, enter a summary of your ***tax liability*** by month.

PART 3

16. and **17.** Complete if either situation applies.

PART 4 Complete if the employer wants to allow an employee, a paid tax preparer, or another person to discuss Form 941 with the IRS.

In addition, semiweekly and next-day depositors must complete Schedule B of ***Form 941, Report of Tax Liability for Semiweekly Schedule Depositors,*** instead of Form 941, line 15. The employer's tax liability is listed by each payday (see Figure 3–11 on page 3-28).

PART 5 The form must be signed by the employer or other person who is required to withhold and pay the tax. If the employer is:

1. An ***individual,*** the return should be signed by that person.
2. A ***corporation,*** the return should be signed by its president, vice president, or other principal officer authorized to sign the return. Corporate officers or duly authorized agents may use facsimile signatures under certain conditions.
3. A ***partnership*** or ***other unincorporated organization,*** a responsible and duly authorized partner or officer having knowledge of the firm's affairs should sign the return.
4. A ***trust*** or ***estate,*** the return should be signed by the fiduciary of the trust or estate.
5. A ***political body,*** such as a state or territory, the return should be signed by the officer or employee having control of the wage payments or officer properly designated for that purpose.
6. An ***agent,*** who pays the wages for the employer, may be authorized by the employer to sign the appropriate tax returns.

Employment tax forms can be signed by a facsimile-rubber stamp, mechanical device, or computer software program.

Employers can use credit cards to pay the balance due as shown on Form 941—this does not apply to tax deposits.

on the *JOB*

If an employer does not deposit social security, Medicare, and withheld income taxes on time, the IRS can require the employer to file monthly returns for these taxes on **Form 941-M, Employer's Monthly Federal Tax Return.**

on the *JOB*

The balance due on Form 941 can now be paid by credit card. This *does not* apply to making federal tax deposits.

***IRS* CONNECTION**

Internal Revenue Service forms and publications are available by calling 1-800-829-3676 or by accessing its Internet Web site at http://www.irs.gov/formspubs/

FIGURE 3–11

Report of Tax Liability for Semiweekly Schedule Depositors

Schedule B (Form 941):

Report of Tax Liability for Semiweekly Schedule Depositors

(Rev. January 2006) Department of the Treasury — Internal Revenue Service

OMB No. 1545-0029

(EIN) Employer identification number: 89 – 1787779

Name (*not your trade name*): JOHN GRANATELLI

Calendar year: 2008 (Also check quarter)

Report for this Quarter ... (Check one.)

- [x] 1: January, February, March
- [ ] 2: April, May, June
- [ ] 3: July, August, September
- [ ] 4: October, November, December

Use this schedule to show your TAX LIABILITY for the quarter; DO NOT use it to show your deposits. You must fill out this form and attach it to Form 941 (or Form 941-SS) if you are a semiweekly schedule depositor or became one because your accumulated tax liability on any day was $100,000 or more. Write your daily tax liability on the numbered space that corresponds to the date wages were paid. See Section 11 in *Pub. 15 (Circular E), Employer's Tax Guide,* for details.

Month 1

1	.	9	.	17	.	25	3819.35
2	.	10	.	18	.	26	.
3	.	11	4019.12	19	.	27	.
4	.	12	.	20	.	28	.
5	.	13	.	21	.	29	.
6	.	14	.	22	.	30	.
7	.	15	.	23	.	31	.
8	.	16	.	24	.		

Tax liability for Month 1: 7838.47

Month 2

1	.	9	.	17	.	25	.
2	.	10	.	18	.	26	.
3	.	11	.	19	.	27	.
4	.	12	.	20	.	28	.
5	.	13	.	21	.	29	.
6	.	14	.	22	3913.96	30	.
7	.	15	.	23	.	31	.
8	4026.82	16	.	24	.		

Tax liability for Month 2: 7940.78

Month 3

1	.	9	.	17	.	25	.
2	.	10	.	18	.	26	.
3	.	11	.	19	.	27	.
4	.	12	.	20	.	28	.
5	.	13	.	21	3944.61	29	.
6	.	14	.	22	.	30	.
7	4107.19	15	.	23	.	31	.
8	.	16	.	24	.		

Tax liability for Month 3: 8051.80

Fill in your total liability for the quarter (Month 1 + Month 2 + Month 3) = Total tax liability for the quarter ▶
Total must equal line 10 on Form 941 (or line 8 on Form 941-SS).

Total liability for the quarter: 23831.05

For Paperwork Reduction Act Notice, see separate instructions. Cat. No. 11967Q **Schedule B (Form 941)** Rev. 1-2006

FIGURE 3–12

Sources of Information for Completing Form 941

Line Number	Source of Information
1	Payroll register.
2	General ledger accounts for wages and salaries; Forms 4070, or employees' written statements reporting cash tips.
3	General ledger accounts.
4	General ledger balances.
5a	Payroll register; include any social security taxes (OASDI) paid for employees, sick pay, and taxable fringe benefits subject to OASDI. Do not include any tips. Do not report any employees' wages that exceed $102,300, the taxable wage base for 2008.
5b	Forms 4070, or employees' written statements to report cash tips. Enter all tips reported until tips and wages for each employee reach $102,300. Report this information even if you are unable to withhold the employee OASDI tax. Do not include allocated tips, which should be reported on Form 8027.
5c	Payroll register; Forms 4070, or employees' written statements to report cash tips. Report amounts paid to certain federal, state, and local government employees who are subject only to the HI portion of the FICA tax.
5d	Add lines 5a, 5b, and 5c.
7a	To adjust for fractions of cents: If there is a difference between the total tax on line 5d and the total deducted from your employees' wages or tips plus the employer's tax on those wages or tips (general ledger accounts) because of fractions of cents added or dropped in collecting the tax, report the difference. Enter this difference in the space for "Fractions of Cents." If a negative number is to be used, use a minus sign –.
7b	To adjust for the tax on third-party sick pay: Deduct the social security tax on third-party sick pay for which you are not responsible. Enter the amount of the adjustment in the space for "Sick Pay."
7c	To adjust for the tax on tips and group-term life insurance: Include the total uncollected employee social security tax for lines 5b and 5c.
7d	Forms 941 previously filed and general ledger accounts—to determine amount of errors made in income tax withheld from wages paid in earlier quarters of the calendar year.
7e	Forms 941 previously filed. Correct errors in social security taxes reported on earlier return or correct errors in credits for overpayments of penalty or interest paid on tax for an earlier quarter. If you report both an underpayment and an overpayment, show only the difference.
7f, 7g	Use Form 941c to explain any amount on line 7, other than adjustments for fractions of cents or third-party sick pay. Or, you may attach a statement that shows the nature of error(s) being corrected.
7h	Total of lines 7a through 7g.
8	Record total taxes by adding lines 6 and 7h.
9	If applicable, show the amount of any advance earned income credit (EIC) payments made (discussed in Chapter 4). The amount of the advance EIC payments does not change the amount deducted and withheld from employees' pay for income tax and employee FICA taxes. Advance EIC payments that you make are treated as made from the amounts withheld as income tax and employee FICA taxes and your FICA tax contributions.
10	Determine net taxes by subtracting line 9 from line 8.
11	General ledger accounts, previous Form 941; record the total deposits for the quarter, including any overpayment applied from previous quarter.
12	Compute balance due by subtracting line 11 from line 10. Pay the balance due IRS.
13	Compute overpayment by subtracting line 10 from line 11 and indicate if amount is to be applied to the next return or refunded.

FILING FORM 941

The law requires employers to file Form 941 on or before the last day of the month following the close of the calendar quarter for which the return applies. If an employer makes timely tax deposits for the quarter, the employer may file Form 941 on or before the 10th day of the second month following the close of the calendar quarter.

Payments can be made with Form 941 only if either the net taxes for the quarter (line 13) are less than $2,500 or the payment serves as a deposit for a monthly depositor in accordance with the accuracy of deposits rule (can be more than $2,500). In both cases, a Form 941-V (Payment Voucher) must be filed with Form 941.

If the last day for filing a quarterly return falls on Saturday, Sunday, or a legal holiday, the employer may file the return on the next business day. If the return is filed by mailing, the employer should mail the return in sufficient time for it to reach the IRS Center no later than the next business day under ordinary handling of the mail.

EXAMPLE

1. An employer files a return by May 1 (if April 30 is a Sunday) for the calendar quarter ending March 31.
2. An employer makes timely deposits for the quarter ending March 31. The form can be filed on or before May 10.
3. The Pruit Company was not required to make any deposits for FICA taxes during the quarter ending March 31. The company makes its deposit for the first quarter taxes on April 25 for taxes due. Pruit can still file Form 941 on or before May 10 for the first quarter return.

on the JOB

You can correct errors on prior period Forms 941 by making an adjustment on the current Form 941 being filed. For example, if an error was made in reporting social security taxes in the 3rd quarter of 2007 and discovered in the 1st quarter of 2008, the error may be adjusted when filing Form 941 for the first quarter of 2008.

Prior period adjustments require supporting information. File **Form 941c, Supporting Statement to Correct Information,** with Form 941. Do not file Form 941c separately.

Individual employers file quarterly returns with the IRS Center of the region in which the employer's principal place of business or office or agency is located. The return may still be filed at the local office of the district director of the IRS if the taxpayer hand delivers the return.

After filing their first Form 941, employers must file returns for each quarter even if there were no taxes to report (unless they had checked box 16—business closed—in their last filing). The exception to this is for ***seasonal employers*** who do not have to file for quarters when they have no tax liability (they must check line 17 for every quarter that they do file).

ELECTRONIC FILING OF FORM 941

Using an electronic data interchange format, employers can now file Form 941 electronically using a personal computer, modem, and specialized tax preparation software. This option is available to any business taxpayer who can meet the program's requirements. Currently, it is a two-step process:

1. Electronic submission of the Form 941 data.
2. Mailing of a paper signature document ***(Form 4996, Electronic/Magnetic Media Filing Transmittal for Wage and Withholding Tax Returns).***

Interested filers must submit a letter of application through a third-party transmitter to the IRS center in Memphis at least 15 days prior to the beginning of the tax quarter. The taxpayer must also make a test transmission at least 20 days prior to the due date of the first electronically filed Form 941.

Once filed electronically, the employer will no longer be sent the quarterly 941 mailings.

FORM 944

NEWS//ALERT//

Approximately 17 percent of tax filers are eligible to file Form 944.

Employer's Annual Federal Tax Return can be used by employers who owe $1,000 or less in employment taxes per year and have not been late with any deposits for two years. These employers have to *file* the form and *pay* their employment taxes *only once a year.* Eligible employers who exceed the $1,000 threshold during the year can still file Form 944 for that year. However, they must start filing Form 941 at the beginning of the next year.

This return can also be used by ***new employers*** who expect to pay wages of $4,000 or less this year.

The form (which is not illustrated) is basically the same as Form 941. The first filing of Form 944 will be due January 31, 2008.

Failure-to-Comply Penalties

7 LEARNING OBJECTIVE

Employers act as collection agents for the government by collecting employment taxes and paying them to the appropriate government agency. Employers who fail to carry out their duties as collection agents are subject to civil and criminal penalties. The penalties may be additions to the tax, interest charges, and fines and imprisonment. Penalties also apply to federal income taxes (Chapter 4) and federal unemployment taxes (Chapter 5) and are imposed on employers who fail to do the following:

1. File employment tax returns.
2. Fully pay taxes when due.
3. Make timely deposits.
4. Furnish wage and tax statements.
5. File or provide information returns.
6. Supply identification numbers.

The penalty depends on the degree of willfulness present in the employer's conduct. Persons other than the employer who have the duty or responsibility for collecting, accounting for, and paying any taxes may also be assessed penalties. Passing bad checks in payment of any employment tax also carries a penalty.

Once Form 941 is received, it usually takes the IRS about five weeks to notify an employer of any tax delinquencies.

NEWS // ALERT//

Over $49 billion in unpaid payroll taxes is owed by nearly 2 million businesses. Many of these businesses are insolvent or defunct.

FAILURE TO FILE EMPLOYMENT TAX RETURNS

If an employer fails to file an employment tax return on the date prescribed for filing, a certain percentage of the amount of tax required to be reported will be added to the tax. Employers may avoid this addition if they show to the satisfaction of the IRS that failure to file was due to reasonable cause and not willful conduct.

IRS CONNECTION

The IRS reports that over 6.6 million employers file more than 23 million 941s every year.

Additions to the Tax	5 percent combined penalty of the net amount of tax that should have been reported less any amounts timely paid; an additional 5 percent for each additional month or fraction of a month during which failure continues, not to exceed 25 percent.
	15 percent per month, not to exceed 75 percent, for fraudulent failure to file.
Criminal Penalties	Not more than $25,000 ($100,000 for corporations), imprisonment of not more than one year, or both.
	Not more than $100,000, imprisonment of no more than three years, or both for willfully signing a return not true and correct as to every material statement.

EXAMPLE

Ned Fromton, an employer, files his employment tax return 20 days after the due date of the return. The amount of tax that was unpaid is $6,000. Fromton's penalty is:

Failure to file (5% × $6,000) = $300 *Note:* Any fraction of a month counts as a whole month.

FAILURE TO FULLY PAY EMPLOYMENT TAXES

Employers who fail to pay the amount as shown on a return by the due date are faced with the following civil and criminal penalties.

Additions to the Tax	0.5 percent of the amount shown as tax on a return per month or fraction of a month, not to exceed 25 percent. The amount on which the penalty is calculated can be reduced by payments made on or before the beginning of the month. If both penalties for filing a late return and for not fully paying the tax apply in the same month, the failure to file penalty is reduced by the amount of the failure to pay full penalty. There is also a separate 0.5 percent per month penalty for failing to pay a tax amount due that was not shown on the return within 21 days of the notice and demand from the IRS. The penalty is based on the amount in the IRS notice. In addition, any taxes due will bear *interest at the rate of 8 percent* per year. Large corporate underpayments ($100,000) will carry the rate of 10 percent.[2]
Additions to the Tax	20 percent of the underpayment for negligence (failure to make a reasonable attempt to comply) or intentional disregard (careless, reckless, or intentional disregard of the law) of the payment rules. 75 percent of the underpayment if underpayment is due to fraud with the intent to evade the tax.
The 100% Penalty	100 percent of the tax due for willfully failing to collect, account for, or pay employment taxes or willfully attempting to evade or defeat the taxes.
Tax Levies	Levy on and seize any property and property rights held by the employer at the time of levy for failure of the employer to pay any taxes, 10 days after notice and demand for payment.
Criminal Penalties	Not more than $10,000, imprisonment of no more than five years, or both, for willful failure to pay the tax. These penalties are in addition to the 75 percent fraud penalty.

***IRS* CONNECTION**

The IRS has estimated that 30 percent of all employers incur penalties for insufficient or late deposits of payroll taxes.

EXAMPLE

The Yeld Company failed to pay its employment taxes of $5,000 for March (due April 15) until May 20. The failure to pay penalty assessed against the Yeld Company is:

Failure to Pay Tax ($5,000 × 0.5% × 2) =	$50.00
Interest on Taxes Due ($5,000 × 0.08 × 35/365) =	38.36
Total Penalty	$88.36

Note: In addition, a penalty for failure to make a timely deposit will also be assessed.

FAILURE TO MAKE TIMELY DEPOSITS

Penalties may apply if employers do not make required deposits on time in an authorized government depository.

Deposits made 1 to 5 calendar days late	2 percent of the undeposited taxes
Deposits made 6 to 15 days late	5 percent of the undeposited taxes
Deposits made 16 or more days late	10 percent of the undeposited taxes
Deposits made at unauthorized financial institutions or directly to IRS	10 percent of the undeposited taxes
Deposits subject to electronic deposit requirements but not deposited by EFTPS	10 percent of the tax deposit required
Amounts unpaid more than 10 days after IRS notice	15 percent of the undeposited taxes

on the *JOB*

Deposits are applied to the most recent tax liabilities within the quarter; however, a depositor can designate to the IRS the period to which a deposit is to be applied. The employer has 90 days from the date of a penalty notice to make the designation.

2 The IRS sets the interest rate each calendar quarter, based on the short-term Treasury bill rate for the first month in each calendar quarter, plus three percentage points, and applies it for the following calendar quarter. The rate stated is for the second quarter of 2007.

EXAMPLE

Greerson Inc. must make a deposit of $1,800 on June 15. The deposit was made 12 days late. The penalty assessed against Greerson is:

Failure to make timely deposit ($1,800 × 5%) = $90

FAILURE TO FURNISH PAYEE STATEMENTS

If employers willfully fail to furnish ***their employees*** with properly executed wage and tax statements or willfully furnish false or fraudulent statements (employee's copy of W-2 or recipient's Form 1099—discussed in Chapter 4), the civil penalty is $50 for each statement.

Maximum Penalty	$100,000 in any calendar year.
Intentional Disregard	$100 per statement or, if greater, 10 percent of the amount required to be shown on the statement. No limit on the maximum penalty for the calendar year.
Criminal Penalties	$1,000 fine, imprisonment for not more than one year, or both, for each offense.

FAILURE TO FURNISH INFORMATION RETURNS

Employers who fail to timely file their information returns ***with the government*** (any 1099 series or Forms W-2) are subject to $50 for each failure. These penalties also apply to failures to include all required information on the forms, to supply only correct information, to file magnetically if required, and to report correct taxpayer identification numbers.

Correction within 30 days	$15 per failure, maximum fine $75,000.
Correction after 30 days, before August 1	$30 per failure, maximum fine $150,000.
Not filed correctly by August 1	$50 per return, maximum fine $250,000.
Intentional disregard	$100 per statement or, if greater, 10 percent of the amount to be shown on the statement. No limit on the maximum penalty for the calendar year.

BAD CHECKS

Checks or money orders not tendered in good faith	2 percent of the amount. If the check is less than $750, penalty is $15 or the amount of the check, whichever is less.

KEY TERMS

Educational assistance *(p. 3-10)*
Employer *(p. 3-4)*
Employment *(p. 3-4)*
Immediate credit item *(p. 3-24)*
Independent contractors *(p. 3-7)*
Lookback period *(p. 3-18)*
Monthly depositor *(p. 3-20)*
Person *(p. 3-4)*
Safe harbor rule *(p. 3-21)*
Self-employment income *(p. 3-13)*
Semiweekly depositor *(p. 3-20)*
Shortfall *(p. 3-21)*
Sick pay *(p. 3-10)*
Taxable wage base *(p. 3-11)*

CHAPTER SUMMARY

Social Security (FICA) taxes apply to all classes of employees—full-time, part-time, seasonal, etc. And they also affect the self-employed based on their net earnings. Tips reported are also taxed.

The tax is made up of two parts:

- Old-age, survivors, disability insurance (OASDI), 6.2% on first $102,300 of earnings.
- Hospital insurance, 1.45% on total wages

Not only is this tax taken out of employees' pays, but the employer must match the employees' contributions. In the case of the self-employed, the tax rate is doubled (12.4% and 2.9%).

The forms discussed in this chapter are:

- Form SS-4—Application for Employer ID Number
- Form SS-5—Application for Social Security Number
- Form 8109—Federal Tax Deposit Coupon
- Form 941—Employer's Quarterly Federal Tax Return
- Form 944—Employer's Annual Federal Tax Return (for employers owing $1,000 or less in employment taxes per year).

Employers' deposits of these taxes (employees' FICA, employers' FICA, and employees' federal income taxes) are made either electronically or at an authorized bank. Based on the annual amount of taxes (under $50,000, or $50,000 and over) paid over a lookback period, an employer could be either a monthly or semiweekly depositor. Exceptions to these requirements are:

1. one-day rule—if accumulated taxes are $100,000 or more on any day during a deposit period,
2. no deposits—less than $2,500 during an entire calendar quarter.

The chapter ends with a review of the penalties imposed on employers for failure to comply with the various requirements of FICA.

MATCHING QUIZ

E ____ 1. Employer's FICA tax rates

D ____ 2. Form SS-4

H ____ 3. Semiweekly depositor

A ____ 4. Taxable for FICA

J ____ 5. Nontaxable for FICA

I ____ 6. Self-employed's FICA tax rates

C ____ 7. Form 941

B ____ 8. Monthly depositor

G ____ 9. Taxable wage base

F ____ 10. Form SS-5

A. Cash value of meals provided for employees' convenience

B. By the 15th day of the following month

C. Employer's Quarterly Federal Tax Return

D. Application for Employer Identification Number

E. 6.2% and 1.45%

F. Employee's application for social security card

G. Applies only to the OASDI portion of the FICA tax

H. More than $50,000 in employment taxes in the lookback period

I. 12.4% and 2.9%

J. Employer's matching contributions into employees' deferred compensation arrangements

QUESTIONS FOR REVIEW

1. For social security purposes, what conditions must an individual meet to be classified as a "covered" employer?
2. For social security purposes, what conditions must an individual meet to be classified as a "covered" employee?
3. Under what conditions does a common-law relationship exist between an employee and an employer?
4. Summarize the test conditions under which a worker is classified as an independent contractor.

5. What are an employer's responsibilities for FICA taxes on:
   a. Tips reported by employees?
   b. Wages paid tipped employees?
6. What conditions exclude sick pay from the definition of wages for FICA tax purposes?
7. What is the FICA tax liability status of pretax contributions to a qualified deferred compensation arrangement?
8. John Luis receives wages from three employers during 2007. Is he entitled to a refund on the OASDI taxes paid on wages in excess of the $102,300 limit? If so, how can he receive a refund?
9. What are the self-employment tax rates for 2008? Explain how the tax is computed.
10. How does an employer file an application for an employer identification number?
11. Summarize the deposit rules for nonagricultural employers.
12. Which employers must deposit their employment taxes electronically?
13. How are the electronic tax deposits transferred from the employer's account to the IRS?
14. How often must an employer file Form 941?
15. List the penalties imposed on the employer for the following:
    a. Filing Form 941 late.
    b. Seven days late making a deposit.
    c. Issuing a bad check to the IRS.

QUESTIONS FOR DISCUSSION

1. In order to improve the cash flow of the company, Neal Emerald decided to postpone depositing all employment taxes a few months ago. He told his sales manager, "I'll pay up before the IRS catches up with me." What risks does Emerald face by not upholding his responsibility for the collection and payment of employment taxes?
2. On Wednesday, June 14, 20--, Jacon Company had employment taxes of $25,000 that were required to be deposited on or before Wednesday, June 21. The deposit was mailed and postmarked Wednesday, June 21, and delivered on Thursday, June 22. What deposit rule is Jacon following? Was the deposit made in a timely manner?
3. During a recent strike at the Ultima Hotel, union members were paid strike benefits by their union. Don Volmer, a union representative, participates in negotiations with the hotel. Are the payments Volmer receives for his services as a union negotiator subject to FICA taxes?
4. When employees of the County Bank are summoned to serve on jury duty, the firm pays its workers the difference between their regular wages and the amount received for jury duty. One such employee has been receiving $365 per week. She just completed a five-day week of jury duty, for which she was paid $65 ($9 per day plus 20 cents per mile from her house to the courthouse, a 20-mile round trip). How much of the employee's earnings are subject to FICA tax?

DATE ____________ NAME ____________

PRACTICAL PROBLEMS—SERIES A

3-1A LO 3.

The biweekly taxable wages for the employees of Stork Foods follow.

Compute the FICA taxes for each employee and the employer's FICA taxes.

Employee No.	Employee Name	Biweekly Taxable Wages	FICA Taxes OASDI (6.2)	FICA Taxes HI (1.45)
711	Burke, Mark	$479.68	$29.74	$6.96
512	Celeo, Mary	495.00	30.69	7.18
624	Filmore, Juanita	385.25	23.89	5.59
325	Harrison, Bob	397.25	24.63	5.76
422	Lang, Will	785.00	48.67	11.38
210	Pagat, Mel	775.50	48.08	11.24
111	Troy, Sheila	495.25	30.71	7.18
		Totals	$236.41	$55.29

Employer's OASDI $3812.93 (Total Taxable Wages) $236.40 (Employer's OASDI Tax)

Employer's HI Tax $3812.93 (Total Taxable Wages) $55.29 (Employer's HI Tax)

3-2A LO 3.

During 2008, Rachael Parkins, president of Mathieson Company, was paid a semimonthly salary of $6,800. Compute the amount of FICA taxes that should be withheld from her:

	OASDI	HI
a. 9th paycheck	$421.60	$98.60
b. 16th paycheck	$18.60	$98.60
c. 24th paycheck	$0	$98.60

3-3A LO 3.

Ernie Gilmore began working as a part-time waiter on June 1, 2008, at Sporthouse Restaurant. The cash tips of $390 that he received during June were reported on Form 4070, which he submitted to his employer on July 1. During July, he was paid wages of $525 by the restaurant. Compute:

	OASDI	HI
a. The amount of FICA taxes that the employer should withhold from Gilmore's wages during July.	$	$
b. The amount of the employer's FICA taxes on Gilmore's wages and tips during July.	$	$

3-4A LO 2.

Ken Gorman is a maitre d' at Carmel Dinner Club. On February 6, his gross pay was $800 (three days working, one paid vacation day, and one paid sick day). He also reported to his employer tips of $900 for the previous month (applicable taxes to be deducted out of this pay). Ken belongs to the company's 401(k) plan and has 5% of his gross pay ($800) deducted each week (salary reduction). Carmel Dinner Club also provides a matching contribution ($40) into the plan for Ken. This week's pay would have a:

a. Deduction for OASDI tax $__________

b. Deduction for HI tax $__________

3-5A LO 3.

The annual salaries paid each of the officers of Maxtun, Inc., follow. The officers are paid semimonthly on the 15th and the last day of the month. Compute the FICA taxes to be withheld from each officer's pay on (a) November 14 and (b) December 31.

November 14

Name and Title	Annual Salary	OASDI Taxable Earnings	OASDI Tax	HI Taxable Earnings	HI Tax
Tate, Jack, President	$120,000	2300	142.60	5000	72.50
Green, Sue, VP Finance	100,800	4200	260.40	4200	60.90
Jones, Al, VP Sales	69,600	2900	179.80	2900	42.05
David, James, VP Mfg.	54,000	2250	139.50	2250	32.63
Wong, Pam, VP Personnel	51,600	2150	133.30	2150	31.18
Molt, Mary, VP Secretary	49,200	2050	127.10	2050	29.73

December 31

Name and Title	Annual Salary	OASDI Taxable Earnings	OASDI Tax	HI Taxable Earnings	HI Tax
Tate, Jack, President	$120,000	0	0	5000	72.50
Green, Sue, VP Finance	100,800	4200	260.40	4200	60.90
Jones, Al, VP Sales	69,600	2900	179.80	2900	42.05
David, James, VP Mfg.	54,000	2250	139.50	2250	32.63
Wong, Pam, VP Personnel	51,600	2150	133.30	2150	31.18
Molt, Mary, VP Secretary	49,200	2050	127.10	2050	29.73

3-6A LO 3.

Audrey Martin and Beth James are partners in the Country Gift Shop, which employs the individuals listed below. Paychecks are distributed every Friday to all employees. Based on the information given, compute the amounts listed below for a weekly payroll period.

Name and Position	Salary	OASDI Taxable Earnings	OASDI Tax	HI Taxable Earnings	HI Tax
Zena Vertin, Office	$ 535 per week				
Nicole Norge, Sales	2,980 per month				
Bob Mert, Delivery	485 per week				
Audrey Martin, Partner	950 per week				
Beth James, Partner	950 per week				
	Totals	$	$	$	$

Employer's OASDI Tax $__________

Employer's HI Tax $__________

3-7A LO 3.

Volpe Corporation has only five employees who are all paid $850 per week. Compute the total FICA taxes that the employer would withhold from the five employees each week and the amount the company would pay as its own liability for the employer's share of the FICA taxes on the weekly wages of the five employees:

Employees' total OASDI .... $ ________
Employees' total HI .... $ ________
Employer's total OASDI .... $ ________
Employer's total HI .... $ ________

3-8A LO 3.

Ralph Henwood was paid a salary of $64,600 during 2008 by Odesto Company. In addition, during the year Henwood started his own business as a public accountant and reported a net business income of $48,000 on his income tax return for 2008. Compute the following:

a. The amount of FICA taxes that was withheld from his earnings during 2008 by Odesto Company.
OASDI $ ________
HI $ ________

b. Henwood's self-employment taxes on the income derived from the public accounting business for 2008.
OASDI $ ________
HI $ ________

3-9A LO 3.

Silver Gym Company pays its salaried employees monthly on the last day of each month. The annual salary payroll for 2008 follows. Compute the following for the payroll of December 31.

Employee	Annual Salary	OASDI Taxable Wages	OASDI Tax	HI Tax
Maggert, June	$ 22,150			
Leonard, Kathy	18,900			
Ferris, Demi	24,000			
Stewart, Sam	102,480			
Wilton, Harriet	20,900			
Hopkins, Louis	19,500			
Singh, Sonja	18,540			
Keith, Karen	56,900			
Pierce, Ted	17,850			
Daven, Maria	51,200			
Totals		$	$	$

Employer's OASDI Tax $ ________
Employer's HI Tax $ ________

3-10A LO 3.

The monthly and hourly wage schedule for the employees of Quirk, Inc., follows. No employees are due overtime pay. Compute the following for the last monthly pay of the year:

a. The total wages of each part-time employee for December 2008.
b. The OASDI and HI taxable wages for each employee.
c. The FICA taxes withheld from each employee's wages for December.
d. Totals of columns.
e. The employer's FICA taxes for the month.

Employees			Total Monthly Payroll	OASDI Taxable Wages	HI Taxable Wages	OASDI Tax	HI Tax
Full-Time Office:							
Adaiar, Gene			$1,400.00	______	______	______	______
Crup, Jason			1,300.00	______	______	______	______
Essex, Joan			1,975.00	______	______	______	______
Garza, Irma			1,985.00	______	______	______	______
Leason, Mel			1,900.00	______	______	______	______
Pruit, Marne			7,000.00	______	______	______	______
Rubble, Deanne			2,400.00	______	______	______	______
Simpson, Dick			3,985.00	______	______	______	______
Truap, Ann			5,000.00	______	______	______	______
Wilson, Trudy			1,500.00	______	______	______	______
	Hours Worked	Hourly Rate	Total Part-Time Wages				
Part-Time Office:							
Kyle, Judy	170	$5.25	______	______	______	______	______
Laird, Sharon	170	5.35	______	______	______	______	______
Maxwell, Sara	140	6.10	______	______	______	______	______
Nelson, Donna	145	5.20	______	______	______	______	______
Scott, Kim	162	5.65	______	______	______	______	______
Totals			$ ______	$ ______	$ ______	$ ______	$ ______

Employer's FICA taxes OASDI $ ______ HI $ ______

3-11A LO 6.

Cruz Company has gathered the information needed to complete its Form 941 for the quarter ended September 30, 2008. Using the information presented below, complete Part 1 of Form 941, reproduced on the next page.

# of employees for pay period that included September 12—14 employees

Wages paid third quarter—$79,750.17
Federal income tax withheld in the third quarter—$9,570.00
Taxable social security and medicare wages—$79,750.17
Total tax deposits for the quarter—$21,771.83
Advance earned income credit payments—0

3-12A LO 6.

Refer to Problem 3–11A. Complete Parts 2, 4, and 5 of Form 941 (on page 3-42) for Cruz Company for the third quarter of 2008. Cruz Company is a monthly depositor with the following monthly tax liabilities for this quarter:

July	$7,193.10
August	7,000.95
September	7,577.78

State unemployment taxes are only paid to California. The company does not use a third-party designee and the tax returns are signed by the president, Carlos Cruz (Phone: 916–555–9739).

3-11A (continued)

Form **941 for 20--: Employer's QUARTERLY Federal Tax Return** 990107

(Rev. January 2007) Department of the Treasury — Internal Revenue Service OMB No. 1545-0029

(EIN) Employer identification number: 2 9 – 9 9 7 6 5 0 9

Name (not your trade name): CARLOS CRUZ

Trade name (if any): CRUZ COMPANY

Address: 901 KEYSTONE (Number, Street, Suite or room number)

SACRAMENTO (City) CA (State) 95916 (ZIP code)

Report for this Quarter of 20-- (Check one.)

☐ **1:** January, February, March

☐ **2:** April, May, June

☐ **3:** July, August, September

☐ **4:** October, November, December

Read the separate instructions before you fill out this form. Please type or print within the boxes.

Part 1: Answer these questions for this quarter.

1 **Number of employees who received wages, tips, or other compensation for the pay period including:** ***Mar. 12*** **(Quarter 1),** ***June 12*** **(Quarter 2),** ***Sept. 12*** **(Quarter 3),** ***Dec. 12*** **(Quarter 4)** . . . 1 ______

2 **Wages, tips, and other compensation** . . . 2 ______ .

3 **Total income tax withheld from wages, tips, and other compensation** . . . 3 ______ .

4 **If no wages, tips, and other compensation are subject to social security or Medicare tax** . . ☐ Check and go to line 6.

5 **Taxable social security and Medicare wages and tips:**

	Column 1		Column 2
5a **Taxable social security wages**	.	× .124 =	.
5b **Taxable social security tips**	.	× .124 =	.
5c **Taxable Medicare wages & tips**	.	× .029 =	.

5d **Total social security and Medicare taxes** (*Column 2,* lines 5a + 5b + 5c = line 5d) . . 5d ______ .

6 **Total taxes before adjustments** (lines 3 + 5d = line 6) . . . 6 ______ .

7 **TAX ADJUSTMENTS** (Read the instructions for line 7 before completing lines 7a through 7h.):

7a **Current quarter's fractions of cents** . . . ______ .

7b **Current quarter's sick pay** . . . ______ .

7c **Current quarter's adjustments for tips and group-term life insurance** ______ .

7d **Current year's income tax withholding** (attach Form 941c) . . . ______ .

7e **Prior quarters' social security and Medicare taxes** (attach Form 941c) ______ .

7f **Special additions to federal income tax** (attach Form 941c) . . . ______ .

7g **Special additions to social security and Medicare** (attach Form 941c) ______ .

7h **TOTAL ADJUSTMENTS** (Combine all amounts: lines 7a through 7g.) . . . 7h ______ .

8 **Total taxes after adjustments** (Combine lines 6 and 7h.) . . . 8 ______ .

9 **Advance earned income credit (EIC) payments made to employees** . . . 9 ______ .

10 **Total taxes after adjustment for advance EIC** (line 8 – line 9 = line 10) . . . 10 ______ .

11 **Total deposits for this quarter, including overpayment applied from a prior quarter** . . . 11 ______ .

12 **Balance due** (If line 10 is more than line 11, write the difference here.) . . . 12 ______ .
Follow the Instructions for Form 941-V, Payment Voucher.

13 **Overpayment** (If line 11 is more than line 10, write the difference here.) ______ . Check one ☐ Apply to next return. ☐ Send a refund.

▶ You **MUST** fill out both pages of this form and **SIGN** it.

Next ➔

For Privacy Act and Paperwork Reduction Act Notice, see the back of the Payment Voucher. Cat. No. 17001Z Form **941** (Rev. 1-2007)

990207

Name (*not your trade name*) | Employer identification number (EIN)

Part 2: Tell us about your deposit schedule and tax liability for this quarter.

If you are unsure about whether you are a monthly schedule depositor or a semiweekly schedule depositor, see *Pub. 15 (Circular E),* section 11.

14 ☐☐ Write the state abbreviation for the state where you made your deposits OR write "MU" if you made your deposits in *multiple* states.

15 Check one: ☐ Line 10 is less than $2,500. Go to Part 3.

☐ You were a monthly schedule depositor for the entire quarter. Fill out your tax liability for each month. Then go to Part 3.

Tax liability: Month 1 ______ .

Month 2 ______ .

Month 3 ______ .

Total liability for quarter ______ . Total must equal line 10.

☐ You were a semiweekly schedule depositor for any part of this quarter. Fill out *Schedule B (Form 941): Report of Tax Liability for Semiweekly Schedule Depositors,* and attach it to this form.

Part 3: Tell us about your business. If a question does NOT apply to your business, leave it blank.

16 If your business has closed or you stopped paying wages . . . . ☐ Check here, and

enter the final date you paid wages ___ / ___ / ___ .

17 If you are a seasonal employer and you do not have to file a return for every quarter of the year . . ☐ Check here.

Part 4: May we speak with your third-party designee?

Do you want to allow an employee, a paid tax preparer, or another person to discuss this return with the IRS? (See the instructions for details.)

☐ Yes. Designee's name ______

Select a 5-digit Personal Identification Number (PIN) to use when talking to IRS. ☐☐☐☐☐

☐ No.

Part 5: Sign here. You MUST fill out both pages of this form and SIGN it.

Under penalties of perjury, I declare that I have examined this return, including accompanying schedules and statements, and to the best of my knowledge and belief, it is true, correct, and complete.

X Sign your name here ______

Print your name here ______

Print your title here ______

Date ___ / ___ / ___

Best daytime phone ( ) –

Part 6: For paid preparers only *(optional)*

Paid Preparer's Signature ______

Firm's name ______

Address ______ EIN ______

ZIP code ______

Date ___ / ___ / ___ Phone ( ) – SSN/PTIN ______

☐ Check if you are self-employed.

Page **2** Form **941** (Rev. 1-2007)

3-13A LO 6.

Stan Barker opened Quik-Stop Market on January 2, 2008. The business is subject to FICA taxes. At the end of the first quarter of 2008, Barker, as president of the company, must file Form 941, Employer's Quarterly Federal Tax Return. Using Form 941 (Parts 1 through 5), reproduced on pages 3-44 and 3-45, prepare, sign, and date the return on the basis of the information shown below.

Employer's address:	**234 Oak, Austin, TX 78711-0234**
Employer's ID number:	**61-1325874**
Phone number:	**(512) 555–1111**

Each employee is paid semimonthly on the 15th and last day of each month. Shown below is the payroll information for the first quarter of 2008. All pay periods were the same.

PAYROLL INFORMATION FOR JANUARY–MARCH

Employee	**SSN**	Quarterly Wage	OASDI Tax	HI Tax	Federal Income Tax	Total Deductions	Net Pay
Albert Greer	384-10-7233	$ 3,480	$ 215.76	$ 50.46	$ 264	$ 530.22	$ 2,949.78
Patty Dilts	345-90-8451	3,510	217.62	50.88	528	796.50	2,713.50
Jerod Hughs	528-09-3668	7,740	479.88	112.26	1,212	1,804.14	5,935.86
Denise Eaton	766-43-6527	3,900	241.80	56.58	552	850.38	3,049.62
Totals		$18,630	$1,155.06	$270.18	$2,556	$3,981.24	$14,648.76

	OASDI	HI
Employer's FICA taxes For the Quarter	$1,155.06	$270.12

The total taxes per payday are:

Employees' FICA Tax—OASDI	$192.51
Employer's FICA Tax—OASDI	192.51
Employees' FICA Tax—HI	45.03
Employer's FICA Tax—HI	45.02
Employees' FIT Tax	426.00
Total	$901.07 × 6 deposits = $5,406.42 for the quarter

None of the employees reported tips during the quarter. No advance earned income credit (EIC) payments were made to the workers.

Note: Lines 5a and 5c of Form 941, tax on total taxable wages, are computed by multiplying by the combined tax rate for both employer and employee. Small differences due to rounding may occur between this total and the total taxes withheld from employees each pay period and the amount of the employer's taxes calculated each pay period. This difference is reported on line 7a as a deduction or an addition as "Fractions of Cents."

Form **941 for 20--: Employer's QUARTERLY Federal Tax Return** 990107
(Rev. January 2007) Department of the Treasury — Internal Revenue Service OMB No. 1545-0029

(EIN) Employer identification number: 6 1 – 1 3 2 5 8 7 4

Name (*not your trade name*): STAN BARKER

Trade name (*if any*): QUIK - STOP MARKET

Address: 234 OAK
Number Street Suite or room number
AUSTIN TX 78711
City State ZIP code

Report for this Quarter of 20-- (Check one.)
- ☐ 1: January, February, March
- ☐ 2: April, May, June
- ☐ 3: July, August, September
- ☐ 4: October, November, December

Read the separate instructions before you fill out this form. Please type or print within the boxes.

Part 1: Answer these questions for this quarter.

Line	Description	Column 1	Column 2	Line	Amount
1	**Number of employees who received wages, tips, or other compensation for the pay period including:** *Mar. 12* (Quarter 1), *June 12* (Quarter 2), *Sept. 12* (Quarter 3), *Dec. 12* (Quarter 4)			1	
2	**Wages, tips, and other compensation**			2	.
3	**Total income tax withheld from wages, tips, and other compensation**			3	.
4	**If no wages, tips, and other compensation are subject to social security or Medicare tax**				☐ Check and go to line 6.
5	**Taxable social security and Medicare wages and tips:**				
5a	**Taxable social security wages**	. × .124 =	.		
5b	**Taxable social security tips**	. × .124 =	.		
5c	**Taxable Medicare wages & tips**	. × .029 =	.		
5d	**Total social security and Medicare taxes** (*Column 2,* lines 5a + 5b + 5c = line 5d)			5d	.
6	**Total taxes before adjustments** (lines 3 + 5d = line 6)			6	.
7	**TAX ADJUSTMENTS** (Read the instructions for line 7 before completing lines 7a through 7h.):				
7a	**Current quarter's fractions of cents**		.		
7b	**Current quarter's sick pay**		.		
7c	**Current quarter's adjustments for tips and group-term life insurance**		.		
7d	**Current year's income tax withholding** (attach Form 941c)		.		
7e	**Prior quarters' social security and Medicare taxes** (attach Form 941c)		.		
7f	**Special additions to federal income tax** (attach Form 941c)		.		
7g	**Special additions to social security and Medicare** (attach Form 941c)		.		
7h	**TOTAL ADJUSTMENTS** (Combine all amounts: lines 7a through 7g.)			7h	.
8	**Total taxes after adjustments** (Combine lines 6 and 7h.)			8	.
9	**Advance earned income credit (EIC) payments made to employees**			9	.
10	**Total taxes after adjustment for advance EIC** (line 8 – line 9 = line 10)			10	.
11	**Total deposits for this quarter, including overpayment applied from a prior quarter**			11	.
12	**Balance due** (If line 10 is more than line 11, write the difference here.) Follow the Instructions for Form 941-V, Payment Voucher.			12	.
13	**Overpayment** (If line 11 is more than line 10, write the difference here.)		.		Check one ☐ Apply to next return. ☐ Send a refund.

▶ You **MUST** fill out both pages of this form and **SIGN** it.

Next ➔

For Privacy Act and Paperwork Reduction Act Notice, see the back of the Payment Voucher. Cat. No. 17001Z Form **941** (Rev. 1-2007)

3-13A (concluded)

990207

Name *(not your trade name)* | Employer identification number (EIN)

Part 2: Tell us about your deposit schedule and tax liability for this quarter.

If you are unsure about whether you are a monthly schedule depositor or a semiweekly schedule depositor, see *Pub. 15 (Circular E)*, section 11.

14 ☐☐ **Write the state abbreviation for the state where you made your deposits** OR **write "MU" if you made your deposits in *multiple* states.**

15 **Check one:** ☐ **Line 10 is less than $2,500.** Go to Part 3.

☐ **You were a monthly schedule depositor for the entire quarter. Fill out your tax liability for each month.** Then go to Part 3.

Tax liability: Month 1 ______ .

Month 2 ______ .

Month 3 ______ .

Total liability for quarter ______ . **Total must equal line 10.**

☐ **You were a semiweekly schedule depositor for any part of this quarter.** Fill out *Schedule B (Form 941): Report of Tax Liability for Semiweekly Schedule Depositors,* and attach it to this form.

Part 3: Tell us about your business. If a question does NOT apply to your business, leave it blank.

16 **If your business has closed or you stopped paying wages** . . . . ☐ Check here, and

enter the final date you paid wages ___/___/___ .

17 **If you are a seasonal employer and you do not have to file a return for every quarter of the year** . . ☐ Check here.

Part 4: May we speak with your third-party designee?

Do you want to allow an employee, a paid tax preparer, or another person to discuss this return with the IRS? (See the instructions for details.)

☐ Yes. Designee's name ______

Select a 5-digit Personal Identification Number (PIN) to use when talking to IRS. ☐☐☐☐☐

☐ No.

Part 5: Sign here. You MUST fill out both pages of this form and SIGN it.

Under penalties of perjury, I declare that I have examined this return, including accompanying schedules and statements, and to the best of my knowledge and belief, it is true, correct, and complete.

X Sign your name here ______

Print your name here ______

Print your title here ______

Date ___/___/___

Best daytime phone ( ) –

Part 6: For paid preparers only *(optional)*

Paid Preparer's Signature ______

Firm's name ______

Address ______ EIN ______

ZIP code ______

Date ___/___/___ Phone ( ) – SSN/PTIN ______

☐ Check if you are self-employed.

Page **2** Form **941** (Rev. 1-2007)

3-14A LO 6.

During the fourth calendar quarter of 2008, Bayview Inn, owned by Diane R. Peters, employed the persons listed below. Also given are the employees' salaries or wages and the amount of tips reported to the owner. The tips were reported by the 10th of each month. The Federal Income Tax and FICA tax to be withheld from the tips were estimated by the owner and withheld equally over the 13 weekly pay periods. The employer's portion of FICA tax on the tips was estimated as the same amount.

Employee	Salary or Wage	Quarter's Wages	Quarter's Tips	Quarter's OASDI	Quarter's HI	Quarter's FIT
Grant Frazier	$25,000/year	$ 6,250.01		$ 387.53	$ 90.61	$ 845.00
Joseph LaVanga	18,000/year	4,499.95		278.98	65.26	546.00
Susanne Ayers	250/week	3,250.00	$ 2,240.90	340.47	79.69	520.00
Howard Cohen	225/week	2,925.00	2,493.10	335.92	78.52	611.00
Lee Soong	250/week	3,250.00	2,640.30	365.17	85.41	650.00
Mary Yee	250/week	3,250.00	2,704.00	369.20	86.45	663.00
Helen Woods	325/week	4,225.00		261.95	61.23	429.00
Koo Shin	325/week	4,225.00		261.95	61.23	533.00
Aaron Abalis	400/week	5,200.00		322.40	75.40	689.00
David Harad	170/week	2,210.00		137.02	32.11	234.00
		$39,284.96	$10,078.30	$3,060.59	$715.91	$5,720.00

Employees are paid weekly on Friday. The following paydays occurred during this quarter:

October	November	December
5 weekly paydays	4 weekly paydays	4 weekly paydays

Taxes withheld for the 13 paydays in the fourth quarter follow:

Weekly Employees' Federal Income Tax	Weekly Employees' and Employer's FICA Taxes Withheld		Weekly Employees' and Employer's FICA Taxes on Tips	
	OASDI	HI	OASDI	HI
$440 per week	$187.36	$43.83	$48.07	$11.24
	187.36	43.82	48.07	11.24

Based on the information given, complete Form 941 on the following pages for Diane R. Peters.
Phone number: (901) 555-7959

DATE ____________ NAME ____________________

3-14A (continued)

Form **941 for 20--: Employer's QUARTERLY Federal Tax Return** 990107

(Rev. January 2007) Department of the Treasury — Internal Revenue Service OMB No. 1545-0029

(EIN) Employer identification number: 6 5 – 4 2 6 3 6 0 7

Name (*not your trade name*): DIANE PETERS

Trade name (*if any*): BAYVIEW INN

Address: 404 UNION AVE (Number, Street, Suite or room number)

MEMPHIS (City) TN (State) 38112 (ZIP code)

Report for this Quarter of 20-- (Check one.)

- ☐ **1:** January, February, March
- ☐ **2:** April, May, June
- ☐ **3:** July, August, September
- ☐ **4:** October, November, December

Read the separate instructions before you fill out this form. Please type or print within the boxes.

Part 1: Answer these questions for this quarter.

1 Number of employees who received wages, tips, or other compensation for the pay period including: *Mar. 12* (Quarter 1), *June 12* (Quarter 2), *Sept. 12* (Quarter 3), *Dec. 12* (Quarter 4) . . . 1 ______

2 Wages, tips, and other compensation . . . 2 ______

3 Total income tax withheld from wages, tips, and other compensation . . . 3 ______

4 If no wages, tips, and other compensation are subject to social security or Medicare tax . . ☐ Check and go to line 6.

5 Taxable social security and Medicare wages and tips:

	Column 1		Column 2
5a Taxable social security wages	.	× .124 =	.
5b Taxable social security tips	.	× .124 =	.
5c Taxable Medicare wages & tips	.	× .029 =	.

5d Total social security and Medicare taxes (*Column 2,* lines 5a + 5b + 5c = line 5d) . . 5d ______

6 Total taxes before adjustments (lines 3 + 5d = line 6) . . . 6 ______

7 TAX ADJUSTMENTS (Read the instructions for line 7 before completing lines 7a through 7h.):

7a Current quarter's fractions of cents . . . ______

7b Current quarter's sick pay . . . ______

7c Current quarter's adjustments for tips and group-term life insurance ______

7d Current year's income tax withholding (attach Form 941c) . . . ______

7e Prior quarters' social security and Medicare taxes (attach Form 941c) ______

7f Special additions to federal income tax (attach Form 941c) . . . ______

7g Special additions to social security and Medicare (attach Form 941c) ______

7h TOTAL ADJUSTMENTS (Combine all amounts: lines 7a through 7g.) . . . 7h ______

8 Total taxes after adjustments (Combine lines 6 and 7h.) . . . 8 ______

9 Advance earned income credit (EIC) payments made to employees . . . 9 ______

10 Total taxes after adjustment for advance EIC (line 8 – line 9 = line 10) . . . 10 ______

11 Total deposits for this quarter, including overpayment applied from a prior quarter . . . 11 ______

12 Balance due (If line 10 is more than line 11, write the difference here.) . . . 12 ______
Follow the Instructions for Form 941-V, Payment Voucher.

13 Overpayment (If line 11 is more than line 10, write the difference here.) ______ Check one ☐ Apply to next return. ☐ Send a refund.

▶ You **MUST** fill out both pages of this form and **SIGN** it.

Next ➔

For Privacy Act and Paperwork Reduction Act Notice, see the back of the Payment Voucher. Cat. No. 17001Z Form **941** (Rev. 1-2007)

990207

Name *(not your trade name)* | Employer identification number (EIN)

Part 2: Tell us about your deposit schedule and tax liability for this quarter.

If you are unsure about whether you are a monthly schedule depositor or a semiweekly schedule depositor, see *Pub. 15 (Circular E)*, section 11.

14 ☐☐ Write the state abbreviation for the state where you made your deposits OR write "MU" if you made your deposits in *multiple* states.

15 Check one: ☐ **Line 10 is less than $2,500.** Go to Part 3.

☐ **You were a monthly schedule depositor for the entire quarter. Fill out your tax liability for each month.** Then go to Part 3.

Tax liability: Month 1 ________ .

Month 2 ________ .

Month 3 ________ .

Total liability for quarter ________ . **Total must equal line 10.**

☐ **You were a semiweekly schedule depositor for any part of this quarter.** Fill out *Schedule B (Form 941): Report of Tax Liability for Semiweekly Schedule Depositors,* and attach it to this form.

Part 3: Tell us about your business. If a question does NOT apply to your business, leave it blank.

16 **If your business has closed or you stopped paying wages** . . . . ☐ Check here, and

enter the final date you paid wages ___ / ___ / ___ .

17 **If you are a seasonal employer and you do not have to file a return for every quarter of the year** . . ☐ Check here.

Part 4: May we speak with your third-party designee?

Do you want to allow an employee, a paid tax preparer, or another person to discuss this return with the IRS? (See the instructions for details.)

☐ Yes. Designee's name ________

Select a 5-digit Personal Identification Number (PIN) to use when talking to IRS. ☐☐☐☐☐

☐ No.

Part 5: Sign here. You MUST fill out both pages of this form and SIGN it.

Under penalties of perjury, I declare that I have examined this return, including accompanying schedules and statements, and to the best of my knowledge and belief, it is true, correct, and complete.

X Sign your name here ________

Print your name here ________

Print your title here ________

Date ___ / ___ / ___

Best daytime phone ( ) –

Part 6: For paid preparers only *(optional)*

Paid Preparer's Signature ________

Firm's name ________

Address ________ EIN ________

ZIP code ________

Date ___ / ___ / ___ Phone ( ) – SSN/PTIN ________

☐ Check if you are self-employed.

Page **2** Form **941** (Rev. 1-2007)

3-15A **LO 5,6.**

The taxable wages and withheld taxes for Stafford Company (EIN 25-7901462), semiweekly depositor, for the first quarter of 2008 follow.

Semimonthly Paydays	Gross and Taxable Wages	FICA Withheld OASDI	FICA Withheld HI	Federal Income Tax Withheld
1/15	$ 24,500	$1,519.00	$ 355.25	$ 3,185.00
1/31	23,985	1,487.07	347.78	3,090.00
2/15	25,190	1,561.78	365.26	3,410.00
2/29	25,530	1,582.86	370.19	3,497.00
3/14	24,950	1,546.90	361.78	3,385.00
3/31	25,100	1,556.20	363.95	3,400.00
	$149,255	$9,253.81	$2,164.21	$19,967.00

a. Complete Schedule B of Form 941 on page 3-50 for the first quarter for Steve Hazelton, the owner of Stafford Company.

b. List the due dates of each deposit in the first quarter.

Paydays	Deposit Due Dates
January 15	____________
January 31	____________
February 15	____________
February 29	____________
March 14	____________
March 31	____________

3-16A **LO 6,7.**

Vulcan Company is a monthly depositor whose tax liability for March 2008 is $2,505.

1. Complete the Federal Tax Deposit Coupon for the March taxes.

MONTH TAX YEAR ENDS → [ ][ ]

AMOUNT OF DEPOSIT (Do NOT type, please print.)

DOLLARS | CENTS

EMPLOYER IDENTIFICATION NUMBER → 73 1456654

BANK NAME/ DATE STAMP

Name Vulcan Company

Address 4713 Henderson Ave.

City South Bend

State IN ZIP 46624-4530

Telephone number (219) 555-7331

IRS USE ONLY

Darken only one TYPE OF TAX		and	Darken only one TAX PERIOD
◄ 941	◄ 945		◄ 1st Quarter
◄ 990-C	◄ 1120		◄ 2nd Quarter
◄ 943	◄ 990-T		◄ 3rd Quarter
◄ 720	◄ 990-PF		◄ 4th Quarter
◄ CT-1	◄ 1042		
◄ 940	◄ 944		

76

FOR BANK USE IN MICR ENCODING

Federal Tax Deposit Coupon
Form 8109 (Rev. 12-2005)

(Continued)

Schedule B (Form 941):

Report of Tax Liability for Semiweekly Schedule Depositors

(Rev. January 2006) Department of the Treasury — Internal Revenue Service

OMB No. 1545-0029

(EIN)
Employer identification number ☐☐ – ☐☐☐☐☐☐☐

Name *(not your trade name)* ____________

Calendar year ☐☐☐☐ (Also check quarter)

Report for this Quarter ...
(Check one.)

☐ **1:** January, February, March
☐ **2:** April, May, June
☐ **3:** July, August, September
☐ **4:** October, November, December

Use this schedule to show your TAX LIABILITY for the quarter; DO NOT use it to show your deposits. You must fill out this form and attach it to Form 941 (or Form 941-SS) if you are a semiweekly schedule depositor or became one because your accumulated tax liability on any day was $100,000 or more. Write your daily tax liability on the numbered space that corresponds to the date wages were paid. See Section 11 in *Pub. 15 (Circular E), Employer's Tax Guide,* for details.

Month 1

1 .	9 .	17 .	25 .	**Tax liability for Month 1** .
2 .	10 .	18 .	26 .	
3 .	11 .	19 .	27 .	
4 .	12 .	20 .	28 .	
5 .	13 .	21 .	29 .	
6 .	14 .	22 .	30 .	
7 .	15 .	23 .	31 .	
8 .	16 .	24 .		

Month 2

1 .	9 .	17 .	25 .	**Tax liability for Month 2** .
2 .	10 .	18 .	26 .	
3 .	11 .	19 .	27 .	
4 .	12 .	20 .	28 .	
5 .	13 .	21 .	29 .	
6 .	14 .	22 .	30 .	
7 .	15 .	23 .	31 .	
8 .	16 .	24 .		

Month 3

1 .	9 .	17 .	25 .	**Tax liability for Month 3** .
2 .	10 .	18 .	26 .	
3 .	11 .	19 .	27 .	
4 .	12 .	20 .	28 .	
5 .	13 .	21 .	29 .	
6 .	14 .	22 .	30 .	
7 .	15 .	23 .	31 .	
8 .	16 .	24 .		

Fill in your total liability for the quarter (Month 1 + Month 2 + Month 3) = Total tax liability for the quarter ▶ **Total liability for the quarter** .

Total must equal line 10 on Form 941 (or line 8 on Form 941-SS).

For Paperwork Reduction Act Notice, see separate instructions. Cat. No. 11967Q **Schedule B (Form 941)** Rev. 1-2006

2. What is the due date for the deposit of these taxes? ____________
3. Assume that no deposit was made until May 5. Compute the following penalties:
   a. Penalty for failure to make timely deposit. $ ____________
   b. Penalty for failure to fully pay tax. $ ____________
   c. Interest on taxes due and unpaid. $ ____________
   d. Total penalty imposed. $ ____________

3-17A LO 3.

At Edwards Cap Company, office workers are employed for a 40-hour workweek on either an annual or a monthly salary basis.

Given on the form on the following page are the current annual and monthly salary rates for five office workers for the week ended December 12, 2008 (50th payday of the year). In addition, with this pay, these employees are paid their sliding-scale annual bonuses. The bonuses are listed on the register.

For each worker, compute:

1. Regular earnings for the weekly payroll ended December 12, 2008.
2. Overtime earnings (if applicable).
3. Total regular, overtime earnings, and bonus.
4. FICA taxable wages for this pay period.
5. FICA taxes to be withheld for this pay period.

EDWARDS CAP COMPANY

Employee	Salary	Hours Worked	Annual Bonus	Regular Earnings	Overtime Earnings	Total Earnings
Luk, J.	97,240 /yr.	40	$30,000			
Bradley, B.	91,000 /yr.	40	25,000			
Livel, F.	6,240 /mo.	40	20,000			
Ross, T.	4,680 /mo.	40	15,000			
Lange, V.	2,900 /mo.	48	8,000			
Totals						

(left side)

EDWARDS CAP COMPANY

Cumulative Earnings as of Last Pay Period	FICA Taxable Wages This Pay Period		FICA Taxes to Be Withheld		Employee
	OASDI	HI	OASDI	HI	
$91,630.00					Luk, J.
85,750.00					Bradley, B.
70,560.00					Livel, F.
52,920.00					Ross, T.
34,890.00					Lange, V.

(right side)

Employer's FICA taxes for week ended December 12, 2008: $ ____________ (OASDI) $ ____________ (HI)

PRACTICAL PROBLEMS—SERIES B

3-1B LO 3.

The biweekly taxable wages for the employees of Wee-Ones Foods follow.

Compute the FICA taxes for each employee and the employer's FICA taxes.

Employee No.	Employee Name	Biweekly Taxable Wages	FICA Taxes OASDI	FICA Taxes HI
711	Murray, Ken	$581.39	$ ______	$ ______
512	Cala, Arnie	695.00	______	______
624	Gomez, Andy	391.75	______	______
325	Harris, Wilma	593.23	______	______
422	Little, Lucy	990.00	______	______
210	Paget, Rao	825.50	______	______
111	Button, Cam	519.45	______	______
		Totals	$ ______	$ ______

Employer's OASDI $______ (Total Taxable Wages) $______ (Employer's OASDI Tax)

Employer's HI Tax $______ (Total Taxable Wages) $______ (Employer's HI Tax)

3-2B LO 3.

During 2008, Matti Conners, president of Maggert Company, was paid a semimonthly salary of $5,200. Compute the amount of FICA taxes that should be withheld from her:

	OASDI	HI
a. 9th paycheck	$ ______	$ ______
b. 20th paycheck	$ ______	$ ______
c. 24th paycheck	$ ______	$ ______

3-3B LO 3.

Eric Sherm began working as a part-time waiter on April 1, 2008, at Yardville Restaurant. The cash tips of $475 that he received during April were reported on Form 4070, which he submitted to his employer on May 1. During May, he was paid wages of $630 by the restaurant. Compute:

	OASDI	HI
a. The amount of FICA taxes that the employer should withhold from Sherm's wages during May.	$ ______	$ ______
b. The amount of the employer's FICA taxes on Sherm's wages and tips during May.	$ ______	$ ______

3-4B **LO 2.**

Moisa Evans is a maitre d' at Red Rock Club. On September 6, his gross pay was $900 (three days working, one paid vacation day, and one paid sick day). He also reported to his employer tips of $860 for the previous month (applicable taxes to be deducted out of this pay). Moisa belongs to the company's 401(k) plan and has 5% of his gross pay ($900) deducted each week (salary reduction). Red Rock Club also provides a matching contribution ($45) into the plan for Moisa. This week's pay would have a:

a. Deduction for OASDI tax $ ____________

b. Deduction for HI tax $ ____________

3-5B **LO 3.**

The annual salaries paid each of the officers of Maxtun, Inc., follow. The officers are paid semimonthly on the 15th and the last day of the month. Compute the FICA taxes to be withheld from each officer's pay on (a) October 15 and (b) December 31.

		October 15			
Name and Title	Annual Salary	OASDI Taxable Earnings	OASDI Tax	HI Taxable Earnings	HI Tax
Nelson, Jack, President	$132,000				
Gift, Sue, VP Finance	100,800				
Grant, Al, VP Sales	76,800				
Ham, James, VP Mfg.	92,400				
Morey, Pam, VP Personnel	78,000				
Davis, Mary, VP Secretary	52,800				

		December 31			
Name and Title	Annual Salary	OASDI Taxable Earnings	OASDI Tax	HI Taxable Earnings	HI Tax
Nelson, Jack, President	$132,000				
Gift, Sue, VP Finance	100,800				
Grant, Al, VP Sales	76,800				
Ham, James, VP Mfg.	92,400				
Morey, Pam, VP Personnel	78,000				
Davis, Mary, VP Secretary	52,800				

3-6B **LO 3.**

Amanda Autry and Carley Wilson are partners in A & W Gift Shop, which employs the individuals listed below. Paychecks are distributed every Friday to all employees. Based on the information given, compute the amounts listed below for a weekly payroll period.

Name and Position	Salary	OASDI Taxable Earnings	OASDI Tax	HI Taxable Earnings	HI Tax
Kelly Simon, Office	$ 650 per week				
Jim Tress, Sales	3,450 per month				
May Aha, Delivery	520 per week				
Amanda Autry, Partner	1,900 per week				
Carley Wilson, Partner	1,900 per week				
	Totals	$	$	$	$

Employer's OASDI Tax $ ____________

Employer's HI Tax $ ____________

3-7B LO 3.

Funke Corporation has only five employees who are all paid \$1,050 per week. Compute the total FICA taxes that the employer would withhold from the five employees each week and the amount the company would pay as its own liability for the employer's share of the FICA taxes on the weekly wages of the five employees:

Employees' total OASDI . . . . \$ ________
Employees' total HI . . . . \$ ________
Employer's total OASDI . . . . \$ ________
Employer's total HI . . . . \$ ________

3-8B LO 3.

George Parker was paid a salary of \$74,700 during 2008 by Umberger Company. In addition, during the year, Parker started his own business as a public accountant and reported a net business income of \$38,900 on his income tax return for 2008. Compute the following:

a. The amount of FICA taxes that was withheld from his earnings during 2008 by Umberger Company. OASDI \$ ______ HI \$ ______

b. Parker's self-employment taxes on the income derived from the public accounting business for 2008. OASDI \$ ______ HI \$ ______

3-9B LO 3.

Livnisch Company pays its salaried employees monthly on the last day of each month. The annual salary payroll for 2008 follows. Compute the following for the payroll of December 31.

Employee	Annual Salary	OASDI Taxable Wages	OASDI Tax	HI Tax
Stern, Myra	\$ 42,150			
Lundy, Hal	30,500			
Franks, Rob	36,000			
Sewal, Ron	101,280			
Ward, Randy	40,800			
Hoskin, Al	29,600			
Wee, Pam	28,700			
Prince, Harry	76,800			
Maven, Mary	24,000			
Harley, David	68,960			
Totals		\$	\$	\$

Employer's OASDI Tax \$ ________
Employer's HI Tax \$ ________

3-10B LO 3.

The monthly and hourly wage schedule for the employees of Quincy, Inc., follows. No employees are due overtime pay. Compute the following for the last monthly pay of the year:

a. The total wages of each part-time employee for December 2008.
b. The OASDI and HI taxable wages for each employee.
c. The FICA taxes withheld from each employee's wages for December.
d. Totals of columns.
e. The employer's FICA taxes for the month.

Employees	Total Monthly Payroll	OASDI Taxable Wages	HI Taxable Wages	OASDI Tax	HI Tax
Full-Time Office:					
Hutchings, Jean	$ 2,300.00				
Florio, Anne	1,900.00				
Trabert, Judy	3,500.00				
Williams, Justin	2,875.00				
Galzano, Jared	4,250.00				
Sussex, Jude	8,000.00				
Robinson, Dave	6,300.00				
Prender, Hank	4,985.00				
Sorenson, Deb	5,600.00				
Hutchinson, Wendy	5,200.00				

Employees	Hours Worked	Hourly Rate	Total Part-Time Wages	OASDI Taxable Wages	HI Taxable Wages	OASDI Tax	HI Tax
Part-Time Office:							
Fox, Mandy	180	$ 8.25					
Billings, Clara	160	10.90					
Nau, Kevin	170	9.75					
Millis, Toby	142	12.10					
Cummings, Cheryl	162	13.40					
Totals			$	$	$	$	$

Employer's FICA taxes OASDI $ ______ HI $ ______

3-11B LO 6.

Gallagher Company has gathered the information needed to complete its Form 941 for the quarter ended September 30, 2008. Using the information presented below, complete Part 1 of Form 941, reproduced on the next page.

# of employees for pay period that included September 12—15 employees

Wages paid third quarter—$89,352.18
Federal income tax withheld in the third quarter—$10,195.00
Taxable social security and medicare wages—$89,352.18
Total tax deposits for the quarter—$23,865.92
Advance earned income credit payments—0

3-12B LO 6.

Refer to Problem 3–11B. Complete Parts 2, 4, and 5 of Form 941 (on page 3-58) for Gallagher Company for the third quarter of 2008. Gallagher Company is a monthly depositor with the following monthly tax liabilities for this quarter:

July	$7,891.75
August	7,984.90
September	7,989.27

State unemployment taxes are only paid to California. The company does not use a third-party designee, and the tax returns are signed by the president, James Gallagher (Phone: 916–555–9739).

3-11B (continued)

Form **941 for 20--: Employer's QUARTERLY Federal Tax Return** 990107

(Rev. January 2007) Department of the Treasury — Internal Revenue Service OMB No. 1545-0029

(EIN) Employer identification number 2 9 – 9 9 7 6 5 0 9

Name *(not your trade name)* JAMES GALLAGHER

Trade name *(if any)* GALLAGHER COMPANY

Address 901 KEYSTONE

Number Street Suite or room number

SACRAMENTO CA 95916

City State ZIP code

Report for this Quarter of 20--
(Check one.)

- ☐ **1:** January, February, March
- ☐ **2:** April, May, June
- ☐ **3:** July, August, September
- ☐ **4:** October, November, December

Read the separate instructions before you fill out this form. Please type or print within the boxes.

Part 1: Answer these questions for this quarter.

1 **Number of employees who received wages, tips, or other compensation for the pay period including:** ***Mar. 12*** **(Quarter 1),** ***June 12*** **(Quarter 2),** ***Sept. 12*** **(Quarter 3),** ***Dec. 12*** **(Quarter 4)** . . . 1 ______

2 **Wages, tips, and other compensation** . . . . 2 ______ .

3 **Total income tax withheld from wages, tips, and other compensation** . . . . 3 ______ .

4 **If no wages, tips, and other compensation are subject to social security or Medicare tax** . . ☐ Check and go to line 6.

5 **Taxable social security and Medicare wages and tips:**

	Column 1		*Column 2*
5a Taxable social security wages	.	× .124 =	.
5b Taxable social security tips	.	× .124 =	.
5c Taxable Medicare wages & tips	.	× .029 =	.

5d **Total social security and Medicare taxes** (*Column 2*, lines 5a + 5b + 5c = line 5d) . . 5d ______ .

6 **Total taxes before adjustments** (lines 3 + 5d = line 6) . . . . 6 ______ .

7 **TAX ADJUSTMENTS** (Read the instructions for line 7 before completing lines 7a through 7h.):

7a **Current quarter's fractions of cents** . . . . ______ .

7b **Current quarter's sick pay** . . . . ______ .

7c **Current quarter's adjustments for tips and group-term life insurance** ______ .

7d **Current year's income tax withholding** (attach Form 941c) . . . ______ .

7e **Prior quarters' social security and Medicare taxes** (attach Form 941c) ______ .

7f **Special additions to federal income tax** (attach Form 941c) . . . ______ .

7g **Special additions to social security and Medicare** (attach Form 941c) ______ .

7h **TOTAL ADJUSTMENTS** (Combine all amounts: lines 7a through 7g.) . . . . 7h ______ .

8 **Total taxes after adjustments** (Combine lines 6 and 7h.) . . . . 8 ______ .

9 **Advance earned income credit (EIC) payments made to employees** . . . . 9 ______ .

10 **Total taxes after adjustment for advance EIC** (line 8 – line 9 = line 10) . . . . 10 ______ .

11 **Total deposits for this quarter, including overpayment applied from a prior quarter** . . . 11 ______ .

12 **Balance due** (If line 10 is more than line 11, write the difference here.) . . . . 12 ______ .
Follow the Instructions for Form 941-V, Payment Voucher.

13 **Overpayment** (If line 11 is more than line 10, write the difference here.) ______ . Check one ☐ Apply to next return. ☐ Send a refund.

▶ You **MUST** fill out both pages of this form and **SIGN** it.

Next ➔

For Privacy Act and Paperwork Reduction Act Notice, see the back of the Payment Voucher. Cat. No. 17001Z Form **941** (Rev. 1-2007)

990207

Name *(not your trade name)*	Employer identification number (EIN) 29-9976509

Part 2: Tell us about your deposit schedule and tax liability for this quarter.

If you are unsure about whether you are a monthly schedule depositor or a semiweekly schedule depositor, see *Pub. 15 (Circular E)*, section 11.

14 ☐☐ **Write the state abbreviation for the state where you made your deposits** OR **write "MU" if you made your deposits in *multiple* states.**

15 **Check one:** ☐ **Line 10 is less than $2,500.** Go to Part 3.

☐ **You were a monthly schedule depositor for the entire quarter. Fill out your tax liability for each month.** Then go to Part 3.

Tax liability: Month 1 ______ .

Month 2 ______ .

Month 3 ______ .

Total liability for quarter ______ . **Total must equal line 10.**

☐ **You were a semiweekly schedule depositor for any part of this quarter.** Fill out *Schedule B (Form 941): Report of Tax Liability for Semiweekly Schedule Depositors,* and attach it to this form.

Part 3: Tell us about your business. If a question does NOT apply to your business, leave it blank.

16 **If your business has closed or you stopped paying wages** . . . . ☐ Check here, and

enter the final date you paid wages ___/___/___ .

17 **If you are a seasonal employer and you do not have to file a return for every quarter of the year** . ☐ Check here.

Part 4: May we speak with your third-party designee?

Do you want to allow an employee, a paid tax preparer, or another person to discuss this return with the IRS? (See the instructions for details.)

☐ Yes. Designee's name ______

Select a 5-digit Personal Identification Number (PIN) to use when talking to IRS. ☐☐☐☐☐

☐ No.

Part 5: Sign here. You MUST fill out both pages of this form and SIGN it.

Under penalties of perjury, I declare that I have examined this return, including accompanying schedules and statements, and to the best of my knowledge and belief, it is true, correct, and complete.

X Sign your name here ______

Print your name here ______

Print your title here ______

Date ___/___/___

Best daytime phone (   )   –

Part 6: For paid preparers only *(optional)*

Paid Preparer's Signature ______

Firm's name ______

Address ______ EIN ______

ZIP code ______

Date ___/___/___ Phone (   )   – SSN/PTIN ______

☐ Check if you are self-employed.

Page **2** Form **941** (Rev. 1-2007)

3-13B LO 6.

Karen Kluster opened Lube and Wash on January 3, 2008. The business is subject to FICA taxes. At the end of the first quarter of 2008, Kluster, as president of the company, must file Form 941, Employer's Quarterly Federal Tax Return. Using Form 941 (Parts 1 through 5), reproduced on pages 3-60 and 3-61, prepare, sign, and date the return on the basis of the information shown below.

Employer's address: **234 Oak, Austin, TX 78711-0234**
Employer's ID number: **61-1325874**
Phone number: **(512) 555–1111**

Each employee is paid semimonthly on the 15th and last day of each month. Shown below is the payroll information for the first quarter of 2008. All pay periods were the same.

PAYROLL INFORMATION FOR JANUARY–MARCH

Employee	SSN	Quarterly Wage	OASDI Tax	HI Tax	Federal Income Tax	Total Deductions	Net Pay
Paul Purson	384-10-7233	$ 4,590	$ 284.58	$ 66.56	$ 366	$ 717.14	$ 3,872.86
Matt Dirkson	345-90-8451	8,110	502.82	117.60	960	1,580.42	6,529.58
Joan Howard	528-09-3668	8,500	527.00	123.25	1,080	1,730.25	6,769.75
Dorrie Smith	766-43-6527	10,090	625.58	146.31	1,140	1,911.89	8,178.11
Totals		$31,290	$1,939.98	$453.72	$3,546	$5,939.70	$25,350.30

Employer's FICA taxes For the Quarter	$1,940.10 OASDI	$453.78 HI

The total taxes per payday are:

Employees' FICA Tax—OASDI	$ 323.33
Employer's FICA Tax—OASDI	323.35
Employees' FICA Tax—HI	75.62
Employer's FICA Tax—HI	75.63
Employees' FIT Tax	591.00
Total	$1,388.93 × 6 deposits = $8,333.58 for the quarter

None of the employees reported tips during the quarter. No advance earned income credit (EIC) payments were made to the workers.

Note: Lines 5a and 5c of Form 941, tax on total taxable wages, are computed by multiplying by the combined tax rate for both employer and employee. Small differences due to rounding may occur between this total and the total taxes withheld from employees each pay period and the amount of the employer's taxes calculated each pay period. This difference is reported on line 7a as a deduction or an addition as "Fractions of Cents."

Form **941 for 20--: Employer's QUARTERLY Federal Tax Return** 990107

(Rev. January 2007) Department of the Treasury — Internal Revenue Service OMB No. 1545-0029

(EIN) Employer identification number: 6 1 – 1 3 2 5 8 7 4

Name (*not your trade name*): KAREN KLUSTER

Trade name (*if any*): LUBE AND WASH

Address: 234 OAK
Number Street Suite or room number

AUSTIN TX 78711
City State ZIP code

Report for this Quarter of 20--
(Check one.)

- ☐ **1:** January, February, March
- ☐ **2:** April, May, June
- ☐ **3:** July, August, September
- ☐ **4:** October, November, December

Read the separate instructions before you fill out this form. Please type or print within the boxes.

Part 1: Answer these questions for this quarter.

1 **Number of employees who received wages, tips, or other compensation for the pay period including:** ***Mar. 12*** **(Quarter 1),** ***June 12*** **(Quarter 2),** ***Sept. 12*** **(Quarter 3),** ***Dec. 12*** **(Quarter 4)** . . . 1 ______

2 **Wages, tips, and other compensation** . . . . 2 ______ .

3 **Total income tax withheld from wages, tips, and other compensation** . . . . 3 ______ .

4 **If no wages, tips, and other compensation are subject to social security or Medicare tax** . . ☐ Check and go to line 6.

5 **Taxable social security and Medicare wages and tips:**

	Column 1		*Column 2*
5a **Taxable social security wages**	.	× .124 =	.
5b **Taxable social security tips**	.	× .124 =	.
5c **Taxable Medicare wages & tips**	.	× .029 =	.

5d **Total social security and Medicare taxes** (*Column 2,* lines 5a + 5b + 5c = line 5d) . . 5d ______ .

6 **Total taxes before adjustments** (lines 3 + 5d = line 6) . . . . 6 ______ .

7 **TAX ADJUSTMENTS** (Read the instructions for line 7 before completing lines 7a through 7h.):

7a **Current quarter's fractions of cents** . . . . ______ .

7b **Current quarter's sick pay** . . . . ______ .

7c **Current quarter's adjustments for tips and group-term life insurance** ______ .

7d **Current year's income tax withholding** (attach Form 941c) . . . ______ .

7e **Prior quarters' social security and Medicare taxes** (attach Form 941c) ______ .

7f **Special additions to federal income tax** (attach Form 941c) . . . ______ .

7g **Special additions to social security and Medicare** (attach Form 941c) ______ .

7h **TOTAL ADJUSTMENTS** (Combine all amounts: lines 7a through 7g.) . . . . 7h ______ .

8 **Total taxes after adjustments** (Combine lines 6 and 7h.) . . . . 8 ______ .

9 **Advance earned income credit (EIC) payments made to employees** . . . . 9 ______ .

10 **Total taxes after adjustment for advance EIC** (line 8 – line 9 = line 10) . . . . 10 ______ .

11 **Total deposits for this quarter, including overpayment applied from a prior quarter** . . . 11 ______ .

12 **Balance due** (If line 10 is more than line 11, write the difference here.) . . . . 12 ______ .
Follow the Instructions for Form 941-V, Payment Voucher.

13 **Overpayment** (If line 11 is more than line 10, write the difference here.) ______ . Check one ☐ Apply to next return. ☐ Send a refund.

▶ You **MUST** fill out both pages of this form and **SIGN** it.

Next ➔

For Privacy Act and Paperwork Reduction Act Notice, see the back of the Payment Voucher. Cat. No. 17001Z Form **941** (Rev. 1-2007)

3-13B (concluded)

990207

Name *(not your trade name)* | Employer identification number (EIN)

Part 2: Tell us about your deposit schedule and tax liability for this quarter.

If you are unsure about whether you are a monthly schedule depositor or a semiweekly schedule depositor, see ***Pub. 15 (Circular E),*** **section 11.**

14 ☐☐ **Write the state abbreviation for the state where you made your deposits** OR **write "MU" if you made your deposits in** ***multiple*** **states.**

15 Check one: ☐ **Line 10 is less than $2,500.** Go to Part 3.

☐ **You were a monthly schedule depositor for the entire quarter. Fill out your tax liability for each month.** Then go to Part 3.

Tax liability: Month 1 ________ .

Month 2 ________ .

Month 3 ________ .

Total liability for quarter ________ . **Total must equal line 10.**

☐ **You were a semiweekly schedule depositor for any part of this quarter.** Fill out *Schedule B (Form 941): Report of Tax Liability for Semiweekly Schedule Depositors,* and attach it to this form.

Part 3: Tell us about your business. If a question does NOT apply to your business, leave it blank.

16 If your business has closed or you stopped paying wages . . . . ☐ Check here, and

enter the final date you paid wages ___ / ___ / ___ .

17 If you are a seasonal employer and you do not have to file a return for every quarter of the year . . ☐ Check here.

Part 4: May we speak with your third-party designee?

Do you want to allow an employee, a paid tax preparer, or another person to discuss this return with the IRS? (See the instructions for details.)

☐ Yes. Designee's name ____________

Select a 5-digit Personal Identification Number (PIN) to use when talking to IRS. ☐☐☐☐☐

☐ No.

Part 5: Sign here. You MUST fill out both pages of this form and SIGN it.

Under penalties of perjury, I declare that I have examined this return, including accompanying schedules and statements, and to the best of my knowledge and belief, it is true, correct, and complete.

X Sign your name here ____________

Print your name here ____________

Print your title here ____________

Date ___ / ___ / ___

Best daytime phone ( ) –

Part 6: For paid preparers only ***(optional)***

Paid Preparer's Signature ____________

Firm's name ____________

Address ____________ EIN ____________

ZIP code ____________

Date ___ / ___ / ___ Phone ( ) – SSN/PTIN ____________

☐ Check if you are self-employed.

Page **2** Form **941** (Rev. 1-2007)

3-14B LO 6.

During the fourth calendar quarter of 2008, the Beechtree Inn, owned by Dawn Smedley, employed the persons listed below. Also given are the employees' salaries or wages and the amount of tips reported to the owner. The tips were reported by the 10th of each month. The Federal Income Tax and FICA tax to be withheld from the tips were estimated by the owner and withheld equally over the 13 weekly pay periods. The employer's portion of FICA tax on the tips was estimated as the same amount.

Employee	Salary or Wage	Quarter's Wages	Quarter's Tips	Quarter's OASDI	Quarter's HI	Quarter's FIT
Grant Frazier	$55,000/year	$ 13,750.00		$ 852.50	$ 199.38	$1,980.00
Joseph LaVanga	42,000/year	10,500.00		651.00	152.25	1,290.00
Susanne Ayers	240/week	3,120.00	$ 3,240.90	394.35	92.22	600.00
Howard Cohen	220/week	2,860.00	3,493.10	393.87	92.11	630.00
Lee Soong	240/week	3,120.00	3,640.30	419.12	98.01	690.00
Mary Yee	230/week	2,990.00	3,704.00	415.01	97.05	540.00
Helen Woods	625/week	8,125.00		503.75	117.81	910.00
Koo Shin	550/week	7,150.00		443.30	103.68	653.00
Aaron Abalis	490/week	6,370.00		394.94	92.36	364.00
David Harad	530/week	6,890.00		427.18	99.91	559.00
		$64,875.00	$14,078.30	$4,895.02	$1,144.78	$8,216.00

Employees are paid weekly on Friday. The following paydays occurred during this quarter:

October	November	December
5 weekly paydays	4 weekly paydays	4 weekly paydays

Taxes withheld for the 13 paydays in the fourth quarter follow:

Weekly Employees' Federal Income Tax	Weekly Employees' and Employer's FICA Taxes Withheld on Wages		Weekly Employees' and Employer's FICA Taxes on Tips	
	OASDI	HI	OASDI	HI
$632 per week	$309.40	$72.36	$67.14	$15.70
	309.40	72.36	67.14	15.70

Based on the information given, complete Form 941 on the following pages for Dawn Smedley
Phone number: (901) 555-7959

3-14B (continued)

Form **941 for 20--: Employer's QUARTERLY Federal Tax Return** 990107

(Rev. January 2007) Department of the Treasury — Internal Revenue Service OMB No. 1545-0029

(EIN) Employer identification number: 6 5 – 4 2 6 3 6 0 7

Name (*not your trade name*): DAWN SMEDLEY

Trade name (*if any*): BEECHTREE INN

Address: 404 UNION AVE.
Number Street Suite or room number

MEMPHIS TN 38112
City State ZIP code

Report for this Quarter of 20--
(Check one.)

- ☐ **1:** January, February, March
- ☐ **2:** April, May, June
- ☐ **3:** July, August, September
- ☐ **4:** October, November, December

Read the separate instructions before you fill out this form. Please type or print within the boxes.

Part 1: Answer these questions for this quarter.

1 **Number of employees who received wages, tips, or other compensation for the pay period including:** ***Mar. 12*** **(Quarter 1),** ***June 12*** **(Quarter 2),** ***Sept. 12*** **(Quarter 3),** ***Dec. 12*** **(Quarter 4)** . . . 1 ________

2 **Wages, tips, and other compensation** . . . . 2 ________ .

3 **Total income tax withheld from wages, tips, and other compensation** . . . . 3 ________ .

4 **If no wages, tips, and other compensation are subject to social security or Medicare tax** . . ☐ Check and go to line 6.

5 **Taxable social security and Medicare wages and tips:**

	Column 1		*Column 2*
5a **Taxable social security wages**	.	× .124 =	.
5b **Taxable social security tips**	.	× .124 =	.
5c **Taxable Medicare wages & tips**	.	× .029 =	.

5d **Total social security and Medicare taxes** (*Column 2,* lines 5a + 5b + 5c = line 5d) . . 5d ________ .

6 **Total taxes before adjustments** (lines 3 + 5d = line 6) . . . . 6 ________ .

7 **TAX ADJUSTMENTS** (Read the instructions for line 7 before completing lines 7a through 7h.):

7a **Current quarter's fractions of cents** . . . . ________ .

7b **Current quarter's sick pay** . . . . ________ .

7c **Current quarter's adjustments for tips and group-term life insurance** ________ .

7d **Current year's income tax withholding** (attach Form 941c) . . . ________ .

7e **Prior quarters' social security and Medicare taxes** (attach Form 941c) ________ .

7f **Special additions to federal income tax** (attach Form 941c) . . . ________ .

7g **Special additions to social security and Medicare** (attach Form 941c) ________ .

7h **TOTAL ADJUSTMENTS** (Combine all amounts: lines 7a through 7g.) . . . . 7h ________ .

8 **Total taxes after adjustments** (Combine lines 6 and 7h.) . . . . 8 ________ .

9 **Advance earned income credit (EIC) payments made to employees** . . . . 9 ________ .

10 **Total taxes after adjustment for advance EIC** (line 8 – line 9 = line 10) . . . . 10 ________ .

11 **Total deposits for this quarter, including overpayment applied from a prior quarter** . . . 11 ________ .

12 **Balance due** (If line 10 is more than line 11, write the difference here.) . . . . 12 ________ .
Follow the Instructions for Form 941-V, Payment Voucher.

13 **Overpayment** (If line 11 is more than line 10, write the difference here.) ________ . Check one ☐ Apply to next return. ☐ Send a refund.

▶ You **MUST** fill out both pages of this form and **SIGN** it.

Next ➔

For Privacy Act and Paperwork Reduction Act Notice, see the back of the Payment Voucher. Cat. No. 17001Z Form **941** (Rev. 1-2007)

990207

Name *(not your trade name)*	Employer identification number (EIN)

Part 2: Tell us about your deposit schedule and tax liability for this quarter.

If you are unsure about whether you are a monthly schedule depositor or a semiweekly schedule depositor, see ***Pub. 15 (Circular E),*** **section 11.**

14 ☐☐ **Write the state abbreviation for the state where you made your deposits** OR **write "MU" if you made your deposits in** ***multiple*** **states.**

15 Check one: ☐ **Line 10 is less than $2,500.** Go to Part 3.

☐ **You were a monthly schedule depositor for the entire quarter. Fill out your tax liability for each month.** Then go to Part 3.

Tax liability: Month 1 ______ .

Month 2 ______ .

Month 3 ______ .

Total liability for quarter ______ . **Total must equal line 10.**

☐ **You were a semiweekly schedule depositor for any part of this quarter.** Fill out *Schedule B (Form 941): Report of Tax Liability for Semiweekly Schedule Depositors,* and attach it to this form.

Part 3: Tell us about your business. If a question does NOT apply to your business, leave it blank.

16 If your business has closed or you stopped paying wages . . . . ☐ Check here, and

enter the final date you paid wages ___ / ___ / ___ .

17 If you are a seasonal employer and you do not have to file a return for every quarter of the year . . ☐ Check here.

Part 4: May we speak with your third-party designee?

Do you want to allow an employee, a paid tax preparer, or another person to discuss this return with the IRS? (See the instructions for details.)

☐ Yes. Designee's name ______

Select a 5-digit Personal Identification Number (PIN) to use when talking to IRS. ☐☐☐☐☐

☐ No.

Part 5: Sign here. You MUST fill out both pages of this form and SIGN it.

Under penalties of perjury, I declare that I have examined this return, including accompanying schedules and statements, and to the best of my knowledge and belief, it is true, correct, and complete.

X **Sign your name here** ______

Print your name here ______

Print your title here ______

Date ___ / ___ / ___

Best daytime phone ( ) –

Part 6: For paid preparers only *(optional)*

Paid Preparer's Signature ______

Firm's name ______

Address ______ EIN ______

______ ZIP code ______

Date ___ / ___ / ___ Phone ( ) – SSN/PTIN ______

☐ Check if you are self-employed.

Page **2** Form **941** (Rev. 1-2007)

3-15B **LO 5,6.**

The taxable wages and withheld taxes for Hamilton Company (EIN 25-7901462), semiweekly depositor, for the first quarter of 2008 follow.

Semimonthly Paydays	Gross and Taxable Wages	FICA Withheld OASDI	FICA Withheld HI	Federal Income Tax Withheld
1/15	$ 34,200	$ 2,120.40	$ 495.90	$ 4,180.00
1/31	32,900	2,039.80	477.05	4,090.00
2/15	31,750	1,968.50	460.38	3,996.00
2/29	28,970	1,796.14	420.07	3,797.00
3/14	28,800	1,785.60	417.60	3,790.00
3/31	29,400	1,822.80	426.30	3,999.00
	$186,020	$11,533.24	$2,697.30	$23,852.00

a. Complete Schedule B of Form 941 on page 3-66 for the first quarter for Harry Conway, the owner of Hamilton Company.

b. List the due dates of each deposit in the first quarter.

Paydays	Deposit Due Dates
January 15	______________
January 31	______________
February 15	______________
February 29	______________
March 14	______________
March 31	______________

Schedule B (Form 941):
Report of Tax Liability for Semiweekly Schedule Depositors

(Rev. January 2006) Department of the Treasury — Internal Revenue Service

OMB No. 1545-0029

(EIN)
Employer identification number ☐☐ – ☐☐☐☐☐☐☐

Name *(not your trade name)*

Calendar year ☐☐☐☐ (Also check quarter)

Report for this Quarter ...
(Check one.)

☐ **1:** January, February, March
☐ **2:** April, May, June
☐ **3:** July, August, September
☐ **4:** October, November, December

Use this schedule to show your TAX LIABILITY for the quarter; DO NOT use it to show your deposits. You must fill out this form and attach it to Form 941 (or Form 941-SS) if you are a semiweekly schedule depositor or became one because your accumulated tax liability on any day was $100,000 or more. Write your daily tax liability on the numbered space that corresponds to the date wages were paid. See Section 11 in *Pub. 15 (Circular E), Employer's Tax Guide,* for details.

Month 1

1 .	9 .	17 .	25 .	**Tax liability for Month 1** .
2 .	10 .	18 .	26 .	
3 .	11 .	19 .	27 .	
4 .	12 .	20 .	28 .	
5 .	13 .	21 .	29 .	
6 .	14 .	22 .	30 .	
7 .	15 .	23 .	31 .	
8 .	16 .	24 .		

Month 2

1 .	9 .	17 .	25 .	**Tax liability for Month 2** .
2 .	10 .	18 .	26 .	
3 .	11 .	19 .	27 .	
4 .	12 .	20 .	28 .	
5 .	13 .	21 .	29 .	
6 .	14 .	22 .	30 .	
7 .	15 .	23 .	31 .	
8 .	16 .	24 .		

Month 3

1 .	9 .	17 .	25 .	**Tax liability for Month 3** .
2 .	10 .	18 .	26 .	
3 .	11 .	19 .	27 .	
4 .	12 .	20 .	28 .	
5 .	13 .	21 .	29 .	
6 .	14 .	22 .	30 .	
7 .	15 .	23 .	31 .	
8 .	16 .	24 .		

Fill in your total liability for the quarter (Month 1 + Month 2 + Month 3) = Total tax liability for the quarter ▶ **Total liability for the quarter** .

Total must equal line 10 on Form 941 (or line 8 on Form 941-SS).

For Paperwork Reduction Act Notice, see separate instructions. Cat. No. 11967Q **Schedule B (Form 941)** Rev. 1-2006

3-16B LO 6,7.

Yelman Company is a monthly depositor whose tax liability for June 2008 is $3,930.

1. Complete the Federal Tax Deposit Coupon for the June taxes.

AMOUNT OF DEPOSIT (Do NOT type, please print.)
DOLLARS | CENTS

MONTH TAX YEAR ENDS →

EMPLOYER IDENTIFICATION NUMBER → 73 1456654

BANK NAME/ DATE STAMP

Name Yelman Company

Address 4713 Henderson Ave.

City South Bend

State IN ZIP 46624-4530

Telephone number (219) 555-7331

IRS USE ONLY

Darken only one TYPE OF TAX		Darken only one TAX PERIOD
941	945	1st Quarter
990-C	1120	2nd Quarter
943	990-T	3rd Quarter
720	990-PF	4th Quarter
CT-1	1042	
940	944	

76

FOR BANK USE IN MICR ENCODING

Federal Tax Deposit Coupon
Form 8109 (Rev. 12-2005)

2. What is the due date for the deposit of these taxes? ____________
3. Assume that no deposit was made until August 4. Compute the following penalties:
   a. Penalty for failure to make timely deposit. $ ____________
   b. Penalty for failure to fully pay tax. $ ____________
   c. Interest on taxes due and unpaid. $ ____________
   d. Total penalty imposed. $ ____________

3-17B LO 3.

At Gleeson Brewing Company, office workers are employed for a 40-hour workweek on either an annual or a monthly salary basis.

Given on the form on the following page are the current annual and monthly salary rates for five office workers for the week ended December 12, 2008 (50th payday of the year). In addition, with this pay, these employees are paid their sliding-scale annual bonuses. The bonuses are listed on the register.

For each worker, compute:

1. Regular earnings for the weekly payroll ended December 12, 2008.
2. Overtime earnings (if applicable).
3. Total regular, overtime earnings, and bonus.
4. FICA taxable wages for this pay period.
5. FICA taxes to be withheld for this pay period.

3-17B (Concluded on page 3-69)

GLEESON BREWING

Employee	Salary	Hours Worked	Annual Bonus	Regular Earnings	Overtime Earnings	Total Earnings
Won, H.	99,840/yr.	40	$30,000			
Park, B.	96,200/yr.	40	25,000			
James, R.	7,280/mo.	40	20,000			
Oho, J.	5,265/mo.	40	15,000			
Mack, K.	3,400/mo.	46	8,000			
Totals						

Employer's FICA taxes for week ended December 12, 2008: $______ OASDI $______ HI

(left side)

CONTINUING PAYROLL PROBLEM

Refer to the partially completed payroll register you started at the end of Chapter 2. You will now determine the amount of FICA taxes to be withheld from each employee's pay for the pay period ending January 7.

1. In the Taxable Earnings columns, record the amount of each employee's weekly earnings that is subject to FICA taxes.
2. Using the amount recorded in step (1), compute the taxes for each employee and record in the appropriate column.

Note: Keep your partially completed payroll register for use at the end of Chapter 4.

CASE PROBLEMS

C1. Auditing Form 941. LO 5,6.

Your assistant has just completed a rough draft of Form 941, shown on pages 3-71 and 3-72, for the quarter ending March 31, 20--. As the supervisor and authorized signer, you are auditing the form before it is mailed to ensure its accuracy.

Four of the company's general ledger accounts are shown on the following pages. Employees are paid on the 15th and last day of each month. The company is a semiweekly depositor. Indicate any changes that should be made on the form before it is signed, dated, and mailed.

GLEESON BREWING COMPANY (Concluded)

Cumulative Earnings as of Last Pay Period	FICA Taxable Wages This Pay Period		FICA Taxes to Be Withheld		Employee
	OASDI	HI	OASDI	HI	
$94,080.00					Won, H.
90,650.00					Park, B.
82,320.00					James, R.
59,535.00					Oho, J.
38,446.38					Mack, K.

(right side)

C1. (Continued)

	FICA TAXES PAYABLE—OASDI		Account No. 214	
			Balance	
Date	Debit	Credit	Debit	Credit
20—				
Jan. 15		773.96		773.96
15		773.94		1,547.90
19	1,547.90			—
31		843.78		843.78
31		843.78		1,687.56
Feb. 2	1,687.56			—
15		833.74		833.74
15		833.72		1,667.46
22	1,667.46			—
28		803.79		803.79
28		803.79		1,607.58
Mar. 3	1,607.58			—
15		786.72		786.72
15		786.73		1,573.45
20	1,573.45			—
31		787.88		787.88
31		787.87		1,575.75
Apr. 5	1,575.75			—

C1. (Continued)

FICA TAXES PAYABLE—HI Account No. 215

Date		Debit	Credit	Balance Debit	Balance Credit
20--					
Jan.	15		181.01		181.01
	15		181.01		362.02
	19	362.02			—
	31		197.34		197.34
	31		197.32		394.66
Feb.	2	394.66			—
	15		194.98		194.98
	15		194.98		389.96
	22	389.96			—
	28		187.98		187.98
	28		187.98		375.96
Mar.	3	375.96			—
	15		184.01		184.01
	15		183.99		368.00
	20	368.00			—
	31		184.26		184.26
	31		184.24		368.50
Apr.	5	368.50			—

EMPLOYEES FEDERAL INCOME TAX PAYABLE Account No. 216

Date		Debit	Credit	Balance Debit	Balance Credit
20--					
Jan.	15		1,980.00		1,980.00
	19	1,980.00			—
	31		2,217.00		2,217.00
Feb.	2	2,217.00			—
	15		2,016.00		2,016.00
	22	2,016.00			—
	28		2,007.00		2,007.00
Mar.	3	2,007.00			—
	15		1,970.00		1,970.00
	20	1,970.00			—
	31		1,887.00		1,887.00
Apr.	5	1,887.00			—

WAGES AND SALARIES Account No. 511

Date		Debit	Credit	Balance Debit	Balance Credit
20--					
Jan.	15	12,483.16		12,483.16	
	31	13,609.40		26,092.56	
Feb.	15	13,447.13		39,539.69	
	28	12,964.43		52,504.12	
Mar.	15	12,689.02		65,193.14	
	31	12,707.69		77,900.83	

C1. (Continued)

Form **941 for 20--: Employer's QUARTERLY Federal Tax Return** 990107
(Rev. January 2007) Department of the Treasury — Internal Revenue Service OMB No. 1545-0029

(EIN) Employer identification number: 7 7 – 2 2 6 7 1 4 2

Name (*not your trade name*):

Trade name (*if any*): COASTAL COMPANY

Address: 77 CASTRO
Number Street Suite or room number

SAN FRANCISCO | CA | 94117
City State ZIP code

Report for this Quarter of 20-- (Check one.)

- [x] 1: January, February, March
- [ ] 2: April, May, June
- [ ] 3: July, August, September
- [ ] 4: October, November, December

Read the separate instructions before you fill out this form. Please type or print within the boxes.

Part 1: Answer these questions for this quarter.

1 **Number of employees who received wages, tips, or other compensation for the pay period including:** ***Mar. 12*** (Quarter 1), ***June 12*** (Quarter 2), ***Sept. 12*** (Quarter 3), ***Dec. 12*** (Quarter 4)	1	17
2 **Wages, tips, and other compensation**	2	77900 . 38
3 **Total income tax withheld from wages, tips, and other compensation**	3	12077 . 00
4 **If no wages, tips, and other compensation are subject to social security or Medicare tax**		☐ Check and go to line 6.

5 **Taxable social security and Medicare wages and tips:**

	Column 1		Column 2
5a **Taxable social security wages**	77900 . 38	× .124 =	9659 . 65
5b **Taxable social security tips**	.	× .124 =	.
5c **Taxable Medicare wages & tips**	77900 . 38	× .029 =	2259 . 11

5d **Total social security and Medicare taxes** (*Column 2,* lines 5a + 5b + 5c = line 5d)	5d	11918 . 76
6 **Total taxes before adjustments** (lines 3 + 5d = line 6)	6	23995 . 76

7 **TAX ADJUSTMENTS** (Read the instructions for line 7 before completing lines 7a through 7h.):

7a **Current quarter's fractions of cents**	. 04	
7b **Current quarter's sick pay**	.	
7c **Current quarter's adjustments for tips and group-term life insurance**	.	
7d **Current year's income tax withholding** (attach Form 941c)	.	
7e **Prior quarters' social security and Medicare taxes** (attach Form 941c)	.	
7f **Special additions to federal income tax** (attach Form 941c)	.	
7g **Special additions to social security and Medicare** (attach Form 941c)	.	
7h **TOTAL ADJUSTMENTS** (Combine all amounts: lines 7a through 7g.)	7h	. 04
8 **Total taxes after adjustments** (Combine lines 6 and 7h.)	8	23995 . 80
9 **Advance earned income credit (EIC) payments made to employees**	9	.
10 **Total taxes after adjustment for advance EIC** (line 8 – line 9 = line 10)	10	23995 . 80
11 **Total deposits for this quarter, including overpayment applied from a prior quarter**	11	23997 . 80
12 **Balance due** (If line 10 is more than line 11, write the difference here.) Follow the Instructions for Form 941-V, Payment Voucher.	12	18 . 00
13 **Overpayment** (If line 11 is more than line 10, write the difference here.)	.	Check one ☐ Apply to next return. ☐ Send a refund.

▶ You **MUST** fill out both pages of this form and **SIGN** it.

Next ➔

For Privacy Act and Paperwork Reduction Act Notice, see the back of the Payment Voucher. Cat. No. 17001Z Form **941** (Rev. 1-2007)

C1. (Concluded)

990207

Name *(not your trade name)* | **Employer identification number (EIN)** 77-2267142

Part 2: Tell us about your deposit schedule and tax liability for this quarter.

If you are unsure about whether you are a monthly schedule depositor or a semiweekly schedule depositor, see *Pub. 15 (Circular E),* section 11.

14 C A **Write the state abbreviation for the state where you made your deposits** OR **write "MU" if you made your deposits in *multiple* states.**

15 Check one: ☐ **Line 10 is less than $2,500.** Go to Part 3.

☑ **You were a monthly schedule depositor for the entire quarter. Fill out your tax liability for each month.** Then go to Part 3.

Tax liability:	**Month 1**	8189.14
	Month 2	8063.96
	Month 3	7742.70
Total liability for quarter		23995.80

Total must equal line 10.

☐ **You were a semiweekly schedule depositor for any part of this quarter.** Fill out *Schedule B (Form 941): Report of Tax Liability for Semiweekly Schedule Depositors,* and attach it to this form.

Part 3: Tell us about your business. If a question does NOT apply to your business, leave it blank.

16 If your business has closed or you stopped paying wages . . . . ☐ Check here, and

enter the final date you paid wages / / .

17 If you are a seasonal employer and you do not have to file a return for every quarter of the year . ☐ Check here.

Part 4: May we speak with your third-party designee?

Do you want to allow an employee, a paid tax preparer, or another person to discuss this return with the IRS? (See the instructions for details.)

☐ Yes. Designee's name

Select a 5-digit Personal Identification Number (PIN) to use when talking to IRS. ☐☐☐☐☐

☑ No.

Part 5: Sign here. You MUST fill out both pages of this form and SIGN it.

Under penalties of perjury, I declare that I have examined this return, including accompanying schedules and statements, and to the best of my knowledge and belief, it is true, correct, and complete.

X Sign your name here

Print your name here

Print your title here

Date / /

Best daytime phone ( ) –

Part 6: For paid preparers only *(optional)*

Paid Preparer's Signature

Firm's name

Address

EIN

ZIP code

Date / /   Phone ( ) –

SSN/PTIN

☐ Check if you are self-employed.

Page **2**

Form **941** (Rev. 1-2007)

C2. Household Employee? LO 1.

Nelson operates a placement service for companionsitting for the elderly. He placed Martha Jackson with Mrs. Mock, an elderly woman who needed a person to assist with her personal needs, household care, and companionship. Jackson is paid directly from Mrs. Mock. Jackson had to pay a placement fee of $50 to Nelson. Is Jackson an employee of Nelson or a household employee of Mrs. Mock? Explain.

chapter

4

Income Tax Withholding

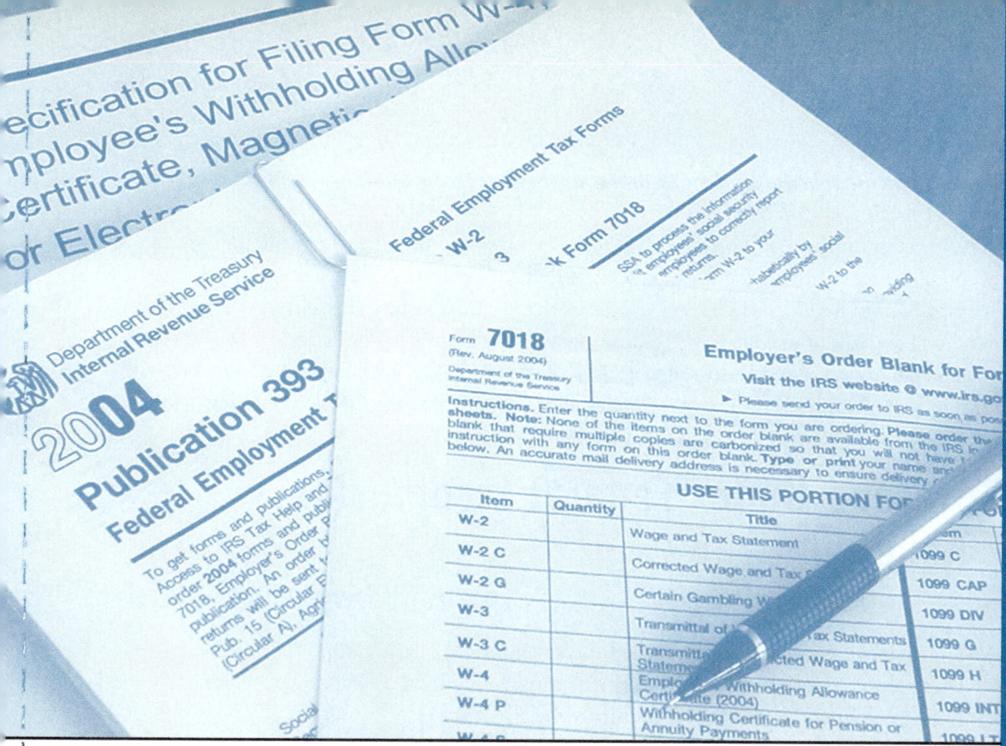

Now what do we take out of the employees' pay for federal income taxes? The IRS gives us charts to use! That should be easy! Some fringe benefits are taxed? Some deductions are pretax? What's an allowance? How about supplemental pays? It's bad enough filing an individual income tax return—being an employer is worse!

LEARNING OBJECTIVES

After studying this chapter, you should be able to:

1. Explain coverage under the federal income tax withholding law by determining: (a) the employer-employee relationship, (b) the kinds of payments defined as wages, and (c) the kinds of employment excluded under the law.
2. Explain the types of withholding allowances that may be claimed by employees for income tax withholding purposes.
3. Explain the purpose of Form W-4 and list the proper procedures for using the information contained on the form.
4. Compute the amount of federal income tax to be withheld using: (a) the percentage method and (b) the wage-bracket method.
5. Compute the amount of federal income tax to be withheld using alternative methods such as quarterly averaging, annualizing of wages, and part-year employment.
6. Compute the withholding of federal income taxes on supplementary wage payments.
7. Explain how employees may receive advance earned income credit and how the employer computes the amount of the advance.
8. Complete Form W-2 and become familiar with other wage and tax statements.
9. Review completion of ***Form 941, Employer's Quarterly Federal Tax Return***.
10. Describe the major types of information returns.
11. Explain the impact of state and local income taxes on the payroll accounting process.

Due to printing schedules, the tax tables at the end of the book are the tables that were in effect until December 31, 2007.

At the beginning of World War II, the income tax became the principal source of revenue to finance government operations. The Ruml plan put the collection of this tax on a pay-as-you-go basis. This chapter describes the employer's responsibility for withholding income taxes from employees' wages and paying these taxes to the federal government. In addition, many employers must also comply with state, city, and county income tax withholding laws. Employers must be aware of these laws to avoid possible penalties.

Coverage Under Federal Income Tax Withholding Laws

LEARNING OBJECTIVE 1

Before an individual withholds any tax under the tax law, the following conditions must exist:

1. There must be, or have been, an employer-employee relationship.
2. The payments received by the employee must be defined as wages under the law.
3. The employment must not be exempted by the law.

EMPLOYER-EMPLOYEE RELATIONSHIP

As discussed in Chapter 3, establishing the correct relationship between the employer and employee is a very important factor in complying with the Social Security Tax Law. This also applies to the Federal Income Tax Withholding Law.

If a business has the right to control and direct the worker, it meets the definition of an employer under the common-law criteria.

Employers can be sole proprietorships, partners, corporations, not-for-profit corporations, and federal and state governments. No distinctions are made between classes or grades of employees—from executives to entry-level personnel. Directors of a corporation are not considered employees unless they perform services other than participation in board meetings. Partners are also eliminated from the definition of an employee.

If the employer-employee relationship exists, the pay is subject to federal income tax withholding.

> ***IRS* CONNECTION**
>
> Since the Income Tax Reform Act of 1986, it has been estimated that the Internal Revenue Code has been amended some 4,000 times. The original Income Tax Code of 1914 contained 14 pages of law, and the forms consisted of four pages, including the instructions to complete the forms. There were 4,000 employees of the IRS in 1914. Today there are 9,400 pages of laws, 4,000 pages of IRS forms, and 115,000 employees.

STATUTORY EMPLOYEES/NONEMPLOYEES

If a worker does not qualify as an employee under the Common Law Test, federal income taxes are not withheld. However, by statute, under certain conditions he or she may be considered ***an employee*** for FICA and FUTA taxes. As discussed in Chapter 3, this applies to agent drivers, full-time life insurance salespersons, homeworkers, and traveling or city salespersons.

Direct sellers and qualified real estate agents are considered ***nonemployees*** by statute. They are treated as self-employed for ***all*** federal tax purposes.

TAXABLE WAGES

For withholding purposes, the term **wages** includes the total compensation paid to employees for services. Employers withhold federal income taxes on the ***gross amount*** of wages before deductions such as state and local taxes, insurance premiums, savings bonds, profit-sharing contributions, and union dues. Examples of employee compensation subject to withholding include:

- Wages and salaries
- Vacation allowances
- Supplemental payments
- Bonuses and commissions
- Taxable fringe benefits
- Tips
- Cash awards

Employees may receive compensation in ways other than their regular wage payments. Figure 4–1 shows some special types of payments that are also subject to federal income tax withholding.

Payments to employees in a medium other than cash are also taxed. Payments in the form of goods, lodging, food, clothing, or services are taxed at their fair market value at the time that they are given.

FRINGE BENEFITS

Unless the law says otherwise, fringe benefits are subject to federal income tax withholding. In general, the taxable portion is the amount by which the fair market value of the benefits exceeds what the employee paid, plus any amount the law excludes. Fringe benefits include employer-provided items such as those listed at the top of page 4-6.

FIGURE 4–1

Taxable Payments to Employees

Disabled Worker's Wages	Withhold for wages paid after the year in which the worker became entitled to disability insurance under the Social Security Act.
Drawing Account Advances	Advance payments to salespersons against their commissions or unearned salaries for which they are to perform services, but for which they are not legally obligated to repay.
Gift Certificates (cards)	Considered cash equivalent, and therefore taxable.
Meals and Lodging	Unless furnished for the employer's convenience and on the employer's premises, as a condition of employment. Cash allowances for meals and lodging are taxable. If more than half of the meals provided to employees on the employer's premises are for the convenience of the employer, then these meals are treated as for the employer's convenience.
Moving Expenses	Nonqualified reimbursed and employer-paid expenses are subject to withholding. Nonqualified expenses include cost of sale of old residence, purchase of new residence, house hunting, temporary living expenses, and meals.
Partially Exempt Employment	If the employee spends half or more time in a pay period performing services subject to employment taxes, all pay in that pay period is taxable.
Payments to Nonresident Aliens	Subject to withholding (unless excepted by regulations).
Sick Pay	Subject to withholding whether paid by the employer or third party (to the extent of the employer's contribution into the plan).
Supplemental Unemployment Compensation	To the extent it is includible in an employee's gross income. It does not include separation due to disciplinary problems or age.
Travel and Business Expenses (non-accountable plans)	If (1) the employee is not required to or does not substantiate expenses with receipts or (2) the employee receives travel advances and does not or is not required to return any unused amount of the advance.

- Cars
- Free or discounted flights
- Discounts on property or services
- Vacations
- Memberships in social or country clubs
- Tickets for entertainment and sporting events

WITHHOLDING ON FRINGE BENEFITS Determination of the value of the fringe benefit must be made by January 31 of the following year. For withholding and depositing purposes, reasonable estimates may be used before that date. The employer may add the value of fringe benefits to regular wages for a payroll period and figure withholding taxes on the total or may withhold the tax on the value of the benefits at the *flat 25* percent supplemental wage rate.

The employer may choose not to withhold income tax on the value of an employee's personal use of a vehicle. The employer must, however, withhold social security, Medicare, or railroad retirement taxes on the use of the vehicle.

FLEXIBLE REPORTING With noncash fringe benefits, the employer has the option of treating the benefits as being paid on any basis (paying monthly, at year-end, etc.). As long as the benefits are treated as paid by December 31, the employer can choose any option.

Due to a ***special period rule,*** employers can even use October 31 as the cutoff date for valuing the noncash fringe benefit. This rule allows employers to treat noncash fringe benefits of November and December as being provided in the following year and therefore taxed in the next year.

If this special rule is applied to a particular benefit, it must apply to all employees who receive this benefit. Also, if applied, the employer must notify the employees of this special rule treatment prior to giving them their W-2 forms.

EXAMPLE

Employers may treat the value of a single fringe benefit as paid on one or more dates in the same calendar year even if the employee receives the entire benefit at one time.

A one-time receipt of a $1,000 fringe benefit in 2008 can be treated as four payments of $250, each in a different pay period of 2008.

on the *JOB*

If you need to determine if a certain type of payment or individual is subject to income tax withholding, check **Circular E, Employer's Tax Guide.** Special classes of employment and payments are listed, along with their treatment under employment tax laws.

NONTAXABLE FRINGE BENEFITS

Fringe benefits that are nontaxable include:

- Services provided at no additional cost
- Qualified employee discounts
- Working condition fringes
- Minimal value fringes
- Qualified transportation fringes
- Use of on-premises athletic facilities
- Reduced tuition for education
- Job-placement assistance

Services the employer provides at no additional cost, qualified employee discounts, meals at employer-run eating establishments, and reduced tuition are excluded from their income only if the benefits are given to employees on a nondiscriminatory basis.

TAXABLE TIPS

As reported in Chapter 3, employees must report cash tips to the employer by the 10th of the month following the month they receive the tips. This report includes tips paid by the employer for charge customers and tips the employee receives directly from the customers. Tips of *less than $20* in a month and noncash tips need not be reported.

WITHHOLDING FROM TIPS The employer collects income tax, as well as social security taxes, on reported tips. The following procedures apply to withholding income tax on reported tips:

1. The employer collects the tax from the employee's wages or from other funds the employee makes available.
2. When tips are reported in connection with employment where the employee also receives a regular wage, compute the withholding tax on the aggregate—treat tips as a supplemental wage payment.
3. If the withholding tax exceeds the amount of wages paid to the employee, the employee must pay the uncollected portion of the taxes directly to the IRS when filing the annual income tax return (Form 1040).
4. The employer is not required to audit or verify the accuracy of the tip income reported.

ALLOCATED TIPS Large food and beverage establishments that have customary tipping and normally had more than 10 employees on a typical business day in the preceding year may be required to allocate tips among employees if:

> *The total tips reported by the employees during any payroll period are less than 8 percent of the establishment's gross receipts for that period.*

The amount of allocated tips to employees equals:

> *The difference between tips reported and 8 percent of gross receipts, other than carryout sales and sales with at least a 10 percent service charge added.*

The tip allocation may be made using one of three methods: hours worked, gross receipts, good faith agreement. Federal income taxes are to be withheld only on the tips reported to the employer; no taxes are withheld on the tips that are merely allocated.

TRAVELING EXPENSES

ACCOUNTABLE PLAN Employee expense reimbursement amounts paid under an accountable plan are not subject to income tax withholding. An accountable plan requires the employer's reimbursement or allowance arrangement to meet all three of the following rules:

1. Business connected.
2. Adequate accounting within a reasonable time period (generally, 60 days).
3. Employee return of excess of substantiated amounts (generally, 120 days).

NONACCOUNTABLE PLAN A nonaccountable plan is an arrangement that does not meet all of the previous requirements. All amounts paid under this plan are considered wages and are subject to income tax withholding.

PAYMENTS EXEMPT FROM WITHHOLDING

The law excludes certain payments and payments to certain individuals from federal income tax withholding, as shown in Figure 4–2.

SELF-STUDY QUIZ 4-1 *Check any item of employee compensation not subject to withholding:*

√ **a.** Company-provided lunches at the plant to reduce tardiness by keeping employees on the premises.
___ **b.** Year-end bonuses to managers and supervisors.
√ **c.** Work-out room for employee use during lunch hours.
√ **d.** Travel advances to salespersons for overnight sales calls out of town.
___ **e.** Employer-paid sick pay.
___ **f.** Memberships in the local country club for department managers.
√ **g.** Meals provided by a local restaurant for its employees.

FIGURE 4–2

Exempt Payments

Type of Payment or Individual	Conditions
Advances	For travel and other business expenses reasonably expected to be incurred.
Accident and Health Insurance Payments	Exempt except 2% shareholder-employees of S corporations.
De Minimus Fringe Benefits	Benefits of so little value as to make accounting for the benefit unreasonable and administratively impractical.
Deceased Person's Wages	Paid to the person's beneficiary or estate.
Dependent Care Assistance	To the extent it is reasonable to believe the amounts will be excludable from gross income. Up to $5,000 can be excluded from an employee's gross income without being subject to social security, medicare, or income tax withholding.
Domestic Service	Private home, local college club, or local chapter of college fraternity or sorority.
Educational Assistance	If education maintains or improves employee's skills required by the job. For the non-job-related educational assistance, up to $5,250 per year of employer-provided assistance for undergraduate and graduate education is tax-free. Also applies to "downsized" employees and can be used after voluntary or involuntary termination.
Employee Business Expense Reimbursements	Accountable plans for amounts not exceeding specified government rates for mileage, lodging, meals, and incidental expenses.
Employee-Safety and Length-of-Service Awards	If merchandise costs $400 or less. Rises to $1,600 for a written nondiscriminatory plan.
Employer-Provided Parking	Up to $205 per month.
Foreign Service by U.S. Citizens	As employees for affiliates of American employers if entitled to exclusion under section 911 or required by law of foreign country to withhold income tax on such payment.
Group-Term Life Insurance Costs	The employer's cost of group-term life insurance less than $50,000.
Health Reimbursement Arrangements (HRA)	As long as no person has the right to receive cash or any other taxable or nontaxable benefit other than medical care reimbursement.
Individuals Under 18	For delivery or distribution of newspapers, shopping news, and vendors of newspapers and magazines where payment is the difference between the purchase and sales price.
Long-Term Care Insurance Premiums	Employer-paid premiums for long-term care insurance up to a limit. For example, for an employee age 40 or under, the first $260 of premiums are nontaxable.
Ministers of Churches, Members of Religious Orders	Performing services for the order agency of the supervising church or associated institution.
Moving Expense Reimbursements	For qualified expenses, if the employee is entitled to a deduction for these expenses on the individual's federal income tax return.
Public Officials	For fees only, not salaries.
Retirement and Pension Plans	• Employer contributions to a qualified plan. • Employer contributions to IRA accounts under an SEP [see section 402(g) for salary reduction limitation]. • Employer contributions to section 403(b) annuity contract [see section 402(g) for limitation]. • Elective contributions and deferrals to plans containing a qualified cash or deferred compensation arrangement, such as 401(k).
Sickness or Injury Payments	Payments made under worker's compensation law or contract of insurance.

PRETAX SALARY REDUCTIONS

An employee can authorize an employer to deduct certain withholdings from his or her pay on a pretax basis. These withholdings are taken from the gross pay and therefore reduce the amount of pay that is subject to federal income tax.

CAFETERIA PLANS Some employers offer their employees a choice between cash (pay) or qualified (nontaxable) benefits. Employees can select various levels of health, accident, and life insurance coverage or choose to contribute to cash or deferred plans. The salary reductions are used to pay for the desired benefit, and these pretax contributions are not included in taxable wages for FIT. These salary reductions, which are allowed under a cafeteria plan, are also exempt from FICA and FUTA taxes and from most states' taxes.

The following benefits may be included in the plan:

- Accident and health insurance
- Self-insured medical reimbursement plan
- Group-term life insurance (first $50,000 of coverage)
- Dependent care assistance (first $5,000)
- Health savings accounts (discussed below)

These benefits cannot be included in a cafeteria plan:

- Transportation fringe benefits
- Educational assistance
- Scholarships and fellowship grants
- Meals and lodging for the convenience of employer
- Dependent group-term life insurance
- Deferred compensation except for 401(k) contributions

NEWS // ALERT//
Employer cash incentives for employees purchasing hybrid cars are treated as compensation and are taxable.

FLEXIBLE-SPENDING ACCOUNTS These accounts allow employees to have money deducted from their paychecks to cover their out-of-pocket medical expenses. The deductions from the employees' pays are made with pretax dollars. Regulations now allow employers the option to extend the time period to spend the unused money in these accounts from the end of the year until March 15 of the following year. Unused monies in these flexible-spending accounts are forfeited by the participants.

HEALTH SAVINGS ACCOUNTS These accounts are used by employees who have high-deductible health insurance to pay for medical expenses for themselves and their dependents. Contributions made into the plan by the employer are excluded from the employees' taxable income. For a single person, the maximum contribution is $2,850 or the amount of the annual deductible, if less (for family coverage—$5,650). Employee contributions into the account (through payroll deductions) must be included in wages and are subject to withholding taxes. However, if these contributions are part of a salary reduction arrangement in a qualified cafeteria plan, they are not subject to withholding taxes.

ARCHER MEDICAL SAVINGS ACCOUNTS These accounts are for employees of small businesses (50 or fewer employees) and are set up in conjunction with high-deductible insurance plans. Employees' payroll deductions are subject to federal income tax withholding (FICA also). However, employees can deduct the contributions on their tax returns. Employer contributions are not subject to tax withholding. Unused monies in this type of account carry over from year to year.

DEFERRED ARRANGEMENTS Many deferred arrangements are usually set up as retirement plans. The most common of these is the **defined contribution plan** that provides future benefits based solely on the amount paid by each employee and employer into the account, plus investment gains. These plans are tax-deferred savings or stock accounts held in trust for employees. The most popular types of retirement accounts are the 401(k) and IRAs.

EXAMPLE

Carl Jamison, an employee for the Scharman School, belongs to a tax-deferred retirement plan to which he contributes 3 percent of his pay which is matched by the school. His biweekly pay is $2,500. Because of the deferral (3% × $2,500 = $75), $2,425 is subject to federal income tax withholding.

Tax-Deferred Retirement Accounts

These types of accounts allow employees to contribute amounts from their wages into retirement accounts. These contributions reduce the amount of the employees' wages that are subject to federal income tax. These tax-deferred plans set limits on the amounts that employees can contribute tax free and also provide for additional contributions to be made into the accounts by the employers. Upon retirement, the employees will receive their contributions back in the form of regular payments from their retirement plans. These payments are then subject to federal income tax. The advantage to tax-deferred retirement accounts is that the taxpayer may be in a lower tax bracket when the income is taxed.

- ***401(k) Plan.*** A standard tax-deferred retirement plan. A set percentage of an employee's wages is contributed on a pretax basis. Employers can limit the percentage of an employee's pay that can be contributed. This limit can be lower than the maximum set by law. Employees can add after-tax contributions to this total, and the employer can contribute to the employees' plan.
- ***Simple Plans.*** A small company plan for a company with up to 100 employees. The employer can offer a SIMPLE plan as part of a 401(k) plan. This plan allows employees to contribute a percentage of their pay toward retirement.
- ***Section 403(b) Plan.*** A plan for employees of tax-exempt organizations.
- ***Section 457 Plan.*** A plan for employees of state and local governments and of tax-exempt organizations other than churches.

The following information applies to 2007:

401(k) 403(b) 457	$15,500 or 100% of pay	lesser is maximum employee-deferred contribution
	$5,000	extra deferred if age 50 or over
	100% of pay or $45,000	maximum contribution by employer
	$45,000	maximum total combined contribution
SIMPLE	$10,500	maximum employee-deferred contribution
	$2,500	extra deferred if age 50 or over
	3% of pay	employer must match employee's contribution up to this amount

INDIVIDUAL RETIREMENT ACCOUNTS

Beyond the various payroll-related tax deferred accounts, individuals can set up their own retirement accounts. In 2008, under certain conditions, an employee may put aside each year the lesser of $5,000 or 100% of their compensation without paying federal income taxes on their contributions. Eligible employees may make an additional $5,000 contribution on behalf of a nonworking or low-earning spouse provided the combined compensation is at least equal to the total combined IRA contribution. For years after 2008, the limit will be adjusted for inflation in $500 increments. To be eligible for such deductible (tax-free) contributions, either of the following two conditions must be met (for 2007):

1. The individual does not belong to a company-funded retirement plan.
2. The individual has modified adjusted gross income less than $52,000. (In the case of a married employee, the combined adjusted gross income must be less than $83,000.)

If the employee belongs to another qualified plan, full and partial tax-free deductions are allowed if:

1. The employee is single or head of household and has modified adjusted gross income less than $52,000 with phaseout at $62,000.
2. The employee is married, filing a joint return, and has modified adjusted gross income less than $83,000 with phaseout at $103,000.
3. The employee is married, filing separately, and has zero adjusted gross income with phaseout at $10,000.

If an employee's spouse belongs to a company-funded retirement plan, the employee is not considered an active participant in the plan. However, the nonactive spouse's tax-free IRA deduction ($5,000) will begin to phase out between $156,000 to $166,000 of their total adjusted gross income.

Even though these contributions can be made through payroll deductions, the employer is not considered a pension plan sponsor and is not subject to ERISA as long as the following guidelines are met:

1. The employer makes no matching contributions.
2. Participation is not mandatory.
3. The employer does not endorse any IRA sponsors.

ROTH IRA

Another type of IRA that allows taxpayers and their spouses to make annual ***nondeductible*** contributions of up to $5,000 is the Roth IRA. The amount that may be contributed is reduced by the amount contributed into other IRAs. Allowable contributions are phased out for those with adjusted gross income of between $99,000 to $114,000 for single taxpayers, $156,000 to $166,000 for joint taxpayers, and $0 to $10,000 for married taxpayers filing separately.

2 LEARNING OBJECTIVE

The advantage of this type of IRA is that distributions made out of the fund at retirement are tax-free.

Withholding Allowances

The law entitles employees to exempt a portion of their earnings from withholding by claiming a personal allowance and allowances for their dependents if they furnish their employers with a claim for the allowances. Employees may also claim special allowances and allowances for itemized deductions and tax credits. However, employees cannot claim the same withholding allowances with more than one employer at the same time.

PERSONAL ALLOWANCES

Employees can claim a **personal allowance** for themselves and each qualified dependent, provided they are not claimed on another person's tax return. In 2007, the amount of the personal allowance was $3,400, and this was treated as a deduction in computing taxable income. A married employee may also claim one personal allowance for his or her spouse if the spouse is not claimed as a dependent on another person's tax return.

If the employee has a second job or if the spouse also works, the personal allowances that the employee is entitled to should not also be claimed on the other job.

In 2007, the amount of personal exemptions begins to be phased out at $156,400 for single taxpayers, $234,600 for married couples filing joint returns or surviving spouses, $195,500 for heads of households, and $117,300 if married filing separately.

ALLOWANCES FOR DEPENDENTS

Employees may claim one allowance for each dependent (other than a spouse) who will be claimed on their federal income tax returns. To qualify as a dependent, the person must meet specific requirements that are listed in the instructions accompanying the individual's federal income tax return (six tests are involved—relationship, support, domicile, age, joint return, and citizenship).

ADDITIONAL WITHHOLDING ALLOWANCE

Employees can also reduce the amount of withholding by claiming a **special withholding allowance,** whether or not they plan to itemize deductions on their tax returns. An additional withholding allowance can be claimed by a person under any one of the following situations:

1. Single person who has only one job.
2. Married person who has only one job with nonworking spouse.
3. Person's wages from a second job or the spouse's wages (or both) equal $1,000 or less.

This allowance is only used to compute the employee's income tax withholding. The employee ***cannot claim*** this allowance on his or her income tax return.

OTHER WITHHOLDING ALLOWANCES

Withholding allowances reduce the overwithholding of income taxes on employees' wages. In addition to the allowances already discussed, employees may be entitled to withholding allowances based on estimated tax credits, such as child care, and itemized deductions for medical expenses, mortgage interest, and charitable contributions. Employees take these credits when filing their federal income tax returns. The number of withholding allowances is determined on the worksheet that accompanies ***Form W-4, Employee's Withholding Allowance Certificate,*** and is then reported on that form.

FORM W-4 (EMPLOYEE'S WITHHOLDING ALLOWANCE CERTIFICATE)

LEARNING OBJECTIVE 3

The employer uses the information from ***Form W-4, Employee's Withholding Allowance Certificate,*** to compute the amount of income tax to withhold from employees' wages. The employer must have Form W-4 on file for each employee. This form contains the withholding allowance certificate (shown in Figure 4–3), detailed instructions, and worksheets for employees to use in completing the certificate.

FIGURE 4–3

W-4 Employee's Withholding Allowance Certificate

Form **W-4**
Department of the Treasury
Internal Revenue Service

Employee's Withholding Allowance Certificate

▶ Whether you are entitled to claim a certain number of allowances or exemption from withholding is subject to review by the IRS. Your employer may be required to send a copy of this form to the IRS.

OMB No. 1545-0074
20- -

1 Type or print your first name and middle initial.	Last name	2 Your social security number
Harry M.	Weir	542 ; 13 ; 6921

Home address (number and street or rural route): 421 Eastmont

3 ☒ Single ☐ Married ☐ Married, but withhold at higher Single rate.
Note. If married, but legally separated, or spouse is a nonresident alien, check the "Single" box.

City or town, state, and ZIP code: Richland, WA 99352

4 **If your last name differs from that shown on your social security card, check here. You must call 1-800-772-1213 for a replacement card.▶** ☐

5 Total number of allowances you are claiming (from line **H** above **or** from the applicable worksheet on page 2) . . . 5 | 4

6 Additional amount, if any, you want withheld from each paycheck . . . . 6 | $ 0

7 I claim exemption from withholding for 2007, and I certify that I meet **both** of the following conditions for exemption.
- Last year I had a right to a refund of **all** federal income tax withheld because I had **no** tax liability **and**
- This year I expect a refund of **all** federal income tax withheld because I expect to have **no** tax liability.

If you meet both conditions, write "Exempt" here . . . . ▶ 7

Under penalties of perjury, I declare that I have examined this certificate and to the best of my knowledge and belief, it is true, correct, and complete.
Employee's signature
(Form is not valid unless you sign it.) ▶ *Harry M. Weir* **Date ▶** *January 2, 20– –*

8 Employer's name and address (Employer: Complete lines 8 and 10 only if sending to the IRS.)	9 Office code (optional)	10 Employer identification number (EIN)

For Privacy Act and Paperwork Reduction Act Notice, see page 2. Cat. No. 10220Q Form **W-4** (2007)

COMPLETING FORM W-4 The employee completes Form W-4 when he or she begins work for an employer. Employers must retain the withholding certificate as a supporting record of the withholding allowances used in deducting income taxes from the employees' salaries and wages. Once filed, the certificate remains in effect until an amended certificate takes effect. Withholding certificates should be retained as long as they are in effect and for four years thereafter. If the employee does not complete the W-4, the employer withholds taxes as if the employee is ***single, with no withholding allowances.***

Since the employers are required to get each employee's social security number on Form W-4, they can request to see the employee's social security card, and they can photocopy the card for their files.

WITHHOLDING ALLOWANCES The number of withholding allowances claimed on Form W-4 may differ from the number of exemptions claimed on the employee's tax return. The process of determining the correct number of withholding allowances begins with the number of personal exemptions the employee expects to claim on his or her tax return. The employee then increases or decreases this number based on the employee's eligibility and desire for a higher paycheck or a higher tax refund. The worksheets provided with Form W-4 enable the employee to determine the exact number of allowances to enter on the certificate.

CHANGING FORM W-4 If the status of an employee changes with respect to the number of withholding allowances or marital status, the employee files an amended W-4. If there is a ***decrease*** in the number of allowances, the employee must furnish the employer with a new certificate within 10 days. If there is an increase in the number of allowances, the employee can either file a new certificate or allow the current certificate to remain in effect.

The employer makes the certificate effective no later than the start of the first payroll period ending on or after the 30th day from the date the replacement Form W-4 is received. The employer may not repay or reimburse the employee for income taxes overwithheld before the effective date of the new certificate but may reimburse the employee after that date if the employer failed to implement the new certificate.

EXEMPTION FROM INCOME TAX WITHHOLDING Employees may claim exemption from income tax withholding if they had no income tax liability last year and expect none in the current year. The exemption is valid for one year and must be claimed on a new Form W-4 filed by February 15 of each succeeding year. If a new certificate is not filed, taxes are withheld at the single rate with zero withholding allowances.

EXAMPLE

Single persons who made less than $8,750 in 2007 owed no federal income tax. Married couples filing jointly with combined wages up to $17,500 incurred no tax liability.

Employees may not claim exemption from withholding if (1) another person claims the employee as a dependent on his or her tax return ***and*** (2) income exceeds $850 annually and includes more than $300 of unearned income (interest or dividends).

ADDITIONAL AND VOLUNTARY WITHHOLDING AGREEMENTS In some instances, employees want additional federal income taxes withheld from their wages, such as a person with two or more jobs, or a married couple where both work. The simplest way to increase the amount of tax withheld is to reduce the number of withholding allowances claimed. Another method is to request that the employer withhold an additional amount from the employee's pay. These requests must be done on Forms W-4 by filling in the additional amounts to be withheld on line 6. There is a worksheet on the back of Form W-4 that can be used to calculate the additional amount to be withheld.

If an employee receives payments not classified as wages, or an employer-employee relationship does not exist, individuals can voluntarily request that the employer or the one making the payments withhold federal income taxes from their payments. These individuals need only furnish a Form W-4. Requests for additional and voluntary withholding become effective when the employer accepts them and begins to withhold tax. The agreements remain in effect until the specified termination date or until the termination is mutually agreed upon. Either party may terminate an agreement prior to a specified date or mutual agreement by furnishing the other party with a signed, written notice of termination.

EXAMPLE

Individuals who may wish to request additional withholding or a voluntary agreement to withhold include:

- Clergy
- Two wage-earner married couples
- Domestic workers in a private home
- Individuals receiving significant amounts of interest or dividends
- Individuals receiving self-employment income

INVALID W-4S Employers are not required to verify the authenticity of the information on employees' W-4s. However, if the form is altered in any way or if the employee acknowledges that the information is false, the employer cannot accept the invalid W-4. The employer can ask for a new W-4. If the employee refuses to submit a new one, the employer can use the employee's most recent correct W-4 on file or, if a new hire, withhold as if the employee were single with no allowances.

REQUESTED FORMS W-4 Regulations require employers to only submit copies of employees' Forms W-4 that are requested in a written notice from the IRS.

Figure 4–4 outlines the procedures to follow in submitting Forms W-4 to the IRS.

EMPLOYEE PENALTIES Employees who willfully file false information statements (Form W-4) are, in addition to any other penalty, subject to fines of up to $1,000 or imprisonment for up to one year or both.

Employees claiming excess deductions are subject to a $500 civil penalty for each offense.

WITHHOLDING ON NONRESIDENT ALIENS Resident aliens (those with green cards) are lawful citizens and are taxed similar to U.S. citizens. To avoid underwithholding, nonresident aliens (who cannot claim the standard exemption and are limited to one allowance when filing their personal U.S. income tax returns) should (1) not claim exemption from income tax withholding; (2) request withholding as single, regardless of actual status; (3) claim only one allowance (residents of Canada, Mexico, Japan, or Korea may claim

FIGURE 4–4

Procedures for Submitting Forms W-4

- Send copies of Forms W-4 only after the IRS requests them in writing.
- IRS can also issue "lock-in" letters to employers specifying the maximum number of withholding exemptions permitted for an employee without obtaining a copy of the employee's W-4.
- An "employee notice" is sent along with the lock-in letter. This notice must be given to the employee within 10 business days of the receipt. If no longer employed, the employer must notify the IRS in writing.
- Withhold federal income tax based on lock-in letter starting with the first pay period 60 days after the date of the letter, unless the IRS contacts the employer.
- Challenges to the lock-in letter must be sent in writing along with a new Form W-4 by the employee directly to the IRS.
- Employer should disregard any new W-4 (unless claiming fewer exemptions than the IRS notice) submitted by the employee until notified to do so by the IRS.

more than one allowance); (4) add an extra amount to wages, then determine withholding based on the total amount (e.g., $51.00 for a weekly payroll period); and (5) write "Nonresident Alien" on dotted line on line 6 on Form W-4.

OTHER WITHHOLDINGS

Federal income taxes are also withheld from other kinds of payments made to current and former employees, as described below.

WITHHOLDING FOR PENSION OR ANNUITY PAYMENTS Generally, the withholding of federal income taxes applies to payments made from pension, profit-sharing, stock bonus, annuity, and certain deferred compensation plans and individual retirement arrangements. You treat the payments from any of these sources as wages for the purpose of withholding. Unless the recipients of pension or annuity payments elect ***not*** to have federal income taxes withheld from such payments, the taxes will be withheld. Payers must withhold on monthly pension and annuity payments exceeding $19,000 a year, unless the payees elect otherwise. If the recipients do not instruct the payers to the contrary, the payers are required to withhold income taxes as if the recipients were ***married and claiming three withholding allowances.***

By completing Form W-4P or a substitute form furnished by the payer, an employee can elect to have no income tax withheld from the payments received. The form may also be used to change the amount of tax that would ordinarily be withheld by the payers. Once completed, Form W-4P remains in effect until the recipient changes or revokes the certificate. The payer must notify the recipients each year of their right to elect to have no taxes withheld or to revoke their election.

WITHHOLDING FROM SICK PAY ***Form W-4S, Request for Federal Income Tax Withholding from Sick Pay,*** must be filed with the payer of sick pay if the employee wants federal income taxes to be withheld from the payments. Form W-4S is filed only if the payer is a third party, such as an insurance company. The form should not be filed with the worker's employer, who makes such payments, since employers already must withhold income taxes from sick pay.

WITHHOLDING ON GOVERNMENT PAYMENTS Form W-4V can be used to request federal income tax withholding on government payments (such as social security benefits or unemployment compensation). This request is voluntary.

SELF-STUDY QUIZ 4-2

1. Grace Kyle submitted a new Form W-4 claiming one additional withholding allowance. Kyle also requested to be reimbursed for the overwithholding prior to the change. How should the payroll manager respond to Kyle?
2. Bob Bradley is upset because his paycheck on February 22, 2008, has federal income tax withheld, even though he filed a W-4 in 2007 claiming exemption from withholding. What should the payroll manager say to Bradley?
3. Greg Volmer, married with a nonemployed spouse, has three dependent children. How many allowances can Volmer claim on his W-4?

Federal Income Tax Withholding

4 LEARNING OBJECTIVE

After the employer learns from Form W-4 the number of withholding allowances for an employee, the employer selects a withholding method. Employers usually choose either the **percentage method** or the **wage-bracket method**. Both distinguish between married and unmarried persons, and both methods provide the full benefit of the allowances claimed by the employee on Form W-4.

The choice of methods is usually based on the number of employees and the payroll accounting system used. The employer can change from one method to another at any time, and different methods may be used for different groups of employees.

Both methods take into account a **standard deduction,** an amount of money used to reduce an individual's adjusted gross income in arriving at the taxable income. For 2007, the following standard deductions apply:

Joint return filers and surviving spouses	$10,700
Married persons filing separately	5,350
Head of household filers	7,850
Single filers	5,350

These amounts are increased for single and married individuals or surviving spouses age 65 or older or blind. Each year, the standard deductions are adjusted for inflation. The adjustment also applies to the additional standard deductions available to elderly or blind persons.

PERCENTAGE METHOD

To compute the tax using the percentage method, follow these steps:

on the *JOB*

The basic income tax rates for 2007 are 10%, 15%, 25%, 28%, 33%, and 35%.

Step 1

Determine the amount of gross wages earned. If the wage ends in a fractional dollar amount, you may round the gross pay to the nearest dollar. →

Wilson Goodman, single, claims two allowances and earns $915.60 semimonthly.

Round Gross Wages to $916.00

Step 2

Multiply the number of allowances claimed by the amount of one allowance for the appropriate payroll period, as shown in the Table of Allowance Values in Figure 4–5. →

Table of Allowance Values for semimonthly payroll period shows $141.67.

Multiply $141.67 × 2 = $283.34

Step 3

Subtract the amount for the number of allowances claimed from the employee's gross pay to find the excess of wages over allowances claimed. →

Gross pay	$916.00
Less: Allowances	283.34
Excess wages	$632.66

Step 4

Determine the withholding tax on the excess of wages over allowances claimed by referring to the appropriate Percentage Method Withholding Table (rates in effect for January 1, 2007). →

Compute tax from Tax Table 3(a), page T–3.

15% of ($632.66 − $422.00) + $31.20 = $62.80

FIGURE 4–5

Table of Allowance Values for 2007

Weekly	65.38	Biweekly	130.77	Semimonthly	141.67	Monthly	283.33
Quarterly	850.00	Semiannual	1,700.00	Annual	3,400.00	Daily/Misc.	13.08

SELF-STUDY QUIZ 4-3 *Tiffany Moulder, married and claiming three allowances, receives a salary of $1,100.25 each week. Compute the amount to withhold for federal income tax using the percentage method and Figure 4–5. Show the results of each step, as described for figuring withholding using the percentage method.*

Step 1 Result __________ Step 2 Result __________

Step 3 Result __________ Step 4 Result __________

WAGE-BRACKET METHOD

The IRS provides statutory wage-bracket tables for weekly, biweekly, semimonthly, monthly, and daily or miscellaneous pay periods. Copies may be obtained from the District Director of Internal Revenue. Tax Table B at the end of the textbook provides tables for weekly, biweekly, semimonthly, monthly, and daily pay periods for single and married persons effective January 1, 2007.

To use the wage-bracket method, follow these steps:

NEWS // ALERT //

The top 1 percent of taxpayers by income paid 34.3 percent of federal taxes collected, while the bottom half of taxpayers paid 3.5 percent.

Step 1

Select the withholding table that applies to the employee's marital status and pay period. → Adrienne Huff is married and claims 3 allowances. She is paid weekly at a rate of $810.

Step 2

Locate the wage bracket (the first two columns of the table) in which the employee's gross wages fall. → Locate the appropriate wage bracket (see Figure 4–6):

At least $810 but less than $820

Step 3

Follow the line for the wage bracket across to the right to the column showing the appropriate number of allowances. Withhold this amount of tax. → Move across the line to the column showing 3 allowances.

The tax to withhold is $55.

If the employee's wages are higher than the last amount listed on the appropriate wage-bracket table, the percentage method must be used for that employee.

In cases where an employee claims more than 10 allowances, the employer has two methods for determining the amount to withhold when using the wage-bracket tables.

1. Withhold as if the employee claimed only 10 allowances, or
2. Multiply the value of one allowance for the applicable payroll period by the number of withholding allowances exceeding 10. Take this figure from the employee's gross wage that is subject to federal income tax withholding. Use the resulting amount and column 10 for allowances in the wage-bracket table to determine the tax to withhold.

FIGURE 4–6

Married Persons—Weekly Payroll Period

If the wages are—		And the number of withholding allowances claimed is—										
At least	But less than	0	1	2	3	4	5	6	7	8	9	10
		The amount of income tax to be withheld is—										
$740	$750	$74	$64	$54	$44	$35	$26	$20	$13	$7	$0	$0
750	760	75	66	56	46	36	27	21	14	8	1	0
760	770	77	67	57	47	38	28	22	15	9	2	0
770	780	78	69	59	49	39	29	23	16	10	3	0
780	790	80	70	60	50	41	31	24	17	11	4	0
790	800	81	72	62	52	42	32	25	18	12	5	0
800	810	83	73	63	53	44	34	26	19	13	6	0
810	820	84	75	65	(55)	45	35	27	20	14	7	1
820	830	86	76	66	56	47	37	28	21	15	8	2
830	840	87	78	68	58	48	38	29	22	16	9	3

EXAMPLE

WITHHOLDING WITH OVER 10 ALLOWANCES. Genevieve Minster is married and claims 12 allowances. She is paid $2,490 semimonthly. To determine her federal tax withholding using the wage-bracket tables, do the following:

Step 1—Multiply the amount of a withholding allowance for a semimonthly payroll period by 2.

$141.67 × 2 = $283.34

Step 2—Subtract that number from the gross wages.

$2,490.00 − $283.34 = $2,206.66

Step 3—Go to the wage-bracket table for a semimonthly pay period for a married person under the column for 10 allowances. (Page T-10)

$46

SELF-STUDY QUIZ 4-4 *Quirk Motors uses the wage-bracket method to withhold from the semimonthly earnings of its employees. For each employee, compute the amount to be withheld from their earnings for the payroll period ending March 15.*

Employee	Marital Status	No. of Allowances	Salary	Federal Income Tax Withheld
Kyle Lamb	S	1	$1,100	________
Zed Nurin	S	0	850	________
Carol Hogan	M	4	975	________
Marla Vick	M	2	3,000	________
Al Marks	S	3	1,200	________

Other Methods of Withholding

LEARNING OBJECTIVE 5

In addition to the two principal methods of withholding previously described, employers may use other methods such as **quarterly averaging, annualizing wages**, and **part-year employment**.

EXAMPLE

QUARTERLY AVERAGING. Jackson, Inc., estimates that Cal Hudson will be paid $6,690 during the second quarter of the year. Hudson is married, claims five withholding allowances, and is paid semimonthly.

Step 1—Divide the estimated quarterly wages by 6 (the number of semimonthly pay periods in the quarter).

$6,690 ÷ 6 = $1,115

Step 2—Find the amount of federal income tax to withhold from each semimonthly payment.

MARRIED Persons—SEMIMONTHLY Payroll Period
Wages at least $1,100 but not more than $1,120 for 5 allowances = $7

The withholding is based on the average payment instead of the actual payment.

EXAMPLE

ANNUALIZING WAGES. Marc Field, married with three allowances, receives $1,050 semimonthly. Under the annualizing method, do the following:

Step 1—Multiply the semimonthly wage by 24 pay periods to compute his annual wage.

$1,050 × 24 = $25,200

Step 2—Subtract withholding allowances of $10,200 (3 × $3,400).

$25,200 − $10,200 = $15,000

Step 3—Use Tax Table 7(b) and apply the percentage method to the taxable wages.

10% of the excess over $8,000 ($15,000 − $8,000) × 0.10 = $700.

$700 ÷ 24 semimonthly payrolls = $29.17 per paycheck

EXAMPLE

PART-YEAR EMPLOYMENT METHOD. Jack Matthews, previously unemployed for the calendar year, has agreed to begin temporary employment on September 15. He has made a written request for the part-year employment method of withholding. He claims single with one allowance on his W-4. For the biweekly period from September 15 to September 26, he earns a total of $7,600.

Step 1—Wages for the current payroll period are added to the wages paid previously.

$7,600 + 0 = $7,600

Step 2—The number of payroll periods worked in step 1 is added to the number of payroll periods between the employee's past and current employment.

1 + 19 = 20

Step 3—Divide the step 1 amount by the total number of payroll periods.

$7,600 ÷ 20 = $380

Step 4—Tax on the step 3 amount (from wage-bracket table for single/biweekly, one allowance).

$15

Step 5—Total number of payroll periods from step 2 multiplied by step 4 equals the withholding for the pay period.

20 × $15 = $300

Supplemental Wage Payments

6 LEARNING OBJECTIVE

Supplemental wage payments include items such as vacation pay, bonuses, commissions, and dismissal pay. Since these types of payments may be paid at a different time from the regular payroll and not related to a particular payroll, the employer must decide whether to lump the regular wages and supplemental wages together or withhold from the supplemental wages separately. The first distinction is the treatment of vacation pays versus other types of supplemental pays.

VACATION PAY

Vacation pay is subject to withholding as though it were a regular payment made for the payroll period or periods occurring during the vacation. If the vacation pay is for a time longer than your usual payroll period, spread it over the pay period(s) for which you pay it. If an employee is paid weekly and is paid for two weeks of vacation, treat each vacation week separately and calculate the tax on each vacation week using the weekly tax tables or wage brackets.

However, if vacation pay is in lieu of taking vacation time, treat it as a regular supplemental wage payment and calculate the tax on the total as a single payment. A lump-sum vacation payment on termination of employment is also treated as a supplemental wage payment.

SUPPLEMENTAL WAGES PAID WITH REGULAR WAGES

If the employer pays supplemental wages with regular wages but does not specify the amount of each type of wage, the employer withholds as if the total were a single payment for a regular payroll period.

EXAMPLE

Mandi Robinson, married with three allowances, earns a monthly salary of $1,800. She also receives a bonus on sales that exceed her quota for the year. For this year, her bonus amounts to $4,600. Robinson's employer pays her the regular monthly salary and the bonus together on her December paycheck. The withholding for the December pay is computed on the total amount of $6,400 ($1,800 + $4,600). After deducting the allowances, using the percentage Tax Table 4(b), the amount to withhold is $668.50

However, if the employer indicates specifically the amount of each payment, the employer may withhold at a ***flat 25 percent rate*** on the supplemental wages if the tax is withheld on the employee's regular wages at the appropriate rate.

EXAMPLE

If you indicate separately on Robinson's paycheck stub the amount of each payment, the amount of federal income tax to be withheld is computed as follows:

		Taxes Withheld	
Regular monthly earnings	$1,800	$ 30.00	(from wage-bracket tax tables*)
Annual bonus	4,600	1,150.00	($4,600 × 25%)
Totals	$6,400	$1,180.00	

*The percentage table could also be used.

If the employee has already received supplemental wages for the year in excess of $1 million, ***a new 35 percent*** withholding rate must be used for the amount above $1 million (the aggregate method cannot be used).

States that have income taxes usually set up their own flat rate for withholding on these supplemental pays. Some require that the supplemental pay be added to a regular pay and the total taxed.

SUPPLEMENTAL WAGES PAID SEPARATELY FROM REGULAR WAGES

If the supplemental wages are paid separately, the income tax withholding method depends on whether or not you withheld income tax from the employee's last regular wage payment. If you withheld income tax from the employee's regular wages, you can use either of the following methods for supplemental wages.

METHOD A Add the supplemental wages and regular wages for the most recent payroll period. Then, figure the income tax as if the total were a single payment. Subtract the tax already withheld from the regular wage. Withhold the remaining tax from the supplemental wage.

EXAMPLE

Louis Ernst, married with two allowances, is paid $985 semimonthly. The tax to be withheld under the wage-bracket method on each semimonthly pay is $37. Ernst is paid his regular wage on June 15. On June 18, he receives a bonus of $500. The tax on the bonus is computed as follows:

Regular wage payment	$ 985
Bonus	500
Total	$1,485
Tax on total from the wage-bracket table in Tax Table B	$99
Less: Tax already withheld on $985	37
Tax to be withheld from $500 bonus	$ 62

If you did not withhold income tax from the employee's regular wage payment, use Method A.

METHOD B Withhold a flat 25 percent (35 percent if over $1 million) on the supplemental pay.

EXAMPLE

The tax withheld on Louis Ernst's June 18 bonus of $500 is computed as follows:

Bonus	$500
Tax rate	× 25%
Tax withheld on bonus	$125

If a supplemental payment is paid in a year where no regular wages are paid, the payment is treated as a regular wage payment, and withholding is determined by the rules that apply to a miscellaneous payroll period.

SELF-STUDY QUIZ 4-5 *Fred Burdette, married with two allowances, received his regular semimonthly wage of $1,450 on June 15. On June 20, he received a semiannual bonus of $500. Compute the amount of federal income tax to be withheld on the bonus using each method for computing supplemental wage payments. The employer uses the wage-bracket tables.*

Method A ____________

Method B ____________

GROSS-UP SUPPLEMENTALS

In order to give an employee the intended amount of a supplemental payment, the employer will need to gross up the payment so that after the appropriate payroll taxes are withheld, the net amount left is equal to the original intended payment.

A special "**gross-up**" formula can be applied in this situation:

$$\text{Grossed-up amount} = \frac{\text{Intended payment}}{1 - \text{Applicable tax rates (FICA, 25\% Federal Income Tax rate, and state tax rate)}}$$

EXAMPLE

GROSSING-UP. Cotter Company wants to award a $4,000 bonus to Donna D'Amico. In addition, it wants the net bonus payment to equal $4,000. Assuming D'Amico is still under the OASDI/FICA limit, the calculation would be:

A. $$\frac{\$4{,}000}{1 - 0.25\ (\text{supplemental W/H rate}) - 0.062\ (\text{OASDI}) - 0.0145\ (\text{HI})}$$

B. $$\frac{\$4{,}000}{0.6735} = \$5{,}939.12 \text{ grossed-up bonus}$$

If state or local taxes apply, they must also be included in the formula.

Advance Earned Income Credit

LEARNING OBJECTIVE 7

The **earned income credit (EIC)** reduces federal income taxes and is intended to offset living expenses for an eligible employee (see Figure 4–7) who has a qualifying child and for the low-income taxpayers who have no qualifying children. The credit can be claimed at the time of filing their individual income tax returns, and they receive a lump-sum tax refund. For 2007, the refund, as calculated at the time of filing Form 1040, could be as much as $2,853 if the employee had one qualifying child; with two or more qualifying children, $4,716. However, to get these payments in advance with his or her paycheck, the employee must give the employer a properly completed ***Form W-5, Earned Income Credit Advance Payment Certificate.*** The employer must make advance EIC payments to employees who complete and sign Form W-5. For 2007, the maximum ***advance*** payment (up to 60 percent of the credit available) was $1,712. Employees will receive the balance of the credit when they file their federal income tax returns.

For joint filers with two or more children, the credit is phased out at an income of $39,783.

NEWS // ALERT //

Due to "high errors" in the program, the IRS has started to require some claimants to submit proof of their eligible children's residency status and relationship to them.

FORM W-5

Eligible employees who want to receive advance EIC payments must file Form W-5 with their employer. On this form, the employee shows the following:

- Expected eligibility for the credit in 2007.
- If they have a qualifying child.
- If they are married.
- If married, whether their spouse has a certificate in effect with any other employer.
- If another W-5 is on file with another current employer.

An employee can have only one certificate in effect with a current employer. If the employee is married and the employee's spouse works, each spouse files a separate Form W-5. This form remains in effect until the end of the calendar year or until the employee revokes the certificate or files another one. A new certificate must be filed by December 31 in order to continue receiving payment in the new year. Figure 4–8 shows an example of a filled-in Form W-5.

FIGURE 4–7

Employees Eligible for Advance EIC

Only eligible employees can receive advance EIC payments. The eligibility requirements are summarized below.

1. Employee must have a qualifying child, as defined on Form W-5;
2. Employee's expected 2007 earned income and adjusted gross income must each be less than $33,241 ($35,241 if filing jointly); and
3. Expect to be able to claim the EIC for 2007.

FIGURE 4–8

Earned Income Credit Advance Payment Certificate

Form **W-5**
Department of the Treasury
Internal Revenue Service

Earned Income Credit Advance Payment Certificate
▶ **Use the current year's certificate only.**
▶ **Give this certificate to your employer.**
▶ **This certificate expires on December 31, 20--.**

OMB No. 1545-1342
20--

Print or type your full name: Mary Sue Graser
Your social security number: 269 11 0001

Note: *If you get advance payments of the earned income credit for 20--, you **must** file a 20-- Federal income tax return. To get advance payments, you **must** have a qualifying child and your filing status must be any status **except** married filing a separate return.*

1 I expect to have a qualifying child and be able to claim the earned income credit for 20--, I do not have another Form W-5 in effect with any other current employer, and I choose to get advance EIC payments . ☒ **Yes** ☐ **No**
2 Check the box that shows your expected filing status for 20--:
☒ Single, head of household, or qualifying widow(er) ☐ Married filing jointly
3 If you are married, does your spouse have a Form W-5 in effect for 20-- with any employer? . . . . . ☐ **Yes** ☐ **No**

Under penalties of perjury, I declare that the information I have furnished above is, to the best of my knowledge, true, correct, and complete.

Signature ▶ Mary Sue Graser **Date** ▶ 1/24/--

Cat. No. 10227P

EMPLOYEE'S CHANGE OF STATUS

If circumstances change after an employee has submitted a signed Form W-5 that make the employee ineligible for the credit, he or she must revoke the certificate within 10 days after learning of the change. The employee then gives the employer a new Form W-5, stating that he or she is no longer eligible for advance EIC payments. If the employee's situation changes because his or her spouse files a Form W-5, the employee must file a new certificate showing that his or her spouse has a certificate in effect with an employer.

on the *JOB*

For 2007, taxpayers with no qualifying children and incomes between $7,000 and $12,590 ($9,000 and $14,590 if married filing jointly) can receive a maximum EIC of $428 (with their tax return filing).

EMPLOYER RESPONSIBILITIES

Employers must notify employees who have no income tax withheld that they may be eligible for EIC payments. The employer may use any of the following methods to notify employees:

1. The IRS Form W-2, which has the required statement about the EIC on the back of Copy C.
2. A substitute Form W-2 with the same EIC statement on the back of the employee's copy.
3. Notice 797, Possible Federal Refund Due to the Earned Income Credit (EIC).
4. Your written statement with the same wording as Notice 797.

***IRS* CONNECTION**

An employee receiving advance earned income credit payments in the paycheck, who finds out that he or she is ineligible, must pay back the advance payments when filing the federal income tax return (Form 1040).

COMPUTING THE ADVANCE EIC

Employers must include the advance EIC payment with wages paid to their eligible employees who have filed Form W-5. In determining the advance payment, the employer considers the following factors:

1. Wages and reported tips for the pay period.
2. Whether the employee is married or single.
3. Whether a married employee's spouse has a Form W-5 in effect with an employer.

To figure the amount of the advance payment, the employer uses either the ***Tables for Percentage Method of Advance EIC Payments*** or ***Tables for Wage-Bracket Method of Advance EIC Payments.*** There are separate tables for employees whose spouses have a certificate in effect, without spouses filing certificate, or single/head of household.

FIGURE 4–9

MARRIED with Both Spouses Filing Certificate—Weekly Payroll Period

MARRIED With Both Spouses Filing Certificate

Wages— At least	Wages— But less than	Payment to be made	Wages— At least	Wages— But less than	Payment to be made	Wages— At least	Wages— But less than	Payment to be made	Wages— At least	Wages— But less than	Payment to be made	Wages— At least	Wages— But less than	Payment to be made
$0	**$5**	$0	**$35**	**$40**	$7	**$70**	**$75**	$14	**$205**	**$215**	$12	**$275**	**$285**	$5
5	**10**	1	**40**	**45**	8	**75**	**80**	15	**215**	**225**	11	**285**	**295**	4
10	**15**	2	**45**	**50**	9	**80**	**165**	16	**225**	**235**	10	**295**	**305**	3
15	**20**	3	**50**	**55**	10	**165**	**175**	16	**235**	**245**	9	**305**	**315**	2
20	**25**	4	**55**	**60**	11	**175**	**185**	15	**245**	**255**	8	**315**	**325**	1
25	**30**	5	**60**	**65**	12	**185**	**195**	14	**255**	**265**	7	**325**	**- - -**	0
30	**35**	6	**65**	**70**	13	**195**	**205**	13	**265**	**275**	6			

EXAMPLE

Renee Riley is paid $150 per week. She has filed Form W-5 showing that she is married and that her husband has given his employer Form W-5. Using the "Married With Both Spouses Filing Certificate" in Figure 4–9, the advance EIC payment is $16.

on the *JOB*

Studies done by the General Accounting Office have revealed massive losses to the federal government in the EIC program due to fraud and errors. Losses have been estimated to range from 20 to 30 percent of all EIC benefits.

PAYING THE ADVANCE EIC

The advance EIC payments do not affect the amount of income taxes or FICA taxes withheld from employees' wages. Since the EIC payments are not compensation for services rendered, they are not subject to payroll taxes. Generally, the employer pays the amount of the advance EIC payment from withheld income taxes and FICA taxes. It is possible that for a payroll period the advance EIC payments may be more than the withheld income taxes and the FICA taxes. In such cases, the employer can:

1. Reduce each advance EIC payment proportionately, or
2. Elect to make full payment of the advance EIC amount and treat such full amounts as an advance payment of the company's employment payroll taxes.

The amount of the advance EIC payments does not change the amount that employers must withhold from their employees' wages for income taxes and FICA. Advance EIC payments made by the employer are treated as having been made from amounts withheld as income tax, employee FICA taxes, and from the employer's FICA taxes. The amount of advance EIC payments is considered to have been paid over to the IRS on the day the wages are paid to employees.

EXAMPLE

Nolan Inc. has 10 employees who are each entitled to advance EIC payments of $12. The total advance payments made by Nolan for the payroll period amount to $120. The total income tax withheld for the payroll period is $110. The total FICA taxes for employees and employer are $128.

Nolan is considered to have made a deposit of $120 from the advance EIC payments on the day the wages are paid. The $120 is treated as if the company has paid the total $110 in income tax withholding and $10 of the employee FICA taxes to the IRS. The company must deposit only $118 of the remaining FICA taxes.

EMPLOYER'S RETURNS AND RECORDS

The employer takes into account the amount of the advance EIC payments when completing Form 941. The amount of the advance EIC payments is subtracted from the total amount of income taxes and FICA taxes in order to determine the net taxes due for the quarter. All records of advance EIC payments should be retained four years and be available for review by the IRS. These records include:

1. Copies of employees' Forms W-5.
2. Amounts and dates of all wage payments and advance EIC payments.

3. Dates of each employee's employment.
4. Dates and amounts of tax deposits made.
5. Copies of returns filed.

SELF-STUDY QUIZ 4-6

1. During one week, Georgia Brewer earned $175. She and her spouse have both filed Form W-5. Using the information presented in Figure 4–9, compute the amount of advance EIC payment Brewer is entitled to receive.
   $ 15.00
2. On a certain payday, Gregory Company made advance EIC payments to its employees that amounted to more than the federal income taxes withheld. Does the company have to make a tax deposit for this payday? Explain.

Wage and Tax Statements

8 LEARNING OBJECTIVE

Employers must furnish **wage and tax statements** to employees informing them of the wages paid during the calendar year and the amount of taxes withheld from those wages. The employer sends copies of these statements to the federal government and, in many cases, to state, city, and local governments.

on the JOB

On Form W-2, enter name exactly as shown on employee's social security card. Do not include titles (Mr., Mrs., Dr., etc.), suffixes (RN, MD, CPA, etc.), or Jr. or Sr.

FORM W-2

Form W-2, Wage and Tax Statement (2007 version), shown in Figure 4–10, is prepared if any of the following items apply to an employee during the calendar year:

FIGURE 4–10

W-2 Wage and Tax Statement

22222 Void ☐	a Employee's social security number 382-13-7478	For Official Use Only ▶ OMB No. 1545-0008	
b Employer identification number (EIN) 13-5407221		1 Wages, tips, other compensation 29360.18	2 Federal income tax withheld 4610.00
c Employer's name, address, and ZIP code Keevey Motors, 600 Third Avenue, Philadelphia, PA 19103-5600		3 Social security wages 29360.18	4 Social security tax withheld 1820.33
		5 Medicare wages and tips 29360.18	6 Medicare tax withheld 425.72
		7 Social security tips	8 Allocated tips
d Control number		9 Advance EIC payment	10 Dependent care benefits
e Employee's first name and initial Richard M.	Last name Cabor Suff.	11 Nonqualified plans	12a See instructions for box 12 Code C 78.00
		13 Statutory employee ☐ Retirement plan ☒ Third-party sick pay ☐	12b Code
483 Monroe Street, Philadelphia, PA 19119-4821		14 Other BC/BS Premium w/h 296.00	12c Code
f Employee's address and ZIP code			12d Code

15 State	Employer's state ID number	16 State wages, tips, etc.	17 State income tax	18 Local wages, tips, etc.	19 Local income tax	20 Locality name
PA	46-8-0013	29282.18	898.96	29282.18	1259.43	Phila

Form **W-2** **Wage and Tax Statement** 20--

Department of the Treasury—Internal Revenue Service

For Privacy Act and Paperwork Reduction Act Notice, see back of Copy D.

Cat. No. 10134D

Copy A For Social Security Administration — Send this entire page with Form W-3 to the Social Security Administration; photocopies are not acceptable.

Do Not Cut, Fold, or Staple Forms on This Page — Do Not Cut, Fold, or Staple Forms on This Page

on the *JOB*

Employers can create "fill-in" versions of forms W-2 and W-3 for filing with the Social Security Administration and print out copies for employees at http://www.socialsecurity.gov/employer.

1. Income tax or social security taxes were withheld.
2. Income tax would have been withheld if the employee had not claimed more than one withholding allowance or had not claimed exemption from withholding on Form W-4.
3. Any amount was paid for services if the employer is in a trade or business. The cash value of any noncash payments made should be included.
4. Any advance EIC payments were made.

Figure 4–11 summarizes the instructions for completing each of the boxes on Form W-2. If an entry does not apply to the firm or employee, leave the box blank. Employers must give employees Form W-2 on or before *January 31* following the close of the calendar year. When employees leave the service of the employer, you may give them Form W-2 any time after employment ends. If employees ask for Form W-2, the employer should give it to them within 30 days of their request or the final wage payment, whichever is later. In instances where terminated workers may be rehired at some time before the year ends, the employer may delay furnishing the form until January 31 following the close of the calendar year. Employers distribute Form W-2 copies as follows:

IRS CONNECTION

Time extensions for filing W-2s can be requested by sending Form 8809 (Request for Extension of Time to File Information Returns) to the IRS by February 28. An additional 30-day extension can be requested by submitting another Form 8809 before the end of the initial extension period.

Copy A—To the Social Security Administration ***by the end of February*** following the year for which Form W-2 is applicable. If filed *electronically, March 31* is the due date.
Copy 1—To the state, city, or local tax department.
Copy B—To employees for filing with their federal income tax return.
Copy C—To employees for their personal records.
Copy 2—To employees for filing with their state, city, or local income tax returns.
Copy D—Retained by the employer.

If 250 or more Forms W-2 are being filed, reporting must be done electronically. An extended deadline of March 31 applies to any W-2s filed electronically.

Employers that are going out of business must send W-2 forms to the employees by the date the final Form 941 is due. One month later, the W-2 forms are due at the Social Security Administration.

If Form W-2 has been lost or destroyed, employers are authorized to furnish substitute copies to the employee. The substitute form should be clearly marked **REISSUED STATEMENT.** Do not send Copy A of the substitute statement to the Social Security Administration. If, after a reasonable effort, the employer cannot deliver a Form W-2, the employer retains the employee's copies of the form for a four-year period. A "reasonable effort" means the forms were mailed to the last known address of the employee.

The IRS allows employers to put W-2s on a secure Web site and provide employees with passwords to access their individual W-2s. As long as an employee has affirmatively consented, his or her W-2 can be sent electronically. The consent by the employee must also be made electronically in a manner that indicates that the employee will be able to access the W-2. The W-2 must be posted on or before January 31 (kept until October 15), and the employee must be notified of its availability and must be given instructions on how to access and print the W-2.

FORM W-2C

To correct errors in previously filed Forms W-2, employers file ***Form W-2c, Statement of Corrected Income and Tax Amounts,*** shown in Figure 4–12. File Copy A with the Social Security Administration and the remaining copies as noted on the bottom of each form. Form W-3c should accompany all corrected wage and tax statements unless the correction is for only one employee or to correct employees' names, addresses, or social security numbers. In the case of an incorrect address, the employer can mail the "incorrect" W-2 in an envelope bearing the corrected address.

on the *NET*

For access to all federal tax forms, see the **Forms and Publications** download page: http://www.irs.gov/formspubs/

FORM W-3

Form W-3, Transmittal of Wage and Tax Statements, must be filed with the Social Security Administration by employers and other payers as a transmittal for Forms W-2. On Form W-3, the employer indicates the number of documents being transmitted. Form W-3 and the

FIGURE 4–11

How to Complete Form W-2

Box A—Employee's social security number: An employee who does not have an SSN should apply for one by completing Form SS-5.

Void: Put an X in this box when an error has been made. Amounts shown on void forms should not be included in your subtotal Form W-2.

Box B—Employer nor Employer's identification number (EIN): Enter the number assigned to you by the IRS. Do not use a prior owner's EIN. If you do not have an EIN when filing Forms W-2, enter "Applied For." You can get an EIN by filing Form SS-4.

Box C—Employer's name, address, and ZIP code: This entry should be the same as shown on your Form 941 or 943.

Box D—Control number: For the employer to identify the individual Forms W-2. Up to 7 digits may be used to assign the number, which the employer uses when writing the Social Security Administration about the form. The employer does not have to use this box.

Box E—Employee's name: The name should be entered exactly as shown on the employee's social security card.

Box F— Employee's address and ZIP code: This box is combined with Box E on all copies except Copy A, to allow you to mail employee's copies in a window envelope or as a self-mailer.

Box 1—Wages, tips, other compensation: Record, before any payroll deductions, the total of (1) wages, prizes, and awards paid; (2) noncash payments (including certain fringe benefits); (3) tips reported by employee to employer (not allocated tips); (4) certain employee business expense reimbursements; (5) cost of accident and health insurance premiums paid on behalf of 2% or more shareholder employees by an S corporation; (6) taxable benefits made from a Section 125 (cafeteria plan); and (7) all other compensation including certain scholarships and fellowship grants and payments for moving expenses. Other compensation is an amount you pay your employee from which federal income tax is not withheld. You may show other compensation on a separate Form W-2.

Box 2—Federal income tax withheld: Record the amount of federal income tax withheld from the employee's wages for the year.

Box 3—Social security wages: Enter the total wages paid (before payroll deductions) subject to employee social security (OASDI) tax. Do not include social security tips and allocated tips. Generally, noncash payments are considered wages. Include employee business expenses reported in Box 1. Include employer contributions to qualified cash or deferred compensation plans and to retirement arrangements described in Box 12 (Codes D, E, F, and G), even though the deferrals are not includible in Box 1 as wages, tips, and other compensation. Include any employee OASDI and HI taxes and employee state unemployment compensation taxes you paid for your employee rather than deducting it from wages. Report in this box the cost of group-term life insurance coverage over $50,000 that is taxable to former employees. Report the cost of accident and health insurance premiums paid on behalf of 2% or more shareholder-employees by an S corporation only if the exclusion under Section 312(a)(2)(B) is not satisfied. Do not enter more than the maximum OASDI taxable wage base for the year.

Box 4—Social security tax withheld: Record the total social security (OASDI) tax (not your share) withheld or paid by you for the employee. Include only taxes withheld for the year's wages.

Box 5—Medicare wages and tips: Enter the medicare (HI) wages and tips. Be sure to enter tips the employee reported even if you did not have enough employee funds to collect the HI tax for those tips. Report in this box the cost of group-term life insurance coverage over $50,000 that is taxable to former employees.

Box 6—Medicare tax withheld: Enter the total employee medicare (HI) tax (not your share) withheld or paid by you for your employee. Include only taxes withheld for the year's wages.

Box 7—Social security tips: Record the amount the employee reported even if you did not have enough employee funds to collect the social security (OASDI) tax for the tips. The total of Boxes 3 and 7 should not be more than the maximum OASDI wage base for the year. But report all tips in Box 1 along with wages and other compensation.

Box 8—Allocated tips: If you are a large food or beverage establishment, record the amount of tips allocated to the employee. Do not include this amount in Boxes 1, 3, 5, or 7.

Box 9—Advance EIC payment: Record the total amount paid to the employee as advance earned income credit payments.

Box 10—Dependent care benefits: Record the total amount of dependent care benefits paid or incurred by you for your employee. This total should include any amount in excess of the exclusion ($5,000).

Box 11—Nonqualified plans: Enter the amount from a nonqualified deferred compensation plan or Section 457 plan that was distributed or became taxable because the substantial risk of forfeiture lapsed. Include this amount in Box 11 only if it is also includible in Boxes 1, 3, and 5. Report distributions to beneficiaries of deceased employees on Form 1099-R.

(Continued)

FIGURE 4–11 *(Concluded)*

How to Complete Form W-2

Box 12—Complete and code this box for all applicable items listed below in the Reference Guide. Additional information about any coded item may be found in the IRS's Instructions for Form W-2. Do not enter more than four codes in this box. If you are reporting more than four items, use a separate Form W-2 or a substitute Form W-2 to report the additional items.

Use a capital letter when entering each code and enter the dollar amount on the same line. Use decimal points.

Box 13—Mark the boxes that apply.

Statutory employee: Mark this box for statutory employees whose earnings are subject to social security (OASDI) and medicare (HI) taxes but not subject to federal income tax withholding.

Retirement plan: Mark this box if the employee was an active participant (for any part of the year) in a retirement plan such as 401(k) and SEP.

Third-party sick plan: Mark this box only if you are a third-party, sick-pay payer filing a Form W-2 for an insured's employee.

Box 14—Other: Use this box for any other information you want to give your employee. Label each item. Examples are union dues, health insurance premiums deducted, moving expenses paid, nontaxable income, or educational assistance payments.

Boxes 15 through 20—State or local income tax information: You do not have to complete these boxes, but you may want to if you use copies of this form for your state and local returns. The ID number is assigned by each individual state. The state and local information boxes can be used to report wages and taxes on two states and two localities. Keep each state's and locality's information separated by the dotted line.

Reference Guide for Box 12 Codes

A—Uncollected social security (OASDI) tax on tips
B—Uncollected medicare (HI) tax on tips
C—Group-term life insurance over $50,000
D—Elective deferrals to a Section 401(k) cash or deferred arrangement
E—Elective deferrals to a Section 403(b) salary reduction agreement
F—Elective deferrals to a Section 408(k)(6) salary reduction SEP
G—Elective and nonelective deferrals to a Section 457(b) deferred compensation plan (state and local government and tax-exempt employers)
H—Elective deferrals to a Section 501(c)(18)(D) tax-exempt organization plan
J—Nontaxable sick pay
K—20% excise tax on excess golden parachute payments
L—Substantiated employee business expense (federal rate)
M—Uncollected social security (OASDI) tax on group-term life insurance coverage
N—Uncollected medicare (HI) tax on group-term life insurance coverage
P—Excludable reimbursed moving expenses
Q—Military employee basic housing, subsistence and combat zone pay
R—Employer contributions to medical savings account
S—Employee salary reduction contributions to a 408(p) SIMPLE retirement plan
T—Employer-provided qualified adoption benefits
V—Exercise of nonstatutory stock options
W—Employer contributions to an employee's health savings account (HSA)
Y—Deferrals under a Section 409A nonqualified deferred compensation plan
Z—Income under Section 409A on a nonqualified deferred compensation plan
AA—Designated Roth contributions to a 401(k) plan
BB—Designated Roth contributions under a 403(b) salary reduction agreement

on the *JOB*

The Social Security Administration processes close to 240 million W-2s a year, and about 10 percent have names and numbers that do not match.

accompanying documents enable the Social Security Administration and the IRS to compare the totals to the amounts for the income tax withholdings, social security wages, social security tips, medicare wages and tips, and the advanced earned income credits, as reported on the employer's 941s for the year. The IRS will require explanations of any differences and corrections to any errors. Figure 4–13, on page 4-30, shows a completed Form W-3. The employer files all Forms W-2 with one W-3. Forms W-3 and the related documents are filed with the Social Security Administration by the end of February each year. Form W-3 is mailed to employers during the fourth quarter.

FIGURE 4–12

Form W-2c, Statement of Corrected Income and Tax Amounts

a Tax year/Form corrected 20-- / W-2	44444	**For Official Use Only** ▶ OMB No. 1545-0008	
b Employee's correct SSN 911-12-6399		**c** Corrected SSN and/or name (if checked, enter incorrect SSN and/or name in box **h** and/or box i) ☐	**d** Employer's Federal EIN 13-5407221
e Employee's first name and initial Marge A.	Last name Mangano	Suff.	**g** Employer's name, address, and ZIP code Comcart Company 1600 Fourth Avenue Princeton, NJ 09109
8911 State Street Trenton, NJ 08033 **f** Employee's address and ZIP code			
Complete boxes h and/or i only if incorrect on last form filed. ▶	**h** Employee's **incorrect** SSN		**i** Employee's name (as **incorrectly** shown on previous form)

Note: Only complete money fields that are being corrected (except MQGE).

Previously reported	Correct information	Previously reported	Correct information
1 Wages, tips, other compensation	1 Wages, tips, other compensation	2 Federal income tax withheld 3,293.00	2 Federal income tax withheld 3,923.00
3 Social security wages	3 Social security wages	4 Social security tax withheld	4 Social security tax withheld
5 Medicare wages and tips	5 Medicare wages and tips	6 Medicare tax withheld	6 Medicare tax withheld
7 Social security tips	7 Social security tips	8 Allocated tips	8 Allocated tips
9 Advance EIC payment	9 Advance EIC payment	10 Dependent care benefits	10 Dependent care benefits
11 Nonqualified plans	11 Nonqualified plans	12a See instructions for box 12 Code	12a See instructions for box 12 Code
13 Statutory employee ☐ Retirement plan ☐ Third-party sick pay ☐	13 Statutory employee ☐ Retirement plan ☐ Third-party sick pay ☐	12b Code	12b Code
14 Other (see instructions)	14 Other (see instructions)	12c Code	12c Code
		12d Code	12d Code

State Correction Information

Previously reported	Correct information	Previously reported	Correct information
15 State	15 State	15 State	15 State
Employer's state ID number	Employer's state ID number	Employer's state ID number	Employer's state ID number
16 State wages, tips, etc.	16 State wages, tips, etc.	16 State wages, tips, etc.	16 State wages, tips, etc.
17 State income tax	17 State income tax	17 State income tax	17 State income tax

Locality Correction Information

18 Local wages, tips, etc.	18 Local wages, tips, etc.	18 Local wages, tips, etc.	18 Local wages, tips, etc.
19 Local income tax	19 Local income tax	19 Local income tax	19 Local income tax
20 Locality name	20 Locality name	20 Locality name	20 Locality name

For Privacy Act and Paperwork Reduction Act Notice, see separate instructions. **Copy A—For Social Security Administration**

Form **W-2c** (Rev. 1-2006) **Corrected Wage and Tax Statement** Cat. No. 61437D Department of the Treasury Internal Revenue Service

FIGURE 4–13

Form W-3, Transmittal of Wage and Tax Statements

DO NOT STAPLE

33333 | a Control number | For Official Use Only ► OMB No. 1545-0008

b Kind of Payer ► 941 [X] Military [ ] 943 [ ] 944 [ ] CT-1 [ ] Hshld. emp. [ ] Medicare govt. emp. [ ] Third-party sick pay [ ]

1 Wages, tips, other compensation 2620736.40	2 Federal income tax withheld 330317.19
3 Social security wages 2485210.05	4 Social security tax withheld 154083.02
5 Medicare wages and tips 2620736.40	6 Medicare tax withheld 38000.68
7 Social security tips	8 Allocated tips
9 Advance EIC payments 778.00	10 Dependent care benefits
11 Nonqualified plans	12 Deferred compensation
13 For third-party sick pay use only	
14 Income tax withheld by payer of third-party sick pay	
16 State wages, tips, etc. 2620736.40	17 State income tax $ 111381.29
18 Local wages, tips, etc.	19 Local income tax

c Total number of Forms W-2 132 | d Establishment number

e Employer identification number (EIN) 88-1936281

f Employer's name
Grove Electronics
33 Vista Road
Vallejo, CA 94590-0033

g Employer's address and ZIP code

h Other EIN used this year

15 State CA | Employer's state ID number 16-794132

Contact person Roger Damron | Telephone number (415) 555-3200 | For Official Use Only

Email address RDamron@grove.com | Fax number (415) 555-2229

Under penalties of perjury, I declare that I have examined this return and accompanying documents, and, to the best of my knowledge and belief, they are true, correct, and complete.

Signature ► *Carl W. Tolan* Title ► President Date ► 3/2/2009

Form **W-3 Transmittal of Wage and Tax Statements** 20-- Department of the Treasury Internal Revenue Service

The information shown on Form W-3 is matched against the employer's Forms 941 for the year. If the totals do not match, the IRS notifies the employer of the discrepancy, and the employer is required to provide additional information.

PENALTIES

The following penalties are imposed for late or incorrect filing of W-2s:

1. If filed correctly within 30 days after the due date, $15 per return ($75,000 maximum penalty/$25,000 for small businesses).
2. If filed between 30 days after the due date and August 1, $30 per return ($150,000 maximum penalty/$50,000 for small businesses).
3. After August 1, $50 per return ($250,000 maximum penalty/$100,000 for small businesses).
4. Penalties of $100 per return, or if greater, 10 percent of the amount to be reported correctly for intentional disregard of the requirements for filing, providing payee statements, and reporting incorrect information (no maximum penalty).
5. Filing W-2s with mismatched names and social security numbers, $50 per form.

FORM W-3C

The ***Transmittal of Corrected Income and Tax Statements, Form W-3c,*** is used to accompany copies of Form W-2c, sent to the Social Security Administration. This form can also be used to correct a previously filed Form W-3.

PRIVATELY PRINTED FORMS

Employers may use their own forms by obtaining specifications for the private printing of Forms W-2 from any IRS center or district office. To the extent that the privately printed forms meet the specifications, the employer may use them without prior approval of the IRS.

SELF-STUDY QUIZ 4-7

1. Marquat Company deducts union dues from its employees' paychecks each month during the year and sends them to the local union office. How should the company report this deduction on the employees' Forms W-2?
2. Gringle's terminated 10 of its employees on July 15. The company informed each employee that it may rehire them again during its peak season in September. When should the company furnish each employee with a W-2 statement?
3. While preparing her 2007 personal income tax return, Connie Becker, an employee of Trident Mills, discovered that she had lost her Form W-2. What procedures should the company follow to prepare a new Form W-2 for Becker?

Returns Employers Must Complete

9 LEARNING OBJECTIVE

Employers must file returns reporting the amount of wages paid and the amount of taxes withheld at designated times, beginning with the first quarter in which taxable wages are paid. Rules that require different returns for different types of employees further complicate the accounting tasks and payroll procedures. Figure 4–14 briefly summarizes the major returns completed by employers.

FIGURE 4–14

Major Returns Filed by Employers

Form 941, Employer's Quarterly Federal Tax Return	For reporting federal income taxes withheld during the calendar quarter and the employer and employee portions of the FICA taxes. Form 941 is illustrated in Chapter 3.
Form 941-M, Employer's Monthly Federal Tax Return	For reporting federal income taxes withheld and FICA taxes on a monthly basis. The IRS may require monthly returns and payments of taxes from employers who have not complied with the requirements for filing returns or the paying or depositing of taxes reported on quarterly returns. You are not required to file this return unless notified by the IRS.
Form 942, Employer's Quarterly Tax Return for Household Employees	For reporting federal income taxes withheld as a result of voluntary withholding agreements between employers and their domestic employees. Form 942 is also completed by employers who are liable for FICA taxes on wages paid to domestic workers.
Form 943, Employer's Annual Tax Return for Agricultural Employees	For reporting the withholding of federal income taxes and FICA taxes on wages paid to agricultural workers. Form 943 is used for agricultural employees even though the employer may employ nonagricultural workers.
Form 944, Employer's Annual Federal Tax Return	Replaces Form 941 for employers who owe $1,000 or less in employment taxes for the year.
Form 945, Annual Return of Withheld Federal Income Tax	Used to report tax liability for nonpayroll items such as backup withholding and withholding on gambling winnings, pensions, and annuities, and deposits made for the year. **Backup withholding** occurs when an individual receives taxable interest, dividends, and certain other payments and fails to furnish the payer with the correct taxpayer identification numbers. Payers are then required to withhold 28 percent of those payments. Backup withholding does not apply to wages, pensions, annuities, or IRAs.

The most recent information with regard to withholding, deposit, and payment and reporting of federal income taxes, FICA taxes, and FUTA taxes is available in ***Circular E, Employer's Tax Guide.*** This circular is sent to employers prior to the start of the new year and is also available at district offices of the IRS.

Information Returns

LEARNING OBJECTIVE 10

The IRS requires employers to file **information returns** to report compensation paid to certain individuals who are not employees. These returns allow the IRS to determine if taxpayers are reporting their true income. Figure 4–15 briefly summarizes the major information returns required by the IRS. The employer sends copies of the returns to the payee by the end of January. These forms can be sent to the contractors electronically as long as they agree in advance to this method of delivery.

FIGURE 4–15

Major Information Returns

Form 1099-DIV, Dividends and Distributions	For reporting dividends totaling $10 or more to any person; foreign tax withheld and paid on dividends and other distributions on stock for a person; distributions made by corporations and regulated investment companies (including money market funds) as part of liquidation.
Form 1099-G, Certain Government Payments	For reporting unemployment compensation payments, state and local income tax refunds of $10 or more, taxable grants, income tax refunds, and agricultural subsidy payments.
Form 1099-INT, Interest Income	For reporting payments of (a) interest of $10 or more paid or credited on earnings from savings and loans, credit unions, bank deposits, corporate bonds, etc.; (b) interest of $600 or more from other sources; (c) forfeited interest due on premature withdrawals of time deposits; (d) foreign tax eligible for the recipient's foreign tax credit withheld and paid on interest; (e) payments of any interest on bearer certificates of deposit.
Form 1099-MISC, Miscellaneous Income (See Figure 4–16)	For reporting miscellaneous income, such as rents, royalties, commissions, fees, prizes, and awards of at least $600 paid to nonemployees, and any backup withholding. Gross royalty payments of $10 or more must also be reported on this form. Life insurance companies may use either 1099-MISC or Form W-2 to report payments to full-time life insurance sales agents.
Form 1099-PATR, Taxable Distributions Received from Cooperatives	For cooperatives to report patronage dividends paid and other distributions made that total $10 or more during the year.
Form 1099-R, Distributions from Pensions, Annuities, Retirement or Profit-Sharing Plans, IRAs, Insurance Contracts, etc.	For reporting all distributions from pensions, annuities, profit-sharing and retirement plans, and individual retirement arrangements made by employees' trusts or funds; federal, state, or local government retirement system; life insurance companies.
Form 5498, Individual Retirement Arrangement Information *Form 8027, Employer's Annual Information Return of Tip Income and Allocated Tips*	For reporting contributions received from each person to an IRA or simplified employee pension plan (SEP) and qualified deductible voluntary employee contributions to a plan maintained by the employer.

To transmit each type of Form 1099 to the IRS, the employer uses ***Form 1096, Annual Summary and Transmittal of U.S. Information Returns.*** Employers use a separate Form 1096 to transmit each type of information return. For example, one Form 1096 is used to transmit all Forms 1099-MISC (see Figure 4–16), and another Form 1096 is used to transmit all Forms 1099-INT. The employer files Form 1096 and all accompanying forms to the IRS on or before the last day of February of the year following the payment. For returns filed electronically, the due date is March 31. Penalties previously listed for late submission of Forms W-2 also apply to the Form 1099 series (see page 4-30).

IRS CONNECTION

The IRS estimates that self-employed taxpayers are underpaying their taxes by at least $81 billion. These nonwage workers are not caught because payers do not always report these payments to the IRS.

Independent Contractor Payments

Payments made to independent contractors (individuals or partnerships) of at least $600 must be reported on Form 1099-Miscellaneous Income. This does not apply to contractors who are incorporated unless the payments are medical or health-care related. Since payments to these independent contractors are not generated by payroll departments, the accounts payable departments usually complete the appropriate 1099 forms.

Form 1099-MISC can also be provided electronically to any recipient who has consented to receive the form in this manner.

Backup Withholding

Independent contractors must provide taxpayer identification numbers (TIN) to their employers (orally, in writing, or on Form W-9). If this is not done and the company anticipates paying the contractor $600 or more, the company must withhold federal income

FIGURE 4–16

Form 1099-MISC, Miscellaneous Income

9595 ☐ VOID ☐ CORRECTED

PAYER'S name, street address, city, state, ZIP code, and telephone no.
Worldwide Publishing Co.
40 Fifth Avenue
New York, NY 10011-4000
(212) 555-2000

1 Rents $

2 Royalties $ 34,970.65

OMB No. 1545-0115

20--

Form **1099-MISC**

Miscellaneous Income

3 Other income $

4 Federal income tax withheld $

Copy A

For Internal Revenue Service Center

File with Form 1096.

PAYER'S federal identification number 75-4013736

RECIPIENT'S identification number 461-91-4821

5 Fishing boat proceeds $

6 Medical and health care payments $

RECIPIENT'S name
Laurie T. Musberger

7 Nonemployee compensation $

8 Substitute payments in lieu of dividends or interest $

For Privacy Act and Paperwork Reduction Act Notice, see the **20-- General Instructions for Forms 1099, 1098, 5498, and W-2G.**

Street address (including apt. no.)
1043 Maple Drive

9 Payer made direct sales of $5,000 or more of consumer products to a buyer (recipient) for resale ► ☐

10 Crop insurance proceeds $

City, state, and ZIP code
Chicago, IL 60615-3443

11

12

Account number (see instructions)

2nd TIN not. ☐

13 Excess golden parachute payments $

14 Gross proceeds paid to an attorney $

15a Section 409A deferrals $

15b Section 409A income $

16 State tax withheld $ $

17 State/Payer's state no. 85-33378

18 State income $ $

Form **1099-MISC**

Department of the Treasury - Internal Revenue Service

taxes of *28 percent* of the payments made. This withholding must continue until the number is reported. Failure to withhold will result in the payer being held liable by the IRS for the 28 percent withholding.

NONPAYROLL REPORTING

Payroll income tax withholdings are reported on Form 941, while nonpayroll items are reported on Form 945, ***Annual Return of Withheld Federal Income Tax.*** Nonpayroll items include backup withholdings and withholdings on pensions, IRAs, gambling winnings, and military retirement pay. Generally, all income tax witholdings that are reported on Form 1099 or Form W-2G belong on Form 945.

Electronic Filing Form W-2 and Information Returns

on the *NET*

For electronic filing of tax return and payment options, go to: **Electronic Filing for Businesses:** http://www.eftps.gov/eftps/.

If employers file 250 or more Forms W-2 or other information returns (for each type of information return), they must use electronic filing instead of paper forms. Filing Forms W-2 does not require approval of the medium by the Social Security Administration. The employer must complete ***Form 4419, Application for Filing Information Returns Electronically,*** and file it with the IRS.

Withholding State Income Tax

LEARNING OBJECTIVE 11

In addition to federal income taxes, many states also have income tax withholding requirements. The situation is further complicated if an employer has employees in several states. This requires employers to know how much tax to withhold, what types of employees and payments are exempt, and how to pay the tax.

In general, state income taxes should be withheld based on where the services are performed unless there is a reciprocal agreement between the states. If there is no such agreement and the employee works in one state and lives in another, the laws of both states must be considered.

on the *JOB*

Only nine states do not have a state income tax—Alaska, Florida, Nevada, New Hampshire, South Dakota, Tennessee, Texas, Washington, and Wyoming.

The three different methods of withholding are:

1. Full taxation—both resident's state and work state calculate the taxes without any credits.
2. Leftover taxation—pay the full tax to the work state, and then pay the rest to the resident state.
3. Reciprocity—withhold only for the work state or resident state depending on the reciprocal agreement between the states.[1]

Employers must also be informed about each state's regulations regarding:

1. The required frequency of making wage payments.
2. The acceptable media of payment.
3. The maximum interval between the end of a pay period and the payday for that period.
4. The time limits for making final wage payments to employees who are discharged, laid off, quit, or go on strike.
5. How often to inform employees of the deductions made from their wages.
6. The maximum amount of unpaid wages to pay the surviving spouse or family of a deceased worker.

1 "State Tax Issues for Travelling and Telecommuting Employees," *Pay State Update,* American Payroll Association, May 30, 2002, Issue 11, p. 2.

Wage-bracket tables and percentage method formulas are used in many states to determine the amount of state income taxes to withhold from their employees' wages. Each state also determines for state income tax purposes the taxability status of the various fringe benefits discussed in this chapter. Even though most states do not tax deductions made for cafeteria plans and 401(k) accounts, some states do not allow for the tax sheltering of these deductions from employees' wages. Once again, it is the employers' responsibility to know the laws of the states in which they conduct business.

Most states having income tax laws require employers to withhold tax from both nonresidents and residents, unless a **reciprocal agreement** exists with one or more states to the contrary. For example, a reciprocal agreement may exist between two states where both states grant an exemption to nonresidents who work in each of those states.

Even though there is no law requiring an employer to withhold income tax from the employee's home state if the employer has no physical presence in that state, most employers do this as a courtesy to their out-of-state employees.

STATE INCOME TAX RETURNS AND REPORTS

Payroll managers should be familiar with four main types of state income tax returns or reports:

1. **Periodic withholding returns** on which you report the wages paid and the state tax withheld during the reporting period. Figure 4–17 shows the ***Payroll Tax Deposit Coupon*** used by employers in California. Depending on the amount of state income taxes withheld for each quarterly period, employers may be required to pay the taxes semimonthly, monthly, or quarterly. Some states require employers to deposit their withheld income taxes through electronic funds transfer (EFT).
2. **Reconciliation returns** that compare the total amount of state tax paid as shown on the periodic returns with the amounts of state tax declared to have been withheld from employees' wages. Figure 4–18 shows the ***Quarterly Wage and Withholding Report*** for use by employers in California. Employers may submit their information on magnetic media.

FIGURE 4–17

Form DE 88ALL, California Payroll Tax Deposit

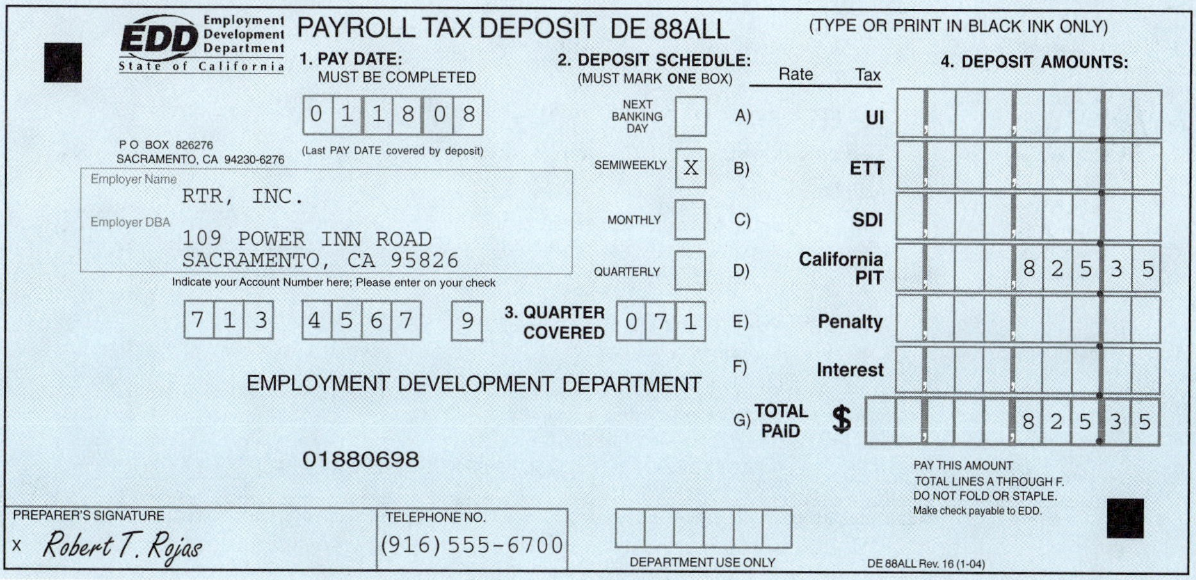

EDD Employment Development Department State of California

PAYROLL TAX DEPOSIT DE 88ALL (TYPE OR PRINT IN BLACK INK ONLY)

1. PAY DATE: MUST BE COMPLETED
0 1 1 8 0 8
(Last PAY DATE covered by deposit)

2. DEPOSIT SCHEDULE: (MUST MARK **ONE** BOX)

			Rate	Tax	4. DEPOSIT AMOUNTS:
NEXT BANKING DAY		A)		UI	
SEMIWEEKLY	X	B)		ETT	
MONTHLY		C)		SDI	
QUARTERLY		D)		California PIT	825.35
		E)		Penalty	
		F)		Interest	
		G)		TOTAL PAID $	825.35

P O BOX 826276
SACRAMENTO, CA 94230-6276

Employer Name
RTR, INC.
Employer DBA
109 POWER INN ROAD
SACRAMENTO, CA 95826

Indicate your Account Number here; Please enter on your check
713 4567 9

3. QUARTER COVERED 071

EMPLOYMENT DEVELOPMENT DEPARTMENT

01880698

PAY THIS AMOUNT
TOTAL LINES A THROUGH F.
DO NOT FOLD OR STAPLE.
Make check payable to EDD.

PREPARER'S SIGNATURE
x Robert T. Rojas

TELEPHONE NO.
(916) 555-6700

DEPARTMENT USE ONLY

DE 88ALL Rev. 16 (1-04)

FIGURE 4-18

Form DE 6, California Quarterly Wage and Withholding Report

EDD Employment Development Department State of California

Page number ______ of ______

QUARTERLY WAGE AND WITHHOLDING REPORT

PLEASE TYPE THIS FORM PER INSTRUCTIONS ON REVERSE

You must FILE this report even if you had no payroll. If you had no payroll, complete Items C or D and P.

00060198

YR QTR

QUARTER ENDED 331

DUE 04 30 08

DELINQUENT IF NOT POSTMARKED OR RECEIVED BY 04 30 08

EMPLOYER ACCOUNT NO.

VIRENG COMPANY
1817 KRESSON ROAD
SACRAMENTO CA 95826

DO NOT ALTER THIS AREA

P1 C T S W A

EFFECTIVE DATE Mo. Day Yr. WIC

A. **EMPLOYEES** full-time and part-time who worked during or received pay subject to UI for the payroll period **which includes the 12th** of the month.

1st Mo. 2nd Mo. 3rd Mo.

B. Check this box if you are reporting ONLY Voluntary Plan DI wages on this page. Report PIT Wages and PIT Withheld, if appropriate. (See instructions for Item B.)

C. NO PAYROLL

D. OUT OF BUSINESS/FINAL REPORT Date ______

E. SOCIAL SECURITY NUMBER	F. EMPLOYEE NAME (FIRST NAME)	(M.I.)	(LAST NAME)	G. TOTAL SUBJECT WAGES	H. PIT WAGES	I. PIT WITHHELD
199 87 6399	MARIA	L	GOSHEN	5009.25	5009.25	55.25
199 16 7931	CARMEN	M	RODGERS	7195.00	7195.00	95.03
199 80 8001	JOSEPH	N	NYUGEN	10319.00	10319.00	120.77
199 91 9114	ELAINE	M	SCHMIDT	15910.00	15910.00	724.62
199 16 4091	JOHN	V	VIRENG	28350.00	28350.00	1383.98

J. TOTAL SUBJECT WAGES THIS PAGE 0.00

K. TOTAL PIT WAGES THIS PAGE 0.00

L. TOTAL PIT WITHHELD THIS PAGE 0.00

M. GRAND TOTAL SUBJECT WAGES

N. GRAND TOTAL PIT WAGES

O. GRAND TOTAL PIT WITHHELD

P. *I declare that the information herein is true and correct to the best of my knowledge and belief.*

Preparer's Signature *John V. Vireng* Title PRESIDENT (Owner, Accountant, Preparer, etc.) Phone (916) 555-8121 Date 4/30/08

DE 6 Rev. 4 (2-04) MAIL TO: State of California / Employment Development Department / P.O. Box 826288 / Sacramento, CA 94230-6288

CU

3. **Annual statements** to employees showing the amount of wages paid during the year and the state tax withheld from those wages.
4. **Information returns** used to report payments to individuals that are not subject to withholding and/or are not reported on the annual employee wage and tax statements. See Figure 4–15, on page 4-32, for a listing of the major information returns.

Since the requirements for transmitting returns and reports vary from state to state, employers should become familiar with the tax regulations of the state in which their business is located and of the state or states in which their employees reside. Because federal regulations require filing of information returns on magnetic media, many states permit employers to submit wage information on magnetic disk or tape. Also, many states take part in the Combined Federal/State Filing Program, which enables employers to file information returns with the federal government and authorize release of the information to the applicable state. To participate in this program, employers must first obtain permission from the IRS.

WITHHOLDING LOCAL INCOME TAXES

In addition to state income tax laws, many cities and counties have passed local income tax legislation requiring employers to deduct and withhold income taxes or license fees on salaries or wages paid. In Alabama, several cities have license fee ordinances that require the withholding of the fees from employees' wages. Certain employees in Denver, Colorado, are subject to the withholding of the Denver Occupational Privilege Tax from their compensation. In Kentucky, a number of cities and counties impose a license fee (payroll tax).

Figure 4–19 shows the coupon that must be completed by employers in Philadelphia. All must withhold the city income tax from compensation paid their employees. Depending upon the amount of taxes withheld, employers may be required to make deposits weekly, monthly, or quarterly. For any late payments of the tax, the city imposes a penalty on the underpayment. Employers must file annual reconciliation returns by the end of February, reporting the amount of taxes deducted during the preceding calendar year.

FIGURE 4–19

Philadelphia Wage Tax Coupon

Monthly Wage Tax

WEINER, INC.
820 ALLEN DRIVE
AMBLER, PA 19002-0882

Account #: **3256301** From: **12/1**

Tax Type: **01** To: **12/31**

Period/Yr: **4/--** Due Date: **1/15**

Signature: Robert T. Rojas
I hereby certify that I have examined this return and that it is correct to the best of my knowledge.

Phone #: (215) 555-6700

Philadelphia Revenue Department
P.O. Box 8040
Philadelphia, PA 19101-8040

1. TAX DUE PER WORKSHEET, *Line 8* — 1,088 | 50
2. INTEREST AND PENALTY — -0-
3. TOTAL DUE (LINE 1 & 2) — 1,088 | 50

Make checks payable to:
CITY OF PHILADELPHIA

33301043097000000000610004400000000000000000000000092978010000000000002

KEY TERMS

Annualizing wages *(p. 4-18)*
Backup withholding *(p. 4-31)*
Defined contribution plan *(p. 4-9)*
Earned income credit (EIC) *(p. 4-22)*
Gross-up supplementals *(p. 4-21)*
Information returns *(p. 4-32)*
Part-year employment *(p. 4-18)*
Percentage method *(p. 4-15)*
Personal allowance *(p. 4-11)*
Quarterly averaging *(p. 4-18)*
Reciprocal agreement *(p. 4-35)*
Special withholding allowance *(p. 4-12)*
Standard deduction *(p. 4-16)*
Supplemental wage payments *(p. 4-19)*
Wage and tax statements *(p. 4-25)*
Wage-bracket method *(p. 4-15)*
Wages *(p. 4-4)*

CHAPTER SUMMARY

This unit begins with a detailed examination of taxable and nontaxable fringe benefits and the withholding of income taxes on these benefits. The effect of pretax salary reductions for cafeteria plans and retirement accounts was then discussed along with the amount of contributions that could be made by the employee and employer into these types of accounts.

The major focus of this chapter is the determination of the amount of federal income tax to withhold from employees' paychecks. The two main methods (the Percentage and Wage-Bracket) use the gross pay, the marital status, and the number of withholding allowances (each allowance is a $3,400 deduction from taxable earnings) to determine the tax to be withheld. Form W-4, which must be completed by each employee, provides the marital status, allowance information, and also the status as exempt from tax or additional amounts to be withheld.

Supplemental pays (vacation, bonuses, commissions, etc.) must also be taxed—either lumped in with the regular pay or as a straight percent (25% or 35%). The formula used to gross-up supplemental pays to an intended amount was also applied.

The completion of Form W-5, the addition of the earned income credits into eligible employees' paychecks, and the actual payments to the employees along with the source of the funds for these payments are the basics of the Advanced Earned Income Credit discussion.

The reporting of information from Form W-2, Form W-3, Form 1099, and the filing of and corrections to these forms completes Chapter 4.

MATCHING QUIZ

J 1. Taxable tips
E 2. Personal allowance
I 3. Backup withholding
A 4. Form W-5
B 5. Roth IRA
F 6. Standard deduction
H 7. Pretax salary reductions
C 8. Form 1096
G 9. Nontaxable fringe benefits
D 10. Flexible reporting

A. Earned Income Credit Advance Payment Certificate
B. Annual nondeductible contributions of up to $5,000
C. Annual summary and transmittal of U.S. information returns
D. Allows employers to use any basis as the time period for payment of noncash fringe benefits
E. $3,400 deduction in computing taxable income
F. Withholdings from gross pay that reduce the amount of pay subject to federal income tax
G. Qualified employee discounts
H. Amount of money used to reduce an individual's adjusted gross income to taxable income
I. Withhold federal income taxes of 28 percent of payments made
J. $20 or more in a month

QUESTIONS FOR REVIEW

NOTE: Use Tax Tables A and B at the back of this textbook and the tax regulations presented in this chapter to answer all questions and solve all problems.

1. How is the amount of a fringe benefit that is taxable to an employee determined?
2. To what extent are cash tips treated as remuneration subject to federal income tax withholding?
3. For each of the following kinds of wage payments, indicate whether or not the wages are exempt from the withholding of federal income taxes:
   a. Three weeks' vacation pay.
   b. Weekly advance to a sales representative for traveling expenses to be incurred.
   c. Weekly wages paid the housekeeper in a college fraternity.
   d. Monthly salary received by Rev. Cole Carpenter.
   e. Payments under a worker's compensation law for sickness or injury.
4. What is the maximum contribution that an employer can make to an employee's SIMPLE account?
5. What is the maximum amount that an employee can shelter into a 401(k) plan?
6. What is a personal allowance? What was the amount of a personal allowance for 2007?
7. Orrin D'Amato, single, participates in his firm's pension retirement plan. This year, his modified adjusted gross income will be about $70,000. How much of his compensation may D'Amato contribute to an IRA this year without paying federal income taxes on the contribution?
8. Are employer contributions into employees' health savings accounts taxed as earnings of the employees?
9. Under what conditions may employees be exempt from the withholding of federal income taxes during 2007? How do such employees indicate their no-tax-liability status?
10. How is the ***special period rule*** for the reporting of fringe benefits applied?
11. Commencing in June, Alan Oldt is eligible to receive monthly payments from a pension fund. What procedure should Oldt follow if he does not wish to have federal income taxes withheld from his periodic pension payments?
12. Rhonda Gramm is single, and her wages are paid weekly. Under the percentage method, what is the amount of Gramm's one weekly withholding allowance? Howard Heinz, married, claims two withholding allowances, and his wages are paid semimonthly. What is the total amount of his semimonthly withholding allowances?
13. What formula is used to "gross-up" supplemental payments in order to cover the taxes on the supplemental payments?
14. Trowbridge Company has just completed the processing of its year-end payroll and distributed all the weekly paychecks. The payroll department is now computing the amount of the annual bonus to be given each worker. What methods may be used by the company in determining the amount of federal income taxes to be withheld from the annual bonus payments?
15. From what source do employers obtain the funds needed to make advance EIC payments to their eligible employees?
16. What is Form 944?
17. Why must some employers file Form 1096?
18. What is the penalty for filing W-2s with mismatched names and social security numbers?
19. What are the penalties imposed on employees for filing false information on Form W-4?
20. Under what conditions must employers submit copies of Form W-4 to the IRS?

QUESTIONS FOR DISCUSSION

1. Alex Oberstar, a cook in the Lagomarsino Company cafeteria, is furnished two meals each day during his eight-hour shift. Oberstar's duties require him to have his meals on the company's premises. Should the cash value of Oberstar's meals be included as part of his taxable wages? Explain.
2. Barbri Company ordinarily pays its employees on a weekly basis. Recently, one of the employees, Bernard Nagle, was sent from the home office on a three-week trip. Nagle has now returned to the office, and you are preparing a single check covering his three-week services. Should you withhold federal income taxes on the total gross earnings for the three-week period, or should you compute the federal income taxes as if Nagle were receiving three separate weekly wage payments?
3. Investigate your state's income tax withholding law (or that of some other state assigned by your instructor), and find the answers to the following questions:
   a. Who must withhold the tax?
   b. How are covered employers and covered employees defined?
   c. Are there any reciprocal agreements into which the state has entered? If so, describe them.
   d. How is the withholding rate determined?
   e. What payments are subject to withholding?
   f. What payments are not subject to withholding?
   g. Are there any employee withholding exemptions?
   h. What methods of withholding are permitted?
   i. Describe each of the returns required by the state.
   j. What kinds of information must be retained by employers in their withholding tax records?

k. What penalties are imposed for failure to comply with the withholding law?

l. Are any employers required to deposit their withheld income taxes through electronic funds transfer (EFT)? If so, what requirements does the state impose?

4. Rena Reynolds, one of your firm's workers, has just come into the payroll department and says to you: "I am thinking of amending my Form W-4 so that an additional $10 is withheld each week. That way I will get a fat refund next year. What do you think of my idea?" How would you reply to Reynolds?

5. Anita Leland, a waitress in Atlantis Casino, reported tips of $467 to her employer last year. Two months after she filed her federal income tax return, Leland received a letter from the IRS informing her that she had earned $5,260 in tips rather than the $467 reported and that she owed the government $1,872.94 in back taxes.
   a. How is the IRS able to determine the amount of tips received by a waitress in a casino?
   b. If the IRS is correct in its determination of the tips received, is Atlantis subject to a penalty for not having withheld payroll taxes on all the tips Leland received during the year?

6. Justin Holmes, an ex-employee, is entitled to a taxable fringe benefit during the first part of this year. Because he wasn't paid any wages this year, can his employer report the taxable fringe benefit on Form 1099?

PRACTICAL PROBLEMS—SERIES A

4-1A LO 4.

Jeremy Rymes is a waiter at the Duluxe Lounge. In his first weekly pay in March, he earned $120.00 for the 40 hours he worked. In addition, he reports his tips for February to his employer ($450.00), and the employer withholds the appropriate taxes for the tips from this first pay in March.

Calculate his net take-home pay assuming the employer withheld federal income tax (***wage-bracket,*** married, 2 allowances), social security taxes, and state income tax (2%).

4-2A LO 4.

Use the ***percentage method*** to compute the federal income taxes to withhold from the wages or salaries of each employee.

Employee No.	Employee Name	Marital Status	No. of Withholding Allowances	Gross Wage or Salary	Amount to Be Withheld
1	Amoroso, A.	M	4	$1,610 weekly	________
2	Finley, R.	S	0	$825 biweekly	________
3	Gluck, E.	S	5	$9,630 quarterly	________
4	Quinn, S.	M	8	$925 semimonthly	________
5	Treave, Y.	M	3	$1,975 monthly	________

4-3A LO 4.

Use (a) the percentage method and (b) the wage-bracket method to compute the federal income taxes to withhold from the wages or salaries of each employee.

Employee	Marital Status	No. of Withholding Allowances	Gross Wage or Salary	Amount to Be Withheld: Percentage Method	Amount to Be Withheld: Wage-Bracket Method
Corn, A.	S	2	$675 weekly	________	________
Fogge, P.	S	1	$1,960 weekly	________	________
Felps, S.	M	6	$1,775 biweekly	________	________
Carson, W.	M	4	$2,480 semimonthly	________	________
Helm, M.	M	9	$5,380 monthly	________	________

4-4A LO 4.

Eaton Enterprises uses the ***wage-bracket method*** to determine federal income tax withholding on its employees.

Determine the amount to withhold from the wages paid each employee.

Employee	Marital Status	No. of Withholding Allowances	Payroll Period W=Weekly S=Semimonthly M=Monthly D=Daily	Wage	Amount to Be Withheld
Hal Bower	M	1	W	$1,350	________
Ruth Cramden	S	1	W	590	________
Gil Jones	S	3	W	675	________
Teresa Kern	M	6	M	4,090	________
Ruby Long	M	2	M	2,730	________
Katie Luis	M	8	S	955	________
Susan Martin	S	1	D	96	________
Jim Singer	S	4	S	2,610	________
Martin Torres	M	4	M	3,215	________

4-5A LO 4.

The names of the employees of Hogan Thrift Shop are listed on the following payroll register. Employees are paid weekly. The marital status and the number of allowances claimed are shown on the payroll register, along with each employee's weekly salary, which has remained the same all year. Complete the payroll register for the payroll period ending December 19, the 51st weekly payday. The state income tax rate is 2% of total earnings, the city income tax rate is 1.5% of the total gross earnings, and the ***wage-bracket method*** is used for federal income taxes.

HOGAN THRIFT SHOP

PAYROLL REGISTER

FOR PERIOD ENDING 20

EMPLOYEE NAME	MARITAL STATUS	NO. OF W/H ALLOW.	TOTAL EARNINGS	DEDUCTIONS (a) FICA 6.2% OASDI	(a) FICA 1.45% HI	(b) FIT	(c) SIT 2%	(d) CIT 1.5%	(e) NET PAY
Green, Tom	*M*	*3*	*2,060 00*	0	29 87	292 12	41 20	30 90	1,665 91
Morris, Maive	*S*	*1*	*285 00*	17 67	4 13	18 00	5 70	4 28	235 22
Schmidt, Beth	*M*	*0*	*255 00*	15 81	3 70	10 00	5 10	3 83	216 56
Carr, Herman	*S*	*3*	*324 25*	20 10	4 70	8 00	6 49	4 86	280 10
Hadt, Ronnie	*S*	*1*	*475 00*	29 45	6 89	47 00	9 50	7 13	375 03
Camp, Kevin	*S*	*2*	*558 50*	34 63	8 10	49 00	11 17	8 38	447 22
Wilson, Ronda	*S*	*1*	*470 50*	29 17	6 82	47 00	9 41	7 08	371 02
Gleason, Wendy	*M*	*3*	*880 00*	54 56	12 76	65 00	17 60	13 20	716 88
Totals			5,307.75	201 39	76 97	536 12	106 17	79 66	4,307 94

Compute the employer's FICA taxes for the pay period ending December 19.

OASDI Taxes

OASDI taxable earnings $ 3248.25

OASDI taxes $ 201.39

HI Taxes

HI taxable earnings $ 5307.75

HI taxes $ 76.96

4-6A LO 4.

Damerly Company (a California employer) wants to give a holiday bonus check of $250 to each employee. Since it wants the check amount to be $250, it will need to gross up the amount of the bonus. Calculate the withholding taxes and the gross amount of the bonus to be made to John Rolen if his cumulative earnings for the year are $46,910. Besides being subject to social security taxes and federal income tax (supplemental rate), a 6% California income tax must be withheld on supplemental payments.

4-7A LO 4.

Julie Whiteweiler made $930 this week. Only social security (fully taxable) and federal income taxes attach to her pay. Julie contributes $100 each week to her company's 401(k) plan and has $25 put into her health savings account (nonqualified) each week. Her employer matches this $25 each week. Determine Julie's take-home pay if she is single and claims 2 allowances (use the wage-bracket method).

4-8A LO 4,6.

The names of the employees of Cox Security Systems and their regular salaries are shown in the following payroll register. Note that Hill and Van Dyne are paid monthly on the last payday, while all others are paid weekly.

In addition to the regular salaries, the company pays an annual bonus based on the amount of earnings for the year. For the current year, the bonus amounts to 8% of the annual salary paid to each employee. The bonus is to be paid along with the regular salaries on December 26, but the amount of the bonus and the amount of the regular salary will be shown separately on each employee's earnings statement. Assume that all employees received their regular salary during the entire year.

Prepare the payroll for the pay period ending December 26, showing the following for each employee:

- Use the ***wage-bracket method*** to withhold federal income tax from the regular salaries.
- Withhold a flat 25% on the annual bonus.
- Total salaries and bonuses are subject to a 2% state income tax and a 1% city income tax.

FOR PERIOD ENDING ____________ 20__

EMPLOYEE NAME	MARITAL STATUS	NO. OF W/H ALLOW.	EARNINGS			DEDUCTIONS					(g) NET PAY
			REGULAR	(a) SUPP'L.	(b) TOTAL	(c) FICA		(d) FIT	(e) SIT	(f) CIT	
						OASDI	HI				
Hill, J. Harvey	*M*	*5*	*5,500.00* (M)*								
Van Dyne, Joyce S.	*M*	*2*	*2,850.00* (M)*								
Abbott, Leslie N.	*S*	*1*	*520.00*								
Bunger, Russel L.	*M*	*4*	*465.00*								
Noblet, Thomas D.	*M*	*2*	*380.00*								
Short, Frank C.	*S*	*1*	*350.00*								
Toban, Harriette O.	*M*	*2*	*575.00*								
Wyeth, Amy R.	*S*	*0*	*425.00*								
Totals											

Compute the employer's FICA taxes for the pay period ending December 26.

OASDI Taxes
OASDI taxable earnings $ ____________
OASDI taxes $ ____________

HI Taxes
HI taxable earnings $ ____________
HI taxes $ ____________

(M)* indicates monthly pay.

4-9A LO 4,6.

During the quarter ending December 31 of the current year, Cox Security Systems had 13 weekly paydays and three monthly paydays.

a. Total earnings paid during the quarter, including both the regular and the supplemental earnings.

b. Total amount of FICA taxes withheld during the quarter.

c. Total amount of federal income taxes withheld during the quarter.

Using the data given in Problem 4–8A, complete the following form to show:

d. Total amount of state income taxes withheld during the quarter.

e. Total amount of city income taxes withheld during the quarter.

f. Total net amount paid each employee during the quarter.

EMPLOYEE NAME	(a) TOTAL EARNINGS	DEDUCTIONS					(f) NET PAY
		(b) FICA		(c) FIT	(d) SIT	(e) CIT	
		OASDI	HI				
Hill, J. Harvey							
Van Dyne, Joyce S.							
Abbott, Leslie N.							
Bunger, Russel L.							
Noblet, Thomas D.							
Short, Frank C.							
Toban, Harriette O.							
Wyeth, Amy R.							
Totals							

4-10A LO 4,7.

The employees of Greevale Landscape Center are paid weekly. The names of five employees of the company are given on the following payroll register. The payroll register also shows the marital status and number of withholding allowances claimed and the total weekly earnings for each worker. Assume that each employee is paid the same weekly wage on each payday in 2008. Also shown below is the wage-bracket table for advance earned income credit (EIC) payments for a weekly payroll period. Each employee listed on the payroll register has completed a Form W-5 indicating that the worker is not married. Complete the payroll register for the weekly period ending November 14, 2008. The state income tax rate is 1.5% on total earnings and the ***wage-bracket tables*** are used for federal income tax.

EMPLOYEE NAME	MARITAL STATUS	NO. OF W/H ALLOW.	TOTAL EARNINGS	DEDUCTIONS (a) FICA OASDI	HI	(b) FIT	(c) SIT	(d) ADVANCE EIC PAYMENT	(e) NET PAY
Arnold, C.	*S*	*4*	*229 00*						
Catus, M.	*S*	*1*	*412 00*						
Farland, R.	*S*	*2*	*215 00*						
McMann, W.	*S*	*3*	*376 00*						
Rudolph, A.	*S*	*1*	*125 00*						
Totals									

WEEKLY Payroll Period

SINGLE or HEAD OF HOUSEHOLD

Wages— At least	But less than	Payment to be made	Wages— At least	But less than	Payment to be made	Wages— At least	But less than	Payment to be made	Wages— At least	But less than	Payment to be made	Wages— At least	But less than	Payment to be made
$0	$5	$0	$70	$75	$14	$140	$145	$29	$385	$395	$23	$525	$535	$10
5	10	1	75	80	15	145	150	30	395	405	22	535	545	9
10	15	2	80	85	16	150	155	31	405	415	22	545	555	8
15	20	3	85	90	17	155	160	32	415	425	21	555	565	7
20	25	4	90	95	18	160	295	33	425	435	20	565	575	6
25	30	5	95	100	19	295	305	32	435	445	19	575	585	5
30	35	6	100	105	20	305	315	31	445	455	18	585	595	4
35	40	7	105	110	21	315	325	30	455	465	17	595	605	3
40	45	8	110	115	22	325	335	29	465	475	16	605	615	2
45	50	9	115	120	23	335	345	28	475	485	15	615	625	1
50	55	10	120	125	24	345	355	27	485	495	14	625	- - -	0
55	60	11	125	130	26	355	365	26	495	505	13			
60	65	12	130	135	27	365	375	25	505	515	12			
65	70	13	135	140	28	375	385	24	515	525	11			

4-11A LO 4.

Mattola Company is giving each of its employees a holiday bonus of $100 on December 24 (a nonpayday). The company wants each employee's check to be $100. The supplemental tax percent is used.

a. What will be the gross amount of each bonus if each employee pays a state income tax of 2.8% (besides the other payroll taxes)? $________

b. What would the net amount of each bonus check be if the company did not gross up the bonus? $________

4-12A LO 4.

George Clausen (age 48) is employed by Kline Company and is paid a salary of $42,640. He has just decided to join the company's Simple Retirement Account (IRA form) and has a few questions. Answer the following for Clausen:

a. What is the maximum that he can contribute into this retirement fund? $________

b. What would be the company's contribution? $________

c. What would be his weekly take-home pay with the retirement contribution deducted (married, 2 allowances, ***wage-bracket method,*** and a 2.3% state income tax on total wages)? $________

d. What would be his weekly take-home pay without the retirement contribution deduction? $________

4-13A LO 9.

During the fourth quarter of 2008, there were seven biweekly paydays on Friday (October 3, 17, 31; November 14, 28; December 12, 26) for Emerald City Repair. Using the forms supplied below and on pages 4-47–50, complete the following for the fourth quarter:

a. Federal Tax Deposit Coupons (monthly depositor), Forms 8109. The employer's phone number is (501) 555-7331. Federal Deposit Liability Each Pay, $401.28.

b. Employer's Quarterly Federal Tax Return, Form 941. The form is signed by you.

c. Employer's Report of State Income Tax Withheld for the quarter, due on or before February 2, 2009.

Quarterly Payroll Data

Total Earnings 5 Employees	OASDI	HI	FIT	SIT	EIC Payments
$18,725.00	$1,160.95	$271.53	$1,701.00	$1,310.75	$1,757.00

Employer's OASDI	$1,160.95	
Employer's HI	$271.53	
Federal Deposit Liability Each Pay		$401.28

EMPLOYER'S REPORT OF STATE INCOME TAX WITHHELD

(DO NOT WRITE IN THIS SPACE)

IMPORTANT: PLEASE REFER TO THIS NUMBER IN ANY CORRESPONDENCE →

WITHHOLDING IDENTIFICATION NUMBER	MONTH OF OR QUARTER ENDING
42-7-3301	DEC 08

IF YOU ARE A SEASONAL EMPLOYER AND THIS IS YOUR FINAL REPORT FOR THIS SEASON, CHECK HERE ☐ AND SHOW THE NEXT MONTH IN WHICH YOU WILL PAY WAGES.

EMERALD CITY REPAIR
10 SUMMIT SQUARE
CITY, STATE 00000-0000

IF NAME OR ADDRESS IS INCORRECT, PLEASE MAKE CORRECTIONS.

THIS REPORT MUST BE RETURNED EVEN IF NO AMOUNT HAS BEEN WITHHELD

1. GROSS PAYROLL THIS PERIOD	$	
2. STATE INCOME TAX WITHHELD	$	
3. ADJUSTMENT FOR PREVIOUS PERIOD(S). (ATTACH STATEMENT)	$	
4. TOTAL ADJUSTED TAX (LINE 2 PLUS OR MINUS LINE 3)	$	
5. PENALTY (35% OF LINE 4)		
6. INTEREST		
7. TOTAL AMOUNT DUE AND PAYABLE	$	

Under penalties prescribed by law, I hereby affirm that to the best of my knowledge and belief this return, including any accompanying schedules and statements, is true and complete. If prepared by a person other than taxpayer, his affirmation is based on all information of which he has any knowledge.

SIGNATURE: TITLE: DATE:

MAIL THIS REPORT WITH CHECK OR MONEY ORDER PAYABLE TO THE DEPT. OF REVENUE ON OR BEFORE DUE DATE TO AVOID PENALTY.

4-13A (continued)

AMOUNT OF DEPOSIT (Do NOT type, please print.)

DOLLARS | CENTS

MONTH TAX YEAR ENDS → 12

EMPLOYER IDENTIFICATION NUMBER → 70 2204701

BANK NAME/ DATE STAMP

Name EMERALD CITY REPAIR

Address 10 SUMMIT SQUARE

City CITY

State STATE ZIP 00000-0000

Telephone number ( )

IRS USE ONLY

Darken only one TYPE OF TAX		Darken only one TAX PERIOD
941	945	1st Quarter
990-C	1120	2nd Quarter
943	990-T	3rd Quarter
720	990-PF	4th Quarter
CT-1	1042	
940	944	

76

FOR BANK USE IN MICR ENCODING

Federal Tax Deposit Coupon
Form 8109 (Rev. 12-2005)

To be deposited on or before ____________

AMOUNT OF DEPOSIT (Do NOT type, please print.)

DOLLARS | CENTS

MONTH TAX YEAR ENDS → 12

EMPLOYER IDENTIFICATION NUMBER → 70 2204701

BANK NAME/ DATE STAMP

Name EMERALD CITY REPAIR

Address 10 SUMMIT SQUARE

City CITY

State STATE ZIP 00000-0000

Telephone number ( )

IRS USE ONLY

Darken only one TYPE OF TAX		Darken only one TAX PERIOD
941	945	1st Quarter
990-C	1120	2nd Quarter
943	990-T	3rd Quarter
720	990-PF	4th Quarter
CT-1	1042	
940	944	

76

FOR BANK USE IN MICR ENCODING

Federal Tax Deposit Coupon
Form 8109 (Rev. 12-2005)

To be deposited on or before ____________

4-13A (continued)

AMOUNT OF DEPOSIT (Do NOT type, please print.)	DOLLARS / CENTS
MONTH TAX YEAR ENDS	1 2
EMPLOYER IDENTIFICATION NUMBER	70 2204701
BANK NAME/ DATE STAMP	
Name	EMERALD CITY REPAIR
Address	10 SUMMIT SQUARE
City	CITY
State	STATE
ZIP	00000-0000
Telephone number	( )
IRS USE ONLY	

Darken only one TYPE OF TAX		Darken only one TAX PERIOD
941	945	1st Quarter
990-C	1120	2nd Quarter
943	990-T	3rd Quarter
720	990-PF	4th Quarter
CT-1	1042	
940	944	

76

FOR BANK USE IN MICR ENCODING

Federal Tax Deposit Coupon
Form 8109 (Rev. 12-2005)

To be deposited on or before ____________

4-13A (continued)

Form **941 for 20--: Employer's QUARTERLY Federal Tax Return** 990107

(Rev. January 2007) Department of the Treasury — Internal Revenue Service OMB No. 1545-0029

(EIN) Employer identification number: 7 0 – 2 2 0 4 7 0 1

Name (*not your trade name*): EMERALD CITY REPAIR

Trade name (*if any*):

Address: 10 SUMMIT SQUARE
Number Street Suite or room number

CITY ST 00000
City State ZIP code

Report for this Quarter of 20-- (Check one.)

☐ **1:** January, February, March
☐ **2:** April, May, June
☐ **3:** July, August, September
☐ **4:** October, November, December

Read the separate instructions before you fill out this form. Please type or print within the boxes.

Part 1: Answer these questions for this quarter.

1 **Number of employees who received wages, tips, or other compensation for the pay period including:** ***Mar. 12*** **(Quarter 1),** ***June 12*** **(Quarter 2),** ***Sept. 12*** **(Quarter 3),** ***Dec. 12*** **(Quarter 4)** . . . 1 ______

2 **Wages, tips, and other compensation** . . . 2 ______ .

3 **Total income tax withheld from wages, tips, and other compensation** . . . 3 ______ .

4 **If no wages, tips, and other compensation are subject to social security or Medicare tax** . . ☐ Check and go to line 6.

5 **Taxable social security and Medicare wages and tips:**

	Column 1		*Column 2*
5a **Taxable social security wages**	.	× .124 =	.
5b **Taxable social security tips**	.	× .124 =	.
5c **Taxable Medicare wages & tips**	.	× .029 =	.

5d **Total social security and Medicare taxes** (*Column 2*, lines 5a + 5b + 5c = line 5d) . . 5d ______ .

6 **Total taxes before adjustments** (lines 3 + 5d = line 6) . . . 6 ______ .

7 **TAX ADJUSTMENTS** (Read the instructions for line 7 before completing lines 7a through 7h.):

7a **Current quarter's fractions of cents** . . . ______ .

7b **Current quarter's sick pay** . . . ______ .

7c **Current quarter's adjustments for tips and group-term life insurance** ______ .

7d **Current year's income tax withholding** (attach Form 941c) . . . ______ .

7e **Prior quarters' social security and Medicare taxes** (attach Form 941c) ______ .

7f **Special additions to federal income tax** (attach Form 941c) . . . ______ .

7g **Special additions to social security and Medicare** (attach Form 941c) ______ .

7h **TOTAL ADJUSTMENTS** (Combine all amounts: lines 7a through 7g.) . . . 7h ______ .

8 **Total taxes after adjustments** (Combine lines 6 and 7h.) . . . 8 ______ .

9 **Advance earned income credit (EIC) payments made to employees** . . . 9 ______ .

10 **Total taxes after adjustment for advance EIC** (line 8 – line 9 = line 10) . . . 10 ______ .

11 **Total deposits for this quarter, including overpayment applied from a prior quarter** . . . 11 ______ .

12 **Balance due** (If line 10 is more than line 11, write the difference here.) . . . 12 ______ .
Follow the Instructions for Form 941-V, Payment Voucher.

13 **Overpayment** (If line 11 is more than line 10, write the difference here.) ______ . Check one ☐ Apply to next return. ☐ Send a refund.

▶ You **MUST** fill out both pages of this form and **SIGN** it.

Next ➔

For Privacy Act and Paperwork Reduction Act Notice, see the back of the Payment Voucher. Cat. No. 17001Z Form **941** (Rev. 1-2007)

990207

Name *(not your trade name)* | Employer identification number (EIN)

Part 2: Tell us about your deposit schedule and tax liability for this quarter.

If you are unsure about whether you are a monthly schedule depositor or a semiweekly schedule depositor, see *Pub. 15 (Circular E),* section 11.

14 ☐☐ **Write the state abbreviation for the state where you made your deposits** OR **write "MU" if you made your deposits in *multiple* states.**

15 **Check one:** ☐ **Line 10 is less than $2,500.** Go to Part 3.

☐ **You were a monthly schedule depositor for the entire quarter. Fill out your tax liability for each month.** Then go to Part 3.

Tax liability: Month 1 ______ .

Month 2 ______ .

Month 3 ______ .

Total liability for quarter ______ . **Total must equal line 10.**

☐ **You were a semiweekly schedule depositor for any part of this quarter.** Fill out *Schedule B (Form 941): Report of Tax Liability for Semiweekly Schedule Depositors,* and attach it to this form.

Part 3: Tell us about your business. If a question does NOT apply to your business, leave it blank.

16 **If your business has closed or you stopped paying wages** . . . . ☐ Check here, and

enter the final date you paid wages ___ / ___ / ___ .

17 **If you are a seasonal employer and you do not have to file a return for every quarter of the year** . . ☐ Check here.

Part 4: May we speak with your third-party designee?

Do you want to allow an employee, a paid tax preparer, or another person to discuss this return with the IRS? (See the instructions for details.)

☐ Yes. Designee's name ______

Select a 5-digit Personal Identification Number (PIN) to use when talking to IRS. ☐☐☐☐☐

☐ No.

Part 5: Sign here. You MUST fill out both pages of this form and SIGN it.

Under penalties of perjury, I declare that I have examined this return, including accompanying schedules and statements, and to the best of my knowledge and belief, it is true, correct, and complete.

X Sign your name here ______

Print your name here ______

Print your title here ______

Date ___ / ___ / ___

Best daytime phone ( ) –

Part 6: For paid preparers only *(optional)*

Paid Preparer's Signature ______

Firm's name ______

Address ______ EIN ______

______ ZIP code ______

Date ___ / ___ / ___ Phone ( ) – SSN/PTIN ______

☐ Check if you are self-employed.

Page **2** | Form **941** (Rev. 1-2007)

4-14A LO 4,8.

During the first week of 2009, the Payroll Department of Quigley Corporation is preparing the Forms W-2 for distribution to its employees along with their payroll checks on January 9. In this problem, you will complete six of the forms in order to gain some experience in recording the different kinds of information required.

Assume each employee earned the same weekly salary for each of the 52 paydays in 2008.

Using the following information obtained from the personnel and payroll records of the firm, complete Copy A of the six Forms W-2 reproduced on the following pages. Also complete Form W-3. The form is to be signed by the president, Kenneth T. Ford, and is prepared by Ralph I. Volpe.

Company Information:

Address: 4800 River Road
Philadelphia, PA 19113-5548
Telephone number: (215) 555-0017
Fax number: (215) 555-0010

Pennsylvania State identification number:	46-3-1066
Federal identification number:	13-7490972
Philadelphia identification number:	4731895

Income Tax Information:

The wage-bracket method is used to determine federal income tax withholding. Calculate the annual federal income tax withheld by using the weekly wage-bracket table and multiply the answer by 52. The other taxes withheld are shown below.

Employee Data	Payroll Data	Annual Taxes Withheld	
Kelly B. Roach	Single, 1 allowance	1,337.96	Social security tax withheld
54 Gradison Place	$415 per week	313.04	Medicare tax withheld
Philadelphia, PA 19113-4054	SS#: 376-72-4310	662.48	State income tax withheld
	Deduction for 401(k) plan: $50/week	928.20	Local income tax withheld
Ralph I. Volpe	Married, 1 allowance	1,563.64	Social security tax withheld
56 Andrews Court, Apt. 7	$485 per week	365.56	Medicare tax withheld
Philadelphia, PA 19103-3356	SS#: 272-33-8804	774.28	State income tax withheld
	Dependent care payment: $950	1,084.72	Local income tax withheld
	$70/week—401(k)		
Randi A. Myer	Single, 0 allowances	1,176.76	Social security tax withheld
770 Camac Street	$365 per week	275.08	Medicare tax withheld
Philadelphia, PA 19101-3770	SS#: 178-92-3316	582.92	State income tax withheld
	Union dues withheld: $102	816.40	Local income tax withheld
Kenneth T. Ford	Married, 7 allowances	4,368.69	Social security tax withheld
338 North Side Avenue	$1,350	1,021.96	Medicare tax withheld
Philadelphia, PA 19130-6638	SS#: 269-01-6839	2,155.40	State income tax withheld
	Cost of group-term life insurance exceeding $50,000: $262.75	3,019.12	Local income tax withheld
	No income tax withheld on insurance cost, but FICA taxes are withheld.		
	$100/week—401(k)		
Chrissy C. Carman	Married, 2 allowances	1,031.68	Social security tax withheld
4900 Gladwynne Terrace	$320 per week	241.28	Medicare tax withheld
Philadelphia, PA 19127-0049	SS#: 368-14-5771	510.64	State income tax withheld
	Advance EIC payments: $16 per week	715.52	Local income tax withheld
	Union dues withheld: $102		
Hal B. Zuber	Single, 1 allowance	1,257.36	Social security tax withheld
480-A Hopkinson Tower	$390 per week	294.32	Medicare tax withheld
Philadelphia, PA 19101-3301	SS#: 337-99-8703	622.44	State income tax withheld
	Educational assistance payments (job-required): $675	872.04	Local income tax withheld
	$50/week—401(k)		

4-14A (continued)

22222	Void ☐	a Employee's social security number	For Official Use Only ▶ OMB No. 1545-0008	
b Employer identification number (EIN)			1 Wages, tips, other compensation	2 Federal income tax withheld
c Employer's name, address, and ZIP code			3 Social security wages	4 Social security tax withheld
			5 Medicare wages and tips	6 Medicare tax withheld
			7 Social security tips	8 Allocated tips
d Control number			9 Advance EIC payment	10 Dependent care benefits
e Employee's first name and initial	Last name	Suff.	11 Nonqualified plans	12a See instructions for box 12 Code
			13 Statutory employee ☐ Retirement plan ☐ Third-party sick pay ☐	12b Code
			14 Other	12c Code
f Employee's address and ZIP code				12d Code

15 State	Employer's state ID number	16 State wages, tips, etc.	17 State income tax	18 Local wages, tips, etc.	19 Local income tax	20 Locality name

Form **W-2** **Wage and Tax Statement** **20- -**

Department of the Treasury—Internal Revenue Service

For Privacy Act and Paperwork Reduction Act Notice, see back of Copy D.

Copy A For Social Security Administration — Send this entire page with Form W-3 to the Social Security Administration; photocopies are **not** acceptable.

Cat. No. 10134D

Do Not Cut, Fold, or Staple Forms on This Page — Do Not Cut, Fold, or Staple Forms on This Page

22222	Void ☐	a Employee's social security number	For Official Use Only ▶ OMB No. 1545-0008	
b Employer identification number (EIN)			1 Wages, tips, other compensation	2 Federal income tax withheld
c Employer's name, address, and ZIP code			3 Social security wages	4 Social security tax withheld
			5 Medicare wages and tips	6 Medicare tax withheld
			7 Social security tips	8 Allocated tips
d Control number			9 Advance EIC payment	10 Dependent care benefits
e Employee's first name and initial	Last name	Suff.	11 Nonqualified plans	12a See instructions for box 12 Code
			13 Statutory employee ☐ Retirement plan ☐ Third-party sick pay ☐	12b Code
			14 Other	12c Code
f Employee's address and ZIP code				12d Code

15 State	Employer's state ID number	16 State wages, tips, etc.	17 State income tax	18 Local wages, tips, etc.	19 Local income tax	20 Locality name

Form **W-2** **Wage and Tax Statement** **20- -**

Department of the Treasury—Internal Revenue Service

For Privacy Act and Paperwork Reduction Act Notice, see back of Copy D.

Copy A For Social Security Administration — Send this entire page with Form W-3 to the Social Security Administration; photocopies are **not** acceptable.

Cat. No. 10134D

Do Not Cut, Fold, or Staple Forms on This Page — Do Not Cut, Fold, or Staple Forms on This Page

4-14A (continued)

22222	Void ☐	a Employee's social security number	For Official Use Only ▶ OMB No. 1545-0008
b Employer identification number (EIN)		1 Wages, tips, other compensation	2 Federal income tax withheld
c Employer's name, address, and ZIP code		3 Social security wages	4 Social security tax withheld
		5 Medicare wages and tips	6 Medicare tax withheld
		7 Social security tips	8 Allocated tips
d Control number		9 Advance EIC payment	10 Dependent care benefits
e Employee's first name and initial	Last name / Suff.	11 Nonqualified plans	12a See instructions for box 12 (Code)
		13 Statutory employee ☐ Retirement plan ☐ Third-party sick pay ☐	12b (Code)
		14 Other	12c (Code)
f Employee's address and ZIP code			12d (Code)

15 State / Employer's state ID number	16 State wages, tips, etc.	17 State income tax	18 Local wages, tips, etc.	19 Local income tax	20 Locality name

Form **W-2** **Wage and Tax Statement** 20- -

Department of the Treasury—Internal Revenue Service

For Privacy Act and Paperwork Reduction Act Notice, see back of Copy D.

Cat. No. 10134D

Copy A For Social Security Administration — Send this entire page with Form W-3 to the Social Security Administration; photocopies are **not** acceptable.

Do Not Cut, Fold, or Staple Forms on This Page — Do Not Cut, Fold, or Staple Forms on This Page

22222	Void ☐	a Employee's social security number	For Official Use Only ▶ OMB No. 1545-0008
b Employer identification number (EIN)		1 Wages, tips, other compensation	2 Federal income tax withheld
c Employer's name, address, and ZIP code		3 Social security wages	4 Social security tax withheld
		5 Medicare wages and tips	6 Medicare tax withheld
		7 Social security tips	8 Allocated tips
d Control number		9 Advance EIC payment	10 Dependent care benefits
e Employee's first name and initial	Last name / Suff.	11 Nonqualified plans	12a See instructions for box 12 (Code)
		13 Statutory employee ☐ Retirement plan ☐ Third-party sick pay ☐	12b (Code)
		14 Other	12c (Code)
f Employee's address and ZIP code			12d (Code)

15 State / Employer's state ID number	16 State wages, tips, etc.	17 State income tax	18 Local wages, tips, etc.	19 Local income tax	20 Locality name

Form **W-2** **Wage and Tax Statement** 20- -

Department of the Treasury—Internal Revenue Service

For Privacy Act and Paperwork Reduction Act Notice, see back of Copy D.

Cat. No. 10134D

Copy A For Social Security Administration — Send this entire page with Form W-3 to the Social Security Administration; photocopies are **not** acceptable.

Do Not Cut, Fold, or Staple Forms on This Page — Do Not Cut, Fold, or Staple Forms on This Page

4-14A (continued)

22222 Void ☐ | a Employee's social security number | For Official Use Only ▶ OMB No. 1545-0008

b Employer identification number (EIN)
1 Wages, tips, other compensation
2 Federal income tax withheld
c Employer's name, address, and ZIP code
3 Social security wages
4 Social security tax withheld
5 Medicare wages and tips
6 Medicare tax withheld
7 Social security tips
8 Allocated tips
d Control number
9 Advance EIC payment
10 Dependent care benefits
e Employee's first name and initial | Last name | Suff.
11 Nonqualified plans
12a See instructions for box 12 Code
13 Statutory employee ☐ Retirement plan ☐ Third-party sick pay ☐
12b Code
14 Other
12c Code
12d Code
f Employee's address and ZIP code

15 State | Employer's state ID number | 16 State wages, tips, etc. | 17 State income tax | 18 Local wages, tips, etc. | 19 Local income tax | 20 Locality name

Form **W-2** **Wage and Tax Statement** **20- -**

Department of the Treasury—Internal Revenue Service

For Privacy Act and Paperwork Reduction Act Notice, see back of Copy D.

Cat. No. 10134D

Copy A For Social Security Administration — Send this entire page with Form W-3 to the Social Security Administration; photocopies are **not** acceptable.

Do Not Cut, Fold, or Staple Forms on This Page — Do Not Cut, Fold, or Staple Forms on This Page

22222 Void ☐ | a Employee's social security number | For Official Use Only ▶ OMB No. 1545-0008

b Employer identification number (EIN)
1 Wages, tips, other compensation
2 Federal income tax withheld
c Employer's name, address, and ZIP code
3 Social security wages
4 Social security tax withheld
5 Medicare wages and tips
6 Medicare tax withheld
7 Social security tips
8 Allocated tips
d Control number
9 Advance EIC payment
10 Dependent care benefits
e Employee's first name and initial | Last name | Suff.
11 Nonqualified plans
12a See instructions for box 12 Code
13 Statutory employee ☐ Retirement plan ☐ Third-party sick pay ☐
12b Code
14 Other
12c Code
12d Code
f Employee's address and ZIP code

15 State | Employer's state ID number | 16 State wages, tips, etc. | 17 State income tax | 18 Local wages, tips, etc. | 19 Local income tax | 20 Locality name

Form **W-2** **Wage and Tax Statement** **20- -**

Department of the Treasury—Internal Revenue Service

For Privacy Act and Paperwork Reduction Act Notice, see back of Copy D.

Cat. No. 10134D

Copy A For Social Security Administration — Send this entire page with Form W-3 to the Social Security Administration; photocopies are **not** acceptable.

Do Not Cut, Fold, or Staple Forms on This Page — Do Not Cut, Fold, or Staple Forms on This Page

4-14A (concluded)

DO NOT STAPLE

33333	a Control number	For Official Use Only ▶ OMB No. 1545-0008	
b Kind of Payer: 941 ☐ Military ☐ 943 ☐ 944 ☐ CT-1 ☐ Hshld. emp. ☐ Medicare govt. emp. ☐ Third-party sick pay ☐		1 Wages, tips, other compensation	2 Federal income tax withheld
		3 Social security wages	4 Social security tax withheld
c Total number of Forms W-2	d Establishment number	5 Medicare wages and tips	6 Medicare tax withheld
e Employer identification number (EIN)		7 Social security tips	8 Allocated tips
f Employer's name		9 Advance EIC payments	10 Dependent care benefits
		11 Nonqualified plans	12 Deferred compensation
		13 For third-party sick pay use only	
g Employer's address and ZIP code		14 Income tax withheld by payer of third-party sick pay	
h Other EIN used this year			
15 State	Employer's state ID number	16 State wages, tips, etc.	17 State income tax
		18 Local wages, tips, etc.	19 Local income tax
Contact person		Telephone number ( )	For Official Use Only
Email address		Fax number ( )	

Under penalties of perjury, I declare that I have examined this return and accompanying documents, and, to the best of my knowledge and belief, they are true, correct, and complete.

Signature ▶ Title ▶ Date ▶

Form **W-3 Transmittal of Wage and Tax Statements** 20- -

Department of the Treasury
Internal Revenue Service

Send this entire page with the entire Copy A page of Form(s) W-2 to the Social Security Administration. Photocopies are not acceptable.

4-1B LO 4.

Herman Swayne is a waiter at the Dixie Hotel. In his first weekly pay in March, he earned $160.00 for the 40 hours he worked. In addition, he reports his tips for February to his employer ($700.00), and the employer withholds the appropriate taxes for the tips from this first pay in March.

Calculate his net take-home pay assuming the employer withheld federal income tax (***wage-bracket,*** married, 2 allowances), social security taxes, and state income tax (2%).

4-2B LO 4.

Use the ***percentage method*** to compute the federal income taxes to withhold from the wages or salaries of each employee.

Employee No.	Employee Name	Marital Status	No. of Withholding Allowances	Gross Wage or Salary	Amount to Be Withheld
1	Skymer, A.	M	4	$ 1,575 weekly	________
2	Wolfe, T.	S	0	990 biweekly	________
3	Klein, G.	S	5	12,600 quarterly	________
4	Carey, P.	M	8	1,090 semimonthly	________
5	Wu, M.	M	3	3,120 monthly	________

4-3B LO 4.

Use (a) the percentage method and (b) the wage-bracket method to compute the federal income taxes to withhold from the wages or salaries of each employee.

				Amount to Be Withheld	
Employee	Marital Status	No. of Withholding Allowances	Gross Wage or Salary	Percentage Method	Wage-Bracket Method
Ruiz, S.	S	2	$1,040 weekly	________	________
Flume, X.	S	1	2,190 weekly	________	________
Farley, H.	M	6	1,890 biweekly	________	________
Comey, P.	M	4	2,315 semimonthly	________	________
Hanks, R.	M	9	4,200 monthly	________	________

4-4B LO 4.

Ernesto Enterprises uses the ***wage-bracket method*** to determine federal income tax withholding on its employees. Determine the amount to withhold from the wages paid each employee.

Employee	Marital Status	No. of Withholding Allowances	Payroll Period W = Weekly S = Semimonthly M = Monthly D = Daily	Wage	Amount to Be Withheld
Ed Boone	M	1	W	$1,250	________
Ray Ortega	S	1	W	695	________
Carl Lopez	S	3	W	915	________
Terri Kim	M	6	M	5,070	________
Kathy Horace	M	2	M	3,730	________
John Gleam	M	8	S	995	________
Rob Abreu	S	1	D	115	________
Carmen Sanchez	S	4	S	3,040	________
Howard Nee	M	4	M	4,500	________

4-5B LO 4.

The names of the employees of Hogan Thrift Shop are listed on the following payroll register. Employees are paid weekly. The marital status and the number of allowances claimed are shown on the payroll register, along with each employee's weekly salary, which has remained the same all year. Complete the payroll register for the payroll period ending December 19, the 51st weekly payday. The state income tax rate is 3.1% of total earnings, the city income tax rate is 1% of the total gross earnings, and the ***wage-bracket method*** is used for federal income taxes.

HOGAN THRIFT SHOP

PAYROLL REGISTER

FOR PERIOD ENDING 20

EMPLOYEE NAME	MARITAL STATUS	NO. OF W/H ALLOW.	TOTAL EARNINGS	DEDUCTIONS (a) FICA OASDI	HI	(b) FIT	(c) SIT	(d) CIT	(e) NET PAY
Gold, Ken	*M*	*3*	*2,080.00*						
Morton, Cam	*S*	*1*	*490.00*						
Wendal, Hal	*M*	*0*	*675.00*						
Cox, Debbie	*S*	*3*	*510.00*						
Hurley, Don	*S*	*1*	*1,010.00*						
Hand, Cheryl	*S*	*2*	*850.00*						
Welsh, Ronda	*S*	*1*	*490.90*						
Ruiz, Stacy	*M*	*3*	*611.15*						
Totals									

Compute the employer's FICA taxes for the pay period ending December 19.

OASDI Taxes
- OASDI taxable earnings $ ______
- OASDI taxes $ ______

HI Taxes
- HI taxable earnings $ ______
- HI taxes $ ______

4-6B LO 4.

Youngston Company (a Kansas employer) wants to give a holiday bonus check of $750 to each employee. Since it wants the check amount to be $750, it will need to gross up the amount of the bonus. Calculate the withholding taxes and the gross amount of the bonus to be made to Genna Fredrich if her earnings for the year are $55,920. Besides being subject to social security taxes and federal income tax (supplemental rate), a 5% Kansas income tax must be withheld on supplemental payments.

4-7B LO 4.

Jen Miller made $1,090 this week. Only social security (fully taxable) and federal income taxes attach to her pay. Jen contributes $125 each week to her company's 401(k) plan and has $40 put into her health savings account (nonqualified) each week. Her employer matches this $40 each week. Determine Jen's take-home pay if she is married and claims 2 allowances (use the wage-bracket method).

4-8B LO 4,6.

The names of the employees of Matson Office Systems and their regular salaries are shown in the following payroll register. Note that Wayne and Young are paid monthly on the last payday, while all others are paid weekly.

In addition to the regular salaries, the company pays an annual bonus based on the amount of earnings for the year. For the current year, the bonus amounts to 8% of the annual salary paid to each employee. The bonus is to be paid along with the regular salaries on December 26, but the amount of the bonus and the amount of the regular salary will be shown separately on each employee's earnings statement. Assume that all employees received their regular salary during the entire year.

Prepare the payroll for the pay period ending December 26, showing the following for each employee:

- Use the ***wage-bracket method*** to withhold federal income tax from the regular salaries.
- Withhold a flat 25% on the annual bonus.
- Total salaries and bonuses are subject to a 2% state income tax and a 1% city income tax.

FOR PERIOD ENDING 20

EMPLOYEE NAME	MARITAL STATUS	NO. OF W/H ALLOW.	EARNINGS			DEDUCTIONS					(g) NET PAY
			REGULAR	(a) SUPP'L.	(b) TOTAL	(c) FICA OASDI	(c) FICA HI	(d) FIT	(e) SIT	(f) CIT	
Wayne, Bret	*M*	*5*	*6,200.00* (M)*								
Young, Gina	*M*	*2*	*4,150.00* (M)*								
Course, Rudy	*S*	*1*	*810.00*								
Dickson, Emile	*M*	*4*	*715.00*								
Woodrow, Walt	*M*	*2*	*695.00*								
Noblet, Jim	*S*	*1*	*525.00*								
Ono, Joan	*M*	*2*	*800.00*								
Jones, Carrie	*S*	*0*	*645.00*								
Totals											

Compute the employer's FICA taxes for the pay period ending December 26.

OASDI Taxes
- OASDI taxable earnings $________
- OASDI taxes $________

HI Taxes
- HI taxable earnings $________
- HI taxes $________

(M)* indicates monthly pay.

4-9B LO 4,6.

During the quarter ending December 31 of the current year, Matson Office Systems had 13 weekly paydays and three monthly paydays. Using the data given in Problem 4–8B, complete the following form to show:

a. Total earnings paid during the quarter, including both the regular and the supplemental earnings.
b. Total amount of FICA taxes withheld during the quarter.
c. Total amount of federal income taxes withheld during the quarter.
d. Total amount of state income taxes withheld during the quarter.
e. Total amount of city income taxes withheld during the quarter.
f. Total net amount paid each employee during the quarter.

EMPLOYEE NAME	(a) TOTAL EARNINGS	DEDUCTIONS: (b) FICA					(f) NET PAY
		OASDI	HI	(c) FIT	(d) SIT	(e) CIT	
Wayne, Bret							
Young, Gina							
Course, Rudy							
Dickson, Emile							
Woodrow, Walt							
Noblet, Jim							
Ono, Joan							
Jones, Carrie							
Totals							

4-10B LO 4,7.

The employees of Bowen Supply Center are paid weekly. The names of five employees of the company are given on the following payroll register. The payroll register also shows the marital status and number of withholding allowances claimed and the total weekly earnings for each worker. Assume that each employee is paid the same weekly wage on each payday in 2008. Also shown below is the wage-bracket table for advance earned income credit (EIC) payments for a weekly payroll period. Each employee listed on the payroll register has completed a Form W-5 indicating that the worker is not married. Complete the payroll register for the weekly period ending November 14, 2008. The state income tax rate is 1.5% on total earnings and the ***wage-bracket tables*** are used for federal income tax.

EMPLOYEE NAME	MARITAL STATUS	NO.OFW/H ALLOW.	TOTAL EARNINGS	DEDUCTIONS (a) FICA OASDI	HI	(b) FIT	(c) SIT	(d) ADVANCE EIC PAYMENT	(e) NET PAY
Chung, P.	*S*	*4*	*395 00*						
Ruiz, H.	*S*	*1*	*325 00*						
Lloyd, C.	*S*	*2*	*290 00*						
Lewis, J.	*S*	*3*	*415 00*						
Chen, B.	*S*	*1*	*195 00*						
Totals									

WEEKLY Payroll Period

SINGLE or HEAD OF HOUSEHOLD

Wages— At least	But less than	Payment to be made	Wages— At least	But less than	Payment to be made	Wages— At least	But less than	Payment to be made	Wages— At least	But less than	Payment to be made	Wages— At least	But less than	Payment to be made
$0	**$5**	$0	**$70**	**$75**	$14	**$140**	**$145**	$29	**$385**	**$395**	$23	**$525**	**$535**	$10
5	**10**	1	**75**	**80**	15	**145**	**150**	30	**395**	**405**	22	**535**	**545**	9
10	**15**	2	**80**	**85**	16	**150**	**155**	31	**405**	**415**	22	**545**	**555**	8
15	**20**	3	**85**	**90**	17	**155**	**160**	32	**415**	**425**	21	**555**	**565**	7
20	**25**	4	**90**	**95**	18	**160**	**295**	33	**425**	**435**	20	**565**	**575**	6
25	**30**	5	**95**	**100**	19	**295**	**305**	32	**435**	**445**	19	**575**	**585**	5
30	**35**	6	**100**	**105**	20	**305**	**315**	31	**445**	**455**	18	**585**	**595**	4
35	**40**	7	**105**	**110**	21	**315**	**325**	30	**455**	**465**	17	**595**	**605**	3
40	**45**	8	**110**	**115**	22	**325**	**335**	29	**465**	**475**	16	**605**	**615**	2
45	**50**	9	**115**	**120**	23	**335**	**345**	28	**475**	**485**	15	**615**	**625**	1
50	**55**	10	**120**	**125**	24	**345**	**355**	27	**485**	**495**	14	**625**	**- - -**	0
55	**60**	11	**125**	**130**	26	**355**	**365**	26	**495**	**505**	13			
60	**65**	12	**130**	**135**	27	**365**	**375**	25	**505**	**515**	12			
65	**70**	13	**135**	**140**	28	**375**	**385**	24	**515**	**525**	11			

4-11B LO 4.

Harrington Company is giving each of its employees a holiday bonus of $250 on December 24 (a nonpayday). The company wants each employee's check to be $250. The supplemental tax percent is used.

a. What will be the gross amount of each bonus if each employee pays a state income tax of 3.01% (besides the other payroll taxes)? $________

b. What would the net amount of each bonus check be if the company did not gross up the bonus? $________

4-12B LO 4.

Samantha Montgomery (age 52) is employed by Canon Company and is paid a salary of $62,430. She has just decided to join the company's Simple Retirement Account (IRA form) and has a few questions. Answer the following for Montgomery:

a. What is the maximum that she can contribute into this retirement fund? $________

b. What would be the company's contribution? $________

c. What would be her weekly take-home pay with the retirement contribution deducted (married, 2 allowances, ***wage-bracket method,*** and a 2.3% state income tax on total wages)? $________

d. What would be her weekly take-home pay without the retirement contribution deduction? $________

4-13B LO 9.

During the fourth quarter of 2008, there were seven biweekly paydays on Friday (October 3, 17, 31; November 14, 28; December 12, 26) for Clarke's Roofing. Using the forms supplied below and on pages 4-62–65, complete the following for the fourth quarter:

a. Federal Tax Deposit Coupons (monthly depositor), Forms 8109. The employer's phone number is (501) 555-7331. Federal Deposit Liability Each Pay, $1,176.58.

b. Employer's Quarterly Federal Tax Return, Form 941. The form is signed by you.

c. Employer's Report of State Income Tax Withheld for the quarter, due on or before February 2, 2009.

Quarterly Payroll Data

Total Earnings 5 Employees	OASDI	HI	FIT	SIT	EIC Payments
$37,450.00	$2,321.90	$543.06	$3,402.00	$2,621.50	$896.00

Employer's OASDI	$2,321.90	
Employer's HI	$543.06	
Federal Deposit Liability Each Pay		$1,176.58

EMPLOYER'S REPORT OF STATE INCOME TAX WITHHELD

(DO NOT WRITE IN THIS SPACE)

IMPORTANT: PLEASE REFER TO THIS NUMBER IN ANY CORRESPONDENCE →

WITHHOLDING IDENTIFICATION NUMBER	MONTH OF OR QUARTER ENDING
42-7-3301	DEC 08

IF YOU ARE A SEASONAL EMPLOYER AND THIS IS YOUR FINAL REPORT FOR THIS SEASON, CHECK HERE ☐ AND SHOW THE NEXT MONTH IN WHICH YOU WILL PAY WAGES.

CLARKE'S ROOFING
10 SUMMIT SQUARE
CITY, STATE 00000-0000

IF NAME OR ADDRESS IS INCORRECT, PLEASE MAKE CORRECTIONS.

THIS REPORT MUST BE RETURNED EVEN IF NO AMOUNT HAS BEEN WITHHELD

1. GROSS PAYROLL THIS PERIOD	$
2. STATE INCOME TAX WITHHELD	$
3. ADJUSTMENT FOR PREVIOUS PERIOD(S). (ATTACH STATEMENT)	$
4. TOTAL ADJUSTED TAX (LINE 2 PLUS OR MINUS LINE 3)	$
5. PENALTY (35% OF LINE 4)	
6. INTEREST	
7. TOTAL AMOUNT DUE AND PAYABLE	$

Under penalties prescribed by law, I hereby affirm that to the best of my knowledge and belief this return, including any accompanying schedules and statements, is true and complete. If prepared by a person other than taxpayer, his affirmation is based on all information of which he has any knowledge.

SIGNATURE: TITLE: DATE:

MAIL THIS REPORT WITH CHECK OR MONEY ORDER PAYABLE TO THE DEPT. OF REVENUE ON OR BEFORE DUE DATE TO AVOID PENALTY.

4-13B (continued)

AMOUNT OF DEPOSIT (Do NOT type, please print.)

DOLLARS | CENTS

MONTH TAX YEAR ENDS → 1 2

EMPLOYER IDENTIFICATION NUMBER → 70 2204701

BANK NAME/ DATE STAMP

Name CLARKE'S ROOFING

Address 10 SUMMIT SQUARE

City CITY

State STATE ZIP 00000-0000

Telephone number ( )

IRS USE ONLY

Darken only one TYPE OF TAX: 941, 945, 990-C, 1120, 943, 990-T, 720, 990-PF, CT-1, 1042, 940, 944

and

Darken only one TAX PERIOD: 1st Quarter, 2nd Quarter, 3rd Quarter, 4th Quarter

76

FOR BANK USE IN MICR ENCODING

Federal Tax Deposit Coupon
Form 8109 (Rev. 12-2005)

To be deposited on or before ____________

AMOUNT OF DEPOSIT (Do NOT type, please print.)

DOLLARS | CENTS

MONTH TAX YEAR ENDS → 1 2

EMPLOYER IDENTIFICATION NUMBER → 70 2204701

BANK NAME/ DATE STAMP

Name CLARKE'S ROOFING

Address 10 SUMMIT SQUARE

City CITY

State STATE ZIP 00000-0000

Telephone number ( )

IRS USE ONLY

Darken only one TYPE OF TAX: 941, 945, 990-C, 1120, 943, 990-T, 720, 990-PF, CT-1, 1042, 940, 944

and

Darken only one TAX PERIOD: 1st Quarter, 2nd Quarter, 3rd Quarter, 4th Quarter

76

FOR BANK USE IN MICR ENCODING

Federal Tax Deposit Coupon
Form 8109 (Rev. 12-2005)

To be deposited on or before ____________

4-13B (continued)

MONTH TAX YEAR ENDS →	1 2
AMOUNT OF DEPOSIT (Do NOT type, please print.)	DOLLARS ___,___,___ . CENTS ___
EMPLOYER IDENTIFICATION NUMBER →	70 2204701
BANK NAME/ DATE STAMP	
Name	CLARKE'S ROOFING
Address	10 SUMMIT SQUARE
City	CITY
State	STATE
ZIP	00000-0000
Telephone number	( )
IRS USE ONLY	

Darken only one TYPE OF TAX		and	Darken only one TAX PERIOD
941	945		1st Quarter
990-C	1120		2nd Quarter
943	990-T		3rd Quarter
720	990-PF		4th Quarter
CT-1	1042		
940	944		

76

FOR BANK USE IN MICR ENCODING

Federal Tax Deposit Coupon
Form 8109 (Rev. 12-2005)

To be deposited on or before ____________

Form **941 for 20--: Employer's QUARTERLY Federal Tax Return** 990107

(Rev. January 2007) Department of the Treasury — Internal Revenue Service OMB No. 1545-0029

(EIN) Employer identification number: 7 0 – 2 2 0 4 7 0 1

Name (*not your trade name*): CLARKE'S ROOFING

Trade name (*if any*):

Address: 10 SUMMIT SQUARE
Number Street Suite or room number

CITY ST 00000
City State ZIP code

Report for this Quarter of 20--
(Check one.)

- ☐ **1:** January, February, March
- ☐ **2:** April, May, June
- ☐ **3:** July, August, September
- ☐ **4:** October, November, December

Read the separate instructions before you fill out this form. Please type or print within the boxes.

Part 1: Answer these questions for this quarter.

1 **Number of employees who received wages, tips, or other compensation for the pay period including:** ***Mar. 12*** **(Quarter 1),** ***June 12*** **(Quarter 2),** ***Sept. 12*** **(Quarter 3),** ***Dec. 12*** **(Quarter 4)** . . . 1 ______

2 **Wages, tips, and other compensation** . . . . 2 ______ .

3 **Total income tax withheld from wages, tips, and other compensation** . . . . 3 ______ .

4 **If no wages, tips, and other compensation are subject to social security or Medicare tax** . . ☐ Check and go to line 6.

5 **Taxable social security and Medicare wages and tips:**

	Column 1		*Column 2*
5a Taxable social security wages	.	× .124 =	.
5b Taxable social security tips	.	× .124 =	.
5c Taxable Medicare wages & tips	.	× .029 =	.

5d **Total social security and Medicare taxes** (*Column 2,* lines 5a + 5b + 5c = line 5d) . . 5d ______ .

6 **Total taxes before adjustments** (lines 3 + 5d = line 6) . . . . 6 ______ .

7 **TAX ADJUSTMENTS** (Read the instructions for line 7 before completing lines 7a through 7h.):

7a **Current quarter's fractions of cents** . . . . ______ .

7b **Current quarter's sick pay** . . . . ______ .

7c **Current quarter's adjustments for tips and group-term life insurance** ______ .

7d **Current year's income tax withholding** (attach Form 941c) . . . ______ .

7e **Prior quarters' social security and Medicare taxes** (attach Form 941c) ______ .

7f **Special additions to federal income tax** (attach Form 941c) . . . ______ .

7g **Special additions to social security and Medicare** (attach Form 941c) ______ .

7h **TOTAL ADJUSTMENTS** (Combine all amounts: lines 7a through 7g.) . . . . 7h ______ .

8 **Total taxes after adjustments** (Combine lines 6 and 7h.) . . . . 8 ______ .

9 **Advance earned income credit (EIC) payments made to employees** . . . . 9 ______ .

10 **Total taxes after adjustment for advance EIC** (line 8 – line 9 = line 10) . . . . 10 ______ .

11 **Total deposits for this quarter, including overpayment applied from a prior quarter** . . . 11 ______ .

12 **Balance due** (If line 10 is more than line 11, write the difference here.) . . . . 12 ______ .
Follow the Instructions for Form 941-V, Payment Voucher.

13 **Overpayment** (If line 11 is more than line 10, write the difference here.) ______ . Check one ☐ Apply to next return. ☐ Send a refund.

▶ You **MUST** fill out both pages of this form and **SIGN** it.

Next ➔

For Privacy Act and Paperwork Reduction Act Notice, see the back of the Payment Voucher. Cat. No. 17001Z Form **941** (Rev. 1-2007)

4-13B (concluded)

990207

Name *(not your trade name)* | Employer identification number (EIN)

Part 2: Tell us about your deposit schedule and tax liability for this quarter.

If you are unsure about whether you are a monthly schedule depositor or a semiweekly schedule depositor, see *Pub. 15 (Circular E)*, section 11.

14 ☐☐ **Write the state abbreviation for the state where you made your deposits** OR **write "MU" if you made your deposits in *multiple* states.**

15 **Check one:** ☐ **Line 10 is less than $2,500.** Go to Part 3.

☐ **You were a monthly schedule depositor for the entire quarter. Fill out your tax liability for each month.** Then go to Part 3.

Tax liability: Month 1 ______ .

Month 2 ______ .

Month 3 ______ .

Total liability for quarter ______ . **Total must equal line 10.**

☐ **You were a semiweekly schedule depositor for any part of this quarter.** Fill out *Schedule B (Form 941): Report of Tax Liability for Semiweekly Schedule Depositors,* and attach it to this form.

Part 3: Tell us about your business. If a question does NOT apply to your business, leave it blank.

16 **If your business has closed or you stopped paying wages** . . . . ☐ Check here, and

enter the final date you paid wages ___/___/___ .

17 **If you are a seasonal employer and you do not have to file a return for every quarter of the year** . . ☐ Check here.

Part 4: May we speak with your third-party designee?

Do you want to allow an employee, a paid tax preparer, or another person to discuss this return with the IRS? (See the instructions for details.)

☐ Yes. Designee's name ______

Select a 5-digit Personal Identification Number (PIN) to use when talking to IRS. ☐☐☐☐☐

☐ No.

Part 5: Sign here. You MUST fill out both pages of this form and SIGN it.

Under penalties of perjury, I declare that I have examined this return, including accompanying schedules and statements, and to the best of my knowledge and belief, it is true, correct, and complete.

X **Sign your name here** ______

Print your name here ______

Print your title here ______

Date ___/___/___

Best daytime phone (   )   –

Part 6: For paid preparers only *(optional)*

Paid Preparer's Signature ______

Firm's name ______

Address ______ EIN ______

ZIP code ______

Date ___/___/___ Phone (   )   – SSN/PTIN ______

☐ Check if you are self-employed.

Page **2** Form **941** (Rev. 1-2007)

4-14B LO 4,8.

During the first week of 2009, the Payroll Department of Omni Corporation is preparing the Forms W-2 for distribution to its employees along with their payroll checks on January 11. In this problem, you will complete six of the forms in order to gain some experience in recording the different kinds of information required.

Assume each employee earned the same weekly salary for each of the 52 paydays in 2008.

Using the following information obtained from the personnel and payroll records of the firm, complete Copy A of the six Forms W-2 reproduced on the following pages. Also complete Form W-3. The form is to be signed by the president, Frank Kent, and is prepared by Vince Roper.

Company Information:

Address:	4800 River Road Philadelphia, PA 19113-5548	Pennsylvania State identification number:	46-3-1066
Telephone number: (215) 555-0017		Federal identification number:	13-7490972
Fax number: (215) 555-0010		Philadelphia identification number:	4731895

Income Tax Information:

The wage-bracket method is used to determine federal income tax withholding. Calculate the annual federal income tax withheld by using the weekly wage-bracket table and multiply the answer by 52. The other taxes withheld are shown below.

Employee Data	Payroll Data	Annual Taxes Withheld	
Randy A. Kellison	Single, 2 allowances	1,982.76	Social security tax withheld
54 Gradison Place	$615 per week	463.84	Medicare tax withheld
Philadelphia, PA 19113-4054	SS#: 376-72-4310	981.76	State income tax withheld
	Deduction for 401(k) plan: $50/week	1,375.40	Local income tax withheld
Vince T. Roper	Married, 3 allowances	3,175.64	Social security tax withheld
56 Andrews Court, Apt. 7	$985 per week	742.56	Medicare tax withheld
Philadelphia, PA 19103-3356	SS#: 272-33-8804	1,572.48	State income tax withheld
	Dependent care payment: $950 $70/week—401(k)	2,203.24	Local income tax withheld
Murray T. Rodson	Single, 0 allowances	1,821.56	Social security tax withheld
770 Camac Street	$565 per week	425.88	Medicare tax withheld
Philadelphia, PA 19101-3770	SS#: 178-92-3316	902.20	State income tax withheld
	Union dues withheld: $102	1,263.60	Local income tax withheld
Frank A. Kent	Married, 6 allowances	6,061.29	Social security tax withheld
338 North Side Avenue	$1,875	1,417.69	Medicare tax withheld
Philadelphia, PA 19130-6638	SS#: 269-01-6839	2,993.12	State income tax withheld
	Cost of group-term life insurance exceeding $50,000: $262.75 No income tax withheld on insurance cost, but FICA taxes are withheld.* $100/week—401(k)	4,193.28	Local income tax withheld
Carlie C. Christian	Married, 5 allowances	1,547.52	Social security tax withheld
4900 Gladwynne Terrace	$480 per week	361.92	Medicare tax withheld
Philadelphia, PA 19127-0049	SS#: 368-14-5771	766.48	State income tax withheld
	Advance EIC payments: $16 per week Union dues withheld: $102	1,073.80	Local income tax withheld
Zana W. Amelia	Single, 1 allowance	1,579.76	Social security tax withheld
480-A Hopkinson Tower	$490 per week	369.72	Medicare tax withheld
Philadelphia, PA 19101-3301	SS#: 337-99-8703	782.08	State income tax withheld
	Educational assistance payments (job-required): $675 $50/week—401(k)	1,096.16	Local income tax withheld

*Must use percent table to calculate federal income tax.

4-14B (continued)

22222	Void ☐	a Employee's social security number	For Official Use Only ▶ OMB No. 1545-0008

b Employer identification number (EIN)	1 Wages, tips, other compensation	2 Federal income tax withheld
c Employer's name, address, and ZIP code	3 Social security wages	4 Social security tax withheld
	5 Medicare wages and tips	6 Medicare tax withheld
	7 Social security tips	8 Allocated tips
d Control number	9 Advance EIC payment	10 Dependent care benefits
e Employee's first name and initial / Last name / Suff.	11 Nonqualified plans	12a See instructions for box 12 Code
	13 Statutory employee ☐ Retirement plan ☐ Third-party sick pay ☐	12b Code
	14 Other	12c Code
f Employee's address and ZIP code		12d Code

15 State Employer's state ID number	16 State wages, tips, etc.	17 State income tax	18 Local wages, tips, etc.	19 Local income tax	20 Locality name

Form **W-2** **Wage and Tax Statement** **20- -**

Department of the Treasury—Internal Revenue Service

For Privacy Act and Paperwork Reduction Act Notice, see back of Copy D.

Cat. No. 10134D

Copy A For Social Security Administration — Send this entire page with Form W-3 to the Social Security Administration; photocopies are **not** acceptable.

Do Not Cut, Fold, or Staple Forms on This Page — Do Not Cut, Fold, or Staple Forms on This Page

22222	Void ☐	a Employee's social security number	For Official Use Only ▶ OMB No. 1545-0008

b Employer identification number (EIN)	1 Wages, tips, other compensation	2 Federal income tax withheld
c Employer's name, address, and ZIP code	3 Social security wages	4 Social security tax withheld
	5 Medicare wages and tips	6 Medicare tax withheld
	7 Social security tips	8 Allocated tips
d Control number	9 Advance EIC payment	10 Dependent care benefits
e Employee's first name and initial / Last name / Suff.	11 Nonqualified plans	12a See instructions for box 12 Code
	13 Statutory employee ☐ Retirement plan ☐ Third-party sick pay ☐	12b Code
	14 Other	12c Code
f Employee's address and ZIP code		12d Code

15 State Employer's state ID number	16 State wages, tips, etc.	17 State income tax	18 Local wages, tips, etc.	19 Local income tax	20 Locality name

Form **W-2** **Wage and Tax Statement** **20- -**

Department of the Treasury—Internal Revenue Service

For Privacy Act and Paperwork Reduction Act Notice, see back of Copy D.

Cat. No. 10134D

Copy A For Social Security Administration — Send this entire page with Form W-3 to the Social Security Administration; photocopies are **not** acceptable.

Do Not Cut, Fold, or Staple Forms on This Page — Do Not Cut, Fold, or Staple Forms on This Page

4-14B (continued)

22222	Void ☐	a Employee's social security number	For Official Use Only ▶ OMB No. 1545-0008	
b Employer identification number (EIN)			1 Wages, tips, other compensation	2 Federal income tax withheld
c Employer's name, address, and ZIP code			3 Social security wages	4 Social security tax withheld
			5 Medicare wages and tips	6 Medicare tax withheld
			7 Social security tips	8 Allocated tips
d Control number			9 Advance EIC payment	10 Dependent care benefits
e Employee's first name and initial	Last name	Suff.	11 Nonqualified plans	12a See instructions for box 12 Code
			13 Statutory employee ☐ Retirement plan ☐ Third-party sick pay ☐	12b Code
			14 Other	12c Code
				12d Code
f Employee's address and ZIP code				

15 State	Employer's state ID number	16 State wages, tips, etc.	17 State income tax	18 Local wages, tips, etc.	19 Local income tax	20 Locality name

Form **W-2** **Wage and Tax Statement** **20- -**

Department of the Treasury—Internal Revenue Service

For Privacy Act and Paperwork Reduction Act Notice, see back of Copy D.

Cat. No. 10134D

Copy A For Social Security Administration — Send this entire page with Form W-3 to the Social Security Administration; photocopies are **not** acceptable.

Do Not Cut, Fold, or Staple Forms on This Page — Do Not Cut, Fold, or Staple Forms on This Page

22222	Void ☐	a Employee's social security number	For Official Use Only ▶ OMB No. 1545-0008	
b Employer identification number (EIN)			1 Wages, tips, other compensation	2 Federal income tax withheld
c Employer's name, address, and ZIP code			3 Social security wages	4 Social security tax withheld
			5 Medicare wages and tips	6 Medicare tax withheld
			7 Social security tips	8 Allocated tips
d Control number			9 Advance EIC payment	10 Dependent care benefits
e Employee's first name and initial	Last name	Suff.	11 Nonqualified plans	12a See instructions for box 12 Code
			13 Statutory employee ☐ Retirement plan ☐ Third-party sick pay ☐	12b Code
			14 Other	12c Code
				12d Code
f Employee's address and ZIP code				

15 State	Employer's state ID number	16 State wages, tips, etc.	17 State income tax	18 Local wages, tips, etc.	19 Local income tax	20 Locality name

Form **W-2** **Wage and Tax Statement** **20- -**

Department of the Treasury—Internal Revenue Service

For Privacy Act and Paperwork Reduction Act Notice, see back of Copy D.

Cat. No. 10134D

Copy A For Social Security Administration — Send this entire page with Form W-3 to the Social Security Administration; photocopies are **not** acceptable.

Do Not Cut, Fold, or Staple Forms on This Page — Do Not Cut, Fold, or Staple Forms on This Page

4-14B (continued)

22222	Void ☐	a Employee's social security number	For Official Use Only ► OMB No. 1545-0008	
b Employer identification number (EIN)			1 Wages, tips, other compensation	2 Federal income tax withheld
c Employer's name, address, and ZIP code			3 Social security wages	4 Social security tax withheld
			5 Medicare wages and tips	6 Medicare tax withheld
			7 Social security tips	8 Allocated tips
d Control number			9 Advance EIC payment	10 Dependent care benefits
e Employee's first name and initial	Last name	Suff.	11 Nonqualified plans	12a See instructions for box 12 Code
			13 Statutory employee ☐ Retirement plan ☐ Third-party sick pay ☐	12b Code
			14 Other	12c Code
				12d Code
f Employee's address and ZIP code				

15 State	Employer's state ID number	16 State wages, tips, etc.	17 State income tax	18 Local wages, tips, etc.	19 Local income tax	20 Locality name

Form **W-2** **Wage and Tax Statement** **20--**

Department of the Treasury—Internal Revenue Service

For Privacy Act and Paperwork Reduction Act Notice, see back of Copy D.

Copy A For Social Security Administration — Send this entire page with Form W-3 to the Social Security Administration; photocopies are **not** acceptable.

Cat. No. 10134D

Do Not Cut, Fold, or Staple Forms on This Page — Do Not Cut, Fold, or Staple Forms on This Page

22222	Void ☐	a Employee's social security number	For Official Use Only ► OMB No. 1545-0008	
b Employer identification number (EIN)			1 Wages, tips, other compensation	2 Federal income tax withheld
c Employer's name, address, and ZIP code			3 Social security wages	4 Social security tax withheld
			5 Medicare wages and tips	6 Medicare tax withheld
			7 Social security tips	8 Allocated tips
d Control number			9 Advance EIC payment	10 Dependent care benefits
e Employee's first name and initial	Last name	Suff.	11 Nonqualified plans	12a See instructions for box 12 Code
			13 Statutory employee ☐ Retirement plan ☐ Third-party sick pay ☐	12b Code
			14 Other	12c Code
				12d Code
f Employee's address and ZIP code				

15 State	Employer's state ID number	16 State wages, tips, etc.	17 State income tax	18 Local wages, tips, etc.	19 Local income tax	20 Locality name

Form **W-2** **Wage and Tax Statement** **20--**

Department of the Treasury—Internal Revenue Service

For Privacy Act and Paperwork Reduction Act Notice, see back of Copy D.

Copy A For Social Security Administration — Send this entire page with Form W-3 to the Social Security Administration; photocopies are **not** acceptable.

Cat. No. 10134D

Do Not Cut, Fold, or Staple Forms on This Page — Do Not Cut, Fold, or Staple Forms on This Page

4-14B (concluded)

DO NOT STAPLE

33333	a Control number	For Official Use Only ▶ OMB No. 1545-0008

b Kind of Payer ▶ 941 ☐ Military ☐ 943 ☐ 944 ☐ CT-1 ☐ Hshld. emp. ☐ Medicare govt. emp. ☐ Third-party sick pay ☐	1 Wages, tips, other compensation	2 Federal income tax withheld
	3 Social security wages	4 Social security tax withheld
c Total number of Forms W-2 / d Establishment number	5 Medicare wages and tips	6 Medicare tax withheld
e Employer identification number (EIN)	7 Social security tips	8 Allocated tips
f Employer's name	9 Advance EIC payments	10 Dependent care benefits
	11 Nonqualified plans	12 Deferred compensation
	13 For third-party sick pay use only	
g Employer's address and ZIP code	14 Income tax withheld by payer of third-party sick pay	
h Other EIN used this year		
15 State / Employer's state ID number	16 State wages, tips, etc.	17 State income tax
	18 Local wages, tips, etc.	19 Local income tax
Contact person	Telephone number ( )	For Official Use Only
Email address	Fax number ( )	

Under penalties of perjury, I declare that I have examined this return and accompanying documents, and, to the best of my knowledge and belief, they are true, correct, and complete.

Signature ▶ Title ▶ Date ▶

Form **W-3 Transmittal of Wage and Tax Statements** 20- -

Department of the Treasury
Internal Revenue Service

Send this entire page with the entire Copy A page of Form(s) W-2 to the Social Security Administration.
Photocopies are not acceptable.

CONTINUING PAYROLL PROBLEM

Refer to the partially completed payroll register which you worked on at the end of Chapter 3. You will now determine the amount of income tax to withhold for each employee, proceeding as follows:

1. In the appropriate columns of your payroll register, record the marital status and number of withholding allowances claimed for each employee, using the information provided.
2. Record the payroll deductions for the SIMPLE plan that the employer has established for participating employees. All of the employees are participating and their weekly contributions are listed below. The tax deferral on these deductions applies only to the federal income tax.
3. Record the amount of federal income taxes using the wage-bracket method.
4. Record the state income taxes on the gross weekly earnings for each employee. The rate is 3.07% for the state of Pennsylvania.
5. Record the city income taxes on the gross weekly earnings of each employee. The rate is 1% for the city of Pittsburgh residents.

Time Card No.	Marital Status	No. of Allowances	SIMPLE Deductions
11	S	1	$20
12	S	0	50
13	M	2	40
21	M	4	50
22	S	2	20
31	M	3	40
32	M	6	50
33	S	1	60
51	M	5	30
99	M	7	80

CASE PROBLEMS

C1. Answering Employees' Questions About Wage Reporting.

During the past week, one of your newly employed payroll associates dropped into your office to ask several questions regarding wage reporting for federal income and social security tax purposes. If you were the payroll supervisor, how would you answer each of the following questions raised by your associate?

1. I just noticed that the social security number is wrong on three of the employees' W-2 forms. How do I go about correcting the forms? Will the employees be penalized for filing incorrect forms?
2. Eileen Huang informed me today that we had withheld too much Medicare tax from her pay last year. She is right! What forms do I use to make the correction?
3. You asked me last week to locate one of our former employees, Warren Bucks. I can't seem to track him down. What should I do with his Form W-2?
4. Is it okay to use titles like "M.D." and "Esq." when I keyboard data in the W-2 forms?

C2. Classified as an Employee and Independent Contractor.

Yeager Company pays John Kerr a salary as an employee and also fees for work he does as an independent contractor. Does this violate IRS rules?

chapter

5

Unemployment Compensation Taxes

LEARNING OBJECTIVES

After studying this chapter, you should be able to:

1. Describe the basic requirements for an individual to be classified as an employer or an employee under the Federal Unemployment Tax Act.
2. Describe the factors considered in determining the coverage of interstate employees.
3. Identify generally what is defined as taxable wages by the Federal Unemployment Tax Act.
4. Compute the federal unemployment tax and the credit against this tax.
5. Describe how an experience-rating system is used in determining employers' contributions to state unemployment compensation funds.
6. Complete the reports required by the Federal Unemployment Tax Act.
7. Describe the types of information reports under the various state unemployment compensation laws.

Are there any more taxes that the employer has to pay out of the employer's own pocket? Are there taxable wage limits for both federal and state unemployment taxes? How are the tax rates determined? Are there more forms to be filed and more deposits to be made? When are we finished?

Welcome to the world of unemployment taxes.

The Social Security Act of 1935 ordered every state to set up an unemployment compensation program in order to provide payments to workers during periods of temporary unemployment. Payroll taxes at both the federal and state levels fund this unemployment insurance program. The Federal Unemployment Tax Act (FUTA) imposes a tax on employers based on wages paid for covered employment. It is ***not*** collected or deducted from employees' wages. The funds collected by the federal government as a result of this tax pay the cost of administering both the federal and the state unemployment insurance programs. The FUTA tax is ***not*** used for the payment of weekly benefits to unemployed workers. Such benefits are paid by the states in accordance with each state's unemployment tax law (SUTA). These unemployment benefits are paid out of each state's trust fund, which is financed by state unemployment taxes. Because all states conform to standards specified in FUTA, considerable uniformity exists in the provisions of the state unemployment compensation laws. However, many variations in eligibility requirements, rates of contributions, benefits paid, and duration of benefits exist. All the states, Puerto Rico, the Virgin Islands, and the District of Columbia have enacted unemployment compensation laws that have been approved by the Social Security Administration.

You can realize the extent of the federal-state unemployment insurance program in terms of the people involved by the fact that in July 2007 the number of unemployed persons was 7.1 million out of a civilian labor force of about 153.2 million. At that time, the jobless rate was 4.6 percent. ***Unemployed persons*** include young people seeking positions for the first time, seasonal workers unemployed a part of each year, and workers who lost their jobs through various causes and cannot find other suitable employment.

Coverage Under FUTA and SUTA

LEARNING OBJECTIVE 1

Other than a few significant exceptions as explained in this section, the coverage under FUTA is similar to that under FICA, as described in Chapter 3.

EMPLOYERS—FUTA

The federal law levies a payroll tax on employers for the purpose of providing more uniform administration of the various state unemployment compensation laws. The federal law considers a person or a business an employer if ***either*** of the following two tests applies:

1. Pays wages of $1,500 or more during any calendar quarter in the current or preceding calendar year, or
2. Employs one or more persons, on at least some portion of one day, in each of 20 or more calendar weeks during the current or preceding taxable year.

A number of points serve to clarify the meaning of the two alternative tests: (a) a calendar week is defined as seven successive days beginning with Sunday; (b) the 20 weeks need not be consecutive; (c) the employees need not be the same employees; (d) regular, part-time, and temporary workers are considered employees; (e) in determining the employer's status, employees include individuals on vacation or sick leave; and (f) members of a partnership are not considered to be employees. As soon as an employer meets either test, the employer becomes liable for the FUTA tax for the entire calendar year.

EXAMPLE

For Vemor Company (a new employer), the 20th week of having one or more employees does not occur until November of 2008. The company becomes liable for FUTA tax on all taxable wages paid beginning with January 1, 2008.

Other covered employers are:

1. *Agricultural employers* who in the present or previous year paid $20,000 or more to farm workers in any calendar quarter and/or employed 10 or more farm workers during some part of a day during any 20 different weeks.

2. A *household employer* who during the present or previous year paid $1,000 or more during any quarter for household services in a private home, college club, or local fraternity or sorority club.

Once attained, the employer status continues until the employer fails to meet the test for coverage during a year. In this case, liability under FUTA would end as of January 1 of the next year.

Generally, the nature of the business organization has no relevance in determining employer status. Thus, the employer may be an individual, corporation, partnership, company, association, trust, or estate. There may be instances where it is difficult to determine which of two entities is the employer for purposes of FUTA. As under FICA, the question is answered by determining which entity has the ultimate right to direct and control the employees' activities. It is not necessary that the employer actually direct or control the manner in which the services are performed; it is sufficient if the employer has the right to do so. Other factors characteristic of an employer include the right to discharge and the furnishing of tools and a place to work.

EMPLOYERS—SUTA

In general, employers specifically excluded under the federal law are also excluded under the state laws. However, as a result of variations found in state unemployment compensation laws, not all employers covered by the unemployment compensation laws of one or more states are covered by FUTA. For example, the services performed by some charitable organizations may be covered by a state's unemployment compensation act, but these same services may be exempt from FUTA coverage.

on the *NET*

http://www.itsc.state.md.us/maps_charts/maps_charts.asp
This site provides a variety of interactive maps concerning individual state's status on unemployment-related issues.

EMPLOYEES—FUTA

Every individual is considered an employee if the relationship between the worker and the person for whom the services are performed is the legal common-law relationship of employer and employee. This individual would then be counted in determining whether the employer is subject to FUTA. Chapters 3 and 4 cover the nature of this common-law relationship.

For the purpose of the FUTA tax, the term "employee" also means any of the following who perform service for remuneration:

1. An *agent-driver* or a *commission-driver* who distributes food or beverages (other than milk) or laundry or dry-cleaning services for the principal.
2. A *traveling* or a *city salesperson* engaged in full-time soliciting and transmitting to the principal orders for merchandise for resale or supplies for use in business operations.

If a person in one of these categories has a substantial investment in facilities used to perform the services (not including transportation facilities), the individual is an independent contractor and not a covered employee. Also, individuals are not covered if their services are a single transaction that is not part of a continuing relationship with the persons for whom they are performed.

The work performed by the employee for the employer includes any services of whatever nature performed within the United States, regardless of the citizenship or residence of either. FUTA coverage also includes service of any nature performed outside the United States by a citizen of the United States for an American employer. The major exception is that service performed in Canada or in any other adjoining country with which the United States has an agreement relating to unemployment does not constitute covered employment.

An employee may perform both included and excluded employment for the same employer during a pay period. In such a case, the services that predominate in the pay period determine the employee's status with that employer for the period. FUTA wholly exempts some services from coverage. Among those *excluded* from coverage in 2008 are:

1. Casual laborers, unless cash remuneration paid for such service is $50 or more in a calendar quarter and the person to whom it is paid is regularly employed by the one for whom the services were performed during that period.

2. Directors of corporations, unless they perform services for the corporation other than those required by attending and participating in meetings of the board of directors.
3. Foreign students and exchange visitors who are carrying out the purposes for which they are admitted into the United States, such as studying, teaching, or conducting research. If employed for other purposes, they would not be excluded.
4. Government employees of international organizations, such as the United Nations.
5. Independent contractors, such as physicians, lawyers, dentists, veterinarians, contractors, subcontractors, public stenographers, auctioneers, and others who follow an independent trade, business, or profession in which they offer their services to the public.
6. Individuals under 18 years of age who deliver or distribute newspapers or shopping news (other than delivery or distribution to any point for subsequent delivery and distribution) and retail vendors of any age who sell and distribute newspapers and magazines to the ultimate consumer.
7. Insurance agents or solicitors paid solely on a commission basis.
8. Members of partnerships.
9. Service performed by an individual for a son, daughter, or spouse, or by a child under the age of 21 for a parent.
10. Services performed by a student who is enrolled and regularly attending classes at a school, college, or university, if service is performed for that school, college, or university.
11. Services performed by employees or employee representatives for employers covered by either the Railroad Retirement Tax Act or the Railroad Unemployment Insurance Act.
12. Services performed by individuals in fishing and related activities if the vessel is less than ten net tons.
13. Services performed in the employ of a religious, educational, or charitable organization that is exempt from federal income tax. This exemption includes service in church-sponsored elementary and secondary schools.
14. Services performed in the employ of foreign, federal, state, or local governments and certain of their instrumentalities. However, taxes imposed by FUTA apply to these federal instrumentalities: federal reserve banks, federal loan banks, and federal credit unions.
15. Students enrolled full-time in a work-study or internship program, for work that is an integral part of the student's academic program.
16. Student nurses and hospital interns.

EMPLOYEES—SUTA

The definition of "employee" as established by FUTA applies to a majority of the states, although minor variations exist in the state laws. Many states apply a simple "ABC" test to determine exclusion from coverage. All of the following requirements must be met for exclusion:

1. Free from control or direction.
2. Performed outside usual course of business.
3. Customarily engaged in an independent trade or business.

All states extend coverage to U.S. citizens working abroad for American employers (except in Canada).

LEARNING OBJECTIVE 2

COVERAGE OF INTERSTATE EMPLOYEES

An **interstate employee** is an individual who works in more than one state. To prevent duplicate contributions on the services of interstate employees, all states have adopted a uniform four-part definition of employment to determine which state will cover such employees. This definition covers the entire services of an interstate worker in one state only—that state in which the worker will most likely look for a job if he or she becomes unemployed. Several factors that must be considered in determining coverage of interstate employees, in their order of application, include:

1. Place where the work is ***localized.***
2. Location of ***base of operations.***
3. Location of place from which operations are ***directed or controlled.***
4. Location of ***employee's residence.***

PLACE WHERE THE WORK IS LOCALIZED Under this main criterion of coverage adopted by the states, if all the work is performed within one state, it is clearly "localized" in that state and constitutes "employment" under the law of that state. In some cases, however, part of the person's work may be performed outside the state. In such instances, the entire work may be treated as localized within the state if the services performed in other states are temporary or transitory in nature.

EXAMPLE

Carlin Parker is a sales representative whose regular sales territory lies within Arizona. Parker is covered by the laws of Arizona, with respect to his total employment, even though he makes frequent trips to the firm's showrooms in Los Angeles to attend sales meetings and to look over new lines of goods.

LOCATION OF BASE OF OPERATIONS Often, a worker may perform services continually in two or more states. In such situations, the employment in one state is not incidental to the employment in the other state. Thus, the test of localization does not apply, and the base of operations test must be considered. Under this test, the employee's services may be covered by the laws of a single state even though the services are not localized within that state. The base of operation is the place of a more or less permanent nature from which the employee starts work and to which the employee customarily returns. It could be a particular place where his or her (a) instructions are received, (b) business records are maintained, (c) supplies are sent, or (d) office is maintained (may be in the employee's home).

EXAMPLE

Mathew Hinges travels through four southern states for Irwin Company, which is headquartered in Georgia. His work is equally divided among the four states. When working in Georgia, he reports to the main office for instructions. The location of his base of operations is clearly Georgia, and his services are subject to the Georgia laws.

LOCATION OF PLACE FROM WHICH OPERATIONS ARE DIRECTED OR CONTROLLED Often an employee's services are not localized in any state. Or, it may be impossible to determine any base of operations. If the place of control can be fixed in a particular state in which some service is performed, that will be the state in which the individual is covered.

EXAMPLE

Joyce Mendes is a sales representative whose sales territory is so widespread that she does not retain any fixed business address or office. She receives all orders or instructions by mail or wire wherever she may happen to be. Clearly, the work is not localized in any state, and no fixed base of operations exists. However, the services performed by Mendes may still come under the provisions of a single state law—the law of that state in which is located the place of direction or control, provided that some of Mendes's work is also performed in that state.

LOCATION OF EMPLOYEE'S RESIDENCE If an employee's coverage cannot be determined by any of the three tests described, a final test, that of the employee's residence, is used. Thus, the worker's service is covered in its entirety in the state in which the employee lives, provided some of the service is performed in that state.

EXAMPLE

Randy Mueller is employed by Prang Company of Illinois. He lives in Iowa, and his work territory includes Iowa, Minnesota, and Wisconsin. Since neither the base of operations nor the place from which his work is directed is in a state in which he works, he is covered in his state of residence (Iowa).

on the JOB

The only states that do not participate in reciprocal arrangements are Alaska, Kentucky, Mississippi, New Jersey, and New York, plus Puerto Rico.

RECIPROCAL ARRANGEMENTS AND TRANSFERS OF EMPLOYMENT If coverage of interstate employees cannot be determined using these factors, states may enter into arrangements under which the employer may elect coverage of the employee in one state.

These agreements, known as **reciprocal arrangements,** provide unemployment insurance coverage and payment of benefits to interstate workers. The most widely accepted type of interstate coverage arrangement is the Interstate Reciprocal Coverage Arrangement. Under this arrangement, an employer can elect to cover all of the services of a worker in any one state in which (a) the employee performs any work, (b) the employee maintains a residence, or (c) the employer maintains the place of business.

EXAMPLE

Morris Davidson is a salesperson for Tannenbaum Company. His sales territory includes parts of Connecticut and Massachusetts, and his services can be considered localized in both states. Under the Interstate Reciprocal Coverage Arrangement, the company elects to cover Davidson under the law of Massachusetts.

Instead of paying into two or more of the 50 states, an employer can elect a state based on such factors as low wage bases and contribution rates. Once the employer chooses the state in which all the services of the interstate workers are to be covered and the employee consents to the coverage, this state approves the election of coverage. Then, the appropriate agencies of the other states in which services are performed are notified so that they can agree to the coverage in the state of election. Since they are usually done on a case-by-case basis, new arrangements must be agreed upon for each employee.

Another aspect of reciprocal arrangements concerns the transfer of an employee from one state to another during the same calendar year. An employer can include, for purposes of determining the taxable wage base in the second state, wages paid an employee with respect to employment covered by the unemployment compensation law of the previous state.

EXAMPLE

Parlone Company has paid wages of $4,000 to an employee in State A. During the year, the employee is transferred to State B, which has a $7,000 taxable salary limitation for its state unemployment tax. The company has a credit of $4,000 against this $7,000 limit. Thus, the company has to pay State B's unemployment tax on only the next $3,000 of wages earned by that worker in State B during the remainder of the calendar year.

COVERAGE OF AMERICANS WORKING OVERSEAS As mentioned before, coverage extends to U.S. citizens working abroad for American employers. The state of the employer's principal place of business would provide the coverage. If the principal place of business cannot be determined, the state of incorporation or the state of residence of the individual owner would be the state of coverage.

WAGES—FUTA

LEARNING OBJECTIVE 3

Generally, ***wages*** means all remuneration for employment, including the cash value of all remuneration paid in any medium other than cash, with certain exceptions.

During 2008, taxable wages include only the first $7,000 of remuneration paid by an employer to an employee with respect to employment during any calendar year. The basis upon which the remuneration is paid is immaterial. It may be paid on a piece-work basis or it may be a percentage of profits; it may be paid hourly, daily, weekly, biweekly, semimonthly, monthly, or annually. Some of the more common types of payments made to employees and the taxability status of these payments include the following:

on the JOB

Wages paid by a previous employer can be counted by the successor in figuring the wage limit if both are covered employers in the year that the acquisition took place.

TAXABLE WAGES FOR UNEMPLOYMENT PURPOSES

1. Advance payment for work to be done in the future.
2. Bonuses as remuneration for services.

3. Cash and noncash prizes and awards for doing outstanding work, for exceeding sales quotas, or for contributing suggestions that increase productivity or efficiency.
4. Christmas gifts, excluding noncash gifts of nominal value.
5. Commissions as compensation for covered employment.
6. Contributions by an employer to a supplemental unemployment individual-account plan to which the employee has a fully vested and nonforfeitable right.
7. Dismissal payments.
8. Employer contributions to cash or deferred arrangements to the extent that the contributions are not included in the employee's gross income.
9. Idle time and standby payments.
10. Payment by the employer of the employee's FICA tax or the employee's share of any state unemployment compensation tax without deduction from the employee's wages.
11. Payments representing compensation for services by an employee paid to the dependents after an employee's death. Payments in the nature of a gratuity rather than compensation for services are nontaxable. Any payments made by an employer to an employee's estate or to the employee's survivors after the calendar year in which the employee died are excluded from the definition of wages and thus may not be taxed.
12. Payments to employees or their dependents on account of sickness or accident disability. These payments are ***not*** taxable after the expiration of six months following the last calendar month in which the employee worked. Payments for work missed due to pregnancy are not classified as taxable wages during the first six months of absence.
13. Payments under a guaranteed annual wage plan.
14. Retroactive wage increases.
15. Tips, including charged tips, reported by the employee to the employer.
16. Transfer of stock by an employer to the employees as remuneration for services. (The fair market value of the stock at the time of payment is the taxable base.)
17. Vacation pay.

NONTAXABLE WAGES FOR UNEMPLOYMENT PURPOSES

1. Advances or reimbursement of ordinary and necessary business expenses incurred in the business of the employer.
2. Allowances made to an individual by a prospective employer for expenses incurred in connection with interviews for possible employment.
3. Bonuses under a supplemental compensation plan paid upon retirement, death, or disability of an employee.
4. Caddy fees.
5. Commissions paid to insurance agents and solicitors who are paid solely by commission. Such persons are classified as independent contractors, not employees.
6. Courtesy discounts to employees and their families.
7. Educational assistance payments to workers.
8. Payments made by an employer under a plan established by the employer for health, accident, or life insurance, or retirement benefits on behalf of the employees or their dependents.
9. Reimbursement of an employee's moving expenses if, at the time of payment, it is reasonable to believe that the employee will be entitled to a deduction for those expenses at the time of filing his or her federal income tax return.
10. Retirement pay.
11. Strike benefits paid by a union to its members.
12. Value of meals and lodging furnished employees for the convenience of the employer.
13. Workers' compensation payments.

WAGES—SUTA

The definition of taxable wages is fairly uniform under the various state unemployment compensation laws. However, some variations exist among the states as to the status of particular kinds of payments. For example, about one-sixth of the states have ruled that Christmas bonuses or gifts are "wages" when substantial, contractual, or based on a percentage of the employee's wages or length of service. New Hampshire, however, does not include gifts or gratuities of $25 or less as wages, unless paid under a contract related to past or future employment. A further variation in defining taxable wages among the states arises in the treatment of **dismissal payments.** Generally, such payments are considered wages whether or not the employer must legally make the payments. However, in some states, dismissal payments do not constitute wages unless the employer must legally make them. Puerto Rico does not consider any type of dismissal payment to be wages. In Puerto Rico, tips are also not considered taxable wages.

Unemployment Compensation Taxes and Credits

The base of the unemployment compensation tax is wages *paid* rather than *wages payable.* Thus, an employer is liable for the unemployment compensation tax in the year in which wages are paid employees, not necessarily in the year in which the services are rendered. Thus, if an employee performs services in 2007 but is not paid for them until 2008, the employer is liable for the tax in 2008, and the 2008 tax rates apply. Wages are considered paid when actually paid or when **constructively paid.** Wages are considered constructively paid when credited to the account of, or set apart for, an employee so that they may be drawn upon at any time, even though they are not actually possessed by the employee.

TAX RATE—FUTA

Under FUTA, all employers, as defined earlier, are subject to a tax with respect to having individuals in their employ. For 2008, the employer's tax rate is 6.2 percent of the first $7,000 wages paid each employee during the calendar year. Thus, an employer is liable for the FUTA tax on wages paid each employee until the employee's wages reach the $7,000 level. If an employee has more than one employer during the current year, the taxable wage base *applies separately* to each of those employers, unless one employer has transferred the business to the second.

EXAMPLE

Assume that in 2008, an employer had charged the wages account for $79,850. Of this amount, $720 will not be paid until the first payday in 2009. Further, the wages actually paid to employees in 2008 in excess of $7,000 each amounted to $29,840. The gross FUTA tax imposed on the employer is computed as follows:

Total amount charged to wages during 2008		$79,850.00
Less:		
Wages not to be paid until 2009	$ 720	
Wages paid in excess of $7,000 limit	29,840	30,560.00
Total taxable wages		$49,290.00
Rate of tax		×6.2%
Amount of gross FUTA tax		$ 3,055.98

LEARNING OBJECTIVE 4

CREDITS AGAINST FUTA TAX The actual FUTA tax paid is usually only *0.8 percent,* since employers are entitled to a credit against their FUTA tax liability for contributions made under approved state unemployment compensation laws. The maximum credit permitted is 5.4 percent (90% of 6%). Thus, in the preceding example where the ***gross*** FUTA tax rate is 6.2 percent, the ***net*** FUTA rate would be 0.8 percent if the full 5.4 percent credit applied. Even if employers pay a SUTA rate of less than 5.4 percent, they still get the full credit against the FUTA tax.

EXAMPLE

Total taxable earnings (above example)	$49,290.00
Net rate of tax (6.2% – 5.4%)	×0.8%
Amount of net FUTA tax	$ 394.32

To obtain the maximum credit of 5.4 percent against the federal tax, the employer must make the state contributions on or before the due date for filing the annual return under FUTA (see page 5-20)—February 2, 2009. If the employer is late in paying the state contributions, the credit is limited to 90 percent of the amount of the deposit that would have been allowed as a credit if the late contributions had been paid on time.

EXAMPLE

Sutcliffe Company had taxable wages totaling $87,500 in 2008. During the year, the company paid some of its state contributions after the February 2, 2009 cutoff—January 31 is a Saturday. The penalty for tardiness is shown in the following calculation of the firm's net FUTA tax for 2008:

Amount of gross FUTA tax ($87,500 × 6.2%)		$ 5,425.00
State taxable wages	$87,500	
Sutcliffe's SUTA tax rate	×5.4%	
Sutcliffe's SUTA tax	$ 4,725	
Breakdown of Sutcliffe's SUTA tax payments:		
Before 2/2/09—$3,000 × 100% credit		(3,000.00)
After 2/2/09—$1,725 × 90% credit		(1,552.50)
Amount of net FUTA tax		$ 872.50

If the company had made timely payments of its state contributions, the amount of its net FUTA tax would have been reduced to $700, for a savings of $172.50, as follows:

Amount of gross FUTA tax ($87,500 × 6.2%)		$ 5,425.00
Total taxable wages	$87,500	
Credit against tax	×5.4%	
Total credit		4,725.00
Amount of net FUTA tax ($87,500 × 0.8%)		$ 700.00

$872.50 – $700.00 = $172.50 savings

The credit against the FUTA tax for state contributions does not apply to any SUTA payments deducted from employees' pay and penalties and interest not included in the contribution rate assigned by the state.

EXPERIENCE RATING In some cases, employers may pay contributions into their state unemployment fund at a rate lower than 5.4 percent. The method by which the employer contributions may be adjusted because of a favorable employment record is referred to as **experience rating** or **merit rating**. Thus, an employer's favorable experience rate (employment record) qualifies the employer for a SUTA rate lower than 5.4 percent. As noted before, FUTA provides for a credit equal to the employer's SUTA rate plus an additional credit so that the ***full 5.4 percent credit*** still applies. In this way, employers who have steady employment histories, and therefore lower SUTA tax rates, are not penalized when the FUTA tax is paid.

SELF-STUDY QUIZ 5-1 *Garo Company pays taxable wages (FUTA and SUTA) of $188,000 during 2008. Garo Company has a state unemployment tax rate of 4.1% for 2008 because of its past employment record. Compute Garo Company's 2008 FUTA and SUTA taxes.*

$ 1504.00 FUTA

$ 7708.00 SUTA

If an employer receives an additional credit against the FUTA tax because the state experience rate is less than 5.4 percent, the additional credit is not subject to the 90 percent

FUTA credit limitation for late SUTA payments. The credit reduction applies only to actual SUTA tax payments made after February 2, 2009.

EXAMPLE

Yeldon Company has a $70,000 federal and state taxable payroll and has earned a reduced state tax rate of 4 percent. If none of its state tax payments are timely, the FUTA tax calculation is as follows:

Gross FUTA tax ($70,000 × 0.062)		$4,340
Less 90% credit for state taxes paid late ($70,000 × 0.04 × 90%). . .	$2,520	
Less additional credit for state tax if rate were 5.4% [$70,000 × (0.054 − 0.04)]	980	
Total credit.		3,500
Net FUTA tax		$ 840

If Yeldon Company had made its SUTA payments before the due date of Form 940, the credit for the payments (4%) and the additional credit (1.4%) would have provided a total credit of $3,780 and a FUTA tax savings of $280.

Where contributions are paid into more than one state unemployment compensation fund, the credit against the federal tax is still limited to 5.4 percent.

EXAMPLE

The contribution rate of Domski Supply in Kansas is 5.5 percent and in Missouri, 2 percent. The credit against the gross FUTA tax on the wages paid is 5.4 percent in each state.

The unemployment compensation laws of certain states set the taxable wage base at a figure higher than the first $7,000 paid to each employee. For example, in Arkansas, the wage base for 2007 was the first $10,000. In such states, the total contributions that the employer must pay into the state fund may exceed 5.4 percent of the taxable wages as established by FUTA (first $7,000 of each employee's earnings). However, the maximum credit that can be claimed against the gross FUTA tax for the state contributions is 5.4 percent of the first $7,000 of each individual employee's earnings.

TITLE XII ADVANCES States that experience financial difficulties and are unable to pay their unemployment compensation benefits may borrow funds from the federal government under Title XII of the Social Security Act. The states use these funds, called **Title XII advances,** to pay their regular unemployment benefits. Under the repayment provisions established by the federal government, if a state defaults in its payments, the credit against the gross FUTA tax is reduced by 0.3 percent beginning the ***second taxable year after the advance.*** This penalty increases by an additional 0.3 percent for each succeeding year in which there is a balance due the federal government. Thus, employers in those states have their gross FUTA tax rate increased by 0.3 percent the second year after the advance, then by 0.6 percent. The credit reduction is capped if certain solvency requirements are met by the state. The credit reduction applicable to employers in the affected states is limited to either 0.6 percent of wages paid or the percentage credit reduction in effect in the state for the preceding taxable year if greater than 0.6 percent. The credit reduction can be avoided if the state repays the loan by November 10 of the year in which the reduction is scheduled to take effect.

TAX RATES—SUTA

Figure 5–1 presents a summary of each state's 2007 unemployment compensation laws, including the tax rates and the wage limitations. The tax rate applied to each employer within a particular state yields the funds used by that state in paying benefits to its unemployed

FIGURE 5–1

Summary of State Unemployment Compensation Laws (2007)
Warning: The Provisions of the state laws are subject to change at any time.

State	Size of Firm (One employee in specified time and/or size of payroll[1])	Contributions (On first $7,000 unless otherwise indicated) Employer Min.–Max.	Contributions Employee	Benefits (Excluding dependency allowances) Waiting Period (weeks)	Max. per Week	Min. per Week	Max. Duration (weeks)
ALABAMA	20 weeks	0.5%–6.1% on first $8,000		none	$230	$45	26
ALASKA	any time	1.0%–5.4% on first $30,100	0.5% on first $30,100	1	248	44	26
ARIZONA	20 weeks	0.02%–5.4%*		1	240	60	26
ARKANSAS	10 days	0.8%–10.7% on first $10,000*		1	395	71	26
CALIFORNIA	over $100 in any calendar quarter	1.5%–6.2%*	0.6% on first $83,389 (disability ins.)	1	450	40	26
COLORADO	any time	0.0%–8.92% on first $10,000*		1	435	25	26
CONNECTICUT	20 weeks	1.2%–6.1% on first $15,000		none	483	15	26
DELAWARE	20 weeks	0.3%–8.2% on first $8,500		none	330	20	26
DISTRICT OF COLUMBIA	any time	1.3%–6.6% on first $9,000		1	359	50	26
FLORIDA	20 weeks	0.12%–5.4%		1	275	32	26
GEORGIA	20 weeks	0.03%–5.4% on first $8,500*		none	320	42	26
HAWAII	any time	0.0%–5.4% on first $35,300	0.5% of maximum weekly wages of $820.26, not to exceed $4.10 per week (disability ins.)	1	459	5	26
IDAHO	20 weeks or $300 in any calendar quarter	0.372%–5.4% on first $30,200		1	322	51	26
ILLINOIS	20 weeks	1.0%–8.2% on first $11,500		1	350	51	26
INDIANA	20 weeks	1.1%–5.6%*		1	390	50	26
IOWA	20 weeks	0.0%–8.0% on first $22,000		none	334	50	26
KANSAS	20 weeks	0.0%–7.4% on first $8,000*		1	386	96	26
KENTUCKY	20 weeks	0.5%–9.5% on first $8,000*		none	401	39	26

1 This is $1,500 in any calendar quarter in current or preceding calendar year unless otherwise specified.
*Allow voluntary contributions

(Continued)

FIGURE 5–1 (Continued)

Summary of State Unemployment Compensation Laws (2007)
Warning: The Provisions of the state laws are subject to change at any time.

State	Size of Firm (One employee in specified time and/or size of payroll[1])	Contributions (On first $7,000 unless otherwise indicated)		Benefits (Excluding dependency allowances)			
		Employer Min.–Max.	Employee	Waiting Period (weeks)	Max. per Week	Min. per Week	Max. Duration (weeks)
LOUISIANA	20 weeks	0.1%–6.2%*		1	$258	$10	26
MAINE	20 weeks	0.54%–5.4% on first $12,000*		1	320	56	26
MARYLAND	any time	0.3%–7.5% on first $8,500		none	340	25	26
MASSACHUSETTS	13 weeks	1.12%–10.96% on first $14,000*		1	575	31	30
MICHIGAN	20 weeks or $1,000 in calendar year	0.6%–10.3% on first $9,000*		none	362	81	26
MINNESOTA	20 weeks	0.4%–9.3% on first $24,000*		1	521	38	26
MISSISSIPPI	20 weeks	0.7%–5.4%		1	210	30	26
MISSOURI	20 weeks	0.0%–8.4% on first $11,000*		1	270	48	26
MONTANA	over $1,000 in current or preceding year	0.13%–6.5% on first $22,700		1	362	103	26
NEBRASKA	20 weeks	0.24%–5.4%*		1	288	30	26
NEVADA	$225 in any quarter	0.25%–5.4% on first $24,600		none	362	16	26
NEW HAMPSHIRE	20 weeks	0.05%–6.5% on first $8,000		none	372	32	26
NEW JERSEY	$1,000 in any year	0.3%–5.4% on first $26,600*	0.925% (0.5% for disability ins.; 0.425% for unempl. comp.)	1	521	73	26
NEW MEXICO	20 weeks or $450 in any quarter	0.03%–5.4% on first $18,600*		1	360	62	26
NEW YORK	$300 in any quarter	1.1%–9.5% on first $8,500*	0.5% of weekly wages, not to exceed 60¢ per week (disability ins.)	1	405	40	26
NORTH CAROLINA	20 weeks	0.00%–6.84% on first $17,800*		1	457	36	26
NORTH DAKOTA	20 weeks	0.34%–8.09% on first $21,300*		1	351	43	26
OHIO	20 weeks	0.4%–9.0% on first $9,000*		1	355	96	26

1 This is $1,500 in any calendar quarter in current or preceding calendar year unless otherwise specified.
*Allow voluntary contributions

(Continued)

FIGURE 5–1 (Concluded)

Summary of State Unemployment Compensation Laws (2007)
Warning: The Provisions of the state laws are subject to change at any time.

State	Size of Firm (One employee in specified time and/or size of payroll[1])	Contributions (On first $7,000 unless otherwise indicated)		Benefits (Excluding dependency allowances)			
		Employer Min.–Max.	Employee	Waiting Period (weeks)	Max. per Week	Min. per Week	Max. Duration (weeks)
OKLAHOMA		0.2%–5.8% on first $13,200		1	$342	$16	26
OREGON	20 weeks	.9%–5.4% on first $29,000		1	445	104	26
PENNSYLVANIA	18 weeks or $225 in any quarter	2.008%–10.2624% on first $8,000*	0.09% on total wages	1	520	35	26
PUERTO RICO	any time	1.4%–5.4%	0.3% on first $9,000 (disability ins.)	1	133	7	26
RHODE ISLAND	any time	1.9%–10.0% on first $14,000	1.3% on first $52,100 (disability ins.)	1	492	65	26
SOUTH CAROLINA	any time	1.24%–6.1%		1	303	20	26
SOUTH DAKOTA	20 weeks	0.0%–9.1%* on first $8,500		1	274	28	26
TENNESSEE	20 weeks	0.3%–10.0%		1	275	30	26
TEXAS	20 weeks	0.29%–7.7% on first $9,000*		1	364	56	26
UTAH	$140 in calendar quarter in current or preceding calendar year	0.3%–9.3% on first $25,400		1	383	25	26
VERMONT	20 weeks	0.8%–6.5% on first $8,000		1	394	59	26
VIRGIN ISLANDS	any time	0.0%–6.0% on first $20,500		1	426	33	26
VIRGINIA	20 weeks	0.17%–6.27% on first $8,000		1	347	54	26
WASHINGTON	any time	0.3%–6.02% on first $31,400*		1	496	116	30
WEST VIRGINIA	20 weeks	1.5%–8.5% on first $8,000*		1	391	24	28
WISCONSIN	20 weeks	0.05%–9.8% on first $10,500*		none	355	53	26
WYOMING	$500 in current or preceding calendar year	0.47%–8.97% on first $18,100		1	349	25	26

1 This is $1,500 in any calendar quarter in current or preceding calendar year unless otherwise specified.
*Allow voluntary contributions

workers. Currently, all states have enacted **pooled-fund laws** as a basis for their unemployment insurance systems. By means of pooled funds, the cost of unemployment benefits is spread among all the employers in a particular state.

EMPLOYER CONTRIBUTIONS Every state has its own unemployment compensation law with varying tax rates and taxable wage bases. As with FUTA tax, if an employee has more than one employer during the year, the taxable wage base (same state) or bases (different states) applies separately to each employer.

To minimize the impact of unemployment insurance taxes on newly covered employers, each state sets an initial contribution rate for new employers that will apply for a specific period of time. During this period of time, the new employer's employment record can be developed and an experience rating can later be established. A state may assign a contribution rate of not less than 1 percent to newly covered employers on some "reasonable basis" other than employment experience. Once the new employer has accumulated the experience required under the provisions of the state law, a new rate will be assigned. For example, New York applies 4.1 percent to new employers.

EMPLOYEE CONTRIBUTIONS Some states, as shown in Figure 5–1, impose a contributions requirement on employees in addition to the contributions made by the employer.

EXAMPLE

1. Fay Nannen earns $320 during the first week of February while working for Dango, Inc. Since the company is located in New Jersey, Nannen would have $2.96 deducted from her pay (0.925% of $320). This 0.925 percent tax would be deducted on the first $24,900 paid to her during the year. (In New Jersey, 0.5 percent of the employees' contributions is for the disability benefit plan and 0.425 percent for the unemployment insurance fund.)
2. Donald Drury works in Puerto Rico and earns $450 each week. He would contribute $1.35 (0.3% of $450) of each pay to a disability fund. This 0.3 percent deduction would continue until his cumulative pay for the year reached $9,000.

SELF-STUDY QUIZ 5-2 *Moss Company paid wages of $6,000 to John Castellano in Arizona. During the year, Castellano transferred to the company's office in Colorado, and he received $26,000 for the rest of the year. The company's unemployment tax rate for Colorado is 2.9 percent. What would Moss Company pay to Colorado for unemployment taxes on John's wages?*
$ 10,000 - 6,000 = 4000 x 2.9% = 116.00

LEARNING OBJECTIVE 5

EXPERIENCE RATING As indicated earlier, the concept of experience rating is based upon the payment of state unemployment taxes according to the employer's stability of employment. As an employer experiences a lower employee turnover, generally the state unemployment tax rate will lower.

In all states, some type of experience-rating plan provides for a reduction in the employer's tax contributions based on the employer's experience with the risk of unemployment. Of the several formulas used to determine the contribution rates, the most commonly used is the **reserve-ratio formula**:

$$\text{Reserve Ratio} = \frac{\text{Contributions} - \text{Benefits Paid}}{\text{Average Payroll}}$$

The amount of the unemployment compensation contributions (taxes paid), the benefits paid by the state, and the employer's payroll are entered by the state on each employer's record. The benefits paid are subtracted from the contributions, and the balance of the employer's account is divided by the average payroll for a stated period of time to determine the reserve ratio. Under this plan, the balance carried forward each year equals the difference between the employer's total contributions and the total benefits paid to former employees by the state. The contribution rates are then established according to a schedule under which the higher the reserve ratio, the lower the tax rate.

Employers who have built up a balance in their reserve account (contributions paid in less benefits charged) are sometimes referred to as **positive-balance employers.** The larger the positive balance in a company's reserve account, the lower its tax rate will be. Employers whose reserve accounts have been charged for more benefits paid out than contributions paid in are referred to as **negative-balance employers,** and their high tax rates reflect this fact.

COMPUTING THE CONTRIBUTION RATE In an experience-rating system, the rate of contributions for employers is based on the employment experience of the employer. The rate is determined by computing the total of the reserve built up by employer contributions over a certain period of time and by computing the ratio of the amount in the reserve account to the employer's average annual payroll as determined under the state's formula.

EXAMPLE

Spencili Company is an employer located in a state with an unemployment compensation law containing merit-rating provisions for employers who meet certain requirements. Below is a summary of the total wages for the years 2004 to 2007, inclusive. For the purpose of the illustration, assume that the total wages and taxable wages are the same amount.

Quarter	2004	2005	2006	2007
1st	$11,000	$10,000	$ 8,500	$10,500
2nd	10,000	9,000	9,500	11,000
3rd	10,000	9,500	10,000	11,000
4th	10,500	9,750	9,500	9,500
Total	$41,500	$38,250	$37,500	$42,000

The State Unemployment Compensation Commission maintains a separate account for each employer. The account is credited with contributions paid into the unemployment compensation fund by the employer and is charged with unemployment benefits paid from the fund.

For 2008, the state law set up the following contribution rate schedule for employers:

Reserve Ratio	Rate
Negative reserve balance	6.7%
0% to less than 8%	5.9%
8% to less than 10%	5.0%
10% to less than 12%	4.1%
12% to less than 15%	3.2%
15% and over	2.5%

The state law under discussion defines: *average annual payroll*—average of last three years, *annual payroll*—wages paid from October 1 to September 30 each year.

The following computations show the state contributions made by Spencili Company for the calendar years 2004 to 2007, inclusive, the federal tax imposed under FUTA, and the method of arriving at the contribution rate for the calendar year 2008:

2004

Taxable wages	$41,500	
Rate (SUTA)	×2.7%	
State contributions		$1,120.50
Federal tax: 0.8% of $41,500		332.00
Total unemployment tax		$1,452.50

(Continued)

2005

Taxable wages	$38,250	
Rate (SUTA)	×2.7%	
State contributions		$1,032.75
Federal tax: 0.8% of $38,250		306.00
Total unemployment tax		$1,338.75

2006

Taxable wages	$37,500	
Rate (SUTA)	×3.4%	
State contributions		$1,275.00
Federal tax: 0.8% of $37,500		300.00
Total unemployment tax		$1,575.00

2007

Taxable wages	$42,000	
Rate (SUTA)	×3.7%	
State contributions		$1,554.00
Federal tax: 0.8% of $42,000		336.00
Total unemployment tax		$1,890.00

Remember that the average annual payroll is the average of the last three annual payrolls, with each annual payroll period running from October 1 to September 30.

Assume that Spencili Company paid state contributions of $960 in 2002 and $1,010 in 2003 and that $1,850 was charged to the employer's account for unemployment compensation benefits during 2006 and 2007. The contribution rate for 2008 is computed as follows:

Computation of rate for 2008:

Annual payroll period ending 9/30/05	$ 39,000
Annual payroll period ending 9/30/06	37,750
Annual payroll period ending 9/30/07	42,000
Total of last 3 annual payroll periods	$118,750

Average annual payroll:

$118,750 divided by 3 = $39,583

Contributions for 2002	$ 960.00
Contributions for 2003	1,010.00
Contributions for 2004	1,120.50
Contributions for 2005	1,032.75
Contributions for 2006	1,275.00
Contributions for 2007 (first nine months)	1,202.50
Total contributions	$6,600.75
Less amount of benefits paid	1,850.00
Balance in reserve account 9/30/07	$4,750.75

$4,750.75, divided by average annual payroll, $39,583 = 12%

Since the reserve is 12 percent of the average annual payroll, the tax rate for 2008 is 3.2 percent (the ratio is between 12% and 15%).

VOLUNTARY CONTRIBUTIONS In some states (see Figure 5–1, page 5-13), employers may obtain reduced unemployment compensation rates by making **voluntary contributions** to the state fund. Employers deliberately make these contributions in addition to their regularly required payments of state unemployment taxes. The voluntary contributions increase the balance in the employer's reserve account so that a lower contribution rate may be assigned for the following year. Thus, the new lower tax rate will save the employer more in future state unemployment tax payments than the amount of the voluntary contribution itself.

An employer who desires to make a voluntary contribution usually must determine the amount of the contribution needed in order to obtain a lower contribution rate. In some states, the agencies provide worksheets that aid employers in determining the amount of

EXAMPLE

To illustrate the tax saving that may be realized as a result of making voluntary contributions, consider the following case of Krane Company, which is subject to the unemployment compensation law of a state that uses the reserve-ratio formula to determine experience ratings. The following contribution rate schedule applies for 2009:

Reserve Ratio	Rate
0% to less than 1%	6.2%
1% to less than 1.4%	5.6%
1.4% to less than 1.8%	5.0%
1.8% to less than 2.2%	4.4%
2.2% to less than 2.6%	3.8%
2.6% to less than 3.0%	3.2%
3.0% and over	2.6%

For the three 12-month periods ending on June 30, 2008, the company had an average annual taxable payroll of $330,000. This is the base that the state uses as the average payroll. As of June 30, 2008, the credits to the employer's account exceeded the benefits paid by $6,800. Thus, the 2008 reserve ratio is 2.06 percent ($6,800 ÷ $330,000), which would result in the assignment of a 4.4 percent tax rate, as shown in the preceding table. If the employer's 2009 total taxable payroll were $390,000, the SUTA contribution would amount to $17,160.

If Krane Company makes a voluntary contribution into the state fund within the time period specified by the state law, the tax for 2009 will be less. For example, if the company contributes $460, the reserve ratio will be 2.2 percent ($7,260 ÷ $330,000). As a result, the tax rate will be reduced to 3.8 percent, with the following savings realized in 2009:

Tax Payment with No Voluntary Contribution (4.4% × $390,000) =		$17,160
Tax Payment with Voluntary Contribution	$ 460	
(3.8% × $390,000) =	14,820	15,280
Tax Savings		$ 1,880

voluntary contributions required. Ohio computes the voluntary contribution amount needed and includes it in the rate notices sent to all employers. As with the regular contributions, the state must receive the voluntary contributions by a certain date before they can be credited to the employer's account and be used in computing a new tax rate. In some states, the employer may have a certain number of days following the mailing of the tax rate notice to make the voluntary contributions. For instance, in Arizona, the voluntary contributions must be paid by January 31.

NEWS// ALERT//

If there are unpaid taxes and penalties due, states may apply the voluntary contributions to these amounts first.

Since these payments are not required payments, these voluntary contributions do not count as part of the credit against the FUTA tax.

NONPROFITS A federal law allows nonprofits the option to reimburse the state for the actual amount of unemployment benefits paid to their former employees, instead of paying a set percentage for state unemployment taxes. The reimbursement takes place on a dollar-for-dollar basis when the state pays the benefits to the former employees.

DUMPING *The SUTA Dumping Prevention Act* requires states to enact laws that stop businesses from changing their business structure to avoid paying their proper amount of SUTA taxes. This law is designed to stop companies with poor experience ratings from forming new companies with lower new employer tax rates and then transferring the employees to the new company ("dumping" the original company's high tax rates).

Unemployment Compensation Reports Required of the Employer

6 LEARNING OBJECTIVE

Employers liable for both the FUTA and the SUTA tax must file periodic reports with both the federal and the state governments. For FUTA tax reporting, employers file an annual return (Form 940) and generally make quarterly tax payments. Also, employers covered by state unemployment compensation laws generally submit two major kinds of reports. One is a tax return, on which the employer reports the tax due the state. The other is a wage report, which reflects the amount of taxable wages paid to each of the employer's covered employees.

ANNUAL FUTA RETURN—FORM 940

Form 940, Employer's Annual Federal Unemployment (FUTA) Tax Return, is the prescribed form for making the return required of employers in reporting the tax imposed under FUTA. Figure 5–2 shows a filled-in copy of this form.

COMPLETING THE RETURN Employers who pay SUTA tax to only one state, enter that state in box 1a. Those who pay unemployment tax to more than one state, check box 1b and complete Schedule A along with Form 940. The information needed to complete the rest of Form 940 may be obtained from the sources listed in Figure 5–3 (on page 5-23).

PRETAX CONTRIBUTIONS Contributions made on a pretax basis to a cafeteria plan are included in line 3 on Form 940 (total payments), and then, line 4 as exempt payments (and check box 4e). This also applies to the value of group-term life insurance in excess of $50,000 (taxable for FICA, federal income tax, but not FUTA).

PAYMENT OF BALANCE DUE After computing the final net FUTA tax (Line 12), the employer compares the net tax with the total deposits for the year in order to determine the balance due. Depending on the amount of the liability, the employer either deposits the balance due, electronically transfers, or remits it directly to the IRS with Form 940. Employers may now use a major credit card to pay the balance due on the form.

NOT LIABLE If an employer who is not liable for FUTA tax receives a Form 940, check box C in the top corner of the form and sign and return the form to the IRS.

SIGNING FORM 940 Form 940 must be signed by:

1. The individual, if a sole proprietorship.
2. The president, vice president, or other principal officer, if a corporation.
3. A responsible and duly authorized member, if a partnership or other unincorporated organization.
4. A fiduciary, if a trust or estate.

Officers and authorized agents may sign the return by rubber stamp, mechanical device, or computer software.

SCHEDULE A This schedule (Figure 5–4, on page 5-24) is only completed by employers who were required to pay state unemployment taxes in more than one state. The boxes for the appropriate states are checked off, and the schedule is mailed along with Form 940.

FILING THE RETURN The employer must file the annual return no later than January 31 following the close of the calendar year. If, however, the employer has made timely deposits that pay the FUTA tax liability in full, as discussed later, the company may delay the filing of Form 940 until February 10. The return must be filed on a calendar-year basis even though the company operates on a fiscal-year basis different from the calendar year. If January 31 falls on Saturday, Sunday, or a legal holiday, the return may be filed on the following business day. A mailed return bearing a postmark indicating it was mailed on or before the due date will be considered to have been timely filed even though received after the due date.

Upon application of the employer, the district director or the director of a service center may grant a reasonable extension of time in which to file the return, but not for payment of the tax. However, no extension will be granted for a period of more than 90 days. Generally, the application for an extension must be written on or before the filing due date. The return must be

FIGURE 5–2

Form 940, Employer's Annual Federal Unemployment (FUTA) Tax Return (Page 1)

Form **940 for 20--: Employer's Annual Federal Unemployment (FUTA) Tax Return**

Department of the Treasury — Internal Revenue Service

OMB No. 1545-0028

(EIN) Employer identification number 7 9 – 2 3 6 0 3 2 0

Name *(not your trade name)* SHANNON HEATING COMPANY

Trade name *(if any)*

Address P.O. BOX 1803
Number Street Suite or room number

LANSDOWNE PA 19019-3636
City State ZIP code

Type of Return
(Check all that apply.)

☐ **a.** Amended
☐ **b.** Successor employer
☐ **c.** No payments to employees in 20--
☐ **d.** Final: Business closed or stopped paying wages

Read the separate instructions before you fill out this form. Please type or print within the boxes.

Part 1: Tell us about your return. If any line does NOT apply, leave it blank.

1 **If you were required to pay your state unemployment tax in ...**

1a **One state only,** write the state abbreviation . . . . **1a** ☐☐

- OR -

1b **More than one state** (You are a multi-state employer) . . . . **1b** ☑ Check here. Fill out Schedule A.

2

Part 2: Determine your FUTA tax before adjustments for 20--. If any line does NOT apply, leave it blank.

3 **Total payments to all employees** **3** 98230.42

4 **Payments exempt from FUTA tax** . . . . **4** .

Check all that apply: **4a** ☐ Fringe benefits **4c** ☐ Retirement/Pension **4e** ☐ Other
4b ☐ Group term life insurance **4d** ☐ Dependent care

5 **Total of payments made to each employee in excess of $7,000** **5** 25317.62

6 **Subtotal** (line 4 + line 5 = line 6) **6** 25317.62

7 **Total taxable FUTA wages** (line 3 – line 6 = line 7) **7** 72912.80

8 **FUTA tax before adjustments** (line 7 × .008 = line 8) **8** 583.30

Part 3: Determine your adjustments. If any line does NOT apply, leave it blank.

9 **If ALL of the taxable FUTA wages you paid were excluded from state unemployment tax, multiply line 7 by .054** (line 7 × .054 = line 9). Then go to line 12 . . . . **9** .

10 **If SOME of the taxable FUTA wages you paid were excluded from state unemployment tax, OR you paid ANY state unemployment tax late** (after the due date for filing Form 940), fill out the worksheet in the instructions. Enter the amount from line 7 of the worksheet onto line 10 . . **10** .

11

Part 4: Determine your FUTA tax and balance due or overpayment for 20--. If any line does NOT apply, leave it blank.

12 **Total FUTA tax after adjustments** (lines 8 + 9 + 10 = line 12) **12** 583.30

13 **FUTA tax deposited for the year, including any payment applied from a prior year** **13** 583.30

14 **Balance due** (If line 12 is more than line 13, enter the difference on line 14.)
- If line 14 is more than $500, you must deposit your tax.
- If line 14 is $500 or less and you pay by check, make your check payable to the United States Treasury and write your EIN, *Form 940,* and *20--* on the check . . . . **14** 0.

15 **Overpayment** (If line 13 is more than line 12, enter the difference on line 15 and check a box below.) . . . . **15** .

Check one ☐ Apply to next return.
☐ Send a refund.

▶ You **MUST** fill out both pages of this form and **SIGN** it.

Next ➔

For Privacy Act and Paperwork Reduction Act Notice, see the back of Form 940-V, Payment Voucher. Cat. No. 11234O Form **940** (2006)

(Continued)

FIGURE 5–2 *(Concluded)*

Form 940, Employer's Annual Federal Unemployment (FUTA) Tax Return (Page 2)

Name *(not your trade name)*	**Employer identification number (EIN)**
SHANNON HEATING COMPANY	79-2360320

Part 5: Report your FUTA tax liability by quarter only if line 12 is more than $500. If not, go to Part 6.

16 **Report the amount of your FUTA tax liability for each quarter; do NOT enter the amount you deposited. If you had no liability for a quarter, leave the line blank.**

16a **1st quarter** (January 1 – March 31)	**16a**	203.42
16b **2nd quarter** (April 1 – June 30)	**16b**	259.95
16c **3rd quarter** (July 1 – September 30)	**16c**	98.83
16d **4th quarter** (October 1 – December 31)	**16d**	21.10
17 **Total tax liability for the year** (lines 16a + 16b + 16c + 16d = line 17)	**17**	583.30 **Total must equal line 12.**

Part 6: May we speak with your third-party designee?

Do you want to allow an employee, a paid tax preparer, or another person to discuss this return with the IRS? See the instructions for details.

☐ **Yes.** Designee's name ____________

Select a 5-digit Personal Identification Number (PIN) to use when talking to IRS ☐☐☐☐☐

☑ **No.**

Part 7: Sign here.

You MUST fill out both pages of this form and SIGN it.

Under penalties of perjury, I declare that I have examined this return, including accompanying schedules and statements, and to the best of my knowledge and belief, it is true, correct, and complete, and that no part of any payment made to a state unemployment fund claimed as a credit was, or is to be, deducted from the payments made to employees.

X Sign your name here	*J.D. Shannon*	Print your name here	J.D. SHANNON
		Print your title here	PRESIDENT
Date	1 / 31 / --	Best daytime phone	(215) 691 - 5555

Part 8: For PAID preparers only (optional)

If you were paid to prepare this return and are not an employee of the business that is filing this return, you may choose to fill out Part 8.

Paid Preparer's name		Preparer's SSN/PTIN	
Paid Preparer's signature		Date	/ /
	☐ Check if you are self-employed.		
Firm's name		Firm's EIN	
Street address			
City	State	ZIP code	

FIGURE 5–3

Sources of Information for Completing Form 940

Line No.	Source of Information
Part I—About Your Return	
1	State unemployment tax forms
Part 2—Determine Your FUTA Tax	
3	General ledger account(s) for wages and salaries
4	Employee earnings records
5	Employee earnings records
6	Follow directions for addition.
7	Follow directions for subtraction.
8	Follow directions for multiplication.
Part 3—Determine Your Adjustments	
9 and 10	From the appropriate states' unemployment tax returns
Part 4—Determine Your FUTA Tax	
12	Follow directions for addition.
13	From the debit postings to the FUTA taxes payable account in the general ledger
14, 15	Difference between lines 12 and 13
Part 5—FUTA Tax Liability for Each Quarter	
16	From the quarterly balances in the FUTA taxes payable account in the general ledger
17	Follow directions for addition.
Part 6—Third-Party Designee	
	Check the yes or no box.
Part 7—Sign Here.	
	Sign, date, and list phone number.

filed with the IRS center for the district in which the employer's principal place of business or office or agency is located. The instructions for Form 940 list the addresses of the IRS centers.

Once an employer has filed Form 940, the IRS will send the employer a preaddressed Form 940 near the close of each subsequent calendar year.

ELECTRONIC FILING Under the 940 e-filing program, businesses can use a personal computer, modem, and specialized software to file Forms 940. They must submit their electronic forms through a third-party transmitter. Filers must first submit an electronic letter of application to the IRS through their transmitter.

AMENDING THE RETURN When filing a corrected return, the employer must complete a new Form 940 for the year being amended. The "Amended" box on Form 940 should be checked, and the correct figures should be completed on the form. The return must be signed, and an explanation of the reasons for filing an amended return should be attached.

FIGURE 5–4

Required Form for Multi-State Employers

Schedule A (Form 940) for 20--:

Multi-State Employer and Credit Reduction Information

OMB No. 1545-0028

Department of the Treasury — Internal Revenue Service

Employer identification number (EIN) 7 9 - 2 3 6 0 3 2 0

Name *(not your trade name)* SHANNON HEATING COMPANY

About this schedule:

- You must fill out Schedule A (Form 940) if you were required to pay your state unemployment tax in ***more than one state*** or if you paid wages in any state that is subject to ***credit reduction.*** FOR 20--, THERE ARE NO STATES SUBJECT TO CREDIT REDUCTION.
- File Schedule A (Form 940) as an attachment to your Form 940.

For more information, read the Instructions for Schedule A (Form 940) on the back.

Part 1: Fill out this part if you were required to pay state unemployment taxes in more than one state (including the District of Columbia, Puerto Rico, and the U.S. Virgin Islands). If any states do NOT apply to you, leave them blank.

1 **Check the box for every state in which you were required to pay state unemployment tax this year.** For a list of state names and their abbreviations, see the Instructions for Schedule A (Form 940).

☐ AK	☐ CO	☐ GA	☑ IN	☐ MD	☐ MS	☐ NH	☐ OH	☐ SC	☐ VA	☐ WY
☐ AL	☐ CT	☐ HI	☐ KS	☐ MI	☐ MT	☐ NJ	☐ OK	☐ SD	☐ VT	☐ PR
☐ AR	☐ DC	☐ IA	☑ KY	☐ MN	☐ NC	☐ NM	☐ OR	☐ TN	☐ WA	☐ VI
☐ AZ	☐ DE	☐ ID	☐ LA	☐ MO	☐ ND	☐ NV	☑ PA	☐ TX	☐ WI	
☐ CA	☐ FL	☐ IL	☐ MA	☐ ME	☐ NE	☐ NY	☐ RI	☐ UT	☐ WV	

Part 2: Fill out this part to tell us about wages you paid in any state (including the District of Columbia, Puerto Rico, and the U.S. Virgin Islands) that is subject to credit reduction. If any lines do NOT apply, leave them blank.

2

3

For Privacy Act and Paperwork Reduction Act Notice, see back of Form 940-V. Cat. No. 16997C **Schedule A (Form 940) (Rev. 12-2006)**

FINAL RETURN If a company has ceased doing business, a final Form 940 must be completed (check box on Form 940 to indicate a final return) and the balance of the tax paid. In addition, a statement giving the name and address of the person(s) in charge of the required payroll records must be included with Form 940. If the business was sold or transferred, the name and address of the acquiring company should be included in the statement.

QUARTERLY DEPOSIT FORM—FUTA

The employer computes the net FUTA tax on a quarterly basis during the month following the end of each calendar quarter by multiplying 0.8 percent by that part of the first $7,000 of each of the employee's annual wages that the employer paid during the quarter. If the employer's tax liability exceeds $500, the employer must deposit it with an authorized depository on or before the last day of the month following the end of the quarter. If the employer deposits social security (FICA) and withheld federal income taxes (FIT) electronically, the employer is required to deposit all federal depository tax liabilities (including FUTA) electronically. Chapter 3 enumerated the requirements for each employer.

A similar computation and deposit for each of the first three quarters of the year is made. Each quarterly deposit for the coupon-based deposit system is to be accompanied by a preinscribed ***Federal Tax Deposit Coupon (Form 8109).*** Figure 5–5 shows a filled-in copy of this deposit form. If the tax liability for the first quarter is $500 or less, a deposit is not required; however, the employer must add the amount of the liability to the amount subject to deposit for the next quarter in order to compare the total tax due with the $500 minimum for that quarter.

EXAMPLE

As shown in Figure 5–2, on page 5-21, the accumulated tax liabilities of Shannon Heating Company for the 1st and 2nd quarter of 2008 were less than $500; no deposit was made for the first two quarters. Since the accumulated liability at the end of the 3rd quarter exceeded the $500 limit, a deposit of $562.20 was made on October 31, 2008, as shown on Form 8109 in Figure 5–5.

If the employer is required to deposit employment taxes electronically (see Chapter 3), the quarterly FUTA taxes must also be paid using the EFTPS.

At the time of filing the annual return on Form 940, the employer pays the balance of tax owed for the prior year and not yet deposited. If the amount of tax reportable on Form 940 exceeds by more than $500 the sum of amounts deposited each quarter, the employer must deposit the total amount owed either electronically or by using Form 8109 on or before January 31 following the year for which Form 940 is filed. If the amount owed is $500 or less, the employer may remit it with the annual form. A payment voucher form,

FIGURE 5–5

Form 8109, Federal Tax Deposit Coupon

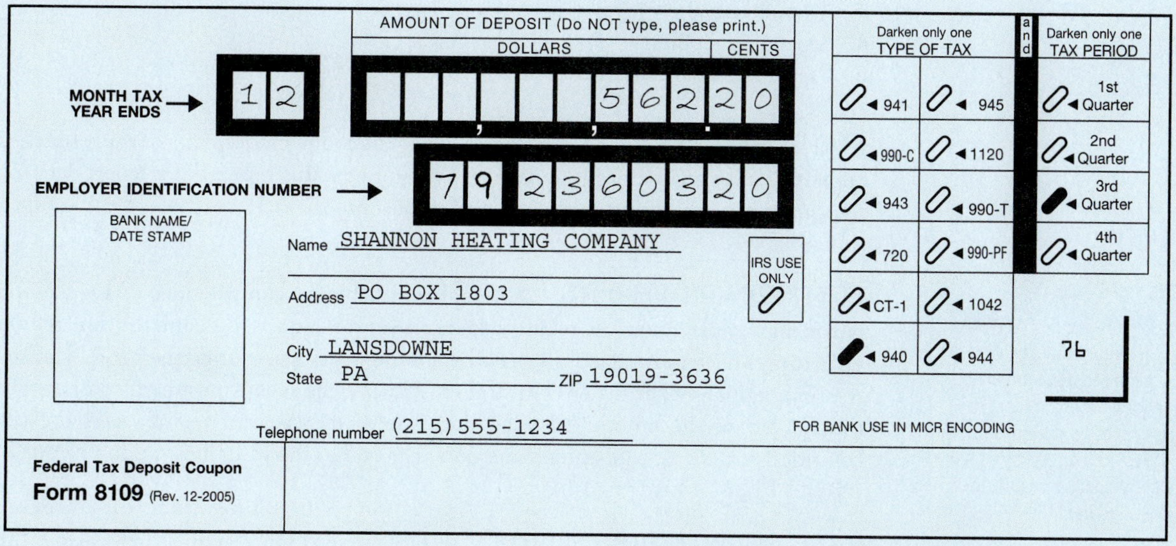
AMOUNT OF DEPOSIT (Do NOT type, please print.)
DOLLARS | CENTS
MONTH TAX YEAR ENDS → 12
562 20
EMPLOYER IDENTIFICATION NUMBER → 79 2360320
BANK NAME/ DATE STAMP
Name SHANNON HEATING COMPANY
Address PO BOX 1803
City LANSDOWNE
State PA ZIP 19019-3636
Telephone number (215) 555-1234
IRS USE ONLY
Darken only one TYPE OF TAX: 941, 945, 990-C, 1120, 943, 990-T, 720, 990-PF, CT-1, 1042, 940 (darkened), 944
Darken only one TAX PERIOD: 1st Quarter, 2nd Quarter, 3rd Quarter (darkened), 4th Quarter
76
FOR BANK USE IN MICR ENCODING
Federal Tax Deposit Coupon
Form 8109 (Rev. 12-2005)

Form 940V, is completed and filed along with Form 940 and the check or money order. This form allows the government to process the payment more efficiently.

SELF-STUDY QUIZ 5-3 *The FUTA taxable wages of Davies Company during 2008 follow. List the amount and the due date of each deposit of FUTA taxes for the year.*

	Amount	Due Date
1st Quarter—$66,000	$________	________
2nd Quarter—$64,000	$________	________
3rd Quarter—$42,000	$________	________
4th Quarter—$25,000	$________	________

TAXES—HOUSEHOLD EMPLOYERS Household employers both report and pay their federal unemployment taxes for their household employees with their personal income tax return (Form 1040). Schedule H, *Household Employment Taxes,* is attached to their tax returns, and payment of the unemployment taxes for the previous year is due by April 15.

PENALTIES—FUTA

As indicated in Chapter 3, the Internal Revenue Code subjects employers to civil and criminal penalties for failing to file returns, pay the employment taxes when due, and make timely deposits. These penalties apply, generally, without regard to the type of tax or return involved. The last section of Chapter 3 presents all of the penalties.

INFORMATION REPORTS—SUTA

LEARNING OBJECTIVE 7

A wide variation exists in the official forms that the states provide for filing the reports required under the unemployment compensation laws. Therefore, the employer must become familiar with the law and regulations of each state in which liability might be incurred.

The reports required of the employers by the individual states determine (1) the employer's liability for the contributions, (2) the amount of the contribution due on a quarterly basis, and (3) the amount of benefits to which employees will be entitled if they become unemployed. The most important of the required reports follow:

1. Status reports
2. Contribution reports
3. Wage information reports
4. Separation reports
5. Partial unemployment notices

STATUS REPORTS Under the unemployment compensation laws of most states, new employers must register or file an initial statement or **status report**. This report determines the employer's liability for making contributions into the state unemployment compensation fund.

CONTRIBUTION REPORTS All employers liable for contributions under the unemployment compensation law of any state must submit a quarterly **contribution report** or tax return. This report provides a summary of the wages paid during the period and shows the computation of the tax or contribution. Usually, the report must be filed on or before the last day of the month following the close of the calendar quarter, and the tax or contribution must be paid at the same time. Figure 5–6 shows an illustration of a quarterly tax calculation report (Part I).

NEWS // ALERT//

As part of a feasibility study, employers in Montana are filing just one form for both federal and state unemployment purposes. The form is filed with the state, which then electronically forwards the federal data to the IRS.

WAGE INFORMATION REPORTS In most state employers must make **wage information reports** concerning individual employees. Usually, employers file these reports

FIGURE 5–6

Pennsylvania Form, UC-2. Employer's Report for Unemployment Compensation—Part I

PA Form UC-2, REV 9-00, Employer's Report for Unemployment Compensation

Read Instructions – Answer Each Item

QTR./YEAR 1/20--

DUE DATE 04/30/20--

I INV. EXAMINED BY:

Signature certifies that the information contained herein is true and correct to the best of the signer's knowledge.

John Kiel

10. SIGN HERE-DO NOT PRINT

TITLE President DATE 4/23/-- PHONE # (555)555-5555

11. FILED ☐ PAPER UC-2A ☐ MAGNETIC MEDIA UC-2A

EMPLOYER'S CONTRIBUTION RATE .018734 EMPLOYER'S ACCT. NO. 79-16093-0 CHECK DIGIT &

Item	1ST MONTH	2ND MONTH	3RD MONTH
1. TOTAL COVERED EMPLOYEES IN PAY PERIOD INCL. 12TH OF MONTH	5	6	6

Item	Amount	FOR DEPT. USE
2. GROSS WAGES	31,790.00	
3. EMPLOYEE CONTRIBUTIONS	6.36	XXXXX
4. TAXABLE WAGES FOR EMPLOYER CONTRIBUTIONS	29,290.00	
5. EMPLOYER CONTRIBUTIONS DUE (RATE X ITEM 4)	548.72	
6. TOTAL CONTRIBUTIONS DUE (ITEMS 3 + 5)	555.08	
7. INTEREST DUE SEE INSTRUCTIONS		
8. PENALTY DUE SEE INSTRUCTIONS		
9. TOTAL REMITTANCE (ITEMS 6 + 7 + 8)	$ 555.08	

MAKE CHECKS PAYABLE TO: PA UC FUND

Employer name and address
Make any corrections on Form UC-2B

Kielso Company
23 Carriage Lane
Lansdale, PA 17094

DATE PAYMENT RECEIVED MMDDYY SUBJECTIVITY DATE MMDDYY REPORT DELINQUENT DATE MMDDYY

with the quarterly contribution reports. Figure 5–7 on page 5-28 shows an example of a quarterly wage information report (Part II). On the report are listed all employee names, SSNs, taxable wages, taxable tips, and the employer's federal account number. In addition, the number of credit weeks earned by each employee during the quarter could be required. (A ***credit week*** is defined by the state's unemployment compensation law; for example, Pennsylvania defines a credit week as any calendar week in the quarter during which the person earned remuneration of not less than $50.)

Most states permit the use of the same magnetic tape for reporting state wage information that is used for federal social security reporting purposes. The payroll manager should contact the state agency to determine whether federal-state combined magnetic tape reporting is acceptable.

SEPARATION REPORTS Whenever a worker becomes separated from employment, a **separation report**, providing a wage and employment record of the separated employee and the reason for leaving, might be required. Usually, a copy of the report is given to the worker in order that the individual may be informed of any entitlement to unemployment insurance benefits.

PARTIAL UNEMPLOYMENT NOTICES Most states require employers to give **partial unemployment notices** to those workers who become "partially unemployed," so that they are informed of their potential eligibility for partial unemployment benefits. **Partial unemployment** refers to employment by the individual's regular employer but on a reduced scale because of lack of work. In most states, the notice must be given to the worker immediately after a week of partial employment has been completed. After that, the employer ordinarily furnishes the worker with some kind of low-earnings report during each week of partial employment so that the worker will be assured of the receipt of supplemental or partial benefits.

on the *JOB*

State unemployment insurance records must be preserved by employers for a certain number of years based on each state's requirements. The minimum periods range from a low in Mississippi of three years to a high in Tennessee of seven years.

PENALTIES—SUTA

All states have some form of penalty for failure to pay, for the late payment of contributions, and also for failure to file reports. Some states impose a 10 percent penalty if the failure to pay the tax is due to negligence, and in a few states, a 50 percent penalty is

FIGURE 5–7

Pennsylvania Form, UC-2A. Employer's Report for Unemployment Compensation—Part II

PA Form UC-2A, Rev 6-2000, Employer's Quarterly Report of Wages Paid to Each Employee

See instructions on separate sheet. Information MUST be typewritten or printed in BLACK ink. Do NOT use commas (,) or dollar signs ($).
If typed, disregard vertical bars and type a consecutive string of characters. If hand printed, print in CAPS and within the boxes as below:

SAMPLE Typed: 123456.00 **SAMPLE Handwritten:** 123456.00 **SAMPLE Filled-in:** → ●

Employer name (make corrections on Form UC-2B)	Employer PA UC account no.	Check digit	Quarter and year Q/YYYY	Quarter ending date MM/DD/YYYY
Kielso Company	79-16093-0	&	1/20--	03/31/20--

1. Name and telephone number of preparer: Nancy Heller (555) 555-5555

2. Total number of pages in this report: 1

3. Total number of employees listed in item 8 on all pages of Form UC-2A: 7

4. Plant number (if approved):

5. Gross wages, MUST agree with item 2 on UC-2 and the sum of item 11 on all pages of Form UC-2A: 31790.00

6. Fill in this circle if you would like the Department to preprint your employees names & SSNs on Form UC-2A next quarter → ●

7. Employee's social security number	8. Employee's name FI	MI	LAST	9. Gross wages paid this qtr Example:***123456.00	10. Credit weeks
111098271	J	L	CARROLL	6300.00	13
095191918	C	H	LONG	1900.00	5
212163790	H	M	DORSEY	2990.00	13
091786510	M	F	ERNST	2100.00	13
109050093	J	B	KIEL	10500.00	13
170919008	A	W	PINKETT	4100.00	13
089871792	L	B	GOLIC	3900.00	13

List any additional employees on continuation sheets in the required format (see instructions).

Batch # For Dept. Use Only

11. Total gross wages for this page: → 31790.00

12. Page 1 of 1

imposed if the failure to pay is due to fraud. Many states also deny experience rates to employers who are delinquent in filing reports or paying contributions. In some states, employers who have been delinquent in paying their contributions may be required to pay the contributions monthly rather than quarterly.

KEY TERMS

Constructively paid *(p. 5-10)*
Contribution report *(p. 5-26)*
Dismissal payments *(p. 5-10)*
Experience rating *(p. 5-11)*
Interstate employee *(p. 5-6)*
Merit rating *(p. 5-11)*
Negative-balance employers *(p. 5-17)*
Partial unemployment *(p. 5-27)*
Partial unemployment notices *(p. 5-27)*
Pooled-fund laws *(p. 5-16)*
Positive-balance employers *(p. 5-17)*
Reciprocal arrangements *(p. 5-8)*
Reserve-ratio formula *(p. 5-16)*
Separation report *(p. 5-27)*
Status report *(p. 5-26)*
Title XII advances *(p. 5-12)*
Voluntary contributions *(p. 5-18)*
Wage information reports *(p. 5-26)*

CHAPTER SUMMARY

This chapter on FUTA and SUTA begins with the definition of an employer—the $1,500 wages or the one-day employment in 20 weeks tests. The coverage of employees (legal common-law relationship) applies for both FUTA and SUTA. SUTA coverage of interstate (working in more than one state) employees is based on localized work, base of operations, base of direction, or residence. Reciprocal arrangements between the states can override the previous factors—the employer elects the state of coverage. FUTA tax rates are a net tax of 0.8% (6.2% gross less 5.4% credit) on the first $7,000 of earnings. Each state sets its own range of rates and taxable wage limit (e.g., New York—1.1% to 9.5% on the first $8,500). States base the rate they charge an employer on past experience.

$$\text{Reserve Ratio} = \frac{\text{Contributions} - \text{Benefits Paid}}{\text{Average Payroll}}$$

Employers have to file an annual federal unemployment tax return (Form 940)—due January 31. The deposit of the FUTA taxes is done on a quarterly basis (if over $500 is due). The states also require that reports be filed and tax payments made on a quarterly basis.

MATCHING QUIZ

______ 1. Reciprocal arrangements
______ 2. Title XII advances
______ 3. Negative-balance employers
______ 4. Dumping
______ 5. Over $500
______ 6. Merit rating
______ 7. Form 8109
______ 8. Household employers
______ 9. Wage information reports
______ 10. Voluntary contributions

A. Extra state unemployment contributions in addition to employers' regular SUTA tax payments
B. Favorable employment records results in a lower SUTA tax
C. Federal tax deposit coupon
D. Poor experience-rated companies form new companies with lower unemployment tax rates
E. Pay FUTA tax with Schedule H of Form 1040
F. Provide unemployment insurance coverage and payment of benefits to interstate workers
G. Borrowings from federal government to pay unemployment compensation benefits
H. Employers whose reserve account has been charged with more benefits paid out than contributions made
I. Quarterly threshold for mandatory depositing of FUTA taxes
J. Quarterly reports submitted to the state listing employees, SSNs, and taxable wages

QUESTIONS FOR REVIEW

1. What two alternative tests are applied to a business in order to judge whether it is an "employer" and therefore subject to the FUTA tax?
2. What condition would make a household employer a covered employer under FUTA?
3. Charlie Carlson is a full-time student at Wenonah College and works part-time in the school's maintenance department. Must the college pay a FUTA tax on Charlie's earnings?
4. Under the Interstate Reciprocal Coverage Arrangement, the services of a worker can be covered in the state of the election of the employer as long as one of three factors exists. What are those three conditions?
5. To what extent does FUTA coverage extend to services that a citizen of the United States performs for an American employer outside the United States?
6. Which of the following types of payments are taxable under FUTA?
   a. Commissions as compensation for covered employment.
   b. Christmas gifts of nominal value.
   c. Courtesy discounts to employees.
   d. Reimbursement of ordinary and necessary business expenses.
   e. Dismissal payments.
7. What is an employer required to do in order to obtain the maximum credit of 5.4% against the FUTA tax?
8. An employer, because of a favorable experience rating, is permitted to pay a state contribution at a reduced rate of 1.5%. What percentage of taxable wages must be paid in the aggregate to the federal and state governments?
9. What are two situations in which an employer could be liable for a net FUTA tax greater than 0.8%?
10. What is the purpose of Title XII advances?
11. In 2007:
    a. Which state had the widest range of SUTA tax rates for employers?
    b. Which state paid the highest weekly maximum benefit (excluding dependency allowances) to qualified unemployed workers?
    c. Which state had the highest taxable wage base for the SUTA tax?
12. How is the SUTA tax rate determined for a new employer?
13. a. For an employer who is subject to FUTA, what are the basic forms that must be filed with the federal government?
    b. When must these forms be filed?
    c. How are taxable wages computed on the annual return?
14. How are pretax contributions by employees into cafeteria plans presented on Form 940?
15. How does an employer file an amended Form 940?
16. What special steps must be taken when completing Form 940 for a company that has ceased operations during the year?
17. When does an employer have to pay the FUTA taxes?
18. When is an employer required to deposit FUTA taxes electronically?
19. How often do employers file wage and contribution reports with their states?
20. What is a separation report?

QUESTIONS FOR DISCUSSION

1. Can the owner of a small business receive unemployment compensation? Explain.
2. What arguments could be made for raising the upper limits of the SUTA tax rates?
3. Check the unemployment compensation law of your state and determine the answers to the following questions:
   a. How do nonprofit organizations, subject to coverage, make payments to the unemployment compensation fund?
   b. Can part-time teachers collect unemployment compensation between school terms?
   c. Can professional athletes receive unemployment compensation?
   d. Are aliens covered by the unemployment compensation law?
   e. How do employers protest or appeal benefit determinations and charges against their accounts?
   f. Briefly describe how a person's weekly benefit rate and maximum benefit amount are determined.
   g. Can an unemployed worker collect additional benefits if he or she has dependents? If so, how much is paid for each dependent?
   h. Does the state provide payment of partial benefits?
   i. Are benefits payable to a female during pregnancy?
   j. Can employers make voluntary contributions to their state unemployment reserve accounts?
   k. For what reasons may an unemployed worker be disqualified from receiving unemployment benefits?
   l. What steps are taken by the state unemployment agency to prevent the improper payment of claims?

4. As a way of curbing the unemployment rate, California has instituted a "shared-work compensation" program. Under this program, a company faced with a layoff of its workers may place its entire workforce on a four-day workweek during the period of hardship. During this period of reduced workweeks, the employees collect partial unemployment benefits. When business rebounds, the firm returns to its normal five-day workweek, and the unemployment compensation benefits cease. Participation in the program must be approved by both the employer and the unions. If, however, the firm is not unionized, management has the discretion of putting the plan into effect.
   a. What are the benefits of such a shared-work compensation program to (1) the employer and (2) the employees?
   b. What disadvantages do you see in the operation of a shared-work compensation program, especially from the viewpoint of organized labor?

PRACTICAL PROBLEMS—SERIES A

5-1A LO 4,5.

During the year, Nunzio Company has a SUTA tax rate of 5.9%. The taxable payroll for the year for FUTA and SUTA is $67,000. Compute:

a. Net FUTA tax . . . . $ ________
b. Net SUTA tax . . . . ________
c. Total unemployment taxes . . . $ ________

5-2A LO 4,5.

Peyton Company's payroll for the year is $737,910. Of this amount, $472,120 is for wages paid in excess of $7,000 to each individual employee. The SUTA rate in Peyton Company's state is 2.9% on the first $7,000 of each employee's earnings. Compute:

a. Net FUTA tax . . . . $ ________
b. Net SUTA tax . . . . ________
c. Total unemployment taxes . . . $ ________

5-3A LO 4,5.

Garrison Shops had a SUTA tax rate of 3.7%. The state's taxable limit was $8,000 of each employee's earnings. For the year, Garrison Shops had FUTA taxable wages of $67,900 and SUTA taxable wages of $83,900. Compute:

a. Net FUTA tax . . . . $ ________
b. Net SUTA tax . . . . $ ________

5-4A LO 4,5.

Due to its experience rating, Ianelli, Inc., is required to pay unemployment taxes on its payroll as follows:

1. Under SUTA for Illinois on taxable payroll of $18,000, the contribution rate is 4%.
2. Under SUTA for Indiana on taxable payroll of $24,000, the contribution rate is 2.65%.
3. Under SUTA for Ohio on taxable payroll of $79,000, the contribution rate is 2.9%.
4. Under FUTA, the taxable payroll is $103,500.

Compute:

a. SUTA taxes paid to Illinois . . . . $ ________
b. SUTA taxes paid to Indiana . . . $ ________
c. SUTA taxes paid to Ohio . . . . . $ ________
d. FUTA taxes paid . . . . $ ________

5-5A LO 1,4.

Boxon Company began its operations in August of the current year. During August and September, the company paid wages of $6,950. For the last quarter of the year, the taxable wages paid amounted to $12,910. None of the employees were paid more than $7,000 this year.

a. Is Boxon Company liable for FUTA tax this year? Explain.
b. If so, what is the ***net*** FUTA tax before any credit is granted for the SUTA tax?
. . . . $ ________

5-6A LO 1,3,4,5.

In September 2008, Manson Paint Corporation began operations in a state that requires new employers of one or more individuals to pay a state unemployment tax of 3.5% of the first $7,000 of wages paid each employee.

An analysis of the company's payroll for the year shows total wages paid of $177,610. The salaries of the president and the vice president of the company were $20,000 and $15,000, respectively, for the four-month period, but there were no other employees who received wages in excess of $7,000 for the four months. Included in the total wages were $900 paid to a director who only attended director meetings during the year and $6,300 paid to the factory superintendent and $2,000 in employee contributions to a cafeteria plan made on a pretax basis—for both federal and state.

In addition to the total wages of $177,610, a payment of $2,430 was made to Andersen Accounting Company for an audit it performed on the company's books in December 2008. Compute:

a. Net FUTA tax . . . . $ ________
b. SUTA tax . . . . $ ________

5-7A LO 2,3,4,5.

In April of the current year, Freeman Steel Company transferred Herb Porter from its factory in Tennessee to its plant in South Carolina. The company's SUTA tax rates based on its experience ratings are 3.2% in Tennessee and 3.8% in South Carolina. Both states base the tax on the first $7,000 of each employee's earnings. This year, Freeman Steel Company paid Herb Porter wages of $9,900; $2,800 were paid in Tennessee and the remainder in South Carolina. Compute:

a. Amount of SUTA tax the company must pay to Tennessee on Porter's wages . . . $__________

b. Amount of SUTA tax the company must pay to South Carolina on Porter's wages . . . . $__________

c. Amount of the net FUTA tax on Porter's wages . . . . $__________

5-8A LO 5.

During 2008, Jeff Smallwood worked for two different employers. Until May, he worked for Rowland Construction Company in Cincinnati, Ohio, and earned $22,000. The state unemployment rate for Rowland is 4.6%. He then changed jobs and worked for Ford Improvement Company in Louisville, Kentucky, and earned $29,500. The state unemployment rate for Ford is 5.1%. Determine the unemployment taxes (FUTA and SUTA) that would be paid by:

a. Rowland Construction Company $__________

b. Ford Improvement Company. . $__________

5-9A LO 3,4.

The partnership of Edward and Farnam paid the following wages during this year:

M. Edward (partner)	$21,000
S. Farnam (partner)	19,000
N. Pearson (supervisor).	12,500
T. Grunhart (factory worker)	9,700
R. Rice (factory worker)	9,200
D. Brown (factory worker)	7,900
S. Koenig (bookkeeper).	10,900
C. Chang (maintenance).	4,500

In addition, the partnership owed $200 to Chang for work he performed during December. However, payment for this work will not be made until January of the following year. The state unemployment tax rate for the company is 2.15% on the first $9,000 of each employee's earnings. Compute:

a. Net FUTA tax for the partnership for this year . . . . $__________

b. SUTA tax for this year . . . . $__________

5-10A LO 4,5.

Peroni Company paid wages of $170,900 this year. Of this amount, $114,000 was taxable for net FUTA and SUTA purposes. The state's contribution tax rate is 3.1% for Peroni Company. Due to cash flow problems, the company did not make any SUTA payments until after the Form 940 filing date. Compute:

a. Amount of credit the company would receive against the FUTA tax for its SUTA contributions. . . . . $__________

b. Amount that Peroni Company would pay to the federal government for its FUTA tax . . $__________

c. Amount that the company lost because of its late payments . . . . $__________

5-11A LO 4,5.

During 2008, Jordan Company was subject to the Alaska state unemployment tax of 4.2%. The company's taxable earnings for FUTA were $86,700 and for SUTA, $171,000. Compute:

a. SUTA tax that Jordan Company would pay to the state of Alaska . . . . $__________

b. Net FUTA tax for 2008 . . . . . . $__________

c. Amount of employees' unemployment tax for 2008 (use the employee's tax rate shown in Figure 5–1 on p. 5-13) . . . . $__________

5-12A LO 5.

The following unemployment tax rate schedule is in effect for the calendar year 2008 in State A, which uses the reserve-ratio formula in determining employer contributions:

Reserve Ratio	Contribution Rate
0.0% or more, but less than 1.0%	6.7%
1.0% or more, but less than 1.2%	6.4%
1.2% or more, but less than 1.4%	6.1%
1.4% or more, but less than 1.6%	5.8%
1.6% or more, but less than 1.8%	5.5%
1.8% or more, but less than 2.0%	5.2%
2.0% or more, but less than 2.2%	4.9%
2.2% or more, but less than 2.4%	4.6%
2.4% or more, but less than 2.6%	4.3%
2.6% or more, but less than 2.8%	4.0%
2.8% or more, but less than 3.0%	3.7%
3.0% or more, but less than 3.2%	3.4%
3.2% or more	3.1%

Hyram Company, which is located in State A, had an average annual payroll of $850,000 for the three 12-month periods ending on June 30, 2007 (the computation date for the tax year 2008). As of June 30, 2007, the total contributions that had been made to Hyram Company's reserve account, in excess of the benefits charged, amounted to $17,440. Compute:

a. Hyram Company's reserve ratio for 2007 . . . . ____________%

b. 2008 contribution rate for the company . . . . ____________%

c. Smallest contribution that the company can make in order to reduce its tax rate if State A permits voluntary contributions. . . . . $____________

d. Tax savings realized by the company, taking into consideration the voluntary contribution made in (c) if the taxable payroll in 2008 is $980,000 . . . . $____________

5-13A LO 5.

As of June 30, 2007 (the computation date for the 2008 tax rate), Zimfer Company had a negative balance of $867 in its unemployment reserve account in State A. The company's average payroll over the last three 12-month periods amounted to $360,000. The unemployment compensation law of State A provides that the tax rate of an employer who has a negative balance on the computation date shall be 7.2% during the following calendar year. Using the tax rate schedule presented in Problem 5–12A, compute:

a. The smallest voluntary contribution that Zimfer Company should make in order to effect a change in its tax rate . . . . $____________

b. The amount of the tax savings as a result of the voluntary contribution if Zimfer Company's taxable payroll for 2008 is $420,000 . . $____________

5-14A LO 3,4,5.

Marlene Grady and Pauline Monroe are partners engaged in operating The G&M Doll Shop, which has employed the following persons since the beginning of the year:

V. Hoffman (general office worker)	$1,700 per month
A. Drugan (saleswoman)	$15,000 per year
G. Beiter (stock clerk)	$180 per week
S. Egan (deliveryman)	$220 per week
B. Lin (cleaning and maintenance, part-time)	$160 per week

Grady and Monroe are each paid a weekly salary allowance of $950.

The doll shop is located in a state that requires unemployment compensation contributions of employers of one or more individuals. The company is subject to state contributions at a rate of 3.1% for wages not in excess of $8,100. Compute each of the following amounts based upon the 41st weekly payroll period for the week ending October 10, 2008:

a. Amount of FICA taxes (OASDI and HI) to be withheld from the earnings of each person. (Refer to Chapter 3.)

	OASDI	HI
M. Grady	$ ________	$ ________
P. Monroe	________	________
V. Hoffman	________	________
A. Drugan	________	________
G. Beiter	________	________
S. Egan	________	________
B. Lin	________	________

b. Amount of the employer's FICA taxes for the weekly payroll .... ________ ________

c. Amount of state unemployment contributions for the weekly payroll .... $ ________

d. Amount of the net FUTA tax on the payroll .... $ ________

e. Total amount of the employer's payroll taxes for the weekly payroll .... $ ________

5-15A LO 5.

Karlson Software Company is located in State H, which enables employers to reduce their contribution rates under the experience-rating system. From 1994 to 2003, inclusive, the company's total contributions to state unemployment compensation amounted to $14,695. For the calendar years 2004 to 2007, inclusive, the contribution rate for employers was 2.7%.

The contributions of each employer are credited to an account maintained by the State Unemployment Compensation Commission. This account is credited with contributions paid into the account by the employer and is charged with unemployment benefits that are paid from the account. Starting January 1, 2008, the contributions rate for all employers in State H will be based on the following tax-rate schedule:

Reserve Ratio	Contribution Rate
Contributions falling below benefits paid	7.0%
0.0% to 7.9%	5.5%
8.0% to 9.9%	4.5%
10.0% to 11.9%	3.5%
12.0% to 14.9%	2.5%
15.0% or more	1.5%

The annual payroll for calculation purposes is the total wages payable during a 12-month period ending with the last day of the third quarter of any calendar year. The average annual payroll is the average of the last three annual payrolls. The SUTA tax rate for the year is computed using the information available (benefits received and taxes paid) as of September 30 of the preceding year.

The schedule below shows the total payroll and the taxable payroll for the calendar years 2004 to 2007.

Calendar Year

	2004		2005		2006		2007	
	Total Payroll	Taxable Payroll	Total Payroll	Taxable Payroll	Total Payroll	Taxable Payroll	Total Payroll	Taxable Payroll
First Quarter	$12,000	$12,000	$11,000	$11,000	$13,000	$13,000	$10,000	$10,000
Second Quarter	11,750	11,750	11,500	11,400	12,750	12,700	9,300	9,300
Third Quarter	12,500	12,250	12,750	12,400	12,200	12,000	9,350	9,350
Fourth Quarter	13,000	12,500	12,500	12,200	14,000	13,750	—	—

Unemployment benefits became payable to the company's qualified unemployed workers on January 1, 1994. Between that time and September 30, 2007, total benefits amounting to $15,100.90 were charged against the employer's account. Compute:

a. Contribution rate for 2008 ... ________%

b. Rate for 2008 if $2,000 additional benefits had been charged by mistake to the account of Karlson Software Company by the State Unemployment Compensation Commission .... ________%

5-16A LO 6.

As the accountant for Monroe Trucking Company, you are preparing the company's annual return, Form 940 and Schedule A. Use the following information to complete Form 940, Schedule A on pages 5-38 to 5-40.

The net FUTA tax liability for each quarter of 2008 was as follows: 1st, $97; 2nd, $87; 3rd, $69.70; and 4th, $59.50.

Since the net FUTA tax liability did not exceed $500, the company was not required to make its first deposit of FUTA taxes until February 2, 2009. Assume that the federal tax deposit coupon (Form 8109) was completed and the deposit was made on that date.

a. One of the employees performs all of his duties in another state—Florida.

b. Total payments made to employees during calendar year 2008:

South Carolina.	$53,450
Florida.	9,100
Total	$62,550

c. Payments made to employees in excess of $7,000: $23,400.

d. Amount contributed to unemployment compensation fund of South Carolina under merit rating, 1.8% of $32,150, or $578.70, for calendar year 2008. For Florida, the contribution was 3.6% of $7,000 (the taxable salary limit), or $252.

e. Form is to be signed by Vernon Scott, Vice President.

f. Phone number – (834) 555-5551.

Form **940 for 20--: Employer's Annual Federal Unemployment (FUTA) Tax Return**

Department of the Treasury — Internal Revenue Service

OMB No. 1545-0028

(EIN) Employer identification number: 5 4 – 0 6 6 3 7 9 3

Name (*not your trade name*): MONROE TRUCKING COMPANY

Trade name (*if any*):

Address: 423 BRISTOL PIKE
Number Street Suite or room number

NEWTON | F | 18940-4523
City State ZIP code

Type of Return
(Check all that apply.)

- ☐ **a.** Amended
- ☐ **b.** Successor employer
- ☐ **c.** No payments to employees in 20--
- ☐ **d.** Final: Business closed or stopped paying wages

Read the separate instructions before you fill out this form. Please type or print within the boxes.

Part 1: Tell us about your return. If any line does NOT apply, leave it blank.

1 **If you were required to pay your state unemployment tax in ...**

1a **One state only,** write the state abbreviation . . . . 1a ☐☐

- OR -

1b **More than one state** (You are a multi-state employer) . . . . 1b ☐ Check here. Fill out Schedule A.

2

Part 2: Determine your FUTA tax before adjustments for 20--. If any line does NOT apply, leave it blank.

3 **Total payments to all employees** . . . . 3 ______ .

4 **Payments exempt from FUTA tax** . . . . 4 ______ .

Check all that apply: 4a ☐ Fringe benefits 4c ☐ Retirement/Pension 4e ☐ Other
4b ☐ Group term life insurance 4d ☐ Dependent care

5 **Total of payments made to each employee in excess of $7,000** . . . . 5 ______ .

6 **Subtotal** (line 4 + line 5 = line 6) . . . . 6 ______ .

7 **Total taxable FUTA wages** (line 3 – line 6 = line 7) . . . . 7 ______ .

8 **FUTA tax before adjustments** (line 7 × .008 = line 8) . . . . 8 ______ .

Part 3: Determine your adjustments. If any line does NOT apply, leave it blank.

9 **If ALL of the taxable FUTA wages you paid were excluded from state unemployment tax, multiply line 7 by .054** (line 7 × .054 = line 9). Then go to line 12 . . . . 9 ______ .

10 **If SOME of the taxable FUTA wages you paid were excluded from state unemployment tax, OR you paid ANY state unemployment tax late** (after the due date for filing Form 940), fill out the worksheet in the instructions. Enter the amount from line 7 of the worksheet onto line 10 . . 10 ______ .

11

Part 4: Determine your FUTA tax and balance due or overpayment for 20--. If any line does NOT apply, leave it blank.

12 **Total FUTA tax after adjustments** (lines 8 + 9 + 10 = line 12) . . . . 12 ______ .

13 **FUTA tax deposited for the year, including any payment applied from a prior year** . . . . 13 ______ .

14 **Balance due** (If line 12 is more than line 13, enter the difference on line 14.)

- If line 14 is more than $500, you must deposit your tax.
- If line 14 is $500 or less and you pay by check, make your check payable to the United States Treasury and write your EIN, *Form 940,* and *20--* on the check . . . . 14 ______ .

15 **Overpayment** (If line 13 is more than line 12, enter the difference on line 15 and check a box below.) . . . . 15 ______ .

Check one ☐ Apply to next return.
☐ Send a refund.

▶ You **MUST** fill out both pages of this form and **SIGN** it.

Next ➔

For Privacy Act and Paperwork Reduction Act Notice, see the back of Form 940-V, Payment Voucher. Cat. No. 11234O Form **940** (2006)

5-16A (continued)

Name *(not your trade name)* | Employer identification number (EIN)

Part 5: Report your FUTA tax liability by quarter only if line 12 is more than $500. If not, go to Part 6.

16 Report the amount of your FUTA tax liability for each quarter; do NOT enter the amount you deposited. If you had no liability for a quarter, leave the line blank.

16a 1st quarter (January 1 – March 31) . . . . **16a** ______ .

16b 2nd quarter (April 1 – June 30) . . . . **16b** ______ .

16c 3rd quarter (July 1 – September 30) . . . . **16c** ______ .

16d 4th quarter (October 1 – December 31) . . . . **16d** ______ .

17 Total tax liability for the year (lines 16a + 16b + 16c + 16d = line 17) **17** ______ . **Total must equal line 12.**

Part 6: May we speak with your third-party designee?

Do you want to allow an employee, a paid tax preparer, or another person to discuss this return with the IRS? See the instructions for details.

☐ **Yes.** Designee's name ______

Select a 5-digit Personal Identification Number (PIN) to use when talking to IRS ☐☐☐☐☐

☐ **No.**

Part 7: Sign here.

You MUST fill out both pages of this form and SIGN it.

Under penalties of perjury, I declare that I have examined this return, including accompanying schedules and statements, and to the best of my knowledge and belief, it is true, correct, and complete, and that no part of any payment made to a state unemployment fund claimed as a credit was, or is to be, deducted from the payments made to employees.

✗ **Sign your name here** ______

Print your name here ______

Print your title here ______

Date ___ / ___ / ___

Best daytime phone ( ) –

Part 8: For PAID preparers only (optional)

If you were paid to prepare this return and are not an employee of the business that is filing this return, you may choose to fill out Part 8.

Paid Preparer's name ______ Preparer's SSN/PTIN ______

Paid Preparer's signature ______ Date ___ / ___ / ___

☐ Check if you are self-employed.

Firm's name ______ Firm's EIN ______

Street address ______

City ______ State ______ ZIP code ______

Page **2** Form **940** (2006)

5-16A (concluded)

Schedule A (Form 940) for 20--:

Multi-State Employer and Credit Reduction Information

OMB No. 1545-0028

Department of the Treasury — Internal Revenue Service

Employer identification number (EIN) ☐☐ - ☐☐☐☐☐☐☐

Name *(not your trade name)* ________________

About this schedule:

- You must fill out Schedule A (Form 940) if you were required to pay your state unemployment tax in ***more than one state*** or if you paid wages in any state that is subject to ***credit reduction.*** FOR 20--, THERE ARE NO STATES SUBJECT TO CREDIT REDUCTION.
- File Schedule A (Form 940) as an attachment to your Form 940.

For more information, read the Instructions for Schedule A (Form 940) on the back.

Part 1: Fill out this part if you were required to pay state unemployment taxes in more than one state (including the District of Columbia, Puerto Rico, and the U.S. Virgin Islands). If any states do NOT apply to you, leave them blank.

1 **Check the box for every state in which you were required to pay state unemployment tax this year.** For a list of state names and their abbreviations, see the Instructions for Schedule A (Form 940).

☐ AK	☐ CO	☐ GA	☐ IN	☐ MD	☐ MS	☐ NH	☐ OH	☐ SC	☐ VA	☐ WY
☐ AL	☐ CT	☐ HI	☐ KS	☐ MI	☐ MT	☐ NJ	☐ OK	☐ SD	☐ VT	☐ PR
☐ AR	☐ DC	☐ IA	☐ KY	☐ MN	☐ NC	☐ NM	☐ OR	☐ TN	☐ WA	☐ VI
☐ AZ	☐ DE	☐ ID	☐ LA	☐ MO	☐ ND	☐ NV	☐ PA	☐ TX	☐ WI	
☐ CA	☐ FL	☐ IL	☐ MA	☐ ME	☐ NE	☐ NY	☐ RI	☐ UT	☐ WV	

Part 2: Fill out this part to tell us about wages you paid in any state (including the District of Columbia, Puerto Rico, and the U.S. Virgin Islands) that is subject to credit reduction. If any lines do NOT apply, leave them blank.

2

3

For Privacy Act and Paperwork Reduction Act Notice, see back of Form 940-V. Cat. No. 16997C **Schedule A (Form 940) (Rev. 12-2006)**

5-17A LO 6,7.

The information listed below refers to the employees of Lemonica Company for the year ended December 31, 2008. The wages are separated into the quarters in which they were paid to the individual employees.

Name	Social Security #	1st Qtr.	2nd Qtr.	3rd Qtr.	4th Qtr.	Total
Robert G. Cramer	173-68-0001	$ 1,800	$ 2,000	$ 2,000	$ 2,200	$ 8,000
Daniel M. English (Foreman)	168-95-0003	3,000	3,400	3,400	3,400	13,200
Ruth A. Small	199-99-1998	2,000	2,300	2,300	2,400	9,000
Harry B. Klaus	168-75-7413	1,600	1,700	1,700	1,700	6,700
Kenneth N. George (Manager)	179-18-6523	3,600	4,000	4,500	5,000	17,100
Mavis R. Jones	123-45-6789	1,600	1,700	1,700	-0-	5,000
Marshall T. McCoy	131-35-3334	1,400	1,400	-0-	-0-	2,800
Bertram A. Gompers (President) . . .	153-00-1014	4,500	5,000	5,500	6,300	21,300
Arthur S. Rooks	171-71-7277	-0-	700	1,700	1,700	4,100
Mary R. Bastian	186-83-8111	3,000	3,200	3,200	3,200	12,600
Klaus C. Werner	143-21-2623	2,300	2,500	2,500	2,500	9,800
Kathy T. Tyler	137-36-3534	-0-	-0-	1,300	1,700	3,000
Totals		$24,800	$27,900	$29,800	$30,100	$112,600

For 2008, State D's contributions rate for Lemonica Company, based on the experience-rating system of the state, was 2.8% of the first $7,000 of each employee's earnings. The state tax returns are due one month after the end of each calendar quarter. During 2008, the company paid $1,976.80 of contributions to State D's unemployment fund.

Employer's phone number: (613) 555-0029. Employer's State D reporting number: 80596.

Using the forms supplied on pages 5-42 to 5-44, complete the following for 2008:

a. Federal Tax Deposit Coupons—Form 8109

b. Employer's Report for Unemployment Compensation, State D—4th quarter only. Item I is the number of employees employed in the pay period that includes the 12th of each month in the quarter. For Lemonica Company, the number of employees is eight in October, seven in November, and eight in December. All employees earned 13 credit weeks during the last quarter except for Rooks (8) and Tyler (9).

c. Employer's Annual Federal Unemployment (FUTA) Tax Return—Form 940

Indicate on each form the date that the form should be submitted and the amount of money that must be paid.

The president of the company prepares and signs all tax forms.

5-17A (continued)

AMOUNT OF DEPOSIT (Do NOT type, please print.)

DOLLARS | CENTS

MONTH TAX YEAR ENDS → 1 2

EMPLOYER IDENTIFICATION NUMBER → 5 3 0 0 6 4 2 1

BANK NAME/ DATE STAMP

Name LEMONICA COMPANY

Address 123 SWAMP ROAD

City PIKESVILLE

State D STATE ZIP 10777-2017

Telephone number ( )

IRS USE ONLY

Darken only one TYPE OF TAX: 941, 945, 990-C, 1120, 943, 990-T, 720, 990-PF, CT-1, 1042, 940, 944

and

Darken only one TAX PERIOD: 1st Quarter, 2nd Quarter, 3rd Quarter, 4th Quarter

76

FOR BANK USE IN MICR ENCODING

Federal Tax Deposit Coupon

Form 8109 (Rev. 12-2005)

AMOUNT OF DEPOSIT (Do NOT type, please print.)

DOLLARS | CENTS

MONTH TAX YEAR ENDS → 1 2

EMPLOYER IDENTIFICATION NUMBER → 5 3 0 0 6 4 2 1

BANK NAME/ DATE STAMP

Name LEMONICA COMPANY

Address 123 SWAMP ROAD

City PIKESVILLE

State D STATE ZIP 10777-2017

Telephone number ( )

IRS USE ONLY

Darken only one TYPE OF TAX: 941, 945, 990-C, 1120, 943, 990-T, 720, 990-PF, CT-1, 1042, 940, 944

and

Darken only one TAX PERIOD: 1st Quarter, 2nd Quarter, 3rd Quarter, 4th Quarter

76

FOR BANK USE IN MICR ENCODING

Federal Tax Deposit Coupon

Form 8109 (Rev. 12-2005)

5-17A (continued)

D State Form UC-2, Rev 6-2000, Employer's Report for Unemployment Compensation QTR./YEAR 4/20--
Read Instructions—Answer Each Item DUE DATE 01/31/20--

DETACH HERE

INV. ☐ EXAMINED BY: ☐

Signature certifies that the information contained herein is true and correct to the best of the signer's knowledge.

10. SIGN HERE-DO NOT PRINT

TITLE ________ DATE ________ PHONE # ________

11. FILED ☐ PAPER UC-2A ☐ MAGNETIC MEDIA UC-2A

EMPLOYER'S CONTRIBUTION RATE	EMPLOYER'S ACCT. NO.	CHECK DIGIT
2.8%	80596	1

Employer name and address
Make any corrections on Form UC-2B

Lemonica Company
123 Swamp Road
Pikesville, D State 10777-2017

	1ST MONTH	2ND MONTH	3RD MONTH	FOR DEPT. USE
1. TOTAL COVERED EMPLOYEES IN PAY PERIOD INCL. 12TH OF MONTH				
2. GROSS WAGES				
3. EMPLOYEE CONTRIBUTIONS	XXXXXXXX XX			XXXXX
4. TAXABLE WAGES FOR EMPLOYER CONTRIBUTIONS				
5. EMPLOYER CONTRIBUTIONS DUE (RATE X ITEM 4)				
6. TOTAL CONTRIBUTIONS DUE (ITEMS 3 + 5)				
7. INTEREST DUE SEE INSTRUCTIONS				
8. PENALTY DUE SEE INSTRUCTIONS				
9. TOTAL REMITTANCE (ITEMS 6 + 7 + 8)	$.			

DETACH HERE

MAKES CHECKS PAYABLE TO: D UC FUND

DATE PAYMENT RECEIVED SUBJECTIVITY DATE REPORT DELINQUENT DATE

D State Form UC-2A, Rev 6-2000, Employer's for Unemployment Compensation

See instructions on separate sheet. Information MUST be typewritten or printed in BLACK ink. Do NOT use commas (,) or dollar signs ($). If typed, disregard vertical bars and type a consecutive string of characters. If hand printed, print in CAPS and within the boxes as below:

SAMPLE Typed: 1 2 3 4 5 6 . 0 0 **SAMPLE Handwritten:** 1 2 3 4 5 6 . 0 0 **SAMPLE Filled-in:** → ●

Employer name (make corrections on Form UC-2B)	Employer D UC account no.	Check digit	Quarter and year Q/YYYY	Quarter ending date MM/DD/YYYY
		1	4/20--	12/31/20--

1. Name and telephone number of preparer

2. Total number of pages in this report

3. Total number of employees listed in item 8 on all pages of Form UC-2A

4. Plant number (if approved)

5. Gross wages, MUST agree with item 2 on UC-2 and the sum of item 11 on all pages of Form UC-2A

6. Fill in this circle if you would like the Department to preprint your employees' names & SSNs on Form UC-2A next quarter → ○

7. Employee's social security number	8. Employee's name FI	MI	LAST	9. Gross wages paid this qtr Example: 123456.00	10. Credit weeks
				.	
				.	
				.	
				.	
				.	
				.	
				.	
				.	
				.	
				.	

List any additional employees on continuation sheets in the required format (see instructions).

Batch # For Dept. Use Only

11. Total gross wages for this page: → .

12. Page ____ of ____

Form **940 for 20--: Employer's Annual Federal Unemployment (FUTA) Tax Return**
Department of the Treasury — Internal Revenue Service
OMB No. 1545-0028

(EIN)
Employer identification number 5 4 – 0 0 0 6 4 2 1

Name (*not your trade name*) LEMONICA COMPANY

Trade name (*if any*)

Address 123 SWAMP ROAD
Number Street Suite or room number

PIKESVILLE D 10777-2017
City State ZIP code

Type of Return
(Check all that apply.)

- ☐ **a.** Amended
- ☐ **b.** Successor employer
- ☐ **c.** No payments to employees in 20--
- ☐ **d.** Final: Business closed or stopped paying wages

Read the separate instructions before you fill out this form. Please type or print within the boxes.

Part 1: Tell us about your return. If any line does NOT apply, leave it blank.

1 **If you were required to pay your state unemployment tax in ...**

1a **One state only,** write the state abbreviation . . . . 1a ☐☐

- OR -

1b **More than one state** (You are a multi-state employer) . . . . 1b ☐ Check here. Fill out Schedule A.

2

Part 2: Determine your FUTA tax before adjustments for 20--. If any line does NOT apply, leave it blank.

3 **Total payments to all employees** . . . . 3 ______ .

4 **Payments exempt from FUTA tax** . . . . 4 ______ .

Check all that apply: 4a ☐ Fringe benefits 4c ☐ Retirement/Pension 4e ☐ Other
4b ☐ Group term life insurance 4d ☐ Dependent care

5 **Total of payments made to each employee in excess of $7,000** . . . . 5 ______ .

6 **Subtotal** (line 4 + line 5 = line 6) . . . . 6 ______ .

7 **Total taxable FUTA wages** (line 3 – line 6 = line 7) . . . . 7 ______ .

8 **FUTA tax before adjustments** (line 7 × .008 = line 8) . . . . 8 ______ .

Part 3: Determine your adjustments. If any line does NOT apply, leave it blank.

9 **If ALL of the taxable FUTA wages you paid were excluded from state unemployment tax, multiply line 7 by .054** (line 7 × .054 = line 9). Then go to line 12 . . . . 9 ______ .

10 **If SOME of the taxable FUTA wages you paid were excluded from state unemployment tax, OR you paid ANY state unemployment tax late** (after the due date for filing Form 940), fill out the worksheet in the instructions. Enter the amount from line 7 of the worksheet onto line 10 . . 10 ______ .

11

Part 4: Determine your FUTA tax and balance due or overpayment for 20--. If any line does NOT apply, leave it blank.

12 **Total FUTA tax after adjustments** (lines 8 + 9 + 10 = line 12) . . . . 12 ______ .

13 **FUTA tax deposited for the year, including any payment applied from a prior year** . . . . 13 ______ .

14 **Balance due** (If line 12 is more than line 13, enter the difference on line 14.)
- If line 14 is more than $500, you must deposit your tax.
- If line 14 is $500 or less and you pay by check, make your check payable to the United States Treasury and write your EIN, *Form 940,* and *20--* on the check . . . . 14 ______ .

15 **Overpayment** (If line 13 is more than line 12, enter the difference on line 15 and check a box below.) . . . . 15 ______ .

Check one ☐ Apply to next return.
☐ Send a refund.

▶ You **MUST** fill out both pages of this form and **SIGN** it.

Next ➔

For Privacy Act and Paperwork Reduction Act Notice, see the back of Form 940-V, Payment Voucher. Cat. No. 11234O Form **940** (2006)

5-17A (concluded)

Name *(not your trade name)* | **Employer identification number (EIN)**

Part 5: Report your FUTA tax liability by quarter only if line 12 is more than $500. If not, go to Part 6.

16 **Report the amount of your FUTA tax liability for each quarter; do NOT enter the amount you deposited. If you had no liability for a quarter, leave the line blank.**

16a **1st quarter** (January 1 – March 31) . . . . **16a** ________ .

16b **2nd quarter** (April 1 – June 30) . . . . **16b** ________ .

16c **3rd quarter** (July 1 – September 30) . . . . **16c** ________ .

16d **4th quarter** (October 1 – December 31) . . . . **16d** ________ .

17 **Total tax liability for the year** (lines 16a + 16b + 16c + 16d = line 17) **17** ________ . **Total must equal line 12.**

Part 6: May we speak with your third-party designee?

Do you want to allow an employee, a paid tax preparer, or another person to discuss this return with the IRS? See the instructions for details.

☐ **Yes.** Designee's name ________

Select a 5-digit Personal Identification Number (PIN) to use when talking to IRS ☐☐☐☐☐

☐ **No.**

Part 7: Sign here.

You MUST fill out both pages of this form and SIGN it.

Under penalties of perjury, I declare that I have examined this return, including accompanying schedules and statements, and to the best of my knowledge and belief, it is true, correct, and complete, and that no part of any payment made to a state unemployment fund claimed as a credit was, or is to be, deducted from the payments made to employees.

✗ Sign your name here ________

Print your name here ________

Print your title here ________

Date ___ / ___ / ___

Best daytime phone ( ) –

Part 8: For PAID preparers only (optional)

If you were paid to prepare this return and are not an employee of the business that is filing this return, you may choose to fill out Part 8.

Paid Preparer's name ________ Preparer's SSN/PTIN ________

Paid Preparer's signature ________ Date ___ / ___ / ___

☐ Check if you are self-employed.

Firm's name ________ Firm's EIN ________

Street address ________

City ________ State ________ ZIP code ________

Page **2** Form **940** (2006)

PRACTICAL PROBLEMS—SERIES B

5-1B LO 4,5.

During the year, Zeno Company has a SUTA tax rate of 6.3%. The taxable payroll for the year for FUTA and SUTA is $77,000. Compute:

a. Net FUTA tax . . . . $ ________
b. Net SUTA tax . . . . ________
c. Total unemployment taxes . . . $ ________

5-2B LO 4,5.

Yengling Company's payroll for the year is $593,150. Of this amount, $211,630 is for wages paid in excess of $7,000 to each individual employee. The SUTA rate in Yengling Company's state is 2.9% on the first $7,000 of each employee's earnings. Compute:

a. Net FUTA tax . . . . $ ________
b. Net SUTA tax . . . . ________
c. Total unemployment taxes . . . $ ________

5-3B LO 4,5.

Garrison Shops had a SUTA tax rate of 2.7%. The state's taxable limit was $8,000 of each employee's earnings. For the year, Garrison Shops had FUTA taxable wages of $77,900 and SUTA taxable wages of $93,900. Compute:

a. Net FUTA tax . . . . $ ________
b. Net SUTA tax . . . . $ ________

5-4B LO 4,5.

Due to its experience rating, Ianelli, Inc., is required to pay unemployment taxes on its payroll as follows:

1. Under SUTA for Illinois on taxable payroll of $28,000, the contribution rate is 3.9%.
2. Under SUTA for Indiana on taxable payroll of $23,000, the contribution rate is 2.95%.
3. Under SUTA for Ohio on taxable payroll of $65,000, the contribution rate is 4.1%.
4. Under FUTA, the taxable payroll is $94,500.

Compute:

a. SUTA taxes paid to Illinois . . . . $ ________
b. SUTA taxes paid to Indiana . . . $ ________
c. SUTA taxes paid to Ohio . . . . . $ ________
d. FUTA taxes paid . . . . $ ________

5-5 LO 1,4.

Cowen Company began its operations in August of the current year. During August and September, the company paid wages of $2,450. For the last quarter of the year, the taxable wages paid amounted to $3,900. None of the employees were paid more than $7,000 this year.

a. Is Cowen Company liable for FUTA tax this year? Explain.
b. If so, what is the ***net*** FUTA tax before any credit is granted for the SUTA tax?
. . . . $ ________

5-6B LO 1,3,4,5.

In September 2008, Painter Wax Corporation began operations in a state that requires new employers of one or more individuals to pay a state unemployment tax of 4.1% of the first $7,000 of wages paid each employee.

An analysis of the company's payroll for the year shows total wages paid of $212,640. The salaries of the president and the vice president of the company were $25,000 and $15,000, respectively, for the four-month period, but there were no other employees who received wages in excess of $7,000 for the four months. Included in the total wages were $900 paid to a director who only attended director meetings during the year, $6,300 paid to the factory superintendent, and $2,000 in employee contributions to a cafeteria plan made on a pretax basis—for both federal and state.

In addition to the total wages of $212,640, a payment of $2,000 was made to Andersen Accounting Company for an audit it performed on the company's books in December 2008. Compute:

a. Net FUTA tax . . . . $ ________
b. SUTA tax . . . . $ ________

5-7B **LO 2,3,4,5.**

In April of the current year, Steelman Press Company transferred Ken Sherm from its factory in Louisiana to its plant in Florida. The company's SUTA tax rates based on its experience ratings are 3.2% in Louisiana and 3.8% in Florida. Both states base the tax on the first $7,000 of each employee's earnings. This year, Steelman Press Company paid Ken Sherm wages of $14,190; $4,950 were paid in Louisiana and the remainder in Florida. Compute:

a. Amount of SUTA tax the company must pay to Louisiana on Sherm's wages . . . $ ________

b. Amount of SUTA tax the company must pay to Florida on Sherm's wages. . . . . $ ________

c. Amount of the net FUTA tax on Sherm's wages . . . . $ ________

5-8B **LO 5.**

During 2008, Jake Gore worked for two different employers. Until May, he worked for Wonderman Construction Company in Kansas City, Kansas, and earned $21,500. The state unemployment rate for Wonderman is 4.6%. He then changed jobs and worked for Buxmont Improvement Company in Atlanta, Georgia, and earned $33,100. The state unemployment rate for Buxmont is 5.1%. Determine the unemployment taxes (FUTA and SUTA) that would be paid by:

a. Wonderman Construction Company . . . . $ ________

b. Buxmont Improvement Company $ ________

5-9B **LO 3,4.**

The partnership of Cox and Cohen paid the following wages during this year:

M. Cox (partner)	$45,000
S. Cohen (partner)	26,000
N. Tate (supervisor)	14,350
T. Gerenski (factory worker)	9,900
R. Sobowski (factory worker)	9,450
D. Brunder (factory worker)	8,910
S. Carsoni (bookkeeper)	11,100
C. Chu (maintenance)	3,900

In addition, the partnership owed $200 to Chu for work he performed during December. However, payment for this work will not be made until January of the following year. The state unemployment tax rate for the company is 2.95% on the first $9,000 of each employee's earnings. Compute:

a. Net FUTA tax for the partnership for this year. . . . . $ ________

b. SUTA tax for this year. . . . . . . $ ________

5-10B **LO 4,5.**

Roofling Company paid wages of $319,600 this year. Of this amount, $193,900 was taxable for net FUTA and SUTA purposes. The state's contribution tax rate is 4.3% for Roofling Company. Due to cash flow problems, the company did not make any SUTA payments until after the Form 940 filing date. Compute:

a. Amount of credit the company would receive against the FUTA tax for its SUTA contributions. . . . . $ ________

b. Amount that Roofling Company would pay to the federal government for its FUTA tax . . $ ________

c. Amount that the company lost because of its late payments . . . . $ ________

5-11B **LO 4,5.**

During 2008, Shoupe Company was subject to the Alaska state unemployment tax of 5.1%. The company's taxable earnings for FUTA were $93,400 and for SUTA, $194,300. Compute:

a. SUTA tax that Shoupe Company would pay to the state of Alaska. . . . . $ ________

b. Net FUTA tax for 2008. . . . . . $ ________

c. Amount of employees' unemployment tax for 2008 (use the employee's tax rate shown in Figure 5–1 on p. 5-13) . . . . $ ________

5-12B LO 5.

The following unemployment tax rate schedule is in effect for the calendar year 2008 in State A, which uses the reserve-ratio formula in determining employer contributions:

Reserve Ratio	Contribution Rate
0.0% or more, but less than 1.0%	6.7%
1.0% or more, but less than 1.2%	6.4%
1.2% or more, but less than 1.4%	6.1%
1.4% or more, but less than 1.6%	5.8%
1.6% or more, but less than 1.8%	5.5%
1.8% or more, but less than 2.0%	5.2%
2.0% or more, but less than 2.2%	4.9%
2.2% or more, but less than 2.4%	4.6%
2.4% or more, but less than 2.6%	4.3%
2.6% or more, but less than 2.8%	4.0%
2.8% or more, but less than 3.0%	3.7%
3.0% or more, but less than 3.2%	3.4%
3.2% or more	3.1%

Conrad Company, which is located in State A, had an average annual payroll of $1,150,000 for the three 12-month periods ending on June 30, 2007 (the computation date for the tax year 2008). As of June 30, 2007, the total contributions that had been made to Conrad Company's reserve account, in excess of the benefits charged, amounted to $21,560. Compute:

a. Conrad Company's reserve ratio for 2007 . . . . ____________ %

b. 2008 contribution rate for the company . . . . ____________ %

c. Smallest contribution that the company can make in order to reduce its tax rate if State A permits voluntary contributions. . . . . $ ____________

d. Tax savings realized by the company, taking into consideration the voluntary contribution made in (c) if the taxable payroll in 2008 is $1,295,000 . . . . $ ____________

5-13B LO 5.

As of June 30, 2007 (the computation date for the 2008 tax rate), Amanda Company had a negative balance of $1,015 in its unemployment reserve account in State A. The company's average payroll over the last three 12-month periods amounted to $525,000. The unemployment compensation law of State A provides that the tax rate of an employer who has a negative balance on the computation date shall be 7.2% during the following calendar year. Using the tax rate schedule presented in Problem 5–12B, compute:

a. The smallest voluntary contribution that Amanda Company should make in order to effect a change in its tax rate . . . . $ ____________

b. The amount of the tax savings as a result of the voluntary contribution if Amanda Company's taxable payroll for 2008 is $650,000 . . $ ____________

5-14B LO 3,4,5.

Mary Givens and Peggy Moser are partners engaged in operating The G&M Doll Shop, which has employed the following persons since the beginning of the year:

T. Binn (general office worker)	$3,100 per month
W. Ashworth (saleswoman)	$30,000 per year
K. Bitner (stock clerk)	$280 per week
J. Vern (deliveryman)	$350 per week
A. Axel (cleaning and maintenance, part-time)	$240 per week

Givens and Moser are each paid a weekly salary allowance of $1,000.

The doll shop is located in a state that requires unemployment compensation contributions of employers of one or more individuals. The company is subject to state contributions at a rate of 3.25% for wages not in excess of $10,000. Compute each of the following amounts based upon the 41st weekly payroll period for the week ending October 10, 2008:

a. Amount of FICA taxes (OASDI and HI) to be withheld from the earnings of each person. (Refer to Chapter 3.)

	OASDI	HI
M. Givens	$______	$______
P. Moser	______	______
T. Binn	______	______
W. Ashworth	______	______
K. Bitner	______	______
J. Vern	______	______
A. Axel	______	______

b. Amount of the employer's FICA taxes for the weekly payroll. . . . . . . ______ ______

c. Amount of state unemployment contributions for the weekly payroll. . . . . $______

d. Amount of the net FUTA tax on the payroll. . . . . $______

e. Total amount of the employer's payroll taxes for the weekly payroll . . . . $______

5-15B LO 5.

Applebaum Security Company is located in State H, which enables employers to reduce their contribution rates under the experience-rating system. From 1994 to 2003, inclusive, the company's total contributions to state unemployment compensation amounted to $18,135. For the calendar years 2004 to 2007, inclusive, the contribution rate for employers was 3.7%.

The contributions of each employer are credited to an account maintained by the State Unemployment Compensation Commission. This account is credited with contributions paid into the account by the employer and is charged with unemployment benefits that are paid from the account. Starting January 1, 2008, the contributions rate for all employers in State H will be based on the following tax-rate schedule:

Reserve Ratio	Contribution Rate
Contributions falling below benefits paid	7.0%
0.0% to 7.9%	5.5%
8.0% to 9.9%	4.5%
10.0% to 11.9%	3.5%
12.0% to 14.9%	2.5%
15.0% or more	1.5%

The annual payroll for calculation purposes is the total wages payable during a 12-month period ending with the last day of the third quarter of any calendar year. The average annual payroll is the average of the last three annual payrolls. The SUTA tax rate for the year is computed using the information available (benefits received and taxes paid) as of September 30 of the preceding year.

The schedule below shows the total payroll and the taxable payroll for the calendar years 2004 to 2007.

Calendar Year

	2004		2005		2006		2007	
	Total Payroll	Taxable Payroll	Total Payroll	Taxable Payroll	Total Payroll	Taxable Payroll	Total Payroll	Taxable Payroll
First Quarter	$12,000	$12,000	$11,000	$11,000	$13,000	$13,000	$10,000	$10,000
Second Quarter	11,750	11,750	11,500	11,400	12,750	12,700	9,300	9,300
Third Quarter	12,500	12,250	12,750	12,400	12,200	12,000	9,350	9,350
Fourth Quarter	13,000	12,500	12,500	12,200	14,000	13,750	—	—

Unemployment benefits became payable to the company's qualified unemployed workers on January 1, 1994. Between that time and September 30, 2007 total benefits amounting to $23,194.15 were charged against the employer's account. Compute:

a. Contribution rate for 2008 . . . ______%

b. Rate for 2008 if $2,000 additional benefits had been charged by mistake to the account of Applebaum Security Company by the State Unemployment Compensation Commission . . . . ______%

5-16B LO 6.

As the accountant for Runson Moving Company, you are preparing the company's annual return, Form 940 and Schedule A. Use the following information to complete Form 940 and Schedule A on pages 5-52 to 5-54.

The net FUTA tax liability for each quarter of 2008 was as follows: 1st, $220.10; 2nd, $107.60; 3rd, $101.00; and 4th, $56.10.

Since the net FUTA tax liability did not exceed $500, the company was not required to make its first deposit of FUTA taxes until Feburary 2, 2009. Assume that the federal tax deposit coupon (Form 8109) was completed and the deposit was made on that date.

a. One of the employees performs all of his duties in another state—Arizona.

b. Total payments made to employees during calendar year 2008:

California	$ 82,110
Arizona	18,490
Total	$100,600

c. Payments made to employees in excess of $7,000: $40,000.

d. Amount contributed to unemployment compensation fund of California under merit rating, 2.2% of $53,600, or $578.70, for calendar year 2008. For Arizona, the contribution was 4.2% of $7,000 (the taxable salary limit), or $294.

e. Form is to be signed by Mickey Vixon, Vice President.

f. Phone number – (219) 555-8310.

Form **940 for 20--: Employer's Annual Federal Unemployment (FUTA) Tax Return**
Department of the Treasury — Internal Revenue Service
OMB No. 1545-0028

(EIN)
Employer identification number 5 4 – 0 6 6 3 7 9 3

Name *(not your trade name)* RUNSON MOVING COMPANY

Trade name *(if any)*

Address 423 BRISTOL PIKE
Number Street Suite or room number

SACRAMENTO CA 18940-4523
City State ZIP code

Type of Return
(Check all that apply.)

☐ **a.** Amended
☐ **b.** Successor employer
☐ **c.** No payments to employees in 20--
☐ **d.** Final: Business closed or stopped paying wages

Read the separate instructions before you fill out this form. Please type or print within the boxes.

Part 1: Tell us about your return. If any line does NOT apply, leave it blank.

1 **If you were required to pay your state unemployment tax in ...**

1a **One state only,** write the state abbreviation . . . . **1a** ☐ ☐

- OR -

1b **More than one state** (You are a multi-state employer) . . . . **1b** ☐ Check here. Fill out Schedule A.

2

Part 2: Determine your FUTA tax before adjustments for 20--. If any line does NOT apply, leave it blank.

3 **Total payments to all employees** . . . . **3** ______ .

4 **Payments exempt from FUTA tax** . . . . **4** ______ .

Check all that apply: **4a** ☐ Fringe benefits **4c** ☐ Retirement/Pension **4e** ☐ Other
4b ☐ Group term life insurance **4d** ☐ Dependent care

5 **Total of payments made to each employee in excess of $7,000** . . . . **5** ______ .

6 **Subtotal** (line 4 + line 5 = line 6) . . . . **6** ______ .

7 **Total taxable FUTA wages** (line 3 – line 6 = line 7) . . . . **7** ______ .

8 **FUTA tax before adjustments** (line 7 × .008 = line 8) . . . . **8** ______ .

Part 3: Determine your adjustments. If any line does NOT apply, leave it blank.

9 **If ALL of the taxable FUTA wages you paid were excluded from state unemployment tax, multiply line 7 by .054** (line 7 × .054 = line 9). Then go to line 12 . . . . **9** ______ .

10 **If SOME of the taxable FUTA wages you paid were excluded from state unemployment tax, OR you paid ANY state unemployment tax late** (after the due date for filing Form 940), fill out the worksheet in the instructions. Enter the amount from line 7 of the worksheet onto line 10 . . **10** ______ .

11

Part 4: Determine your FUTA tax and balance due or overpayment for 20--. If any line does NOT apply, leave it blank.

12 **Total FUTA tax after adjustments** (lines 8 + 9 + 10 = line 12) . . . . **12** ______ .

13 **FUTA tax deposited for the year, including any payment applied from a prior year** . . . . **13** ______ .

14 **Balance due** (If line 12 is more than line 13, enter the difference on line 14.)
- If line 14 is more than $500, you must deposit your tax.
- If line 14 is $500 or less and you pay by check, make your check payable to the United States Treasury and write your EIN, *Form 940,* and *20--* on the check . . . . **14** ______ .

15 **Overpayment** (If line 13 is more than line 12, enter the difference on line 15 and check a box below.) . . . . **15** ______ .

Check one ☐ Apply to next return.
☐ Send a refund.

▶ You **MUST** fill out both pages of this form and **SIGN** it.

Next ➔

For Privacy Act and Paperwork Reduction Act Notice, see the back of Form 940-V, Payment Voucher. Cat. No. 11234O Form **940** (2006)

5-16B (continued)

Name *(not your trade name)* | Employer identification number (EIN)

Part 5: Report your FUTA tax liability by quarter only if line 12 is more than $500. If not, go to Part 6.

16 Report the amount of your FUTA tax liability for each quarter; do NOT enter the amount you deposited. If you had no liability for a quarter, leave the line blank.

16a 1st quarter (January 1 – March 31) . . . . **16a** ________ .

16b 2nd quarter (April 1 – June 30) . . . . **16b** ________ .

16c 3rd quarter (July 1 – September 30) . . . . **16c** ________ .

16d 4th quarter (October 1 – December 31) . . . . **16d** ________ .

17 Total tax liability for the year (lines 16a + 16b + 16c + 16d = line 17) **17** ________ . **Total must equal line 12.**

Part 6: May we speak with your third-party designee?

Do you want to allow an employee, a paid tax preparer, or another person to discuss this return with the IRS? See the instructions for details.

☐ **Yes.** Designee's name ________

Select a 5-digit Personal Identification Number (PIN) to use when talking to IRS ☐☐☐☐☐

☐ **No.**

Part 7: Sign here.

You MUST fill out both pages of this form and SIGN it.

Under penalties of perjury, I declare that I have examined this return, including accompanying schedules and statements, and to the best of my knowledge and belief, it is true, correct, and complete, and that no part of any payment made to a state unemployment fund claimed as a credit was, or is to be, deducted from the payments made to employees.

✗ **Sign your name here** ________

Print your name here ________

Print your title here ________

Date ___ / ___ / ___

Best daytime phone ( ) –

Part 8: For PAID preparers only (optional)

If you were paid to prepare this return and are not an employee of the business that is filing this return, you may choose to fill out Part 8.

Paid Preparer's name ________

Preparer's SSN/PTIN ________

Paid Preparer's signature ________

Date ___ / ___ / ___

☐ Check if you are self-employed.

Firm's name ________

Firm's EIN ________

Street address ________

City ________ State ________ ZIP code ________

Page **2** Form **940** (2006)

Schedule A (Form 940) for 20--:

Multi-State Employer and Credit Reduction Information

OMB No. 1545-0028

Department of the Treasury — Internal Revenue Service

Employer identification number (EIN) ☐☐ - ☐☐☐☐☐☐☐

Name *(not your trade name)* ____________________

About this schedule:

- You must fill out Schedule A (Form 940) if you were required to pay your state unemployment tax in ***more than one state*** or if you paid wages in any state that is subject to ***credit reduction.*** FOR 20--, THERE ARE NO STATES SUBJECT TO CREDIT REDUCTION.
- File Schedule A (Form 940) as an attachment to your Form 940.

For more information, read the Instructions for Schedule A (Form 940) on the back.

Part 1: Fill out this part if you were required to pay state unemployment taxes in more than one state (including the District of Columbia, Puerto Rico, and the U.S. Virgin Islands). If any states do NOT apply to you, leave them blank.

1 **Check the box for every state in which you were required to pay state unemployment tax this year.** For a list of state names and their abbreviations, see the Instructions for Schedule A (Form 940).

☐ AK	☐ CO	☐ GA	☐ IN	☐ MD	☐ MS	☐ NH	☐ OH	☐ SC	☐ VA	☐ WY
☐ AL	☐ CT	☐ HI	☐ KS	☐ MI	☐ MT	☐ NJ	☐ OK	☐ SD	☐ VT	☐ PR
☐ AR	☐ DC	☐ IA	☐ KY	☐ MN	☐ NC	☐ NM	☐ OR	☐ TN	☐ WA	☐ VI
☐ AZ	☐ DE	☐ ID	☐ LA	☐ MO	☐ ND	☐ NV	☐ PA	☐ TX	☐ WI	
☐ CA	☐ FL	☐ IL	☐ MA	☐ ME	☐ NE	☐ NY	☐ RI	☐ UT	☐ WV	

Part 2: Fill out this part to tell us about wages you paid in any state (including the District of Columbia, Puerto Rico, and the U.S. Virgin Islands) that is subject to credit reduction. If any lines do NOT apply, leave them blank.

2

3

For Privacy Act and Paperwork Reduction Act Notice, see back of Form 940-V. Cat. No. 16997C **Schedule A (Form 940) (Rev. 12-2006)**

5-17B LO 6,7.

The information listed below refers to the employees of Brennan Company for the year ended December 31, 2008. The wages are separated into the quarters in which they were paid to the individual employees.

Name	Social Security #	1st Qtr.	2nd Qtr.	3rd Qtr.	4th Qtr.	Total
May S. Sun	173-68-0001	$ -0-	$ 6,100	$ 6,300	$ 4,100	$ 16,500
David R. Maro (Foreman)	168-95-0003	4,000	3,800	4,200	4,700	16,700
Randy A. Wade	199-99-1998	2,900	2,700	2,900	3,200	11,700
Hilary B. Cahn	168-75-7413	3,800	4,100	4,900	5,500	18,300
Paul C. Morse (Manager)	179-18-6523	9,000	8,800	9,500	10,000	37,300
Morrie T. Black	123-45-6789	6,500	4,100	-0-	-0-	10,600
Kelly K. Woods	131-35-3334	2,500	2,300	1,900	1,800	8,500
Terry M. Brennan (President)	153-00-1014	15,000	14,700	15,500	16,900	62,100
Art A. Mintz	171-71-7277	-0-	-0-	6,000	10,800	16,800
Megan T. Rudolph	186-83-8111	8,800	8,400	8,900	-0-	26,100
Kurt A. Weiner	143-21-2623	-0-	7,500	7,700	8,400	23,600
Ryan C. Harrow	137-36-3534	5,300	5,700	6,100	2,400	19,500
Totals		$57,800	$68,200	$73,900	$67,800	$267,700

For 2008, State D's contributions rate for Brennan Company, based on the experience-rating system of the state, was 3.6% of the first $7,000 of each employee's earnings. The state tax returns are due one month after the end of each calendar quarter. During 2008, the company paid $3,024.00 of contributions to State D's unemployment fund.

Employer's phone number: (613) 555-0029. Employer's State D reporting number: 80596.

Using the forms supplied on pages 5-55 to 5-58, complete the following for 2008:

a. Federal Tax Deposit Coupon—Form 8109. The last coupon of the year is used to pay the FUTA tax for the third and fourth quarters combined (the third-quarter liability was less than the $500 threshold).

b. Employer's Report for Unemployment Compensation, State D—4th quarter only. Item I is the number of employees employed in the pay period that includes the 12th of each month in the quarter. For Brennan Company, the number of employees is ten in October, nine in November, and eight in December. All employees earned 13 credit weeks during the last quarter except for Sun (8) and Harrow (9).

c. Employer's Annual Federal Unemployment (FUTA) Tax Return—Form 940

Indicate on each form the date that the form should be submitted and the amount of money that must be paid.

The president of the company prepares and signs all tax forms.

AMOUNT OF DEPOSIT (Do NOT type, please print.)
DOLLARS | CENTS

MONTH TAX YEAR ENDES → 1 2

EMPLOYER IDENTIFICATION NUMBER → 5 3 0 0 6 4 2 1

BANK NAME/ DATE STAMP

Name BRENNAN COMPANY

Address 123 SWAMP ROAD

City PIKESVILLE

State D STATE ZIP 10777-2017

Telephone number ( )

IRS USE ONLY

Darken only one TYPE OF TAX: 941, 945, 990-C, 1120, 943, 990-T, 720, 990-PF, CT-1, 1042, 940, 944

Darken only one TAX PERIOD: 1st Quarter, 2nd Quarter, 3rd Quarter, 4th Quarter

76

FOR BANK USE IN MICR ENCODING

Federal Tax Deposit Coupon
Form 8109 (Rev. 12-2005)

D State Form UC-2, Rev 6-2000, Employer's Report for Unemployment Compensation QTR./YEAR 4/20--

Read Instructions—Answer Each Item DUE DATE 01/31/20--

DETACH HERE

INV. ☐ EXAMINED BY: ☐

Signature certifies that the information contained herein is true and correct to the best of the signer's knowledge.

10. SIGN HERE-DO NOT PRINT

TITLE ______ DATE ______ PHONE # ______

11. FILED ☐ PAPER UC-2A ☐ MAGNETIC MEDIA UC-2A

EMPLOYER'S CONTRIBUTION RATE	EMPLOYER'S ACCT. NO.	CHECK DIGIT
3.6%	80596	1

Employer name and address
Make any corrections on Form UC-2B

Brennan Company
123 Swamp Road
Pikesville, D State 10777-2017

	1ST MONTH	2ND MONTH	3RD MONTH
1. TOTAL COVERED EMPLOYEES IN PAY PERIOD INCL. 12TH OF MONTH			

		FOR DEPT. USE
2. GROSS WAGES		
3. EMPLOYEE CONTRIBUTIONS	XXXXXXXX XX	XXXXX
4. TAXABLE WAGES FOR EMPLOYER CONTRIBUTIONS		
5. EMPLOYER CONTRIBUTIONS DUE (RATE X ITEM 4)		
6. TOTAL CONTRIBUTIONS DUE (ITEMS 3 + 5)		
7. INTEREST DUE SEE INSTRUCTIONS		
8. PENALTY DUE SEE INSTRUCTIONS		
9. TOTAL REMITTANCE (ITEMS 6 + 7 + 8)	$.	

MAKES CHECKS PAYABLE TO: D UC FUND

DATE PAYMENT RECEIVED SUBJECTIVITY DATE REPORT DELINQUENT DATE

DETACH HERE

D State Form UC-2A, Rev 6-2000, Employer's for Unemployment Compensation

See instructions on separate sheet. Information MUST be typewritten or printed in BLACK ink. Do NOT use commas (,) or dollar signs ($). If typed, disregard vertical bars and type a consecutive string of characters. If hand printed, print in CAPS and within the boxes as below:

SAMPLE Typed: 123456.00 **SAMPLE Handwritten:** 123456.00 **SAMPLE Filled-in:** → ●

Employer name (make corrections on Form UC-2B)	Employer D UC account no.	Check digit	Quarter and year Q/YYYY	Quarter ending date MM/DD/YYYY
		1	4/20--	12/31/20--

1. Name and telephone number of preparer

2. Total number of pages in this report

3. Total number of employees listed in item 8 on all pages of Form UC-2A

4. Plant number (if approved)

5. Gross wages, MUST agree with item 2 on UC-2 and the sum of item 11 on all pages of Form UC-2A

6. Fill in this circle if you would like the Department to preprint your employees' names & SSNs on Form UC-2A next quarter → ○

7. Employee's social security number	8. Employee's name FI	MI	LAST	9. Gross wages paid this qtr Example: 123456.00	10. Credit weeks
				.	
				.	
				.	
				.	
				.	
				.	
				.	
				.	
				.	
				.	

List any additional employees on continuation sheets in the required format (see instructions).

Batch # For Dept. Use Only

11. Total gross wages for this page: → .

12. Page ____ of ____

5-17B (continued)

Form **940 for 20--: Employer's Annual Federal Unemployment (FUTA) Tax Return**
Department of the Treasury — Internal Revenue Service
OMB No. 1545-0028

(EIN) Employer identification number 5 3 – 0 0 0 6 4 2 1

Name *(not your trade name)* BRENNAN COMPANY

Trade name *(if any)*

Address 123 SWAMP ROAD
Number Street Suite or room number
PIKESVILLE D 10777-2017
City State ZIP code

Type of Return
(Check all that apply.)

- ☐ **a.** Amended
- ☐ **b.** Successor employer
- ☐ **c.** No payments to employees in 20--
- ☐ **d.** Final: Business closed or stopped paying wages

Read the separate instructions before you fill out this form. Please type or print within the boxes.

Part 1: Tell us about your return. If any line does NOT apply, leave it blank.

1 **If you were required to pay your state unemployment tax in ...**

1a **One state only,** write the state abbreviation . . . . 1a ☐☐

- OR -

1b **More than one state** (You are a multi-state employer) . . . . 1b ☐ Check here. Fill out Schedule A.

2

Part 2: Determine your FUTA tax before adjustments for 20--. If any line does NOT apply, leave it blank.

3 **Total payments to all employees** . . . . 3 ____ .

4 **Payments exempt from FUTA tax** . . . . 4 ____ .

Check all that apply: 4a ☐ Fringe benefits 4c ☐ Retirement/Pension 4e ☐ Other
4b ☐ Group term life insurance 4d ☐ Dependent care

5 **Total of payments made to each employee in excess of $7,000** . . . . 5 ____ .

6 **Subtotal** (line 4 + line 5 = line 6) . . . . 6 ____ .

7 **Total taxable FUTA wages** (line 3 – line 6 = line 7) . . . . 7 ____ .

8 **FUTA tax before adjustments** (line 7 × .008 = line 8) . . . . 8 ____ .

Part 3: Determine your adjustments. If any line does NOT apply, leave it blank.

9 **If ALL of the taxable FUTA wages you paid were excluded from state unemployment tax, multiply line 7 by .054** (line 7 × .054 = line 9). Then go to line 12 . . . . 9 ____ .

10 **If SOME of the taxable FUTA wages you paid were excluded from state unemployment tax, OR you paid ANY state unemployment tax late** (after the due date for filing Form 940), fill out the worksheet in the instructions. Enter the amount from line 7 of the worksheet onto line 10 . . 10 ____ .

11

Part 4: Determine your FUTA tax and balance due or overpayment for 20--. If any line does NOT apply, leave it blank.

12 **Total FUTA tax after adjustments** (lines 8 + 9 + 10 = line 12) . . . . 12 ____ .

13 **FUTA tax deposited for the year, including any payment applied from a prior year** . . . . 13 ____ .

14 **Balance due** (If line 12 is more than line 13, enter the difference on line 14.)

- If line 14 is more than $500, you must deposit your tax.
- If line 14 is $500 or less and you pay by check, make your check payable to the United States Treasury and write your EIN, *Form 940,* and *20--* on the check . . . . 14 ____ .

15 **Overpayment** (If line 13 is more than line 12, enter the difference on line 15 and check a box below.) . . . . 15 ____ .

Check one ☐ Apply to next return.
☐ Send a refund.

▶ You **MUST** fill out both pages of this form and **SIGN** it.

Next ➡

For Privacy Act and Paperwork Reduction Act Notice, see the back of Form 940-V, Payment Voucher. Cat. No. 11234O Form **940** (2006)

Name *(not your trade name)* | Employer identification number (EIN)

Part 5: Report your FUTA tax liability by quarter only if line 12 is more than $500. If not, go to Part 6.

16 **Report the amount of your FUTA tax liability for each quarter; do NOT enter the amount you deposited. If you had no liability for a quarter, leave the line blank.**

16a **1st quarter** (January 1 – March 31) . . . . 16a ______ .

16b **2nd quarter** (April 1 – June 30) . . . . 16b ______ .

16c **3rd quarter** (July 1 – September 30) . . . . 16c ______ .

16d **4th quarter** (October 1 – December 31) . . . . 16d ______ .

17 **Total tax liability for the year** (lines 16a + 16b + 16c + 16d = line 17) **17** ______ . **Total must equal line 12.**

Part 6: May we speak with your third-party designee?

Do you want to allow an employee, a paid tax preparer, or another person to discuss this return with the IRS? See the instructions for details.

☐ **Yes.** Designee's name ______

Select a 5-digit Personal Identification Number (PIN) to use when talking to IRS ☐☐☐☐☐

☐ **No.**

Part 7: Sign here.

You MUST fill out both pages of this form and SIGN it.

Under penalties of perjury, I declare that I have examined this return, including accompanying schedules and statements, and to the best of my knowledge and belief, it is true, correct, and complete, and that no part of any payment made to a state unemployment fund claimed as a credit was, or is to be, deducted from the payments made to employees.

X Sign your name here ______

Print your name here ______

Print your title here ______

Date ___ / ___ / ___

Best daytime phone ( ) –

Part 8: For PAID preparers only (optional)

If you were paid to prepare this return and are not an employee of the business that is filing this return, you may choose to fill out Part 8.

Paid Preparer's name ______ Preparer's SSN/PTIN ______

Paid Preparer's signature ______ Date ___ / ___ / ___

☐ Check if you are self-employed.

Firm's name ______ Firm's EIN ______

Street address ______

City ______ State ______ ZIP code ______

Page **2** Form **940** (2006)

CONTINUING PAYROLL PROBLEM

Refer to the partially completed payroll register that you worked on at the end of Chapter 4. You will now compute the employer's liability for unemployment taxes (FUTA and SUTA) for the pay of January 14. These computations will be used at the end of Chapter 6 in recording the payroll tax entries.

To compute the employer's liability for unemployment taxes, proceed as follows:

1. Enter each employee's gross earnings in the Taxable Earnings—FUTA and SUTA columns.
2. Total the Taxable Earnings—FUTA and SUTA columns.
3. At the bottom of your payroll register, compute the following for the total payroll:

a. Net FUTA tax. Since this is the first pay period of the year, none of the employees are near the $7,000 ceiling; therefore, each employee's gross earnings is subject to the FUTA tax.

b. SUTA tax. Since Kipley Company is a new employer, Pennsylvania has assigned the company a contribution rate of 3.5% on the first $8,000 of each employee's earnings. Employees pay 0.09% on total gross pay.

NOTE: Retain your partially completed payroll register for use at the end of Chapter 6.

CASE PROBLEM

C1. Reducing a High Unemployment Tax Rate.

Over the past two years, Kermit Stone, the controller of Hilton Company, has been concerned that the company has been paying a large amount of money for state unemployment taxes. On reviewing the "unemployment file" with the head accountant, Deborah Murtha, he learns that the company's tax rate is near the top of the range of the state's experience-rating system.

After calling the local unemployment office, Stone realizes that the turnover of employees at Hilton Company has had an adverse effect on the company's tax rates. In addition, after consulting with Murtha, he discovers that the eligibility reports that come from the state unemployment office are just signed and sent back to the state without any review.

The eligibility reports are notices that an ex-employee has filed a claim for unemployment benefits. By signing these reports "blindly," the company, in effect, tells the state that the employee is eligible for the benefits. Any benefits paid are charged by the state against Hilton Company's account.

Stone is convinced that the rates the company is paying are too high, and he feels that part of the reason is the "blind" signing of the eligibility reports. Besides this, he wonders what other steps the company can take to lower its contributions rate and taxes.

Submit recommendations that might help Stone reduce the "unfair" burden that the unemployment compensation taxes are leveling on Hilton Company.

chapter

6

Analyzing and Journalizing Payroll Transactions

© PHOTODISC COLLECTION/GETTY IMAGES

LEARNING OBJECTIVES

After studying this chapter, you should be able to:

1. Record payrolls in payroll registers and post to employees' earnings records.
2. Understand the various deductions—both voluntary and involuntary (garnishments)—that are taken out of employees' gross pay.
3. Journalize the entries to record the payroll, payroll taxes, and payment of payroll-related liabilities.
4. Post to the various general ledger accounts that are used to accumulate information from the payroll entries.
5. Explain the payment and the recording of the payroll tax deposits.
6. Understand the need for end-of-period adjustments.
7. Identify the general ledger accounts used to record payroll transactions.

Now is the time to discuss the accounting part of payroll accounting. In this chapter, the costs of the payroll will be recorded in the journal and ledger of the company. The payments of various payroll-related liabilities will also be illustrated.

Get ready to prepare payroll registers, employees' earnings records, and then journalize and post payroll entries. Also, learn what adjustments must be made at the end of the fiscal period. It is time for the wonderful world of debits and credits.

This chapter presents the procedures for recording the payroll in a payroll register, transferring information from the payroll register to the employees' earnings records, recording these transactions in the company's book of original entry, and posting them to the proper ledger accounts. Today, many of these functions are done by sophisticated computer programs. However, the payroll professional must understand the steps that the computer is performing.

We will also look at the various withholdings that can come out of an employee's pay and some issues that the employer must be aware of in making these deductions. In addition, the methods of paying employees are detailed in this chapter.

The Payroll Register

LEARNING OBJECTIVE 1

As you have seen in Figure 1–9 and in completing the Continuing Payroll Problem, the payroll register gives detailed information about the payroll for each pay period. To summarize, the payroll register may provide the following types of information:

1. The title of the form.
2. The period covered by the payroll and the paydate.
3. Department or branch. Some large businesses with many departments or branches prepare a separate sheet in the payroll register for each department or branch on each payday. Other firms provide "distribution" columns such as "Sales Salaries," "Office Salaries," and "Plant Wages" for classifying the gross wages and salaries according to the nature of the wage and salary expense. The total of each distribution column shows the total amount of that department's wage expense.
4. A column to record the name of each employee. Many businesses provide a column to record an identifying number such as the time clock number for each employee.
5. Marital status and number of withholding allowances. This information determines the income tax deductions. In some cases, this information is presented only in the employees' earnings records.
6. A record of time worked. Many companies show detailed information in the payroll register as to hours worked each day by each employee. Separate columns can be used to show a total of regular hours worked and a total of overtime hours worked during the pay period. This information helps a business that schedules much overtime work.
7. The regular rate of pay and the amount earned at the regular rate.

FIGURE 6–1

Payroll Register (left side)

FOR WEEK ENDING *January 17, 20--* Payday January 17, 20—

					TIME RECORD						REGULAR EARNINGS			OVERTIME EARNINGS		
	NO.	NAME	MARITAL STATUS	NO. W/H ALLOW.	M	T	W	T	F	S	HOURS	RATE PER HOUR	AMOUNT	HOURS	RATE PER HOUR	AMOUNT
1	*10*	*Collins, Chris R.*	*M*	*2*	*8*	*8*	*8*	*8*	*8*	*4*	*40*	*15 20*	*6 0 8 00*	*4*	*22 80*	*9 1 20*
2	*12*	*Banks, Carolyn B.*	*M*	*4*	*8*	*8*	*8*	*8*	*10*		*40*	*17 10*	*6 8 4 00*	*2*	*25 65*	*5 1 30*
3	*13*	*Carson, Henry S.*	*S*	*1*	*8*	*8*	*8*	*8*	*8*		*40*	*16 30*	*6 5 2 00*			
4	*23*	*O'Brien, LuAnn T.*	*M*	*2*	*8*	*8*	*8*	*8*	*8*	*8*	*40*	*15 90*	*6 3 6 00*	*8*	*23 85*	*1 9 0 80*
5	*24*	*Rudolph, Beth M.*	*S*	*1*	*8*	*8*	*8*	*0*	*8*		*32*	*16 10*	*5 1 5 20*			
36		*Totals*											*224 9 7 20*			*22 6 5 50*

8. A space to record the overtime rate and the total earnings at the overtime rate. Some companies prefer to show an Overtime Premium Earnings column in place of the Overtime Earnings column. With this approach, as discussed in Chapter 2, the regular earnings is equal to the regular hourly rate of pay multiplied by the total hours worked, and the overtime premium is equal to the extra one-half rate of pay multiplied by the overtime hours.

[e.g., Collins ($15.20 × 44 hours) + ($7.60 × 4 hours)]

9. A column to record the total earnings.

10. Information about deductions from total earnings. A separate column may be provided for each type of deduction. The various deductions will be discussed later in this chapter.

11. A column to show the net amount paid (total earnings less deductions). When paying by check, a company usually provides a column for the number of each employee's paycheck.

12. Some firms provide special columns in the payroll register to indicate that portion of the employee's wages taxable under the Federal Insurance Contributions Act (OASDI and HI) and other laws that require payment of taxes only on wages up to the taxable limits.

The partial payroll register shown in Figure 6–1 contains most of the information outlined above. This register is used to compute the pay for hourly workers for a weekly pay period. The layout of the section devoted to time or hours worked will vary, depending on the payroll period and the work schedules of each individual business. Although a few small businesses still prepare the payroll manually, most businesses use computers to process their payrolls.

on the JOB

According to a survey done by the American Payroll Association, close to 20 percent of large employers outsource their payroll operations, while 44 percent have their tax filings done by contractors.

PROVING THE TOTALS OF THE PAYROLL REGISTER

As shown later in this chapter, the payroll register provides the information needed in preparing the **journal entries** to record (1) the wages earned, deductions from wages, and net amount paid each payday and (2) the employer's payroll taxes. Prior to making the journal entry to record the payroll, check the accuracy of the amounts entered in the payroll register by proving the totals of the money columns. Prove the partial payroll register shown in Figure 6–1 as follows:

FIGURE 6–1

Payroll Register (right side)

DEPT. ACCOUNTING—10

TOTAL EARNINGS	DEDUCTIONS: FICA OASDI	DEDUCTIONS: FICA HI	DEDUCTIONS: FED. INCOME TAX	DEDUCTIONS: STATE INCOME TAX	DEDUCTIONS: GROUP INS.	NET PAID: CHECK NO.	NET PAID: AMOUNT	TAXABLE EARNINGS: FICA OASDI	TAXABLE EARNINGS: FICA HI	TAXABLE EARNINGS: FUTA & SUTA	
6 9 9 20	4 3 35	10 14	47 00	4 78	9 00	898	5 8 4 93	6 9 9 20	6 9 9 20	6 9 9 20	1
7 3 5 30	4 5 59	10 66	33 00	6 11	9 00	899	6 3 0 94	7 3 5 30	7 3 5 30	7 3 5 30	2
6 5 2 00	4 0 42	9 45	74 00	5 04	3 90	900	5 1 9 19	6 5 2 00	6 5 2 00	6 5 2 00	3
8 2 6 80	5 1 26	11 99	66 00	6 14	9 00	901	6 8 2 41	8 2 6 80	8 2 6 80	8 2 6 80	4
5 1 5 20	3 1 94	7 47	53 00	3 90	3 90	902	4 1 4 99	5 1 5 20	5 1 5 20	5 1 5 20	5
247 6 2 70	153 5 29	3 59 06	37 14 00	5 5 25	5 4 70		190 4 4 40	247 6 2 70	247 6 2 70	247 6 2 70	36

Proof:

Regular earnings	$22,497.20	
Overtime earnings	2,265.50	
Total earnings		$24,762.70
FICA tax withheld—OASDI	$ 1,535.29	
FICA tax withheld—HI	359.06	
Federal income taxes withheld	3,714.00	
State income taxes withheld	55.25	
Group insurance withheld	54.70	
Total deductions		$ 5,718.30
Total net pay		19,044.40
Total earnings		$24,762.70

In preparing the journal entry to record a payroll, you make an entry each payday to record the aggregate amount of wages earned, deductions made, and net payments to all employees, as determined from the Totals line of the payroll register. After making the journal entry, you must transfer, or post, the information from the journal to the appropriate general ledger accounts.

In most companies having computer-driven payroll systems, the payroll programs are interfaced with the general ledger programs. In these systems, computers generate the payroll entries into a printed journal-entry format and post to the various general ledger accounts automatically from these entries.

USING THE INFORMATION IN THE PAYROLL REGISTER

In addition to serving as the source for preparing journal entries to record the payroll and the employer's payroll taxes, the payroll register provides information that meets some of the recordkeeping requirements of the various payroll acts. Also, the register provides data used in preparing periodic reports required by various laws (e.g., hours worked each day as required by the Fair Labor Standards Act).

Besides the information contained in the payroll register, businesses must provide information about the accumulated earnings of each employee. Therefore, companies keep a separate payroll record on each employee—the employee's earnings record. This record, introduced in Figure 1–10, on page 1-21, is discussed in the following section.

The Employee's Earnings Record

The employee's earnings record, a supplementary record, provides information for:

1. *Preparing the payroll register.* The earnings record contains the information needed to compute gross earnings and to determine the amount to withhold for income tax purposes.
2. *Preparing reports* required by state unemployment compensation or disability laws.
3. *Determining when the accumulated wages of an employee reach the cutoff level* for purposes of FICA (OASDI), FUTA, or SUTA. As shown in Figure 6–2, a special "Cumulative Earnings" column is provided so that the total amount of accumulated wages can be recorded each pay period. Thus, when the FICA (OASDI), FUTA, or SUTA cutoff has been reached, the record shows that the employee or the employer no longer has a liability for that particular tax during the rest of the calendar year. (In Figure 6–1, the FUTA and SUTA taxable wage cutoffs are the same [$7,000]. However, another separate column would be needed in the payroll register if there were a different cutoff for the SUTA tax.)
4. *Preparing payroll analyses* for governmental agencies and for internal management control. Information such as the department in which the employee works and the job title serves as the basis for such analyses.

FIGURE 6–2

Employee's Earnings Record (page 1)

WEEK	20– WEEK ENDING	TOTAL WORKED		REGULAR EARNINGS			OVERTIME EARNINGS			DEDUCTIONS					NET PAID		CUMULATIVE EARNINGS	TIME LOST
										FICA		FEDERAL INCOME TAX	STATE INCOME TAX	GROUP INSURANCE				
		DAYS	HRS.	HRS.	RATE	AMOUNT	HRS.	RATE	AMOUNT	OASDI	HI				CK. NO.	AMOUNT		
1	*1/3*	*5*	*44*	*40*	*15 20*	*6 0 8 00*	*4*	*22 80*	*9 1 20*	*4 3 35*	*1 0 14*	*4 7 00*	*4 78*	*9 00*	*510*	*5 8 4 93*	*6 9 9 20*	
2	*1/10*	*5*	*42*	*40*	*15 20*	*6 0 8 00*	*2*	*22 80*	*4 5 60*	*4 0 52*	*9 48*	*4 1 00*	*4 47*	*9 00*	*706*	*5 4 9 13*	*13 5 2 80*	
3	*1/17*	*6*	*44*	*40*	*15 20*	*6 0 8 00*	*4*	*22 80*	*9 1 20*	*4 3 35*	*1 0 14*	*4 7 00*	*4 78*	*9 00*	*898*	*5 8 4 93*	*20 5 2 00*	
4																		
5																		
6																		
7																		
8																		
9																		
10																		
11																		
12																		
13																		
QUARTER TOTAL																		
1																		
2																		
13																		
QUARTER TOTAL																		
SEMIANNUAL TOTAL																		

SEX F	SEX M	DEPARTMENT	OCCUPATION	WORKS IN (STATE)	S.S. ACCOUNT NO.	NAME–LAST	FIRST	MIDDLE	NO. W/H ALLOW.	MARITAL STATUS
X		*A-10*	*Adm. Ass't*	*XXX*	*204-43-1186*	*Collins*	*Chris*	*Ruth*	*2*	*M*

5. ***Settling employee grievances*** regarding regular pay and overtime pay calculations and the withholding of amounts for income taxes and other purposes.
6. ***Completing Forms W-2,*** which show for each employee the annual gross earnings, income taxes withheld, wages subject to FICA taxes, and FICA taxes withheld.

A business keeps an employee's earnings record for each employee whose wages are recorded in the payroll register. Each payday, after the information has been recorded in the payroll register, the information for each employee is posted to the employee's earnings record. The columns are arranged so that the information can be transferred easily. The earnings record shown in Figure 6–2 is arranged for weekly pay periods. You will note that totals are provided for each quarter so that you can enter information easily on the quarterly tax returns. The bottom of page 1 of the earnings record shows a line for semiannual totals. The bottom of page 2 of the form, which is not illustrated, shows a line for annual totals, which you will need in preparing Form 940, W-2s, and other annual reports.

Recording the Gross Payroll and Withholdings

LEARNING OBJECTIVE 2

After you have recorded the payroll in the payroll register and posted to the employees' earnings records, you must enter the information in the employer's accounting system. An entry for the totals of each payroll period should be made in the general journal and posted to the general ledger. You can obtain the amounts needed for this entry from the Totals line at the bottom of the last payroll register sheet.

The following journal entry to record the payroll includes a debit to the appropriate expense account(s) for the gross payroll and credits to the various liability accounts for the withholdings from the pay and for the net amount to be paid employees:

	Debit	Credit
Salary Expense	XXX	
Liabilities (Withholdings).		XXX
Cash or Salaries Payable (Net Pay)		XXX
To record the payment of salaries and the liabilities for the employees' taxes withheld.		

GROSS PAYROLL

You should record the total gross payroll (regular earnings and overtime earnings) as the debit portion of the payroll entry. The account has a title such as *Wages Expense* or *Salaries Expense.* In the case of a company with many departments or cost centers, the accounts would have titles such as *Wages Expense—Department A, Wages Expense—Maintenance,* and *Wages Expense—Residential Services.* These accounts show the total gross earnings that the employer incurs as an *expense* each payday.

FICA TAXES—EMPLOYEE

The employer must withhold FICA taxes for each employee. Since the employer has withheld these taxes from the pay of the employees and now owes this amount to the IRS, the taxes withheld represent a *liability* of the employer. When recording the payroll, you should credit accounts entitled *FICA Taxes Payable—OASDI* and *FICA Taxes Payable—HI* for the amounts withheld.

FEDERAL INCOME TAXES

Employers must withhold a percentage of their employees' wages for income tax purposes. Chapter 4 presented the methods of determining the amounts to be withheld from wages for income tax purposes. As with FICA taxes withheld, the employer also owes to the IRS the federal income taxes withheld from the employees' pay. You should keep a separate account in the general ledger for recording the employer's ***liability*** for the amount of federal income taxes withheld. A suitable title for this account, ***Employees Federal Income Taxes Payable,*** may be abbreviated to read ***Employees FIT Payable.*** The account is credited for the total amount of federal income taxes withheld each payday and is subsequently debited for the amounts paid to a depositary or to the IRS.

STATE AND CITY INCOME TAXES

Employers may be required to withhold state and city income taxes in addition to the federal income taxes. You should keep a separate account in the general ledger for recording the employer's ***liability*** for the amount of each kind of income tax withheld. Account titles that may be used include ***Employees State Income Taxes (SIT) Payable*** and ***Employees City Income Taxes (CIT) Payable.***

EMPLOYEES' CONTRIBUTIONS TO STATE FUNDS

A few states require employees to contribute to state unemployment compensation or disability funds. In states requiring employee contributions, the employer deducts the amount of the contributions from the employees' wages at the time the wages are paid. The ***liability*** for employees' contributions may be recorded in the same account as the employer's SUTA contributions; namely, ***SUTA Taxes Payable.*** If employees make contributions to a disability benefit fund, this amount is usually reported separately to the state and should be recorded in a separate liability account such as ***Employees Disability Contributions Payable.***

ADVANCE EARNED INCOME CREDIT

As discussed in Chapter 4, advance EIC payments can be paid to eligible employees in their paychecks. These payments are added to the employees' net pay, and the employer pays these advances out of the withheld taxes for social security (FICA) and federal income tax (FIT).

Since these advances increase the net pay, they increase the credit to cash in the payroll entry. These advances also reduce the employer's liability for the payment of FICA taxes and FIT taxes to the IRS, since these monies are used to pay the employees. The tax liability accounts should be reduced by the total of these EIC payments to the employees. Therefore, the liability account (usually FIT Payable) should be reduced and the credit to that account in the payroll entry will be less than the amount actually withheld from the employees for that payday. If the total amount of the advances is greater than the total FIT withheld, the excess should reduce the amount of the credit to the FICA liability accounts (OASDI and HI) in the payroll entry.

EXAMPLE

Evergreen Company's payroll data for the first pay in January are:

Total earnings	$1,357.00
Deductions:	
OASDI	(84.13)
HI	(19.67)
FIT	(85.00)
SIT	(20.37)
Addition:	
EIC	59.00
Net pay	$1,206.83

(Continued)

The entry to record the payroll is:

Wages Expense	1,357.00	
FICA Taxes Payable—OASDI		84.13
FICA Taxes Payable—HI		19.67
FIT Taxes Payable		26.00 ($85.00 – $59.00)
SIT Taxes Payable		20.37
Cash		1,206.83

OTHER PAYROLL DEDUCTIONS

Besides FICA taxes, state unemployment contributions, and income taxes, most companies have other deductions that must be taken into consideration when preparing the payroll. Regardless of the number or the types of deductions made from employees' wages, we must provide a systematic means of keeping a record of the total wages for each employee, the deductions for each purpose, and the net amount paid.

Although you should have a separate column in the payroll register for each deduction, the payroll register may become too cumbersome if there are too many columns for deductions. Many businesses, therefore, use a payroll register with a separate column for each of the major deductions and lump all other deductions together in one column headed "Other Deductions." Some companies use only one column for deductions and place the entire total in that column. If this practice is followed, it is usually necessary to have a supplementary record of deductions showing a detailed breakdown of the total for each employee. This supplementary record serves as the basis for obtaining the figure for total deductions shown in the payroll register.

Many payroll deductions result from company policies, collective bargaining agreements, court orders, or employee authorizations. Some of the purposes for making deductions include:

1. Group insurance.
2. Health insurance.
3. Purchase of government savings bonds.
4. Union dues.
5. Garnishment of wages.
    a. Child support.
    b. Federal tax levy.
6. Pension and retirement contributions.

GROUP INSURANCE Many companies have a **group insurance** program for employees. Such programs usually permit employees to obtain life insurance at a much lower rate than would be possible if the employee purchased the insurance as an individual. Under some group insurance plans, the employer and the employee share the cost of the insurance premium. The employees' share may be deducted from their wages every payday, every month, or every quarter.

When recording a payroll which makes deductions from employees' wages for group insurance, the amount withheld from their wages is applied toward the payment of their share of the premium. The total amount withheld is credited to a ***liability*** account with a title such as *Group Insurance Premiums Collected* or *Group Insurance Payments Withheld.* This general ledger account serves the same purpose as the accounts used to record payroll taxes withheld from employees' wages. When the premiums are paid to the insurance company, the liability account will be debited.

HEALTH INSURANCE Many companies have developed their own health insurance plans for employees or are members of private insurance groups that provide coverage for employees of companies that are members of the group. If employees bear the cost or a portion of the cost of such insurance, the portion paid by the employees is usually deducted every payday from the wages of the employees. The amounts withheld from the employees' wages for health insurance are credited to a ***liability*** account such as ***Health Insurance Premiums Collected.***

Employers often pay the premium for health insurance in advance to the insurance carrier. At the time of paying the premium, a prepaid expense account such as ***Prepaid Health Insurance*** is debited for the amount paid the carrier. This account is adjusted periodically through the health insurance or fringe benefit expense account and, if applicable, the employees' withholding account.

PURCHASE OF GOVERNMENT SAVINGS BONDS Employees are encouraged to invest a certain amount of their wages in government savings bonds. Such plans or similar savings plans encourage employees to save a certain amount of each salary payment. The theory behind such deductions is that most employees will not miss a small amount that is set aside each payday, and over a period of time the deductions accumulate into a sizable amount.

Employees authorize their employer to make payroll deductions for the purchase of savings bonds by completing authorization forms that indicate the amount to be withheld and the frequency. The amounts withheld from the paychecks are set aside by the employer, acting in a trustee position, until a sufficient amount has been accumulated for the purchase of savings bonds for the employees. The minimum denomination for Series EE savings bonds for new participants in a payroll savings plan is $100. A $100 bond can be purchased as soon as the participant has accumulated the $50 purchase price in his or her withholding account.

EXAMPLE

Ruth Hayes has authorized her employer to withhold $10 from her pay every two weeks toward the purchase of a Series EE U.S. savings bond, which has a maturity value of $100. At the time of preparing each biweekly payroll, the employer credits the liability account *U.S. Savings Bonds Deductions Payable* for $10. After the employer has recorded five similar entries, the balance of the liability account will be $50, the amount required for the purchase of one $100 Series EE U.S. savings bond. At this time, the employer purchases the bond, which is later delivered to the employee. The journal entry to record this transaction includes a debit of $50 to the liability account *U.S. Savings Bonds Deductions Payable* and a corresponding credit to the cash account.

UNION DUES In companies in which employees are members of unions that require employees to pay dues to the union, many employees pay their dues, assessments, and initiation fees through deductions from wages, known as a **check-off system.** Amounts withheld from union members' wages are credited to a ***liability*** account such as ***Union Dues Payable.*** Monthly, or as agreed upon by the union and the employer, the amounts withheld are turned over to the treasurer of the union. At this time, a journal entry is made in which the payment of union dues is recorded by debiting the liability account and crediting the cash account.

GARNISHMENT OF WAGES **Garnishment** refers to the legal or equitable procedure by which a portion of the wages of any person must be withheld for payment of a debt. Through the garnishment process, a creditor, with the aid of the courts, may require the employer to hold back a portion of the debtor's wages and pay that amount to the court or to the creditor. In some companies, the amounts to be held back are deducted each payday from the employee's wages. Generally, the following priority withholding order applies to these wage attachments: (1) bankruptcy, (2) federal tax levy or child support order, whichever is delivered first, and (3) creditor, student loan, or federal administrative wage garnishments.

The Consumer Credit Protection Act limits the amount of wages subject to garnishment, in general, to

- Child support: 50%–65% of disposable earnings
- Creditor garnishment: 25% of disposable earnings
- Administrative wage garnishment: 15% of disposable earnings
- Student loan garnishment: 15% of disposable earnings

These maximum deductions apply regardless of the number of garnishments received on an employee.

Disposable earnings are the earnings remaining after withholding for federal and state income taxes, FICA taxes, state unemployment and disability taxes, and deductions required for state employees' retirement systems.

Federal tax levies are not subject to the limits of the Consumer Credit Protection Act. In practice, the IRS instructs employers to withhold the difference between the employee's take-home pay and the exempt amount. This allows the employee's voluntary deductions to continue. Likewise, state tax levies are not subject to federal garnishment limits.

The Social Security Administration (SSA) has started to use the administrative wage garnishment to collect delinquent overpayments owed by former beneficiaries of the social security program. Unlike other credits, the SSA does not need a court order to initiate this garnishment process.

The provisions of the Consumer Credit Protection Act prohibit an employer from discharging an employee simply because the employee's wages are subject to garnishment for one indebtedness. If another garnishment for a second indebtedness should arise, the worker could be discharged, provided a considerable amount of time had ***not*** elapsed between the two occasions of indebtedness.

The payroll manager should also be aware that state garnishment laws that are more favorable to employees have priority over the federal law.

IRS CONNECTION

Seventy percent of the nearly $23 billion of child support payments were made through withholding by employers.

CHILD SUPPORT The Family Support Act requires the immediate withholding for child-support payments for all cases supported by a court order. The amount withheld is equal to the amount of the delinquency, subject to the limits prescribed in the federal garnishment law. Employers may withhold a fee, set by each state, for administrative costs. (In cases of support orders, the limits on the amounts that can be taken from an employee's pay are 50 percent of disposable income if the employee supports a second family and 60 percent if not. These limits increase to 55 percent and 65 percent if the employee is in arrears for 12 weeks or more.) Tips are part of the disposable earnings for child support purposes—whether in the form of cash, debit or credit card receipts, or a set service charge.

Child support takes precedence over most voluntary and involuntary deductions. In the case of multiple support orders, the employer is to allocate monies to each order from the employee's available disposable income.

In the case of competing orders, the process begins with the deduction of the child support order. Then, the other garnishment is satisfied by taking the lesser of:

1. 25 percent of the weekly disposable income (prior to the child support deduction), or
2. The difference between the weekly disposable income and 30 times the minimum wage.

EXAMPLE

Huffman Company has a child support order outstanding on one of its employees (Charles Suffert—$170 per week). Charles Suffert's disposable income is $950 per week. A new garnishment is received for a $5,000 debt to a credit card company. The company would take an additional $237.50 out of Suffert's pay.

Lesser of:

25% × $950	= $237.50	or
$950 − (30 × $5.15)	= $795.50	

FEDERAL TAX LEVY Federal tax levies take second priority after wages withheld for child support (if received prior to the tax levy). If a tax levy is in place prior to the child support order, the employer must call the issuing agency so that an alternate payment plan can be worked out with the IRS. The only portions of wages that are exempt from a federal tax levy are the taxpayer's standard deduction and the personal exemptions allowed for the tax year divided by the number of pay periods in the year.

The IRS uses Form 668-W (not illustrated) to notify an employer of a tax levy. Copies of the form must then be forwarded to the employee for completion of a statement of filing status and exemptions. This information will then allow the employer to compute the actual levy. If the employee fails to return the signed statement within three working days to the employer, the exempt amount is based on married-filing-separately status with one personal exemption.

Although the gross pay less the amounts exempted can be seized, the IRS wants employers to withhold the difference between the take-home pay and the exempt amount. The take-home pay is the gross pay less taxes and the deductions in effect before the levy was received.

The employer must continue to withhold until Form 668-D (Release of Levy/Release of Property from Levy) is received.

EXAMPLE

Booz Company received a federal tax levy on John Parlini. John is single, claims two personal exemptions, and had a take-home pay of $535.00 this week. The amount of the tax levy would be:

Take-home pay		$535.00
Standard deduction	$ 5,350	
Personal exemptions ($3,400 × 2)	6,800	
	$12,150 ÷ 52 weeks =	233.65
Federal tax levy		$301.35

PENSION AND RETIREMENT CONTRIBUTIONS Since in many instances social security benefits are inadequate for retired employees and their dependents, many firms provide pension and retirement plans that will supplement the government benefits. Although the benefit formulas and eligibility rules vary, the coverage is about the same for production workers, office employees, and managers. Many pension plans are financed solely by employer contributions, but other plans involve employee contributions. Once these contributions are deducted from the employees' pay, they become a liability for the employer and are recorded as such in the payroll entry. This would also apply to employee contributions into 401(k) plans.

Some employers also provide their employees with the opportunity to set up their own Individual Retirement Accounts (IRA) through a payroll deduction plan (see page 4-10). These voluntary contributions are deducted from the paychecks of the employees who set up their own retirement accounts. These deductions are recorded as a liability in the payroll entry. This liability account will be cleared as the employer pays the contributions to the financial institution that is in charge of each employee's retirement account.

NET PAY

The total of the net amount paid to the employees each payday is credited to either the ***cash*** account or the ***salaries payable*** account.

The journal entry to record the payroll from Figure 6–1 on pages 6-4 and 6-5 would be:

	Debit	Credit
Wage Expense	24,762.70	
FICA Payable—OASDI		1,535.29
FICA Payable—HI		359.06
FIT Payable		3,714.00
SIT Payable		55.25
Group Insurance Payments W/H.		54.70
Cash		19,044.40

SELF-STUDY QUIZ 6-1 *The totals from the payroll register of Olt Company for the week of January 25 show:*

Gross earnings	$95,190.00
Withholdings:	
FICA taxes—OASDI	(5,901.78)
FICA taxes—HI	(1,380.26)
Federal income tax	(14,270.00)
State income tax	(1,427.85)
State unemployment tax—employee portion	(951.90)
Net pay	$71,258.21

Journalize the entry to record the payroll of January 25.

Methods of Paying Wages and Salaries

The three main methods used in paying wages and salaries include (1) cash, (2) check, and (3) electronic transfer.

PAYING IN CASH

When a company pays wages and salaries in cash, a common procedure is used, as follows:

1. Compute the total wages earned, the deductions, and the net amount to be paid and record this information in the payroll register, as shown in Figure 1–9.
2. Prepare a supplementary payroll sheet showing the various denominations of bills and coins needed to pay the salary of each employee. The form in Figure 6–3 provides columns to list the names of the employees, the net amount to be paid, the denominations needed to pay each employee, the total amount needed to pay all employees, and the total number of each denomination needed to pay all employees.
3. Prepare a payroll slip by using the total amount of each denomination needed for the payroll.
4. Write a check for the total amount of the payroll and present it to the bank with the payroll slip to obtain the proper denominations.
5. Place the amount due to each employee in an envelope with a receipt showing the total earnings, the deductions, and the net amount paid. Distribute the prepared envelopes to the employees.

on the *JOB*

In a survey conducted by KPMG Consulting, more than 72 percent of employers were found to have paid their employees on a biweekly basis.

PAYING BY CHECK

When paying wages and salaries by check, the employer prepares and signs the checks in the usual way. The check preparer should ensure the accuracy of the names of the payees and the net amounts of the checks. Employers must give employees a periodic statement showing the deductions that have been made from their wages for tax purposes. The employer may distribute these statements each payday or give them out monthly, quarterly, or annually. Also, employees receive a statement at the time they leave the employ of the company. Most employers who pay wages and salaries by check indicate on each check issued or on the check stub or earnings statement the various deductions made. (See Figure 6–4 on page 6-16.)

on the *JOB*

The National Automated Clearing House Association estimated that employees spend an average of 8 to 24 hours per year depositing or cashing paychecks. In many cases, these transactions are made on company time.

Many businesses maintain a payroll account at their bank in addition to their regular checking account. In such a case, all checks to pay wages and salaries are issued against the payroll account rather than against the regular checking account. When the company maintains a separate payroll account, the usual procedure is as follows:

1. Sets up a payroll account with a certain balance to be maintained at all times. A transfer from the regular checking account is made to the payroll account. A small balance is desirable in the payroll account because it may be necessary to issue payroll checks before the regular payday. For example, if mistakes were made in an employee's paycheck, an additional check must be issued. These types of corrections will be shown in the next payday's payroll register.

FIGURE 6–3

Supplementary Payroll Sheet

HENDRIX, INC.

SUPPLEMENTARY PAYROLL SHEET June 30, 20--

Name of Employee	Net Amount to Be Paid	Bills					Coins				
		$50	$20	$10	$5	$1	50¢	25¢	10¢	5¢	1¢
Brandon, Paul C.	$ 268.62	5		1	1	3	1		1		2
Connor, Rose T.	271.40	5	1			1		1	1	1	
Day, Joseph R.	297.28	5	2		1	2		1			3
Gee, Margaret F.	704.92	14				4	1	1	1	1	2
Hawke, Sidney O.	271.64	5	1			1	1		1		4
Kirk, Evelyn A.	788.24	15	1	1	1	3			2		4
Lerro, Doris B.	268.12	5		1	1	3			1		2
Pesiri, Armand G.	878.80	17	1		1	3	1	1		1	
Topkis, Christine W.	284.65	5	1	1		4	1		1	1	
Vogel, John C.	724.10	14	1			4			1		
Total	$4,757.77	90	8	4	5	28	5	4	9	4	17

2. Makes a transfer to payroll, drawn on the regular checking account, equal to the total net pay, and deposited in the special payroll account at the bank.
3. Prepares individual checks, drawn against the special payroll account, and records the numbers of the payroll checks in the payroll register. Many companies having a large number of employees may use automatic means of signing the checks.

By maintaining a separate payroll account at the bank, the canceled payroll checks, accompanied by a statement of the payroll account balance, are returned separately from the canceled checks drawn upon the regular checking account, making it easier to reconcile both accounts. The payroll account balance as shown on the bank statement should always be equal to the sum of the total of the outstanding payroll checks and any maintained balance, less any service charge.

on the *JOB*

Studies have shown that the cost to produce one check is close to $1.30 (annual cost per employee: approximately $70).

PAYING BY ELECTRONIC TRANSFER

Under an **electronic funds transfer system (EFTS),** employers do not have to issue a paycheck to each worker, although the worker is given a stub showing the amounts deducted. Instead, the employer creates a computerized record for each employee. This record indicates:

1. The employee's bank.
2. The account number at the bank.
3. The net amount to be paid.

A day or two before payday the employer sends the information to the company's bank where the amounts due to any employees who also keep their accounts at that bank are removed and deposited to the appropriate accounts. That bank sends the remaining names to an automated clearinghouse which sorts out the other bank names and prepares a computer tape for each bank to receive funds electronically. For banks unable to receive entries in electronic form, the clearinghouse creates a printed statement showing the customers' names and the amounts for which their accounts are to be credited. The actual crediting of accounts and the settlement occur on payday.

Under a "paperless" deposit and bill-paying system, employers may deposit wages in bank accounts designated by the employees if the deposits are voluntarily authorized by the

FIGURE 6–4

Earnings Statement (Check Stub) Showing Payroll Deductions

EMPLOYEE'S NAME ARTHUR T. COCO — PENLAND EQUIPMENT COMPANY, SAN MATEO, FL 32088-2279

PAY PERIOD ENDING	HOURS	RATE	GROSS EARNINGS	OASDI TAX	HI TAX	FED. WITH. TAX	STATE WITH. TAX	UNION DUES		NET EARNINGS PAID
5/16/--	REG. T. 40 O.T. 12	5.50 8.25	319.00	19.78	4.63	14.00		3.00		277.59

EMPLOYEE: THIS IS A STATEMENT OF YOUR EARNINGS AND DEDUCTIONS FOR PERIOD INDICATED. KEEP THIS FOR YOUR PERMANENT RECORD.

employees. Millions of written checks may be eliminated each month. After electronically transferring each employee's net pay directly into the worker's account, the employee can pay bills by authorizing the bank to automatically transfer funds from that account to the accounts of creditors such as the utility company and department stores.

PAY CARDS

The major problem of direct deposit is to obtain up-to-date and timely banking information—employees changing accounts without notifying their employer, gathering information in time to make payroll for new employees, and paying into closed accounts.

Over 15 million American households do not have bank accounts; however, by using debit card-based accounts, the "unbanked" employees can opt for direct deposit of their paychecks. All transactions are completed electronically by using a pay card to make purchases at any point-of-sale terminal or to access cash at automated teller machines (ATMs).[1]

Leading banks are now offering VISA and MasterCard payroll cards. These cards allow employers to deposit employees' pay directly into a prepaid card issued to the employee. The card is then used like any debit or credit card and can also be used to access cash at certain automated teller machines (ATMs). Employees will then receive a monthly statement detailing their transactions.[2] These cards are reusable, and each payday the cards will be "loaded-up" with the pays without the employees needing to be anywhere near their employers.

Over 7 million pay cards were in use in the United States in 2006, and more than 30 states allow employers to use this method of payment.

on the JOB

One hundred percent of Canadian employees use direct deposit, while the rate in Germany is 95 percent, and the United States is only 46 percent.

ELECTRONIC PAYSTUB

Cost savings can also be realized by offering employees **electronic paystubs**. In these cases, the company will make the information that is usually found on a paper paystub available through a secured Web site, kiosk, or interactive voice response system.

As with electronic payments, one can eliminate paper, postage, and distribution costs.

FINAL PAY

Many states set a time limit after notice of termination for the payment of an employee's final wage. The deadline depends on whether or not the worker is leaving voluntarily. Most states allow a lag time in which to process the final check. However, if fired, California and Michigan require immediate payment. If the employee quits, California requires payment within 72 hours, while Michigan requires payment as soon as the final wages can be calculated.

1 "Pay Card Pays Off for Employees and Employers," *PAYTECH*, May/June 2000, p. 36.
2 "Card-Based Payroll Solutions," *PAYTECH*, April 2002, p. 22.

UNCLAIMED WAGES

Occasionally, a worker may terminate employment or be terminated and not claim the final wage payment. The payroll manager is then faced with the question of what to do with the worker's unclaimed wages. Even though a uniform law exists on the subject of unclaimed or abandoned property, varying practices occur in those states that provide for the disposition of unclaimed property, such as unclaimed wages. The uniform law, followed by most states, provides that the holder of any unclaimed property must file a report after a specified statutory period and then surrender the money to the state as abandoned property. The length of the statutory period varies widely from state to state. In other states, the holder of unclaimed property files a report with the state, and the state then files suit for possession of the property. Because of the different practices among states, payroll managers must be well acquainted with the laws of their own states in the event they are faced with the difficult problem of disposing of unclaimed wages.

Recording Payroll Taxes

3 LEARNING OBJECTIVE

In this section, we will analyze the journal entries that record the ***employer's*** payroll taxes, each of which has been discussed in preceding chapters:

1. *FICA:* Taxes imposed under the Federal Insurance Contributions Act for old-age, survivors, and disability insurance (OASDI) and hospital insurance (HI) benefits.
2. *FUTA:* Taxes imposed under the Federal Unemployment Tax Act.
3. *SUTA:* Contributions to the unemployment compensation funds of one or more states.

The following accounts will be needed in the general ledger if the employer is subject to FICA taxes, FUTA taxes, and SUTA taxes:

1. *Payroll Taxes:* An expense account for the FICA, FUTA, and SUTA taxes on the employer.
2. *FICA Taxes Payable—OASDI:* A liability account for the tax withheld from employees' wages plus the employer's portion of the tax.
3. *FICA Taxes Payable—HI:* A liability account for the tax withheld from employees' wages plus the employer's portion of the tax.
4. *FUTA Taxes Payable:* A liability account for the accumulation of the employer's federal unemployment taxes payable to the federal government.
5. *SUTA Taxes Payable:* A liability account for the amount payable to state unemployment compensation fund(s).

The following journal entry to record the payroll taxes includes a debit to the tax expense account for the total of the employer's payroll taxes and a credit to the various tax liability accounts:

	Debit	Credit
Payroll Taxes	XXX	
Liabilities (various taxes)		XXX
To record the payroll taxes and liabilities of the employer.		

FICA TAXES—EMPLOYER

The law states specifically that deductions made from the wages of employees under FICA should be recorded immediately as liabilities on the books of the company. The law does not require that employers record their part of the FICA taxes at the time the ***wages are paid.*** However, in order to place the tax expense in the proper accounting period, the common practice is to also record the employer's FICA tax liabilities each payday.

The taxes on the employer represent both business expenses and liabilities of the employer. The employer may deduct the employer's FICA contributions as a **business expense** in the calculation of the company's net income for federal income tax purposes (and the costs of all other payroll taxes).

SUTA TAXES

Under the state unemployment compensation laws, employers must pay contributions into one or more state unemployment compensation funds. When an employer must make contributions to the state unemployment compensation funds of more than one state, it may be advisable to keep a separate liability account for the contributions payable to each state.

FUTA TAX

An employer subject to the gross FUTA tax of 6.2 percent may be able to claim credit in paying the federal tax because of contributions made to state unemployment compensation funds. As discussed in Chapter 5, the maximum credit is 5.4 percent, even though the amount of state contributions is more or less than 5.4 percent. Thus, the net FUTA tax (6.2% – 5.4%) is 0.8 percent. Although you do not actually claim the credit against the FUTA tax until Form 940 is filed with the Internal Revenue Service, you may record the FUTA tax at the net amount (0.8%) at the time you make the entry to record the employer's payroll taxes for each payroll period.

EXAMPLE

The employees of Richardson Company earn wages during the year amounting to $26,400, all of which is subject to the gross FUTA tax of 6.2 percent. The company must make contributions to the unemployment compensation fund of the state in which the business is located at the rate of 2.8 percent of the wages paid each employee. Richardson computes the federal and state unemployment taxes as follows:

SUTA tax, 2.8% of $26,400		$739.20	
Gross FUTA tax, 6.2% of $26,400	$1,636.80		
Less: Credit for SUTA tax, 5.4% of $26,400	–1,425.60	211.20	(net FUTA tax)
Total unemployment taxes		$950.40	

More simply, the net FUTA tax is computed by multiplying the taxable wages, $26,400, by the net FUTA tax rate, 0.8 percent, yielding $211.20.

The FUTA tax, like the FICA taxes and the contributions to the state for unemployment compensation purposes, is a social security tax. Thus, the FUTA tax can be charged to the same expense account as the other payroll taxes on the employer, the payroll taxes account. However, since employers may be required to pay the net FUTA tax quarterly and to pay the FICA taxes more frequently, an employer should keep separate liability accounts for recording these two taxes.

SELF-STUDY QUIZ 6-2 *Olt Company's gross payroll for the week of January 25 was $95,190.00. This total pay was taxable for federal (0.8%) and state (3.15%) unemployment taxes.*

Journalize the entry to record Olt Company's payroll taxes for this pay.

ENTRIES TO RECORD WAGES AND PAYROLL TAXES

In the following illustrations of recording (or journalizing) wages and the payroll taxes imposed under both the federal and state laws, the employer is responsible for the following taxes:

1. FICA tax—OASDI on employees: 6.2%.
2. FICA tax—HI on employees: 1.45%.
3. FIT withheld from employees.
4. FICA tax—OASDI on employers: 6.2%.
5. FICA tax—HI on employers: 1.45%.

6. Net FUTA tax: 0.8%.
7. SUTA tax: 2.4%.

The weekly payroll amounts to $3,200, and the entire amount is subject to all social security and unemployment taxes. You record this information in two separate journal entries. In the first entry, you record the wages expense of the employer and the liabilities for the FICA taxes and FIT withheld in a two-column general journal as follows:

	Debit	Credit
Wages Expense	3,200.00	
FICA Taxes Payable—OASDI		198.40[3]
FICA Taxes Payable—HI		46.40[4]
Employees FIT Payable		230.00[5]
Cash		2,725.20[6]
To record the payment of wages and the liability for the employees' FICA taxes and FIT withheld.		

We can analyze this entry in T-accounts as follows:

WAGES EXPENSE

Debit	Credit
3,200.00	
This debit represents the employees' gross earnings for the pay period. This results in an increase in the operating expenses of the employer.	

FICA TAXES PAYABLE—OASDI

Debit	Credit
	198.40
	This credit results in an increase in a liability of the employer.

FICA TAXES PAYABLE—HI

Debit	Credit
	46.40
	This credit results in an increase in a liability of the employer.

EMPLOYEES FIT PAYABLE

Debit	Credit
	230.00
	This credit results in an increase in a liability of the employer.

CASH

Debit	Credit
	2,725.20
	This credit results in a decrease in an asset.

3 The amount credited to FICA Taxes Payable—OASDI is computed as follows: 6.2% of $3,200 = $198.40, amount deducted from employees' wages.

4 The amount credited to FICA Taxes Payable—HI is computed as follows: 1.45% of $3,200 = $46.40, amount deducted from employees' wages.

5 The amount credited to Employees FIT Payable is obtained by using one of the withholding methods explained in Chapter 4.

6 The amount credited to Cash is computed as follows:

$3,200.00	gross wages earned
−474.80	employees' taxes withheld
$2,725.20	net amount paid employees

In the second entry, you record the employer's payroll taxes as follows:

	Debit	Credit
Payroll Taxes	347.20[7]	
FICA Taxes Payable—OASDI		198.40
FICA Taxes Payable—HI		46.40
FUTA Taxes Payable		25.60
SUTA Taxes Payable		76.80
To record the payroll taxes and the employer's liability for the taxes.		

Let's analyze this entry by means of T-accounts as shown below.

PAYROLL TAXES

347.20	
This debit results in an increase in the operating expenses.	

FICA TAXES PAYABLE—OASDI

	198.40
	198.40
	The second credit amount, representing the employer's OASDI tax, also increases the employer's liability. The amount is determined as shown in the computation of the payroll taxes.

FICA TAXES PAYABLE—HI

	46.40
	46.40
	The second credit amount, representing the employer's HI tax, also increases the employer's liability. The amount is determined as shown in the computation of the payroll taxes.

FUTA TAXES PAYABLE

	25.60
	This credit results in an increase in a liability of the employer. The amount is determined as shown in the computation of the payroll taxes.

SUTA TAXES PAYABLE

	76.80
	This credit results in an increase in a liability of the employer. The amount is determined as shown in the computation of the payroll taxes.

In the preceding illustration, no contributions were required of employees for state unemployment compensation purposes. Assume that the employees had been required to make contributions of 1 percent to state unemployment compensation funds. The payroll entry would then appear as shown on the next page.

7 The amount debited to Payroll Taxes is computed as follows:

6.2% of $3,200 =	$198.40	employer's OASDI tax
1.45% of $3,200 =	46.40	employer's HI tax
0.8% of $3,200 =	25.60	employer's net FUTA tax
2.4% of $3,200 =	76.80	employer's SUTA tax
Total payroll taxes	$347.20	

	Debit	Credit
Wages Expense	3,200.00	
FICA Taxes Payable—OASDI		198.40
FICA Taxes Payable—HI.		46.40
Employees FIT Payable.		230.00
SUTA Taxes Payable		32.00
Cash		2,693.20
To record the payment of wages and the liability for the employees' FICA, FIT, and SUTA taxes withheld.		

In a small company with few employees, you can compute the hours worked, determine net pay, and prepare the paychecks or pay envelopes in a relatively short period of time. For such companies, a journal entry crediting the cash account for the total net pay is a logical, efficient procedure.

In larger companies, however, the calculation of hours worked, the determination of net pay, and the preparation of paychecks may extend over the greater part of a workday, or even longer. In such companies, because of the workload involved in meeting each payroll and especially when the paychecks must be mailed to far-flung branch offices, the paychecks may be prepared several days in advance of their actual distribution to the workers. Further, the preparation of the workers' paychecks may occur in one accounting period, although the actual payment is made in the following accounting period. Thus, to show an accurate picture of the firm's liability for the payroll, at the time of recording the payroll, the net pay is accrued and credited to a liability account such as Salaries Payable or Accrued Salaries Payable, instead of to the cash account. Later, when the paychecks are given to the workers, an entry is made to record the payment of the payroll.

	Debit	Credit
Salaries Payable	XXX	
Cash		XXX
To record the payment of wages for the pay period ended July 20, 20--.		

Recording Workers' Compensation Insurance Expense

As indicated in Chapter 1, most states have passed laws that require employers to provide workers' compensation insurance to protect their employees against losses due to injury or death incurred during employment. The expense account, ***Workers' Compensation Insurance Expense,*** can be used to record the premiums paid by the company to provide this coverage. Usually, the employer estimates and pays the premium in advance. The insurance premium, often based upon the total gross payroll of the business, may be stated in terms of an amount for each $100 of weekly wages paid to employees. At the end of the year, all the payrolls are audited, and the company pays an additional premium or receives credit for an overpayment. Since the premium rate varies with the hazard involved in the work performed, your personnel and payroll records should provide for a careful classification of employees by kind or grade of work and a summary of labor costs according to the insurance premium classifications.

NEWS // ALERT //

Illinois has the highest payout of workers' compensation benefits—a maximum of $1,034.56 a week to temporarily disabled workers.

EXAMPLE

McMahon Company has only two different grades of work—office clerical and machine shop. The premium rates for the year are $0.18 per $100 of payroll for the office clerical workers and $2.90 per $100 of payroll for the machine-shop workers. Based upon past experience and budgetary projections for the year, the company estimates its annual premium to be $8,900

(Continued)

and sends a check for that amount to the insurance carrier at the beginning of the year. The entry to record this transaction is as follows:

Workers' Compensation Insurance Expense	8,900.00	
Cash		8,900.00

The effect of this entry, when posted to the ledger accounts, increases the operating expenses of the company and decreases the assets.

At the end of the year, the payrolls for the year are audited and analyzed and the current rates are applied to determine the actual premium as follows:

Work Grade	Total Payroll	Rate per $100	Premium
Office clerical	$ 81,000	$0.18	$ 145.80
Machine shop	312,000	2.90	9,048.00
Total	$393,000		$9,193.80
Less: Estimated premium paid in January			8,900.00
Balance due			$ 293.80

A check is written for the balance due the insurance company, and the following entry is made in the journal:

Workers' Compensation Insurance Expense	293.80	
Cash		293.80

Recording the Deposit or Payment of Payroll Taxes

LEARNING OBJECTIVE 4

The journal entries required to record the deposit or payment of FICA taxes and income taxes withheld and the payment of FUTA and SUTA taxes are explained below.

DEPOSITING FICA TAXES AND FEDERAL INCOME TAXES WITHHELD

As explained in Chapter 3, the requirements for depositing FICA taxes and federal income taxes withheld from employees' wages and the employer's FICA match vary.

EXAMPLE

On April 15, the ledger accounts FICA Taxes Payable—OASDI, FICA Taxes Payable—HI, and Employees FIT Payable of Goosen Company appear as follows:

FICA TAXES PAYABLE—OASDI

	4/15	697.07
	4/15	697.07
		1,394.14

FICA TAXES PAYABLE—HI

	4/15	163.02
	4/15	163.02
		326.04

EMPLOYEES FIT PAYABLE

	4/15	1,601.19

The company must deposit or electronically transfer the FICA and the federal income taxes. The following journal entry records this transaction:

FICA Taxes Payable—OASDI	1,394.14	
FICA Taxes Payable—HI	326.04	
Employees FIT Payable	1,601.19	
Cash		3,321.37

When posted, the debits of $1,394.14 and $326.04 to FICA Taxes Payable—OASDI and FICA Taxes Payable—HI remove the liabilities for the employer's share, as well as the employees' share, of the FICA taxes imposed. The debit to Employees FIT Payable removes the liability for the total amount of federal income taxes withheld from the employees' wages during the period. The credit to Cash reduces the assets of the company.

PAYING STATE OR CITY INCOME TAXES

When the employer turns over to the state or city the amount of income taxes withheld from employees' wages, the appropriate journal entry would be recorded as follows:

	Debit	Credit
Employees SIT Payable	XXX	
or		
Employees CIT Payable	XXX	
Cash		XXX

PAYING FUTA AND SUTA TAXES

At the time of depositing the FUTA taxes that have accumulated during the preceding calendar quarter, an entry is made as follows:

	Debit	Credit
FUTA Taxes Payable	XXX	
Cash		XXX

The quarterly payment of state unemployment contributions is recorded as follows:

	Debit	Credit
SUTA Taxes Payable	XXX	
Cash		XXX

Recording End-of-Period Adjustments

5 LEARNING OBJECTIVE

In most cases, the end of the fiscal (accounting) period does not coincide with the end of the payroll period. Therefore, adjustments are commonly made to record the end-of-period wages and accrued vacation pay.

WAGES

To record the adjustment for end-of-period wages, the wages for this last payroll period must be split between the fiscal period just ending (accrued wages) and the fiscal period just beginning. For instance, if the fiscal period ends on Wednesday (e.g., December 31) and payday takes place every Friday, the wages earned by the employees on Monday, Tuesday, and Wednesday are an expense of the fiscal period just ended. However, the wages earned on Thursday and Friday (payday) apply to the new fiscal period.

In order to record the wage expense properly for the fiscal period ended, an adjusting entry must be made on the last day of the fiscal period. However, since there is no actual wage payment and, therefore, no withholding, there is no need to credit any withholding accounts. The debit part of the entry would be based on the gross pay for the workdays to be accrued. The credit part of the entry involves a single liability account for the total wage expense. In the case above, the wage expenses of Monday, Tuesday, and Wednesday would be recorded in the following ***adjusting entry:***

	Debit	Credit
Wages Expense	XXX	
Wages Payable		XXX
To record wages incurred but unpaid as of the end of the fiscal period.		

Since the accumulation of payroll data (timesheets, registers, etc.) is such a time-consuming process, the amount of the adjustment could be based on a percentage of the previous period's payroll. For instance, if the accrual is for three workdays out of a five-workday week, 60 percent of the prior week's gross pay could be used as the amount of the adjustment.

In a situation where the employer holds back one week's pay (earnings for the current week are not paid until the following Friday), the adjusting entry for the example shown above would accrue eight days of expense (one full workweek plus Monday, Tuesday, and Wednesday).

NEWS// ALERT//

More employers are pooling vacation and sick leave. This saves employers money on overtime and temporary help because it avoids the unapproved use of sick time.

VACATION PAY

Another adjustment required at the end of the accounting period concerns vacation pay. If a company has a vacation policy, the employees earn the right for paid future absences during the current period. Therefore, an expense account should be created for the amount of the vacation time earned by the employees and a liability should be accrued at the end of the current period. Whether making the adjustment each payday, each month, or each year, the expense must be recorded when the liability is created, which is in the period when the employees earn it.

EXAMPLE

The employees of Carr Company are entitled to one day's vacation for each month worked. The average daily pay for each of the 50 employees is $130. The adjusting entry to record the vacation expense of $6,500 ($130 × 50) at the end of each month is:

Vacation Benefits Expense	6,500.00	
Vacation Benefits Payable		6,500.00

on the JOB

According to the World Tourism Organization, the average number of vacation days provided to workers is 42 in Italy, 37 in France, 28 in Britain, 26 in Canada, and 13 in the United States.

When employees eventually use their vacation time, the payment entry debits Vacation Benefits Payable, not Wages Expense, since the expense was previously recorded in the adjusting entry, as shown above. Another method that is used by most companies ignores the split between regular pay and vacation pay in the payroll entry. Instead, an adjusting entry is made at the end of each month for the expense and the liability to bring the balance in the liability account (Vacation Benefits Payable) either up to or down to the current total of unused vacation for the company, with the offsetting debit or credit made to a vacation expense account.

Postretirement benefits such as health care and pensions also require adjusting entries of this type. These benefits must be reported as expenses during the employees' working years when they earn the entitlements.

Summary of Accounts Used in Recording Payroll Transactions

6 LEARNING OBJECTIVE

The following listing summarizes some of the general ledger accounts that may be used to record payroll transactions:

1. *Wages and Salaries:* An operating expense account in which the gross payroll is recorded.
2. *Payroll Taxes:* An operating expense account in which are recorded all payroll taxes on the employer under FICA, FUTA, and the various state unemployment compensation laws.
3. *Workers' Compensation Insurance Expense:* An operating expense account in which are recorded the premiums paid by the company to provide coverage for employees against employment-related injury or death.
4. *Vacation Benefits Expense:* An operating expense account in which are recorded the costs of the vacation time that has been earned by employees.
5. *FICA Taxes Payable—OASDI:* A current liability account in which are recorded deductions made from employees' wages and the employer's portion of the OASDI tax.
6. *FICA Taxes Payable—HI:* A current liability account in which are recorded deductions made from employees' wages and the employer's portion of the HI tax.
7. *FUTA Taxes Payable:* A current liability account in which are recorded the employer's federal unemployment taxes.
8. *SUTA Taxes Payable:* A current liability account in which are recorded the amounts due the states for the employer's unemployment compensation contributions. This account may also be credited for amounts deducted from employees' wages, if employees must contribute to state unemployment compensation funds.
9. *Employees FIT Payable:* A current liability account in which are recorded deductions made from employees' wages for federal income taxes.
10. *Employees SIT Payable:* A current liability account in which are recorded deductions made from employees' wages for state income taxes.
11. *Health Insurance Premiums Collected:* A current liability account in which are recorded deductions made from employees' wages for their share of the premiums paid for health insurance coverage.
12. *Union Dues Payable:* A current liability account in which are recorded the deductions made from union members' wages for their union dues, assessments, or initiation fees.
13. *Wages Payable:* A current liability account in which are recorded the net wages that have been earned by employees but not yet paid to them.
14. *Vacation Benefits Payable:* A current liability account in which are recorded the costs of the vacation time that has been earned by employees but not yet used.

Illustrative Case

The following illustrative case shows the accounting procedures used by Brookins Company in recording payroll transactions during the third quarter of its fiscal year. The fiscal year of the company ends on June 30, 20—. Brookins pays employees semimonthly on the 15th and the last day of the month. When the 15th or the last day of the month falls on Saturday or Sunday, employees are paid on the preceding Friday.

On January 1, 20—, the balances of the accounts used in recording payroll transactions follow. These account balances are shown in the general ledger on pages 6-31 through 6-33.

Acct. No.	Account Title	Account Balance
11	Cash	$85,000.00
20	FICA Taxes Payable—OASDI	734.29
21	FICA Taxes Payable—HI	171.73
22	FUTA Taxes Payable	122.00
23	SUTA Taxes Payable	40.50
25	Employees FIT Payable	1,472.00
26	Employees SIT Payable	474.42
28	Union Dues Payable	80.00
51	Wages and Salaries	46,500.00
55	Payroll Taxes	4,254.50

The first $102,300 in wages and salaries paid is subject to the OASDI tax on both the employer (6.2%) and the employees (6.2%). The total wages and salaries paid are subject to the HI tax on both the employer (1.45%) and the employees (1.45%). The employer is also subject to a net FUTA tax of 0.8 percent, based on the first $7,000 in earnings paid each employee during a calendar year, and a SUTA tax of 2.3 percent, based on the first $7,000 in earnings paid during a calendar year. The state does not require contributions of employees for unemployment compensation or disability insurance.

The wage-bracket method is used to determine the amount of federal income taxes to be withheld from the employees' earnings. The state income tax law requires that a graduated percentage of the gross earnings of each employee be withheld each payday. Under the check-off system, union dues are withheld each payday from the union workers who are employed in the plant. On or before the fourth of each month, the dues collected during the preceding month are turned over to the treasurer of the union.

In the following narrative of transactions, the January 14 (Friday) payroll transaction is explained in detail on page 6-27. All other transactions are stated briefly. Adjacent to the narrative are the journal entries to record the transactions. The ledger accounts showing the transactions posted are on pages 6-31 through 6-33.

Narrative of Transactions		Journal	P.R.	Debit	Page 15 Credit
	20—				
Jan. 4. Paid the treasurer of the union $80, representing the union dues withheld from the workers' earnings during the month of December.	Jan. 4	Union Dues Payable	28	80.00	
		Cash	11		80.00
		To record payment of union dues withheld during December.			
Jan. 14. Paid total wages and salaries of all employees, $3,890. All the earnings are taxable under FICA. In addition to the social security taxes, the company withheld $455 from the employees' earnings for federal income taxes, $85.58 for state income taxes, and $45 for union dues. (See the explanation of the January 14 payroll transaction given below.)	14	Wages and Salaries	51	3,890.00	
		FICA Taxes Payable—OASDI	20		241.18
		FICA Taxes Payable—HI	21		56.41
		Employees FIT Payable	25		455.00
		Employees SIT Payable	26		85.58
		Union Dues Payable	28		45.00
		Cash	11		3,006.83
		To record the payment of wages and the liabilities for the employees' taxes withheld.			
Jan. 14. Recorded the employer's payroll taxes for the first pay in January. All the earnings are taxable under FICA, FUTA, and SUTA.	14	Payroll Taxes	55	418.18	
		FICA Taxes Payable—OASDI	20		241.18
		FICA Taxes Payable—HI	21		56.41
		FUTA Taxes Payable	22		31.12
		SUTA Taxes Payable	23		89.47
		To record the payroll taxes and liabilities of the employer.			
Jan. 18. Electronically transferred to the IRS the FICA taxes and employees' federal income taxes withheld on the two December payrolls. At the end of December, the total liability for FICA taxes and federal income taxes withheld was $2,378.02. (January 17 is Martin Luther King, Jr.'s birthday, which is a bank holiday.)	18	FICA Taxes Payable—OASDI	20	734.29	
		FICA Taxes Payable—HI	21	171.73	
		Employees FIT Payable	25	1,472.00	
		Cash	11		2,378.02
		To record deposit of FICA taxes and federal income taxes withheld for the 12/15 and 12/31 payrolls.			
Jan. 18. Paid to the state the amount of state income taxes withheld from employees' pays for the quarter just ended.	18	Employees SIT Payable	26	474.42	
		Cash	11		474.42
		To record payment of state income taxes withheld during 4th quarter.			

Analysis of the January 14 payroll transaction follows:

1. Wages and Salaries is debited for $3,890, the total of the employees' gross earnings.
2. FICA Taxes Payable—OASDI is credited for $241.18, the amount withheld from the employees' earnings for OASDI taxes.
3. FICA Taxes Payable—HI is credited for $56.41, the amount withheld from the employees' earnings for HI taxes.
4. Employees FIT Payable is credited for $455, the amount withheld from employees' earnings for federal income tax purposes.
5. Employees SIT Payable is credited for $85.58, the amount withheld from employees' earnings for state income taxes.
6. Union Dues Payable is credited for $45, the amount withheld from union members' earnings.
7. Cash is credited for $3,006.83, the net amount paid the employees ($3,890 gross earnings – $241.18 OASDI – $56.41 HI – $455 FIT – $85.58 SIT – $45 union dues).
8. Payroll Taxes is debited for $418.18, the amount of taxes imposed on the employer under FICA, FUTA, and SUTA. The computation of the total payroll taxes is:

FICA—OASDI:	6.2% of $3,890 =	$241.18
FICA—HI:	1.45% of $3,890 =	56.41
FUTA:	0.8% of $3,890 =	31.12
SUTA:	2.3% of $3,890 =	89.47
Total payroll taxes		$418.18

9. FICA Taxes Payable—OASDI is credited for the amount of tax on the employer, which is 6.2% of $3,890, or $241.18.
10. FICA Taxes Payable—HI is credited for the amount of tax on the employer, which is 1.45% of $3,890, or $56.41.
11. FUTA Taxes Payable is credited for $31.12, the liability incurred because of the taxes imposed on the employer under FUTA.
12. SUTA Taxes Payable is credited for $89.47, the amount of the contributions payable to the state.

Narrative of Transactions		Journal	P.R.	Debit	Page 16 Credit
Jan. 31. Paid total wages and salaries, $4,100. All of this amount constitutes taxable earnings under FICA. Withheld $483 for federal income taxes, $90.20 for state income taxes, and $45 for union dues.	Jan. 31	Wages and Salaries	51	4,100.00	
		FICA Taxes Payable—OASDI	20		254.20
		FICA Taxes Payable—HI	21		59.45
		Employees FIT Payable	25		483.00
		Employees SIT Payable	26		90.20
		Union Dues Payable	28		45.00
		Cash	11		3,168.15
		To record the payment of wages and the liabilities for the employees' taxes withheld.			
Jan. 31. Recorded the employer's payroll taxes for this payroll. All the earnings are taxable under FICA, FUTA, and SUTA.	31	Payroll Taxes	55	440.75	
		FICA Taxes Payable—OASDI	20		254.20
		FICA Taxes Payable—HI	21		59.45
		FUTA Taxes Payable	22		32.80
		SUTA Taxes Payable	23		94.30
		To record the payroll taxes and liabilities of the employer.			
Jan. 31. Filed the Employer's Annual Federal Unemployment (FUTA) Tax Return, Form 940, for the preceding calendar year. Electronically transferred $122 to remove the liability for FUTA taxes for the fourth quarter of the previous year.	31	FUTA Taxes Payable	22	122.00	
		Cash	11		122.00
		To record the deposit of FUTA taxes for the 4th quarter.			
Jan. 31. Filed the state unemployment contributions return for the quarter ending December 31, and paid $40.50 to the state unemployment compensation fund.	31	SUTA Taxes Payable	23	40.50	
		Cash	11		40.50
		To record payment of contributions to state unemployment compensation fund for the 4th quarter.			
Jan. 31. Filed the quarterly return (Form 941) with the IRS Center for the period ended December 31. No journal entry is required since the liability for FICA taxes and employees' federal income taxes withheld was removed by the timely transfer on January 18, 20—. No taxes were paid or deposited at the time of filing Form 941.					
Feb. 4. Paid the treasurer of the union $90, representing the union dues withheld from the workers' earnings during the month of January.	Feb. 4	Union Dues Payable	28	90.00	
		Cash	11		90.00
		To record the payment of the union dues withheld during January.			

Page 17

Narrative of Transactions		Journal	P.R.	Debit	Credit
	Feb. 15	Wages and Salaries	51	4,000.00	
Feb. 15. Paid total wages and salaries, $4,000. All of this amount is taxable under FICA. Withheld $470 for federal income taxes, $88 for state income taxes, and $45 for union dues.		FICA Taxes Payable—OASDI	20		248.00
		FICA Taxes Payable—HI	21		58.00
		Employees FIT Payable	25		470.00
		Employees SIT Payable	26		88.00
		Union Dues Payable	28		45.00
		Cash	11		3,091.00
		To record the payment of wages and the liabilities for the employees' taxes withheld.			
Feb. 15. Recorded the employer's payroll taxes. All the earnings are taxable under FICA, FUTA, and SUTA.	15	Payroll Taxes	55	430.00	
		FICA Taxes Payable—OASDI	20		248.00
		FICA Taxes Payable—HI	21		58.00
		FUTA Taxes Payable	22		32.00
		SUTA Taxes Payable	23		92.00
		To record the payroll taxes and liabilities of the employer.			
Feb. 15. Electronically transferred $2,160.48 to remove the liability for the FICA taxes and the employees' federal income taxes withheld on the January 14 and January 31 payrolls.	15	FICA Taxes Payable—OASDI	20	990.76	
		FICA Taxes Payable—HI	21	231.72	
		Employees FIT Payable	25	938.00	
		Cash	11		2,160.48
		To record the deposit of FICA taxes and federal income taxes withheld for the January 14 and January 31 payrolls.			
Feb. 28. Paid total wages and salaries, $4,250. All of this amount is taxable under FICA. Withheld $502 for federal income taxes, $93.50 for state income taxes, and $50 for union dues.	28	Wages and Salaries	51	4,250.00	
		FICA Taxes Payable—OASDI	20		263.50
		FICA Taxes Payable—HI	21		61.63
		Employees FIT Payable	25		502.00
		Employees SIT Payable	26		93.50
		Union Dues Payable	28		50.00
		Cash	11		3,279.37
		To record the payment of wages and the liabilities for the employees' taxes withheld.			
Feb. 28. Recorded the employer's payroll taxes. All the earnings are taxable under FICA, FUTA, and SUTA.	28	Payroll Taxes	55	456.88	
		FICA Taxes Payable—OASDI	20		263.50
		FICA Taxes Payable—HI	21		61.63
		FUTA Taxes Payable	22		34.00
		SUTA Taxes Payable	23		97.75
		To record the payroll taxes and liabilities of the employer.			
Mar. 4. Paid the treasurer of the union $95, representing the union dues withheld from the workers' earnings during the month of February.	Mar. 4	Union Dues Payable	28	95.00	
		Cash	11		95.00
		To record the payment of the union dues withheld during February.			

Page 18

Narrative of Transactions	Journal		P.R.	Debit	Credit
Mar. 15. Paid total wages and salaries, $4,300. All of this amount is taxable under FICA. Withheld $554 for federal income taxes, $94.60 for state income taxes, and $50 for union dues.	Mar. 15	Wages and Salaries	51	4,300.00	
		FICA Taxes Payable—OASDI	20		266.60
		FICA Taxes Payable—HI	21		62.35
		Employees FIT Payable	25		554.00
		Employees SIT Payable	26		94.60
		Union Dues Payable	28		50.00
		Cash	11		3,272.45
		To record the payment of wages and the liabilities for the employees' taxes withheld.			
Mar. 15. Recorded the employer's payroll taxes. All the earnings are taxable under FICA, FUTA, and SUTA.	15	Payroll Taxes	55	462.25	
		FICA Taxes Payable—OASDI	20		266.60
		FICA Taxes Payable—HI	21		62.35
		FUTA Taxes Payable	22		34.40
		SUTA Taxes Payable	23		98.90
		To record the payroll taxes and liabilities of the employer.			
Mar. 15. Electronically transferred $2,234.26 to remove the liability for FICA taxes and the employees' federal income taxes withheld on the February 15 and February 28 payrolls.	15	FICA Taxes Payable—OASDI	20	1,023.00	
		FICA Taxes Payable—HI	21	239.26	
		Employees FIT Payable	25	972.00	
		Cash	11		2,234.26
		To record the deposit of FICA taxes and federal income taxes withheld for the February 15 and February 28 payrolls.			
Mar. 31. Paid total wages and salaries, $4,320. All of this amount is taxable under FICA. Withheld $570 for federal income taxes, $95.04 for state income taxes, and $50 for union dues.	31	Wages and Salaries	51	4,320.00	
		FICA Taxes Payable—OASDI	20		267.84
		FICA Taxes Payable—HI	21		62.64
		Employees FIT Payable	25		570.00
		Employees SIT Payable	26		95.04
		Union Dues Payable	28		50.00
		Cash	11		3,274.48
		To record the payment of wages and the liabilities for the employees' taxes withheld.			
Mar. 31. Recorded the employer's payroll taxes. All of the earnings are taxable under FICA, FUTA, and SUTA.	31	Payroll Taxes	55	464.40	
		FICA Taxes Payable—OASDI	20		267.84
		FICA Taxes Payable—HI	21		62.64
		FUTA Taxes Payable	22		34.56
		SUTA Taxes Payable	23		99.36
		To record the payroll taxes and liabilities of the employer.			

After journalizing and posting the transactions for January through March, the general ledger payroll accounts as shown on the next two pages carry the following balances:

1. ***FICA Taxes Payable—OASDI:*** $1,068.88, the amount of the liability for the taxes imposed on both the employer and the employees with respect to wages and salaries paid on March 15 and March 31. The FICA taxes, along with the employees' federal income taxes withheld, must be deposited by April 15.
2. ***FICA Taxes Payable—HI:*** $249.98, the amount of the liability for the taxes imposed on both the employer and the employees with respect to wages and salaries paid on March 15 and March 31. The FICA taxes, along with the employees' federal income taxes withheld, must be paid by April 15.
3. ***FUTA Taxes Payable:*** $198.88, the accumulation of the amounts credited to this account each payday during the first three months of the calendar year. The balance of the account on March 31 need not be deposited since it is $500 or less. The $198.88 will be added to the second quarter's liability and deposited if the $500 threshold is passed.
4. ***SUTA Taxes Payable:*** $571.78, the amount due to the state unemployment compensation fund. This liability must be paid on or before May 2.
5. ***Employees FIT Payable:*** $1,124, the amount due for federal income taxes withheld from employees' earnings on March 15 and March 31. This amount, along with the balances of the FICA taxes payable accounts, represents a liability that must be paid by April 15.
6. ***Employees SIT Payable:*** $546.92, the amount due for state income taxes withheld from employees' earnings during the first three months of the calendar year. This amount must be paid to the treasurer of the state on the date specified in the state's income tax law.
7. ***Union Dues Payable:*** $100, amount due the treasurer of the union on or before April 4.
8. ***Wages and Salaries:*** $71,360, the total gross earnings for the three quarters of the company's fiscal year. The entire amount is an operating expense of the business.
9. ***Payroll Taxes:*** $6,926.96, the total payroll taxes for the three quarters imposed on the employer under FICA, FUTA, and SUTA. The entire amount is an operating expense of the business.

GENERAL LEDGER

CASH 11

Date		Item	P.R.	Dr.	Cr.	Balance Dr.	Balance Cr.
20—							
Jan.	1	Bal.	✓			85,000.00	
	4		J15		80.00	84,920.00	
	14		J15		3,006.83	81,913.17	
	18		J15		2,378.02	79,535.15	
	18		J15		474.42	79,060.73	
	31		J16		3,168.15	75,892.58	
	31		J16		122.00	75,770.58	
	31		J16		40.50	75,730.08	
Feb.	4		J16		90.00	75,640.08	
	15		J17		3,091.00	72,549.08	
	15		J17		2,160.48	70,388.60	
	28		J17		3,279.37	67,109.23	
Mar.	4		J17		95.00	67,014.23	
	15		J18		3,272.45	63,741.78	
	15		J18		2,234.26	61,507.52	
	31		J18		3,274.48	58,233.04	

FICA TAXES PAYABLE—OASDI 20

Date		Item	P.R.	Dr.	Cr.	Balance Dr.	Balance Cr.
20—							
Jan.	1	Bal.	✓				734.29
	14		J15		241.18		975.47
	14		J15		241.18		1,216.65
	18		J15	734.29			482.36
	31		J16		254.20		736.56
	31		J16		254.20		990.76
Feb.	15		J17		248.00		1,238.76
	15		J17		248.00		1,486.76
	15		J17	990.76			496.00
	28		J17		263.50		759.50
	28		J17		263.50		1,023.00
Mar.	15		J18		266.60		1,289.60
	15		J18		266.60		1,556.20
	15		J18	1,023.00			533.20
	31		J18		267.84		801.04
	31		J18		267.84		1,068.88

FICA TAXES PAYABLE—HI 21

Date		Item	P.R.	Dr.	Cr.	Balance Dr.	Balance Cr.
20—							
Jan.	1	Bal.	✓				171.73
	14		J15		56.41		228.14
	14		J15		56.41		284.55
	18		J15	171.73			112.82
	31		J16		59.45		172.27
	31		J16		59.45		231.72
Feb.	15		J17		58.00		289.72
	15		J17		58.00		347.72
	15		J17	231.72			116.00
	28		J17		61.63		177.63
	28		J17		61.63		239.26
Mar.	15		J18		62.35		301.61
	15		J18		62.35		363.96
	15		J18	239.26			124.70
	31		J18		62.64		187.34
	31		J18		62.64		249.98

FUTA TAXES PAYABLE 22

Date		Item	P.R.	Dr.	Cr.	Balance Dr.	Balance Cr.
20—							
Jan.	1	Bal.	✓				122.00
	14		J15		31.12		153.12
	31		J16		32.80		185.92
	31		J16	122.00			63.92
Feb.	15		J17		32.00		95.92
	28		J17		34.00		129.92
Mar.	15		J18		34.40		164.32
	31		J18		34.56		198.88

SUTA TAXES PAYABLE 23

Date		Item	P.R.	Dr.	Cr.	Balance Dr.	Balance Cr.
20—							
Jan.	1	Bal.	✓				40.50
	14		J15		89.47		129.97
	31		J16		94.30		224.27
	31		J16	40.50			183.77
Feb.	15		J17		92.00		275.77
	28		J17		97.75		373.52
Mar.	15		J18		98.90		472.42
	31		J18		99.36		571.78

EMPLOYEES FIT PAYABLE 25

Date		Item	P.R.	Dr.	Cr.	Balance Dr.	Balance Cr.
20—							
Jan.	1	Bal.	✓				1,472.00
	14		J15		455.00		1,927.00
	18		J15	1,472.00			455.00
	31		J16		483.00		938.00
Feb.	15		J17		470.00		1,408.00
	15		J17	938.00			470.00
	28		J17		502.00		972.00
Mar.	15		J18		554.00		1,526.00
	15		J18	972.00			554.00
	31		J18		570.00		1,124.00

EMPLOYEES SIT PAYABLE 26

Date		Item	P.R.	Dr.	Cr.	Balance Dr.	Balance Cr.
20—							
Jan.	1	Bal.	✓				474.42
	14		J15		85.58		560.00
	18		J15	474.42			85.58
	31		J16		90.20		175.78
Feb.	15		J17		88.00		263.78
	28		J17		93.50		357.28
Mar.	15		J18		94.60		451.88
	31		J18		95.04		546.92

UNION DUES PAYABLE 28

Date		Item	P.R.	Dr.	Cr.	Balance Dr.	Balance Cr.
20—							
Jan.	1	Bal.	✓				80.00
	4		J15	80.00		——	
	14		J15		45.00		45.00
	31		J16		45.00		90.00
Feb.	4		J16	90.00		——	
	15		J17		45.00		45.00
	28		J17		50.00		95.00
Mar.	4		J17	95.00		——	
	15		J18		50.00		50.00
	31		J18		50.00		100.00

WAGES AND SALARIES 51

Date		Item	P.R.	Dr.	Cr.	Balance Dr.	Balance Cr.
20—							
Jan.	1	Bal.	✓			46,500.00	
	14		J15	3,890.00		50,390.00	
	31		J16	4,100.00		54,490.00	
Feb.	15		J17	4,000.00		58,490.00	
	28		J17	4,250.00		62,740.00	
Mar.	15		J18	4,300.00		67,040.00	
	31		J18	4,320.00		71,360.00	

PAYROLL TAXES 55

Date		Item	P.R.	Dr.	Cr.	Balance Dr.	Balance Cr.
20—							
Jan.	1	Bal.	✓			4,254.50	
	14		J15	418.18		4,672.68	
	31		J16	440.75		5,113.43	
Feb.	15		J17	430.00		5,543.43	
	28		J17	456.88		6,000.31	
Mar.	15		J18	462.25		6,462.56	
	31		J18	464.40		6,926.96	

KEY TERMS

Business expense *(p. 6-17)*
Check-off system *(p. 6-11)*
Disposable earnings *(p. 6-12)*
Electronic funds transfer system (EFTS) *(p. 6-15)*
Electronic paystub *(p. 6-16)*
Garnishment *(p. 6-11)*
Group insurance *(p. 6-10)*
Journal entries *(p. 6-5)*

CHAPTER SUMMARY

The completion of the internal payroll records—Payroll Register and Employee's Earnings Record—starts off this chapter. In the discussion of employee payroll deductions, the garnishment of wages was highlighted. The percent of disposable earnings (gross earnings − federal and state income taxes − FICA taxes − state unemployment and disability taxes) subject to the various types of garnishments was examined—from a high of 65 percent for child support to a low of 15 percent for student loan garnishments. Federal tax levies are computed by the employer by taking the take-home pay (gross pay − taxes − deductions in effect before the levy) less the exempt amount (employee's standard deduction + personal exemptions ÷ by number of pay periods in the year).

The actual payroll accounting entries were analyzed from the gross pay entry:

GROSS PAY (DEBIT—EXPENSE)
WITHHOLDINGS (CREDIT—LIABILITIES)
NET PAY (CREDIT—CASH)

to the payroll tax entry:

TOTAL EMPLOYER TAXES (DEBIT—EXPENSE)
FICA PAYABLE (CREDIT—LIABILITY)
FUTA PAYABLE (CREDIT—LIABILITY)
SUTA PAYABLE (CREDIT—LIABILITY)

to the adjusting entries for unpaid benefits:

TYPE OF BENEFIT (DEBIT—EXPENSE)
SPECIFIC LIABILITY (CREDIT—LIABILITY)

to the payment of various liabilities:

SPECIFIC LIABILITY (DEBIT—LIABILITY)
CASH (CREDIT—ASSET)

This was followed by posting the entries to the various general ledger accounts.

At the end of the chapter, a full quarter's worth of payroll accounting entries and postings were illustrated.

MATCHING QUIZ

_____ 1. Employee's earnings record

_____ 2. Advance earned income credit

_____ 3. Disposable earnings

_____ 4. Regular earnings plus overtime earnings

_____ 5. Payroll Taxes

_____ 6. Overtime premium earnings

_____ 7. Wages Payable

_____ 8. Payroll Register

_____ 9. Form 668-W

_____ 10. Garnishment

A. Expense account for FICA, FUTA, and SUTA taxes on the employer

B. Legal procedure by which a portion of wages of a person must be withheld for payment of a debt

C. Reduce employer's liability for the payment of FICA and FIT taxes to the IRS

D. Notifies employer of a tax levy

E. Used to complete Form W-2

F. Provides information needed in preparing the journal entries for payroll

G. Debit portion of payroll entry

H. Earnings remaining after withholding for income taxes and for other amounts required by law

I. One-half regular pay rate multiplied by overtime hours

J. Liability account for wages that have been earned by employees but not yet paid

QUESTIONS FOR REVIEW

1. What are the main kinds of information contained in a payroll register?
2. For what reason are "distribution" columns sometimes provided in the payroll register?
3. Explain the use of the "Cumulative" column in the employee's earnings record.
4. In Philadelphia, Pennsylvania, most workers are subject to three income taxes upon their earnings—federal, state, and city. Should an employer in Philadelphia record the liability for the withholding of all three income taxes in one liability account such as Income Taxes Payable?
5. What is meant by the ***garnishment*** of wages?
6. What is general priority order concerning wage attachments?
7. Under the Consumer Credit Protection Act, what is the maximum percentage that can be deducted from an employee's pay to satisfy a student loan garnishment?
8. What portions of an employee's wages are exempt from a federal tax levy?
9. How will payroll deductions from employees' wages for their portion of 401(k) plans be recorded?
10. How are employees who do not have bank accounts paid by an employer who uses an electronic funds transfer system for payroll?
11. How is the information that is usually on a paper paystub given to an employee if the employer is using electronic paystubs?
12. What must the employer do with unclaimed paychecks?
13. What special accounts must usually be opened in the general ledger to record payroll tax entries?
14. Is it necessary for an employer who is subject to FICA and FUTA taxes to keep a separate expense account for the taxes under each act?
15. What is the effect of each of the following postings upon the assets, liabilities, and owner's equity of a company?
    a. A debit to Wages.
    b. A credit to FICA Taxes Payable—HI.
    c. A debit to SUTA Taxes Payable.
    d. A credit to Cash.
16. Why is it necessary to classify employees by kind of work performed when computing the cost of workers' compensation insurance?

17. What accounts are debited and credited when an employer records the electronic transfer of FICA taxes and federal income taxes that have been withheld?

18. How is the amount of accrual entry for the portion of a weekly payroll that is accrued at the end of an accounting period determined?

19. When are expenses of benefits such as vacation pay and retirement pay recorded? Explain.

20. What payroll-related expenses does an employer incur because of its employees?

QUESTIONS FOR DISCUSSION

1. In what respect does an employee's earnings record resemble a ledger?

2. Freisleven Corporation has undertaken a cost study of its operations. One area of concern to the company is the total cost of labor, particularly the cost of employee benefits. Prepare a list of the different kinds of costs that a company might incur as part of its "total package" salary cost.

3. Along with five payroll deductions required by law (FICA—OASDI and HI, Employees FIT, Employees SIT, and Employees CIT), five other deductions are typically made from the employees' earnings in The Cranston Company. What leeway does the company have as to the level of detail shown in the payroll register in recording these 10 deductions?

DATE ______________ NAME ______________________________

PRACTICAL PROBLEMS—SERIES A

Omit the writing of explanations for the journal entries.

6-1A LO 2.

Cody Wendt has a federal tax levy of $3,200.90 against him. If Cody is married with four personal exemptions and had a take-home pay of $915.00 this week, how much would his employer take from his pay to satisfy part of the tax levy?

6-2A LO 3.

Kalen O'Brien earned $730 this week. The deductions from her pay were as follows:

FIT	$76.00
FICA—OASDI	45.26
FICA—HI	10.59
State income tax	36.50
State disability insurance	8.61
Health insurance premium	19.50
Credit union contribution	$35.00
United fund contribution	5.00

O'Brien's employer just received a garnishment order (credit card debt of $3,500) against her pay. Compute the following:

a. O'Brien's disposable earnings . . . . $________

b. The amount of her pay subject to the garnishment . . . . $________

6-3A LO 3,5.

a. Cal Ruther, an employer, is subject to FICA taxes but exempt from FUTA and SUTA taxes. During the last quarter of the year, his employees earned monthly wages of $8,500, all of which is taxable. The amount of federal income taxes withheld each month is $1,040. Journalize the payment of wages, and record the payroll tax on November 30.

JOURNAL

	DATE	DESCRIPTION	POST. REF.	DEBIT	CREDIT	
1						1
2						2
3						3
4						4
5						5
6						6
7						7
8						8
9						9
10						10

6-3A (concluded)

b. Prior to posting the November 30 payroll transaction, FICA Taxes Payable—OASDI, FICA Taxes Payable—HI, and Employees FIT Payable had zero balances. Ruther must pay the FICA taxes and income taxes withheld on the November 30 payroll. Journalize the electronic transfer of the payroll taxes on December 15.

JOURNAL

	DATE	DESCRIPTION	POST. REF.	DEBIT	CREDIT	
1						1
2						2
3						3
4						4
5						5
6						6

6-4A LO 3.

The employees of Donnelly Music Company earn total wages of $4,690 during January. The total amount is taxable under FICA, FUTA, and SUTA. The state contribution rate for the company is 3.6%. The amount withheld for federal income taxes is $685. Journalize the payment of the monthly wages, and record the payroll taxes.

JOURNAL

	DATE	DESCRIPTION	POST. REF.	DEBIT	CREDIT	
1						1
2						2
3						3
4						4
5						5
6						6
7						7
8						8
9						9
10						10
11						11
12						12
13						13
14						14

6-5A LO 3.

Hambro, Inc., has a semimonthly payroll of $38,000 on September 15. The total payroll is taxable under FICA Taxes—HI; $32,850 is taxable under FICA Taxes—OASDI; and $9,300 is taxable under FUTA and SUTA. The state contribution rate for the company is 3.1%. The amount withheld for federal income taxes is $5,780. The amount withheld for state income taxes is $809.

a. Journalize the payment of the wages, and record the payroll taxes on September 15.

b. Assume that the employees of Hambro, Inc., must also pay state contributions (disability insurance) of 1% on the taxable payroll of $29,300 and that the employees' contributions are to be deducted by the employer. Journalize the September 15 payment of wages, assuming that the state contributions of the employees are kept in a separate account.

JOURNAL

DATE		DESCRIPTION	POST. REF.	DEBIT	CREDIT
(A) Sept	15	Wages & Salaries		38000 00	
		FICA - OASDI			2036 70
		FICA - HI			551 00
		FIT Tax			5780 00
		SIT Tax			809 00
		Cash			28823 30
		Payroll Taxes		2950 40	
		FICA - OASDI			2036 70
		FICA - HI			551 00
		SUTA			288 30
		FUTA			74 40
(B) Sept	15	Wages & Salaries		38000 00	
		FICA - OASDI			2036 70
		FICA - HI			551 00
		FIT Tax			5780 00
		SIT Tax			809 00
		State disability Ins			293 00
		Cash			28530 30

6-6A LO 3.

Pauley, Inc., pays its employees' weekly wages in cash. A supplementary payroll sheet that lists the employees' names and their earnings for a certain week is shown below. Complete the payroll sheet by calculating the total amount of payroll and indicating the least possible number of denominations that can be used in paying each employee. However, no employees are to be given bills in denominations greater than $20.

PAULEY, INC.

For Period Ending August 15, 20—

Supplementary Payroll Sheet

		Bills				Coins				
Name of Employee	Net Amount Paid	$20	$10	$5	$1	50¢	25¢	10¢	5¢	1¢
Chad T. Biskis	$251.75									
Nicole A. Cibik	256.52									
Domingo M. Diaz	384.94									
Laura B. Elias	202.59									
Ari M. Fleischer	253.64									
Diane Y. Germano	296.50									
Arnold B. Herst	594.26									
Edward C. Kenner	399.89									
Kathleen J. Marfia	234.01									
Kimberly A. Picket	595.80									
Total										

6-7A LO 3.

Kip Bowman is owner and sole employee of KB Corporation. He pays himself a salary of $1,500 each week.

Additional tax information includes:

FICA tax—OASDI	6.2% on first $102,300
FICA tax—HI	1.45% on total pay
Federal income tax	$232.00 per pay
State income tax	22% of the federal income tax withholding
Federal unemployment tax	0.8% on first $7,000
State unemployment tax	0.05% on first $14,000

Additional payroll deductions include:

401(k) plan	3% per pay
Child support garnishment	$100 per pay
Health insurance premium	$95 per pay

Record the payroll entry and payroll tax entry for the pay of the week ended June 4 (his year-to-date pay is $31,500).

JOURNAL

	DATE		DESCRIPTION	POST. REF.	DEBIT	CREDIT	
1	June	4	Wages & Salaries		1500 00		1
2			FICA - OASDI			93 00	2
3			FICA - HI			21 75	3
4			FIT Tax			232 00	4
5			SIT Tax			51 04	5
6			401 K			45 00	6
7			Child Support			100 00	7
8			Health Ins.			95 00	8
9			Cash			862 21	9
10							10
11	June	4	Payroll Taxes		114 75		11
12			FICA - OASDI Payable			93 00	12
13			FICA - HI			21 75	13
14			FUTA			0	14
15			SUTA			0	15
16							16
17							17
18							18
19							19
20							20

862.21

6-8A LO 3.

The employees of Pelter Company earn wages of $12,000 for the two weeks ending April 20. FIT taxes of $260 were withheld. The entire amount of wages is subject to the FICA taxes, but only $9,800 is taxable under the federal and state unemployment compensation laws. The state contribution rate of the employer is 2.9%. All employees are subject to state unemployment contributions of 0.5% on the April 20 taxable wages of $9,800, and the employees' contributions are to be deducted by the employer. Journalize the payment of the wages, and record the payroll taxes, assuming that the contributions of the employer and the employees are recorded in one account, SUTA Taxes Payable.

JOURNAL

	DATE	DESCRIPTION	POST. REF.	DEBIT	CREDIT	
1						1
2						2
3						3
4						4
5						5
6						6
7						7
8						8
9						9
10						10
11						11
12						12
13						13
14						14
15						15

6-9A LO 3.

The following information pertains to the payroll of Furphy Textile Company on June 6:

- **a.** The total wages earned by employees are $2,180.
- **b.** The state unemployment insurance contribution rate is 2.5%.
- **c.** The entire amount of wages is taxable under FICA, FUTA, and SUTA.
- **d.** The amount withheld from the employees' wages for federal income taxes is $309; for state income taxes, $43.10; and for group insurance, $16.80.
- **e.** The amount of the advance earned income credit payments made to the employees is $131.

Journalize the payment of wages, and record the payroll taxes on June 6.

1225.31

JOURNAL

	DATE		DESCRIPTION	POST. REF.	DEBIT	CREDIT	
1	June	6	Wages + Salaries		2180		1
2			FICA-OASDI Payable			135 16	2
3			FICA-HI Payable			31 61	3
4			FIT Tax Payable			309 00	4
5			SIT Tax Payable			43 10	5
6			Group Insurance payable			16 80	6
7			AEIC		131		7
8			Cash			1775 33	8
9							9
10	June	6	Payroll Taxes		238 71		10
11			FICA-OASDI			135 16	11
12			FICA-HI			31 61	12
13			FUTA			17 44	13
14			SUTA			54 50	14
15							15
16							16
17							17

6-10A **LO 5.**

On December 31, 2008, Reuter Company has a balance of $98.75 in the FUTA taxes payable account. This represents the employer's liability for the fourth quarter taxes.

Journalize the entry Reuter Company should make in January 2009 to record the last transfer (payment) of FUTA taxes for 2008.

JOURNAL

	DATE		DESCRIPTION	POST. REF.	DEBIT	CREDIT	
1							1
2							2
3							3
4							4
5							5
6							6

6-11A **LO 6.**

On December 31, 20—, Karmansky Company needed to record its accrued wages for year-end. December 31 is a Tuesday, and Karmansky Company must account for two days of wages.

The company operates on a five-day workweek, the prior week's gross pay (December 26 payday) was $32,650, and the net pay was $21,330.

Journalize the adjusting entry to be made on December 31 for the accrued wages.

JOURNAL

	DATE		DESCRIPTION	POST. REF.	DEBIT	CREDIT	
1							1
2							2
3							3
4							4
5							5
6							6

6-12A LO 3.

Kelsey Gunn is the only employee of Arsenault Company. His pay rate is $23.00 per hour with an overtime rate of $1\frac{1}{2}$ times for hours over 40 in a workweek.

For the week ending March 31, 20—, he worked 48 hours. Calculate his gross pay for the week using the overtime premium approach to calculate the overtime pay.

Since the company holds back one week of pay, Gunn will not be paid until April 7, 20—. What adjusting entry would the company make in order to record Gunn's salary in the first quarter of this year?

a. Regular pay ________

b. Overtime premium pay ________

c. Gross pay ________

d. Adjusting entry ________

JOURNAL

	DATE		DESCRIPTION	POST. REF.	DEBIT	CREDIT	
1							1
2							2
3							3

6-13A LO 3.

In Oregon, employers who are covered by the state workers' compensation law withhold employee contributions from the wages of covered employees at the rate of 1.4¢ for each hour or part of an hour that the worker is employed. Every covered employer is also assessed 1.4¢ per hour for each worker employed for each hour or part of an hour. The employer-employee contributions for workers' compensation are collected monthly, quarterly, or annually by the employer's insurance carrier, according to a schedule agreed upon by the employer and the carrier. The insurance carrier remits the contributions to the state's Workers' Compensation Department.

Brunansky Company, a covered employer in Oregon, turns over the employer-employee workers' compensation contributions to its insurance carrier by the 15th of each month for the preceding month. During the month of July, the number of full-time employee-hours worked by the company's employees was 24,190; the number of part-time employee-hours was 2,440.

a. The amount the company should have withheld from its full- and part-time employees during the month of July for workers' compensation insurance is . . . . $____________

b. The title you would give to the general ledger account to which the amount withheld from the employees' earnings would be credited is:

____

c. Journalize the entry on July 31 to record the employer's liability for workers' compensation insurance for the month.

JOURNAL

	DATE		DESCRIPTION	POST. REF.	DEBIT	CREDIT	
1							1
2							2
3							3
4							4
5							5

6-13A (concluded)

d. Journalize the entry on August 15 to record payment to the insurance carrier of the amount withheld from the employees' earnings for workers' compensation insurance and the amount of the employer's liability.

JOURNAL

	DATE	DESCRIPTION	POST. REF.	DEBIT	CREDIT	
1						1
2						2
3						3
4						4
5						5

6-14A LO 6.

At the end of April, Hernandez Company had a balance of $37,910 in the vacation benefits payable account. During May, employees earned an additional $2,790 in vacation benefits, but some employees used vacation days that amounted to $2,050 of the vacation benefits. The $2,050 was charged to Wage Expense when it was paid in May. What adjusting entry would Hernandez Company make at the end of May to bring the vacation benefits payable account up to date?

JOURNAL

	DATE	DESCRIPTION	POST. REF.	DEBIT	CREDIT	
1						1
2						2
3						3

6-15A LO 2.

The form on page 6-47 shows the amounts that appear in the Earnings to Date column of the employees' earnings records for 10 workers in Unger Company. These amounts represent the cumulative earnings for each worker as of October 18, the company's last payday. The form also gives the gross amount of earnings to be paid each worker on the next payday, October 25.

In the state where Unger Company is located, the tax rates and bases are as follows:

Tax on Employees:	
FICA—OASDI	6.2% on first $102,300
FICA—HI	1.45% on ***total earnings***
SUTA	0.5% on first $8,000
Tax on Employer:	
FICA—OASDI	6.2% on first $102,300
FICA—HI	1.45% on ***total earnings***
FUTA	0.8% on first $7,000
SUTA	1.8% on first $8,000

In the appropriate columns of the form on page 6-47, do the following:

1. Compute the amount to be withheld from each employee's earnings on October 25 for (a) FICA—OASDI, (b) FICA—HI, and (c) SUTA, and determine the total employee taxes.

2. Record the portion of each employee's earnings that is taxable under FICA, FUTA, and SUTA, and calculate the total employer's payroll taxes on the October 25 payroll.

DATE ____________ NAME ____________

6-15A (concluded)

UNGER COMPANY

	Employee	Earnings to Date	Gross Earnings, Oct. 25	Taxes to Be Withheld from Employees' Earnings Under			Employer Taxes: Portion of Employees' Earnings Taxable Under			
				FICA		SUTA	FICA		FUTA	SUTA
				OASDI	HI		OASDI	HI		
1.	Weiser, Robert A.	$102,790	$790							
2.	Stankard, Laurie C.	14,950	295							
3.	Grow, Joan L.	4,060	240							
4.	Rowe, Paul C.	8,190	235							
5.	McNamara, Joyce M.	7,460	195							
6.	O'Connor, Roger T.	102,410	810							
7.	Carson, Ronald B.	8,905	280							
8.	Kenny, Ginni C.	4,325	175							
9.	Devery, Virginia S.	57,010	590							
10.	Wilson, Joe W.	3,615	205							
	Total employee taxes			$	$	$				
				1.(a)	1.(b)	1.(c)				
	Total taxable earnings						$	$	$	$
	× Applicable tax rate									
	Totals						$	$	$	$
	Total payroll taxes								$	
									2.	

6-16A LO 3,4,5,6,7.

In the Illustrative Case in this chapter, payroll transactions for Brookins Company were analyzed, journalized, and posted for the third quarter of the fiscal year. In this problem, you are to record the payroll transactions for the last quarter of the firm's fiscal year. The last quarter begins on April 1.

Refer to the Illustrative Case on pages 6-25 to 6-33 and proceed as follows:

a. Analyze and journalize the transactions described in the following narrative. Use the two-column journal paper provided on pages 6-50 to 6-53. Omit the writing of explanations in the journal entries.

b. Post the journal entries to the general ledger accounts on pages 6-54 to 6-59.

Narrative of Transactions:

Apr.	1.	Paid the treasurer of the union the amount of union dues withheld from workers' earnings during March.
	15.	Payroll: $6,105. All wages and salaries taxable. Withheld $565 for federal income taxes, $107.32 for state income taxes, and $50 for union dues.
	15.	Paid the treasurer of the state the amount of state income taxes withheld from workers' earnings during the first quarter.
	15.	Electronically transferred funds to remove the liability for FICA taxes and employees' federal income taxes withheld on the March payrolls.
	29.	Payroll: $5,850. All wages and salaries taxable. Withheld $509 for federal income taxes, $128.90 for state income taxes, and $55 for union dues.
	29.	Filed the Employer's Quarterly Federal Tax Return (Form 941) for the period ended March 31. No journal entry is required, since the FICA taxes and federal income taxes withheld have been timely paid.
	29.	Filed the state contribution return for the quarter ended March 31 and paid the amount to the state unemployment compensation fund.
May	2.	Paid the treasurer of the union the amount of union dues withheld from workers' earnings during April.
	13.	Payroll: $5,810. All wages and salaries taxable. Withheld $507 for federal income taxes, $125.05 for state income taxes, and $55 for union dues.
	16.	Electronically transferred funds to remove the liability for FICA taxes and federal income taxes withheld on the April payrolls.
	31.	Payroll: $6,060. All wages and salaries taxable. Withheld $533 for federal income taxes, $119.00 for state income taxes, and $50 for union dues.
June	3.	Paid the treasurer of the union the amount of union dues withheld from workers' earnings during May.
	15.	Payroll: $6,380. All wages and salaries taxable, except only $5,000 is taxable under FUTA and SUTA. Withheld $549 for federal income taxes, $128.70 for state income taxes, and $50 for union dues.
	15.	Electronically transferred funds to remove the liability for FICA taxes and federal income taxes withheld on the May payrolls.
	30.	Payroll: $6,250. All wages and salaries taxable, except only $4,770 is taxable under FUTA and SUTA. Withheld $538 for federal income taxes, $127.60 for state income taxes, and $50 for union dues.

6-16A (continued)

c. Answer the following questions:

1. The total amount of the liability for FICA taxes and federal income taxes withheld as of June 30 is . . . . . . $ ________
2. The total amount of the liability for state income taxes withheld as of June 30 is . . . . . . $ ________
3. The amount of FUTA taxes that must be paid to the federal government on or before August 1 (July 31 is a Sunday) is . . . . . . $ ________
4. The amount of contributions that must be paid into the state unemployment compensation fund on or before August 1 is . . . . . . $ ________
5. The total amount due the treasurer of the union is . . . . . . $ ________
6. The total amount of wages and salaries expense since the beginning of the fiscal year is . . . . . . $ ________
7. The total amount of payroll taxes expense since the beginning of the fiscal year is . . . . . . $ ________
8. Using the partial journal below, journalize the entry to record the vacation accrual at the end of the company's fiscal year. The amount of Brookins Company's vacation accrual for the fiscal year is $15,000.

JOURNAL

	DATE	DESCRIPTION	POST. REF.	DEBIT	CREDIT	
1						1
2						2
3						3
4						4
5						5
6						6

6-16A (continued)

JOURNAL

DATE		DESCRIPTION	POST. REF.	DEBIT	CREDIT

6-16A (continued)

JOURNAL

	DATE		DESCRIPTION	POST. REF.	DEBIT	CREDIT	
1							1
2							2
3							3
4							4
5							5
6							6
7							7
8							8
9							9
10							10
11							11
12							12
13							13
14							14
15							15
16							16
17							17
18							18
19							19
20							20
21							21
22							22
23							23
24							24
25							25
26							26
27							27
28							28
29							29
30							30
31							31
32							32
33							33
34							34

6-16A (continued)

JOURNAL

DATE		DESCRIPTION	POST. REF.	DEBIT	CREDIT

DATE ____________________ NAME ____

6-16A (continued)

JOURNAL

	DATE		DESCRIPTION	POST. REF.	DEBIT	CREDIT	
1							1
2							2
3							3
4							4
5							5
6							6
7							7
8							8
9							9
10							10
11							11
12							12
13							13
14							14
15							15
16							16
17							17
18							18
19							19
20							20
21							21
22							22
23							23
24							24
25							25
26							26
27							27
28							28
29							29
30							30
31							31
32							32
33							33
34							34

6-16A (continued)

ACCOUNT **CASH** ACCOUNT NO. 11

DATE		ITEM	POST. REF.	DEBIT	CREDIT	BALANCE DEBIT	BALANCE CREDIT
20— Apr.	1	*Balance*	✓			58,233.04	

6-16A (continued)

ACCOUNT **FICA TAXES PAYABLE—OASDI** ACCOUNT NO. 20

DATE		ITEM	POST. REF.	DEBIT	CREDIT	BALANCE DEBIT	BALANCE CREDIT
20— Apr.	1	Balance	✓				1,068.88

6-16A (continued)

ACCOUNT **FICA TAXES PAYABLE—HI** ACCOUNT NO. 21

DATE		ITEM	POST. REF.	DEBIT	CREDIT	BALANCE DEBIT	BALANCE CREDIT
20— Apr.	1	Balance	✓				249 98

6-16A (continued)

ACCOUNT **FUTA TAXES PAYABLE** ACCOUNT NO. 22

DATE		ITEM	POST. REF.	DEBIT	CREDIT	BALANCE DEBIT	BALANCE CREDIT
20— Apr.	1	Balance	✓				198.88

ACCOUNT **SUTA TAXES PAYABLE** ACCOUNT NO. 23

DATE		ITEM	POST. REF.	DEBIT	CREDIT	BALANCE DEBIT	BALANCE CREDIT
20— Apr.	1	Balance	✓				571.78

6-16A (continued)

ACCOUNT **EMPLOYEES FIT PAYABLE** ACCOUNT NO. 25

DATE		ITEM	POST. REF.	DEBIT	CREDIT	BALANCE DEBIT	BALANCE CREDIT
20— Apr.	1	*Balance*	✓				1 1 2 4 00

ACCOUNT **EMPLOYEES SIT PAYABLE** ACCOUNT NO. 26

DATE		ITEM	POST. REF.	DEBIT	CREDIT	BALANCE DEBIT	BALANCE CREDIT
20— Apr.	1	*Balance*	✓				5 4 6 92

6-16A (concluded)

ACCOUNT **UNION DUES PAYABLE** ACCOUNT NO. 28

DATE		ITEM	POST. REF.	DEBIT	CREDIT	BALANCE DEBIT	BALANCE CREDIT
20— Apr.	1	*Balance*	✓				1 0 0 00

ACCOUNT **WAGES AND SALARIES** ACCOUNT NO. 51

DATE		ITEM	POST. REF.	DEBIT	CREDIT	BALANCE DEBIT	BALANCE CREDIT
20— Apr.	1	*Balance*	✓			7 1 3 6 0 00	

ACCOUNT **PAYROLL TAXES** ACCOUNT NO. 55

DATE		ITEM	POST. REF.	DEBIT	CREDIT	BALANCE DEBIT	BALANCE CREDIT
20— Apr.	1	*Balance*	✓			6 9 2 6 96	

DATE ______________ NAME ______________________________

PRACTICAL PROBLEMS—SERIES B

Omit the writing of explanations for the journal entries.

6-1B LO 2.

Karen Most has a federal tax levy of $2,100.50 against her. If Karen is single with two personal exemptions and had a take-home pay of $499.00 this week, how much would her employer take from her pay to satisfy part of the tax levy?

6-2B LO 3.

Garrett Hudson earned $895 this week. The deductions from his pay were as follows:

FIT	$95.00
FICA—OASDI	55.49
FICA—HI	12.98
State income tax	27.75
State disability insurance	6.71
Health insurance premium	31.00
Credit union contribution	$ 50.00
United fund contribution	10.00

Hudson's employer just received a garnishment order (credit card debt of $2,140) against his pay. Compute the following:

a. Hudson's disposable earnings . . . . $__________

b. The amount of his pay subject to the garnishment . . . . $__________

6-3B LO 3,5.

a. Harriet Pandel, an employer, is subject to FICA taxes but exempt from FUTA and SUTA taxes. During the last quarter of the year, his employees earned monthly wages of $16,900, all of which is taxable. The amount of federal income taxes withheld each month is $1,698. Journalize the payment of wages, and record the payroll tax on November 30.

JOURNAL

	DATE	DESCRIPTION	POST. REF.	DEBIT	CREDIT	
1						1
2						2
3						3
4						4
5						5
6						6
7						7
8						8
9						9
10						10

6-3B (concluded)

b. Prior to posting the November 30 payroll transaction, FICA Taxes Payable—OASDI, FICA Taxes Payable—HI, and Employees FIT Payable had zero balances. Pandel must pay the FICA taxes and income taxes withheld on the November 30 payroll. Journalize the electronic transfer of the payroll taxes on December 15.

JOURNAL

	DATE	DESCRIPTION	POST. REF.	DEBIT	CREDIT	
1						1
2						2
3						3
4						4
5						5
6						6

6-4B LO 3.

The employees of Carson Bakery Company earn total wages of $7,780 during January. The total amount is taxable under FICA, FUTA, and SUTA. The state contribution rate for the company is 4.3%. The amount withheld for federal income taxes is $998. Journalize the payment of the monthly wages, and record the payroll taxes.

JOURNAL

	DATE	DESCRIPTION	POST. REF.	DEBIT	CREDIT	
1						1
2						2
3						3
4						4
5						5
6						6
7						7
8						8
9						9
10						10
11						11
12						12
13						13
14						14

DATE ____________ NAME ____________

6-5B LO 3.

Purnell, Inc., has a semimonthly payroll of $53,900 on September 15. The total payroll is taxable under FICA Taxes—HI; $50,400 is taxable under FICA Taxes—OASDI; and $7,300 is taxable under FUTA and SUTA. The state contribution rate for the company is 3.1%. The amount withheld for federal income taxes is $6,995. The amount withheld for state income taxes is $1,010.

a. Journalize the payment of the wages, and record the payroll taxes on September 15.

b. Assume that the employees of Purnell, Inc., must also pay state contributions (disability insurance) of 1% on the taxable payroll of $24,100 and that the employees' contributions are to be deducted by the employer. Journalize the September 15 payment of wages, assuming that the state contributions of the employees are kept in a separate account.

JOURNAL

	DATE		DESCRIPTION	POST. REF.	DEBIT	CREDIT	
1							1
2							2
3							3
4							4
5							5
6							6
7							7
8							8
9							9
10							10
11							11
12							12
13							13
14							14
15							15
16							16
17							17
18							18
19							19
20							20
21							21
22							22
23							23
24							24
25							25
26							26
27							27

6-6B LO 3.

Adams, Inc., pays its employees' weekly wages in cash. A supplementary payroll sheet that lists the employees' names and their earnings for a certain week is shown below. Complete the payroll sheet by calculating the total amount of payroll and indicating the least possible number of denominations that can be used in paying each employee. However, no employees are to be given bills in denominations greater than $20.

ADAMS, INC.

For Period Ending August 15, 20—

Supplementary Payroll Sheet

		Bills				Coins				
Name of Employee	Net Amount Paid	$20	$10	$5	$1	50¢	25¢	10¢	5¢	1¢
Ben Dowd	$639.57									
Erin Martin	248.95									
Dot Ruiz	491.95									
Randi Heavner	832.14									
Rex Sundry	710.15									
Hal Roach	709.13									
Mandy Arnold	519.13									
Faye Montgomery	227.24									
Max Held	473.18									
Pedro Rodries	590.90									
Total										

6-7B **LO 3.**

Carmen Santos is owner and sole employee of CS Corporation. He pays himself a salary of $2,400 this week.

Additional tax information includes:

FICA tax—OASDI	6.2% on first $102,300
FICA tax—HI	1.45% on total pay
Federal income tax	$532.00 per pay
State income tax	22% of the federal income tax withholding
Federal unemployment tax	0.8% on first $7,000
State unemployment tax	0.05% on first $14,000

Additional payroll deductions include:

401(k) plan	3% per pay
Child support garnishment	$125 per pay
Health insurance premium	$110 per pay

Record the payroll entry and payroll tax entry for the pay of the week ended June 4 (his year-to-date pay is $51,500).

JOURNAL

	DATE	DESCRIPTION	POST. REF.	DEBIT	CREDIT	
1						1
2						2
3						3
4						4
5						5
6						6
7						7
8						8
9						9
10						10
11						11
12						12
13						13
14						14
15						15
16						16
17						17
18						18
19						19
20						20

6-8B **LO 3.**

The employees of Portonegra Company earn wages of $15,600 for the two weeks ending April 20. FIT taxes of $424 were withheld. The entire amount of wages is subject to the FICA taxes, but only $10,800 is taxable under the federal and state unemployment compensation laws. The state contribution rate of the employer is 3.9%. All employees are subject to state unemployment contributions of 0.5% on the April 20 taxable wages of $10,800, and the employees' contributions are to be deducted by the employer. Journalize the payment of the wages, and record the payroll taxes, assuming that the contributions of the employer and the employees are recorded in one account, SUTA Taxes Payable.

JOURNAL

	DATE	DESCRIPTION	POST. REF.	DEBIT	CREDIT	
1						1
2						2
3						3
4						4
5						5
6						6
7						7
8						8
9						9
10						10
11						11
12						12
13						13
14						14
15						15

6-9B LO 3.

The following information pertains to the payroll of Fanelli Fashion Company on June 6:

a. The total wages earned by employees are $2,910.

b. The state unemployment insurance contribution rate is 3.75%.

c. The entire amount of wages is taxable under FICA, FUTA, and SUTA.

d. The amount withheld from the employees' wages for federal income taxes is $491; for state income taxes, $49.10; and for group insurance, $87.10.

e. The amount of the advance earned income credit payments made to the employees is $195.

Journalize the payment of wages, and record the payroll taxes on June 6.

JOURNAL

	DATE		DESCRIPTION	POST. REF.	DEBIT	CREDIT	
1							1
2							2
3							3
4							4
5							5
6							6
7							7
8							8
9							9
10							10
11							11
12							12
13							13
14							14
15							15
16							16
17							17

6-10B **LO 5.**

On December 31, 2008, Santucci Company has a balance of $619.24 in the FUTA taxes payable account. This represents the employer's liability for the fourth quarter taxes. Journalize the entry Santucci Company should make in January 2009 to record the last transfer (payment) of FUTA taxes for 2008.

JOURNAL

	DATE		DESCRIPTION	POST. REF.	DEBIT	CREDIT	
1							1
2							2
3							3
4							4
5							5
6							6

6-11B **LO 6.**

On December 31, 20—, Sanchez Company needed to record its accrued wages for year-end. December 31 is a Wednesday, and Sanchez Company must account for three days of wages.

The company operates on a five-day workweek, the prior week's gross pay (December 26 payday) was $29,870, and the net pay was $19,995.

Journalize the adjusting entry to be made on December 31 for the accrued wages.

JOURNAL

	DATE		DESCRIPTION	POST. REF.	DEBIT	CREDIT	
1							1
2							2
3							3
4							4
5							5
6							6

6-12B LO 3.

John Torre is the only employee of Bambert Company. His pay rate is $19.70 per hour with an overtime rate of $1\frac{1}{2}$ times for hours over 40 in a workweek.

For the week ending March 31, 20—, he worked 44 hours. Calculate his gross pay for the week using the overtime premium approach to calculate the overtime pay.

Since the company holds back one week of pay, Torre will not be paid until April 7, 20—. What adjusting entry would the company make in order to record Torre's salary in the first quarter of this year?

a. Regular pay ________

b. Overtime premium pay ________

c. Gross pay ________

d. Adjusting entry ________

JOURNAL

	DATE		DESCRIPTION	POST. REF.	DEBIT	CREDIT	
1							1
2							2
3							3

6-13B LO 3.

In Oregon, employers who are covered by the state workers' compensation law withhold employee contributions from the wages of covered employees at the rate of 1.4¢ for each hour or part of an hour that the worker is employed. Every covered employer is also assessed 1.4¢ per hour for each worker employed for each hour or part of an hour. The employer-employee contributions for workers' compensation are collected monthly, quarterly, or annually by the employer's insurance carrier, according to a schedule agreed upon by the employer and the carrier. The insurance carrier remits the contributions to the state's Workers' Compensation Department.

Umber Company, a covered employer in Oregon, turns over the employer-employee workers' compensation contributions to its insurance carrier by the 15th of each month for the preceding month. During the month of July, the number of full-time employee-hours worked by the company's employees was 26,110; the number of part-time employee-hours was 3,490.

a. The amount the company should have withheld from its full- and part-time employees during the month of July for workers' compensation insurance is . . . . $________

b. The title you would give to the general ledger account to which the amount withheld from the employees' earnings would be credited is:

____

c. Journalize the entry on July 31 to record the employer's liability for workers' compensation insurance for the month.

JOURNAL

	DATE		DESCRIPTION	POST. REF.	DEBIT	CREDIT	
1							1
2							2
3							3
4							4
5							5

6-13B (concluded)

d. Journalize the entry on August 15 to record payment to the insurance carrier of the amount withheld from the employees' earnings for workers' compensation insurance and the amount of the employer's liability.

JOURNAL

	DATE		DESCRIPTION	POST. REF.	DEBIT	CREDIT	
1							1
2							2
3							3
4							4
5							5

6-14B LO 6.

At the end of June, Morton Company had a balance of $49,900 in the vacation benefits payable account. During July, employees earned an additional $3,110 in vacation benefits, but some employees used vacation days that amounted to $2,490 of the vacation benefits. The $2,490 was charged to Wage Expense when it was paid in July. What adjusting entry would Morton Company make at the end of July to bring the vacation benefits payable account up to date?

JOURNAL

	DATE		DESCRIPTION	POST. REF.	DEBIT	CREDIT	
1							1
2							2
3							3

6-15B LO 2.

The form on page 6-71 shows the amounts that appear in the Earnings to Date column of the employees' earnings records for 10 workers in Ranger Company. These amounts represent the cumulative earnings for each worker as of November 7, the company's last payday. The form also gives the gross amount of earnings to be paid each worker on the next payday, November 14.

In the state where Ranger Company is located, the tax rates and bases are as follows:

Tax on Employees:

FICA—OASDI	6.2% on first $102,300
FICA—HI	1.45% on ***total earnings***
SUTA	0.5% on first $8,000

Tax on Employer:

FICA—OASDI	6.2% on first $102,300
FICA—HI	1.45% on ***total earnings***
FUTA	0.8% on first $7,000
SUTA	2.8% on first $8,000

In the appropriate columns of the form on page 6-71, do the following:

1. Compute the amount to be withheld from each employee's earnings on November 14 for (a) FICA—OASDI, (b) FICA—HI, and (c) SUTA, and determine the total employee taxes.

2. Record the portion of each employee's earnings that is taxable under FICA, FUTA, and SUTA, and calculate the total employer's payroll taxes on the November 14 payroll.

DATE ______ NAME ______

6-15B (concluded)

RANGER COMPANY

	Employee	Earnings to Date	Gross Earnings, Nov. 14	Taxes to Be Withheld from Employees' Earnings Under: FICA OASDI	FICA HI	SUTA	Employer Taxes: Portion of Employees' Earnings Taxable Under: FICA OASDI	FICA HI	FUTA	SUTA
1.	Watson, Ruth T.	$102,790	$1,890							
2.	Kinder, Ralph A.	14,950	410							
3.	Sanchez, Robert T.	4,060	395							
4.	Carey, Mary C.	8,190	295							
5.	Cox, Mason M.	6,460	425							
6.	Kenni, Jack T.	102,410	1,850							
7.	Britmayer, Tim A.	8,905	490							
8.	Candi, Mark B.	6,825	325							
9.	Boxer, Barbara C.	57,010	1,150							
10.	McBride, James W.	3,615	195							
	Total employee taxes			$	$	$				
				1.(a)	1.(b)	1.(c)				
	Total taxable earnings						$	$	$	$
	× Applicable tax rate									
	Totals						$	$	$	$

Total payroll taxes .... $______

2.

6-16B LO 3,4,5,6,7.

In the Illustrative Case in this chapter, payroll transactions for Brookins Company were analyzed, journalized, and posted for the third quarter of the fiscal year. In this problem, you are to record the payroll transactions for the last quarter of the firm's fiscal year. The last quarter begins on April 1.

Refer to the Illustrative Case on pages 6-25 to 6-33 and proceed as follows:

a. Analyze and journalize the transactions described in the following narrative. Use the two-column journal paper provided on pages 6-74 to 6-77. Omit the writing of explanations in the journal entries.

b. Post the journal entries to the general ledger accounts on pages 6-78 to 6-83.

Narrative of Transactions:

Apr. 1. Paid the treasurer of the union the amount of union dues withheld from workers' earnings during March.

15. Payroll: $8,310. All wages and salaries taxable. Withheld $890 for federal income taxes, $166.20 for state income taxes, and $140 for union dues.

15. Paid the treasurer of the state the amount of state income taxes withheld from workers' earnings during the first quarter.

15. Electronically transferred funds to remove the liability for FICA taxes and employees' federal income taxes withheld on the March payrolls.

29. Payroll: $7,975. All wages and salaries taxable. Withheld $815 for federal income taxes, $151.50 for state income taxes, and $135 for union dues.

29. Filed the Employer's Quarterly Federal Tax Return (Form 941) for the period ended March 31. No journal entry is required, since the FICA taxes and federal income taxes withheld have been timely paid.

29. Filed the state contribution return for the quarter ended March 31 and paid the amount to the state unemployment compensation fund.

May 2. Paid the treasurer of the union the amount of union dues withheld from workers' earnings during April.

13. Payroll: $8,190. All wages and salaries taxable. Withheld $875 for federal income taxes, $160.05 for state income taxes, and $135 for union dues.

16. Electronically transferred funds to remove the liability for FICA taxes and federal income taxes withheld on the April payrolls.

31. Payroll: $8,755. All wages and salaries taxable. Withheld $971 for federal income taxes, $174.05 for state income taxes, and $140 for union dues.

June 3. Paid the treasurer of the union the amount of union dues withheld from workers' earnings during May.

15. Payroll: $9,110. All wages and salaries taxable, except only $4,210 is taxable under FUTA and SUTA. Withheld $1,029 for federal income taxes, $187.15 for state income taxes, and $145 for union dues.

15. Electronically transferred funds to remove the liability for FICA taxes and federal income taxes withheld on the May payrolls.

30. Payroll: $8,960. All wages and salaries taxable, except only $2,280 is taxable under FUTA and SUTA. Withheld $988 for federal income taxes, $183.95 for state income taxes, and $145 for union dues.

6-16B (continued)

c. Answer the following questions:

1. The total amount of the liability for FICA taxes and federal income taxes withheld as of June 30 is . . . . $ ____________
2. The total amount of the liability for state income taxes withheld as of June 30 is . . . . $ ____________
3. The amount of FUTA taxes that must be paid to the federal government on or before August 1 (assume July 31 is a Sunday) is . . . . $ ____________
4. The amount of contributions that must be paid into the state unemployment compensation fund on or before August 1 is . . . . $ ____________
5. The total amount due the treasurer of the union is . . . . $ ____________
6. The total amount of wages and salaries expense since the beginning of the fiscal year is . . . . $ ____________
7. The total amount of payroll taxes expense since the beginning of the fiscal year is . . . . $ ____________
8. Using the partial journal below, journalize the entry to record the vacation accrual at the end of the company's fiscal year. The amount of Brookins Company's vacation accrual for the fiscal year is $15,000.

JOURNAL

	DATE	DESCRIPTION	POST. REF.	DEBIT	CREDIT	
1						1
2						2
3						3
4						4
5						5
6						6

6-16B (continued)

JOURNAL

	DATE		DESCRIPTION	POST. REF.	DEBIT	CREDIT	
1							1
2							2
3							3
4							4
5							5
6							6
7							7
8							8
9							9
10							10
11							11
12							12
13							13
14							14
15							15
16							16
17							17
18							18
19							19
20							20
21							21
22							22
23							23
24							24
25							25
26							26
27							27
28							28
29							29
30							30
31							31
32							32
33							33
34							34

6-16B (continued)

JOURNAL

	DATE	DESCRIPTION	POST. REF.	DEBIT	CREDIT	
1						1
2						2
3						3
4						4
5						5
6						6
7						7
8						8
9						9
10						10
11						11
12						12
13						13
14						14
15						15
16						16
17						17
18						18
19						19
20						20
21						21
22						22
23						23
24						24
25						25
26						26
27						27
28						28
29						29
30						30
31						31
32						32
33						33
34						34

6-16B (continued)

JOURNAL

DATE		DESCRIPTION	POST. REF.	DEBIT	CREDIT

6-16B (continued)

JOURNAL

	DATE		DESCRIPTION	POST. REF.	DEBIT	CREDIT	
1							1
2							2
3							3
4							4
5							5
6							6
7							7
8							8
9							9
10							10
11							11
12							12
13							13
14							14
15							15
16							16
17							17
18							18
19							19
20							20
21							21
22							22
23							23
24							24
25							25
26							26
27							27
28							28
29							29
30							30
31							31
32							32
33							33
34							34

6-16B (continued)

ACCOUNT **CASH** ACCOUNT NO. 11

DATE		ITEM	POST. REF.	DEBIT	CREDIT	BALANCE DEBIT	BALANCE CREDIT
20— Apr.	1	*Balance*	✓			58,233.04	

6-16B (continued)

ACCOUNT **FICA TAXES PAYABLE—OASDI** ACCOUNT NO. 20

DATE		ITEM	POST. REF.	DEBIT	CREDIT	BALANCE DEBIT	BALANCE CREDIT
20— *Apr.*	*1*	*Balance*	✓				*1 0 6 8 88*

6-16B (continued)

ACCOUNT **FICA TAXES PAYABLE—HI** ACCOUNT NO. 21

DATE		ITEM	POST. REF.	DEBIT	CREDIT	BALANCE DEBIT	BALANCE CREDIT
20— Apr.	*1*	*Balance*	✓				*249 98*

6-16B (continued)

ACCOUNT **FUTA TAXES PAYABLE** ACCOUNT NO. 22

DATE		ITEM	POST. REF.	DEBIT	CREDIT	BALANCE DEBIT	BALANCE CREDIT
20— Apr.	1	*Balance*	✓				1 9 8 88

ACCOUNT **SUTA TAXES PAYABLE** ACCOUNT NO. 23

DATE		ITEM	POST. REF.	DEBIT	CREDIT	BALANCE DEBIT	BALANCE CREDIT
20— Apr.	1	*Balance*	✓				5 7 1 78

6-16B (continued)

ACCOUNT **EMPLOYEES FIT PAYABLE** ACCOUNT NO. 25

DATE		ITEM	POST. REF.	DEBIT	CREDIT	BALANCE DEBIT	BALANCE CREDIT
20— Apr.	1	Balance	✓				1,124.00

ACCOUNT **EMPLOYEES SIT PAYABLE** ACCOUNT NO. 26

DATE		ITEM	POST. REF.	DEBIT	CREDIT	BALANCE DEBIT	BALANCE CREDIT
20— Apr.	1	Balance	✓				546.92

6-16B (concluded)

ACCOUNT **UNION DUES PAYABLE** ACCOUNT NO. 28

DATE		ITEM	POST. REF.	DEBIT	CREDIT	BALANCE DEBIT	BALANCE CREDIT
20— Apr.	1	*Balance*	✓				100.00

ACCOUNT **WAGES AND SALARIES** ACCOUNT NO. 51

DATE		ITEM	POST. REF.	DEBIT	CREDIT	BALANCE DEBIT	BALANCE CREDIT
20— Apr.	1	*Balance*	✓			71,360.00	

ACCOUNT **PAYROLL TAXES** ACCOUNT NO. 55

DATE		ITEM	POST. REF.	DEBIT	CREDIT	BALANCE DEBIT	BALANCE CREDIT
20— Apr.	1	*Balance*	✓			6,926.96	

CONTINUING PAYROLL PROBLEM

In this last phase of your work on the Continuing Payroll Problem, you will record the amounts withheld for group and health insurance and calculate the net pay for each employee. Refer to the partially completed payroll register upon which you were working at the end of Chapter 5, and proceed as follows:

1. In the appropriate column of the payroll register, record the amount to be withheld for group life insurance. Each employee contributes 85¢ each week toward the cost of group insurance coverage, with the exception of Smith and Schork, who are not yet eligible for coverage under the company plan.
2. Record the amount to be withheld for health insurance. Each employee contributes $1.65 each week toward the cost of health insurance.
3. Record the net pay for each employee. The net pay for each employee is obtained by subtracting the total amount of all deductions from the total earnings.
4. Each worker is to be paid by check. Assign check numbers commencing with No. 313.
5. Foot all money columns of the payroll register, and prove the accuracy of the column totals.
6. On a separate sheet of paper:
   a. Prepare the journal entries as of January 12 to record the payroll and the payroll taxes for the week ending January 8. Credit Salaries Payable for the total net pay.

      Use the following tax rates and bases: employer's FICA—OASDI, 6.2% on the first $102,300; employer's FICA—HI, 1.45% on total earnings; FUTA, 0.8% on the first $7,000; and SUTA, 3.5% on the first $8,000.
   b. Prepare the journal entry to record the payment of the payroll on January 14 when the paychecks are distributed to all workers.

Your work on the Continuing Payroll Problem is now completed, and you may be asked to submit your payroll register to your instructor. The experience you have gained in working on each of the succeeding phases of the Continuing Payroll Problem will aid you in undertaking the payroll work involved in Chapter 7. In the Comprehensive Payroll Project, you will be responsible for all aspects of payroll operations for a company for an entire calendar quarter.

CASE PROBLEM

C1. Budgeting for Additional Payroll Costs.

Frank Flynn is the payroll manager for Powlus Supply Company. During the budgeting process, Sam Kinder, Director of Finance, asked Flynn to arrive at a set percentage that could be applied to each budgeted salary figure to cover the additional cost that will be incurred by Powlus Supply for each employee. After some discussion, it was determined that the best way to compute this percentage would be to base these additional costs of payroll on the average salary paid by the company.

Kinder wants this additional payroll cost percentage to cover payroll taxes (FICA, FUTA, and SUTA) and other payroll costs covered by the company (workers' compensation expense, health insurance costs, and vacation pay).

Flynn gathers the following information in order to complete the analysis:

Average annual salary.	$24,000
FICA rates	6.2% and 1.45%
FUTA.	0.8% on 1st $7,000
SUTA.	3.3% on 1st $10,400
Workers' compensation costs	$0.97 per $100 of payroll
Health insurance costs.	$75.15 per month
Vacation pay earned	2 weeks' pay earned each year to be used in following year.

Compute the percentage that can be used in the budget.

chapter 7

Payroll Project

LEARNING OBJECTIVES

Chapter 7 consists of a simulation, or practice set, for payroll accounting. You will apply the knowledge acquired in this course to practical payroll situations. This simulation is a culmination of the information presented in the textbook.

After completing the project, you should be able to:

1. Prepare payroll registers.
2. Maintain employees' earnings records.
3. Journalize and post payroll and payroll tax entries.
4. Complete federal, state, and city tax deposit forms and journalize the transactions.
5. Prepare various quarter-end and year-end payroll tax forms.
6. Make the accrual entries for the payroll at the end of a year.

What now? Can we process a payroll? How about the accounting entries and postings? Can we complete the deposit forms and the "dreaded" payroll tax returns? What have we learned in the previous six chapters? Did I waste this semester?

Let's find out. Here's your real-world test.

The Payroll Project will provide you with extended practice in keeping payroll records and accounting for payroll transactions. Your completion of this project involves an application of the information learned in the preceding chapters. The work provided resembles that prevailing in the office of every employer in the United States subject to the provisions of the Federal Wage and Hour Law, income tax withholding laws, social security laws, and unemployment compensation laws. Even though most payroll systems now employ computers, it is important that the practitioner understand the operations performed by the computer.

If your assignment involves the use of Appendix A (computerized option) to complete this project, it is suggested that you do at least one of the payrolls manually so that you gain a thorough understanding of the steps needed to be completed on a typical payday.

In this project, you are employed by Glo-Brite Paint Company. As the payroll clerk in the Accounting Department, you have been in charge of the payroll records since the company first began operations on January 5 of the current year. The company employs about 800 individuals; but for the purpose of this project, payroll records will be kept for only a dozen or so employees. By understanding the principles of payroll accounting for a few employees, you should be able to keep similar records for several hundred employees.

For purposes of this project, you will assume that the payroll records, tax reports, and deposits have been completed and filed for the first three quarters of this year. Your work will involve the processing of the payrolls for the last quarter of the year and the completion of the last quarterly and annual tax reports and forms.

Books of Account and Payroll Records

The books of account and payroll records that you will use in this project are described below.

JOURNAL

You will use a two-column general journal to record all transactions affecting the accounts in the general ledger. This book of original entry serves as a posting medium for transactions affecting the payroll accounts.

GENERAL LEDGER

A general ledger, used in keeping the payroll accounts, is ruled with balance-column ruling, which makes it possible to keep a continuous record of each account balance. Some of the ledger accounts will have beginning balances carried over from the first three quarters of the year.

The chart of accounts in Figure 7–1 has been used in opening the general ledger accounts (pages 7-35 to 7-42). Glo-Brite Paint Company has other accounts in its general ledger, but those listed in the partial chart of accounts are the only accounts required in completing this project.

PAYROLL REGISTER

The payroll register provides the information needed for journalizing each payroll and for posting to the employees' earnings records.

EMPLOYEE'S EARNINGS RECORD

The employee's earnings record provides a summary of each employee's earnings, deductions, and taxable wages. The information recorded in this record is posted from the payroll register.

From the personnel data given in Figure 7–2 (on page 7-6), an employee's earnings record has been maintained for each employee (pages 7-44 to 7-48). The first line of each

FIGURE 7-1

Partial Chart of Accounts

Account Title	Account No.
Cash	11
Payroll Cash	12
FICA Taxes Payable—OASDI	20.1
FICA Taxes Payable—HI	20.2
FUTA Taxes Payable	21
SUTA Taxes Payable—Employer	22
Employees FIT Payable	24
Employees SIT Payable	25
Employees SUTA Payable	25.1
Employees CIT Payable	26
Group Insurance Premiums Collected	27
Union Dues Payable	28
Administrative Salaries	51
Office Salaries	52
Sales Salaries	53
Plant Wages	54
Payroll Taxes	56

of these records shows the employee's cumulative figures for the first three quarters of the year. Note that only one-half page has been used for each employee's earnings record.

General Information

The home office and the manufacturing plant of Glo-Brite Paint Company are located at 2215 Salvador Street, Philadelphia, PA 19175-0682. The company's federal identification number is 31-0450660; the state account number, 146-3-3300; and the city identifying number, 501-6791855.

REGULAR HOURS OF WORK

The workweek for all employees is 40 hours. The office is open from 8:00 A.M. to 5:00 P.M. each day, except weekends. Glo-Brite allows one hour for lunch, 12:00 P.M. to 1:00 P.M. The plant operates on a five-day workweek of eight hours per day, with normal working hours from 7:00 A.M. to 11:00 A.M. and 12:00 P.M. to 4:00 P.M.

OVERTIME

All employees *except* for the exempt administrative employees—the president (*O'Neill*), the sales manager (*Ferguson*), sales representative (*Mann*), and supervisor (*Sokowski*)—are paid ***time and a half*** for any overtime exceeding 40 hours a week. Workers in the plant (*Bonno and Ryan*) are paid ***time and a half*** for any hours worked over eight each workday and for work on Saturdays and ***twice*** the regular hourly rate of pay for work on Sundays or holidays.

FIGURE 7–2

Glo-Brite Employees

Personnel Data—October 1, 20—

BONNO, Anthony Victor, 694 Bristol Avenue, Philadelphia, PA 19135-0617. Married, claiming 4 withholding allowances. Telephone, 555-9827. Social Security No. 537-10-3481. Position, mixer operator in plant. Wages, $17.65 per hour. Group insurance, $55,000.

FERGUSON, James Claude, 808 Sixth Street, Philadelphia, PA 19106-0995. Married, claiming 5 withholding allowances. Telephone, 555-8065. Social Security No. 486-03-8645. Position, sales manager. Salary, $58,500 per year. Group insurance, $88,000. Department: Sales.

FORD, Catherine Louise, 18 Dundee Avenue, Philadelphia, PA 19151-1919. Divorced, claiming 2 withholding allowances. Telephone, 555-0235. Social Security No. 213-09-4567. Position, executive secretary. Salary, $1,950 per month. Group insurance, $35,000. Department: Office.

MANN, Dewey Wilson, 3007 Bisque Drive, Philadelphia, PA 19199-0718. Married, claiming 4 withholding allowances. Telephone, 555-0774. Social Security No. 282-37-9352. Position, sales representative. Salary, $2,925 per month. Group insurance, $53,000. Department: Sales.

O'NEILL, Joseph Tyler, 2100 Broad Street, Philadelphia, PA 19121-7189. Married, claiming 3 withholding allowances. Telephone, 555-2332. Social Security No. 897-04-1534. Position, president. Salary, $60,000 per year. Group insurance, $90,000. Department: Administrative.

RUSSELL, Virginia Aloise, 8004 Dowling Road, Philadelphia, PA 19135-9001. Single, claiming 1 withholding allowance. Telephone, 555-3681. Social Security No. 314-21-6337. Position, time clerk. Salary, $1,495 per month. Group insurance, $27,000. Department: Office.

RYAN, Norman Allen, 7300 Harrison Street, Philadelphia, PA 19124-6699. Married, claiming 4 withholding allowances. Telephone, 555-6660. Social Security No. 526-23-1223. Position, electrician in plant. Wages, $18.00 per hour. Group insurance, $56,000.

SOKOWSKI, Thomas James, 133 Cornwells Street, Philadelphia, PA 19171-5718. Married, claiming 2 withholding allowances. Telephone, 555-5136. Social Security No. 662-04-8832. Position, supervisor in plant. Salary, $1,025 per week. Group insurance, $80,000.

STUDENT, 7018 Erdrick Street, Philadelphia, PA 19135-8517. Single, claiming 1 withholding allowance. Position, accounting trainee. Salary, $1,170 per month. Group insurance, $21,000. Department: Office.

WILLIAMS, Ruth Virginia, 9433 State Street, Philadelphia, PA 19149-0819. Single, claiming 0 withholding allowances. Telephone, 555-5845. Social Security No. 518-30-6741. Position, programmer. Salary, $2,650 per month. Group insurance, $48,000. Department: Office.

TIMEKEEPING

All office and plant employees, except the president, the sales manager, sales representatives, and supervisors, must ring in and out daily on a time clock. Also, those employees who ring in and out must notify the time clerk of the reason for lost time. (The unemployment compensation laws of some states require this information.) The time clerk prepares a weekly report of the hours worked by each employee.

The calendar for the last quarter of the year is presented below.

October

S	M	T	W	T	F	S
				1	2	3
4	5	6	7	8	9	10
11	12	13	14	15	16	17
18	19	20	21	22	23	24
25	26	27	28	29	30	31

November

S	M	T	W	T	F	S
1	2	3	4	5	6	7
8	9	10	11	12	13	14
15	16	17	18	19	20	21
22	23	24	25	26	27	28
29	30					

December

S	M	T	W	T	F	S
		1	2	3	4	5
6	7	8	9	10	11	12
13	14	15	16	17	18	19
20	21	22	23	24	25	26
27	28	29	30	31		

PAYDAY

Employees are paid biweekly on Friday. The first payday in the fourth quarter is Friday, October 9. Since the weekly time clerk's report is not finished until the Monday following the end of each week, the first pay (October 9) will be for the two weeks September 20–26 and September 27–October 3. The company, in effect, holds back one week's pay. This policy applies to all employees. The next payday (October 23) will cover the days worked in the weeks ending October 10 and October 17.

PAYROLL TAXES—CONTRIBUTIONS AND WITHHOLDINGS

Payroll taxes are levied upon Glo-Brite Paint Company and its employees as shown in Figure 7–3.

DEPOSITING TAXES

The company must deposit federal, state, and city taxes during this quarter. The deposit rules that affect the company appear in Figure 7–4.

GROUP INSURANCE

The company carries group life insurance on all its employees in an amount equal to one and one-half times the annual salary or wages paid each employee (rounded to the nearest thousand). The group insurance program covers full-time employees. A notation has been made on each employee's earnings record to show that each month ***30¢ for each $1,000*** of insurance coverage is deducted from the employee's earnings to pay a portion of the premium cost. The amount withheld is credited to a liability account entitled Group Insurance Premiums Collected.

The employer pays any additional premium, which varies each year depending upon the average age of the employees and other factors. This additional amount will be an extra expense that will be debited to an insurance expense account (part of the employees' fringe benefit cost).

PAY POINTS

Deduct insurance premiums only on the last payday of each month.

FIGURE 7–3

Glo-Brite Payroll Taxes

Payroll Taxes Levied Upon Glo-Brite Paint Company and Its Employees		
Federal Income Taxes (FIT)	Withheld from each employee's gross earnings in accordance with information given on Form W-4 and employee's earnings record. Wage-bracket method is used to determine FIT withholding.*	
Pennsylvania State Income Taxes (SIT)	3.07 percent withheld from each employee's gross earnings during the fourth quarter.*	
Philadelphia City Income Taxes (CIT)	4.26 percent withheld from gross earnings of each resident employee.*	
Pennsylvania State Unemployment Taxes (SUTA)	*Employer:*	3.5 percent on first $8,000 gross earnings paid each employee during the calendar year.
	Employee:	0.09 percent (0.0009) on total gross earnings ($8,000 limit does not apply to the employee portion).*
Federal Unemployment Taxes (FUTA)	Net tax rate of 0.8 percent on first $7,000 gross earnings paid each worker in the calendar year.	
Federal Insurance Contributions Act (FICA)	*OASDI—Employer and Employee:*	6.2 percent on first $102,300 gross earnings paid each worker in the calendar year.
	HI—Employer and Employee:	1.45 percent on total gross earnings paid each worker in the calendar year.

*Tax withholdings for FIT, SIT, CIT, and SUTA are based on rates used in 2007. Rates for 2008 were not available at the time of publishing.

FIGURE 7–4

Deposit Rules

Deposit Rules for Glo-Brite Paint Company	
Federal	The FICA taxes and FIT taxes must be deposited *on or before the 15th of the month following the month* in which the taxes were withheld. Since Glo-Brite is a new employer and has no tax liabilities during the lookback period, the company is subject to the monthly deposit rule.
Pennsylvania	Since the state income taxes withheld total $1,000 or more each quarter, the company must remit the withheld taxes semimonthly. The taxes must be remitted within three banking days after the semimonthly periods ending *on the 15th and the last day of the month.*
Philadelphia	Since the city income taxes withheld are more than $350 but less than $16,000 each month, the company is subject to the monthly rule. The city income taxes withheld during the month must be remitted *by the 15th day of the following month.*

UNION DUES

Both workers in the plant (*Bonno and Ryan*) are union members. Under the check-off system, $8 is deducted ***each payday*** from the plant workers' earnings for union dues, assessments, and initiation fees. A notation to this effect has been made on each plant worker's earnings record. On or before the tenth of each month, the amounts withheld during the preceding month are turned over to the treasurer of the union.

DISTRIBUTION OF LABOR COSTS

Figure 7–5 shows how the salaries and wages are to be charged to the labor cost accounts.

Narrative of Payroll Transactions

OCTOBER 9, 20—

No. 1 The first payroll in October covered the two workweeks that ended on September 26 and October 3. This payroll transaction has been entered for you in the payroll register, the employees' earnings records, the general journal, and the general ledger. By reviewing the calculations of the wages and deductions in the payroll register and the posting of the information to the employees' earnings records, you can see the procedure to be followed each payday.

Wages and salaries are paid by issuing special payroll checks. When the bank on which they are drawn receives such checks, they will be charged against the payroll cash account.

Observe the following rules in computing earnings each pay period:

1. Do not make any deduction from an employee's earnings if the employee loses less than 15 minutes of time in any day. Time lost that exceeds 15 minutes is rounded to the nearest quarter-hour and deducted. If the time lost by an employee is not to be deducted, the time clerk will make a notation to that effect on the Time Clerk's Report.
2. In completing the time record columns of the payroll register for all workers, you should place an 8 in the day column for each full day worked (refer to page PR-2 at the end of the book). If an employee works less than a full day, show the actual hours for which the employee will be paid.
3. In the case of an employee who begins work during a pay period, compute the earnings by paying the employees their weekly rate for ***any full week*** worked.

FIGURE 7–5

Glo-Brite Labor Cost Accounts

Personnel	Accounts to Be Charged
President (O'Neill)	Administrative Salaries
Executive Secretary (Ford) Programmer (Williams) Time Clerk (Russell) Accounting Trainee (Student)	Office Salaries
Sales Manager (Ferguson) Sales Representative (Mann)	Sales Salaries
Workers (Bonno and Ryan) Supervisor (Sokowski)	Plant Wages

Time Clerk's Report No. 38
For the Week Ending September 26, 20—

Employee	Time Record							Time Worked	Time Lost
	S	M	T	W	T	F	S		
Bonno, A. V.		8	8	8	8	8		40 hrs.	...
Ford, C. L.		8	8	8	8	8		40 hrs.	...
Russell, V. A.		8	8	8	8	8		40 hrs.	...
Ryan, N. A.		8	8	8	8	8		40 hrs.	...
Student		8	8	8	8	8		40 hrs.	...
Williams, R. V. ...		8	8	D	8	8		32 hrs.	8 hrs.*

*Time lost because of personal business; charged to personal leave; no deduction for this time lost.
D = lost full day

For any ***partial week***, compute the earnings for that week by multiplying the hours worked by the hourly rate of pay.

4. If time lost is to be deducted from a salaried employee's pay, the employee's pay must be determined by multiplying the actual hours worked for that week by the hourly rate. If hours are missed but no pay is deducted, include those hours in the Time Record columns on the payroll register. The following schedule shows the weekly and hourly wage rates of the salaried employees:

Employee	Weekly Rate	Hourly Rate
Ferguson, James C.	$1,125.00	$28.13
Ford, Catherine L.	450.00	11.25
Mann, Dewey W.	675.00	16.88
O'Neill, Joseph T.	1,153.85	28.85
Russell, Virginia A.	345.00	8.63
Sokowski, Thomas J.	1,025.00	25.63
Student	270.00	6.75
Williams, Ruth V.	611.54	15.29

5. Plant workers (*Bonno and Ryan*), other than supervisors, are employed on an hourly basis. Compute the wages by multiplying the number of hours worked during the pay period by the employee's hourly rate.

6. The information needed and the sequence of steps that are completed for the payroll are presented in the following discussion.

The time clerk prepared Time Clerk's Report Nos. 38 and 39 from the time cards used by the employees for these workweeks. ***Inasmuch as the president,***

Time Clerk's Report No. 39
For the Week Ending October 3, 20—

Employee	Time Record							Time Worked	Time Lost
	S	M	T	W	T	F	S		
Bonno, A. V.		8	8	8	8	8		40 hrs.	...
Ford, C. L.		8	8	8	8	8		40 hrs.	...
Russell, V. A.		8	8	8	8	8		40 hrs.	...
Ryan, N. A.		8	8	8	8	8		40 hrs.	...
Student		8	8	8	8	8		40 hrs.	...
Williams, R. V. ...		8	8	8	8	8		40 hrs.	...

sales manager, sales representatives, and supervisors do not ring in and out on the time clock, their records are not included in the time clerk's report, but their salaries must be included in the payroll.

① The following schedule shows the hourly wage rates of the two hourly employees used in preparing the payroll register for the payday on October 9.

Employee	Hourly Rate
Bonno, Anthony V.	$17.65
Ryan, Norman A.	18.00

② The entry required for each employee is recorded in the payroll register. The names of all employees are listed in alphabetical order, including yours as "Student." The fold-out payroll register forms needed to complete this project are bound at the back of the book (pages PR-2, PR-3, and PR-4).

No deduction has been made for the time lost by *Williams.* Thus, the total number of hours (80) for which payment was made is recorded in the Regular Earnings Hours column of the payroll register. However, a notation of the time lost (D) was made in the Time Record column. When posting to Williams's earnings record, 80 hours is recorded in the Regular Earnings Hours column (no deduction for the time lost).

In computing the federal income taxes to be withheld, the wage-bracket tables in Tax Table B at the back of the book were used (pages T-5 to T-14).

PAY POINTS

Use tax tables for biweekly payroll period.

Each payday, $8 was deducted from the earnings of the two plant workers for union dues (*Bonno and Ryan*).

Payroll check numbers were assigned beginning with check No. 672.

In the Labor Cost Distribution columns at the extreme right of the payroll register, each employee's gross earnings were recorded in the column that identifies the department in which the employee regularly works. The totals of the Labor Cost Distribution columns provide the amounts to be charged to the appropriate salary and wage expense accounts and aid department managers and supervisors in comparing the actual labor costs with the budgeted amounts.

Once the net pay of each employee was computed, all the amount columns in the payroll register were footed, proved, and ruled.

③ An entry was made in the journal (page 7-26) transferring from the regular cash account to the payroll cash account the amount of the check issued to Payroll to cover the net amount of the payroll; next, the entry was posted.

④ Information from the payroll register was posted to the employees' earnings records (see pages 7-44 to 7-48).

Note that when posting the deductions for each employee, a column has been provided in the earnings record for recording each deduction for FICA (OASDI and HI), FIT, SIT, SUTA, and CIT. All other deductions for each employee are to be totaled and recorded as one amount in the Other Deductions column. Subsidiary ledgers are maintained for Group Insurance Premiums Collected and Union Dues Withheld. Thus, any question about the amounts withheld from an employee's earnings may be answered by referring to the appropriate subsidiary ledger. In this project, your work will not involve any recording in or reference to the subsidiary ledgers.

⑤ The proper journal entry recorded salaries, wages, taxes, and the net amount of cash paid from the totals of the payroll register. The journal entry to record the payroll for the first pay in the fourth quarter appears below and in the general journal (page 7-26).

Administrative Salaries	2,307.69	
Office Salaries	3,353.08	
Sales Salaries	3,600.00	
Plant Wages	4,902.00	
FICA Taxes Payable—OASDI		878.09
FICA Taxes Payable—HI		205.37
Employees FIT Payable		1,052.00
Employees SIT Payable		434.82
Employees SUTA Payable		12.77
Employees CIT Payable		603.32
Union Dues Payable		16.00
Payroll Cash		10,960.40

The amounts charged the salary and wage expense accounts were obtained from the totals of the Labor Cost Distribution columns in the payroll register. As shown in the listing of the labor cost accounts, Figure 7–5, the salaries and wages were charged as follows:

Administrative Salaries

Joseph T. O'Neill (President)

Office Salaries

Catherine L. Ford (Executive Secretary)
Virginia A. Russell (Time Clerk)
Student (Accounting Trainee)
Ruth V. Williams (Programmer)

Sales Salaries

James C. Ferguson (Sales Manager)
Dewey W. Mann (Sales Representative)

Plant Wages

Anthony V. Bonno (Mixer Operator)
Norman A. Ryan (Electrician)
Thomas J. Sokowski (Supervisor)

FICA Taxes Payable—OASDI and FICA Taxes Payable—HI were credited for $878.09 and $205.37, respectively, the amounts deducted from employees' wages.

Employees FIT Payable, Employees SIT Payable, Employees SUTA Payable, Employees CIT Payable, and Union Dues Payable were credited for the total amount withheld for each kind of deduction from employees' wages. In subsequent payroll transactions, Group Insurance Premiums Collected will be credited for the amounts withheld from employees' wages for this type of deduction. Finally, Payroll Cash was credited for the sum of the net amounts paid all employees.

⑥ The payroll taxes for this pay were then recorded in the general journal (page 7-26) as follows:

Payroll Taxes	1,231.49	
FICA Taxes Payable—OASDI		878.09
FICA Taxes Payable—HI		205.36
FUTA Taxes Payable		26.24
SUTA Taxes Payable—Employer		121.80

Payroll Taxes was debited for the sum of the employer's FICA, FUTA, and SUTA taxes. The taxable earnings used in computing each of these payroll taxes were obtained from the appropriate column totals of the payroll register. Note that only part of *Ford's* wages are taxable ($700 out of $900 gross pay) for FUTA ($7,000 limit). The computation of the debit to Payroll Taxes was:

FICA—OASDI:	6.2% of $14,162.77 =	$ 878.09
FICA—HI:	1.45% of $14,162.77 =	205.36
FUTA:	0.8% of $3,280.00 =	26.24
SUTA:	3.5% of $3,480.00 =	121.80
Total Payroll Taxes		$1,231.49

FICA Taxes Payable—OASDI was credited for $878.09, the amount of the liability for the employer's portion of the tax. FICA Taxes Payable—HI was credited for $205.36, the amount of the liability for the employer's share of this tax. FUTA Taxes Payable was credited for the amount of the tax on the employer for federal unemployment purposes ($26.24). SUTA Taxes Payable—Employer was credited for the amount of the contribution required of ***the employer*** under the state unemployment compensation law. This same amount, $121.80, was charged as part of the debit to Payroll Taxes.

⑦ The journal entries were posted to the proper ledger accounts (pages 7-35 to 7-42).

OCTOBER 15

This is the day on which the deposits of FICA and FIT taxes and the city of Philadelphia income taxes for the September payrolls are due. However, in order to concentrate on the fourth-quarter payrolls, we will assume that the deposits for the third quarter and the appropriate entries were already completed.

OCTOBER 20

No. 2 On this date, Glo-Brite Paint Company must deposit the Pennsylvania state income taxes withheld from the October 9 payroll.

The deposit rule states that if the employer expects the aggregate amount withheld each quarter to be $1,000 or more, the employer must pay the withheld tax semimonthly. The tax must be remitted within three banking days after the close of the semimonthly periods ending on the 15th and the last day of the month.

① Prepare the journal entry to record the deposit of the taxes, and post to the appropriate ledger accounts.

② Pennsylvania has eliminated the filing of paper forms (replaced by telefile or online filing). The information needed to telefile is listed on page 7-52—complete the information worksheet needed for the first semimonthly period of October. The company's Pennsylvania account number is 146333000, its ID number is 31-0450660, its filing password is GBPCOM, and its telephone number is (215) 555-9559.

OCTOBER 23

No. 3 Prepare the payroll for the last pay period of October from Time Clerk's Report Nos. 40 and 41.

The proper procedure in recording the payroll follows:

① Complete the payroll register.

Inasmuch as only a portion of the payroll register sheet was used in recording the October 9 payroll, the October 23 payroll should be recorded on the same sheet to save space. On the first blank ruled line after the October 9 payroll, insert "Payday October 23—For Period Ending October 17, 20—." On the following lines, record the payroll information for the last pay date of October. When

Time Clerk's Report No. 40
For the Week Ending October 10, 20—

Employee	S	M	T	W	T	F	S	Time Worked	Time Lost
Bonno, A. V.		8	8	8	8	8	4	44 hrs.	...
Ford, C. L.		4	8	8	8	8		36 hrs.	4 hrs.*
Russell, V. A.		8	8	8	8	8		40 hrs.	...
Ryan, N. A.		8	8	8	8	8		40 hrs.	...
Student		8	8	8	8	8		40 hrs.	...
Williams, R. V. ...		8	8	8	8	8		40 hrs.	...

*Time lost on account of death of relative; charged against annual personal leave; no deduction for time lost.

PAY POINTS

Even though they are not on the time clerk's report, remember to pay the president, sales manager, sales representatives, and supervisors.

PAY POINTS

The employees' Pennsylvania State Unemployment Tax (SUTA) is calculated (0.0009) on the total wages of each employee. There is no taxable wage limit on the employees' portion of the tax.

PAY POINTS

Be sure to deduct 30¢ premium for each $1,000 of group insurance carried by each employee (last payday of each month).

recording succeeding payrolls, continue to conserve space by recording two payrolls on each separate payroll register sheet.

The workers in the plant (*Bonno and Ryan*) are paid ***time and a half*** for any hours worked over eight each workday and for work on Saturdays and are paid ***twice*** the regular hourly rate for work on Sundays or holidays.

With this pay period, the ***cumulative earnings*** of several employees exceed the taxable income base set up by FUTA and SUTA. This factor must be considered in preparing the payroll register and in computing the employer's payroll taxes. Refer to each employee's earnings record to see the amount of cumulative earnings.

② Make the entry transferring from Cash to Payroll Cash the net amount of the total payroll, and post.

③ Post the required information from the payroll register to each employee's earnings record.

④ Record in the journal the salaries, wages, taxes withheld, group insurance premiums collected, union dues withheld, and net amount paid, and post to the proper ledger accounts.

The entry required to record the October 23 payroll is the same as that to record the October 9 payroll, except it is necessary to record the liability for the amount withheld from the employees' wages to pay their part of the group insurance premium. The amount withheld should be recorded as a credit to Group Insurance Premiums Collected.

⑤ Record in the journal the employer's payroll taxes and the liabilities created; post to the appropriate ledger accounts.

Time Clerk's Report No. 41
For the Week Ending October 17, 20—

Employee	S	M	T	W	T	F	S	Time Worked	Time Lost
Bonno, A. V.		8	8	8	8	8		40 hrs.	...
Ford, C. L.		8	8	8	8	8		40 hrs.	...
Russell, V. A.		8	8	8	8	8		40 hrs.	...
Ryan, N. A.		8	8	8	8	8	8	48 hrs.	...
Student		8	8	8	8	8		40 hrs.	...
Williams, R. V. ...		8	8	8	8	8		40 hrs.	...

NOVEMBER 4

No. 4 Deposit with the state of Pennsylvania the amount of state income taxes withheld from the October 23 payroll and complete information worksheet.

No. 5 *Virginia Russell* completed a new Form W-4, changing the number of withholding allowances to 2. Change Russell's earnings record (her marital status has not changed).

No. 6 *Thomas J. Sokowski* completed a new Form W-4, showing that his marital status changed to single and that the number of withholding allowances remains at 2. Change Sokowski's earnings record accordingly.

No. 7 *Dewey Mann* completed a new Form W-4, leaving his marital status as married but dropping the number of withholding allowances to 0. Change Mann's earnings record accordingly.

PAY POINTS

Make changes in November 6 pay. Refers to Nos. 5, 6, and 7.

NOVEMBER 6

No. 8 Pay the treasurer of the union the amount of union dues withheld during the month of October.

No. 9 Prepare the payroll for the first pay period in November from Time Clerk's Report Nos. 42 and 43 and record the paychecks issued to all employees. Record this payroll at the top of the second payroll register sheet.

Note: Virginia Russell worked only 38 hours in the week ending October 24. Therefore, compute her pay for that week by multiplying 38 by $8.63 (her hourly rate). *Ruth Williams* worked only 39 hours in the week ending October 24.

Time Clerk's Report No. 42
For the Week Ending October 24, 20—

Employee	Time Record							Time Worked	Time Lost
	S	M	T	W	T	F	S		
Bonno, A. V.		8	8	8	8	8		40 hrs.	...
Ford, C. L.		8	8	8	8	8		40 hrs.	...
Russell, V. A.		8	8	8	8	6		38 hrs.	2 hrs.*
Ryan, N. A.		8	8	8	8	8		40 hrs.	...
Student		8	8	8	8	8		40 hrs.	...
Williams, R. V. ...		8	8	8	7	8		39 hrs.	1 hr.**

*Time lost on account of family function; deduct 2 hours' pay.
**Time lost because of tardiness; deduct 1 hour's pay.

Time Clerk's Report No. 43
For the Week Ending October 31, 20—

Employee	Time Record							Time Worked	Time Lost
	S	M	T	W	T	F	S		
Bonno, A. V.		8	8	8	8	8		40 hrs.	...
Ford, C. L.		8	8	8	8	8		40 hrs.	...
Russell, V. A.		8	8	8	8	8		40 hrs.	...
Ryan, N. A.		8	8	8	8	8		40 hrs.	...
Student		8	8	8	8	8		40 hrs.	...
Williams, R. V. ...		8	8	8	8	8		40 hrs.	...

Therefore, compute her pay for that week by multiplying 39 by $15.29 (her hourly rate).

Also, record the employer's payroll taxes.

NOVEMBER 13

No. 10 Because of her excessive tardiness and absenteeism during the year, the company discharged *Ruth V. Williams* today. For the week ending November 7, she was late a total of six hours; and for this week, she missed two full days and was late two hours on another day. In lieu of two weeks' notice, Williams was given two full weeks' pay ($1,223.08). Along with her dismissal pay ($1,223.08), she was paid for the week ending November 7 (34 hours, or $519.86) and the days worked this current week (22 hours, or $336.38). The total pay for the two partial weeks is $856.24.

① Record a separate payroll register (on one line) to show Williams's total earnings, deductions, and net pay. The two weeks' dismissal pay is subject to all payroll taxes. Include dismissal pay with the total earnings but do not show the hours in the Time Record columns. Use the tax table for the biweekly payroll period for the total gross pay ($2,079.32) of Williams.

The deduction for group insurance premiums is $14.40. In the Time Record column, make a note of Williams's discharge as of this date. Indicate the payroll check number used to prepare the final check for Williams. When posting to the earnings record, make a notation of Williams's discharge on this date.

PAY POINTS

Prepare a Wage and Tax Statement, Form W-2, to be given to Williams.

② Prepare the journal entries to transfer the net cash and to record Williams's final pay and the employer's payroll taxes. Post to the ledger accounts.

③ Use the blank Form W-2 on page 7-62. Box "a" should be left blank, since the Glo-Brite Paint Company does not use a control number to identify individual Forms W-2.

NOVEMBER 16

No. 11 Deposit with City Bank the amount of FICA taxes and federal income taxes for the October payrolls. Since the company is subject to the monthly deposit rule, the deposit is due on the 15th of the following month. See the deposit requirements explained on pages 3-18 to 3-21. November 15 is a Sunday; therefore, the deposit is to be made on the next business day.

① Prepare the journal entry to record the deposit of the taxes, and post to the appropriate ledger accounts.

② Complete the ***Federal Tax Deposit Coupon, Form 8109***, to accompany the remittance, using one of the preinscribed forms on page 7-51. The company's telephone number is (215) 555-9559. For this project, Form 8109 will be used even though the company could be using electronic transfer to pay the payroll taxes.

No. 12 Since Glo-Brite Paint Company withholds the city of Philadelphia income tax, you must deposit the taxes with the Department of Revenue. The deposit rule that affects the Glo-Brite Paint Company states that if the withheld taxes are between $350 and $16,000 per month, the company must deposit the tax monthly by the 15th of the following month. The withheld taxes for the October payrolls were $1,220.36.

PAY POINTS

On all tax and deposit forms requiring a signature, use Joseph O'Neill's name.

① Prepare the journal entry to record the deposit of the taxes, and post to the appropriate ledger accounts.

② Complete one of the Philadelphia Employer's Return of Tax Withheld coupons, which appear on pages 7-54 to 7-55.

NOVEMBER 17

No. 13 Prepare an employee's earnings record for *Beth Anne Woods*, a new employee who began work today, Tuesday. Woods is single and claims one withholding allowance. She is employed as a programmer at a monthly salary of $2,600. Address, 8102 Franklin Court, Philadelphia, PA 19105-0915. Telephone, 555-1128. Social Security No. 724-03-1587. She is eligible for group insurance coverage of $47,000 immediately, although her first deduction for group insurance will not be made until December 18.

Department: Office
Weekly rate: $600.00
Hourly rate: $15.00

NOVEMBER 18

No. 14 Deposit with the state of Pennsylvania the amount of state income taxes withheld from the November 6 and 13 (Ruth V. Williams) payrolls and complete information worksheet.

NOVEMBER 20

No. 15 With this pay, the company has decided to offer employees a Savings Incentive Match Plan (SIMPLE Retirement Plan). Most of the employees opted to wait until the start of the following year to participate. However, the following employees have decided to take part in the plan for the remaining pay periods of the year.

James Ferguson: *$500 contribution per pay period*
Dewey Mann: *$250 contribution per pay period*
Joseph O'Neill: *$700 contribution per pay period*
Norman Ryan: *$200 contribution per pay period*

The contributions are to be deducted from the participating employee's pay and are excluded from the employee's income for Federal Income Tax purposes. The other payroll taxes still apply. On the payroll registers and the earnings record, use the blank column under "Deductions" for these contributions. Use the term "SIMPLE" as the new heading for this deduction column (on both the payroll register and employees' earnings record).

Open a new account in the general ledger (use the blank account on page 7-41) for SIMPLE Contributions Payable—account #29.

The company must match these contributions dollar-for-dollar, up to 3 percent of the employee's compensation. These payments will be processed through the Accounts Payable Department.

Prepare the payroll for the last pay period of November from Time Clerk's Report Nos. 44 and 45, and record the paychecks issued all employees. Also, record the employer's payroll taxes.

Time Clerk's Report No. 44
For the Week Ending November 7, 20—

Employee	Time Record							Time Worked	Time Lost
	S	M	T	W	T	F	S		
Bonno, A. V.		8	8	8	8	8		40 hrs.	...
Ford, C. L.		8	8	8	8	8		40 hrs.	...
Russell, V. A.		6	8	8	8	8		38 hrs.	2 hrs.*
Ryan, N. A.		8	8	8	8	8		40 hrs.	...
Student		8	8	8	8	8		40 hrs.	...
Williams, R. V. ...		6	8	7	7	6		34 hrs.	6 hrs.**

*Time lost for personal business; deduct 2 hours' pay.
**Time lost because of tardiness; deduct 6 hours' pay.

Time Clerk's Report No. 45
For the Week Ending November 14, 20—

Employee	Time Record							Time Worked	Time Lost
	S	M	T	W	T	F	S		
Bonno, A. V.		...	...	8	8	8		24 hrs.	...
Ford, C. L.		8	8	8	8	8		40 hrs.	...
Russell, V. A.		8	8	8	8	8		40 hrs.	...
Ryan, N. A.		8	8	8	8	8		40 hrs.	...
Student		8	8	8	8	8		40 hrs.	...
Williams, R. V. ...		D	D	8	6	8		22 hrs.	18 hrs.*

*Time lost because of tardiness; deduct 2 hours' pay. Unexcused absences; deduct 16 hours' pay.

PAY POINTS

Remember to deduct the premiums on the group insurance for each employee.

PAY POINTS

The new wage rates are effective for the December 4 payroll.

No. 16 Salary increases of $130 per month, ***effective for the two weeks covered in the December 4 payroll***, are given to *Catherine L. Ford* and *Virginia A. Russell.* The group insurance coverage for Ford will be increased to $37,000; for Russell, it will be increased to $29,000. Update the employees' earnings records accordingly. The new wage rates are as follows:

Employee	Weekly Rate	Hourly Rate
Ford, Catherine L.	$480.00	$12.00
Russell, Virginia A.	375.00	9.38

NOVEMBER 30

No. 17 Prepare an employee's earnings record for *Paul Winston Young,* the president's nephew, who began work today. Young is single and claims one withholding allowance. He is training as a field sales representative in the city where the home office is located. His beginning salary is $1,750 per month. Address, 7936 Holmes Drive, Philadelphia, PA 19107-6107. Telephone, 555-2096. Social Security No. 432-07-6057. Young is eligible for group insurance coverage of $32,000.

Department: Sales
Weekly rate: $403.85
Hourly rate: $10.10

DECEMBER 3

No. 18 Deposit with the state of Pennsylvania the amount of state income taxes withheld from the November 20 payroll and complete information worksheet.

DECEMBER 4

No. 19 Prepare the payroll for the first pay period of December from Time Clerk's Report Nos. 46 and 47, and record the paychecks issued all employees. Record this payroll at the top of the third payroll register sheet.

Note: Thursday, November 26, is a paid holiday for all workers.

Also, record the employer's payroll taxes.

No. 20 *Anthony V. Bonno* reports the birth of a son and completes an amended Form W-4, showing his total withholding allowances to be five. Change his earnings record accordingly, ***effective with the December 18 pay.***

No. 21 Both *Anthony Bonno* and *Norman Ryan* have been notified that their union dues will increase to $9 per pay, starting with the last pay period of the year. ***Reflect these increases in the December 18 pay*** and show the changes on their earnings records.

Time Clerk's Report No. 46
For the Week Ending November 21, 20—

Employee	S	M	T	W	T	F	S	Time Worked	Time Lost
Bonno, A. V.		8	8	8	8	8		40 hrs.	...
Ford, C. L.		8	8	8	8	8		40 hrs.	...
Russell, V. A.		8	8	8	8	8		40 hrs.	...
Ryan, N. A.		8	8	8	4	8		36 hrs.	4 hrs.*
Student		8	8	8	8	8		40 hrs.	...
Woods, B. A.		...	8	8	8	8		32 hrs.	...

*Time lost on account of personal business; deduct 4 hours' pay.

Time Clerk's Report No. 47
For the Week Ending November 28, 20—

Employee	S	M	T	W	T	F	S	Time Worked	Time Lost
Bonno, A. V.	8*	8	8	8	PAID HOLIDAY	8		48 hrs.	...
Ford, C. L.		8	8	8		8		40 hrs.	...
Russell, V. A.		8	8	8		8		40 hrs.	...
Ryan, N. A.		9	10	8		8		43 hrs.	...
Student		8	8	8		8		40 hrs.	...
Woods, B. A.		8	8	8		8		40 hrs.	...

*Double time.

DECEMBER 9

No. 22 Pay the treasurer of the union the amount of union dues withheld during the month of November.

DECEMBER 11

No. 23 The Payroll Department was informed that *Virginia A. Russell* died in an automobile accident on her way home from work Thursday, December 10.

DECEMBER 14

No. 24 ① Make a separate entry (on one line) in the payroll register to record the issuance of a check payable to the ***Estate of Virginia A. Russell.*** This check covers Russell's work for the weeks ending December 5 and 12 ($675.16) plus her accrued vacation pay ($750.00). Do not show the vacation hours in the Time Record columns on the payroll register, but include them in the Total Earnings column.

Russell's final biweekly pay for time worked and the vacation pay are subject to FICA, FUTA, and SUTA (employer and employee) taxes. Since Russell's cumulative earnings have surpassed the taxable earnings figures established by FUTA and SUTA, there will not be any unemployment tax on the ***employer***. The deduction for group insurance premiums is $8.70.

② Make a notation of Russell's death in the payroll register and on her earnings record.

③ Prepare journal entries to transfer the net pay and to record Russell's final pay and the employer's payroll taxes. Post to the ledger accounts.

PAY POINTS

This final pay is not subject to withholding for FIT, SIT, or CIT purposes.

PAY POINTS

Prepare a *Wage and Tax Statement, Form W-2,* which will be given to the executor of the estate along with the final paycheck.

④ Include the final gross pay ($1,425.16) in Boxes 3 and 5, but not in Boxes 1, 16, and 18. Use the blank Form W-2 on page 7-62.

In addition, the last wage payment and vacation pay must be reported on Form 1099-MISC. A Form 1096 must also be completed. These forms will be completed in February before their due date. (See Transaction Nos. 41 and 42.)

DECEMBER 15

No. 25 Deposit with City Bank the amount of FICA taxes and federal income taxes for the November payrolls.

No. 26 Deposit with the city of Philadelphia the amount of city income taxes withheld from the November payrolls.

DECEMBER 18

No. 27 Deposit with the state of Pennsylvania the amount of state income taxes withheld from the December 4 payroll and complete information worksheet.

No. 28 Glo-Brite has been notified by the insurance company that there will be no premium charge for the month of December on the policy for *Virginia Russell.* Prepare the entry for the check made payable to the estate of Virginia A. Russell, for the amount that was withheld for insurance from her December 14 pay.

No. 29 Prepare an employee's earnings record for *Richard Lloyd Zimmerman,* who was employed today as time clerk to take the place left vacant by the death of Virginia A. Russell last week. His beginning salary is $1,430 per month. Address, 900 South Clark Street, Philadelphia, PA 19195-6247. Telephone, 555-2104. Social Security No. 897-12-1502. Zimmerman is married and claims one withholding allowance. Zimmerman is eligible for group insurance coverage of $26,000, although no deduction for group insurance premiums will be made until the last payday in January.

Department: Office
Weekly rate: $330.00
Hourly rate: $8.25

No. 30 Prepare the payroll for the latter pay of December from Time Clerk's Report Nos. 48 and 49 and record the paychecks issued all employees. Also, record the employer's payroll taxes.

Effective with this pay, *O'Neill* completed a new Form W-4, changing his total withholding allowances to four. Previously, he had claimed fewer allowances than he had been using on his tax return. Change his earnings record accordingly.

Time Clerk's Report No. 48
For the Week Ending December 5, 20—

Employee	Time Record							Time Worked	Time Lost
	S	M	T	W	T	F	S		
Bonno, A. V.	4	8	8	8	8	8		44 hrs.	. . .
Ford, C. L.		8	8	8	8	8		40 hrs.	. . .
Russell, V. A.		8	8	8	8	8		40 hrs.	. . .
Ryan, N. A.		8	9	9	9	9		44 hrs.	. . .
Student		8	8	7	8	8		39 hrs.	1 hr.*
Woods, B. A.		8	8	8	8	8		40 hrs.	. . .
Young, P. W.		8	8	8	8	8		40 hrs.	. . .

*Time lost because of tardiness; deduct 1 hour's pay.

Time Clerk's Report No. 49
For the Week Ending December 12, 20—

Employee	S	M	T	W	T	F	S	Time Worked	Time Lost
Bonno, A. V.	8	8	8	8	8	8		48 hrs.	...
Ford, C. L.		4	8	8	8	8		36 hrs.	4 hrs.*
Russell, V. A.		8	8	8	8	D		32 hrs.	8 hrs.
Ryan, N. A.		10	8	8	9	8		43 hrs.	...
Student		4	8	8	8	8		36 hrs.	4 hrs.**
Woods, B. A.		8	8	8	8	8		40 hrs.	...
Young, P. W.		8	8	8	8	8		40 hrs.	...

*Time lost for dentist appointment; no deduction for this time lost.
**Time spent in training session; no deduction in pay.

In this pay, the president of the company, *Joseph O'Neill,* is paid his annual bonus. This does not affect O'Neill's insurance coverage, which is based on regular pay. This year, his bonus is ***$50,000.*** For withholding purposes, the bonus is considered a supplemental payment and is added to his gross pay, and the aggregate amount is taxed. For this pay, O'Neill has ***increased his SIMPLE deduction to $4,000.*** To determine the federal income tax, use the ***Table of Allowance Values*** along with ***Tax Table A*** (pages T-2 to T-4). In calculating the tax, do not round the ***aggregate*** to the nearest ***earnings*** dollar.

PAY POINTS

Remember to deduct the premiums on the group insurance for each employee.

Note: After posting the information for this last pay to the employees' earnings records, calculate and enter the quarterly and yearly totals on each earnings record.

NOTE: This completes the project insofar as recording the payroll transactions for the last quarter is concerned. The following additional transactions are given to illustrate different types of transactions arising in connection with the accounting for payrolls and payroll taxes. Record these transactions in the journal, but ***do not*** post to the ledger.

JANUARY 6

No. 31 Deposit with the state of Pennsylvania the amount of state income taxes withheld from the December 18 payroll and complete information worksheet.

JANUARY 8

No. 32 Pay the treasurer of the union the amount of union dues withheld during the month of December.

JANUARY 15

No. 33 Deposit with City Bank the amount of FICA taxes and federal income taxes for the December payrolls.

Complete the ***Federal Tax Deposit Coupon, Form 8109,*** using one of the preinscribed forms on page 7-51.

No. 34 Deposit with the city of Philadelphia the amount of city income taxes withheld from the December payrolls.

FEBRUARY 1

No. 35 Prepare ***Form 941, Employer's Quarterly Federal Tax Return,*** with respect to wages paid during the last calendar quarter. Pages 7-57 and 7-58 contain a blank Form 941. The information needed in preparing the return should be obtained from the ledger accounts, payroll registers, employees' earnings records, and Federal Tax Deposit forms.

Form 941 and all forms that follow are to be signed by the president of the company, Joseph T. O'Neill.

No. 36 ① Complete ***Form 940, Employer's Annual Federal Unemployment (FUTA) Tax Return,*** using the blank form reproduced on pages 7-59 and 7-60, and also ***Form 8109, Federal Tax Deposit Coupon,*** using the blank form reproduced on page 7-51. The information needed in preparing these forms can be obtained from the ledger accounts, the payroll registers, the employees' earnings records, and the following:

a. FUTA taxable wages for the first three quarters: $65,490.00
b. FUTA tax liability by quarter:

1st quarter—$272.71
2nd quarter—$140.33
3rd quarter—$110.88

c. Deposit for the first three quarters was made on the date it was due.

② Journalize the entry to record the deposit included with the fourth quarter Form 8109.

No. 37 ① Prepare ***Form UC-2, Employer's Report for Unemployment Compensation—Fourth Quarter,*** using the blank form reproduced on page 7-61. In Pennsylvania, a credit week is any calendar week during the quarter in which the employee earned at least $50 (without regard to when paid). The maximum number of credit weeks in a quarter is 13. The telephone number of the company is (215) 555-9559. All other information needed in preparing the form can be obtained from the ledger accounts, the payroll registers, and the employees' earnings records.

② Journalize the entry to record the payment of the taxes for the fourth quarter.

No. 38 Complete ***Form W-2, Wage and Tax Statement,*** for each current employee, using the blank statements reproduced on pages 7-62 to 7-67. Use each employee's earnings record to obtain the information needed to complete the forms. The two plant workers (Bonno and Ryan) have had $121.00 in union dues withheld during the year.

No. 39 Complete ***Form W-3, Transmittal of Wage and Tax Statements,*** using the blank form reproduced on page 7-68. Use the information on all Forms W-2 to complete this form.

No. 40 Complete ***Pennsylvania Form REV-1667, W-2 Transmittal,*** using the blank form reproduced on page 7-68. Use the information on Forms W-2 to complete this report.

The wages paid and the Pennsylvania tax withheld for the first three quarters are:

1st	34,088.75	1,046.52
2nd	45,535.62	1,397.94
3rd	62,600.20	1,921.83

No. 41 Complete ***Form 1099-MISC, Miscellaneous Income,*** for the payment to ***the estate of Virginia A. Russell.*** The full amount of the December 14 payment must be reported in Box 3. Page 7-69 contains a blank form.

Note: These wages are to be reported as other income in Box 3 so that the IRS will not seek self-employment tax on such amounts.

No. 42 Complete ***Form 1096, Annual Summary and Transmittal of U.S. Information Returns***, using the blank form on page 7-69. Use the information on Form 1099-MISC to complete this form.

No. 43 Pennsylvania's Quarterly Reconciliation of Income Tax Withheld is filed electronically. The information worksheet to be completed is on page 7-55. The telephone number of the company is (215) 555-9559.

No. 44 Prepare the Annual Reconciliation of Wage Tax for Philadelphia, using the blank form on page 7-56. Tax paid during the first three quarters was $6,058.77.

QUESTIONS ON THE PAYROLL PROJECT

1. The total payroll tax expense incurred by the employer on salaries and wages paid during the quarter ended December 31 was . . . . $____________
2. The total payroll tax expense incurred by the employer on the total earnings of Joseph T. O'Neill during the fourth quarter was . . . . $____________
3. The amount of the group insurance premiums collected from employees during the quarter ended December 31 was . . . . $____________
4. O'Neill has decided to give all current employees (excluding himself) a bonus payment during January equal to 5% of their total gross pay for last year. Determine the total of this bonus payment. . . . . $____________
5. On the financial statements prepared at the end of its first year of operations, the company must show an accurate picture of all expenses and all liabilities incurred. The last payday of the year was December 18. However, the payment to the employees on that day did not include the weeks ending December 19 and 26 and the four days (December 28–31) in the following week. These earnings will be reflected in the January payrolls. Two-column journal paper is provided for use in journalizing the following entry.

   Prepare the adjusting entry as of December 31 to record the salaries and wages that have accrued but remain unpaid as of the end of the year. When calculating the amount of the accrual for each hourly worker, assume each employee worked eight hours on each day during the period with no overtime. For each salaried worker, the accrual will amount to 14/10 of the worker's biweekly earnings, except for Zimmerman who worked only 10 days.

   Each of the labor cost accounts should be debited for the appropriate amount of the accrual, and Salaries and Wages Payable should be credited for the total amount of the accrual. There is no liability for payroll taxes on the accrued salaries and wages until the workers are actually paid. Therefore, the company follows the practice of not accruing payroll taxes.
6. Also prepare the adjusting entry as of December 31 to record the accrued vacation pay as of the end of the year. Record the expense in a vacation benefits expense account, and credit the appropriate liability account. Use the journal paper provided.

   As of December 31, the vacation time earned but not used by each employee is listed below.

Bonno	80 hours
Ferguson	three weeks
Ford	two weeks
Mann	one week
O'Neill	four weeks
Ryan	80 hours
Sokowski	two weeks
Student	two weeks
Woods	none
Young	none
Zimmerman	none

JOURNAL

18

DATE		DESCRIPTION	POST. REF.	DEBIT	CREDIT

ACCOUNTING RECORDS AND REPORTS

Contents

JOURNAL

DATE		DESCRIPTION	POST. REF.	DEBIT	CREDIT
20— Oct.	9	Payroll Cash	12	10960 40	
		Cash	11		10960 40
	9	Administrative Salaries	51	2307 69	
		Office Salaries	52	3353 08	
		Sales Salaries	53	3600 00	
		Plant Wages	54	4902 00	
		FICA Taxes Payable—OASDI	20.1		878 09
		FICA Taxes Payable—HI	20.2		205 37
		Employees FIT Payable	24		1052 00
		Employees SIT Payable	25		434 82
		Employees SUTA Payable	25.1		12 77
		Employees CIT Payable	26		603 32
		Union Dues Payable	28		16 00
		Payroll Cash	12		10960 40
	9	Payroll Taxes	56	1231 49	
		FICA Taxes Payable—OASDI	20.1		878 09
		FICA Taxes Payable—HI	20.2		205 36
		FUTA Taxes Payable	21		26 24
		SUTA Taxes Payable—Employer	22		121 80

JOURNAL Page

	DATE	DESCRIPTION	POST. REF.	DEBIT	CREDIT	
1						1
2						2
3						3
4						4
5						5
6						6
7						7
8						8
9						9
10						10
11						11
12						12
13						13
14						14
15						15
16						16
17						17
18						18
19						19
20						20
21						21
22						22
23						23
24						24
25						25
26						26
27						27
28						28
29						29
30						30
31						31
32						32
33						33
34						34

JOURNAL

Page

	DATE		DESCRIPTION	POST. REF.	DEBIT	CREDIT	
1							1
2							2
3							3
4							4
5							5
6							6
7							7
8							8
9							9
10							10
11							11
12							12
13							13
14							14
15							15
16							16
17							17
18							18
19							19
20							20
21							21
22							22
23							23
24							24
25							25
26							26
27							27
28							28
29							29
30							30
31							31
32							32
33							33
34							34

JOURNAL Page

	DATE		DESCRIPTION	POST. REF.	DEBIT	CREDIT	
1							1
2							2
3							3
4							4
5							5
6							6
7							7
8							8
9							9
10							10
11							11
12							12
13							13
14							14
15							15
16							16
17							17
18							18
19							19
20							20
21							21
22							22
23							23
24							24
25							25
26							26
27							27
28							28
29							29
30							30
31							31
32							32
33							33
34							34

JOURNAL

Page

	DATE		DESCRIPTION	POST. REF.	DEBIT	CREDIT	
1							1
2							2
3							3
4							4
5							5
6							6
7							7
8							8
9							9
10							10
11							11
12							12
13							13
14							14
15							15
16							16
17							17
18							18
19							19
20							20
21							21
22							22
23							23
24							24
25							25
26							26
27							27
28							28
29							29
30							30
31							31
32							32
33							33
34							34

JOURNAL

Page

	DATE		DESCRIPTION	POST. REF.	DEBIT	CREDIT	
1							1
2							2
3							3
4							4
5							5
6							6
7							7
8							8
9							9
10							10
11							11
12							12
13							13
14							14
15							15
16							16
17							17
18							18
19							19
20							20
21							21
22							22
23							23
24							24
25							25
26							26
27							27
28							28
29							29
30							30
31							31
32							32
33							33
34							34

JOURNAL Page

	DATE		DESCRIPTION	POST. REF.	DEBIT	CREDIT	
1							1
2							2
3							3
4							4
5							5
6							6
7							7
8							8
9							9
10							10
11							11
12							12
13							13
14							14
15							15
16							16
17							17
18							18
19							19
20							20
21							21
22							22
23							23
24							24
25							25
26							26
27							27
28							28
29							29
30							30
31							31
32							32
33							33
34							34

JOURNAL

Page

	DATE	DESCRIPTION	POST. REF.	DEBIT	CREDIT	
1						1
2						2
3						3
4						4
5						5
6						6
7						7
8						8
9						9
10						10
11						11
12						12
13						13
14						14
15						15
16						16
17						17
18						18
19						19
20						20
21						21
22						22
23						23
24						24
25						25
26						26
27						27
28						28
29						29
30						30
31						31
32						32
33						33
34						34

JOURNAL

Page

DATE		DESCRIPTION	POST. REF.	DEBIT	CREDIT

GENERAL LEDGER

ACCOUNT **CASH** ACCOUNT NO. **11**

DATE		ITEM	POST. REF.	DEBIT	CREDIT	BALANCE DEBIT	BALANCE CREDIT
20— Oct.	1	*Balance*	✓			19 9 8 4 6 33	
	9		J41		1 0 9 6 0 40	18 8 8 8 5 93	

ACCOUNT **PAYROLL CASH** ACCOUNT NO. **12**

DATE		ITEM	POST. REF.	DEBIT	CREDIT	BALANCE DEBIT	BALANCE CREDIT
20— Oct.	9		J41	10960 40		10960 40	
	9		J41		10960 40	– – – –	– – – –

ACCOUNT **FICA TAXES PAYABLE—OASDI** ACCOUNT NO. **20.1**

DATE		ITEM	POST. REF.	DEBIT	CREDIT	BALANCE DEBIT	BALANCE CREDIT
20— Oct.	9		J41		878 09		878 09
	9		J41		878 09		1756 18

ACCOUNT **FICA TAXES PAYABLE—HI** ACCOUNT NO. **20.2**

DATE		ITEM	POST. REF.	DEBIT	CREDIT	BALANCE DEBIT	BALANCE CREDIT
20— Oct.	9		J41		205 37		205 37
	9		J41		205 36		410 73

ACCOUNT **FUTA TAXES PAYABLE** ACCOUNT NO. **21**

DATE		ITEM	POST. REF.	DEBIT	CREDIT	BALANCE DEBIT	BALANCE CREDIT
20— Oct.	9		J41		26 24		26 24

ACCOUNT **SUTA TAXES PAYABLE—EMPLOYER** ACCOUNT NO. **22**

DATE		ITEM	POST. REF.	DEBIT	CREDIT	BALANCE DEBIT	BALANCE CREDIT
20— Oct.	9		J41		121 80		121 80

ACCOUNT **EMPLOYEES FIT PAYABLE** ACCOUNT NO. **24**

DATE		ITEM	POST. REF.	DEBIT	CREDIT	BALANCE DEBIT	BALANCE CREDIT
20– Oct.	9		J41		1 0 5 2 00		1 0 5 2 00

ACCOUNT **EMPLOYEES SIT PAYABLE** ACCOUNT NO. **25**

DATE		ITEM	POST. REF.	DEBIT	CREDIT	BALANCE DEBIT	BALANCE CREDIT
20– Oct.	9		J41		4 3 4 82		4 3 4 82

ACCOUNT **EMPLOYEES SUTA PAYABLE** ACCOUNT NO. **25.1**

DATE		ITEM	POST. REF.	DEBIT	CREDIT	BALANCE DEBIT	BALANCE CREDIT
20– Oct.	9		J41		12 77		12 77

ACCOUNT **EMPLOYEES CIT PAYABLE** ACCOUNT NO. **26**

DATE		ITEM	POST. REF.	DEBIT	CREDIT	BALANCE DEBIT	BALANCE CREDIT
20– Oct.	9		J41		603 32		603 32

ACCOUNT **GROUP INSURANCE PREMIUMS COLLECTED** ACCOUNT NO. **27**

DATE		ITEM	POST. REF.	DEBIT	CREDIT	BALANCE DEBIT	BALANCE CREDIT

ACCOUNT **UNION DUES PAYABLE** ACCOUNT NO. **28**

DATE		ITEM	POST. REF.	DEBIT	CREDIT	BALANCE DEBIT	BALANCE CREDIT
20– Oct.	9		J41		16 00		16 00

ACCOUNT **SIMPLE CONTRIBUTIONS PAYABLE** ACCOUNT NO. **29**

DATE		ITEM	POST. REF.	DEBIT	CREDIT	BALANCE DEBIT	BALANCE CREDIT

ACCOUNT **ADMINISTRATIVE SALARIES** ACCOUNT NO. **51**

DATE		ITEM	POST. REF.	DEBIT	CREDIT	BALANCE DEBIT	BALANCE CREDIT
20– Oct.	1	*Balance*	✓			42,692 27	
	9		J41	2,307 69		44,999 96	

ACCOUNT **OFFICE SALARIES** ACCOUNT NO. **52**

DATE		ITEM	POST. REF.	DEBIT	CREDIT	BALANCE DEBIT	BALANCE CREDIT
20– Oct.	1	*Balance*	✓			28,350 00	
	9		J41	3,353 08		31,703 08	

ACCOUNT **SALES SALARIES** ACCOUNT NO. **53**

DATE		ITEM	POST. REF.	DEBIT	CREDIT	BALANCE DEBIT	BALANCE CREDIT
20— Oct.	1	*Balance*	✓			28,525 00	
	9		J41	3,600 00		32,125 00	

ACCOUNT **PLANT WAGES** ACCOUNT NO. **54**

DATE		ITEM	POST. REF.	DEBIT	CREDIT	BALANCE DEBIT	BALANCE CREDIT
20— Oct.	1	*Balance*	✓			42,657 30	
	9		J41	4,902 00		47,559 30	

ACCOUNT **PAYROLL TAXES** ACCOUNT NO. **56**

DATE		ITEM	POST. REF.	DEBIT	CREDIT	BALANCE DEBIT	BALANCE CREDIT
20— Oct.	1	*Balance*	✓			13,906 21	
	9		J41	1,231 49		15,137 70	

EMPLOYEES' EARNINGS RECORDS

DEPARTMENT	OCCUPATION	WORKS IN (STATE)	SEX M	SEX F	S.S. ACCOUNT NO.	NAME—LAST	FIRST	MIDDLE
Plant	Mixer Operator	PA	X		537–10–3481	BONNO	Anthony	Victor

OTHER DEDUCTIONS INFORMATION: GROUP INSURANCE	UNION DUES	OTHER	SALARY	WEEKLY RATE	HOURLY RATE	OVERTIME RATE	W/H ALLOW.	MARITAL STATUS
$55,000—30¢/M	$8 each pay		$	$	$ 17.65	$ 26.48	4	M

20___ PAYDAY	REGULAR EARNINGS HRS.	RATE	AMOUNT	OVERTIME EARNINGS HRS.	RATE	AMOUNT	CUMULATIVE EARNINGS	DEDUCTIONS: FICA OASDI	FICA HI	FIT	SIT	SUTA	CIT		OTHER DEDUCTIONS	CK. NO.	NET PAID AMOUNT
YEAR-TO-DATE TOTAL			10293.40			1028.60	11322.00	701.96	164.17	810.00	347.59	10.19	482.32		216.80		8588.97
1 10/9	80	17.65	1412.00				12734.00	87.54	20.47	58.00	43.35	1.27	60.15		8.00	672	1133.22
2																	
3																	
4																	
5																	
6																	
QUARTER TOTAL																	
YEARLY TOTAL																	

DEPARTMENT	OCCUPATION	WORKS IN (STATE)	SEX M	SEX F	S.S. ACCOUNT NO.	NAME—LAST	FIRST	MIDDLE
Sales	Sales Manager	PA	X		486–03–8645	FERGUSON	James	Claude

OTHER DEDUCTIONS INFORMATION: GROUP INSURANCE	UNION DUES	OTHER	SALARY	WEEKLY RATE	HOURLY RATE	OVERTIME RATE	W/H ALLOW.	MARITAL STATUS
$88,000—30¢/M			$ 58,500/yr.	$ 1,125.00	$ 28.13	$	5	M

20___ PAYDAY	REGULAR EARNINGS HRS.	RATE	AMOUNT	OVERTIME EARNINGS HRS.	RATE	AMOUNT	CUMULATIVE EARNINGS	DEDUCTIONS: FICA OASDI	FICA HI	FIT	SIT	SUTA	CIT		OTHER DEDUCTIONS	CK. NO.	NET PAID AMOUNT
YEAR-TO-DATE TOTAL			23125.00				23125.00	1433.75	335.31	2291.00	709.94	20.81	985.13		132.30		17216.76
1 10/9	80		2250.00				25375.00	139.50	32.63	164.00	69.08	2.03	95.85			673	1746.91
2																	
3																	
4																	
5																	
6																	
QUARTER TOTAL																	
YEARLY TOTAL																	

DEPARTMENT	OCCUPATION	WORKS IN (STATE)	SEX M	SEX F	S.S. ACCOUNT NO.	NAME—LAST	FIRST	MIDDLE
Office	Executive Secretary	PA		X	213–09–4567	FORD	Catherine	Louise

OTHER DEDUCTIONS INFORMATION: GROUP INSURANCE	UNION DUES	OTHER	SALARY	WEEKLY RATE	HOURLY RATE	OVERTIME RATE	W/H ALLOW.	MARITAL STATUS
$35,000—30¢/M			$ 1,950/mo.	$ 450.00	$ 11.25	$ 16.88	2	S

	20 ___ PAYDAY	REGULAR EARNINGS HRS.	RATE	AMOUNT	OVERTIME EARNINGS HRS.	RATE	AMOUNT	CUMULATIVE EARNINGS	DEDUCTIONS FICA OASDI	FICA HI	FIT	SIT	SUTA	CIT		OTHER DEDUCTIONS	CK. NO.	NET PAID AMOUNT
YEAR-TO-DATE TOTAL				6,300.00				6,300.00	390.60	91.35	639.00	193.41	5.67	268.38		37.80		4,673.79
1	10/9	80		900.00				7,200.00	55.80	13.05	68.00	27.63	0.81	38.34			674	696.37
2																		
3																		
4																		
5																		
6																		
QUARTER TOTAL																		
YEARLY TOTAL																		

DEPARTMENT	OCCUPATION	WORKS IN (STATE)	SEX M	SEX F	S.S. ACCOUNT NO.	NAME—LAST	FIRST	MIDDLE
Sales	Sales Representative	PA	X		282–37–9352	MANN	Dewey	Wilson

OTHER DEDUCTIONS INFORMATION: GROUP INSURANCE	UNION DUES	OTHER	SALARY	WEEKLY RATE	HOURLY RATE	OVERTIME RATE	W/H ALLOW.	MARITAL STATUS
$53,000—30¢/M			$ 2,925/mo.	$ 675.00	$ 16.88	$	4	M

	20 ___ PAYDAY	REGULAR EARNINGS HRS.	RATE	AMOUNT	OVERTIME EARNINGS HRS.	RATE	AMOUNT	CUMULATIVE EARNINGS	DEDUCTIONS FICA OASDI	FICA HI	FIT	SIT	SUTA	CIT		OTHER DEDUCTIONS	CK. NO.	NET PAID AMOUNT
YEAR-TO-DATE TOTAL				5,400.00				5,400.00	334.80	78.30	332.00	165.78	4.86	230.04		31.50		4,222.72
1	10/9	80		1,350.00				6,750.00	83.70	19.58	52.00	41.45	1.22	57.51			675	1,094.54
2																		
3																		
4																		
5																		
6																		
QUARTER TOTAL																		
YEARLY TOTAL																		

DEPARTMENT	OCCUPATION	WORKS IN (STATE)	SEX M	SEX F	S.S. ACCOUNT NO.	NAME—LAST	FIRST	MIDDLE
Admin.	President	PA	X		897–04–1534	O'NEILL	Joseph	Tyler

OTHER DEDUCTIONS INFORMATION				
GROUP INSURANCE	UNION DUES	OTHER		
$90,000—30¢/M				

SALARY	$ 60,000/yr.
WEEKLY RATE	$ 1,153.85
HOURLY RATE	$ 28.85
OVERTIME RATE	$

W/H ALLOW.	MARITAL STATUS
3	M

	20 ___ PAYDAY	REGULAR EARNINGS HRS.	REGULAR EARNINGS RATE	REGULAR EARNINGS AMOUNT	OVERTIME EARNINGS HRS.	OVERTIME EARNINGS RATE	OVERTIME EARNINGS AMOUNT	CUMULATIVE EARNINGS	DEDUCTIONS FICA OASDI	DEDUCTIONS FICA HI	FIT	SIT	SUTA	CIT		OTHER DEDUCTIONS	CK. NO.	NET PAID AMOUNT
YEAR-TO-DATE TOTAL				426 9 2 27				426 9 2 27	26 4 6 92	6 1 9 04	61 1 6 00	13 1 0 65	3 8 42	18 1 8 69		2 0 2 50		299 4 0 05
1	10/9	80		23 0 7 69				449 9 9 96	1 4 3 08	3 3 46	2 1 2 00	7 0 85	2 08	9 8 31			676	17 4 7 91
2																		
3																		
4																		
5																		
6																		
QUARTER TOTAL																		
YEARLY TOTAL																		

DEPARTMENT	OCCUPATION	WORKS IN (STATE)	SEX M	SEX F	S.S. ACCOUNT NO.	NAME—LAST	FIRST	MIDDLE
Office	Time Clerk	PA		X	314–21–6337	RUSSELL	Virginia	Aloise

OTHER DEDUCTIONS INFORMATION		
GROUP INSURANCE	UNION DUES	OTHER
$27,000—30¢/M		

SALARY	$1,495/mo.
WEEKLY RATE	$ 345.00
HOURLY RATE	$ 8.63
OVERTIME RATE	$ 12.95

W/H ALLOW.	MARITAL STATUS
1	S

	20 ___ PAYDAY	REGULAR EARNINGS HRS.	REGULAR EARNINGS RATE	REGULAR EARNINGS AMOUNT	OVERTIME EARNINGS HRS.	OVERTIME EARNINGS RATE	OVERTIME EARNINGS AMOUNT	CUMULATIVE EARNINGS	DEDUCTIONS FICA OASDI	DEDUCTIONS FICA HI	FIT	SIT	SUTA	CIT		OTHER DEDUCTIONS	CK. NO.	NET PAID AMOUNT
YEAR-TO-DATE TOTAL				62 4 0 00				62 4 0 00	3 8 6 88	9 0 48	6 4 2 00	1 9 1 56	5 61	2 6 5 82		3 1 50		46 2 6 15
1	10/9	80		6 9 0 00				69 3 0 00	4 2 78	1 0 01	5 4 00	2 1 18	0 62	2 9 39			677	5 3 2 02
2																		
3																		
4																		
5																		
6																		
QUARTER TOTAL																		
YEARLY TOTAL																		

DEPARTMENT	OCCUPATION	WORKS IN (STATE)	SEX M	SEX F	S.S. ACCOUNT NO.	NAME—LAST	FIRST	MIDDLE
Plant	Electrician	PA	X		526–23–1223	RYAN	Norman	Allen

OTHER DEDUCTIONS INFORMATION: GROUP INSURANCE	UNION DUES	OTHER	SALARY	WEEKLY RATE	HOURLY RATE	OVERTIME RATE	W/H ALLOW.	MARITAL STATUS
$56,000—30¢/M	$8 each pay		$	$	$ 18.00	$ 27.00	4	M

	20 ___ PAYDAY	REGULAR EARNINGS HRS.	RATE	AMOUNT	OVERTIME EARNINGS HRS.	RATE	AMOUNT	CUMULATIVE EARNINGS	FICA OASDI	FICA HI	FIT	SIT	SUTA	CIT		OTHER DEDUCTIONS	CK. NO.	NET PAID AMOUNT
YEAR-TO-DATE TOTAL				13,287.50			1,397.80	14,685.30	910.49	212.94	1,070.00	450.84	13.22	625.59		235.70		11,166.52
1	10/9	80	18.00	1,440.00				16,125.30	89.28	20.88	63.00	44.21	1.30	61.34		8.00	678	1,151.99
2																		
3																		
4																		
5																		
6																		
QUARTER TOTAL																		
YEARLY TOTAL																		

DEPARTMENT	OCCUPATION	WORKS IN (STATE)	SEX M	SEX F	S.S. ACCOUNT NO.	NAME—LAST	FIRST	MIDDLE
Plant	Supervisor	PA	X		662–04–8832	SOKOWSKI	Thomas	James

OTHER DEDUCTIONS INFORMATION: GROUP INSURANCE	UNION DUES	OTHER	SALARY	WEEKLY RATE	HOURLY RATE	OVERTIME RATE	W/H ALLOW.	MARITAL STATUS
$80,000—30¢/M			$	$ 1,025.00	$ 25.63	$	2	M

	20 ___ PAYDAY	REGULAR EARNINGS HRS.	RATE	AMOUNT	OVERTIME EARNINGS HRS.	RATE	AMOUNT	CUMULATIVE EARNINGS	FICA OASDI	FICA HI	FIT	SIT	SUTA	CIT		OTHER DEDUCTIONS	CK. NO.	NET PAID AMOUNT
YEAR-TO-DATE TOTAL				16,650.00				16,650.00	1,032.30	241.43	2,002.00	511.16	14.99	709.29		94.50		12,044.33
1	10/9	80		2,050.00				18,700.00	127.10	29.73	193.00	62.94	1.85	87.33			679	1,548.05
2																		
3																		
4																		
5																		
6																		
QUARTER TOTAL																		
YEARLY TOTAL																		

DEPARTMENT	OCCUPATION	WORKS IN (STATE)	SEX M	SEX F	S.S. ACCOUNT NO.	NAME—LAST	FIRST	MIDDLE
Office	Accounting Trainee	PA						

OTHER DEDUCTIONS INFORMATION					
GROUP INSURANCE	UNION DUES	OTHER	SALARY $ 1,170/mo. WEEKLY RATE $ 270.00 HOURLY RATE $ 6.75 OVERTIME RATE $ 10.13	W/H ALLOW.	MARITAL STATUS
				1	S

	20 ___ PAYDAY	REGULAR EARNINGS HRS.	RATE	AMOUNT	OVERTIME EARNINGS HRS.	RATE	AMOUNT	CUMULATIVE EARNINGS	DEDUCTIONS FICA OASDI	HI	FIT	SIT	SUTA	CIT		OTHER DEDUCTIONS	CK. NO.	NET PAID AMOUNT
YEAR-TO-DATE TOTAL				5,550.00				5,550.00	344.10	80.48	409.00	170.38	5.00	236.43		32.40		4,272.21
1	10/9	80		540.00				6,090.00	33.48	7.83	33.00	16.58	0.49	23.00			680	425.62
2																		
3																		
4																		
5																		
6																		
QUARTER TOTAL																		
YEARLY TOTAL																		

DEPARTMENT	OCCUPATION	WORKS IN (STATE)	SEX M	SEX F	S.S. ACCOUNT NO.	NAME—LAST	FIRST	MIDDLE
Office	Programmer	PA		X	518–30–6741	WILLIAMS	Ruth	Virginia

OTHER DEDUCTIONS INFORMATION					
GROUP INSURANCE	UNION DUES	OTHER	SALARY $ 2,650/mo. WEEKLY RATE $ 611.54 HOURLY RATE $ 15.29 OVERTIME RATE $ 22.94	W/H ALLOW.	MARITAL STATUS
$48,000—30¢/M				0	S

	20 ___ PAYDAY	REGULAR EARNINGS HRS.	RATE	AMOUNT	OVERTIME EARNINGS HRS.	RATE	AMOUNT	CUMULATIVE EARNINGS	DEDUCTIONS FICA OASDI	HI	FIT	SIT	SUTA	CIT		OTHER DEDUCTIONS	CK. NO.	NET PAID AMOUNT
YEAR-TO-DATE TOTAL				10,260.00				10,260.00	636.12	148.77	1,606.00	314.98	9.23	437.08		59.40		7,048.42
1	10/9	80		1,223.08				11,483.08	75.83	17.73	155.00	37.55	1.10	52.10			681	883.77
2																		
3																		
4																		
5																		
6																		
QUARTER TOTAL																		
YEARLY TOTAL																		

DEPARTMENT	OCCUPATION	WORKS IN (STATE)	SEX M F	S.S. ACCOUNT NO.	NAME—LAST	FIRST	MIDDLE

OTHER DEDUCTIONS INFORMATION					
GROUP INSURANCE	UNION DUES	OTHER	SALARY $____ WEEKLY RATE $____ HOURLY RATE $____ OVERTIME RATE $____	W/H ALLOW.	MARITAL STATUS

20 ___ PAYDAY	REGULAR EARNINGS			OVERTIME EARNINGS			CUMULATIVE EARNINGS	DEDUCTIONS									NET PAID
	HRS.	RATE	AMOUNT	HRS.	RATE	AMOUNT		FICA OASDI	FICA HI	FIT	SIT	SUTA	CIT		OTHER DEDUCTIONS	CK. NO.	AMOUNT
YEAR-TO-DATE TOTAL																	
1																	
2																	
3																	
4																	
5																	
6																	
QUARTER TOTAL																	
YEARLY TOTAL																	

DEPARTMENT	OCCUPATION	WORKS IN (STATE)	SEX M F	S.S. ACCOUNT NO.	NAME—LAST	FIRST	MIDDLE

OTHER DEDUCTIONS INFORMATION					
GROUP INSURANCE	UNION DUES	OTHER	SALARY $____ WEEKLY RATE $____ HOURLY RATE $____ OVERTIME RATE $____	W/H ALLOW.	MARITAL STATUS

20 ___ PAYDAY	REGULAR EARNINGS			OVERTIME EARNINGS			CUMULATIVE EARNINGS	DEDUCTIONS									NET PAID
	HRS.	RATE	AMOUNT	HRS.	RATE	AMOUNT		FICA OASDI	FICA HI	FIT	SIT	SUTA	CIT		OTHER DEDUCTIONS	CK. NO.	AMOUNT
YEAR-TO-DATE TOTAL																	
1																	
2																	
3																	
4																	
5																	
6																	
QUARTER TOTAL																	
YEARLY TOTAL																	

DEPARTMENT	OCCUPATION	WORKS IN (STATE)	SEX		S.S. ACCOUNT NO.	NAME—LAST	FIRST	MIDDLE
			M	F				

OTHER DEDUCTIONS INFORMATION					
GROUP INSURANCE	UNION DUES	OTHER	SALARY $ ____ WEEKLY RATE $ ____ HOURLY RATE $ ____ OVERTIME RATE $ ____	W/H ALLOW.	MARITAL STATUS

20 ___ PAYDAY	REGULAR EARNINGS			OVERTIME EARNINGS			CUMULATIVE EARNINGS	DEDUCTIONS								NET PAID	
	HRS.	RATE	AMOUNT	HRS.	RATE	AMOUNT		FICA OASDI	FICA HI	FIT	SIT	SUTA	CIT		OTHER DEDUCTIONS	CK. NO.	AMOUNT
YEAR-TO-DATE TOTAL																	
1																	
2																	
3																	
4																	
5																	
6																	
QUARTER TOTAL																	
YEARLY TOTAL																	

DEPARTMENT	OCCUPATION	WORKS IN (STATE)	SEX		S.S. ACCOUNT NO.	NAME—LAST	FIRST	MIDDLE
			M	F				

OTHER DEDUCTIONS INFORMATION					
GROUP INSURANCE	UNION DUES	OTHER	SALARY $ ____ WEEKLY RATE $ ____ HOURLY RATE $ ____ OVERTIME RATE $ ____	W/H ALLOW.	MARITAL STATUS

20 ___ PAYDAY	REGULAR EARNINGS			OVERTIME EARNINGS			CUMULATIVE EARNINGS	DEDUCTIONS								NET PAID	
	HRS.	RATE	AMOUNT	HRS.	RATE	AMOUNT		FICA OASDI	FICA HI	FIT	SIT	SUTA	CIT		OTHER DEDUCTIONS	CK. NO.	AMOUNT
YEAR-TO-DATE TOTAL																	
1																	
2																	
3																	
4																	
5																	
6																	
QUARTER TOTAL																	
YEARLY TOTAL																	

Transaction No. 11

AMOUNT OF DEPOSIT (Do NOT type, please print.)
DOLLARS | CENTS

MONTH TAX YEAR ENDS → 1 2

EMPLOYER IDENTIFICATION NUMBER → 31 0450660

BANK NAME/ DATE STAMP

Name Glo-Brite Paint Company

Address 2215 Salvador Street

City Philadelphia

State PA ZIP 19175-0682

Telephone number (215) 555-9559

IRS USE ONLY

Darken only one TYPE OF TAX: 941, 945, 990-C, 1120, 943, 990-T, 720, 990-PF, CT-1, 1042, 940, 944

and

Darken only one TAX PERIOD: 1st Quarter, 2nd Quarter, 3rd Quarter, 4th Quarter

76

FOR BANK USE IN MICR ENCODING

Federal Tax Deposit Coupon
Form 8109 (Rev. 12-2005)

Transaction No. 25

AMOUNT OF DEPOSIT (Do NOT type, please print.)
DOLLARS | CENTS

MONTH TAX YEAR ENDS → 1 2

EMPLOYER IDENTIFICATION NUMBER → 31 0450660

BANK NAME/ DATE STAMP

Name Glo-Brite Paint Company

Address 2215 Salvador Street

City Philadelphia

State PA ZIP 19175-0682

Telephone number (215) 555-9559

IRS USE ONLY

Darken only one TYPE OF TAX: 941, 945, 990-C, 1120, 943, 990-T, 720, 990-PF, CT-1, 1042, 940, 944

and

Darken only one TAX PERIOD: 1st Quarter, 2nd Quarter, 3rd Quarter, 4th Quarter

76

FOR BANK USE IN MICR ENCODING

Federal Tax Deposit Coupon
Form 8109 (Rev. 12-2005)

Transaction No. 33

AMOUNT OF DEPOSIT (Do NOT type, please print.)
DOLLARS | CENTS

MONTH TAX YEAR ENDS → 1 2

EMPLOYER IDENTIFICATION NUMBER → 31 0450660

BANK NAME/ DATE STAMP

Name Glo-Brite Paint Company

Address 2215 Salvador Street

City Philadelphia

State PA ZIP 19175-0682

Telephone number (215) 555-9559

IRS USE ONLY

Darken only one TYPE OF TAX: 941, 945, 990-C, 1120, 943, 990-T, 720, 990-PF, CT-1, 1042, 940, 944

and

Darken only one TAX PERIOD: 1st Quarter, 2nd Quarter, 3rd Quarter, 4th Quarter

76

FOR BANK USE IN MICR ENCODING

Federal Tax Deposit Coupon
Form 8109 (Rev. 12-2005)

Transaction No. 36

AMOUNT OF DEPOSIT (Do NOT type, please print.)

DOLLARS | CENTS

MONTH TAX YEAR ENDS → 1 2

EMPLOYER IDENTIFICATION NUMBER → 31 0450660

BANK NAME/ DATE STAMP

Name Glo-Brite Paint Company

Address 2215 Salvador Street

City Philadelphia

State PA ZIP 19175-0682

Telephone number (215) 555-9559

IRS USE ONLY

Darken only one TYPE OF TAX		and	Darken only one TAX PERIOD
941	945		1st Quarter
990-C	1120		2nd Quarter
943	990-T		3rd Quarter
720	990-PF		4th Quarter
CT-1	1042		
940	944		

76

FOR BANK USE IN MICR ENCODING

Federal Tax Deposit Coupon
Form 8109 (Rev. 12-2005)

Transaction No. 2

STATE FILING INFORMATION WORKSHEET

Company Name	________	Payment Frequency	________
Employer Account #	________	Gross Compensation	________
Employer ID #	________	PA Withholding Tax	________
Employer Password	________	Credits	________
Quarter Ending Date	________	Interest	________
Telephone Number	________	Payment	________

Transaction No. 4

STATE FILING INFORMATION WORKSHEET

Company Name	________	Payment Frequency	________
Employer Account #	________	Gross Compensation	________
Employer ID #	________	PA Withholding Tax	________
Employer Password	________	Credits	________
Quarter Ending Date	________	Interest	________
Telephone Number	________	Payment	________

Transaction No. 14

STATE FILING INFORMATION WORKSHEET

Company Name	__________	Payment Frequency	__________
Employer Account #	__________	Gross Compensation	__________
Employer ID #	__________	PA Withholding Tax	__________
Employer Password	__________	Credits	__________
Quarter Ending Date	__________	Interest	__________
Telephone Number	__________	Payment	__________

Transaction No. 18

STATE FILING INFORMATION WORKSHEET

Company Name	__________	Payment Frequency	__________
Employer Account #	__________	Gross Compensation	__________
Employer ID #	__________	PA Withholding Tax	__________
Employer Password	__________	Credits	__________
Quarter Ending Date	__________	Interest	__________
Telephone Number	__________	Payment	__________

Transaction No. 27

STATE FILING INFORMATION WORKSHEET

Company Name	__________	Payment Frequency	__________
Employer Account #	__________	Gross Compensation	__________
Employer ID #	__________	PA Withholding Tax	__________
Employer Password	__________	Credits	__________
Quarter Ending Date	__________	Interest	__________
Telephone Number	__________	Payment	__________

Transaction No. 31

STATE FILING INFORMATION WORKSHEET

Company Name	________	Payment Frequency	________
Employer Account #	________	Gross Compensation	________
Employer ID #	________	PA Withholding Tax	________
Employer Password	________	Credits	________
Quarter Ending Date	________	Interest	________
Telephone Number	________	Payment	________

Transaction No. 12

GLO-BRITE PAINT COMPANY
2215 SALVADOR STREET
PHILADELPHIA, PA 19175-0682

Signature: ________
I hereby certify that I have examined this return and that it is correct to the best of my knowledge.

Phone #: ________

Monthly Wage Tax

Account #: **6791855** From: **10/01**

Tax Type: **01** To: **10/31**

Period/Yr: **10/—** Due Date: **11/16**

Philadelphia Revenue Department
P.O. Box 8040
Philadelphia, PA 19101-8040

1. TAX DUE PER WORKSHEET, *Line 8* ________
2. INTEREST AND PENALTY ________
3. TOTAL DUE (LINE 1 & 2) ________

Make checks payable to:
CITY OF PHILADELPHIA

Transaction No. 26

GLO-BRITE PAINT COMPANY
2215 SALVADOR STREET
PHILADELPHIA, PA 19175-0682

Signature: ________
I hereby certify that I have examined this return and that it is correct to the best of my knowledge.

Phone #: ________

Monthly Wage Tax

Account #: **6791855** From: **11/01**

Tax Type: **01** To: **11/30**

Period/Yr: **11/—** Due Date: **12/15**

Philadelphia Revenue Department
P.O. Box 8040
Philadelphia, PA 19101-8040

1. TAX DUE PER WORKSHEET, *Line 8* ________
2. INTEREST AND PENALTY ________
3. TOTAL DUE (LINE 1 & 2) ________

Make checks payable to:
CITY OF PHILADELPHIA

Transaction No. 34

Monthly Wage Tax

GLO-BRITE PAINT COMPANY
2215 SALVADOR STREET
PHILADELPHIA, PA 19175-0682

Signature: ______________________
I hereby certify that I have examined this return and that it is correct to the best of my knowledge.

Phone #: ______________________

Account #:	**6791855**	From:	**12/01**
Tax Type:	**01**	To:	**12/31**
Period/Yr:	**12/—**	Due Date:	**1/15**

Philadelphia Revenue Department
P.O. Box 8040
Philadelphia, PA 19101-8040

1. TAX DUE PER WORKSHEET, *Line 8* ______
2. INTEREST AND PENALTY ______
3. TOTAL DUE (LINE 1 & 2) ______

Make checks payable to:
CITY OF PHILADELPHIA

Transaction No. 43

PA Employer's Quarterly Reconciliation Worksheet

Company Name ____________

Account Number ____________

ID # ____________

Telephone # ____________

Quarter Ending Date ____________

Record of PA Withholding Tax:

1st half of month	____________	1. Total Compensation	____________
2nd half of month	____________	2. Total PA W/H Tax	____________
1st half of month	____________	3. Total Deposits/Quarter	____________
2nd half of month	____________	4. Tax Due	____________
1st half of month	____________		
2nd half of month	____________		
TOTAL	____________		

Transaction No. 44

ANNUAL RECONCILIATION OF WAGE TAX

Due Date:
2/28/--

20--

Print your numbers like this:
1 2 3 4 5 6 7 8 9 0

Glo-Brite Paint Company
2215 Salvador Street
Philadelphia, PA 19175-0682

Type Tax: W

ACCOUNT NO. 6 7 9 1 8 5 5

Federal Identification Number
3 1 — 0 4 5 0 6 6 0

SEE INSTRUCTIONS ON BACK

DATE WAGES TERMINATED: (IF APPLICABLE) ____________

DATE BUSINESS TERMINATED: (IF APPLICABLE) ____________

PREPARER'S DAYTIME PHONE : ____________

Number of Residents | Number of Non-Residents

GROSS COMPENSATION PER W2'S ⟶

1. Taxable Residents Compensation

2. Line 1 times .0426 (4.26%)

3. Taxable Non-Residents Compensation

4. Line 3 times .037716 (3.7716%)

5. Total Tax Due (Line 2 plus Line 4)

6. Tax Previously Paid For 20--

---DO NOT DETACH---

NAME:

ACCOUNT NO.
TYPE TAX: PERIOD: YEAR:

If Line 5 is Greater Than Line 6, Use Line 7

7. Tax Due (Line 5 Minus Line 6)
Make Check Payable To: City of Philadelphia

If line 5 is less than line 6, use line 8

8. Tax Overpaid (Line 6 Less Line 5)
(SEE INSTRUCTIONS)

Signature: ______________________________ Date ____________

I certify that all amounts indicated as due the City of Philadelphia on this return were actually withheld from the gross compensation paid by this taxpayer to its employees during the period(s) covered by this filing, and that I am authorized to so state.

Transaction No. 35

Form **941 for 20--: Employer's QUARTERLY Federal Tax Return**
(Rev. January 2007) Department of the Treasury — Internal Revenue Service OMB No. 1545-0029

(EIN) Employer identification number 3 1 – 0 4 5 0 6 6 0

Name *(not your trade name)* GLO-BRITE PAINT COMPANY

Trade name *(if any)*

Address 2215 SALVADOR ST
Number Street Suite or room number
PHILADELPHIA PA 19175-0682
City State ZIP code

Report for this Quarter of 20--
(Check one.)

- ☐ **1:** January, February, March
- ☐ **2:** April, May, June
- ☐ **3:** July, August, September
- ☐ **4:** October, November, December

Read the separate instructions before you fill out this form. Please type or print within the boxes.

Part 1: Answer these questions for this quarter.

1 **Number of employees who received wages, tips, or other compensation for the pay period including:** ***Mar. 12*** **(Quarter 1),** ***June 12*** **(Quarter 2),** ***Sept. 12*** **(Quarter 3),** ***Dec. 12*** **(Quarter 4)** . . . 1

2 **Wages, tips, and other compensation** . . . 2 .

3 **Total income tax withheld from wages, tips, and other compensation** . . . 3 .

4 **If no wages, tips, and other compensation are subject to social security or Medicare tax** . . ☐ Check and go to line 6.

5 **Taxable social security and Medicare wages and tips:**

	Column 1		Column 2
5a **Taxable social security wages**	.	× .124 =	.
5b **Taxable social security tips**	.	× .124 =	.
5c **Taxable Medicare wages & tips**	.	× .029 =	.

5d **Total social security and Medicare taxes** (*Column 2,* lines 5a + 5b + 5c = line 5d) . . 5d .

6 **Total taxes before adjustments** (lines 3 + 5d = line 6) . . . 6 .

7 **TAX ADJUSTMENTS** (Read the instructions for line 7 before completing lines 7a through 7h.):

7a **Current quarter's fractions of cents** . . . .

7b **Current quarter's sick pay** . . . .

7c **Current quarter's adjustments for tips and group-term life insurance** .

7d **Current year's income tax withholding** (attach Form 941c) . . . .

7e **Prior quarters' social security and Medicare taxes** (attach Form 941c) .

7f **Special additions to federal income tax** (attach Form 941c) . . . .

7g **Special additions to social security and Medicare** (attach Form 941c) .

7h **TOTAL ADJUSTMENTS** (Combine all amounts: lines 7a through 7g.) . . . 7h .

8 **Total taxes after adjustments** (Combine lines 6 and 7h.) . . . 8 .

9 **Advance earned income credit (EIC) payments made to employees** . . . 9 .

10 **Total taxes after adjustment for advance EIC** (line 8 – line 9 = line 10) . . . 10 .

11 **Total deposits for this quarter, including overpayment applied from a prior quarter** . . . 11 .

12 **Balance due** (If line 10 is more than line 11, write the difference here.) . . . 12 .
Follow the Instructions for Form 941-V, Payment Voucher.

13 **Overpayment** (If line 11 is more than line 10, write the difference here.) . Check one ☐ Apply to next return. ☐ Send a refund.

▶ You **MUST** fill out both pages of this form and **SIGN** it.

Next ➔

For Privacy Act and Paperwork Reduction Act Notice, see the back of the Payment Voucher. Cat. No. 17001Z Form **941**

Transaction No. 35

Name *(not your trade name)* | Employer identification number (EIN)

Part 2: Tell us about your deposit schedule and tax liability for this quarter.

If you are unsure about whether you are a monthly schedule depositor or a semiweekly schedule depositor, see *Pub. 15 (Circular E),* section 11.

14 ☐☐ **Write the state abbreviation for the state where you made your deposits** OR **write "MU" if you made your deposits in *multiple* states.**

15 **Check one:** ☐ **Line 10 is less than $2,500.** Go to Part 3.

☐ **You were a monthly schedule depositor for the entire quarter. Fill out your tax liability for each month.** Then go to Part 3.

Tax liability: **Month 1** ________ .

Month 2 ________ .

Month 3 ________ .

Total liability for quarter ________ . **Total must equal line 10.**

☐ **You were a semiweekly schedule depositor for any part of this quarter.** Fill out *Schedule B (Form 941): Report of Tax Liability for Semiweekly Schedule Depositors,* and attach it to this form.

Part 3: Tell us about your business. If a question does NOT apply to your business, leave it blank.

16 **If your business has closed or you stopped paying wages** . . . . ☐ Check here, and

enter the final date you paid wages ___/___/___ .

17 **If you are a seasonal employer and you do not have to file a return for every quarter of the year** . . ☐ Check here.

Part 4: May we speak with your third-party designee?

Do you want to allow an employee, a paid tax preparer, or another person to discuss this return with the IRS? (See the instructions for details.)

☐ Yes. Designee's name ________

Select a 5-digit Personal Identification Number (PIN) to use when talking to IRS. ☐☐☐☐☐

☐ No.

Part 5: Sign here. You MUST fill out both pages of this form and SIGN it.

Under penalties of perjury, I declare that I have examined this return, including accompanying schedules and statements, and to the best of my knowledge and belief, it is true, correct, and complete.

X Sign your name here ________

Print your name here ________

Print your title here ________

Date ___/___/___

Best daytime phone ( ) –

Part 6: For paid preparers only *(optional)*

Paid Preparer's Signature ________

Firm's name ________

Address ________ EIN ________

________ ZIP code ________

Date ___/___/___ Phone ( ) – SSN/PTIN ________

☐ Check if you are self-employed.

Page **2** Form **941**

Transaction No. 36

Form **940 for 20--: Employer's Annual Federal Unemployment (FUTA) Tax Return**

Department of the Treasury — Internal Revenue Service

OMB No. 1545-0028

(EIN)
Employer identification number 3 1 – 0 4 5 0 6 6 0

Name *(not your trade name)* GLO-BRITE PAINT COMPANY

Trade name *(if any)*

Address 2215 SALVADOR ST
Number Street Suite or room number

PHILADELPHIA PA 19175-0682
City State ZIP code

Type of Return
(Check all that apply.)

☐ **a.** Amended

☐ **b.** Successor employer

☐ **c.** No payments to employees in 20--

☐ **d.** Final: Business closed or stopped paying wages

Read the separate instructions before you fill out this form. Please type or print within the boxes.

Part 1: Tell us about your return. If any line does NOT apply, leave it blank.

1 **If you were required to pay your state unemployment tax in ...**

1a **One state only,** write the state abbreviation . . . . 1a ☐☐

- OR -

1b **More than one state** (You are a multi-state employer) . . . . 1b ☐ Check here. Fill out Schedule A.

2

Part 2: Determine your FUTA tax before adjustments for 20--. If any line does NOT apply, leave it blank.

3 **Total payments to all employees** . . . . 3 ______ .

4 **Payments exempt from FUTA tax** . . . . 4 ______ .

Check all that apply: 4a ☐ Fringe benefits 4c ☐ Retirement/Pension 4e ☐ Other
4b ☐ Group term life insurance 4d ☐ Dependent care

5 **Total of payments made to each employee in excess of $7,000** . . . . 5 ______ .

6 **Subtotal** (line 4 + line 5 = line 6) . . . . 6 ______ .

7 **Total taxable FUTA wages** (line 3 – line 6 = line 7) . . . . 7 ______ .

8 **FUTA tax before adjustments** (line 7 × .008 = line 8) . . . . 8 ______ .

Part 3: Determine your adjustments. If any line does NOT apply, leave it blank.

9 **If ALL of the taxable FUTA wages you paid were excluded from state unemployment tax, multiply line 7 by .054** (line 7 × .054 = line 9). Then go to line 12 . . . . 9 ______ .

10 **If SOME of the taxable FUTA wages you paid were excluded from state unemployment tax, OR you paid ANY state unemployment tax late** (after the due date for filing Form 940), fill out the worksheet in the instructions. Enter the amount from line 7 of the worksheet onto line 10 . . 10 ______ .

11

Part 4: Determine your FUTA tax and balance due or overpayment for 20--. If any line does NOT apply, leave it blank.

12 **Total FUTA tax after adjustments** (lines 8 + 9 + 10 = line 12) . . . . 12 ______ .

13 **FUTA tax deposited for the year, including any payment applied from a prior year** . . . . 13 ______ .

14 **Balance due** (If line 12 is more than line 13, enter the difference on line 14.)

- If line 14 is more than $500, you must deposit your tax.
- If line 14 is $500 or less and you pay by check, make your check payable to the United States Treasury and write your EIN, *Form 940,* and *20--* on the check . . . . 14 ______ .

15 **Overpayment** (If line 13 is more than line 12, enter the difference on line 15 and check a box below.) . . . . 15 ______ .

Check one ☐ Apply to next return.
☐ Send a refund.

▶ You **MUST** fill out both pages of this form and **SIGN** it.

Next ➔

For Privacy Act and Paperwork Reduction Act Notice, see the back of Form 940-V, Payment Voucher. Cat. No. 11234O Form **940**

Transaction No. 36

Name *(not your trade name)* | **Employer identification number (EIN)**

Part 5: Report your FUTA tax liability by quarter only if line 12 is more than $500. If not, go to Part 6.

16 **Report the amount of your FUTA tax liability for each quarter; do NOT enter the amount you deposited. If you had no liability for a quarter, leave the line blank.**

16a **1st quarter** (January 1 – March 31) . . . . **16a** ______ .

16b **2nd quarter** (April 1 – June 30) . . . . **16b** ______ .

16c **3rd quarter** (July 1 – September 30) . . . . **16c** ______ .

16d **4th quarter** (October 1 – December 31) . . . . **16d** ______ .

17 **Total tax liability for the year** (lines 16a + 16b + 16c + 16d = line 17) **17** ______ . **Total must equal line 12.**

Part 6: May we speak with your third-party designee?

Do you want to allow an employee, a paid tax preparer, or another person to discuss this return with the IRS? See the instructions for details.

☐ **Yes.** Designee's name ______

Select a 5-digit Personal Identification Number (PIN) to use when talking to IRS ☐☐☐☐☐

☐ **No.**

Part 7: Sign here.

You MUST fill out both pages of this form and SIGN it.

Under penalties of perjury, I declare that I have examined this return, including accompanying schedules and statements, and to the best of my knowledge and belief, it is true, correct, and complete, and that no part of any payment made to a state unemployment fund claimed as a credit was, or is to be, deducted from the payments made to employees.

✗ **Sign your name here** ______

Print your name here ______

Print your title here ______

Date ___ / ___ / ___

Best daytime phone ( ) –

Part 8: For PAID preparers only (optional)

If you were paid to prepare this return and are not an employee of the business that is filing this return, you may choose to fill out Part 8.

Paid Preparer's name ______ Preparer's SSN/PTIN ______

Paid Preparer's signature ______ Date ___ / ___ / ___

☐ Check if you are self-employed.

Firm's name ______ Firm's EIN ______

Street address ______

City ______ State ______ ZIP code ______

Page **2** Form **940**

Transaction No. 37

PA Form UC-2, Rev 6-2000, Employer's Report for Unemployment Compensation QTR./YEAR 4/20--
Read Instructions Answer Each Item DUE DATE 01/31/20--

DETACH HERE ▶

INV. [ ] EXAMINED BY: [ ]

Signature certifies that the information contained herein is true and correct to the best of the signer's knowledge.

10. SIGN HERE-DO NOT PRINT

TITLE ________ DATE ________ PHONE # ________

11. FILED ☐ PAPER UC-2A ☐ MAGNETIC MEDIA UC-2A

EMPLOYER'S CONTRIBUTION RATE: .035

EMPLOYER'S ACCT. NO.: 146-3-3300

CHECK DIGIT: 1

Employer name and address
Make any corrections on Form UC-2B

GLO-BRITE PAINT COMPANY
2215 SALVADOR STREET
PHILADELPHIA, PA 19175-0682

	1ST MONTH	2ND MONTH	3RD MONTH
1. TOTAL COVERED EMPLOYEES IN PAY PERIOD INCL. 12TH OF MONTH			

		FOR DEPT. USE
2. GROSS WAGES		
3. EMPLOYEE CONTRIBUTIONS		
4. TAXABLE WAGES FOR EMPLOYER CONTRIBUTIONS		
5. EMPLOYER CONTRIBUTIONS DUE (RATE X ITEM 4)		
6. TOTAL CONTRIBUTIONS DUE (ITEMS 3 + 5)		
7. INTEREST DUE SEE INSTRUCTIONS		
8. PENALTY DUE SEE INSTRUCTIONS		
9. TOTAL REMITTANCE (ITEMS 6 + 7 + 8)	$	

MAKE CHECKS PAYABLE TO:"PA UC FUND

◀ DETACH HERE

PA Form UC-2A, Rev 6-2000, Employer's Quarterly Report of Wages Paid to Each Employee

SAMPLE Typed: 123456.00 **SAMPLE Handwritten:** 123456.00 **SAMPLE Filled-in:** → ●

Employer name (make corrections on Form UC-2B)	Employer PA UC account no.	Check digit	Quarter and year Q/YYYY	Quarter ending date MM/DD/YYYY
Glo-Brite Paint Company	146-3-3300	1	4/20--	12/31/20--

1. Name and telephone number of preparer

2. Total number of pages in this report

3. Total number of employees listed in item 8 on all pages of Form UC-2A

4. Plant number (if approved)

5. Gross wages, MUST agree with item 2 on UC-2 and the sum of item 11 on all pages of Form UC-2A

6. Fill in this circle if you would like the Department to preprint your employees' names & SSNs on Form UC-2A next quarter → ○

7. Employee's social security number	8. Employee's name FI	MI	LAST	9. Gross wages paid this qtr Example: 123456.00	10. Credit weeks

List any additional employees on continuation sheets in the required format (see instructions).

Batch # For Dept. Use Only

11. Total gross wages for this page: →

12. Page 1 of 1

Transaction No. 10

22222	Void ☐	a Employee's social security number	For Official Use Only ▶ OMB No. 1545-0008

b Employer identification number (EIN)	1 Wages, tips, other compensation	2 Federal income tax withheld
c Employer's name, address, and ZIP code	3 Social security wages	4 Social security tax withheld
	5 Medicare wages and tips	6 Medicare tax withheld
	7 Social security tips	8 Allocated tips
d Control number	9 Advance EIC payment	10 Dependent care benefits
e Employee's first name and initial / Last name / Suff.	11 Nonqualified plans	12a See instructions for box 12 Code
	13 Statutory employee ☐ Retirement plan ☐ Third-party sick pay ☐	12b Code
	14 Other	12c Code
		12d Code
f Employee's address and ZIP code		

15 State	Employer's state ID number	16 State wages, tips, etc.	17 State income tax	18 Local wages, tips, etc.	19 Local income tax	20 Locality name

Form **W-2** **Wage and Tax Statement** **20--**

Department of the Treasury—Internal Revenue Service

For Privacy Act and Paperwork Reduction Act Notice, see back of Copy D.

Copy A For Social Security Administration — Send this entire page with Form W-3 to the Social Security Administration; photocopies are **not** acceptable.

Cat. No. 10134D

Do Not Cut, Fold, or Staple Forms on This Page — Do Not Cut, Fold, or Staple Forms on This Page

Transaction No. 24

22222	Void ☐	a Employee's social security number	For Official Use Only ▶ OMB No. 1545-0008

b Employer identification number (EIN)	1 Wages, tips, other compensation	2 Federal income tax withheld
c Employer's name, address, and ZIP code	3 Social security wages	4 Social security tax withheld
	5 Medicare wages and tips	6 Medicare tax withheld
	7 Social security tips	8 Allocated tips
d Control number	9 Advance EIC payment	10 Dependent care benefits
e Employee's first name and initial / Last name / Suff.	11 Nonqualified plans	12a See instructions for box 12 Code
	13 Statutory employee ☐ Retirement plan ☐ Third-party sick pay ☐	12b Code
	14 Other	12c Code
		12d Code
f Employee's address and ZIP code		

15 State	Employer's state ID number	16 State wages, tips, etc.	17 State income tax	18 Local wages, tips, etc.	19 Local income tax	20 Locality name

Form **W-2** **Wage and Tax Statement** **20--**

Department of the Treasury—Internal Revenue Service

For Privacy Act and Paperwork Reduction Act Notice, see back of Copy D.

Copy A For Social Security Administration — Send this entire page with Form W-3 to the Social Security Administration; photocopies are **not** acceptable.

Cat. No. 10134D

Do Not Cut, Fold, or Staple Forms on This Page — Do Not Cut, Fold, or Staple Forms on This Page

Transaction No. 38

22222 Void ☐

a Employee's social security number

For Official Use Only ▶
OMB No. 1545-0008

b Employer identification number (EIN)	1 Wages, tips, other compensation	2 Federal income tax withheld
c Employer's name, address, and ZIP code	3 Social security wages	4 Social security tax withheld
	5 Medicare wages and tips	6 Medicare tax withheld
	7 Social security tips	8 Allocated tips
d Control number	9 Advance EIC payment	10 Dependent care benefits
e Employee's first name and initial / Last name / Suff.	11 Nonqualified plans	12a See instructions for box 12 Code
	13 Statutory employee ☐ Retirement plan ☐ Third-party sick pay ☐	12b Code
	14 Other	12c Code
f Employee's address and ZIP code		12d Code

15 State	Employer's state ID number	16 State wages, tips, etc.	17 State income tax	18 Local wages, tips, etc.	19 Local income tax	20 Locality name

Form **W-2** Wage and Tax Statement **20--**

Department of the Treasury—Internal Revenue Service

For Privacy Act and Paperwork Reduction Act Notice, see back of Copy D.

Cat. No. 10134D

Copy A For Social Security Administration — Send this entire page with Form W-3 to the Social Security Administration; photocopies are **not** acceptable.

Do Not Cut, Fold, or Staple Forms on This Page — Do Not Cut, Fold, or Staple Forms on This Page

22222 Void ☐

a Employee's social security number

For Official Use Only ▶
OMB No. 1545-0008

b Employer identification number (EIN)	1 Wages, tips, other compensation	2 Federal income tax withheld
c Employer's name, address, and ZIP code	3 Social security wages	4 Social security tax withheld
	5 Medicare wages and tips	6 Medicare tax withheld
	7 Social security tips	8 Allocated tips
d Control number	9 Advance EIC payment	10 Dependent care benefits
e Employee's first name and initial / Last name / Suff.	11 Nonqualified plans	12a See instructions for box 12 Code
	13 Statutory employee ☐ Retirement plan ☐ Third-party sick pay ☐	12b Code
	14 Other	12c Code
f Employee's address and ZIP code		12d Code

15 State	Employer's state ID number	16 State wages, tips, etc.	17 State income tax	18 Local wages, tips, etc.	19 Local income tax	20 Locality name

Form **W-2** Wage and Tax Statement **20--**

Department of the Treasury—Internal Revenue Service

For Privacy Act and Paperwork Reduction Act Notice, see back of Copy D.

Cat. No. 10134D

Copy A For Social Security Administration — Send this entire page with Form W-3 to the Social Security Administration; photocopies are **not** acceptable.

Do Not Cut, Fold, or Staple Forms on This Page — Do Not Cut, Fold, or Staple Forms on This Page

Transaction No. 38

22222	Void ☐	a Employee's social security number	For Official Use Only ▶ OMB No. 1545-0008

b Employer identification number (EIN)	1 Wages, tips, other compensation	2 Federal income tax withheld
c Employer's name, address, and ZIP code	3 Social security wages	4 Social security tax withheld
	5 Medicare wages and tips	6 Medicare tax withheld
	7 Social security tips	8 Allocated tips
d Control number	9 Advance EIC payment	10 Dependent care benefits
e Employee's first name and initial / Last name / Suff.	11 Nonqualified plans	12a See instructions for box 12 Code
	13 Statutory employee ☐ Retirement plan ☐ Third-party sick pay ☐	12b Code
	14 Other	12c Code
f Employee's address and ZIP code		12d Code

15 State Employer's state ID number	16 State wages, tips, etc.	17 State income tax	18 Local wages, tips, etc.	19 Local income tax	20 Locality name

Form **W-2** **Wage and Tax Statement** **20--**

Department of the Treasury—Internal Revenue Service

For Privacy Act and Paperwork Reduction Act Notice, see back of Copy D.

Copy A For Social Security Administration — Send this entire page with Form W-3 to the Social Security Administration; photocopies are **not** acceptable.

Cat. No. 10134D

Do Not Cut, Fold, or Staple Forms on This Page — Do Not Cut, Fold, or Staple Forms on This Page

22222	Void ☐	a Employee's social security number	For Official Use Only ▶ OMB No. 1545-0008

b Employer identification number (EIN)	1 Wages, tips, other compensation	2 Federal income tax withheld
c Employer's name, address, and ZIP code	3 Social security wages	4 Social security tax withheld
	5 Medicare wages and tips	6 Medicare tax withheld
	7 Social security tips	8 Allocated tips
d Control number	9 Advance EIC payment	10 Dependent care benefits
e Employee's first name and initial / Last name / Suff.	11 Nonqualified plans	12a See instructions for box 12 Code
	13 Statutory employee ☐ Retirement plan ☐ Third-party sick pay ☐	12b Code
	14 Other	12c Code
f Employee's address and ZIP code		12d Code

15 State Employer's state ID number	16 State wages, tips, etc.	17 State income tax	18 Local wages, tips, etc.	19 Local income tax	20 Locality name

Form **W-2** **Wage and Tax Statement** **20--**

Department of the Treasury—Internal Revenue Service

For Privacy Act and Paperwork Reduction Act Notice, see back of Copy D.

Copy A For Social Security Administration — Send this entire page with Form W-3 to the Social Security Administration; photocopies are **not** acceptable.

Cat. No. 10134D

Do Not Cut, Fold, or Staple Forms on This Page — Do Not Cut, Fold, or Staple Forms on This Page

Transaction No. 38

22222	Void ☐	a Employee's social security number	For Official Use Only ▶ OMB No. 1545-0008	
b Employer identification number (EIN)			1 Wages, tips, other compensation	2 Federal income tax withheld
c Employer's name, address, and ZIP code			3 Social security wages	4 Social security tax withheld
			5 Medicare wages and tips	6 Medicare tax withheld
			7 Social security tips	8 Allocated tips
d Control number			9 Advance EIC payment	10 Dependent care benefits
e Employee's first name and initial	Last name	Suff.	11 Nonqualified plans	12a See instructions for box 12 Code
			13 Statutory employee ☐ Retirement plan ☐ Third-party sick pay ☐	12b Code
			14 Other	12c Code
				12d Code
f Employee's address and ZIP code				

15 State	Employer's state ID number	16 State wages, tips, etc.	17 State income tax	18 Local wages, tips, etc.	19 Local income tax	20 Locality name

Form **W-2** **Wage and Tax Statement** **20--**

Department of the Treasury—Internal Revenue Service

For Privacy Act and Paperwork Reduction Act Notice, see back of Copy D.

Cat. No. 10134D

Copy A For Social Security Administration — Send this entire page with Form W-3 to the Social Security Administration; photocopies are **not** acceptable.

Do Not Cut, Fold, or Staple Forms on This Page — Do Not Cut, Fold, or Staple Forms on This Page

22222	Void ☐	a Employee's social security number	For Official Use Only ▶ OMB No. 1545-0008	
b Employer identification number (EIN)			1 Wages, tips, other compensation	2 Federal income tax withheld
c Employer's name, address, and ZIP code			3 Social security wages	4 Social security tax withheld
			5 Medicare wages and tips	6 Medicare tax withheld
			7 Social security tips	8 Allocated tips
d Control number			9 Advance EIC payment	10 Dependent care benefits
e Employee's first name and initial	Last name	Suff.	11 Nonqualified plans	12a See instructions for box 12 Code
			13 Statutory employee ☐ Retirement plan ☐ Third-party sick pay ☐	12b Code
			14 Other	12c Code
				12d Code
f Employee's address and ZIP code				

15 State	Employer's state ID number	16 State wages, tips, etc.	17 State income tax	18 Local wages, tips, etc.	19 Local income tax	20 Locality name

Form **W-2** **Wage and Tax Statement** **20--**

Department of the Treasury—Internal Revenue Service

For Privacy Act and Paperwork Reduction Act Notice, see back of Copy D.

Cat. No. 10134D

Copy A For Social Security Administration — Send this entire page with Form W-3 to the Social Security Administration; photocopies are **not** acceptable.

Do Not Cut, Fold, or Staple Forms on This Page — Do Not Cut, Fold, or Staple Forms on This Page

Transaction No. 38

22222 | Void ☐ | a Employee's social security number | For Official Use Only ▶ OMB No. 1545-0008

b Employer identification number (EIN)	1 Wages, tips, other compensation	2 Federal income tax withheld
c Employer's name, address, and ZIP code	3 Social security wages	4 Social security tax withheld
	5 Medicare wages and tips	6 Medicare tax withheld
	7 Social security tips	8 Allocated tips
d Control number	9 Advance EIC payment	10 Dependent care benefits
e Employee's first name and initial / Last name / Suff.	11 Nonqualified plans	12a See instructions for box 12 Code
	13 Statutory employee ☐ Retirement plan ☐ Third-party sick pay ☐	12b Code
	14 Other	12c Code
f Employee's address and ZIP code		12d Code

15 State / Employer's state ID number	16 State wages, tips, etc.	17 State income tax	18 Local wages, tips, etc.	19 Local income tax	20 Locality name

Form **W-2** **Wage and Tax Statement** 20- -

Department of the Treasury—Internal Revenue Service

For Privacy Act and Paperwork Reduction Act Notice, see back of Copy D.

Cat. No. 10134D

Copy A For Social Security Administration — Send this entire page with Form W-3 to the Social Security Administration; photocopies are **not** acceptable.

Do Not Cut, Fold, or Staple Forms on This Page — Do Not Cut, Fold, or Staple Forms on This Page

22222 | Void ☐ | a Employee's social security number | For Official Use Only ▶ OMB No. 1545-0008

b Employer identification number (EIN)	1 Wages, tips, other compensation	2 Federal income tax withheld
c Employer's name, address, and ZIP code	3 Social security wages	4 Social security tax withheld
	5 Medicare wages and tips	6 Medicare tax withheld
	7 Social security tips	8 Allocated tips
d Control number	9 Advance EIC payment	10 Dependent care benefits
e Employee's first name and initial / Last name / Suff.	11 Nonqualified plans	12a See instructions for box 12 Code
	13 Statutory employee ☐ Retirement plan ☐ Third-party sick pay ☐	12b Code
	14 Other	12c Code
f Employee's address and ZIP code		12d Code

15 State / Employer's state ID number	16 State wages, tips, etc.	17 State income tax	18 Local wages, tips, etc.	19 Local income tax	20 Locality name

Form **W-2** **Wage and Tax Statement** 20- -

Department of the Treasury—Internal Revenue Service

For Privacy Act and Paperwork Reduction Act Notice, see back of Copy D.

Cat. No. 10134D

Copy A For Social Security Administration — Send this entire page with Form W-3 to the Social Security Administration; photocopies are **not** acceptable.

Do Not Cut, Fold, or Staple Forms on This Page — Do Not Cut, Fold, or Staple Forms on This Page

Transaction No. 38

22222 | Void ☐ | a Employee's social security number | For Official Use Only ▶ OMB No. 1545-0008

b Employer identification number (EIN)

1 Wages, tips, other compensation

2 Federal income tax withheld

c Employer's name, address, and ZIP code

3 Social security wages

4 Social security tax withheld

5 Medicare wages and tips

6 Medicare tax withheld

7 Social security tips

8 Allocated tips

d Control number

9 Advance EIC payment

10 Dependent care benefits

e Employee's first name and initial | Last name | Suff.

11 Nonqualified plans

12a See instructions for box 12 Code

13 Statutory employee ☐ Retirement plan ☐ Third-party sick pay ☐

12b Code

14 Other

12c Code

12d Code

f Employee's address and ZIP code

15 State Employer's state ID number	16 State wages, tips, etc.	17 State income tax	18 Local wages, tips, etc.	19 Local income tax	20 Locality name

Form **W-2** **Wage and Tax Statement** **20--**

Department of the Treasury—Internal Revenue Service

For Privacy Act and Paperwork Reduction Act Notice, see back of Copy D.

Copy A For Social Security Administration — Send this entire page with Form W-3 to the Social Security Administration; photocopies are **not** acceptable.

Cat. No. 10134D

Do Not Cut, Fold, or Staple Forms on This Page — Do Not Cut, Fold, or Staple Forms on This Page

22222 | Void ☐ | a Employee's social security number | For Official Use Only ▶ OMB No. 1545-0008

b Employer identification number (EIN)

1 Wages, tips, other compensation

2 Federal income tax withheld

c Employer's name, address, and ZIP code

3 Social security wages

4 Social security tax withheld

5 Medicare wages and tips

6 Medicare tax withheld

7 Social security tips

8 Allocated tips

d Control number

9 Advance EIC payment

10 Dependent care benefits

e Employee's first name and initial | Last name | Suff.

11 Nonqualified plans

12a See instructions for box 12 Code

13 Statutory employee ☐ Retirement plan ☐ Third-party sick pay ☐

12b Code

14 Other

12c Code

12d Code

f Employee's address and ZIP code

15 State Employer's state ID number	16 State wages, tips, etc.	17 State income tax	18 Local wages, tips, etc.	19 Local income tax	20 Locality name

Form **W-2** **Wage and Tax Statement** **20--**

Department of the Treasury—Internal Revenue Service

For Privacy Act and Paperwork Reduction Act Notice, see back of Copy D.

Copy A For Social Security Administration — Send this entire page with Form W-3 to the Social Security Administration; photocopies are **not** acceptable.

Cat. No. 10134D

Do Not Cut, Fold, or Staple Forms on This Page — Do Not Cut, Fold, or Staple Forms on This Page

Transaction No. 39

DO NOT STAPLE OR FOLD

33333	a Control number	**For Official Use Only ▶** **OMB No. 1545-0008**

b **Kind of Payer** ▶ 941 ☐ Military ☐ 943 ☐ 944 ☐ CT-1 ☐ Hshld. emp. ☐ Medicare govt. emp. ☐ **Third-party sick pay** ☐

1 Wages, tips, other compensation	2 Federal income tax withheld
3 Social security wages	4 Social security tax withheld
5 Medicare wages and tips	6 Medicare tax withheld
7 Social security tips	8 Allocated tips
9 Advance EIC payments	10 Dependent care benefits
11 Nonqualified plans	12 Deferred compensation
13 For third-party sick pay use only	
14 Income tax withheld by payer of third-party sick pay	

c Total number of Forms W-2

d Establishment number

e Employer identification number (EIN)

f Employer's name

g Employer's address and ZIP code

h Other EIN used this year

15 State	Employer's state ID number	16 State wages, tips, etc.	17 State income tax
		18 Local wages, tips, etc.	19 Local income tax
Contact person		Telephone number ( )	For Official Use Only
Email address		Fax number ( )	

Under penalties of perjury, I declare that I have examined this return and accompanying documents, and, to the best of my knowledge and belief, they are true, correct, and complete.

Signature ▶ Title ▶ Date ▶

Form **W-3 Transmittal of Wage and Tax Statements** 20--

Department of the Treasury Internal Revenue Service

Transaction No. 40

REV-1667 R AS (01-04)
PA DEPARTMENT OF REVENUE

YEAR: 2 0 - -   EMPLOYER ACCOUNT ID: 3 1 - 0 4 5 0 6 6 0   ENTITY ID (EIN): 1 0 0 9 - 5 5 5 5

Part I W-2 RECONCILIATION

1a	Number of W-2 forms attached	
1b	Number of W-2(s) reported on magnetic tape(s)	
1c	Number of 1099 forms with PA withholding tax	
1d	Add 1a, 1b, & 1c. Enter total here.	
2	Total compensation subject to PA withholding tax	$
3	PA INCOME TAX WITHHELD	$

Part II ANNUAL RECONCILIATION

	Wages paid subject to PA withholding tax	PA tax withheld
1st Quarter		
2nd Quarter		
3rd Quarter		
4th Quarter		
TOTAL		

W-2 TRANSMITTAL

DUE DATE JANUARY 31

Part III FOR TAPE REPORTING

NUMBER OF TAPES		DENSITY	
TRACKS		PARITY	

BUSINESS NAME AND ADDRESS

GLO-BRITE PAINT COMPANY
LEGAL NAME

TRADE NAME
2215 SALVADOR STREET
ADDRESS
PHILADELPHIA, PA 19175-0682
CITY STATE ZIP

DO NOT SEND PAYMENT WITH THIS FORM.

Attach adding machine tape(s) or some acceptable listing of tax withheld as reported on accompanying paper W-2 form(s) to substantiate reported PA withholding tax. This tape or listing applies only to paper W-2(s), **not** magnetic media reporting.

00022 | DATE | DAYTIME TELEPHONE # ( ) | EXT. | TITLE | SIGNATURE

Transaction No. 41

9595 ☐ VOID ☐ CORRECTED

PAYER'S name, street address, city, state, ZIP code, and telephone no.	1 Rents $ / 2 Royalties $	OMB No. 1545-0115 20-- Form 1099-MISC	**Miscellaneous Income**
	3 Other income $	4 Federal income tax withheld $	**Copy A For Internal Revenue Service Center** File with Form 1096.
PAYER'S federal identification number / RECIPIENT'S identification number	5 Fishing boat proceeds $	6 Medical and health care payments $	
RECIPIENT'S name	7 Nonemployee compensation $	8 Substitute payments in lieu of dividends or interest $	For Privacy Act and Paperwork Reduction Act Notice, see the **2006 General Instructions for Forms 1099, 1098, 5498, and W-2G.**
Street address (including apt. no.)	9 Payer made direct sales of $5,000 or more of consumer products to a buyer (recipient) for resale ▶ ☐	10 Crop insurance proceeds $	
City, state, and ZIP code	11	12	
Account number (see instructions) / 2nd TIN not. ☐	13 Excess golden parachute payments $	14 Gross proceeds paid to an attorney $	
15a Section 409A deferrals $ / 15b Section 409A income $	16 State tax withheld $ $	17 State/Payer's state no.	18 State income $ $

Form **1099-MISC** Department of the Treasury - Internal Revenue Service

Transaction No. 42

Do Not Staple 6969

Form **1096** Department of the Treasury Internal Revenue Service

Annual Summary and Transmittal of U.S. Information Returns

OMB No. 1545-0108 20--

FILER'S name

Street address (including room or suite number)

City, state, and ZIP code

Name of person to contact	Telephone number ( )	**For Official Use Only**
Email address	Fax number ( )	

1 Employer identification number	2 Social security number	3 Total number of forms	4 Federal income tax withheld $	5 Total amount reported with this Form 1096 $

Enter an "X" in only one box below to indicate the type of form being filed. If this is your **final return**, enter an "X" here . . . ▶ ☐

W-2G 32	1098 81	1098-C 78	1098-E 84	1098-T 83	1099-A 80	1099-B 79	1099-C 85	1099-CAP 73	1099-DIV 91	1099-G 86	1099-H 71	1099-INT 92	1099-LTC 93
☐	☐	☐	☐	☐	☐	☐	☐	☐	☐	☐	☐	☐	☐
1099-MISC 95	1099-OID 96	1099-PATR 97	1099-Q 31	1099-R 98	1099-S 75	1099-SA 94	5498 28	5498-ESA 72	5498-SA 27				
☐	☐	☐	☐	☐	☐	☐	☐	☐	☐				

Return this entire page to the Internal Revenue Service. Photocopies are not acceptable.

Under penalties of perjury, I declare that I have examined this return and accompanying documents, and, to the best of my knowledge and belief, they are true, correct, and complete.

Signature ▶ **Title ▶** **Date ▶**

APPENDIX A

The introduction to Appendix A has been renamed "Computerized Payroll Accounting User's Guide" and is available on the Bieg 2008 product Web site: http://www.thomsonedu.com/accounting/bieg.

This edition of *Payroll Accounting* contains two different options for the student solution: the complete, full version of the Payroll Project (which follows) and a short version. Both versions are identical except the short version requires only the completion of the December payrolls (as well as the last quarter and annual tax reports and forms). The short version's step-by-step instructions begin on page A-16 of this appendix. Be sure to ask your instructor which of the two versions you are to complete.

Payroll Project

The Payroll Project that follows is the computerized version of the same project you completed manually in Chapter 7 beginning on page 7-9 of this text. In this project, you are employed by Glo-Brite Paint Company as the person in the Accounting Department responsible for the company's payroll processing using the computerized payroll system described in the preceding material.

Like the manual project in Chapter 7, you will assume that the payroll records, tax reports, and deposits have been completed and filed for the first three quarters of this year. Your work will involve the computer processing of the payrolls for the last quarter of the year and the completion of the last quarter and annual tax reports and forms. You may complete the required deposit, quarterly, yearly, etc., forms described in Chapter 7. If you have already completed these forms for the manual student project, check them as you progress through this project and note any differences.

To help you get started, the first pay period is provided as a tutorial problem that illustrates the principles and procedures required to process payroll transactions using the *Integrated Accounting for Payroll* software. In subsequent pay period processing, whenever a new operational procedure is used for the first time, additional instructions will be provided. Each of the step-by-step instructions below lists a task to be completed at the computer. If you need additional explanation for the task, a page reference is provided from the "Computerized Payroll Accounting User's Guide" via the http://www.thomsonedu.com/accounting/bieg Web site.

Note: Throughout this project, some of the computer-calculated withholding amounts (e.g., Federal Income Tax) will differ slightly from the amounts (from the tax tables) in the manual Payroll Project in Chapter 7. This occurs because the computer uses the annualized method to compute withholding taxes. Also, one- to two-cent differences will occur throughout the solutions because of rounding differences.

October 9 Payroll

Step 1: Remove the Student Project Audit Test found on page A-29. Answer the questions for the October 9 payroll as you complete processing for the pay period.

See User's Guide online.

Step 2: Start up the *Integrated Accounting for Payroll* software (page UG-2).

Step 3: Load the opening balances template file, PAYROLL FILE (Page UG-3).
Pull down the File menu and choose the Open menu command. Select PAYROLL FILE from the File list box and click on OK.

Step 4: Enter your name in the User Name text box and click on OK.

Step 5: Enter the employee maintenance data (page UG-12).
Click on the *Accts.* toolbar button. Select employee number 180 (Student), key your name in the Name field (enter your last name in all capital letters similar to the other employees), and then click on the Change Employee command button.

Note: Do not change any of the other fields. If you do, your solutions will not be correct.

Step 6: **Enter the Payroll transactions. *Do not* deduct Group Ins.—*do* deduct Union Dues for the appropriate employees—*do not* deduct Simple Plan (which is the same as Simple Contributions Payable) (page UG-12).**
Click on the *Payroll* toolbar button. Click on the Deductions button. When the Voluntary Deductions dialog box appears, select only the Union Dues deduction, and then click on OK. Enter the payroll transaction data provided below on the blank line at the bottom of the cell grid (the existing data are beginning balances and should *not* be altered). Have the computer calculate taxes. The Voluntary Deductions dialog box will appear again while entering the first employee's data to let you verify that only the Union Dues deduction has been selected (this will occur whenever the date entered in the Date field is changed).

Note: It is very important that you enter the correct date (10/09/--) when entering the payroll transactions. Payroll processing is date sensitive and will accumulate and display incorrectly if the dates are entered incorrectly. Also, be sure to enter the correct Union Dues ($8.00) for the two appropriate employees. (The $72.00 amounts that are shown are carried over from the opening balances.)

Employees to Be Paid This Pay Period

Employee Number	Employee Name	Salary/ Reg. Hrs.	Overtime @ Time 1½	Overtime @ Double	Group Ins.	Union Dues
100	Bonno, Anthony Victor	80				$8.00
110	Ferguson, James Claude	reg. salary				
120	Ford, Catherine Louise	reg. salary				
130	Mann, Dewey Wilson	reg. salary				
140	O'Neill, Joseph Tyler	reg. salary				
150	Russell, Virginia Aloise	reg. salary				
160	Ryan, Norman Allen	80				$8.00
170	Sokowski, Thomas James	reg. salary				
180	Student (your name)	reg. salary				
190	Williams, Ruth Virginia	reg. salary				

Step 7: **Display the employee list report (page UG-20).**
Click on the *Report* toolbar button. Choose the Payroll Reports option. Select the Employee List report, and then click on OK. The report is shown in Figure A–1. Verify the accuracy of the maintenance input and make any corrections via the Employees tab in the Account Maintenance window.

FIGURE A–1

Employee List Report

Glo-Brite Paint Company
Employee List
10/09/--

Emp. No.	Employee Name/Address	Soc. Sec./ Mar. Stat.	# Pay Periods	G.L. Acct.	Salary/ Rate
100	BONNO, Anthony Victor 694 Bristol Avenue Philadelphia, PA 19135-0617	537-10-3481 Married W/H 4	26	54	17.65
110	FERGUSON, James Claude 808 Sixth Street Philadelphia, PA 19106-0995	486-03-8645 Married W/H 5	26	53	2250.00

(Continued)

FIGURE A–1 *(Concluded)*

Employee List Report

Emp. No.	Employee Name/Address	Soc. Sec./ Mar. Stat.	# Pay Periods	G.L. Acct.	Salary/ Rate
120	FORD, Catherine Louise 18 Dundee Avenue Philadelphia, PA 19151-1919	213-09-4567 Single W/H 2	26	52	900.00
130	MANN, Dewey Wilson 3007 Bisque Drive Philadelphia, PA 19199-0718	282-37-9352 Married W/H 4	26	53	1350.00
140	O'NEILL, Joseph Tyler 2100 Broad Street Philadelphia, PA 19121-7189	897-04-1534 Married W/H 3	26	51	2307.69
150	RUSSELL, Virginia Aloise 8004 Dowling Road Philadelphia, PA 19135-9001	314-21-6337 Single W/H 1	26	52	690.00
160	RYAN, Norman Allen 7300 Harrison Street Philadelphia, PA 19124-6699	526-23-1233 Married W/H 4	26	54	18.00
170	SOKOWSKI, Thomas James 133 Cornwells Street Philadelphia, PA 19171-5718	662-04-8832 Married W/H 2	26	54	2050.00
180	STUDENT 7018 Erdrick Street Philadelphia, PA 19135-8517	555-55-5555 Single W/H 1	26	52	540.00
190	WILLIAMS, Ruth Virginia 9433 State Street Philadelphia, PA 19149-0819	518-30-6741 Single W/H 0	26	52	1223.08

FIGURE A–2

Payroll Report (Employee 100 and Summary)

Glo-Brite Paint Company
Payroll Report
10/09/--

			Current	Quarterly	Yearly
100-BONNO, Anthony Victor		Gross Pay	1412.00	1412.00	12734.00
54-Plant		FIT	58.12	58.12	868.12
Married	Acct. 54	SIT	43.35	43.35	390.94
W/H 4	537-10-3481	Soc. Sec.—OASDI	87.54	87.54	789.50
Pay Periods 26		Medicare—HI	20.47	20.47	184.64
Salary		CIT	60.15	60.15	542.47
Hourly Rate	17.65	Group Ins.			144.80
Reg. Hours	80.00	Union Dues	8.00	8.00	80.00
O.T. Hours		Simple Plan			
Check Number 672		Employee SUTA	1.27	1.27	11.46
Check Date	10/09/--	Net Pay	1133.10	1133.10	9722.07

(Continued)

FIGURE A–2 (Concluded)

Payroll Report (Employee 100 and Summary)

		Current	Quarterly	Yearly
Payroll Summary	Gross Pay	14162.77	14162.77	156387.34
	FIT	1045.78	1045.78	16962.78
	SIT	434.82	434.82	4801.11
	Soc. Sec.—OASDI	878.09	878.09	9696.01
	Medicare—HI	205.37	205.37	2267.64
	CIT	603.32	603.32	6662.09
	Group Ins.			930.40
	Union Dues	16.00	16.00	160.00
	Simple Plan			
	Employee SUTA	12.77	12.77	140.77
	Net Pay	10966.62	10966.62	114766.54

Step 8: Display the payroll report (page UG-20).
Make sure the Run Date is set to 10/09/--; then choose the Payroll Report option and click on OK. The payroll report for Employee 100; Bonno, Anthony Victor, followed by the payroll summary is shown in Figure A–2.

Step 9: Generate and post the journal entry for the current payroll (page UG-13).
Choose the Current Payroll Journal Entry menu item from the Options menu. Click Yes when asked if you want to generate the journal entry. When the entry appears in the Current Payroll Journal Entries dialog box, as shown in Figure A–3, click on Post. The journal entry will reappear, posted, in the general journal.

If your journal entries do not match those shown in Figure A–3, check your employee list and payroll report for keying errors, and make the necessary corrections. Return to the General Journal window, delete the incorrect entries, and generate new entries.

FIGURE A–3

Current Payroll Journal Entry

Current Payroll Journal Entries

Acct. #	Account Title	Debit	Credit
54	Plant Wages	4902.00	
53	Sales Salaries	3600.00	
52	Office Salaries	3353.08	
51	Administrative Salaries	2307.69	
24	Employees FIT Payable		1045.78
25	Employees SIT Payable		434.82
20.1	FICA Taxes Payable--OASDI		878.09
20.2	FICA Taxes Payable--HI		205.37
26	Employees CIT Payable		603.32
28	Union Dues Payable		16.00
25.1	Employees SUTA Payable		12.77
12	Payroll Cash		10966.62

Post   Cancel   Help

Step 10: Generate and post the employer's payroll taxes journal entry (page UG-11). With the General Journal window still displayed, choose Employer's Payroll Taxes from the Options menu. Click Yes when asked if you want to generate the journal entry. When the entries appear in the Payroll Taxes Journal Entries dialog box shown in Figure A–4, click on Post. The journal entries will reappear, posted, in the general journal.

Step 11: Enter and post the October 9 general journal entry to record the deposit of cash for the total net amount owed to employees in the payroll cash account (page UG-16). Click on the *Journal* toolbar button. When the General Journal tab appears, enter the journal entry illustrated in Figure A–5. Be sure to enter a reference of General to indicate that the entry was entered manually in the general journal.

FIGURE A–4

Employer's Payroll Taxes Journal Entry

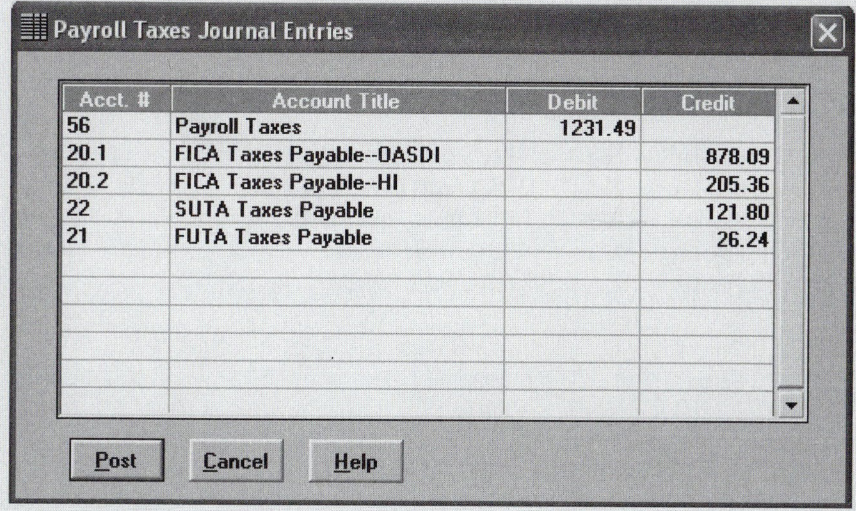

Acct. #	Account Title	Debit	Credit
56	Payroll Taxes	1231.49	
20.1	FICA Taxes Payable--OASDI		878.09
20.2	FICA Taxes Payable--HI		205.36
22	SUTA Taxes Payable		121.80
21	FUTA Taxes Payable		26.24

FIGURE A–5

General Journal Entry to Record Payroll Cash

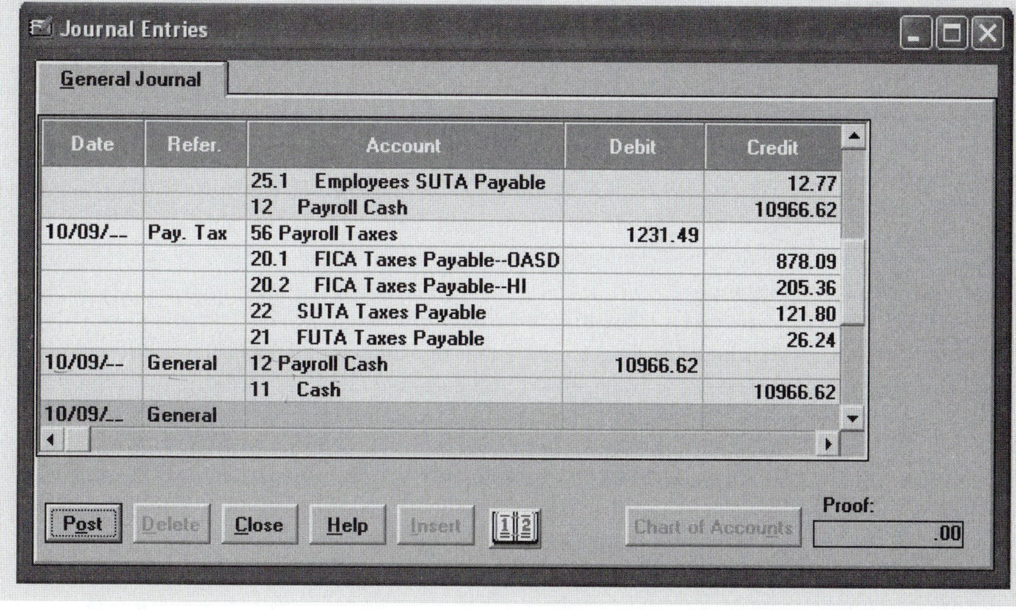

Date	Refer.	Account	Debit	Credit
		25.1 Employees SUTA Payable		12.77
		12 Payroll Cash		10966.62
10/09/--	Pay. Tax	56 Payroll Taxes	1231.49	
		20.1 FICA Taxes Payable--OASD		878.09
		20.2 FICA Taxes Payable--HI		205.36
		22 SUTA Taxes Payable		121.80
		21 FUTA Taxes Payable		26.24
10/09/--	General	12 Payroll Cash	10966.62	
		11 Cash		10966.62
10/09/--	General			

FIGURE A–6

General Journal Report

Glo-Brite Paint Company
General Journal
10/09/--

Date	Refer.	Acct.	Title	Debit	Credit
10/09	Payroll	54	Plant Wages	4902.00	
10/09	Payroll	53	Sales Salaries	3600.00	
10/09	Payroll	52	Office Salaries	3353.08	
10/09	Payroll	51	Administrative Salaries	2307.69	
10/09	Payroll	24	Employees FIT Payable		1045.78
10/09	Payroll	25	Employees SIT Payable		434.82
10/09	Payroll	20.1	FICA Taxes Payable—OASDI		878.09
10/09	Payroll	20.2	FICA Taxes Payable—HI		205.37
10/09	Payroll	26	Employees CIT Payable		603.32
10/09	Payroll	28	Union Dues Payable		16.00
10/09	Payroll	25.1	Employees SUTA Payable		12.77
10/09	Payroll	12	Payroll Cash		10966.62
10/09	Pay. Tax	56	Payroll Taxes	1231.49	
10/09	Pay. Tax	20.1	FICA Taxes Payable—OASDI		878.09
10/09	Pay. Tax	20.2	FICA Taxes Payable—HI		205.36
10/09	Pay. Tax	22	SUTA Taxes Payable		121.80
10/09	Pay. Tax	21	FUTA Taxes Payable		26.24
10/09	General	12	Payroll Cash	10966.62	
10/09	General	11	Cash		10966.62
			Totals	26360.88	26360.88

Step 12: Display the general journal report (page UG-20).
Click on the *Report* toolbar button. Choose the Journal option and the General Journal report, then click on OK. When the Journal Report Selection window appears, choose the Customize Journal Report option. Make sure the Start Date is set to 10/01/-- and the End Date to 10/09/-- (where -- is the current year), and then click on OK. *Note:* If the transactions were entered correctly, the start and end dates will be the default dates set automatically by the computer. The computer uses the first day of the month as the start date and the latest date of the general journal transactions that were entered as the end date. The General Journal report is shown in Figure A–6.

Step 13: Display the general ledger report (page UG-20).
Choose the Ledger Reports option and the General Ledger report, and then click on OK. When the Account Range dialog box appears, click on OK to accept the default range of all accounts. The General Ledger report is shown in Figure A–7.

Step 14: Generate a labor distribution graph (page UG-22).
Click on the *Graphs* toolbar button. Click on the Labor Distribution button to generate the graph shown in Figure A–8.

Step 15: Use the Save As command to save your data to disk (page UG-10).
Choose Save As from the File menu and save the file to your disk and folder with a file name of *10-09 your name* (where 10-09 is the pay period date).

Step 16: End the payroll accounting session (page UG-11).
Choose Exit from the File menu.

FIGURE A–7

General Ledger Report

Glo-Brite Paint Company
General Ledger
10/09/--

Account	Journal	Date Refer.	Debit	Credit	Balance
11-Cash					
	Balance Forward				199846.33Dr
	General	10/09 General		10966.62	188879.71Dr
12-Payroll Cash					
	General	10/09 Payroll		10966.62	10966.62Cr
	General	10/09 General	10966.62		.00
20.1-FICA Taxes Payable—OASDI					
	General	10/09 Payroll		878.09	878.09Cr
	General	10/09 Pay. Tax		878.09	1756.18Cr
20.2-FICA Taxes Payable—HI					
	General	10/09 Payroll		205.37	205.37Cr
	General	10/09 Pay. Tax		205.36	410.73Cr
21-FUTA Taxes Payable					
	General	10/09 Pay. Tax		26.24	26.24Cr
22-SUTA Taxes Payable					
	General	10/09 Pay. Tax		121.80	121.80Cr
24-Employees FIT Payable					
	General	10/09 Payroll		1045.78	1045.78Cr
25-Employees SIT Payable					
	General	10/09 Payroll		434.82	434.82Cr
25.1-Employees SUTA Payable					
	General	10/09 Payroll		12.77	12.77Cr
26-Employees CIT Payable					
	General	10/09 Payroll		603.32	603.32Cr
27-Grp. Ins. Prem. Collected					
	*** No Activity ***				.00
28-Union Dues Payable					
	General	10/09 Payroll		16.00	16.00Cr
29-Simple Contrib. Payable					
	*** No Activity ***				.00
51-Administrative Salaries					
	Balance Forward				42692.27Dr
	General	10/09 Payroll	2307.69		44999.96Dr
52-Office Salaries					
	Balance Forward				28350.00Dr
	General	10/09 Payroll	3353.08		31703.08Dr
53-Sales Salaries					
	Balance Forward				28525.00Dr
	General	10/09 Payroll	3600.00		32125.00Dr
54-Plant Wages					
	Balance Forward				42657.30Dr
	General	10/09 Payroll	4902.00		47559.30Dr
56-Payroll Taxes					
	Balance Forward				13906.21Dr
	General	10/09 Pay. Tax	1231.49		15137.70Dr

FIGURE A–8

Labor Distribution Graph

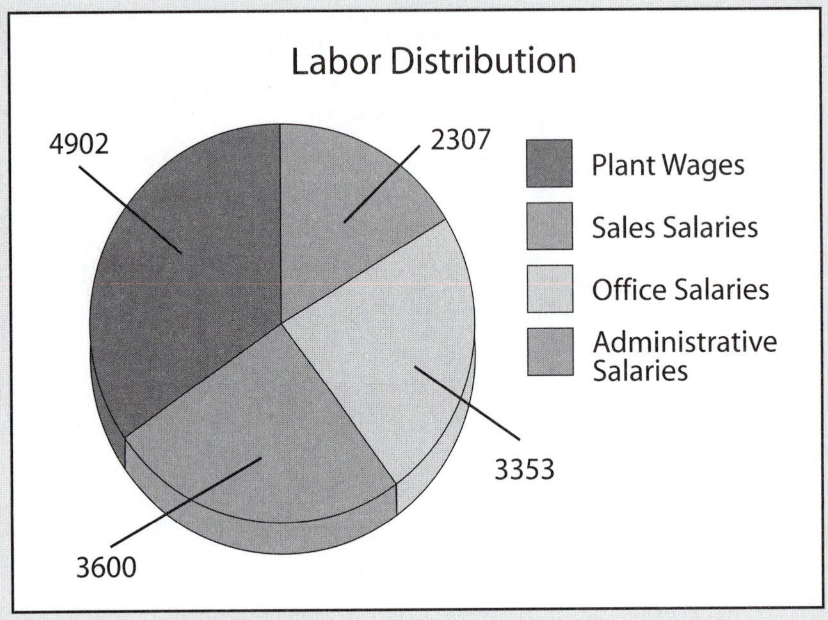

Note: If you are using this product as a distance or online course, and your instructor has provided you with his/her e-mail address, you may e-mail each of your pay period solution files as an e-mail attachment for electronic checking. Simply create an e-mail addressed to your instructor, identifying yourself as a payroll accounting student, and attach your completed pay period solution file (ex. file *10-09 your name*). Your instructor will electronically check your work and then send you a report of the results.

October 23 Payroll

The step-by-step instructions for completing the October 23 payroll (for the period ending October 17 are listed below).

Step 1: Answer the questions for the October 23 payroll on the Student Project Audit Test as you complete processing for the pay period.

Step 2: If you quit the software after processing the previous pay period, perform the following steps:
a. Start up the *Integrated Accounting for Payroll* software.
b. Load your file containing the last pay period data *(10-09 your name).*

Step 3: Enter and post the October 20 transaction required to record the deposit of the Pennsylvania state income taxes withheld from the October 9 payroll.

Step 4: Enter the following payroll transactions. *Do* deduct Group Ins.—*do* deduct Union Dues for the appropriate employees—*do not* deduct Simple Plan (which is the same as Simple Contributions Payable):
Note: Be sure to enter the correct Group Insurance amount for each employee (the amounts that appear are carried over from the opening balances). Also, since the union dues entered in the previous payroll are assumed by the computer to be the same for future pay periods, it will not be necessary to enter these

amounts again. However, it is a good idea to verify that they are the same as those in the payroll transactions below.

Employees to Be Paid This Pay Period

Employee Number	Employee Name	Salary/ Reg. Hrs.	Overtime @ Time 1½	Overtime @ Double	Group Ins.	Union Dues
100	Bonno, Anthony Victor	80	4		$16.50	$8.00
110	Ferguson, James Claude	reg. salary			$26.40	
120	Ford, Catherine Louise	reg. salary			$10.50	
130	Mann, Dewey Wilson	reg. salary			$15.90	
140	O'Neill, Joseph Tyler	reg. salary			$27.00	
150	Russell, Virginia Aloise	reg. salary			$8.10	
160	Ryan, Norman Allen	80	8		$16.80	$8.00
170	Sokowski, Thomas James	reg. salary			$24.00	
180	Student (your name)	reg. salary			$6.30	
190	Williams, Ruth Virginia	reg. salary			$14.40	

Step 5: Display the payroll report.
Step 6: Generate and post the journal entry for the current payroll.
Step 7: Generate and post the journal entry for the employer's payroll taxes.
Step 8: Enter and post the October 23 general journal entry to record the deposit of cash for the total net amount owed to employees in the payroll cash account.
Step 9: Display the journal report for 10/10/-- through 10/23/--.
Step 10: Display the general ledger report.
Step 11: Generate a labor distribution graph.
Note: The graph depicts the distribution of the gross amount of wages paid to each salaries expense account for the current month (sum of the data from the October 9 and October 23 payrolls).
Step 12: Use the Save As command to save the October 23 payroll to disk with a file name of *10-23 your name* (where 10-23 represents month 10, day 23).
Step 13: Proceed to the November 6 payroll. If necessary, end your payroll accounting session.

November 6 Payroll

The step-by-step instructions for completing the November 6 payroll (for the period ending October 31) are listed below.

Step 1: Answer the questions for the November 6 payroll on the Student Project Audit Test as you complete processing for the pay period.
Step 2: If you quit the software after processing the previous pay period, perform the following steps:
a. Start up the *Integrated Accounting for Payroll* software.
b. Load your file containing the last pay period data *(10-23 your name).*
Step 3: Enter and post the following transactions:
November 4: Deposited the Pennsylvania state income taxes withheld from the October 23 payroll.
November 6: Paid the treasurer of the union the amount of union dues withheld during the month of October.

Step 4: Enter the following employee maintenance:
Change Virginia Russell's number of withholding allowances to 2.
Change Thomas J. Sokowski's marital status to Single (his number of withholding allowances remains at 2).
Change Dewey Mann's number of withholding allowances to 0.

Step 5: Enter the following payroll transactions. *Do not* deduct Group Ins.—*do* deduct Union Dues for the appropriate employees—*do not* deduct Simple Plan (which is the same as Simple Contributions Payable). Verify that Group Insurance is not deducted and that Union Dues are deducted for the appropriate employees.
Note: Enter the amounts shown for Virginia Russell and Ruth Williams to override their regular salary amounts.

Employees to Be Paid This Pay Period

Employee Number	Employee Name	Salary/ Reg. Hrs.	Overtime @ Time 1½	Overtime @ Double	Group Ins.	Union Dues
100	Bonno, Anthony Victor	80				$8.00
110	Ferguson, James Claude	reg. salary				
120	Ford, Catherine Louise	reg. salary				
130	Mann, Dewey Wilson	reg. salary				
140	O'Neill, Joseph Tyler	reg. salary				
150	Russell, Virginia Aloise	$672.94 (loss of 2 hours)				
160	Ryan, Norman Allen	80				$8.00
170	Sokowski, Thomas James	reg. salary				
180	Student (your name)	reg. salary				
190	Williams, Ruth Virginia	$1,207.85 (loss of 1 hour)				

Step 6: Display an employee list report.
Step 7: Display the payroll report.
Step 8: Generate and post the journal entry for the current payroll.
Step 9: Generate and post the journal entry for the employer's payroll taxes.
Step 10: Enter and post the November 6 general journal entry to record the deposit of cash for the total net amount owed to employees in the payroll cash account.
Step 11: Display the journal report for 10/24/-- through 11/06/--.
Step 12: Display the general ledger report.
Step 13: Generate a labor distribution graph.
Step 14: Use the Save As command to save the November 6 payroll to disk with a file name of *11-06 your name* (where 11-06 represents month 11, day 06).
Step 15: Proceed to the November 13 payroll. If necessary, end your payroll accounting session.

November 13 Payroll

A special payroll needs to be run to process a discharged employee (Ruth Williams has been discharged because of her excessive tardiness and absenteeism). The step-by-step instructions for completing the November 13 special payroll are listed below.

Step 1: Answer the questions for the November 13 payroll on the Student Project Audit Test as you complete processing for the pay period.

Step 2: If you quit the software after processing the previous pay period, perform the following steps:
a. Start up the *Integrated Accounting for Payroll* software.
b. Load your file containing the last pay period data *(11-06 your name)*.

Step 3: Enter Ruth V. Williams's payroll transaction (*do* deduct Group Ins. of $14.40).
Enter $2,079.32 in her salary (two partial weeks of work ($856.24), plus two full weeks' pay ($1,223.08) in lieu of two weeks' notice for her final pay).

Step 4: Display the payroll report.

Step 5: Generate and post the journal entry for the current payroll.

Step 6: Generate and post the journal entry for the employer's payroll taxes.

Step 7: Enter and post the November 13 general journal entry to record the deposit of cash for the total net amount of Ruth Williams' pay in the payroll cash account.

Step 8: Display the journal report for 11/07/-- through 11/13/--.

Step 9: Display the general ledger report.

Step 10: Use the Save As command to save the November 13 payroll to disk with a file name of *11-13 your name* (where 11-13 represents month 11, day 13).

Step 11: Proceed to the November 20 payroll. If necessary, end your payroll session.

November 20 Payroll

The step-by-step instructions for completing the November 20 payroll (for the period ending November 14) follow.

Step 1: Answer the questions for the November 20 payroll on the Student Project Audit Test as you complete processing for the pay period.

Step 2: If you quit the software after processing the previous pay period, perform the following steps:
a. Start up the *Integrated Accounting for Payroll* software.
b. Load your file containing the last pay period data *(11-13 your name).*

Step 3: Enter and post the following transactions:
November 16: Deposited with City Bank the amount of FICA taxes and federal income taxes for the October payrolls.
Hint: Display the general ledger report to obtain these amounts from the FICA Taxes Payable—OASDI, FICA Taxes Payable—HI, and the Employees FIT payable account balances.
November 16: Deposited the city of Philadelphia employees withheld income tax ($1,220.36) with the Department of Revenue for the October payrolls (see the Employees CIT Payable account balance in the general ledger report).
November 18: Deposited the Pennsylvania state income taxes withheld from the November 6 and 13 (Ruth V. Williams) payrolls.

Step 4: Enter the following employee maintenance:
Add new employee: Employee number 200; WOODS, Beth Anne; 8102 Franklin Court, Philadelphia, PA 19105-0915; social security number, 724-03-1587; single, salaried, $1,200.00, number of pay periods per year, 26; withholding allowances, 1; Account No. 52 (Office Salaries).

Step 5: Enter the following payroll transactions. *Do* deduct Group Ins.—*do* deduct Union Dues for the appropriate employee—*do* deduct Simple Plan (which is the same as Simple Contributions Payable) for the appropriate employees. Verify that Group Insurance is deducted, that Union Dues are deducted, and that Simple Plan (Simple Contributions Payable) is deducted for the appropriate employees. *Note:* This is the first pay in which the company offers a savings incentive match plan. The computer software has been designed to use the key terms "Simple Plan" to instruct it to exclude this deduction from the employee's income for FIT purposes. The general ledger account Simple Contributions Payable is associated with this term for updating during payroll transaction processing.

Employees to Be Paid This Pay Period

Employee Number	Employee Name	Salary/ Reg. Hrs.	Overtime @ Time 1½	Overtime @ Double	Group Ins.	Union Dues	Simple Plan
100	Bonno, Anthony Victor	64			$16.50	$8.00	
110	Ferguson, James Claude	reg. salary			$26.40		$500.00
120	Ford, Catherine Louise	reg. salary			$10.50		
130	Mann, Dewey Wilson	reg. salary			$15.90		$250.00
140	O'Neill, Joseph Tyler	reg. salary			$27.00		$700.00
150	Russell, Virginia Aloise	$672.94 (loss of 2 hours)			$8.10		
160	Ryan, Norman Allen	80			$16.80	$8.00	$200.00
170	Sokowski, Thomas James	reg. salary			$24.00		
180	Student (your name)	reg. salary			$6.30		

Step 6: Display an employee list report.
Step 7: Display a payroll report.
Step 8: Generate and post the journal entry for the current payroll.
Step 9: Generate and post the journal entry for the employer's payroll taxes.
Step 10: Enter and post the November 20 general journal entry to record the deposit of cash for the total net amount owed to employees in the payroll cash account.
Step 11: Display the journal report for 11/14/-- through 11/20/--.
Step 12: Display the general ledger report.
Step 13: Generate a labor distribution graph.
Step 14: Use the Save As command to save the November 20 payroll to disk with a file name of *11-20 your name* (where 11-20 represents month 11, day 20).
Step 15: Proceed to the December 4 payroll. If necessary, end your payroll session.

December 4 Payroll

The step-by-step instructions for completing the December 4 payroll (for the week ending November 28) follow.

Step 1: Answer the questions for the December 4 payroll on the Student Project Audit Test as you complete the processing for the pay period.
Step 2: If you quit the software after processing the previous pay period, perform the following steps:
a. Start up the *Integrated Accounting for Payroll* software.
b. Load your file containing the last pay period data *(11-20 your name).*
Step 3: Enter and post the following transaction:
December 3: Deposited the Pennsylvania state income taxes withheld from the November 20 payroll.
Step 4: Enter the following employee maintenance:
Change Catherine L. Ford's salary amount to $960.00 because of a salary increase.
Change Virginia Russell's salary amount to $750.00 because of a salary increase.
Add new employee: Employee number 210; YOUNG, Paul Winston; 7936 Holmes Drive, Philadelphia, PA 19107-6107; social security number, 432-07-6057; single, salaried, $807.70, number of pay periods per year, 26; withholding allowances, 1; Account No. 53 (Sales Salaries).
Step 5: Enter the following payroll transactions. *Do not* deduct Group Ins.—*do* deduct Union Dues for the appropriate employees—*do* deduct Simple Plan for the appropriate employees.

Employees to Be Paid This Pay Period

Employee Number	Employee Name	Salary/ Reg. Hrs.	Overtime @ Time 1½	Overtime @ Double	Group Ins.	Union Dues	Simple Plan
100	Bonno, Anthony Victor	80		8		$8.00	
110	Ferguson, James Claude	reg. salary					$500.00
120	Ford, Catherine Louise	reg. salary					
130	Mann, Dewey Wilson	reg. salary					$250.00
140	O'Neill, Joseph Tyler	reg. salary					$700.00
150	Russell, Virginia Aloise	reg. salary					
160	Ryan, Norman Allen	76	3			$8.00	$200.00
170	Sokowski, Thomas James	reg. salary					
180	Student (your name)	reg. salary					
200	Woods, Beth Anne	$1,080.00 (first payroll)					

Step 6: Display an employee list report.
Step 7: Display a payroll report.
Step 8: Generate and post the journal entry for the current payroll.
Step 9: Generate and post the journal entry for the employer's payroll taxes.
Step 10: Enter and post the December 4 general journal entry to record the deposit of cash for the total net amount owed to employees in the payroll cash account.
Step 11: Display the journal report for 11/21/-- through 12/04/--.
Step 12: Display the general ledger report.
Step 13: Generate a labor distribution graph.
Step 14: Use the Save As command to save the December 4 payroll to disk with a file name of *12-04 your name* (where 12-04 represents month 12, day 04).
Step 15: Proceed to the December 14 payroll. If necessary, end your payroll session.

December 14 Payroll

A special payroll needs to be run to process the death of an employee (Virginia A. Russell). The step-by-step instructions for completing the December 14 special payroll follow.

Step 1: Answer the questions for the December 14 payroll on the Student Project Audit Test as you complete processing for the pay period.
Step 2: If you quit the software after processing the previous pay period, perform the following steps:
a. Start up the *Integrated Accounting for Payroll* software.
b. Load your file containing the last pay period data *(12-04 your name).*
Step 3: Enter and post the following transaction:
December 9: Paid the treasurer of the union the amount of union dues withheld during the month of November.
Step 4: Enter the employee maintenance:
Change Anthony V. Bonno's number of withholding allowances to 5.
Step 5: Pay Virginia A. Russell (pay will go to her estate). (*Do* deduct $8.70 for her Group Ins.)
Enter $1,425.16 in her salary amount, which is two partial weeks of work ($675.16) plus her accrued vacation pay ($750.00) for her final check.
Note: After clicking on the Calculate Taxes command button, remove the calculated withholding amounts for FIT, SIT, and CIT by keying zeros in these grid cells (final pay is not subject to these withholdings).
Step 6: Display an employee list report.
Step 7: Display a payroll report.
Step 8: Generate and post the journal entry for the current payroll.
Step 9: Generate and post the journal entry for the employer's payroll taxes.

Step 10: Enter and post the December 14 general journal entry to record the deposit of cash for Virginia A. Russell's net amount in the payroll cash account.

Step 11: Display the journal report for 12/05/-- through 12/14/--.

Step 12: Display the general ledger report.

Step 13: Use the Save As command to save the December 14 special payroll to disk with a file name of *12-14 your name* (where 12-14 represents month 12, day 14).

Step 14: Proceed to the December 18 payroll. If necessary, end your payroll session.

December 18 Payroll

The step-by-step instructions for completing the December 18 payroll (for the week ending December 12) follow.

Step 1: Answer the questions for the December 18 payroll on the Student Project Audit Test as you complete processing for the pay period.

Step 2: If you quit the software after processing the previous pay period, perform the following steps:
a. Start up the *Integrated Accounting for Payroll* software.
b. Load your file containing the last pay period data *(12-14 your name).*

Step 3: Enter and post the following transactions:
December 15: Deposited with City Bank the amount of FICA taxes and federal income taxes for the November payrolls.
December 15: Deposited the city of Philadelphia employees income tax withheld by the Department of Revenue from the November payrolls.
December 18: Deposited the Pennsylvania state income taxes withheld from the December 4 payroll.
December 18: Wrote check to Virginia Russell's estate from the regular cash account for the amount withheld from her December 14 pay for insurance.

Step 4: Enter the following employee maintenance:
Change: Employee number 140; O'Neill, Joseph Tyler withholding allowances to 4.
Add new employee: Employee number 220; ZIMMERMAN, Richard Lewis; 900 South Clark Street, Philadelphia, PA 19195-6247; social security number, 897-12-1502; married, salaried, $660.00, number of pay periods per year, 26; withholding allowances, 1; Account No. 52 (Office Salaries).

Step 5: Enter the following payroll transactions. *Do* deduct Group Ins.—*do* deduct Union Dues for the appropriate employees—*do* deduct Simple Plan for the appropriate employees.
Note: Be sure to enter the changes and amounts of Group Ins. deductions for the new employees and the $9.00 Union Dues, as noted below. Also, be sure to enter the change to Joseph O'Neill's Simple Plan deduction.

Employees to Be Paid This Pay Period

Employee Number	Employee Name	Salary/ Reg. Hrs.	Overtime @ Time ½	Overtime @ Double	Group Ins.	Union Dues	Simple Plan
100	Bonno, Anthony Victor	80		12	$16.50	$9.00	
110	Ferguson, James Claude	reg. salary			$26.40		$500.00
120	Ford, Catherine Louise	reg. salary			$11.10		
130	Mann, Dewey Wilson	reg. salary			$15.90		$250.00
140	O'Neill, Joseph Tyler	$52,307.69 (reg. salary + $50,000 bonus)			$27.00		$4,000.00
160	Ryan, Norman Allen	80	7		$16.80	$9.00	$200.00
170	Sokowski, Thomas James	reg. salary			$24.00		
180	Student (your name)	$533.25 (loss of 1 hour)			$6.30		
200	Woods, Beth Anne	reg. salary			$14.10		
210	Young, Paul Winston	reg. salary			$9.60		

Step 6: Display an employee list report.
Step 7: Display the payroll report.
Step 8: Generate and post the journal entry for the current payroll.
Step 9: Generate and post the journal entry for the employer's payroll taxes.
Step 10: Enter and post the December 18 general journal entry to record the deposit of cash for the total net amount owed to employees in the payroll cash account.
Step 11: Display the journal report for 12/15/-- through 12/18/--.
Step 12: Display the general ledger report.
Step 13: Generate a labor distribution graph.
Step 14: Use the Save As command to save the December 18 payroll to disk with a file name of *12-18 your name* (where 12-18 represents month 12, day 18).
Step 15: This completes the project insofar as recording and processing the computerized payroll transactions for the last quarter is concerned. Proceed to the Optional Activities. End your payroll session.

Stop

Optional Activities

This optional, clerical activity is provided to prepare the payroll file for the next calendar year and to follow the manual student project in Chapter 7. The transactions have been included to illustrate different types of transactions arising in connection with the accounting for payrolls and payroll taxes. The information contained in the computerized payroll reports may be referenced in order to complete the forms in this activity.

Step 1: Answer the questions for the additional transactions on the Student Project Audit Test as you complete the journal entries.
Step 2: If you quit the software after processing the previous pay period, perform the following steps:
a. Start up the *Integrated Accounting for Payroll* software.
b. Load your file containing the last pay period data (*12-18 your name*).
Step 3: Purge the payroll transactions (page UG-11).
Choose the Purge Payroll Transactions (Year-End) menu item from the Options menu. When the dialog box appears asking if you want to purge transactions and clear payroll for year-end, click on Yes.
Step 4: Enter the following employee maintenance:
Delete employee number 150 (Virginia A. Russell).
Delete employee number 190 (Ruth V. Williams).
Step 5: Use the Save As command to save the data to disk with a file name of *01-01 your name* (where 01-01 represents month 1, day 01).
Note: This is the payroll file that will be used to begin processing for the new year.
Prepare the various quarter-end and year-end payroll tax forms, and make the accrual entries for the payroll at the end of the year.
Step 6: Load your file containing the last pay period data *(12-18 your name).*
Step 7: Use the information contained in the payroll accounting reports to complete the following forms—if not completed in the student project in Chapter 7. If completed in Chapter 7, check the forms and note any differences. Refer to the February 1 narrative regarding the forms to be completed, on pages 7-22–7-23 in the manual student project in Chapter 7, if necessary.
a. Form 941, Employer's Quarterly Federal Tax Return.
b. Form 940, Employer's Annual Federal Unemployment (FUTA) Tax Return.
c. Form UC-2, Employer's Report for Unemployment Compensation—Fourth Quarter.
d. Form W-2, Wage and Tax Statement for each employee.
e. Form W-3, Transmittal of Wage and Tax Statements.
f. Pennsylvania Form REV1667, W-2 Transmittal.
g. Form 1099-MISC, Miscellaneous Income (for Virginia A. Russell).

h. Form 1096, Annual Summary and Transmittal of U.S. Information Returns.
i. Form PA-W3R, Employer Quarterly Reconciliation Return of Income Tax Withheld.
j. Annual Reconciliation of Wage Tax for Philadelphia.

Step 8: Enter and post the following transactions:

January 6: Deposited the Pennsylvania state income taxes withheld from the December 18 payroll.

January 8: Paid the treasurer of the union the amount of union dues withheld during the month of December.

January 15: Deposited with City Bank, the amount of FICA taxes and federal income taxes for the December payrolls.

January 15: Deposited the City of Philadelphia employees income tax withheld with the Department of Revenue from the December payrolls.

February 1: Deposited FUTA Taxes Payable for the quarter.

Hint: See the FUTA Taxes Payable account balance in the general ledger report.

February 1: Paid the SUTA Taxes Payable and Employees SUTA Payable for the fourth quarter.

Hint: See the SUTA Taxes Payable and the Employees SUTA Payable account balances in the general ledger report.

Step 9: Display the journal report for January 1 of the next year through February 1 of the next year.

Step 10: Use the Save As command to save your data to disk with a file name of *YR-END your name* (where YR-END represents the payroll file containing the accrual entries at the end of the year).

Step 11: End your computer session.

Payroll Project (Short Version)

The Payroll Project that follows is a computerized short version of the same project you completed manually in Chapter 7 beginning on page 7-9 of this text. In this project, you are employed by Glo-Brite Paint Company as the person in the Accounting Department responsible for the company's payroll processing using the computerized payroll system. However, unlike the Payroll Project in Chapter 7, you will only complete the payrolls for the month of December and the optional last quarter and year-end activities. The opening balance file you will use will already contain all the processing for the first two months of the quarter.

Your work will involve the computer processing of the payrolls for the last month of the year and the completion of the last quarter and annual tax reports and forms. You may complete the required deposit, quarterly, yearly, etc., forms described in Chapter 7. If you have already completed these forms for the manual student project, check them as you progress through this project and note any differences.

To help you get started, the first pay period of December is provided as a tutorial problem that illustrates the principles and procedures required to process payroll transactions using the *Integrated Accounting for Payroll* software. If you need additional explanation for the task, a page reference is provided from the "Computerized Payroll Accounting User's Guide" that can be accessed via the Web at http://www.thomsonedu.com/accounting/bieg.

Note: Throughout this project, some of the computer-calculated withholding amounts (e.g., Federal Income Tax) will differ slightly from the amounts (from the tax tables) in the manual Payroll Project in Chapter 7. This occurs because the computer uses the annualized method to compute withholding taxes. Also, one- to two-cent differences will occur throughout the solutions because of rounding differences.

December 4 Payroll

The step-by-step instructions for completing the December 4 payroll (for the week ending November 28) follow.

Step 1: **Remove the Student Project Audit Test found on page A-33. Answer the questions for the December 4 payroll as you complete the processing for the pay period.**

Step 2: **Start up the *Integrated Accounting for Payroll* software (page UG-2).**

Step 3: **Load the opening balances template file, PAYROLL FILE (SHORT VERSION) (page UG-3).**

Pull down the File menu and choose the Open menu command. Select PAYROLL FILE (SHORT VERSION) from the File list box and click on OK.

Step 4: **Enter your name in the User Name text box and click on OK.**

Step 5: **Enter the following employee maintenance (page UG-12):**

Click on the *Accts.* toolbar button. Select the employee to be changed, key the change, and click on the Change Employee command button. Repeat this procedure for each employee that requires a change. To enter the new employee, key all the employee's data at the bottom of the cell grids, and then click on the Add Employee command button.

Change Catherine L. Ford's salary amount to $960.00 because of a salary increase.

Change Virginia Russell's salary amount to $750.00 because of a salary increase.

Change employee number 180 (Student) to your name (Key your last name in all capital letters similar to the other employees).

Add new employee: Employee number 210; YOUNG, Paul Winston; 7936 Holmes Drive, Philadelphia, PA 19107-6107; social security number, 432-07-6057; single, salaried, $807.70, number of pay periods per year, 26; withholding allowances, 1; Account No. 53 (Sales Salaries).

Step 6: **Enter and post the December 3 journal entry to record the deposit for the Pennsylvania state income taxes withheld from the November 20 payroll (page UG-16).**

Click on the *Journal* toolbar button. When the General Journals tab appears, enter the journal entry illustrated in Figure A–9. Be sure to enter a reference of General to indicate that the entry was entered.

FIGURE A–9

Short Version—General Journal Entry to Record November State Income Tax Withheld

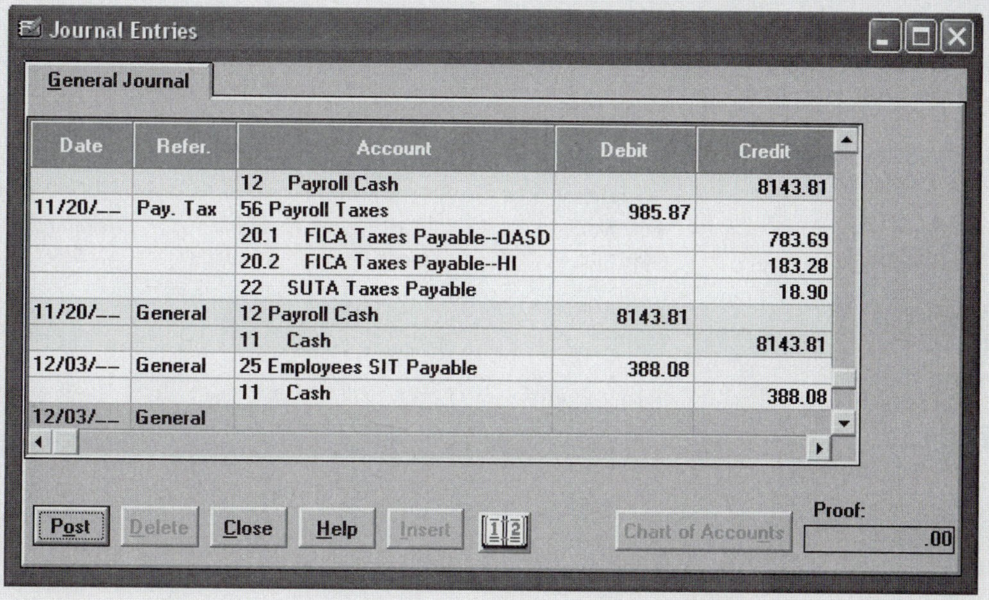

Step 7: Enter the following payroll transactions. *Do not* deduct Group Ins.—*do* deduct Union Dues for the appropriate employees—*do* deduct Simple Plan for the appropriate employees (page UG-12).

Click on the *Payroll* toolbar button. Click on the Deductions button. When the Voluntary Deductions dialog box appears, select only the Union Dues and the Simple Plan deductions, and then click on OK. Enter the payroll transaction data provided below on the blank line at the bottom of the cell grids (the existing data are beginning balances and should *not* be altered). Have the computer calculate taxes. The Voluntary Deductions dialog box will appear again while entering the first employee's data to let you verify that only the Union Dues deduction has been selected (this will occur whenever the date entered in the Date field is changed). *Note:* It is very important that you enter the correct date (12/04/--) when entering the payroll transactions. Payroll processing is date sensitive and will accumulate and display incorrectly if the dates are entered incorrectly.

Employees to Be Paid This Pay Period

Employee Number	Employee Name	Salary/ Reg. Hrs.	Overtime @ Time 1½	Overtime @ Double	Group Ins.	Union Dues	Simple Plan
100	Bonno, Anthony Victor	80		8		$8.00	
110	Ferguson, James Claude	reg. salary					$500.00
120	Ford, Catherine Louise	reg. salary					
130	Mann, Dewey Wilson	reg. salary					$250.00
140	O'Neill, Joseph Tyler	reg. salary					$700.00
150	Russell, Virginia Aloise	reg. salary					
160	Ryan, Norman Allen	76	3			$8.00	$200.00
170	Sokowski, Thomas James	reg. salary					
180	Student (your name)	reg. salary					
200	Woods, Beth Anne	$1,080.00 (first payroll)					

Step 8: Display an employee list report (page UG-20).

Click on the *Report* toolbar button. Choose the Payroll Reports option. Select the Employee List report, and then click on OK. The report is shown in Figure A–10. Verify the accuracy of the maintenance input and make any corrections via the Employees tab in the Account Maintenance window.

FIGURE A–10

Short Version—Employee List Report

Glo-Brite Paint Company
Employee List
12/04/--

Employee Number	Employee Name/Address	Soc. Sec./ Mar. Stat.	# Pay Periods	G.L. Acct.	Salary/ Rate
100	BONNO, Anthony Victor	537-10-3481	26	54	
	694 Bristol Avenue	Married			17.65
	Philadelphia, PA 19135-0617	W/H 4			
110	FERGUSON, James Claude	486-03-8645	26	53	2250.00
	808 Sixth Street	Married			
	Philadelphia, PA 19106-0995	W/H 5			
120	FORD, Catherine Louise	213-09-4567	26	52	960.00
	18 Dundee Avenue	Single			
	Philadelphia, PA 19151-1919	W/H 2			

(Continued)

FIGURE A–10 (Concluded)

Short Version—Employee List Report

Employee Number	Employee Name/Address	Soc. Sec./ Mar. Stat.	# Pay Periods	G.L. Acct.	Salary/ Rate
130	MANN, Dewey Wilson 3007 Bisque Drive Philadelphia, PA 19199-0718	282-37-9352 Married W/H 0	26	53	1350.00
140	O'NEILL, Joseph Tyler 2100 Broad Street Philadelphia, PA 19121-7189	897-04-1534 Married W/H 3	26	51	2307.69
150	RUSSELL, Virginia Aloise 8004 Dowling Road Philadelphia, PA 19135-9001	314-21-6337 Single W/H 2	26	52	750.00
160	RYAN, Norman Allen 7300 Harrison Street Philadelphia, PA 19124-6699	526-23-1233 Married W/H 4	26	54	18.00
170	SOKOWSKI, Thomas James 133 Cornwells Street Philadelphia, PA 19171-5718	662-04-8832 Single W/H 2	26	54	2050.00
180	STUDENT 7018 Erdrick Street Philadelphia, PA 19135-8517	555-55-5555 Single W/H 1	26	52	540.00
190	WILLIAMS, Ruth Virginia 9433 State Street Philadelphia, PA 19149-0819	518-30-6741 Single W/H 0	26	52	1223.08
200	WOODS, Beth Anne 8102 Franklin Court Philadelphia, PA 19105-0915	724-03-1587 Single W/H 1	26	52	1200.00
210	YOUNG, Paul Winston 7936 Holmes Drive Philadelphia, PA 19107-6107	432-07-6057 Single W/H 1	26	53	807.70

Step 9: Display a payroll report (page UG-20).
Make sure the Run Date is set to 12/04/--; then choose the Payroll Report option and click on OK. The payroll report for Employee 100; Bonno, Anthony Victor, followed by the payroll summary is shown in Figure A–11.

FIGURE A–11

Short Version—Payroll Report (Employee 100 and Summary)

Glo-Brite Paint Company
Employee List
12/04/--

			Current	Quarterly	Yearly
100-BONNO, Anthony Victor		Gross Pay	1694.40	7165.90	18487.90
54-Plant	FIT		100.03	319.70	1129.70
Married	Acct. 54	SIT	52.02	220.00	567.59
W/H 4	537-10-3481	Soc. Sec.--OASDI	105.05	444.28	1146.24
Pay Periods 26		Medicare—HI	24.57	103.90	268.07
Salary		CIT	72.18	305.26	787.58
Hourly Rate	17.65	Group Ins.		33.00	177.80

(Continued)

FIGURE A–11 (Concluded)

Short Version—Payroll Report (Employee 100 and Summary)

		Current	Quarterly	Yearly
Reg. Hours 80.00	Union Dues	8.00	40.00	112.00
O.T. Hours 8.00	Simple Plan			
Check Number 712	Employee SUTA	1.53	6.46	16.65
Check Date 12/04/--	Net Pay	1331.02	5693.30	14282.27
Payroll Summary	Gross Pay	14431.09	71928.56	214153.13
	FIT	978.30	5445.07	21362.07
	SIT	443.06	2208.33	6574.62
	Soc. Sec.—OASDI	894.73	4459.58	13277.50
	Medicare—HI	209.27	1043.03	3105.30
	CIT	614.77	3064.13	9122.90
	Group Ins.		331.80	1262.20
	Union Dues	16.00	80.00	224.00
	Simple Plan	1650.00	3300.00	3300.00
	Employee SUTA	13.01	64.87	192.87
	Net Pay	9611.95	51931.75	155731.67

Step 10: Generate and post the journal entry for the current payroll (page UG-11). Choose the Current Payroll Journal Entry menu item from the Options menu. Click Yes when asked if you want to generate the journal entry. When the entry appears in the Current Payroll Journal Entries dialog box, as shown in Figure A–12, click on Post. The journal entry will reappear, posted, in the general journal. If your journal entries do not match those shown in Figure A–12, check your employee list and payroll report for keying errors, and make the necessary corrections. Return to the General Journal window, delete the incorrect entries, and generate new entries.

FIGURE A–12

Short Version—Current Payroll Journal Entry

Current Payroll Journal Entries

Acct. #	Account Title	Debit	Credit
54	Plant Wages	5193.40	
53	Sales Salaries	3600.00	
52	Office Salaries	3330.00	
51	Administrative Salaries	2307.69	
24	Employees FIT Payable		978.30
25	Employees SIT Payable		443.06
20.1	FICA Taxes Payable--OASDI		894.73
20.2	FICA Taxes Payable--HI		209.27
26	Employees CIT Payable		614.77
28	Union Dues Payable		16.00
29	Simple Contrib. Payable		1650.00
25.1	Employees SUTA Payable		13.01
12	Payroll Cash		9611.95

Post Cancel Help

Step 11: Generate and post the journal entry for the employer's payroll taxes (page UG-11).

With the General Journal window still displayed, choose Employer's Payroll Taxes from the Options menu. Click Yes when asked if you want to generate the journal entry. When the entries appear in the Payroll Taxes Journal Entries dialog box shown in Figure A–13, click on Post. The journal entries will reappear.

FIGURE A–13

Short Version—Employer's Payroll Taxes Journal Entry

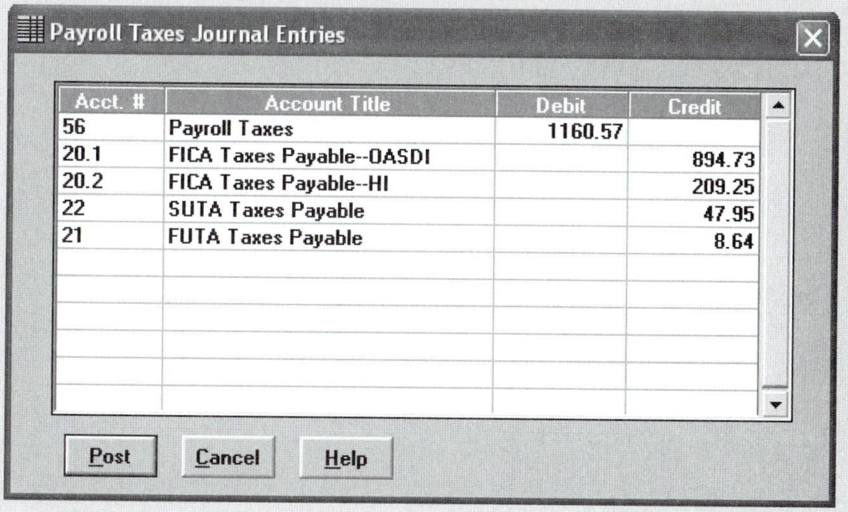

Acct. #	Account Title	Debit	Credit
56	Payroll Taxes	1160.57	
20.1	FICA Taxes Payable--OASDI		894.73
20.2	FICA Taxes Payable--HI		209.25
22	SUTA Taxes Payable		47.95
21	FUTA Taxes Payable		8.64

Step 12: Enter and post the December 4 general journal entry to record the deposit of cash for the total net amount owed to employees in the payroll cash account (page UG-16).

Click on the *Journal* toolbar button. When the General Journal tab appears, enter the journal entry illustrated in Figure A–14. Be sure to enter a reference of General to indicate that the entry was entered manually in the general journal.

FIGURE A–14

Short Version—General Journal Entry to Record Payroll Cash

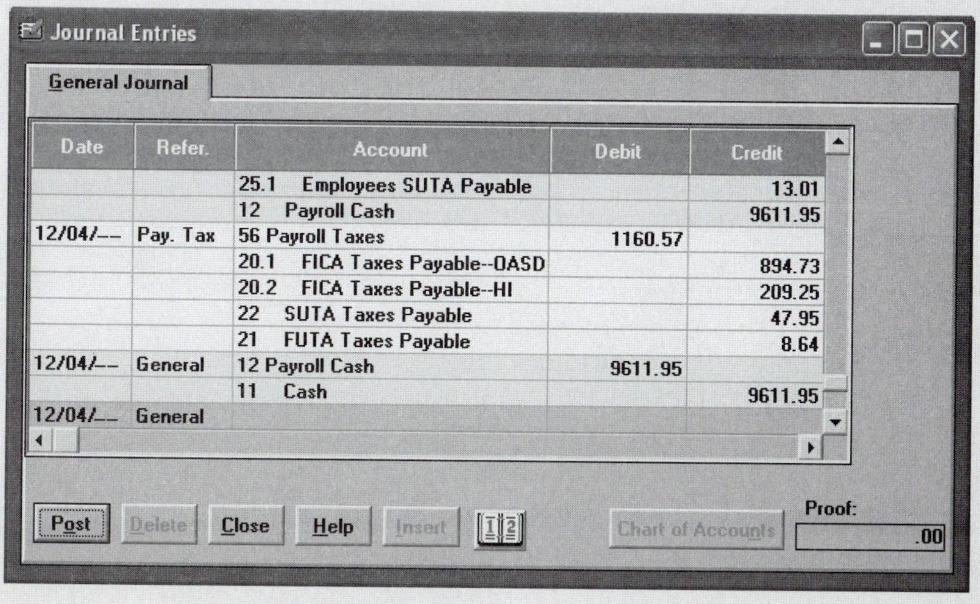

Date	Refer.	Account	Debit	Credit
		25.1 Employees SUTA Payable		13.01
		12 Payroll Cash		9611.95
12/04/––	Pay. Tax	56 Payroll Taxes	1160.57	
		20.1 FICA Taxes Payable--OASD		894.73
		20.2 FICA Taxes Payable--HI		209.25
		22 SUTA Taxes Payable		47.95
		21 FUTA Taxes Payable		8.64
12/04/––	General	12 Payroll Cash	9611.95	
		11 Cash		9611.95
12/04/––	General			

Step 13: Display the journal report for 11/21/-- through 12/04/-- (page UG-20).
Click on the *Report* toolbar button. Choose the Journal option and the General Journal report, and then click on OK. When the Journal Report Selection window appears, choose the Customize Journal Report option. Make sure the Start Date is set to 11/21/-- and the End Date to 12/04/-- (where -- is the current year), and then click on OK. The general journal report is shown in Figure A–15.

FIGURE A–15

Short Version—General Journal Report

Glo-Brite Paint Company
General Journal
12/04/--

Date	Refer.	Acct.	Title	Debit	Credit
12/03	General	25	Employees SIT Payable	388.08	
12/03	General	11	Cash		388.08
12/04	Payroll	54	Plant Wages	5193.40	
12/04	Payroll	53	Sales Salaries	3600.00	
12/04	Payroll	52	Office Salaries	3330.00	
12/04	Payroll	51	Administrative Salaries	2307.69	
12/04	Payroll	24	Employees FIT Payable		978.30
12/04	Payroll	25	Employees SIT Payable		443.06
12/04	Payroll	20.1	FICA Taxes Payable—OASDI		894.73
12/04	Payroll	20.2	FICA Taxes Payable—HI		209.27
12/04	Payroll	26	Employees CIT Payable		614.77
12/04	Payroll	28	Union Dues Payable		16.00
12/04	Payroll	29	Simple Contrib. Payable		1650.00
12/04	Payroll	25.1	Employees SUTA Payable		13.01
12/04	Payroll	12	Payroll Cash		9611.95
12/04	Pay. Tax	56	Payroll Taxes	1160.57	
12/04	Pay. Tax	20.1	FICA Taxes Payable—OASDI		894.73
12/04	Pay. Tax	20.2	FICA Taxes Payable—HI		209.25
12/04	Pay. Tax	22	SUTA Taxes Payable		47.95
12/04	Pay. Tax	21	FUTA Taxes Payable		8.64
12/04	General	12	Payroll Cash	9611.95	
12/04	General	11	Cash		9611.95
			Totals	25591.69	25591.69

Step 14: Display the general ledger report (page UG-20).
Choose the Ledger Reports option and the General Ledger report, and then click on OK. When the Account Range dialog box appears, click on OK to accept the default range of all accounts. A partial general ledger report is shown in Figure A–16.

FIGURE A–16

Short Version—Partial General Ledger Report

Glo-Brite Paint Company
General Ledger
12/04/--

Account	Journal	Date Refer.	Debit	Credit	Balance
11-Cash					
	Balance Forward				199846.33Dr
	General	10/09 General		10966.62	188879.71Dr

(Continued)

FIGURE A–16 *(Concluded)*

Short Version—Partial General Ledger Report

Account	Journal	Date Refer.	Debit	Credit	Balance
	General	10/20 General		434.82	188444.89Dr
	General	10/23 General		11026.27	177418.62Dr
	General	11/04 General		444.70	176973.92Dr
	General	11/06 General		32.00	176941.92Dr
	General	11/06 General		10792.79	166149.13Dr
	General	11/13 General		1390.31	164758.82Dr
	General	11/16 General		6522.47	158236.35Dr
	General	11/16 General		1220.36	157015.99Dr
	General	11/18 General		497.67	156518.32Dr
	General	11/20 General		8143.81	148374.51Dr
	General	12/03 General		388.08	147986.43Dr
	General	12/04 General		9611.95	138374.48Dr
12-Payroll Cash					
	General	10/09 Payroll		10966.62	10966.62Cr
	General	10/09 General	10966.62		.00
	General	10/23 Payroll		11026.27	11026.27Cr
	General	10/23 General	11026.27		.00
	General	11/06 Payroll		10792.79	10792.79Cr
	General	11/06 General	10792.79		.00
	General	11/13 Payroll		1390.31	1390.31Cr
	General	11/13 General	1390.31		.00
	General	11/20 Payroll		8143.81	8143.81Cr
	General	11/20 General	8143.81		.00
	General	12/04 Payroll		9611.95	9611.95Cr
	General	12/04 General	9611.95		.00
54-Plant Wages					
	Balance Forward				42657.30Dr
	General	10/09 Payroll	4902.00		47559.30Dr
	General	10/23 Payroll	5223.90		52783.20Dr
	General	11/06 Payroll	4902.00		57685.20Dr
	General	11/20 Payroll	4619.60		62304.80Dr
	General	12/04 Payroll	5193.40		67498.20Dr
56-Payroll Taxes					
	Balance Forward				13906.21Dr
	General	10/09 Pay. Tax	1231.49		15137.70Dr
	General	10/23 Pay. Tax	1229.76		16367.46Dr
	General	11/06 Pay. Tax	1116.14		17483.60Dr
	General	11/13 Pay. Tax	159.07		17642.67Dr
	General	11/20 Pay. Tax	985.87		18628.54Dr
	General	12/04 Pay. Tax	1160.57		19789.11Dr

Step 15: Generate a labor distribution graph (page UG-22).

Click on the *Graphs* toolbar button. Click on the Labor Distribution button to generate the graph shown in Figure A–17.

FIGURE A–17

Short Version—Labor Distribution Graph

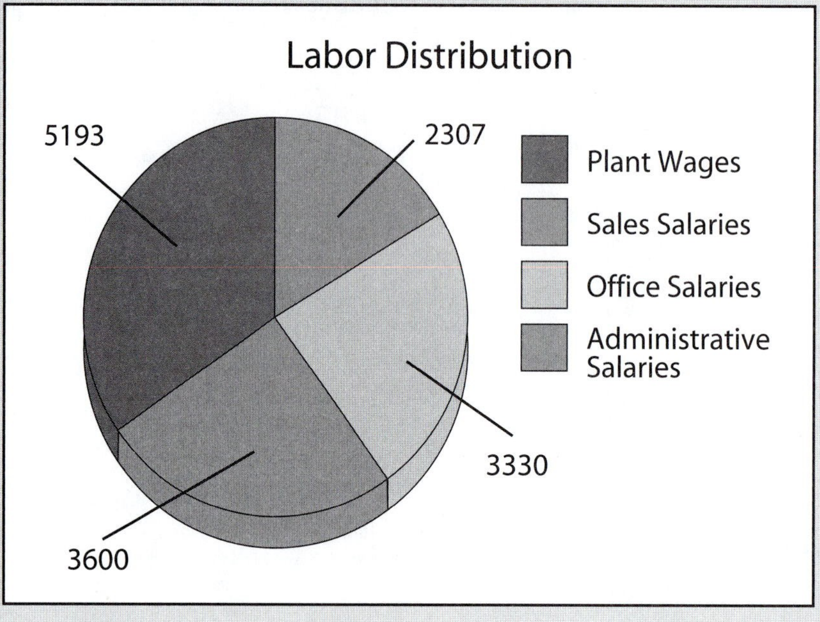

Step 16: **Use the Save As command to save the December 4 payroll to disk with a file name of *12-04 your name* (where 12-04 represents month 12, day 04) (page UG-10).**

Choose Save As from the File menu and save the file to your disk and folder with a file name of *12-04 your name* (where 12-04 is the pay period date).

Step 17: **Proceed to the December 14 payroll. If necessary, end your payroll session (page UG-11).**

Choose Exit from the File menu.

Note: If you are using this product as a distance or online course, and your instructor has provided you with his/her e-mail address, you may e-mail each of your pay period solution files as an e-mail attachment for electronic checking. Simply create an e-mail addressed to your instructor, identifying yourself as a payroll accounting student, and attach your completed pay period solution file (ex. file *10-09 your name*). Your instructor will electronically check your work and then send you a report of the results.

December 14 Payroll

A special payroll needs to be run to process the death of an employee (Virginia A. Russell). The step-by-step instructions for completing the December 14 special payroll follow.

Step 1: Answer the questions for the December 14 payroll on the Student Project Audit Test as you complete the processing for the pay period.

Step 2: If you quit the software after processing the previous pay period, perform the following steps:

a. Start up the *Integrated Accounting for Payroll* software.

b. Load your file containing the last pay period data *(12-04 your name).*

Step 3: Enter and post the following transaction:

December 9: Paid the treasurer of the union the amount of union dues withheld during the month of November.

Step 4: Enter the employee maintenance:
Change Anthony V. Bonno's number of withholding allowances to 5.

Step 5: Pay Virginia A. Russell (pay will go to her estate). (*Do* deduct $8.70 for her Group Ins.)
Enter $1,425.16 in her salary amount, which is two partial weeks of work ($675.16) plus her accrued vacation pay ($750.00) for her final check.
Note: After clicking on the Calculate Taxes command button, remove the calculated withholding amounts for FIT, SIT, and CIT by keying zeros in these grid cells (final pay is not subject to these withholdings).

Step 6: Display an employee list report.

Step 7: Display a payroll report.

Step 8: Generate and post the journal entry for the current payroll.

Step 9: Generate and post the journal entry for the employer's payroll taxes.

Step 10: Enter and post the December 14 general journal entry to record the deposit of cash for Virginia A. Russell's net amount in the payroll cash account.

Step 11: Display the journal report for 12/05/-- through 12/14/--.

Step 12: Display the general ledger report.

Step 13: Use the Save As command to save the December 14 special payroll to disk with a file name of *12-14 your name* (where 12-14 represents month 12, day 14).

Step 14: Proceed to the December 18 payroll. If necessary, end your payroll session.

December 18 Payroll

The step-by-step instructions for completing the December 18 payroll (for the week ending December 12) follow.

Step 1: Answer the questions for the December 18 payroll on the Student Project Audit Test as you complete processing for the pay period.

Step 2: If you quit the software after processing the previous pay period, perform the following steps:
a. Start up the *Integrated Accounting for Payroll* software.
b. Load your file containing the last pay period data *(12-14 your name).*

Step 3: Enter and post the following transactions:
December 15: Deposited with City Bank the amount of FICA taxes and federal income taxes for the November payrolls.
December 15: Deposited the City of Philadelphia employees income tax withheld by the Department of Revenue from the November payrolls.
December 18: Deposited the Pennsylvania state income taxes withheld from the December 4 payroll.
December 18: Wrote check to Virginia Russell's estate from the regular cash account for the amount withheld from her December 14 pay for insurance.

Step 4: Enter the following employee maintenance:
Change: Employee number 140; O'Neill, Joseph Tyler withholding allowances to 4.
Add new employee: Employee number 220; ZIMMERMAN, Richard Lewis; 900 South Clark Street, Philadelphia, PA 19195-6247; social security number, 897-12-1502; married, salaried, $660.00, number of pay periods per year, 26; withholding allowances, 1; Account No. 52 (Office Salaries).

Step 5: Enter the following payroll transactions. *Do* deduct Group Ins.—*do* deduct Union Dues for the appropriate employees—*do* deduct Simple Plan for the appropriate employees.
Note: Be sure to enter the changes and amounts of Group Ins. deductions for the new employees and the $9.00 Union Dues, as noted below. Also, be sure to enter the change to Joseph O'Neill's Simple Plan deduction.

Employees to Be Paid This Pay Period

Employee Number	Employee Name	Salary/ Reg. Hrs.	Overtime @ Time ½	Overtime @ Double	Group Ins.	Union Dues	Simple Plan
100	Bonno, Anthony Victor	80		12	$16.50	$9.00	
110	Ferguson, James Claude	reg. salary			$26.40		$500.00
120	Ford, Catherine Louise	reg. salary			$11.10		
130	Mann, Dewey Wilson	reg. salary			$15.90		$250.00
140	O'Neill, Joseph Tyler	$52,307.69 (reg. salary + $50,000 bonus)			$27.00		$4,000.00
160	Ryan, Norman Allen	80	7		$16.80	$9.00	$200.00
170	Sokowski, Thomas James	reg. salary			$24.00		
180	Student (your name)	$533.25 (loss of 1 hour)			$6.30		
200	Woods, Beth Anne	reg. salary			$14.10		
210	Young, Paul Winston	reg. salary			$9.60		

Step 6: Display an employee list report.
Step 7: Display the payroll report.
Step 8: Generate and post the journal entry for the current payroll.
Step 9: Generate and post the journal entry for the employer's payroll taxes.
Step 10: Enter and post the December 18 general journal entry to record the deposit of cash for the total net amount owed to employees in the payroll cash account.
Step 11: Display the journal report for 12/15/-- through 12/18/--.
Step 12: Display the general ledger report.
Step 13: Generate a labor distribution graph.
Step 14: Use the Save As command to save the December 18 payroll to disk with a file name of *12-18 your name* (where 12-18 represents month 12, day 18).
Step 15: This completes the project insofar as recording and processing the computerized payroll transactions for the last quarter is concerned. Proceed to the Optional Activities. End your payroll session.

Optional Activities

This optional, clerical activity is provided to prepare the payroll file for the next calendar year and to follow the manual student project in Chapter 7. The transactions have been included to illustrate different types of transactions arising in connection with the accounting for payrolls and payroll taxes. The information contained in the computerized payroll reports may be referenced in order to complete the forms in this activity.

Step 1: Answer the questions for the additional transactions on the Student Project Audit Test as you complete the journal entries.
Step 2: If you quit the software after processing the previous pay period, perform the following steps:
a. Start up the *Integrated Accounting for Payroll* software.
b. Load your file containing the last pay period data (*12-18 your name*).
Step 3: Purge the payroll transactions (page UG-11).
Choose the Purge Payroll Transactions (Year-End) menu item from the Options menu. When the dialog box appears asking if you want to purge transactions and clear payroll for year-end, click on Yes.
Step 4: Enter the following employee maintenance:
Delete employee number 150 (Virginia A. Russell).
Delete employee number 190 (Ruth V. Williams).
Step 5: Use the Save As command to save the data to disk with a file name of *01-01 your name* (where 01-01 represents month 1, day 01).

Note: This is the payroll file that will be used to begin processing for the new year.

Prepare the various quarter-end and year-end payroll tax forms, and make the accrual entries for the payroll at the end of the year.

Step 6: Load your file containing the last pay period data *(12-18 your name).*

Step 7: Use the information contained in the payroll accounting reports to complete the following forms—if not completed in the student project in Chapter 7. If completed in Chapter 7, check the forms and note any differences. Refer to the February 1 narrative regarding the forms to be completed, on pages 7-22–7-23 in the manual student project in Chapter 7, if necessary.

a. Form 941, Employer's Quarterly Federal Tax Return.
b. Form 940, Employer's Annual Federal Unemployment (FUTA) Tax Return.
c. Form UC-2, Employer's Report for Unemployment Compensation—Fourth Quarter.
d. Form W-2, Wage and Tax Statement for each employee.
e. Form W-3, Transmittal of Wage and Tax Statements.
f. Pennsylvania Form REV1667, W-2 Transmittal.
g. Form 1099-MISC, Miscellaneous Income (for Virginia A. Russell).
h. Form 1096, Annual Summary and Transmittal of U.S. Information Returns.
i. Form PA-W3R, Employer Quarterly Reconciliation Return of Income Tax Withheld.
j. Annual Reconciliation of Wage Tax for Philadelphia.

Step 8: Enter and post the following transactions:

January 6: Deposited the Pennsylvania state income taxes withheld from the December 18 payroll.

January 8: Paid the treasurer of the union the amount of union dues withheld during the month of December.

January 15: Deposited with City Bank, the amount of FICA taxes and federal income taxes for the December payrolls.

January 15: Deposited the City of Philadelphia employees income tax withheld with the Department of Revenue from the December payrolls.

February 1: Deposited FUTA Taxes Payable for the quarter.

Hint: See the FUTA Taxes Payable account balance in the general ledger report.

February 1: Paid the SUTA Taxes Payable and Employees SUTA Payable for the fourth quarter.

Hint: See the SUTA Taxes Payable and the Employees SUTA Payable account balances in the general ledger report.

Step 9: Display the journal report for January 1 of the next year through February 1 of the next year.

Step 10: Use the Save As command to save your data to disk with a file name of *YR-END your name* (where YR-END represents the payroll file containing the accrual entries at the end of the year).

Step 11: End your computer session.

Name ______________________

Student Project Audit Test

OCTOBER 9 PAYROLL: (Use the payroll file you saved under filename *10-09 your name* to answer the following questions for the October 9 payroll.)

Payroll Report

1. What is the number of withholding allowances for James C. Ferguson? . . . . ______
2. What is the current gross pay for Norman A. Ryan? . . . . ______
3. What is the amount of HI withheld for the current pay period for Ruth V. Williams? . . . . . ______
4. What is the total current net pay for all employees? . . . . ______
5. What is the total yearly SIT withheld for all employees? . . . . ______

Journal Entries Report

6. What is the amount of the debit to Office Salaries? . . . . ______
7. What is the amount of the debit to Payroll Taxes Expense? . . . . ______
8. What is the amount of the credit to Cash? . . . . ______

General Ledger

9. What is the Cash (account number 11) account balance? . . . . ______
10. What is the total Administrative Salaries paid to date? . . . . ______

Name ______________________

Student Project Audit Test

OCTOBER 23 PAYROLL: (Use the payroll file you saved under filename *10-23 your name* to answer the following questions for the October 23 payroll.)

Payroll Report

1. What is the current gross pay for Anthony V. Bonno? . . . . ______
2. What is the current amount of OASDI withheld for Catherine L. Ford? . . . . ______
3. What is the total current net pay for all employees? . . . . ______
4. What is the total quarterly gross pay for all employees? . . . . ______
5. What is the total current amount of group insurance withheld for all employees? . . . . ______

Journal Entries Report

6. What is the amount of the credit to Employees SIT Payable? . . . . ______
7. What is the amount of the debit to Payroll Taxes Expense? . . . . ______

General Ledger

8. What is the amount of FICA Taxes Payable—OASDI for the month of October? . . . . ______
9. What is the amount of Union Dues withheld for the employees for the month of October? ______

Name ____________________

Student Project Audit Test

NOVEMBER 6 PAYROLL: (Use the payroll file you saved under filename *11-06 your name* to answer the following questions for the November 6 payroll.)

Payroll Report

1. What is the current amount of FIT withheld for Joseph T. O'Neill? . . . . ____________
2. What is the total current gross pay for all employees? . . . . ____________
3. What is the total current amount of CIT withheld for all employees? . . . . ____________
4. What is the total current net pay for all employees? . . . . ____________

Journal Entries Report

5. What is the amount of the credit to FICA Taxes Payable—OASDI? . . . . ____________
6. What is the amount of the credit to FICA Taxes Payable—HI? . . . . ____________
7. What is the amount of the debit to Payroll Taxes Expense? . . . . ____________

General Ledger

8. What is the balance in the cash (account number 11) account? . . . . ____________
9. What is the amount of Sales Salaries paid to date? . . . . ____________

Name ____________________

Student Project Audit Test

NOVEMBER 13 PAYROLL: (Use the payroll file you saved under filename *11-13 your name* to answer the following questions for the special November 13 payroll.)

Payroll Report

1. What is the amount of FIT withheld for the year for Ruth V. Williams? . . . . ____________
2. What is Ruth V. Williams' current net pay? . . . . ____________
3. In what department did Ruth V. Williams work? . . . . ____________

Journal Entries Report

4. What is the amount of Ruth V. Williams' Group Insurance withheld? . . . . ____________

General Ledger

5. What is the total amount of Payroll Taxes (account number 56) to date? . . . . ____________

Name ______________________

Student Project Audit Test

NOVEMBER 20 PAYROLL: (Use the payroll file you saved under filename *11-20 your name* to answer the following questions for the November 20 payroll.)

Payroll Report

1. What is the amount of FIT withheld for the current pay period for Dewey W. Mann? . . . . ______
2. What is the total current net pay for all employees? . . . . ______
3. What is the total current gross pay for all employees? . . . . ______

Journal Entries Report

4. What is the November 20 payroll amount of the credit to Cash? . . . . ______
5. What is the amount of the debit to Payroll Taxes Expense? . . . . ______
6. What is the amount of the debit to Plant Wages? . . . . ______

General Ledger

7. What is the amount of Employees SIT Payable? . . . . ______
8. What is the amount of Office Salaries paid to date? . . . . ______
9. What is the amount of Simple Contributions Payable? . . . . ______

Name ______________________

Student Project Audit Test

DECEMBER 4 PAYROLL: (Use the payroll file you saved under filename *12-04 your name* to answer the following questions for the December 4 payroll.)

Payroll Report

1. What is the current gross pay for Joseph T. O'Neill? . . . . ______
2. What is the current amount of OASDI withheld for Norman A. Ryan? . . . . ______
3. What is the total current net pay for all employees? . . . . ______
4. What is the total current CIT withheld for all employees? . . . . ______

Journal Entries Report

5. What is the amount of the debit to Administrative Salaries? . . . . ______
6. What is the amount of the credit to Employees SIT Payable? . . . . ______
7. What is the amount of the debit to Payroll Taxes Expense? . . . . ______

General Ledger

8. What is the amount of SUTA Taxes Payable? . . . . ______
9. What is the amount of Sales Salaries? . . . . ______

Name ______________________

Student Project Audit Test

DECEMBER 14 PAYROLL: (Use the payroll file you saved under file name *12-14 your name* to answer the following questions for the special December 14 payroll.)

Payroll Report

1. What was Virginia A. Russell's social security number? .... ______
2. What was the amount of net pay received by Virginia A. Russell's estate? .... ______

Journal Entries Report

3. What is the amount of the debit to Office Salaries? ______

General Ledger

4. What is the amount that was credited to Group Insurance Premiums Collected (account number 27) during this period? .... ______
5. What is the amount paid to Office Salaries to date? .... ______

Name ______________________

Student Project Audit Test

DECEMBER 18 PAYROLL: (Use the payroll file you saved under file name *12-18 your name* to answer the following questions for the December 18 payroll.)

Payroll Report

1. What is the current amount of SIT withheld for Thomas J. Sokowski? .... ______
2. What is the total current net pay for all employees? .... ______
3. What is the total yearly gross pay for all employees? .... ______

Journal Entries Report

4. What is the amount of the debit to Administrative Salaries? .... ______
5. What is the amount of the debit to Payroll Taxes Expense? .... ______

General Ledger

6. What is the balance in the cash account? .... ______
7. What is the total amount of Plant Wages to date? .... ______
8. What is the total amount of Payroll Taxes to date? .... ______

Name ____________________

Student Project Audit Test

OPTIONAL ACTIVITIES: (Use the payroll file you saved under file name *YR-END your name* to answer the following questions.)

Journal Entries Report

1. What is the amount of the deposit for Pennsylvania state income taxes withheld from the December 18 payroll? . . . . ____________
2. What is the amount of Union Dues withheld during the month of December? . . . . ____________
3. What is the amount of FICA Taxes Payable—OASDI deposited from the December payrolls? . . . . ____________
4. What is the amount of the City of Philadelphia employees' income tax deposited from the December payrolls? . . . . ____________
5. What is the amount of FUTA Taxes Payable deposited for the quarter? . . . . ____________
6. What is the amount of SUTA Taxes Payable for the fourth quarter? . . . . ____________
7. What is the amount of Employee's SUTA Taxes Payable for the fourth quarter? . . . . ____________

The following tables were in effect during 2007.

TABLE OF ALLOWANCE VALUES

Payroll period	One withholding allowance
Weekly	$ 65.38
Biweekly	130.77
Semimonthly	141.67
Monthly	283.33
Quarterly	850.00
Semiannually	1,700.00
Annually	3,400.00
Daily or miscellaneous (each day of the payroll period)	13.08

Tables for Percentage Method of Withholding

(For Wages Paid in 2007)

TABLE 1—WEEKLY Payroll Period

(a) SINGLE person (including head of household)—

If the amount of wages (after subtracting withholding allowances) is:		The amount of income tax to withhold is:	
Not over $51		$0	
Over—	**But not over—**		**of excess over—**
$51	—$195	10%	—$51
$195	—$645	$14.40 plus 15%	—$195
$645	—$1,482	$81.90 plus 25%	—$645
$1,482	—$3,131	$291.15 plus 28%	—$1,482
$3,131	—$6,763	$752.87 plus 33%	—$3,131
$6,763		$1,951.43 plus 35%	—$6,763

(b) MARRIED person—

If the amount of wages (after subtracting withholding allowances) is:		The amount of income tax to withhold is:	
Not over $154		$0	
Over—	**But not over—**		**of excess over—**
$154	—$449	10%	—$154
$449	—$1,360	$29.50 plus 15%	—$449
$1,360	—$2,573	$166.15 plus 25%	—$1,360
$2,573	—$3,907	$469.40 plus 28%	—$2,573
$3,907	—$6,865	$842.92 plus 33%	—$3,907
$6,865		$1,819.06 plus 35%	—$6,865

TABLE 2—BIWEEKLY Payroll Period

(a) SINGLE person (including head of household)—

If the amount of wages (after subtracting withholding allowances) is:		The amount of income tax to withhold is:	
Not over $102		$0	
Over—	**But not over—**		**of excess over—**
$102	—$389	10%	—$102
$389	—$1,289	$28.70 plus 15%	—$389
$1,289	—$2,964	$163.70 plus 25%	—$1,289
$2,964	—$6,262	$582.45 plus 28%	—$2,964
$6,262	—$13,525	$1,505.89 plus 33%	—$6,262
$13,525		$3,902.68 plus 35%	—$13,525

(b) MARRIED person—

If the amount of wages (after subtracting withholding allowances) is:		The amount of income tax to withhold is:	
Not over $308		$0	
Over—	**But not over—**		**of excess over—**
$308	—$898	10%	—$308
$898	—$2,719	$59.00 plus 15%	—$898
$2,719	—$5,146	$332.15 plus 25%	—$2,719
$5,146	—$7,813	$938.90 plus 28%	—$5,146
$7,813	—$13,731	$1,685.66 plus 33%	—$7,813
$13,731		$3,638.60 plus 35%	—$13,731

TABLE 3—SEMIMONTHLY Payroll Period

(a) SINGLE person (including head of household)—

If the amount of wages (after subtracting withholding allowances) is:		The amount of income tax to withhold is:	
Not over $110		$0	
Over—	**But not over—**		**of excess over—**
$110	—$422	10%	—$110
$422	—$1,397	$31.20 plus 15%	—$422
$1,397	—$3,211	$177.45 plus 25%	—$1,397
$3,211	—$6,783	$630.95 plus 28%	—$3,211
$6,783	—$14,652	$1,631.11 plus 33%	—$6,783
$14,652		$4,227.88 plus 35%	—$14,652

(b) MARRIED person—

If the amount of wages (after subtracting withholding allowances) is:		The amount of income tax to withhold is:	
Not over $333		$0	
Over—	**But not over—**		**of excess over—**
$333	—$973	10%	—$333
$973	—$2,946	$64.00 plus 15%	—$973
$2,946	—$5,575	$359.95 plus 25%	—$2,946
$5,575	—$8,465	$1,017.20 plus 28%	—$5,575
$8,465	—$14,875	$1,826.40 plus 33%	—$8,465
$14,875		$3,941.70 plus 35%	—$14,875

TABLE 4—MONTHLY Payroll Period

(a) SINGLE person (including head of household)—

If the amount of wages (after subtracting withholding allowances) is:		The amount of income tax to withhold is:	
Not over $221		$0	
Over—	**But not over—**		**of excess over—**
$221	—$843	10%	—$221
$843	—$2,793	$62.20 plus 15%	—$843
$2,793	—$6,423	$354.70 plus 25%	—$2,793
$6,423	—$13,567	$1,262.20 plus 28%	—$6,423
$13,567	—$29,304	$3,262.52 plus 33%	—$13,567
$29,304		$8,455.73 plus 35%	—$29,304

(b) MARRIED person—

If the amount of wages (after subtracting withholding allowances) is:		The amount of income tax to withhold is:	
Not over $667		$0	
Over—	**But not over—**		**of excess over—**
$667	—$1,946	10%	—$667
$1,946	—$5,892	$127.90 plus 15%	—$1,946
$5,892	—$11,150	$719.80 plus 25%	—$5,892
$11,150	—$16,929	$2,034.30 plus 28%	—$11,150
$16,929	—$29,750	$3,652.42 plus 33%	—$16,929
$29,750		$7,883.35 plus 35%	—$29,750

Tables for Percentage Method of Withholding (Continued)

(For Wages Paid in 2007)

TABLE 5—QUARTERLY Payroll Period

(a) SINGLE person (including head of household)—

If the amount of wages (after subtracting withholding allowances) is: Not over $663 . . . . The amount of income tax to withhold is: $0

Over—	But not over—		of excess over—
$663	—$2,530	10%	—$663
$2,530	—$8,380	$186.70 plus 15%	—$2,530
$8,380	—$19,269	$1,064.20 plus 25%	—$8,380
$19,269	—$40,700	$3,786.45 plus 28%	—$19,269
$40,700	—$87,913	$9,787.13 plus 33%	—$40,700
$87,913	. . . . . .	$25,367.42 plus 35%	—$87,913

(b) MARRIED person—

If the amount of wages (after subtracting withholding allowances) is: Not over $2,000 . . . . The amount of income tax to withhold is: $0

Over—	But not over—		of excess over—
$2,000	—$5,838	10%	—$2,000
$5,838	—$17,675	$383.80 plus 15%	—$5,838
$17,675	—$33,450	$2,159.35 plus 25%	—$17,675
$33,450	—$50,788	$6,103.10 plus 28%	—$33,450
$50,788	—$89,250	$10,957.74 plus 33%	—$50,788
$89,250	. . . . . .	$23,650.20 plus 35%	—$89,250

TABLE 6—SEMIANNUAL Payroll Period

(a) SINGLE person (including head of household)—

If the amount of wages (after subtracting withholding allowances) is: Not over $1,325 . . . . The amount of income tax to withhold is: $0

Over—	But not over—		of excess over—
$1,325	—$5,060	10%	—$1,325
$5,060	—$16,760	$373.50 plus 15%	—$5,060
$16,760	—$38,538	$2,128.50 plus 25%	—$16,760
$38,538	—$81,400	$7,573.00 plus 28%	—$38,538
$81,400	—$175,825	$19,574.36 plus 33%	—$81,400
$175,825	. . . . . .	$50,734.61 plus 35%	—$175,825

(b) MARRIED person—

If the amount of wages (after subtracting withholding allowances) is: Not over $4,000 . . . . The amount of income tax to withhold is: $0

Over—	But not over—		of excess over—
$4,000	—$11,675	10%	—$4,000
$11,675	—$35,350	$767.50 plus 15%	—$11,675
$35,350	—$66,900	$4,318.75 plus 25%	—$35,350
$66,900	—$101,575	$12,206.25 plus 28%	—$66,900
$101,575	—$178,500	$21,915.25 plus 33%	—$101,575
$178,500	. . . . . .	$47,300.50 plus 35%	—$178,500

TABLE 7—ANNUAL Payroll Period

(a) SINGLE person (including head of household)—

If the amount of wages (after subtracting withholding allowances) is: Not over $2,650 . . . . The amount of income tax to withhold is: $0

Over—	But not over—		of excess over—
$2,650	—$10,120	10%	—$2,650
$10,120	—$33,520	$747.00 plus 15%	—$10,120
$33,520	—$77,075	$4,257.00 plus 25%	—$33,520
$77,075	—$162,800	$15,145.75 plus 28%	—$77,075
$162,800	—$351,650	$39,148.75 plus 33%	—$162,800
$351,650	. . . . . .	$101,469.25 plus 35%	—$351,650

(b) MARRIED person—

If the amount of wages (after subtracting withholding allowances) is: Not over $8,000 . . . . The amount of income tax to withhold is: $0

Over—	But not over—		of excess over—
$8,000	—$23,350	10%	—$8,000
$23,350	—$70,700	$1,535.00 plus 15%	—$23,350
$70,700	—$133,800	$8,637.50 plus 25%	—$70,700
$133,800	—$203,150	$24,412.50 plus 28%	—$133,800
$203,150	—$357,000	$43,830.50 plus 33%	—$203,150
$357,000	. . . . . .	$94,601.00 plus 35%	—$357,000

TABLE 8—DAILY or MISCELLANEOUS Payroll Period

(a) SINGLE person (including head of household)—

If the amount of wages (after subtracting withholding allowances) divided by the number of days in the payroll period is: Not over $10.20 . . . . The amount of income tax to withhold per day is: $0

Over—	But not over—		of excess over—
$10.20	—$38.90	10%	—$10.20
$38.90	—$128.90	$2.87 plus 15%	—$38.90
$128.90	—$296.40	$16.37 plus 25%	—$128.90
$296.40	—$626.20	$58.25 plus 28%	—$296.40
$626.20	—$1,352.50	$150.59 plus 33%	—$626.20
$1,352.50	. . . . . .	$390.27 plus 35%	—$1,352.50

(b) MARRIED person—

If the amount of wages (after subtracting withholding allowances) divided by the number of days in the payroll period is: Not over $30.80 . . . . The amount of income tax to withhold per day is: $0

Over—	But not over—		of excess over—
$30.80	—$89.80	10%	—$30.80
$89.80	—$271.90	$5.90 plus 15%	—$89.80
$271.90	—$514.60	$33.22 plus 25%	—$271.90
$514.60	—$781.30	$93.90 plus 28%	—$514.60
$781.30	—$1,373.10	$168.58 plus 33%	—$781.30
$1,373.10	. . . . . .	$363.87 plus 35%	—$1,373.10

WAGE-BRACKET INCOME TAX WITHHOLDING TABLES

WEEKLY SINGLE PERSONS

SINGLE Persons—**WEEKLY** Payroll Period

(For Wages Paid in 2007)

If the wages are–		And the number of withholding allowances claimed is—										
At least	But less than	0	1	2	3	4	5	6	7	8	9	10
		The amount of income tax to be withheld is—										
$0	**$55**	$0	$0	$0	$0	$0	$0	$0	$0	$0	$0	$0
55	**60**	1	0	0	0	0	0	0	0	0	0	0
60	**65**	1	0	0	0	0	0	0	0	0	0	0
65	**70**	2	0	0	0	0	0	0	0	0	0	0
70	**75**	2	0	0	0	0	0	0	0	0	0	0
75	**80**	3	0	0	0	0	0	0				
80	**85**	3	0	0	0	0	0	0				
85	**90**	4	0	0	0	0	0	0				
90	**95**	4	0	0	0	0	0	0				
95	**100**	5	0	0	0	0	0	0				
100	**105**	5	0	0	0	0	0	0				
105	**110**	6	0	0	0	0	0	0				
110	**115**	6	0	0	0	0	0	0				
115	**120**	7	0	0	0	0	0	0				
120	**125**	7	1	0	0	0	0	0				
125	**130**	8	1	0	0	0	0	0	0	0	0	0
130	**135**	8	2	0	0	0	0	0	0	0	0	0
135	**140**	9	2	0	0	0	0	0	0	0	0	0
140	**145**	9	3	0	0	0	0	0	0	0	0	0
145	**150**	10	3	0	0	0	0	0	0	0	0	0
150	**155**	10	4	0	0	0	0	0	0	0	0	0
155	**160**	11	4	0	0	0	0	0	0	0	0	0
160	**165**	11	5	0	0	0	0	0	0	0	0	0
165	**170**	12	5	0	0	0	0	0	0	0	0	0
170	**175**	12	6	0	0	0	0	0	0	0	0	0
175	**180**	13	6	0	0	0	0	0	0	0	0	0
180	**185**	13	7	0	0	0	0	0	0	0	0	0
185	**190**	14	7	1	0	0	0	0	0	0	0	0
190	**195**	14	8	1	0	0	0	0	0	0	0	0
195	**200**	15	8	2	0	0	0	0	0	0	0	0
200	**210**	16	9	2	0	0	0	0	0	0	0	0
210	**220**	17	10	3	0	0	0	0	0	0	0	0
220	**230**	19	11	4	0	0	0	0	0	0	0	0
230	**240**	20	12	5	0	0	0	0	0	0	0	0
240	**250**	22	13	6	0	0	0	0	0	0	0	0
250	**260**	23	14	7	1	0	0	0	0	0	0	0
260	**270**	25	15	8	2	0	0	0	0	0	0	0
270	**280**	26	17	9	3	0	0	0	0	0	0	0
280	**290**	28	18	10	4	0	0	0	0	0	0	0
290	**300**	29	20	11	5	0	0	0	0	0	0	0
300	**310**	31	21	12	6	0	0	0	0	0	0	0
310	**320**	32	23	13	7	0	0	0	0	0	0	0
320	**330**	34	24	14	8	1	0	0	0	0	0	0
330	**340**	35	26	16	9	2	0	0	0	0	0	0
340	**350**	37	27	17	10	3	0	0	0	0	0	0
350	**360**	38	29	19	11	4	0	0	0	0	0	0
360	**370**	40	30	20	12	5	0	0	0	0	0	0
370	**380**	41	32	22	13	6	0	0	0	0	0	0
380	**390**	43	33	23	14	7	1	0	0	0	0	0
390	**400**	44	35	25	15	8	2	0	0	0	0	0
400	**410**	46	36	26	17	9	3	0	0	0	0	0
410	**420**	47	38	28	18	10	4	0	0	0	0	0
420	**430**	49	39	29	20	11	5	0	0	0	0	0
430	**440**	50	41	31	21	12	6	0	0	0	0	0
440	**450**	52	42	32	23	13	7	0	0	0	0	0
450	**460**	53	44	34	24	14	8	1	0	0	0	0
460	**470**	55	45	35	26	16	9	2	0	0	0	0
470	**480**	56	47	37	27	17	10	3	0	0	0	0
480	**490**	58	48	38	29	19	11	4	0	0	0	0
490	**500**	59	50	40	30	20	12	5	0	0	0	0
500	**510**	61	51	41	32	22	13	6	0	0	0	0
510	**520**	62	53	43	33	23	14	7	1	0	0	0
520	**530**	64	54	44	35	25	15	8	2	0	0	0
530	**540**	65	56	46	36	26	16	9	3	0	0	0
540	**550**	67	57	47	38	28	18	10	4	0	0	0
550	**560**	68	59	49	39	29	19	11	5	0	0	0
560	**570**	70	60	50	41	31	21	12	6	0	0	0
570	**580**	71	62	52	42	32	22	13	7	0	0	0
580	**590**	73	63	53	44	34	24	14	8	1	0	0
590	**600**	74	65	55	45	35	25	16	9	2	0	0

SINGLE Persons—**WEEKLY** Payroll Period

(For Wages Paid in 2007)

If the wages are–		And the number of withholding allowances claimed is—										
At least	But less than	0	1	2	3	4	5	6	7	8	9	10
		The amount of income tax to be withheld is—										
$600	**$610**	$76	$66	$56	$47	$37	$27	$17	$10	$3	$0	$0
610	**620**	77	68	58	48	38	28	19	11	4	0	0
620	**630**	79	69	59	50	40	30	20	12	5	0	0
630	**640**	80	71	61	51	41	31	22	13	6	0	0
640	**650**	82	72	62	53	43	33	23	14	7	1	0
650	**660**	84	74	64	54	44	34	25	15	8	2	0
660	**670**	87	75	65	56	46	36	26	16	9	3	0
670	**680**	89	77	67	57	47	37	28	18	10	4	0
680	**690**	92	78	68	59	49	39	29	19	11	5	0
690	**700**	94	80	70	60	50	40	31	21	12	6	0
700	**710**	97	81	71	62	52	42	32	22	13	7	0
710	**720**	99	83	73	63	53	43	34	24	14	8	1
720	**730**	102	86	74	65	55	45	35	25	15	9	2
730	**740**	104	88	76	66	56	46	37	27	17	10	3
740	**750**	107	91	77	68	58	48	38	28	18	11	4
750	**760**	109	93	79	69	59	49	40	30	20	12	5
760	**770**	112	96	80	71	61	51	41	31	21	13	6
770	**780**	114	98	82	72	62	52	43	33	23	14	7
780	**790**	117	101	84	74	64	54	44	34	24	15	8
790	**800**	119	103	87	75	65	55	46	36	26	16	9
800	**810**	122	106	89	77	67	57	47	37	27	18	10
810	**820**	124	108	92	78	68	58	49	39	29	19	11
820	**830**	127	111	94	80	70	60	50	40	30	21	12
830	**840**	129	113	97	81	71	61	52	42	32	22	13
840	**850**	132	116	99	83	73	63	53	43	33	24	14
850	**860**	134	118	102	85	74	64	55	45	35	25	15
860	**870**	137	121	104	88	76	66	56	46	36	27	17
870	**880**	139	123	107	90	77	67	58	48	38	28	18
880	**890**	142	126	109	93	79	69	59	49	39	30	20
890	**900**	144	128	112	95	80	70	61	51	41	31	21
900	**910**	147	131	114	98	82	72	62	52	42	33	23
910	**920**	149	133	117	100	84	73	64	54	44	34	24
920	**930**	152	136	119	103	87	75	65	55	45	36	26
930	**940**	154	138	122	105	89	76	67	57	47	37	27
940	**950**	157	141	124	108	92	78	68	58	48	39	29
950	**960**	159	143	127	110	94	79	70	60	50	40	30
960	**970**	162	146	129	113	97	81	71	61	51	42	32
970	**980**	164	148	132	115	99	83	73	63	53	43	33
980	**990**	167	151	134	118	102	85	74	64	54	45	35
990	**1,000**	169	153	137	120	104	88	76	66	56	46	36
1,000	**1,010**	172	156	139	123	107	90	77	67	57	48	38
1,010	**1,020**	174	158	142	125	109	93	79	69	59	49	39
1,020	**1,030**	177	161	144	128	112	95	80	70	60	51	41
1,030	**1,040**	179	163	147	130	114	98	82	72	62	52	42
1,040	**1,050**	182	166	149	133	117	100	84	73	63	54	44
1,050	**1,060**	184	168	152	135	119	103	86	75	65	55	45
1,060	**1,070**	187	171	154	138	122	105	89	76	66	57	47
1,070	**1,080**	189	173	157	140	124	108	91	78	68	58	48
1,080	**1,090**	192	176	159	143	127	110	94	79	69	60	50
1,090	**1,100**	194	178	162	145	129	113	96	81	71	61	51
1,100	**1,110**	197	181	164	148	132	115	99	83	72	63	53
1,110	**1,120**	199	183	167	150	134	118	101	85	74	64	54
1,120	**1,130**	202	186	169	153	137	120	104	88	75	66	56
1,130	**1,140**	204	188	172	155	139	123	106	90	77	67	57
1,140	**1,150**	207	191	174	158	142	125	109	93	78	69	59
1,150	**1,160**	209	193	177	160	144	128	111	95	80	70	60
1,160	**1,170**	212	196	179	163	147	130	114	98	81	72	62
1,170	**1,180**	214	198	182	165	149	133	116	100	84	73	63
1,180	**1,190**	217	201	184	168	152	135	119	103	86	75	65
1,190	**1,200**	219	203	187	170	154	138	121	105	89	76	66
1,200	**1,210**	222	206	189	173	157	140	124	108	91	78	68
1,210	**1,220**	224	208	192	175	159	143	126	110	94	79	69
1,220	**1,230**	227	211	194	178	162	145	129	113	96	81	71
1,230	**1,240**	229	213	197	180	164	148	131	115	99	82	72
1,240	**1,250**	232	216	199	183	167	150	134	118	101	85	74
$1,250 and over		Use Table 1(a) for a **SINGLE person** on page T-3										

WAGE-BRACKET INCOME TAX WITHHOLDING TABLES

MARRIED Persons—WEEKLY Payroll Period

(For Wages Paid in 2007)

WEEKLY
MARRIED PERSONS

If the wages are—		And the number of withholding allowances claimed is—										
At least	But less than	0	1	2	3	4	5	6	7	8	9	10
		The amount of income tax to be withheld is—										
$0	**$125**	$0	$0	$0	$0	$0	$0	$0	$0	$0	$0	$0
125	**130**	0	0	0	0	0	0	0	0	0	0	0
130	**135**	0	0	0	0	0	0	0	0	0	0	0
135	**140**	0	0	0	0	0	0	0	0	0	0	0
140	**145**	0	0	0	0	0	0	0	0	0	0	0
145	**150**	1	0	0	0	0	0	0	[illegible]	[illegible]	[illegible]	[illegible]
150	**155**	1	0	0	0	0	0	0	[illegible]	[illegible]	[illegible]	[illegible]
155	**160**	1	0	0	0	0	0	0	[illegible]	[illegible]	[illegible]	[illegible]
160	**165**	1	0	0	0	0	0	0	[illegible]	[illegible]	[illegible]	[illegible]
165	**170**	1	0	0	0	0	0	0	[illegible]	[illegible]	[illegible]	[illegible]
170	**175**	2	0	0	0	0	0	0	[illegible]	[illegible]	[illegible]	[illegible]
175	**180**	2	0	0	0	0	0	0	[illegible]	[illegible]	[illegible]	[illegible]
180	**185**	3	0	0	0	0	0	0	[illegible]	[illegible]	[illegible]	[illegible]
185	**190**	3	0	0	0	0	0	0	[illegible]	[illegible]	[illegible]	[illegible]
190	**195**	4	0	0	0	0	0	0	[illegible]	[illegible]	[illegible]	[illegible]
195	**200**	4	0	0	0	0	0	0	0	0	0	0
200	**210**	5	0	0	0	0	0	0	0	0	0	0
210	**220**	6	0	0	0	0	0	0	0	0	0	0
220	**230**	7	1	0	0	0	0	0	0	0	0	0
230	**240**	8	2	0	0	0	0	0	0	0	0	0
240	**250**	9	3	0	0	0	0	0	0	0	0	0
250	**260**	10	4	0	0	0	0	0	0	0	0	0
260	**270**	11	5	0	0	0	0	0	0	0	0	0
270	**280**	12	6	0	0	0	0	0	0	0	0	0
280	**290**	13	7	0	0	0	0	0	0	0	0	0
290	**300**	14	8	1	0	0	0	0	0	0	0	0
300	**310**	15	9	2	0	0	0	0	0	0	0	0
310	**320**	16	10	3	0	0	0	0	0	0	0	0
320	**330**	17	11	4	0	0	0	0	0	0	0	0
330	**340**	18	12	5	0	0	0	0	0	0	0	0
340	**350**	19	13	6	0	0	0	0	0	0	0	0
350	**360**	20	14	7	1	0	0	0	0	0	0	0
360	**370**	21	15	8	2	0	0	0	0	0	0	0
370	**380**	22	16	9	3	0	0	0	0	0	0	0
380	**390**	23	17	10	4	0	0	0	0	0	0	0
390	**400**	24	18	11	5	0	0	0	0	0	0	0
400	**410**	25	19	12	6	0	0	0	0	0	0	0
410	**420**	26	20	13	7	0	0	0	0	0	0	0
420	**430**	27	21	14	8	1	0	0	0	0	0	0
430	**440**	28	22	15	9	2	0	0	0	0	0	0
440	**450**	29	23	16	10	3	0	0	0	0	0	0
450	**460**	30	24	17	11	4	0	0	0	0	0	0
460	**470**	32	25	18	12	5	0	0	0	0	0	0
470	**480**	33	26	19	13	6	0	0	0	0	0	0
480	**490**	35	27	20	14	7	0	0	0	0	0	0
490	**500**	36	28	21	15	8	1	0	0	0	0	0
500	**510**	38	29	22	16	9	2	0	0	0	0	0
510	**520**	39	30	23	17	10	3	0	0	0	0	0
520	**530**	41	31	24	18	11	4	0	0	0	0	0
530	**540**	42	33	25	19	12	5	0	0	0	0	0
540	**550**	44	34	26	20	13	6	0	0	0	0	0
550	**560**	45	36	27	21	14	7	1	0	0	0	0
560	**570**	47	37	28	22	15	8	2	0	0	0	0
570	**580**	48	39	29	23	16	9	3	0	0	0	0
580	**590**	50	40	30	24	17	10	4	0	0	0	0
590	**600**	51	42	32	25	18	11	5	0	0	0	0
600	**610**	53	43	33	26	19	12	6	0	0	0	0
610	**620**	54	45	35	27	20	13	7	0	0	0	0
620	**630**	56	46	36	28	21	14	8	1	0	0	0
630	**640**	57	48	38	29	22	15	9	2	0	0	0
640	**650**	59	49	39	30	23	16	10	3	0	0	0
650	**660**	60	51	41	31	24	17	11	4	0	0	0
660	**670**	62	52	42	32	25	18	12	5	0	0	0
670	**680**	63	54	44	34	26	19	13	6	0	0	0
680	**690**	65	55	45	35	27	20	14	7	1	0	0
690	**700**	66	57	47	37	28	21	15	8	2	0	0
700	**710**	68	58	48	38	29	22	16	9	3	0	0
710	**720**	69	60	50	40	30	23	17	10	4	0	0
720	**730**	71	61	51	41	32	24	18	11	5	0	0
730	**740**	72	63	53	43	33	25	19	12	6	0	0

MARRIED Persons—WEEKLY Payroll Period

(For Wages Paid in 2007)

If the wages are–		And the number of withholding allowances claimed is—										
At least	But less than	0	1	2	3	4	5	6	7	8	9	10
		The amount of income tax to be withheld is—										
$740	**$750**	$74	$64	$54	$44	$35	$26	$20	$13	$7	$0	$0
750	**760**	75	66	56	46	36	27	21	14	8	1	0
760	**770**	77	67	57	47	38	28	22	15	9	2	0
770	**780**	78	69	59	49	39	29	23	16	10	3	0
780	**790**	80	70	60	50	41	31	24	17	11	4	0
790	**800**	81	72	62	52	42	32	25	18	12	5	0
800	**810**	83	73	63	53	44	34	26	19	13	6	0
810	**820**	84	75	65	55	45	35	27	20	14	7	1
820	**830**	86	76	66	56	47	37	28	21	15	8	2
830	**840**	87	78	68	58	48	38	29	22	16	9	3
840	**850**	89	79	69	59	50	40	30	23	17	10	4
850	**860**	90	81	71	61	51	41	32	24	18	11	5
860	**870**	92	82	72	62	53	43	33	25	19	12	6
870	**880**	93	84	74	64	54	44	35	26	20	13	7
880	**890**	95	85	75	65	56	46	36	27	21	14	8
890	**900**	96	87	77	67	57	47	38	28	22	15	9
900	**910**	98	88	78	68	59	49	39	29	23	16	10
910	**920**	99	90	80	70	60	50	41	31	24	17	11
920	**930**	101	91	81	71	62	52	42	32	25	18	12
930	**940**	102	93	83	73	63	53	44	34	26	19	13
940	**950**	104	94	84	74	65	55	45	35	27	20	14
950	**960**	105	96	86	76	66	56	47	37	28	21	15
960	**970**	107	97	87	77	68	58	48	38	29	22	16
970	**980**	108	99	89	79	69	59	50	40	30	23	17
980	**990**	110	100	90	80	71	61	51	41	31	24	18
990	**1,000**	111	102	92	82	72	62	53	43	33	25	19
1,000	**1,010**	113	103	93	83	74	64	54	44	34	26	20
1,010	**1,020**	114	105	95	85	75	65	56	46	36	27	21
1,020	**1,030**	116	106	96	86	77	67	57	47	37	28	22
1,030	**1,040**	117	108	98	88	78	68	59	49	39	29	23
1,040	**1,050**	119	109	99	89	80	70	60	50	40	31	24
1,050	**1,060**	120	111	101	91	81	71	62	52	42	32	25
1,060	**1,070**	122	112	102	92	83	73	63	53	43	34	26
1,070	**1,080**	123	114	104	94	84	74	65	55	45	35	27
1,080	**1,090**	125	115	105	95	86	76	66	56	46	37	28
1,090	**1,100**	126	117	107	97	87	77	68	58	48	38	29
1,100	**1,110**	128	118	108	98	89	79	69	59	49	40	30
1,110	**1,120**	129	120	110	100	90	80	71	61	51	41	31
1,120	**1,130**	131	121	111	101	92	82	72	62	52	43	33
1,130	**1,140**	132	123	113	103	93	83	74	64	54	44	34
1,140	**1,150**	134	124	114	104	95	85	75	65	55	46	36
1,150	**1,160**	135	126	116	106	96	86	77	67	57	47	37
1,160	**1,170**	137	127	117	107	98	88	78	68	58	49	39
1,170	**1,180**	138	129	119	109	99	89	80	70	60	50	40
1,180	**1,190**	140	130	120	110	101	91	81	71	61	52	42
1,190	**1,200**	141	132	122	112	102	92	83	73	63	53	43
1,200	**1,210**	143	133	123	113	104	94	84	74	64	55	45
1,210	**1,220**	144	135	125	115	105	95	86	76	66	56	46
1,220	**1,230**	146	136	126	116	107	97	87	77	67	58	48
1,230	**1,240**	147	138	128	118	108	98	89	79	69	59	49
1,240	**1,250**	149	139	129	119	110	100	90	80	70	61	51
1,250	**1,260**	150	141	131	121	111	101	92	82	72	62	52
1,260	**1,270**	152	142	132	122	113	103	93	83	73	64	54
1,270	**1,280**	153	144	134	124	114	104	95	85	75	65	55
1,280	**1,290**	155	145	135	125	116	106	96	86	76	67	57
1,290	**1,300**	156	147	137	127	117	107	98	88	78	68	58
1,300	**1,310**	158	148	138	128	119	109	99	89	79	70	60
1,310	**1,320**	159	150	140	130	120	110	101	91	81	71	61
1,320	**1,330**	161	151	141	131	122	112	102	92	82	73	63
1,330	**1,340**	162	153	143	133	123	113	104	94	84	74	64
1,340	**1,350**	164	154	144	134	125	115	105	95	85	76	66
1,350	**1,360**	165	156	146	136	126	116	107	97	87	77	67
1,360	**1,370**	167	157	147	137	128	118	108	98	88	79	69
1,370	**1,380**	170	159	149	139	129	119	110	100	90	80	70
1,380	**1,390**	172	160	150	140	131	121	111	101	91	82	72
1,390	**1,400**	175	162	152	142	132	122	113	103	93	83	73

$1,400 and over Use Table 1(b) for a **MARRIED person** on page T-3

WAGE-BRACKET INCOME TAX WITHHOLDING TABLES

SINGLE Persons—BIWEEKLY Payroll Period

(For Wages Paid in 2007)

If the wages are–		And the number of withholding allowances claimed is—										
At least	But less than	0	1	2	3	4	5	6	7	8	9	10
		The amount of income tax to be withheld is—										
$0	$105	$0	$0	$0	$0	$0	$0	$0	$0	$0	$0	$0
105	110	1	0	0	0	0	0	0	0	0	0	0
110	115	1	0	0	0	0	0	0				
115	120	2	0	0	0	0	0	0				
120	125	2	0	0	0	0	0	0				
125	130	3	0	0	0	0	0	0				
130	135	3	0	0	0	0	0	0				
135	140	4	0	0	0	0	0	0				
140	145	4	0	0	0	0	0	0				
145	150	5	0	0	0	0	0	0				
150	155	5	0	0	0	0	0	0				
155	160	6	0	0	0	0	0	0	0	0	0	0
160	165	6	0	0	0	0	0	0	0	0	0	0
165	170	7	0	0	0	0	0	0	0	0	0	0
170	175	7	0	0	0	0	0	0	0	0	0	0
175	180	8	0	0	0	0	0	0	0	0	0	0
180	185	8	0	0	0	0	0	0	0	0	0	0
185	190	9	0	0	0	0	0	0	0	0	0	0
190	195	9	0	0	0	0	0	0	0	0	0	0
195	200	10	0	0	0	0	0	0	0	0	0	0
200	205	10	0	0	0	0	0	0	0	0	0	0
205	210	11	0	0	0	0	0	0	0	0	0	0
210	215	11	0	0	0	0	0	0	0	0	0	0
215	220	12	0	0	0	0	0	0	0	0	0	0
220	225	12	0	0	0	0	0	0	0	0	0	0
225	230	13	0	0	0	0	0	0	0	0	0	0
230	235	13	0	0	0	0	0	0	0	0	0	0
235	240	14	0	0	0	0	0	0	0	0	0	0
240	245	14	1	0	0	0	0	0	0	0	0	0
245	250	15	1	0	0	0	0	0	0	0	0	0
250	260	15	2	0	0	0	0	0	0	0	0	0
260	270	16	3	0	0	0	0	0	0	0	0	0
270	280	17	4	0	0	0	0	0	0	0	0	0
280	290	18	5	0	0	0	0	0	0	0	0	0
290	300	19	6	0	0	0	0	0	0	0	0	0
300	310	20	7	0	0	0	0	0	0	0	0	0
310	320	21	8	0	0	0	0	0	0	0	0	0
320	330	22	9	0	0	0	0	0	0	0	0	0
330	340	23	10	0	0	0	0	0	0	0	0	0
340	350	24	11	0	0	0	0	0	0	0	0	0
350	360	25	12	0	0	0	0	0	0	0	0	0
360	370	26	13	0	0	0	0	0	0	0	0	0
370	380	27	14	1	0	0	0	0	0	0	0	0
380	390	28	15	2	0	0	0	0	0	0	0	0
390	400	30	16	3	0	0	0	0	0	0	0	0
400	410	31	17	4	0	0	0	0	0	0	0	0
410	420	33	18	5	0	0	0	0	0	0	0	0
420	430	34	19	6	0	0	0	0	0	0	0	0
430	440	36	20	7	0	0	0	0	0	0	0	0
440	450	37	21	8	0	0	0	0	0	0	0	0
450	460	39	22	9	0	0	0	0	0	0	0	0
460	470	40	23	10	0	0	0	0	0	0	0	0
470	480	42	24	11	0	0	0	0	0	0	0	0
480	490	43	25	12	0	0	0	0	0	0	0	0
490	500	45	26	13	0	0	0	0	0	0	0	0
500	520	47	28	15	2	0	0	0	0	0	0	0
520	540	50	30	17	4	0	0	0	0	0	0	0
540	560	53	33	19	6	0	0	0	0	0	0	0
560	580	56	36	21	8	0	0	0	0	0	0	0
580	600	59	39	23	10	0	0	0	0	0	0	0
600	620	62	42	25	12	0	0	0	0	0	0	0
620	640	65	45	27	14	1	0	0	0	0	0	0
640	660	68	48	29	16	3	0	0	0	0	0	0
660	680	71	51	32	18	5	0	0	0	0	0	0
680	700	74	54	35	20	7	0	0	0	0	0	0
700	720	77	57	38	22	9	0	0	0	0	0	0
720	740	80	60	41	24	11	0	0	0	0	0	0
740	760	83	63	44	26	13	0	0	0	0	0	0
760	780	86	66	47	28	15	1	0	0	0	0	0
780	800	89	69	50	30	17	3	0	0	0	0	0

BIWEEKLY SINGLE PERSONS

SINGLE Persons—BIWEEKLY Payroll Period

(For Wages Paid in 2007)

If the wages are–		And the number of withholding allowances claimed is—										
At least	But less than	0	1	2	3	4	5	6	7	8	9	10
		The amount of income tax to be withheld is—										
$800	$820	$92	$72	$53	$33	$19	$5	$0	$0	$0	$0	$0
820	840	95	75	56	36	21	7	0	0	0	0	0
840	860	98	78	59	39	23	9	0	0	0	0	0
860	880	101	81	62	42	25	11	0	0	0	0	0
880	900	104	84	65	45	27	13	0	0	0	0	0
900	920	107	87	68	48	29	15	2	0	0	0	0
920	940	110	90	71	51	31	17	4	0	0	0	0
940	960	113	93	74	54	34	19	6	0	0	0	0
960	980	116	96	77	57	37	21	8	0	0	0	0
980	1,000	119	99	80	60	40	23	10	0	0	0	0
1,000	1,020	122	102	83	63	43	25	12	0	0	0	0
1,020	1,040	125	105	86	66	46	27	14	1	0	0	0
1,040	1,060	128	108	89	69	49	30	16	3	0	0	0
1,060	1,080	131	111	92	72	52	33	18	5	0	0	0
1,080	1,100	134	114	95	75	55	36	20	7	0	0	0
1,100	1,120	137	117	98	78	58	39	22	9	0	0	0
1,120	1,140	140	120	101	81	61	42	24	11	0	0	0
1,140	1,160	143	123	104	84	64	45	26	13	0	0	0
1,160	1,180	146	126	107	87	67	48	28	15	2	0	0
1,180	1,200	149	129	110	90	70	51	31	17	4	0	0
1,200	1,220	152	132	113	93	73	54	34	19	6	0	0
1,220	1,240	155	135	116	96	76	57	37	21	8	0	0
1,240	1,260	158	138	119	99	79	60	40	23	10	0	0
1,260	1,280	161	141	122	102	82	63	43	25	12	0	0
1,280	1,300	164	144	125	105	85	66	46	27	14	1	0
1,300	1,320	169	147	128	108	88	69	49	30	16	3	0
1,320	1,340	174	150	131	111	91	72	52	33	18	5	0
1,340	1,360	179	153	134	114	94	75	55	36	20	7	0
1,360	1,380	184	156	137	117	97	78	58	39	22	9	0
1,380	1,400	189	159	140	120	100	81	61	42	24	11	0
1,400	1,420	194	162	143	123	103	84	64	45	26	13	0
1,420	1,440	199	166	146	126	106	87	67	48	28	15	2
1,440	1,460	204	171	149	129	109	90	70	51	31	17	4
1,460	1,480	209	176	152	132	112	93	73	54	34	19	6
1,480	1,500	214	181	155	135	115	96	76	57	37	21	8
1,500	1,520	219	186	158	138	118	99	79	60	40	23	10
1,520	1,540	224	191	161	141	121	102	82	63	43	25	12
1,540	1,560	229	196	164	144	124	105	85	66	46	27	14
1,560	1,580	234	201	169	147	127	108	88	69	49	29	16
1,580	1,600	239	206	174	150	130	111	91	72	52	32	18
1,600	1,620	244	211	179	153	133	114	94	75	55	35	20
1,620	1,640	249	216	184	156	136	117	97	78	58	38	22
1,640	1,660	254	221	189	159	139	120	100	81	61	41	24
1,660	1,680	259	226	194	162	142	123	103	84	64	44	26
1,680	1,700	264	231	199	166	145	126	106	87	67	47	28
1,700	1,720	269	236	204	171	148	129	109	90	70	50	31
1,720	1,740	274	241	209	176	151	132	112	93	73	53	34
1,740	1,760	279	246	214	181	154	135	115	96	76	56	37
1,760	1,780	284	251	219	186	157	138	118	99	79	59	40
1,780	1,800	289	256	224	191	160	141	121	102	82	62	43
1,800	1,820	294	261	229	196	163	144	124	105	85	65	46
1,820	1,840	299	266	234	201	168	147	127	108	88	68	49
1,840	1,860	304	271	239	206	173	150	130	111	91	71	52
1,860	1,880	309	276	244	211	178	153	133	114	94	74	55
1,880	1,900	314	281	249	216	183	156	136	117	97	77	58
1,900	1,920	319	286	254	221	188	159	139	120	100	80	61
1,920	1,940	324	291	259	226	193	162	142	123	103	83	64
1,940	1,960	329	296	264	231	198	165	145	126	106	86	67
1,960	1,980	334	301	269	236	203	170	148	129	109	89	70
1,980	2,000	339	306	274	241	208	175	151	132	112	92	73
2,000	2,020	344	311	279	246	213	180	154	135	115	95	76
2,020	2,040	349	316	284	251	218	185	157	138	118	98	79
2,040	2,060	354	321	289	256	223	190	160	141	121	101	82
2,060	2,080	359	326	294	261	228	195	163	144	124	104	85
2,080	2,100	364	331	299	266	233	200	168	147	127	107	88
$2,100 and over		Use Table 2(a) for a **SINGLE person** on page T-3										

WAGE-BRACKET INCOME TAX WITHHOLDING TABLES

MARRIED Persons—**BIWEEKLY** Payroll Period

(For Wages Paid in 2007)

If the wages are–		And the number of withholding allowances claimed is—										
At least	But less than	0	1	2	3	4	5	6	7	8	9	10
		The amount of income tax to be withheld is—										
$0	$250	$0	$0	$0	$0	$0	$0	$0	$0	$0	$0	$0
250	260	0	0	0	0	0	0	0	0	0	0	0
260	270	0	0	0	0	0	0	0	0	0	0	0
270	280	0	0	0	0	0	0	0	0	0	0	0
280	290	0	0	0	0	0	0	0	0	0	0	0
290	300	0	0	0	0	0	0	0				
300	310	0	0	0	0	0	0	0				
310	320	1	0	0	0	0	0	0				
320	330	2	0	0	0	0	0	0				
330	340	3	0	0	0	0	0	0				
340	350	4	0	0	0	0	0	0				
350	360	5	0	0	0	0	0	0				
360	370	6	0	0	0	0	0	0				
370	380	7	0	0	0	0	0	0				
380	390	8	0	0	0	0	0	0				
390	400	9	0	0	0	0	0	0	0	0	0	0
400	410	10	0	0	0	0	0	0	0	0	0	0
410	420	11	0	0	0	0	0	0	0	0	0	0
420	430	12	0	0	0	0	0	0	0	0	0	0
430	440	13	0	0	0	0	0	0	0	0	0	0
440	450	14	1	0	0	0	0	0	0	0	0	0
450	460	15	2	0	0	0	0	0	0	0	0	0
460	470	16	3	0	0	0	0	0	0	0	0	0
470	480	17	4	0	0	0	0	0	0	0	0	0
480	490	18	5	0	0	0	0	0	0	0	0	0
490	500	19	6	0	0	0	0	0	0	0	0	0
500	520	20	7	0	0	0	0	0	0	0	0	0
520	540	22	9	0	0	0	0	0	0	0	0	0
540	560	24	11	0	0	0	0	0	0	0	0	0
560	580	26	13	0	0	0	0	0	0	0	0	0
580	600	28	15	2	0	0	0	0	0	0	0	0
600	620	30	17	4	0	0	0	0	0	0	0	0
620	640	32	19	6	0	0	0	0	0	0	0	0
640	660	34	21	8	0	0	0	0	0	0	0	0
660	680	36	23	10	0	0	0	0	0	0	0	0
680	700	38	25	12	0	0	0	0	0	0	0	0
700	720	40	27	14	1	0	0	0	0	0	0	0
720	740	42	29	16	3	0	0	0	0	0	0	0
740	760	44	31	18	5	0	0	0	0	0	0	0
760	780	46	33	20	7	0	0	0	0	0	0	0
780	800	48	35	22	9	0	0	0	0	0	0	0
800	820	50	37	24	11	0	0	0	0	0	0	0
820	840	52	39	26	13	0	0	0	0	0	0	0
840	860	54	41	28	15	2	0	0	0	0	0	0
860	880	56	43	30	17	4	0	0	0	0	0	0
880	900	58	45	32	19	6	0	0	0	0	0	0
900	920	61	47	34	21	8	0	0	0	0	0	0
920	940	64	49	36	23	10	0	0	0	0	0	0
940	960	67	51	38	25	12	0	0	0	0	0	0
960	980	70	53	40	27	14	1	0	0	0	0	0
980	1,000	73	55	42	29	16	3	0	0	0	0	0
1,000	1,020	76	57	44	31	18	5	0	0	0	0	0
1,020	1,040	79	59	46	33	20	7	0	0	0	0	0
1,040	1,060	82	62	48	35	22	9	0	0	0	0	0
1,060	1,080	85	65	50	37	24	11	0	0	0	0	0
1,080	1,100	88	68	52	39	26	13	0	0	0	0	0
1,100	1,120	91	71	54	41	28	15	2	0	0	0	0
1,120	1,140	94	74	56	43	30	17	4	0	0	0	0
1,140	1,160	97	77	58	45	32	19	6	0	0	0	0
1,160	1,180	100	80	61	47	34	21	8	0	0	0	0
1,180	1,200	103	83	64	49	36	23	10	0	0	0	0
1,200	1,220	106	86	67	51	38	25	12	0	0	0	0
1,220	1,240	109	89	70	53	40	27	14	1	0	0	0
1,240	1,260	112	92	73	55	42	29	16	3	0	0	0
1,260	1,280	115	95	76	57	44	31	18	5	0	0	0
1,280	1,300	118	98	79	59	46	33	20	7	0	0	0
1,300	1,320	121	101	82	62	48	35	22	9	0	0	0
1,320	1,340	124	104	85	65	50	37	24	11	0	0	0
1,340	1,360	127	107	88	68	52	39	26	13	0	0	0
1,360	1,380	130	110	91	71	54	41	28	15	2	0	0

BIWEEKLY MARRIED PERSONS

MARRIED Persons—**BIWEEKLY** Payroll Period

(For Wages Paid in 2007)

If the wages are–		And the number of withholding allowances claimed is—										
At least	But less than	0	1	2	3	4	5	6	7	8	9	10
		The amount of income tax to be withheld is—										
$1,380	$1,400	$133	$113	$94	$74	$56	$43	$30	$17	$4	$0	$0
1,400	1,420	136	116	97	77	58	45	32	19	6	0	0
1,420	1,440	139	119	100	80	60	47	34	21	8	0	0
1,440	1,460	142	122	103	83	63	49	36	23	10	0	0
1,460	1,480	145	125	106	86	66	51	38	25	12	0	0
1,480	1,500	148	128	109	89	69	53	40	27	14	1	0
1,500	1,520	151	131	112	92	72	55	42	29	16	3	0
1,520	1,540	154	134	115	95	75	57	44	31	18	5	0
1,540	1,560	157	137	118	98	78	59	46	33	20	7	0
1,560	1,580	160	140	121	101	81	62	48	35	22	9	0
1,580	1,600	163	143	124	104	84	65	50	37	24	11	0
1,600	1,620	166	146	127	107	87	68	52	39	26	13	0
1,620	1,640	169	149	130	110	90	71	54	41	28	15	1
1,640	1,660	172	152	133	113	93	74	56	43	30	17	3
1,660	1,680	175	155	136	116	96	77	58	45	32	19	5
1,680	1,700	178	158	139	119	99	80	60	47	34	21	7
1,700	1,720	181	161	142	122	102	83	63	49	36	23	9
1,720	1,740	184	164	145	125	105	86	66	51	38	25	11
1,740	1,760	187	167	148	128	108	89	69	53	40	27	13
1,760	1,780	190	170	151	131	111	92	72	55	42	29	15
1,780	1,800	193	173	154	134	114	95	75	57	44	31	17
1,800	1,820	196	176	157	137	117	98	78	59	46	33	19
1,820	1,840	199	179	160	140	120	101	81	62	48	35	21
1,840	1,860	202	182	163	143	123	104	84	65	50	37	23
1,860	1,880	205	185	166	146	126	107	87	68	52	39	25
1,880	1,900	208	188	169	149	129	110	90	71	54	41	27
1,900	1,920	211	191	172	152	132	113	93	74	56	43	29
1,920	1,940	214	194	175	155	135	116	96	77	58	45	31
1,940	1,960	217	197	178	158	138	119	99	80	60	47	33
1,960	1,980	220	200	181	161	141	122	102	83	63	49	35
1,980	2,000	223	203	184	164	144	125	105	86	66	51	37
2,000	2,020	226	206	187	167	147	128	108	89	69	53	39
2,020	2,040	229	209	190	170	150	131	111	92	72	55	41
2,040	2,060	232	212	193	173	153	134	114	95	75	57	43
2,060	2,080	235	215	196	176	156	137	117	98	78	59	45
2,080	2,100	238	218	199	179	159	140	120	101	81	61	47
2,100	2,120	241	221	202	182	162	143	123	104	84	64	49
2,120	2,140	244	224	205	185	165	146	126	107	87	67	51
2,140	2,160	247	227	208	188	168	149	129	110	90	70	53
2,160	2,180	250	230	211	191	171	152	132	113	93	73	55
2,180	2,200	253	233	214	194	174	155	135	116	96	76	57
2,200	2,220	256	236	217	197	177	158	138	119	99	79	60
2,220	2,240	259	239	220	200	180	161	141	122	102	82	63
2,240	2,260	262	242	223	203	183	164	144	125	105	85	66
2,260	2,280	265	245	226	206	186	167	147	128	108	88	69
2,280	2,300	268	248	229	209	189	170	150	131	111	91	72
2,300	2,320	271	251	232	212	192	173	153	134	114	94	75
2,320	2,340	274	254	235	215	195	176	156	137	117	97	78
2,340	2,360	277	257	238	218	198	179	159	140	120	100	81
2,360	2,380	280	260	241	221	201	182	162	143	123	103	84
2,380	2,400	283	263	244	224	204	185	165	146	126	106	87
2,400	2,420	286	266	247	227	207	188	168	149	129	109	90
2,420	2,440	289	269	250	230	210	191	171	152	132	112	93
2,440	2,460	292	272	253	233	213	194	174	155	135	115	96
2,460	2,480	295	275	256	236	216	197	177	158	138	118	99
2,480	2,500	298	278	259	239	219	200	180	161	141	121	102
2,500	2,520	301	281	262	242	222	203	183	164	144	124	105
2,520	2,540	304	284	265	245	225	206	186	167	147	127	108
2,540	2,560	307	287	268	248	228	209	189	170	150	130	111
2,560	2,580	310	290	271	251	231	212	192	173	153	133	114
2,580	2,600	313	293	274	254	234	215	195	176	156	136	117
2,600	2,620	316	296	277	257	237	218	198	179	159	139	120
2,620	2,640	319	299	280	260	240	221	201	182	162	142	123
2,640	2,660	322	302	283	263	243	224	204	185	165	145	126
2,660	2,680	325	305	286	266	246	227	207	188	168	148	129
2,680	2,700	328	308	289	269	249	230	210	191	171	151	132
$2,700 and over		Use Table 2(b) for a **MARRIED person** on page T-3										

WAGE-BRACKET INCOME TAX WITHHOLDING TABLES

SINGLE Persons—SEMIMONTHLY Payroll Period

(For Wages Paid in 2007)

SEMIMONTHLY SINGLE PERSONS

If the wages are–		And the number of withholding allowances claimed is—										
At least	But less than	0	1	2	3	4	5	6	7	8	9	10
		The amount of income tax to be withheld is—										
$0	$115	$0	$0	$0	$0	$0	$0	$0	$0	$0	$0	$0
115	120	1	0	0	0	0	0	0	0	0	0	0
120	125	1	0	0	0	0	0	0	0	0	0	0
125	130	2	0	0	0	0	0	0	0	0	0	0
130	135	2	0	0	0	0	0	0	0	0	0	0
135	140	3	0	0	0	0	0	0	0	0	0	0
140	145	3	0	0	0	0	0	0				
145	150	4	0	0	0	0	0	0				
150	155	4	0	0	0	0	0	0				
155	160	5	0	0	0	0	0	0				
160	165	5	0	0	0	0	0	0				
165	170	6	0	0	0	0	0	0				
170	175	6	0	0	0	0	0	0				
175	180	7	0	0	0	0	0	0				
180	185	7	0	0	0	0	0	0				
185	190	8	0	0	0	0	0	0	0	0	0	0
190	195	8	0	0	0	0	0	0	0	0	0	0
195	200	9	0	0	0	0	0	0	0	0	0	0
200	205	9	0	0	0	0	0	0	0	0	0	0
205	210	10	0	0	0	0	0	0	0	0	0	0
210	215	10	0	0	0	0	0	0	0	0	0	0
215	220	11	0	0	0	0	0	0	0	0	0	0
220	225	11	0	0	0	0	0	0	0	0	0	0
225	230	12	0	0	0	0	0	0	0	0	0	0
230	235	12	0	0	0	0	0	0	0	0	0	0
235	240	13	0	0	0	0	0	0	0	0	0	0
240	245	13	0	0	0	0	0	0	0	0	0	0
245	250	14	0	0	0	0	0	0	0	0	0	0
250	260	14	0	0	0	0	0	0	0	0	0	0
260	270	15	1	0	0	0	0	0	0	0	0	0
270	280	16	2	0	0	0	0	0	0	0	0	0
280	290	17	3	0	0	0	0	0	0	0	0	0
290	300	18	4	0	0	0	0	0	0	0	0	0
300	310	19	5	0	0	0	0	0	0	0	0	0
310	320	20	6	0	0	0	0	0	0	0	0	0
320	330	21	7	0	0	0	0	0	0	0	0	0
330	340	22	8	0	0	0	0	0	0	0	0	0
340	350	23	9	0	0	0	0	0	0	0	0	0
350	360	24	10	0	0	0	0	0	0	0	0	0
360	370	25	11	0	0	0	0	0	0	0	0	0
370	380	26	12	0	0	0	0	0	0	0	0	0
380	390	27	13	0	0	0	0	0	0	0	0	0
390	400	28	14	0	0	0	0	0	0	0	0	0
400	410	29	15	1	0	0	0	0	0	0	0	0
410	420	30	16	2	0	0	0	0	0	0	0	0
420	430	32	17	3	0	0	0	0	0	0	0	0
430	440	33	18	4	0	0	0	0	0	0	0	0
440	450	35	19	5	0	0	0	0	0	0	0	0
450	460	36	20	6	0	0	0	0	0	0	0	0
460	470	38	21	7	0	0	0	0	0	0	0	0
470	480	39	22	8	0	0	0	0	0	0	0	0
480	490	41	23	9	0	0	0	0	0	0	0	0
490	500	42	24	10	0	0	0	0	0	0	0	0
500	520	44	26	12	0	0	0	0	0	0	0	0
520	540	47	28	14	0	0	0	0	0	0	0	0
540	560	50	30	16	1	0	0	0	0	0	0	0
560	580	53	32	18	3	0	0	0	0	0	0	0
580	600	56	35	20	5	0	0	0	0	0	0	0
600	620	59	38	22	7	0	0	0	0	0	0	0
620	640	62	41	24	9	0	0	0	0	0	0	0
640	660	65	44	26	11	0	0	0	0	0	0	0
660	680	68	47	28	13	0	0	0	0	0	0	0
680	700	71	50	30	15	1	0	0	0	0	0	0
700	720	74	53	32	17	3	0	0	0	0	0	0
720	740	77	56	35	19	5	0	0	0	0	0	0
740	760	80	59	38	21	7	0	0	0	0	0	0
760	780	83	62	41	23	9	0	0	0	0	0	0
780	800	86	65	44	25	11	0	0	0	0	0	0
800	820	89	68	47	27	13	0	0	0	0	0	0
820	840	92	71	50	29	15	1	0	0	0	0	0

SINGLE Persons—SEMIMONTHLY Payroll Period

(For Wages Paid in 2007)

If the wages are–		And the number of withholding allowances claimed is—										
At least	But less than	0	1	2	3	4	5	6	7	8	9	10
		The amount of income tax to be withheld is—										
$840	$860	$95	$74	$53	$32	$17	$3	$0	$0	$0	$0	$0
860	880	98	77	56	35	19	5	0	0	0	0	0
880	900	101	80	59	38	21	7	0	0	0	0	0
900	920	104	83	62	41	23	9	0	0	0	0	0
920	940	107	86	65	44	25	11	0	0	0	0	0
940	960	110	89	68	47	27	13	0	0	0	0	0
960	980	113	92	71	50	29	15	1	0	0	0	0
980	1,000	116	95	74	53	31	17	3	0	0	0	0
1,000	1,020	119	98	77	56	34	19	5	0	0	0	0
1,020	1,040	122	101	80	59	37	21	7	0	0	0	0
1,040	1,060	125	104	83	62	40	23	9	0	0	0	0
1,060	1,080	128	107	86	65	43	25	11	0	0	0	0
1,080	1,100	131	110	89	68	46	27	13	0	0	0	0
1,100	1,120	134	113	92	71	49	29	15	1	0	0	0
1,120	1,140	137	116	95	74	52	31	17	3	0	0	0
1,140	1,160	140	119	98	77	55	34	19	5	0	0	0
1,160	1,180	143	122	101	80	58	37	21	7	0	0	0
1,180	1,200	146	125	104	83	61	40	23	9	0	0	0
1,200	1,220	149	128	107	86	64	43	25	11	0	0	0
1,220	1,240	152	131	110	89	67	46	27	13	0	0	0
1,240	1,260	155	134	113	92	70	49	29	15	1	0	0
1,260	1,280	158	137	116	95	73	52	31	17	3	0	0
1,280	1,300	161	140	119	98	76	55	34	19	5	0	0
1,300	1,320	164	143	122	101	79	58	37	21	7	0	0
1,320	1,340	167	146	125	104	82	61	40	23	9	0	0
1,340	1,360	170	149	128	107	85	64	43	25	11	0	0
1,360	1,380	173	152	131	110	88	67	46	27	13	0	0
1,380	1,400	176	155	134	113	91	70	49	29	15	0	0
1,400	1,420	181	158	137	116	94	73	52	31	17	2	0
1,420	1,440	186	161	140	119	97	76	55	34	19	4	0
1,440	1,460	191	164	143	122	100	79	58	37	21	6	0
1,460	1,480	196	167	146	125	103	82	61	40	23	8	0
1,480	1,500	201	170	149	128	106	85	64	43	25	10	0
1,500	1,520	206	173	152	131	109	88	67	46	27	12	0
1,520	1,540	211	176	155	134	112	91	70	49	29	14	0
1,540	1,560	216	180	158	137	115	94	73	52	31	16	2
1,560	1,580	221	185	161	140	118	97	76	55	33	18	4
1,580	1,600	226	190	164	143	121	100	79	58	36	20	6
1,600	1,620	231	195	167	146	124	103	82	61	39	22	8
1,620	1,640	236	200	170	149	127	106	85	64	42	24	10
1,640	1,660	241	205	173	152	130	109	88	67	45	26	12
1,660	1,680	246	210	176	155	133	112	91	70	48	28	14
1,680	1,700	251	215	180	158	136	115	94	73	51	30	16
1,700	1,720	256	220	185	161	139	118	97	76	54	33	18
1,720	1,740	261	225	190	164	142	121	100	79	57	36	20
1,740	1,760	266	230	195	167	145	124	103	82	60	39	22
1,760	1,780	271	235	200	170	148	127	106	85	63	42	24
1,780	1,800	276	240	205	173	151	130	109	88	66	45	26
1,800	1,820	281	245	210	176	154	133	112	91	69	48	28
1,820	1,840	286	250	215	179	157	136	115	94	72	51	30
1,840	1,860	291	255	220	184	160	139	118	97	75	54	33
1,860	1,880	296	260	225	189	163	142	121	100	78	57	36
1,880	1,900	301	265	230	194	166	145	124	103	81	60	39
1,900	1,920	306	270	235	199	169	148	127	106	84	63	42
1,920	1,940	311	275	240	204	172	151	130	109	87	66	45
1,940	1,960	316	280	245	209	175	154	133	112	90	69	48
1,960	1,980	321	285	250	214	179	157	136	115	93	72	51
1,980	2,000	326	290	255	219	184	160	139	118	96	75	54
2,000	2,020	331	295	260	224	189	163	142	121	99	78	57
2,020	2,040	336	300	265	229	194	166	145	124	102	81	60
2,040	2,060	341	305	270	234	199	169	148	127	105	84	63
2,060	2,080	346	310	275	239	204	172	151	130	108	87	66
2,080	2,100	351	315	280	244	209	175	154	133	111	90	69
2,100	2,120	356	320	285	249	214	179	157	136	114	93	72
2,120	2,140	361	325	290	254	219	184	160	139	117	96	75
$2,140 and over		Use Table 3(a) for a **SINGLE person** on page T-3										

WAGE-BRACKET INCOME TAX WITHHOLDING TABLES

MARRIED Persons—**SEMIMONTHLY** Payroll Period

(For Wages Paid in 2007)

SEMIMONTHLY MARRIED PERSONS

If the wages are–		And the number of withholding allowances claimed is—										
At least	But less than	0	1	2	3	4	5	6	7	8	9	10
		The amount of income tax to be withheld is—										
$0	**$270**	$0	$0	$0	$0	$0	$0	$0	$0	$0	$0	$0
270	**280**	0	0	0	0	0	0	0	0	0	0	0
280	**290**	0	0	0	0	0	0	0	0	0	0	0
290	**300**	0	0	0	0	0	0	0	0	0	0	0
300	**310**	0	0	0	0	0	0	0	0	0	0	0
310	**320**	0	0	0	0	0	0	0	0	0	0	0
320	**330**	0	0	0	0	0	0	0				
330	**340**	0	0	0	0	0	0	0				
340	**350**	1	0	0	0	0	0	0				
350	**360**	2	0	0	0	0	0	0				
360	**370**	3	0	0	0	0	0	0				
370	**380**	4	0	0	0	0	0	0				
380	**390**	5	0	0	0	0	0	0				
390	**400**	6	0	0	0	0	0	0				
400	**410**	7	0	0	0	0	0	0				
410	**420**	8	0	0	0	0	0	0	0	0	0	0
420	**430**	9	0	0	0	0	0	0	0	0	0	0
430	**440**	10	0	0	0	0	0	0	0	0	0	0
440	**450**	11	0	0	0	0	0	0	0	0	0	0
450	**460**	12	0	0	0	0	0	0	0	0	0	0
460	**470**	13	0	0	0	0	0	0	0	0	0	0
470	**480**	14	0	0	0	0	0	0	0	0	0	0
480	**490**	15	1	0	0	0	0	0	0	0	0	0
490	**500**	16	2	0	0	0	0	0	0	0	0	0
500	**520**	18	4	0	0	0	0	0	0	0	0	0
520	**540**	20	6	0	0	0	0	0	0	0	0	0
540	**560**	22	8	0	0	0	0	0	0	0	0	0
560	**580**	24	10	0	0	0	0	0	0	0	0	0
580	**600**	26	12	0	0	0	0	0	0	0	0	0
600	**620**	28	14	0	0	0	0	0	0	0	0	0
620	**640**	30	16	1	0	0	0	0	0	0	0	0
640	**660**	32	18	3	0	0	0	0	0	0	0	0
660	**680**	34	20	5	0	0	0	0	0	0	0	0
680	**700**	36	22	7	0	0	0	0	0	0	0	0
700	**720**	38	24	9	0	0	0	0	0	0	0	0
720	**740**	40	26	11	0	0	0	0	0	0	0	0
740	**760**	42	28	13	0	0	0	0	0	0	0	0
760	**780**	44	30	15	1	0	0	0	0	0	0	0
780	**800**	46	32	17	3	0	0	0	0	0	0	0
800	**820**	48	34	19	5	0	0	0	0	0	0	0
820	**840**	50	36	21	7	0	0	0	0	0	0	0
840	**860**	52	38	23	9	0	0	0	0	0	0	0
860	**880**	54	40	25	11	0	0	0	0	0	0	0
880	**900**	56	42	27	13	0	0	0	0	0	0	0
900	**920**	58	44	29	15	1	0	0	0	0	0	0
920	**940**	60	46	31	17	3	0	0	0	0	0	0
940	**960**	62	48	33	19	5	0	0	0	0	0	0
960	**980**	64	50	35	21	7	0	0	0	0	0	0
980	**1,000**	67	52	37	23	9	0	0	0	0	0	0
1,000	**1,020**	70	54	39	25	11	0	0	0	0	0	0
1,020	**1,040**	73	56	41	27	13	0	0	0	0	0	0
1,040	**1,060**	76	58	43	29	15	1	0	0	0	0	0
1,060	**1,080**	79	60	45	31	17	3	0	0	0	0	0
1,080	**1,100**	82	62	47	33	19	5	0	0	0	0	0
1,100	**1,120**	85	64	49	35	21	7	0	0	0	0	0
1,120	**1,140**	88	66	51	37	23	9	0	0	0	0	0
1,140	**1,160**	91	69	53	39	25	11	0	0	0	0	0
1,160	**1,180**	94	72	55	41	27	13	0	0	0	0	0
1,180	**1,200**	97	75	57	43	29	15	1	0	0	0	0
1,200	**1,220**	100	78	59	45	31	17	3	0	0	0	0
1,220	**1,240**	103	81	61	47	33	19	5	0	0	0	0
1,240	**1,260**	106	84	63	49	35	21	7	0	0	0	0
1,260	**1,280**	109	87	66	51	37	23	9	0	0	0	0
1,280	**1,300**	112	90	69	53	39	25	11	0	0	0	0
1,300	**1,320**	115	93	72	55	41	27	13	0	0	0	0
1,320	**1,340**	118	96	75	57	43	29	15	1	0	0	0
1,340	**1,360**	121	99	78	59	45	31	17	3	0	0	0
1,360	**1,380**	124	102	81	61	47	33	19	5	0	0	0
1,380	**1,400**	127	105	84	63	49	35	21	7	0	0	0
1,400	**1,420**	130	108	87	66	51	37	23	9	0	0	0

MARRIED Persons—**SEMIMONTHLY** Payroll Period

(For Wages Paid in 2007)

If the wages are–		And the number of withholding allowances claimed is—										
At least	But less than	0	1	2	3	4	5	6	7	8	9	10
		The amount of income tax to be withheld is—										
$1,420	**$1,440**	$133	$111	$90	$69	$53	$39	$25	$11	$0	$0	$0
1,440	**1,460**	136	114	93	72	55	41	27	13	0	0	0
1,460	**1,480**	139	117	96	75	57	43	29	15	0	0	0
1,480	**1,500**	142	120	99	78	59	45	31	17	2	0	0
1,500	**1,520**	145	123	102	81	61	47	33	19	4	0	0
1,520	**1,540**	148	126	105	84	63	49	35	21	6	0	0
1,540	**1,560**	151	129	108	87	66	51	37	23	8	0	0
1,560	**1,580**	154	132	111	90	69	53	39	25	10	0	0
1,580	**1,600**	157	135	114	93	72	55	41	27	12	0	0
1,600	**1,620**	160	138	117	96	75	57	43	29	14	0	0
1,620	**1,640**	163	141	120	99	78	59	45	31	16	2	0
1,640	**1,660**	166	144	123	102	81	61	47	33	18	4	0
1,660	**1,680**	169	147	126	105	84	63	49	35	20	6	0
1,680	**1,700**	172	150	129	108	87	65	51	37	22	8	0
1,700	**1,720**	175	153	132	111	90	68	53	39	24	10	0
1,720	**1,740**	178	156	135	114	93	71	55	41	26	12	0
1,740	**1,760**	181	159	138	117	96	74	57	43	28	14	0
1,760	**1,780**	184	162	141	120	99	77	59	45	30	16	2
1,780	**1,800**	187	165	144	123	102	80	61	47	32	18	4
1,800	**1,820**	190	168	147	126	105	83	63	49	34	20	6
1,820	**1,840**	193	171	150	129	108	86	65	51	36	22	8
1,840	**1,860**	196	174	153	132	111	89	68	53	38	24	10
1,860	**1,880**	199	177	156	135	114	92	71	55	40	26	12
1,880	**1,900**	202	180	159	138	117	95	74	57	42	28	14
1,900	**1,920**	205	183	162	141	120	98	77	59	44	30	16
1,920	**1,940**	208	186	165	144	123	101	80	61	46	32	18
1,940	**1,960**	211	189	168	147	126	104	83	63	48	34	20
1,960	**1,980**	214	192	171	150	129	107	86	65	50	36	22
1,980	**2,000**	217	195	174	153	132	110	89	68	52	38	24
2,000	**2,020**	220	198	177	156	135	113	92	71	54	40	26
2,020	**2,040**	223	201	180	159	138	116	95	74	56	42	28
2,040	**2,060**	226	204	183	162	141	119	98	77	58	44	30
2,060	**2,080**	229	207	186	165	144	122	101	80	60	46	32
2,080	**2,100**	232	210	189	168	147	125	104	83	62	48	34
2,100	**2,120**	235	213	192	171	150	128	107	86	65	50	36
2,120	**2,140**	238	216	195	174	153	131	110	89	68	52	38
2,140	**2,160**	241	219	198	177	156	134	113	92	71	54	40
2,160	**2,180**	244	222	201	180	159	137	116	95	74	56	42
2,180	**2,200**	247	225	204	183	162	140	119	98	77	58	44
2,200	**2,220**	250	228	207	186	165	143	122	101	80	60	46
2,220	**2,240**	253	231	210	189	168	146	125	104	83	62	48
2,240	**2,260**	256	234	213	192	171	149	128	107	86	64	50
2,260	**2,280**	259	237	216	195	174	152	131	110	89	67	52
2,280	**2,300**	262	240	219	198	177	155	134	113	92	70	54
2,300	**2,320**	265	243	222	201	180	158	137	116	95	73	56
2,320	**2,340**	268	246	225	204	183	161	140	119	98	76	58
2,340	**2,360**	271	249	228	207	186	164	143	122	101	79	60
2,360	**2,380**	274	252	231	210	189	167	146	125	104	82	62
2,380	**2,400**	277	255	234	213	192	170	149	128	107	85	64
2,400	**2,420**	280	258	237	216	195	173	152	131	110	88	67
2,420	**2,440**	283	261	240	219	198	176	155	134	113	91	70
2,440	**2,460**	286	264	243	222	201	179	158	137	116	94	73
2,460	**2,480**	289	267	246	225	204	182	161	140	119	97	76
2,480	**2,500**	292	270	249	228	207	185	164	143	122	100	79
2,500	**2,520**	295	273	252	231	210	188	167	146	125	103	82
2,520	**2,540**	298	276	255	234	213	191	170	149	128	106	85
2,540	**2,560**	301	279	258	237	216	194	173	152	131	109	88
2,560	**2,580**	304	282	261	240	219	197	176	155	134	112	91
2,580	**2,600**	307	285	264	243	222	200	179	158	137	115	94
2,600	**2,620**	310	288	267	246	225	203	182	161	140	118	97
2,620	**2,640**	313	291	270	249	228	206	185	164	143	121	100
2,640	**2,660**	316	294	273	252	231	209	188	167	146	124	103
2,660	**2,680**	319	297	276	255	234	212	191	170	149	127	106
2,680	**2,700**	322	300	279	258	237	215	194	173	152	130	109
2,700	**2,720**	325	303	282	261	240	218	197	176	155	133	112
2,720	**2,740**	328	306	285	264	243	221	200	179	158	136	115

$2,740 and over Use Table 3(b) for a **MARRIED person** on page T-3

WAGE-BRACKET INCOME TAX WITHHOLDING TABLES

SINGLE Persons—MONTHLY Payroll Period

(For Wages Paid in 2007)

MONTHLY SINGLE PERSONS

If the wages are–		And the number of withholding allowances claimed is—										
At least	But less than	0	1	2	3	4	5	6	7	8	9	10
		The amount of income tax to be withheld is—										
$0	$220	$0	$0	$0	$0	$0	$0	$0	$0	$0	$0	$0
220	230	0	0	0	0	0	0	0	0	0	0	0
230	240	1	0	0	0	0	0	0	0	0	0	0
240	250	2	0	0	0	0	0	0	0	0	0	0
250	260	3	0	0	0	0	0	0	0	0	0	0
260	270	4	0	0	0	0	0	0				
270	280	5	0	0	0	0	0	0				
280	290	6	0	0	0	0	0	0				
290	300	7	0	0	0	0	0	0				
300	320	9	0	0	0	0	0	0				
320	340	11	0	0	0	0	0	0				
340	360	13	0	0	0	0	0	0				
360	380	15	0	0	0	0	0	0				
380	400	17	0	0	0	0	0	0				
400	420	19	0	0	0	0	0	0				
420	440	21	0	0	0	0	0	0	0	0	0	0
440	460	23	0	0	0	0	0	0	0	0	0	0
460	480	25	0	0	0	0	0	0	0	0	0	0
480	500	27	0	0	0	0	0	0	0	0	0	0
500	520	29	1	0	0	0	0	0	0	0	0	0
520	540	31	3	0	0	0	0	0	0	0	0	0
540	560	33	5	0	0	0	0	0	0	0	0	0
560	580	35	7	0	0	0	0	0	0	0	0	0
580	600	37	9	0	0	0	0	0	0	0	0	0
600	640	40	12	0	0	0	0	0	0	0	0	0
640	680	44	16	0	0	0	0	0	0	0	0	0
680	720	48	20	0	0	0	0	0	0	0	0	0
720	760	52	24	0	0	0	0	0	0	0	0	0
760	800	56	28	0	0	0	0	0	0	0	0	0
800	840	60	32	3	0	0	0	0	0	0	0	0
840	880	65	36	7	0	0	0	0	0	0	0	0
880	920	71	40	11	0	0	0	0	0	0	0	0
920	960	77	44	15	0	0	0	0	0	0	0	0
960	1,000	83	48	19	0	0	0	0	0	0	0	0
1,000	1,040	89	52	23	0	0	0	0	0	0	0	0
1,040	1,080	95	56	27	0	0	0	0	0	0	0	0
1,080	1,120	101	60	31	3	0	0	0	0	0	0	0
1,120	1,160	107	64	35	7	0	0	0	0	0	0	0
1,160	1,200	113	70	39	11	0	0	0	0	0	0	0
1,200	1,240	119	76	43	15	0	0	0	0	0	0	0
1,240	1,280	125	82	47	19	0	0	0	0	0	0	0
1,280	1,320	131	88	51	23	0	0	0	0	0	0	0
1,320	1,360	137	94	55	27	0	0	0	0	0	0	0
1,360	1,400	143	100	59	31	3	0	0	0	0	0	0
1,400	1,440	149	106	64	35	7	0	0	0	0	0	0
1,440	1,480	155	112	70	39	11	0	0	0	0	0	0
1,480	1,520	161	118	76	43	15	0	0	0	0	0	0
1,520	1,560	167	124	82	47	19	0	0	0	0	0	0
1,560	1,600	173	130	88	51	23	0	0	0	0	0	0
1,600	1,640	179	136	94	55	27	0	0	0	0	0	0
1,640	1,680	185	142	100	59	31	2	0	0	0	0	0
1,680	1,720	191	148	106	63	35	6	0	0	0	0	0
1,720	1,760	197	154	112	69	39	10	0	0	0	0	0
1,760	1,800	203	160	118	75	43	14	0	0	0	0	0
1,800	1,840	209	166	124	81	47	18	0	0	0	0	0
1,840	1,880	215	172	130	87	51	22	0	0	0	0	0
1,880	1,920	221	178	136	93	55	26	0	0	0	0	0
1,920	1,960	227	184	142	99	59	30	2	0	0	0	0
1,960	2,000	233	190	148	105	63	34	6	0	0	0	0
2,000	2,040	239	196	154	111	69	38	10	0	0	0	0
2,040	2,080	245	202	160	117	75	42	14	0	0	0	0
2,080	2,120	251	208	166	123	81	46	18	0	0	0	0
2,120	2,160	257	214	172	129	87	50	22	0	0	0	0
2,160	2,200	263	220	178	135	93	54	26	0	0	0	0
2,200	2,240	269	226	184	141	99	58	30	2	0	0	0
2,240	2,280	275	232	190	147	105	62	34	6	0	0	0
2,280	2,320	281	238	196	153	111	68	38	10	0	0	0
2,320	2,360	287	244	202	159	117	74	42	14	0	0	0
2,360	2,400	293	250	208	165	123	80	46	18	0	0	0
2,400	2,440	299	256	214	171	129	86	50	22	0	0	0

SINGLE Persons—MONTHLY Payroll Period

(For Wages Paid in 2007)

If the wages are–		And the number of withholding allowances claimed is—										
At least	But less than	0	1	2	3	4	5	6	7	8	9	10
		The amount of income tax to be withheld is—										
$2,440	$2,480	$305	$262	$220	$177	$135	$92	$54	$26	$0	$0	$0
2,480	2,520	311	268	226	183	141	98	58	30	1	0	0
2,520	2,560	317	274	232	189	147	104	62	34	5	0	0
2,560	2,600	323	280	238	195	153	110	68	38	9	0	0
2,600	2,640	329	286	244	201	159	116	74	42	13	0	0
2,640	2,680	335	292	250	207	165	122	80	46	17	0	0
2,680	2,720	341	298	256	213	171	128	86	50	21	0	0
2,720	2,760	347	304	262	219	177	134	92	54	25	0	0
2,760	2,800	353	310	268	225	183	140	98	58	29	1	0
2,800	2,840	361	316	274	231	189	146	104	62	33	5	0
2,840	2,880	371	322	280	237	195	152	110	67	37	9	0
2,880	2,920	381	328	286	243	201	158	116	73	41	13	0
2,920	2,960	391	334	292	249	207	164	122	79	45	17	0
2,960	3,000	401	340	298	255	213	170	128	85	49	21	0
3,000	3,040	411	346	304	261	219	176	134	91	53	25	0
3,040	3,080	421	352	310	267	225	182	140	97	57	29	1
3,080	3,120	431	361	316	273	231	188	146	103	61	33	5
3,120	3,160	441	371	322	279	237	194	152	109	67	37	9
3,160	3,200	451	381	328	285	243	200	158	115	73	41	13
3,200	3,240	461	391	334	291	249	206	164	121	79	45	17
3,240	3,280	471	401	340	297	255	212	170	127	85	49	21
3,280	3,320	481	411	346	303	261	218	176	133	91	53	25
3,320	3,360	491	421	352	309	267	224	182	139	97	57	29
3,360	3,400	501	431	360	315	273	230	188	145	103	61	33
3,400	3,440	511	441	370	321	279	236	194	151	109	66	37
3,440	3,480	521	451	380	327	285	242	200	157	115	72	41
3,480	3,520	531	461	390	333	291	248	206	163	121	78	45
3,520	3,560	541	471	400	339	297	254	212	169	127	84	49
3,560	3,600	551	481	410	345	303	260	218	175	133	90	53
3,600	3,640	561	491	420	351	309	266	224	181	139	96	57
3,640	3,680	571	501	430	359	315	272	230	187	145	102	61
3,680	3,720	581	511	440	369	321	278	236	193	151	108	66
3,720	3,760	591	521	450	379	327	284	242	199	157	114	72
3,760	3,800	601	531	460	389	333	290	248	205	163	120	78
3,800	3,840	611	541	470	399	339	296	254	211	169	126	84
3,840	3,880	621	551	480	409	345	302	260	217	175	132	90
3,880	3,920	631	561	490	419	351	308	266	223	181	138	96
3,920	3,960	641	571	500	429	358	314	272	229	187	144	102
3,960	4,000	651	581	510	439	368	320	278	235	193	150	108
4,000	4,040	661	591	520	449	378	326	284	241	199	156	114
4,040	4,080	671	601	530	459	388	332	290	247	205	162	120
4,080	4,120	681	611	540	469	398	338	296	253	211	168	126
4,120	4,160	691	621	550	479	408	344	302	259	217	174	132
4,160	4,200	701	631	560	489	418	350	308	265	223	180	138
4,200	4,240	711	641	570	499	428	357	314	271	229	186	144
4,240	4,280	721	651	580	509	438	367	320	277	235	192	150
4,280	4,320	731	661	590	519	448	377	326	283	241	198	156
4,320	4,360	741	671	600	529	458	387	332	289	247	204	162
4,360	4,400	751	681	610	539	468	397	338	295	253	210	168
4,400	4,440	761	691	620	549	478	407	344	301	259	216	174
4,440	4,480	771	701	630	559	488	417	350	307	265	222	180
4,480	4,520	781	711	640	569	498	427	356	313	271	228	186
4,520	4,560	791	721	650	579	508	437	366	319	277	234	192
4,560	4,600	801	731	660	589	518	447	376	325	283	240	198
4,600	4,640	811	741	670	599	528	457	386	331	289	246	204
4,640	4,680	821	751	680	609	538	467	396	337	295	252	210
4,680	4,720	831	761	690	619	548	477	406	343	301	258	216
4,720	4,760	841	771	700	629	558	487	416	349	307	264	222
4,760	4,800	851	781	710	639	568	497	426	356	313	270	228
4,800	4,840	861	791	720	649	578	507	436	366	319	276	234
4,840	4,880	871	801	730	659	588	517	446	376	325	282	240
4,880	4,920	881	811	740	669	598	527	456	386	331	288	246
4,920	4,960	891	821	750	679	608	537	466	396	337	294	252
4,960	5,000	901	831	760	689	618	547	476	406	343	300	258
5,000	5,040	911	841	770	699	628	557	486	416	349	306	264
5,040	5,080	921	851	780	709	638	567	496	426	355	312	270

$5,080 and over — Use Table 4(a) for a **SINGLE person** on page T-3

WAGE-BRACKET INCOME TAX WITHHOLDING TABLES

MARRIED Persons—MONTHLY Payroll Period

(For Wages Paid in 2007)

If the wages are–		And the number of withholding allowances claimed is—										
At least	But less than	0	1	2	3	4	5	6	7	8	9	10
		The amount of income tax to be withheld is—										
$0	$540	$0	$0	$0	$0	$0	$0	$0	$0	$0	$0	$0
540	560	0	0	0	0	0	0	0	0	0	0	0
560	580	0	0	0	0	0	0	0	0	0	0	0
580	600	0	0	0	0	0	0	0	0	0	0	0
600	640	0	0	0	0	0	0	0	0	0	0	0
640	680	0	0	0	0	0	0	0				
680	720	3	0	0	0	0	0	0				
720	760	7	0	0	0	0	0	0				
760	800	11	0	0	0	0	0	0				
800	840	15	0	0	0	0	0	0				
840	880	19	0	0	0	0	0	0				
880	920	23	0	0	0	0	0	0				
920	960	27	0	0	0	0	0	0				
960	1,000	31	3	0	0	0	0	0				
1,000	1,040	35	7	0	0	0	0	0				
1,040	1,080	39	11	0	0	0	0	0	0	0	0	0
1,080	1,120	43	15	0	0	0	0	0	0	0	0	0
1,120	1,160	47	19	0	0	0	0	0	0	0	0	0
1,160	1,200	51	23	0	0	0	0	0	0	0	0	0
1,200	1,240	55	27	0	0	0	0	0	0	0	0	0
1,240	1,280	59	31	3	0	0	0	0	0	0	0	0
1,280	1,320	63	35	7	0	0	0	0	0	0	0	0
1,320	1,360	67	39	11	0	0	0	0	0	0	0	0
1,360	1,400	71	43	15	0	0	0	0	0	0	0	0
1,400	1,440	75	47	19	0	0	0	0	0	0	0	0
1,440	1,480	79	51	23	0	0	0	0	0	0	0	0
1,480	1,520	83	55	27	0	0	0	0	0	0	0	0
1,520	1,560	87	59	31	2	0	0	0	0	0	0	0
1,560	1,600	91	63	35	6	0	0	0	0	0	0	0
1,600	1,640	95	67	39	10	0	0	0	0	0	0	0
1,640	1,680	99	71	43	14	0	0	0	0	0	0	0
1,680	1,720	103	75	47	18	0	0	0	0	0	0	0
1,720	1,760	107	79	51	22	0	0	0	0	0	0	0
1,760	1,800	111	83	55	26	0	0	0	0	0	0	0
1,800	1,840	115	87	59	30	2	0	0	0	0	0	0
1,840	1,880	119	91	63	34	6	0	0	0	0	0	0
1,880	1,920	123	95	67	38	10	0	0	0	0	0	0
1,920	1,960	127	99	71	42	14	0	0	0	0	0	0
1,960	2,000	133	103	75	46	18	0	0	0	0	0	0
2,000	2,040	139	107	79	50	22	0	0	0	0	0	0
2,040	2,080	145	111	83	54	26	0	0	0	0	0	0
2,080	2,120	151	115	87	58	30	2	0	0	0	0	0
2,120	2,160	157	119	91	62	34	6	0	0	0	0	0
2,160	2,200	163	123	95	66	38	10	0	0	0	0	0
2,200	2,240	169	127	99	70	42	14	0	0	0	0	0
2,240	2,280	175	133	103	74	46	18	0	0	0	0	0
2,280	2,320	181	139	107	78	50	22	0	0	0	0	0
2,320	2,360	187	145	111	82	54	26	0	0	0	0	0
2,360	2,400	193	151	115	86	58	30	1	0	0	0	0
2,400	2,440	199	157	119	90	62	34	5	0	0	0	0
2,440	2,480	205	163	123	94	66	38	9	0	0	0	0
2,480	2,520	211	169	127	98	70	42	13	0	0	0	0
2,520	2,560	217	175	132	102	74	46	17	0	0	0	0
2,560	2,600	223	181	138	106	78	50	21	0	0	0	0
2,600	2,640	229	187	144	110	82	54	25	0	0	0	0
2,640	2,680	235	193	150	114	86	58	29	1	0	0	0
2,680	2,720	241	199	156	118	90	62	33	5	0	0	0
2,720	2,760	247	205	162	122	94	66	37	9	0	0	0
2,760	2,800	253	211	168	126	98	70	41	13	0	0	0
2,800	2,840	259	217	174	132	102	74	45	17	0	0	0
2,840	2,880	265	223	180	138	106	78	49	21	0	0	0
2,880	2,920	271	229	186	144	110	82	53	25	0	0	0
2,920	2,960	277	235	192	150	114	86	57	29	1	0	0
2,960	3,000	283	241	198	156	118	90	61	33	5	0	0
3,000	3,040	289	247	204	162	122	94	65	37	9	0	0
3,040	3,080	295	253	210	168	126	98	69	41	13	0	0
3,080	3,120	301	259	216	174	131	102	73	45	17	0	0
3,120	3,160	307	265	222	180	137	106	77	49	21	0	0
3,160	3,200	313	271	228	186	143	110	81	53	25	0	0
3,200	3,240	319	277	234	192	149	114	85	57	29	0	0

MONTHLY MARRIED PERSONS

MARRIED Persons—MONTHLY Payroll Period

(For Wages Paid in 2007)

If the wages are–		And the number of withholding allowances claimed is—										
At least	But less than	0	1	2	3	4	5	6	7	8	9	10
		The amount of income tax to be withheld is—										
$3,240	$3,280	$325	$283	$240	$198	$155	$118	$89	$61	$33	$4	$0
3,280	3,320	331	289	246	204	161	122	93	65	37	8	0
3,320	3,360	337	295	252	210	167	126	97	69	41	12	0
3,360	3,400	343	301	258	216	173	131	101	73	45	16	0
3,400	3,440	349	307	264	222	179	137	105	77	49	20	0
3,440	3,480	355	313	270	228	185	143	109	81	53	24	0
3,480	3,520	361	319	276	234	191	149	113	85	57	28	0
3,520	3,560	367	325	282	240	197	155	117	89	61	32	4
3,560	3,600	373	331	288	246	203	161	121	93	65	36	8
3,600	3,640	379	337	294	252	209	167	125	97	69	40	12
3,640	3,680	385	343	300	258	215	173	130	101	73	44	16
3,680	3,720	391	349	306	264	221	179	136	105	77	48	20
3,720	3,760	397	355	312	270	227	185	142	109	81	52	24
3,760	3,800	403	361	318	276	233	191	148	113	85	56	28
3,800	3,840	409	367	324	282	239	197	154	117	89	60	32
3,840	3,880	415	373	330	288	245	203	160	121	93	64	36
3,880	3,920	421	379	336	294	251	209	166	125	97	68	40
3,920	3,960	427	385	342	300	257	215	172	130	101	72	44
3,960	4,000	433	391	348	306	263	221	178	136	105	76	48
4,000	4,040	439	397	354	312	269	227	184	142	109	80	52
4,040	4,080	445	403	360	318	275	233	190	148	113	84	56
4,080	4,120	451	409	366	324	281	239	196	154	117	88	60
4,120	4,160	457	415	372	330	287	245	202	160	121	92	64
4,160	4,200	463	421	378	336	293	251	208	166	125	96	68
4,200	4,240	469	427	384	342	299	257	214	172	129	100	72
4,240	4,280	475	433	390	348	305	263	220	178	135	104	76
4,280	4,320	481	439	396	354	311	269	226	184	141	108	80
4,320	4,360	487	445	402	360	317	275	232	190	147	112	84
4,360	4,400	493	451	408	366	323	281	238	196	153	116	88
4,400	4,440	499	457	414	372	329	287	244	202	159	120	92
4,440	4,480	505	463	420	378	335	293	250	208	165	124	96
4,480	4,520	511	469	426	384	341	299	256	214	171	129	100
4,520	4,560	517	475	432	390	347	305	262	220	177	135	104
4,560	4,600	523	481	438	396	353	311	268	226	183	141	108
4,600	4,640	529	487	444	402	359	317	274	232	189	147	112
4,640	4,680	535	493	450	408	365	323	280	238	195	153	116
4,680	4,720	541	499	456	414	371	329	286	244	201	159	120
4,720	4,760	547	505	462	420	377	335	292	250	207	165	124
4,760	4,800	553	511	468	426	383	341	298	256	213	171	128
4,800	4,840	559	517	474	432	389	347	304	262	219	177	134
4,840	4,880	565	523	480	438	395	353	310	268	225	183	140
4,880	4,920	571	529	486	444	401	359	316	274	231	189	146
4,920	4,960	577	535	492	450	407	365	322	280	237	195	152
4,960	5,000	583	541	498	456	413	371	328	286	243	201	158
5,000	5,040	589	547	504	462	419	377	334	292	249	207	164
5,040	5,080	595	553	510	468	425	383	340	298	255	213	170
5,080	5,120	601	559	516	474	431	389	346	304	261	219	176
5,120	5,160	607	565	522	480	437	395	352	310	267	225	182
5,160	5,200	613	571	528	486	443	401	358	316	273	231	188
5,200	5,240	619	577	534	492	449	407	364	322	279	237	194
5,240	5,280	625	583	540	498	455	413	370	328	285	243	200
5,280	5,320	631	589	546	504	461	419	376	334	291	249	206
5,320	5,360	637	595	552	510	467	425	382	340	297	255	212
5,360	5,400	643	601	558	516	473	431	388	346	303	261	218
5,400	5,440	649	607	564	522	479	437	394	352	309	267	224
5,440	5,480	655	613	570	528	485	443	400	358	315	273	230
5,480	5,520	661	619	576	534	491	449	406	364	321	279	236
5,520	5,560	667	625	582	540	497	455	412	370	327	285	242
5,560	5,600	673	631	588	546	503	461	418	376	333	291	248
5,600	5,640	679	637	594	552	509	467	424	382	339	297	254
5,640	5,680	685	643	600	558	515	473	430	388	345	303	260
5,680	5,720	691	649	606	564	521	479	436	394	351	309	266
5,720	5,760	697	655	612	570	527	485	442	400	357	315	272
5,760	5,800	703	661	618	576	533	491	448	406	363	321	278
5,800	5,840	709	667	624	582	539	497	454	412	369	327	284
5,840	5,880	715	673	630	588	545	503	460	418	375	333	290
$5,880 and over		Use Table 4(b) for a **MARRIED person** on page T-3										

WAGE-BRACKET INCOME TAX WITHHOLDING TABLES

DAILY OR MISC. SINGLE PERSONS

SINGLE Persons—DAILY OR MISCELLANEOUS Payroll Period

(For Wages Paid in 2007)

If the wages are–		And the number of withholding allowances claimed is—										
At least	But less than	0	1	2	3	4	5	6	7	8	9	10
		The amount of income tax to be withheld is—										
$0	$12	$0	$0	$0	$0	$0	$0	$0	$0	$0	$0	$0
12	15	0	0	0	0	0	0	0	0	0	0	0
15	18	1	0	0	0	0	0	0	0	0	0	0
18	21	1	0	0	0	0	0	0	0	0	0	0
21	24	1	0	0	0	0	0	0	0	0	0	0
24	27	2	0	0	0	0	0	0	[illegible]	[illegible]	[illegible]	[illegible]
27	30	2	1	0	0	0	0	0	[illegible]	[illegible]	[illegible]	[illegible]
30	33	2	1	0	0	0	0	0	[illegible]	[illegible]	[illegible]	[illegible]
33	36	2	1	0	0	0	0	0	[illegible]	[illegible]	[illegible]	[illegible]
36	39	3	1	0	0	0	0	0	[illegible]	[illegible]	[illegible]	[illegible]
39	42	3	2	0	0	0	0	0	[illegible]	[illegible]	[illegible]	[illegible]
42	45	4	2	1	0	0	0	0	[illegible]	[illegible]	[illegible]	[illegible]
45	48	4	2	1	0	0	0	0	[illegible]	[illegible]	[illegible]	[illegible]
48	51	4	3	1	0	0	0	0	[illegible]	[illegible]	[illegible]	[illegible]
51	54	5	3	2	0	0	0	0	[illegible]	[illegible]	[illegible]	[illegible]
54	57	5	3	2	1	0	0	0	0	0	0	0
57	60	6	4	2	1	0	0	0	0	0	0	0
60	63	6	4	3	1	0	0	0	0	0	0	0
63	66	7	5	3	2	0	0	0	0	0	0	0
66	69	7	5	3	2	1	0	0	0	0	0	0
69	72	8	6	4	2	1	0	0	0	0	0	0
72	75	8	6	4	2	1	0	0	0	0	0	0
75	78	9	7	5	3	1	0	0	0	0	0	0
78	81	9	7	5	3	2	0	0	0	0	0	0
81	84	9	7	5	4	2	1	0	0	0	0	0
84	87	10	8	6	4	2	1	0	0	0	0	0
87	90	10	8	6	4	3	1	0	0	0	0	0
90	93	11	9	7	5	3	2	0	0	0	0	0
93	96	11	9	7	5	3	2	1	0	0	0	0
96	99	12	10	8	6	4	2	1	0	0	0	0
99	102	12	10	8	6	4	2	1	0	0	0	0
102	105	13	11	9	7	5	3	1	0	0	0	0
105	108	13	11	9	7	5	3	2	0	0	0	0
108	111	13	11	10	8	6	4	2	1	0	0	0
111	114	14	12	10	8	6	4	2	1	0	0	0
114	117	14	12	10	8	7	5	3	1	0	0	0
117	120	15	13	11	9	7	5	3	2	0	0	0
120	123	15	13	11	9	7	5	3	2	1	0	0
123	126	16	14	12	10	8	6	4	2	1	0	0
126	129	16	14	12	10	8	6	4	3	1	0	0
129	132	17	15	13	11	9	7	5	3	2	0	0
132	135	18	15	13	11	9	7	5	3	2	1	0
135	138	18	16	14	12	10	8	6	4	2	1	0
138	141	19	16	14	12	10	8	6	4	2	1	0
141	144	20	16	14	13	11	9	7	5	3	1	0
144	147	21	17	15	13	11	9	7	5	3	2	0
147	150	21	18	15	13	11	10	8	6	4	2	1
150	153	22	19	16	14	12	10	8	6	4	2	1
153	156	23	19	16	14	12	10	8	6	5	3	1
156	159	24	20	17	15	13	11	9	7	5	3	2
159	162	24	21	18	15	13	11	9	7	5	3	2
162	165	25	22	18	16	14	12	10	8	6	4	2
165	168	26	22	19	16	14	12	10	8	6	4	3
168	171	27	23	20	17	15	13	11	9	7	5	3
171	174	27	24	21	17	15	13	11	9	7	5	3
174	177	28	25	21	18	16	14	12	10	8	6	4
177	180	29	25	22	19	16	14	12	10	8	6	4
180	183	30	26	23	20	16	14	12	11	9	7	5
183	186	30	27	24	20	17	15	13	11	9	7	5
186	189	31	28	24	21	18	15	13	11	9	8	6
189	192	32	28	25	22	19	16	14	12	10	8	6
192	195	33	29	26	23	19	16	14	12	10	8	6
195	198	33	30	27	23	20	17	15	13	11	9	7
198	201	34	31	27	24	21	18	15	13	11	9	7
201	204	35	31	28	25	22	18	16	14	12	10	8
204	207	36	32	29	26	22	19	16	14	12	10	8
207	210	36	33	30	26	23	20	17	15	13	11	9
210	213	37	34	30	27	24	21	17	15	13	11	9
213	216	38	34	31	28	25	21	18	15	14	12	10
216	219	39	35	32	29	25	22	19	16	14	12	10

SINGLE Persons—DAILY OR MISCELLANEOUS Payroll Period

(For Wages Paid in 2007)

If the wages are–		And the number of withholding allowances claimed is—										
At least	But less than	0	1	2	3	4	5	6	7	8	9	10
		The amount of income tax to be withheld is—										
$219	$222	$39	$36	$33	$29	$26	$23	$20	$16	$14	$12	$10
222	225	40	37	33	30	27	24	20	17	15	13	11
225	228	41	37	34	31	28	24	21	18	15	13	11
228	231	42	38	35	32	28	25	22	19	16	14	12
231	234	42	39	36	32	29	26	23	19	16	14	12
234	237	43	40	36	33	30	27	23	20	17	15	13
237	240	44	40	37	34	31	27	24	21	18	15	13
240	243	45	41	38	35	31	28	25	22	18	16	14
243	246	45	42	39	35	32	29	26	22	19	16	14
246	249	46	43	39	36	33	30	26	23	20	17	15
249	252	47	43	40	37	34	30	27	24	21	17	15
252	255	48	44	41	38	34	31	28	25	21	18	15
255	258	48	45	42	38	35	32	29	25	22	19	16
258	261	49	46	42	39	36	33	29	26	23	20	16
261	264	50	46	43	40	37	33	30	27	24	20	17
264	267	51	47	44	41	37	34	31	28	24	21	18
267	270	51	48	45	41	38	35	32	28	25	22	19
270	273	52	49	45	42	39	36	32	29	26	23	19
273	276	53	49	46	43	40	36	33	30	27	23	20
276	279	54	50	47	44	40	37	34	31	27	24	21
279	282	54	51	48	44	41	38	35	31	28	25	22
282	285	55	52	48	45	42	39	35	32	29	26	22
285	288	56	52	49	46	43	39	36	33	30	26	23
288	291	57	53	50	47	43	40	37	34	30	27	24
291	294	57	54	51	47	44	41	38	34	31	28	25
294	297	58	55	51	48	45	42	38	35	32	29	25
297	300	59	55	52	49	46	42	39	36	33	29	26
300	303	60	56	53	50	46	43	40	37	33	30	27
303	306	61	57	54	50	47	44	41	37	34	31	28
306	309	61	58	54	51	48	45	41	38	35	32	28
309	312	62	59	55	52	49	45	42	39	36	32	29
312	315	63	59	56	53	49	46	43	40	36	33	30
315	318	64	60	57	53	50	47	44	40	37	34	31
318	321	65	61	57	54	51	48	44	41	38	35	31
321	324	66	62	58	55	52	48	45	42	39	35	32
324	327	66	63	59	56	52	49	46	43	39	36	33
327	330	67	64	60	56	53	50	47	43	40	37	34
330	333	68	64	61	57	54	51	47	44	41	38	34
333	336	69	65	62	58	55	51	48	45	42	38	35
336	339	70	66	62	59	55	52	49	46	42	39	36
339	341	70	67	63	59	56	53	50	46	43	40	36
341	343	71	67	64	60	57	53	50	47	43	40	37
343	345	72	68	64	61	57	54	51	47	44	41	37
345	347	72	68	65	61	58	54	51	48	44	41	38
347	349	73	69	65	62	58	55	52	48	45	42	38
349	351	73	70	66	62	59	55	52	49	45	42	39
351	353	74	70	66	63	59	56	53	49	46	43	39
353	355	74	71	67	63	60	56	53	50	46	43	40
355	357	75	71	68	64	60	57	54	50	47	44	40
357	359	75	72	68	65	61	57	54	51	47	44	41
359	361	76	72	69	65	61	58	55	51	48	45	41
361	363	77	73	69	66	62	58	55	52	48	45	42
363	365	77	74	70	66	63	59	56	52	49	46	42
365	367	78	74	70	67	63	59	56	53	49	46	43
367	369	78	75	71	67	64	60	57	53	50	47	43
369	371	79	75	72	68	64	61	57	54	50	47	44
371	373	79	76	72	68	65	61	58	54	51	48	44
373	375	80	76	73	69	65	62	58	55	51	48	45
375	377	81	77	73	70	66	62	59	55	52	49	45
377	379	81	77	74	70	66	63	59	56	52	49	46
379	381	82	78	74	71	67	63	60	56	53	50	46
381	383	82	79	75	71	68	64	60	57	53	50	47
383	385	83	79	75	72	68	64	61	57	54	51	47
385	387	83	80	76	72	69	65	61	58	54	51	48
387	389	84	80	77	73	69	66	62	58	55	52	48
389	391	84	81	77	73	70	66	62	59	55	52	49

$391 and over Use Table 8(a) for a **SINGLE person** on page T-4

WAGE-BRACKET INCOME TAX WITHHOLDING TABLES

MARRIED Persons—**DAILY OR MISCELLANEOUS** Payroll Period

(For Wages Paid in 2007)

DAILY OR MISC. MARRIED PERSONS

If the wages are–		And the number of withholding allowances claimed is—										
At least	But less than	0	1	2	3	4	5	6	7	8	9	10
		The amount of income tax to be withheld is—										
$0	**$27**	$0	$0	$0	$0	$0	$0	$0	$0	$0	$0	$0
27	**30**	0	0	0	0	0	0	0	0	0	0	0
30	**33**	0	0	0	0	0	0	0	0	0	0	0
33	**36**	0	0	0	0	0	0	0	0	0	0	0
36	**39**	1	0	0	0	0	0	0	0	0	0	0
39	**42**	1	0	0	0	0	0	0				
42	**45**	1	0	0	0	0	0	0				
45	**48**	2	0	0	0	0	0	0				
48	**51**	2	1	0	0	0	0	0				
51	**54**	2	1	0	0	0	0	0				
54	**57**	2	1	0	0	0	0	0				
57	**60**	3	1	0	0	0	0	0				
60	**63**	3	2	0	0	0	0	0				
63	**66**	3	2	1	0	0	0	0				
66	**69**	4	2	1	0	0	0	0				
69	**72**	4	3	1	0	0	0	0	0	0	0	0
72	**75**	4	3	2	0	0	0	0	0	0	0	0
75	**78**	5	3	2	1	0	0	0	0	0	0	0
78	**81**	5	4	2	1	0	0	0	0	0	0	0
81	**84**	5	4	3	1	0	0	0	0	0	0	0
84	**87**	5	4	3	2	0	0	0	0	0	0	0
87	**90**	6	4	3	2	1	0	0	0	0	0	0
90	**93**	6	5	3	2	1	0	0	0	0	0	0
93	**96**	7	5	4	2	1	0	0	0	0	0	0
96	**99**	7	5	4	3	1	0	0	0	0	0	0
99	**102**	8	6	4	3	2	0	0	0	0	0	0
102	**105**	8	6	5	3	2	1	0	0	0	0	0
105	**108**	8	6	5	4	2	1	0	0	0	0	0
108	**111**	9	7	5	4	3	1	0	0	0	0	0
111	**114**	9	7	6	4	3	2	0	0	0	0	0
114	**117**	10	8	6	5	3	2	1	0	0	0	0
117	**120**	10	8	6	5	4	2	1	0	0	0	0
120	**123**	11	9	7	5	4	3	1	0	0	0	0
123	**126**	11	9	7	5	4	3	2	0	0	0	0
126	**129**	12	10	8	6	4	3	2	1	0	0	0
129	**132**	12	10	8	6	5	3	2	1	0	0	0
132	**135**	12	10	9	7	5	4	2	1	0	0	0
135	**138**	13	11	9	7	5	4	3	1	0	0	0
138	**141**	13	11	9	7	6	4	3	2	0	0	0
141	**144**	14	12	10	8	6	5	3	2	1	0	0
144	**147**	14	12	10	8	6	5	4	2	1	0	0
147	**150**	15	13	11	9	7	5	4	3	1	0	0
150	**153**	15	13	11	9	7	6	4	3	2	0	0
153	**156**	16	14	12	10	8	6	5	3	2	1	0
156	**159**	16	14	12	10	8	6	5	4	2	1	0
159	**162**	17	15	13	11	9	7	5	4	3	1	0
162	**165**	17	15	13	11	9	7	5	4	3	2	0
165	**168**	17	15	13	12	10	8	6	4	3	2	0
168	**171**	18	16	14	12	10	8	6	5	3	2	1
171	**174**	18	16	14	12	10	9	7	5	4	2	1
174	**177**	19	17	15	13	11	9	7	5	4	3	1
177	**180**	19	17	15	13	11	9	7	6	4	3	2
180	**183**	20	18	16	14	12	10	8	6	5	3	2
183	**186**	20	18	16	14	12	10	8	6	5	4	2
186	**189**	21	19	17	15	13	11	9	7	5	4	3
189	**192**	21	19	17	15	13	11	9	7	6	4	3
192	**195**	21	19	18	16	14	12	10	8	6	5	3
195	**198**	22	20	18	16	14	12	10	8	6	5	3
198	**201**	22	20	18	16	15	13	11	9	7	5	4
201	**204**	23	21	19	17	15	13	11	9	7	5	4
204	**207**	23	21	19	17	15	13	11	10	8	6	4
207	**210**	24	22	20	18	16	14	12	10	8	6	5
210	**213**	24	22	20	18	16	14	12	10	8	7	5
213	**216**	25	23	21	19	17	15	13	11	9	7	5
216	**219**	25	23	21	19	17	15	13	11	9	7	6
219	**222**	26	24	22	20	18	16	14	12	10	8	6
222	**225**	26	24	22	20	18	16	14	12	10	8	6
225	**228**	26	24	22	21	19	17	15	13	11	9	7
228	**231**	27	25	23	21	19	17	15	13	11	9	7
231	**234**	27	25	23	21	19	18	16	14	12	10	8

MARRIED Persons—**DAILY OR MISCELLANEOUS** Payroll Period

(For Wages Paid in 2007)

If the wages are–		And the number of withholding allowances claimed is—										
At least	But less than	0	1	2	3	4	5	6	7	8	9	10
		The amount of income tax to be withheld is—										
$234	**$237**	$28	$26	$24	$22	$20	$18	$16	$14	$12	$10	$8
237	**240**	28	26	24	22	20	18	16	14	13	11	9
240	**243**	29	27	25	23	21	19	17	15	13	11	9
243	**246**	29	27	25	23	21	19	17	15	13	11	9
246	**249**	30	28	26	24	22	20	18	16	14	12	10
249	**252**	30	28	26	24	22	20	18	16	14	12	10
252	**255**	30	28	27	25	23	21	19	17	15	13	11
255	**258**	31	29	27	25	23	21	19	17	15	13	11
258	**261**	31	29	27	25	24	22	20	18	16	14	12
261	**264**	32	30	28	26	24	22	20	18	16	14	12
264	**267**	32	30	28	26	24	22	20	19	17	15	13
267	**270**	33	31	29	27	25	23	21	19	17	15	13
270	**273**	33	31	29	27	25	23	21	19	17	16	14
273	**276**	34	32	30	28	26	24	22	20	18	16	14
276	**279**	35	32	30	28	26	24	22	20	18	16	14
279	**282**	35	33	31	29	27	25	23	21	19	17	15
282	**285**	36	33	31	29	27	25	23	21	19	17	15
285	**288**	37	34	31	30	28	26	24	22	20	18	16
288	**291**	38	34	32	30	28	26	24	22	20	18	16
291	**294**	38	35	32	30	28	27	25	23	21	19	17
294	**297**	39	36	33	31	29	27	25	23	21	19	17
297	**300**	40	37	33	31	29	27	25	23	22	20	18
300	**303**	41	37	34	32	30	28	26	24	22	20	18
303	**306**	41	38	35	32	30	28	26	24	22	20	18
306	**309**	42	39	36	33	31	29	27	25	23	21	19
309	**312**	43	40	36	33	31	29	27	25	23	21	19
312	**315**	44	40	37	34	32	30	28	26	24	22	20
315	**318**	44	41	38	35	32	30	28	26	24	22	20
318	**321**	45	42	39	35	33	31	29	27	25	23	21
321	**324**	46	43	39	36	33	31	29	27	25	23	21
324	**327**	47	43	40	37	34	31	29	28	26	24	22
327	**330**	47	44	41	38	34	32	30	28	26	24	22
330	**333**	48	45	42	38	35	32	30	28	26	25	23
333	**336**	49	46	42	39	36	33	31	29	27	25	23
336	**339**	50	46	43	40	37	33	31	29	27	25	23
339	**341**	50	47	44	40	37	34	32	30	28	26	24
341	**343**	51	47	44	41	38	34	32	30	28	26	24
343	**345**	51	48	45	41	38	35	32	30	28	26	24
345	**347**	52	48	45	42	39	35	33	31	29	27	25
347	**349**	52	49	46	42	39	36	33	31	29	27	25
349	**351**	53	49	46	43	40	36	33	31	29	27	25
351	**353**	53	50	47	43	40	37	34	32	30	28	26
353	**355**	54	50	47	44	41	37	34	32	30	28	26
355	**357**	54	51	48	44	41	38	35	32	30	28	26
357	**359**	55	51	48	45	42	38	35	32	30	28	27
359	**361**	55	52	49	45	42	39	36	33	31	29	27
361	**363**	56	52	49	46	43	39	36	33	31	29	27
363	**365**	56	53	50	46	43	40	37	33	31	29	27
365	**367**	57	53	50	47	44	40	37	34	32	30	28
367	**369**	57	54	51	47	44	41	38	34	32	30	28
369	**371**	58	54	51	48	45	41	38	35	32	30	28
371	**373**	58	55	52	48	45	42	39	35	33	31	29
373	**375**	59	55	52	49	46	42	39	36	33	31	29
375	**377**	59	56	53	49	46	43	40	36	33	31	29
377	**379**	60	56	53	50	47	43	40	37	34	31	30
379	**381**	60	57	54	50	47	44	41	37	34	32	30
381	**383**	61	57	54	51	48	44	41	38	35	32	30
383	**385**	61	58	55	51	48	45	42	38	35	32	30
385	**387**	62	58	55	52	49	45	42	39	36	33	31
387	**389**	62	59	56	52	49	46	43	39	36	33	31
389	**391**	63	59	56	53	50	46	43	40	37	33	31
391	**393**	63	60	57	53	50	47	44	40	37	34	32
393	**395**	64	60	57	54	51	47	44	41	38	34	32
395	**397**	64	61	58	54	51	48	45	41	38	35	32
397	**399**	65	61	58	55	52	48	45	42	39	35	33
399	**401**	65	62	59	55	52	49	46	42	39	36	33
$401 and over		Use Table 8(b) for a **MARRIED person** on page T-4										

ANSWERS TO SELF-STUDY QUIZZES

Self-Study Quiz 2–1

1. True.
2. False. Live-in domestic workers do not have to be paid overtime.
3. True.
4. False. Individual employee coverage is not affected by the work of fellow employees.
5. True.

Self-Study Quiz 2–2

1. $2.13
2. $58.80

$234.00	($5.85 × 40 hours)
– 85.20	weekly wage
– 90.00	tip credit claimed by employer
$ 58.80	

Self-Study Quiz 2–3

	Hourly Rate	Overtime Rate
1.	$13.13	$19.70
2.	$11.15	$16.73
3.	$16.73	$25.10
4.	$9.23	$13.85

Self-Study Quiz 2–4

1. $276.00
2. $6.00 ($276.00 ÷ 46)
3. $3.00 ($6.00 × 0.50)
4. $18.00 ($3.00 × 6)
5. $294.00

Self-Study Quiz 3–1

1. Yes. Full-time life insurance salespersons are covered as statutory employees for social security, Medicare, and FUTA tax purposes.
2. Yes. Federal government employees hired after 1983 are subject to full FICA coverage.
3. No. Real estate agents are considered independent contractors.
4. No. Schuck offers his services to the general public and is considered an independent contractor.

Self-Study Quiz 3–2

1. No. The gift certificates are of nominal value.
2. Yes. Personal use of a company vehicle for non-business-related activities constitutes a taxable fringe benefit.
3. No. An employer may contribute to an SEP set up by or on behalf of its employees. The employer's contributions are exempt from FICA taxes if reason to believe exists that employees will be entitled to deduct the employer contributions for federal income tax purposes.

4. No. Generally, employers do not have to include in wages or withhold on the value of payment made for job-related training for their employees.
5. Yes. Payments by employers for involuntary separation of an employee from the employer's service are taxable under FICA.

Self-Study Quiz 3–3

Employee	OASDI	HI
Tammy Wolf	13.95	3.26
Bill Young	18.60	4.35
Howard Feldman	10.85	2.54
Carin Clever	62.00	14.50
Bud McAvoy	136.40	31.90
Totals	241.80	56.55
Employer's taxes (based on $3,900 gross wages)	241.80	56.55

Bud McAvoy will earn an annual salary of $114,400, which exceeds the wage base for OASDI taxes.

Through the 46th weekly payday, McAvoy will have cumulative wages of $101,200.

When the payment is made on the 47th payday, McAvoy will exceed the wage base for OASDI taxes:

Cumulative wages	$101,200
Current wage payment	2,200
	$103,400

Therefore, only $1,100 is taxable.

Self-Study Quiz 3–4

1. $54,000 ($1,000 per week × 52 = $52,000 + $2,000 bonus)
2. $82,000 ($54,000 + $28,000)
3. $28,000 (Taxable wage base $102,300)
4. $4,284 ($3,472—OASDI + $812—HI)

Self-Study Quiz 3–5

1. Johnson should deposit its taxes by the following Wednesday.
2. During the first calendar year for a new business, the company is a monthly depositor. However, if during the year it has an undeposited tax liability of $100,000 (which triggers the one-banking-day rule), the company becomes a semiweekly depositor for the remainder of the year.
3. The additional taxes are not accumulated with the previous liability of $105,000. The company should follow the semiweekly deposit rules and deposit the $20,000 by Friday.

Self-Study Quiz 4–1

✓ a. Meals provided to employees for the convenience of the employer on the employer's premises.
___ b. Bonuses to managers and supervisors are considered compensation for services rendered as employees and are subject to withholding.
✓ c. The use of on-site athletic facilities by employees is considered a nontaxable fringe benefit.
✓ d. Advances for business expenses reasonably expected to be incurred.
___ e. Sick pay is subject to withholding.
___ f. Memberships in social or country clubs are taxable fringe benefits and are subject to withholding.
✓ g. No-additional-cost meals provided to employees at an employer-operated eating establishment.

Self-Study Quiz 4–2

1. The payroll manager should inform Kyle that the company cannot reimburse her for any overwithholding that may have occurred prior to her submitting a new W-4. The only circumstances that allow the employer to reimburse an employee for overwithholding is if the employer failed to put a new W-4 into effect that resulted in overwithholding.

2. The payroll manager must inform Bradley that an employee may claim exemption from withholding for only one tax year at a time. The exemption must be claimed each year by February 15. If a new certificate is not filed, the employer must withhold at the single rate with zero withholding allowances.
3. Volmer may claim six personal allowances, as identified on the personal allowance worksheet accompanying Form W-4:
   a. One allowance for himself.
   b. One allowance for his spouse.
   c. One allowance for being married, having one job, and his spouse not working.
   d. One allowance for each dependent child (total of 3).

Self-Study Quiz 4–3

Step 1—Round gross wages:	**$1,100**
Step 2—Multiply the number of allowances by the weekly allowance amount:	**3 × $65.38 = $196.14**
Step 3—Subtract the value of the allowances from the gross pay:	**$1,100 − $196.14 = $903.86**

Step 4—Compute the tax from the percentage tax table for WEEKLY MARRIED person:

Over $449 But not over $1,360 . . . . 15% of excess over $449 plus $29.50

$903.86 – $449.00 = $454.86 × 15% = $68.23 + $29.50 **Total tax to be withheld = $97.73**

Self-Study Quiz 4–4

Employee	Tax
Lamb	$113
Nurin	$95
Hogan	$7
Vick	$325.55
Marks	$86

Self-Study Quiz 4–5

Method A:	Tax previously withheld on semimonthly wage of $1,450 = $93	
	Tax on wage and bonus ($1,950):	$168
	Less tax previously withheld:	93
	Withholding on bonus:	$ 75
Method B:	25% × $500 = $125	

Self-Study Quiz 4–6

1. According to Figure 4–9, Brewer is entitled to an advance EIC payment of $15 per week.
2. Gregory Company can treat the EIC payments as if the company has paid the total amount of income taxes withheld, and it can use any remaining amounts against its deposit of social security taxes. The company must, however, make a deposit for the amount of employment taxes (employees' income taxes, social security taxes, and employer's social security taxes) that exceeds the amount of the EIC payments.

Self-Study Quiz 4–7

1. The company should report the total amount deducted from each employee in Box 14 of Form W-2. This box is to provide "other" information the company wants to give the employees. The company should label the amount as "union dues" in Box 14.
2. If an employee leaves the service of the employer, the employer may furnish Form W-2 any time after employment ends. If the employee requests Form W-2, the employer should give it to him/her within 30 days of the request or final wage payment, whichever is later. If there is a reasonable expectation that the employees may be rehired before the end of the year, the employer may delay providing Form W-2 until January following the close of the calendar year.
3. If Form W-2 has been destroyed or lost, employers are authorized to furnish substitute copies to the employee. Trident should provide a substitute form to Becker. The form should be clearly marked "Reissued Statement," and the company should not send the substitute statement to the Social Security Administration.

Self-Study Quiz 5–1

4.1% of $188,000 = $7,708		SUTA tax
6.2% of $188,000 =	$11,656	Gross FUTA tax
4.1% of $188,000 = $7,708		Credit for SUTA tax paid
1.3% of $188,000 = 2,444	10,152	Additional credit to get to 5.4%
0.8% of $188,000	$ 1,504	Net FUTA tax

Self-Study Quiz 5–2

From the Summary of State Unemployment Compensation Laws (Figure 5–1), the taxable wage in Colorado is $10,000. However, the company receives a credit of $6,000 against this limit because of unemployment taxes paid to Arizona on John's wages in that state. Therefore, the calculation is:

John's wages in Colorado	$26,000
Over taxable limit	16,000
Colorado's SUTA wage limit	$10,000
Credit for wages taxed in Arizona	6,000
John's taxable wages in Colorado	$ 4,000
Moss' SUTA tax rate in Colorado	× 2.9%
Amount of the company's SUTA tax in Colorado	$ 116

Self-Study Quiz 5–3

1st Quarter— $66,000 × 0.008 = $528.00 due on 4/30/08
2nd Quarter— $64,000 × 0.008 = $512.00 due on 7/31/08
3rd Quarter— $42,000 × 0.008 = $336.00 no deposit due
4th Quarter— $25,000 × 0.008 = $200.00 + $336.00 = $536.00 due on 2/2/09

Self-Study Quiz 6–1

January 25	Salary Expense	95,190.00	
	FICA Taxes Payable—OASDI		5,901.78
	FICA Taxes Payable—HI		1,380.26
	Employees FIT Payable		14,270.00
	Employees SIT Payable		1,427.85
	SUTA Taxes Payable		951.90
	Salaries Payable (Cash)		71,258.21

Self-Study Quiz 6–2

January 25	Payroll Taxes	11,042.05	
	FICA Taxes Payable—OASDI		5,901.78
	FICA Taxes Payable—HI		1,380.26
	FUTA Taxes Payable		761.52
	SUTA Taxes Payable		2,998.49

CHECK FIGURES

CHAPTER 2 PROBLEMS

2–1a. (c) $162.77
2–3a. gross earnings, $1,618.60
2–5a. gross pay, $980.77
2–7a. gross pay, $635.04
2–9a. gross earnings, $472.64
2–11a. gross pay, $690.48
2–13a. (a) hourly rate, $16.59
2–15a. gross pay, $729.00
2–17a. total earnings, $473.26
2–19a. annual earnings, $43,250.00

CHAPTER 3 PROBLEMS

3–1a. FICA taxes, $236.41; $55.29
3–3a. FICA taxes, $56.73; $13.27
3–5a. November 14 (TATE), $142.60; $72.50
3–7a. employees' taxes, $263.50; $61.65
3–9a. total FICA taxes, $1,809.67; $425.83
3–11a. total taxes—line 8, $21,771.83
3–13a. total taxes—line 8, $5,406.42
3–15a. last due date, April 4
3–17a. total OASDI taxes, $4,563.82

CHAPTER 4 PROBLEMS

4–1a. net pay, $35.99
4–3a. Corn tax, $66.79; $67.00
4–5a. total FIT, $536.12
4–7a. net, $636.85
4–9a. net, $62,169.46
4–11a. gross, $154.93
4–13a. Form 941, line 8, $4,565.96

CHAPTER 5 PROBLEMS

5–1a. total unemployment taxes, $4,489.00
5–3a. net SUTA tax, $3,104.30
5–5a. FUTA tax—net, $158.88
5–7a. (b), $159.60
5–9a. (b), $1,040.60
5–11a. (c), $855.00
5–13a. voluntary = $867.00
5–15a. tax rate = 4.5%
5–17a. total FUTA tax = $564.80

CHAPTER 6 PROBLEMS

6–1a. tax levy, $447.69
6–3a. (a) payroll tax debit, $650.25
6–5a. a. cash credit, $28,823.30
6–7a. cash credit, $862.21
6–9a. cash credit, $1,775.33
6–11a. wage debit, $13,060.00
6–13a. July w/h, $372.82
6–15a. payroll taxes, $212.28

CHAPTER 7 PROBLEMS

Net pay, October 23, $11,023.90
Net pay, November 6, $10,786.96

GLOSSARY

This glossary includes terms from Appendices B, C, and D. These appendices are available on the Bieg 2008 product Web site at http://www.thomsonedu.com/accounting/bieg and on the Instructor's Resource CD.

A

Annualizing wages method of determining amount of income taxes to be withheld by multiplying the wages for one payroll period by the number of periods in the year, determining the annual amount of withholding required on the total wages, and dividing the annual withholding by the number of payroll periods.

Application form personnel record which gives the applicant an opportunity to provide complete information as to personal qualifications, training, and experience.

Average indexed monthly earnings a worker's average monthly earnings, updated to reflect changes in wage levels.

B

Backup withholding amount of income tax withheld by payers of taxable interest, dividends, and certain other payments made to payees who have failed to furnish the payers with correct identification numbers.

Biweekly every two weeks.

Business expense cost of operating a business that is deductible by the employer for federal income tax purposes.

C

Change in payroll rate form document that notifies the proper departments of a change in the employee's rate of remuneration.

Check-off system withholding of union dues from employees' wages by the employer.

Commission stated percentage of revenue paid an employee who transacts a piece of business or performs a service.

Common-law relationship the state existing when the employer has the right to control both what work will be done and how it will be done.

Constructively paid remunerations that are credited to the account of, or set apart for, an employee so that they may be drawn upon at any time, even though they are not actually possessed by the employee.

Continental system method of recording time on time cards in which the day is divided into one 24-hour period, with time running from 12 midnight to 12 midnight.

Contribution report quarterly tax return filed with the state by the employer that provides a summary of the wages paid during the period and shows the computation of the tax or contribution.

Currently insured criterion used to determine eligibility for social security benefits; persons must have at least six quarters of coverage during the 13-quarter period ending with (1) the quarter in which they died or (2) the quarter in which they became entitled to old-age insurance benefits or most recently became entitled to disability benefits.

D

Defined contribution plan a retirement plan that provides future benefits based solely on the amount paid by each employee and employer into the account, plus investment gains.

Dependency allowance an additional weekly benefit paid to unemployed workers with dependents.

Disability benefits payments to employees who are absent from their jobs because of illness, accident, or disease not arising out of their employment.

Discretionary bonus a bonus not agreed on, announced, or promised before payment.

Dismissal payments amounts paid by employers to workers who have been separated from employment; also known as ***payments in lieu of notice, separation pay***, or ***terminal leave pay***.

Disposable earnings the earnings remaining after withholding for federal and state income taxes, FICA taxes, state unemployment and disability taxes, and deductions required for state employees' retirement systems.

Domestic service services of a household nature performed in or about a private home of the person who employs the domestic.

Drawing account advances advance payments to salespersons against their commissions or unearned salaries for which they are to perform services, but which they are not legally obligated to repay.

E

Earned income credit (EIC) reduction in federal income taxes mostly for workers who have dependent children and maintain a household.

Educational assistance the expenses that an employer pays for an employee's education, such as tuition, fees, and payments for books, supplies, and equipment.

Electronic funds transfer system (EFTS) system whereby the employer transfers employees' net pays to employees' bank accounts with electronic equipment rather than issuing paychecks.

Electronic paystub paystub information made available through a secured Web site, kiosk, or interactive voice response system.

Employee any individual performing services for an employer in the legal relationship of employer and employee.

Employee history record continuous record of the relationship between the employer and the employee.

Employee's earnings record payroll record for each employee that is used to provide complete information about the accumulated earnings of each employee.

Employer any person or organization who employs one or more individuals for the performance of services, unless such services or employment are specifically excepted by law.

Employment any service performed by employees for their employer, regardless of the citizenship or residence of either.

Enterprise coverage applied to determine if employees of an enterprise are covered under the provisions of the FLSA. The test criteria are at least two employees engaged in interstate commerce and an annual gross sales volume of at least $500,000.

Executive orders regulations issued by the federal government that ban, in employment on government contracts, discrimination based on race, color, religion, sex, or national origin.

Exempt employees workers exempt from some, or all, of the FLSA requirements such as minimum wages, equal pay, and overtime pay.

Experience rating method by which employer contribution payments may be adjusted because of a favorable employment record; also known as ***merit rating***.

F

Fair employment practices laws that deal with discrimination on the basis of age, race, color, religion, sex, or national origin as a condition of employment.

Form W-2, Wage and Tax Statement form used by the employer to report the amount of wages paid each worker in the course of the trade or business of the employer.

Fully insured criterion used to determine eligibility for most retirement and disability benefits; generally, a worker needs between 6 and 40 quarters of coverage.

G

Garnishment legal or equitable procedure by means of which a portion of the wages of any person must be withheld for payment of a debt.

Gross earnings total regular earnings and total overtime earnings, also known as ***gross pay***.

Gross-up supplementals gross up amount of payment so that after the appropriate payroll taxes are withheld, the net amount left is equal to the original intended payment.

Group insurance life insurance program for employees at a low cost.

H

Hiring notice form that is sent to the payroll department so that new employees are properly added to the payroll.

Hospital insurance (HI) plan program of medical care that provides protection against costs of certain hospital and related services; also known as ***Basic Medicare*** or ***Part A Medicare***.

Human resources system those procedures and methods related to recruiting, selecting, orienting, training, and terminating personnel.

I

Immediate credit item a check or other instrument of payment for which immediate credit is given the payee by the receiving bank in accordance with its check-collection schedule.

Income tax levy on the earnings of most employees that is deducted from their gross pay.

Independent contractors persons who follow an independent trade, business, or profession where services are offered to the public.

Indexing updating, or adjusting, a dollar amount over any particular time period (such as a calendar year) to reflect changes in wage levels that have occurred since a predetermined base time period.

Individual employee coverage applied to determine if the FLSA covers an employee. The test is that the employee either engages in interstate commerce or produces goods for such commerce.

Individual-account plan supplemental unemployment benefits plan in which the employers' contributions are paid into a separate trust for each employee.

Information returns forms upon which an employer reports compensation paid to individuals who are not employees.

Interstate employee an individual who works in more than one state.

Investigative consumer report study done by a consumer reporting agency on a job applicant or current employee concerning the individual's character, general reputation, and mode of living.

J

Journal entries transactions recorded in the accounting system of a business.

L

Lookback period the block of time, consisting of four quarters beginning July 1 of the second preceding year and ending June 30 of the prior year, used to determine if an employer is a monthly or a semiweekly depositor.

M

Medicaid program of medical assistance provided to aged and needy persons by means of a joint federal-state program.

Merit rating *see* experience rating.

Monthly depositor one who reported employment taxes of $50,000 or less for the four quarters in the lookback period.

N

Negative-balance employers those whose reserve accounts have been charged for more benefits paid out than contributions paid in to the fund.

Nondiscretionary bonus a bonus normally based on hours worked, units produced, production efficiency, or work quality.

O

Overtime premium method of calculating overtime pay by multiplying the total hours worked (including overtime hours) by the regular rate of pay and then multiplying the overtime hours by one-half the regular hourly rate.

P

Partial unemployment employment by the individual's regular employer on a reduced scale because of lack of work.

Partial unemployment notices forms completed by the employer and given to partially unemployed workers so that supplemental unemployment benefits may be obtained.

Part-year employment another method of calculating the withholding of federal income tax from an employee's pay.

Payroll accounting system those procedures and methods related to the disbursement of pay to employees.

Payroll register multicolumn form used to assemble and summarize the data needed at the end of each payroll period. It lists all employees who earned remuneration, the amount of remuneration, the deductions, and the net amount paid.

Percentage method method of determining amount of income taxes to be withheld using Table of Allowance Values and Percentage Method Withholding Table.

Person an entity defined by law as an individual, a trust or estate, a partnership, or a corporation.

Personal allowance a deduction allowed in computing taxable income; also known as a ***personal exemption***.

Piece-rate system compensation plan under which workers are paid according to their output (units or pieces produced).

Pooled-fund laws unemployment insurance system wherein the cost of unemployment benefits is spread among all employers in a particular state.

Pooled-fund plan supplemental unemployment benefits plan financed by employers' contributions into a general fund; also known as the ***auto*** or ***Ford-type plan.***

Positive-balance employers those who have built up a balance in their reserve accounts (contributions paid in less benefits charged).

Prehire inquiries questions asked in the employment interview and on application forms, résumés of experience or education required of an applicant, and any kind of written testing.

Primary insurance amount (PIA) a person's monthly retirement or disability benefit, which is the base upon which monthly benefits of the worker's family and survivors are computed.

Principal activities those tasks employees must perform for the employer.

Profit-sharing plans compensation plans in which employer shares with employees a portion of the profits of the business.

Q

Quarter of coverage criterion used to determine if workers are fully insured, currently insured, or insured for disability benefits; the minimum amount of wages or self-employment income with which individuals must be credited in a calendar quarter if they are to receive credit toward being insured for that period.

Quarterly averaging method of determining the amount of income taxes to be withheld by estimating the employee's average wages for the calendar quarter, computing an average payment, and withholding an amount based on the average payment.

R

Reciprocal agreement arrangement entered into by two or more states whereby the resident of one state working in another state will not be subject to the withholding of income taxes by the state in which the person is employed if that state has entered into a similar agreement with the employee's resident state.

Reciprocal arrangements agreements between states to provide unemployment insurance coverage and payment of benefits to interstate workers.

Reference inquiry form document used by the employer to investigate the references given on the application blank by the job applicant.

Requisition for personnel document submitted by a department head to the Human Resources Department asking for additional or replacement employees.

Reserve-ratio formula experience-rating plan used in most states, based on: Contributions less Benefits Paid ÷ Average Payroll.

S

Safe harbor rule rule that determines if an employer has satisfied the deposit obligations by (a) having no shortfall (under deposit) that exceeds the greater of $100 or 2 percent of the amount of employment taxes required to be deposited and (b) having deposited the shortfall on or before the shortfall make-up date.

Salary remuneration paid on a monthly, biweekly, semimonthly, or yearly basis.

Self-employment income the net earnings derived by individuals from a business or profession carried on as a sole proprietorship or as a partnership.

Semimonthly twice a month.

Semiweekly depositor one who reported employment taxes of more than $50,000 for the four quarters in the lookback period.

Separation report report that provides a wage and employment record of the separated employee and the reason for leaving.

7-minute rule allows companies to set a policy of rounding seven minutes or less to zero and eight minutes or more to a quarter hour. This rule must be administered fairly and consistently.

Shortfall the excess of the amount of employment taxes required to be deposited over the amount deposited on or before the last date prescribed for the deposit.

Sick pay any payment made to individuals because of their personal injury or sickness that does not constitute wages.

Social security benefits payments made under Title II of the Social Security Act to retired workers, their spouses, children and parents, as well as widows, widowers, and some divorced persons; also known as ***OASDI benefits*** and ***Title II benefits***.

Special withholding allowance allowance claimed by employees so that wages which are below the level subject to the income tax will not be subject to withholding.

Standard deduction an amount of money used to reduce an individual's adjusted gross income in computing taxable income.

Status report initial statement filed by new employers with their state unemployment office, which determines their liability to make contributions into the state unemployment compensation fund.

Supplemental Unemployment Benefits (SUB) private supplementation of state unemployment compensation benefits to employees during periods of layoff.

Supplemental wage payments additional compensation such as vacation pay, bonuses, and commissions paid to employees.

Supplementary medical insurance plan program of voluntary medical care for aged and disabled designed to cover costs of doctors' services and other items and services not covered under the basic program; also known as ***supplementary*** or ***voluntary Medicare*** or ***Part B Medicare***.

T

Taxable wage base the maximum amount of wagers during a calendar year that is subject to a particular tax, such as FICA.

Time card form on which employee's time worked is recorded manually by the worker or automatically by a time clock.

Time sheet form that indicates an employee's time of arrival and time of departure.

Tip gift or gratuity given by a customer in recognition of service performed for him or her.

Tipped employee one engaged in an occupation in which tips of more than $30 a month are customarily and regularly received.

Title XII advances funds borrowed from the federal government by states who, due to financial difficulties, cannot pay their unemployment compensation benefits.

U

Unemployment compensation benefits payments made to workers who are temporarily unemployed.

Unemployment insurance a federal-state program that provides economic security for workers during periods of temporary unemployment.

V

Vesting the process of conveying to employees the right to share in a retirement fund in the event they are terminated before the normal retirement age.

Voluntary contributions payments deliberately made by employers to their state funds in order to qualify for a lower unemployment compensation tax rate.

W

Wage remuneration paid on an hourly, weekly, or piece-work basis.

Wage and tax statements statements furnished by employers to their employees informing them of the wages paid during the calendar year and the amount of taxes withheld from those wages.

Wage information reports statements filed by the employer, usually with the quarterly contribution report, which lists employee names, social security numbers, taxable wages, taxable tips, state in which worker was employed during the reported quarter, and employer's federal account number.

Wage-bracket method method of determining amount of income taxes to be withheld by reading amount from tables provided by the IRS, which take into consideration length of payroll period, gross earnings, marital status, and number of withholding allowances claimed.

Wages total compensation paid to employees for services, such as wages, salaries, commissions, or bonuses, including the fair market value of noncash property.

Workers' compensation insurance protection provided to employees and their dependents against losses due to injury or death incurred during employment.

Workweek fixed and regularly recurring period of 168 hours—7 consecutive 24-hour periods.

INDEX

E

F

G

H

I

J

L

M

N

O

P

Q

R

S

T

U

V

W